Capital Markets Law and Compliance

The Markets in Financial Instruments Directive (MiFID) is a detailed re-writing of the regulation of capital markets. To the extent those rules permit, the Financial Services Authority (FSA) is also introducing high-level 'principles-based regulation'. In response to this, Paul Nelson presents practical guidance on the regulation of the capital markets, ranging from new issues and IPOs to investment banking, broker-dealing and asset management. All laws and rules relevant to the regulation of the capital markets are explained and put into context within the economic operation of markets, institutions and products, the European Single Market, the FSA's policies and objectives, the historical evolution of the regulations and the general civil and criminal law. Drawing on 30 years' experience as a practitioner, and referring to a vast range of supporting materials, the author provides an insightful analysis and critique of the rules, the rule makers and the institutions.

PAUL NELSON is a partner at Linklaters, London. He is also the FINRA Professor of Capital Markets Regulation and Compliance at the ICMA Centre, University of Reading.

Law Practitioner Series

The *Law Practitioner Series* offers practical guidance in corporate and commercial law for the practitioner. It offers high-quality comment and analysis rather than simply restating the legislation, providing a critical framework as well as exploring the fundamental concepts which shape the law. Books in the series cover carefully chosen subjects of direct relevance and use to the practitioner.

The series will appeal to experienced specialists in each field, but is also accessible to more junior practitioners looking to develop their understanding of particular fields of practice.

The Consultant Editors and Editorial Board have outstanding expertise in the UK corporate and commercial arena, ensuring academic rigour with a practical approach.

Consultant editors
Charles Allen-Jones, retired senior partner of Linklaters
Mr Justice David Richards, Judge of the High Court of Justice, Chancery Division

Editors
Chris Ashworth – O'Melveny & Myers LLP
Professor Eilis Ferran – University of Cambridge
Nick Gibbon – Allen & Overy
Stephen Hancock – Herbert Smith
Judith Hanratty – BP Corporate Lawyer, retired
Keith Hyman – Clifford Chance
Keith Johnston – Addleshaw Goddard
Vanessa Knapp – Freshfields Bruckhaus Deringer
Charles Mayo – Simmons & Simmons
Andrew Peck – Linklaters
Richard Snowden QC – Erskine Chambers
Richard Sykes QC
William Underhill – Slaughter & May
Sandra Walker – Rio Tinto

Books in the series

Stamp Duty Land Tax
Michael Thomas; Consultant Editor David Goy QC
Accounting Principles for Lawyers
Peter Holgate
The European Company: Volume 1
General editors Dirk Van Gerven and Paul Storm
Capital Markets Law and Compliance: The Implications of MiFID
Paul Nelson

Capital Markets Law and Compliance:
The Implications of MiFID

PAUL NELSON

CAMBRIDGE UNIVERSITY PRESS
Cambridge, New York, Melbourne, Madrid, Cape Town, Singapore,
São Paulo, Delhi

Cambridge University Press
The Edinburgh Building, Cambridge CB2 8RU, UK

Published in the United States of America by Cambridge University Press, New York

www.cambridge.org
Information on this title: www.cambridge.org/9780521889360

© Cambridge University Press 2008
© in the diagrams, Paul Nelson 2008

This publication is in copyright. Subject to statutory exception
and to the provisions of relevant collective licensing agreements,
no reproduction of any part may take place without
the written permission of Cambridge University Press.

First published 2008

Printed in the United Kingdom at the University Press, Cambridge

A catalogue record for this publication is available from the British Library

ISBN   978-0-521-88936-0   hardback

Cambridge University Press has no responsibility for the persistence or
accuracy of URLs for external or third-party internet websites referred to
in this book, and does not guarantee that any content on such
websites is, or will remain, accurate or appropriate.

For Myrtle, Aubrey, Dora, Saul, Joel,
with love and respect

Contents

	Preface	xiii
	List of acronyms	xiv
Part I	**Evolution of capital markets regulation, FSA and the European single market**	**1**
1	Introduction	3
2	FSMA and the single market	8
2.1	Evolution	8
2.2	Up to the 1930s	9
2.2.1	The secondary market and the London Stock Exchange	9
2.2.2	Primary market new issues	10
2.3	The Prevention of Fraud Acts	12
2.4	The Financial Services Act 1986	15
2.4.1	Reform of securities regulation	15
2.4.2	Self-regulation?	17
2.4.3	Rules and principles	19
2.4.4	A complete (functional) regulatory regime	22
2.5	FSMA	27
2.5.1	The statutory objectives	33
2.5.2	Conveyance structure	36
2.5.3	Annual report	37
2.5.4	Practitioner input and consultation	38
2.5.5	Enforcement	39
2.5.6	Complaints commissioner	43
2.5.7	Accountability to Treasury	44
2.5.8	The rulebook	45
2.6	European Union directives	53
Part II	**Licensing and rule application**	**61**
3	Licensing	63
3.1	Analysing the application of regulations	63
3.2	Regulated activities	64

3.2.1	'Investments'	65
3.2.2	'Investment activities'	79
3.2.3	Activities in and/or from a UK place of business	86
3.2.4	Activities into the UK and the overseas persons exclusion	86
3.2.5	Excluded activities	88
3.2.6	The ISD/MiFID override	90
3.2.7	By way of business	92
3.2.8	A licence is required	92
3.3	Process and criteria	94
3.4	Passporting	94
3.5	Non-EEA firms	96
4	The application of FSA MiFID rules	98
4.1	Methodology	98
4.2	Rules of application	98

Part III The firm's infrastructure — 111

5	Systems and controls	113
5.1	Evolution of FSA's approach	113
5.2	Systems and controls rules	117
5.2.1	Overall requirement	118
5.2.2	Apportionment of responsibility	121
5.2.3	Control functions	123
5.2.4	Employees	125
5.2.5	Outsourcing	128
5.3	Senior management responsibility	132
5.3.1	Registration as an Approved Person	132
5.3.2	Rule responsibilities	135
5.4	Approved Persons	139
5.4.1	Registration as an Approved Person	139
5.4.2	Rule responsibilities	140
5.5	Record-keeping	140
5.6	FSA's risk assessment methodology	142
6	Conflicts of interest	146
6.1	Differences in interests and conflicts of interest	146
6.2	The general law of fiduciaries	146
6.2.1	A fiduciary relationship	146
6.2.2	A conflict of interest	148
6.2.3	Solutions	153
6.3	Regulatory rules	158
6.3.1	The general rule	158
6.3.2	Inducements	166
6.3.3	Soft commission and bundling	171

6.3.4	Investment research	178
6.3.5	Corporate finance securities issues	189
6.3.6	Churning	191
6.3.7	Personal account dealing	191
6.3.8	Polarisation	193
7	Client property	194
7.1	Client assets and custody	194
7.1.1	Protecting the client's assets	194
7.1.2	Application of the custody rules	199
7.1.3	Procedures	203
7.2	Client money	208
7.2.1	Protecting the client's money	208
7.2.2	Defining client money	211
7.2.3	Procedures	216

Part IV Conduct of business — 223

8	Client classification and client documentation	225
8.1	Regulatory policy	225
8.2	'Clients' for regulatory purposes	226
8.2.1	The definition of 'client'	226
8.2.2	Clients acting as agent	229
8.3	Client categorisation	230
8.3.1	Private customers and retail clients	231
8.3.2	Intermediate customers and professional clients	231
8.3.3	Market counterparties and eligible counterparties	239
8.4	Terms of business	241
8.4.1	The requirement	241
8.4.2	Content	243
8.4.3	Form	249
8.4.4	Amendments	249
8.4.5	Standard terms and exclusion clauses	250
8.4.6	Enforcement	251
8.4.7	One-way and two-way notifications	251
9	Principles of conduct	254
9.1	The FSA's 11 Principles	254
9.1.1	Policy	254
9.1.2	Application	257
9.2	Treating the customer fairly	259
9.3	The MiFID Principle	264
10	Marketing investments	265
10.1	The different regulatory regimes	265

10.2	Securities	265
10.2.1	Transferable securities	268
10.2.2	Offer to the public	268
10.3	Misleading etc marketing	270
10.4	Marketing by unlicensed persons	272
10.4.1	Marketing up to the end of the 20th century	272
10.4.2	The FSMA regime	276
10.5	Marketing by licensed persons	282
10.5.1	Full disclosure	282
10.5.2	Specific disclosures	289
10.5.3	Real-time promotions	293
10.5.4	Electronic Commerce Directive	293
10.5.5	Distance marketing	296
10.5.6	Collective investment schemes	298
11	Advising clients	306
11.1	General Law	306
11.2	The Regulated Activity	307
11.3	Execution-only services	318
11.4	Appropriateness	320
11.5	Margin Lending	324
11.5.1	Consumer Credit	324
11.5.2	Securities Regulation	324
12	Improper behaviour in dealing and executing orders	326
12.1	Introduction	326
12.2	Insider dealing	326
12.2.1	An individual	327
12.2.2	Territorial jurisdiction	327
12.2.3	Inside information	329
12.2.4	Connection	331
12.2.5	Dealing	332
12.2.6	Encouraging	332
12.2.7	Disclosure	333
12.2.8	Defences	333
12.3	Market manipulation	336
12.3.1	Act or course of conduct	336
12.3.2	False or misleading impression	337
12.3.3	In the UK	338
12.3.4	Purpose	339
12.3.5	Inducing	339
12.3.6	Reasonable belief	339
12.3.7	Defences	339
12.4	A principle of conduct and the need for an administrative remedy	343

12.4.1	An administrative offence	345
12.4.2	The burden of proof	345
12.4.3	Intention	346
12.4.4	Affected persons and certainty	347
12.4.5	Multiple jeopardy	347
12.5	The market abuse regime	347
12.5.1	'Behaviour' in relation to an exchange	349
12.5.2	Territorial ambit	350
12.5.3	Misuse of information	350
12.5.4	False or misleading impression	360
12.5.5	Distortion	364
12.5.6	The reasonable and regular user	371
12.5.7	Requiring or encouraging	373
12.5.8	Safe harbours	374
12.5.9	Mitigating factors	374
12.6	The Principle	375
12.7	The future	376
13	Dealing and executing orders	378
13.1	Transactions	378
13.1.1	Pre-transaction	378
13.1.2	The order to deal	378
13.1.3	The decision on how to deal	379
13.1.4	Executing transactions	380
13.1.5	Own account dealing	388
13.2	Best execution	391
13.2.1	Policy	391
13.2.2	When the best execution obligation applies	391
13.2.3	Achieving best execution	398
13.3	Systematic internalisers	407
13.3.1	Introduction	407
13.3.2	The Investment Services Directive	408
13.3.3	MiFID	409
13.4	Reporting	413
13.4.1	Trade reporting	413
13.4.2	Transaction reporting	415
13.4.3	Reporting to clients	417
14	Exchanges and MTFs	418
14.1	Regulated markets	418
14.2	Multi-lateral trading facilities (Alternative Trading Systems)	418
14.2.1	The need for separate regulation	418
14.2.2	Regulatory standards	419
14.3	Clearing services	422

| Part V | Application of rules to particular businesses | 423 |

15	Corporate finance	425
15.1	Regulatory status	425
15.2	Infrastructure rules	425
15.3	Conduct rules	426
15.3.1	Conduct rules	426
15.3.2	MiFID	427
16	Broker–dealers	429
16.1	Regulatory status	429
16.2	Infrastructure rules	429
16.3	Conduct rules	429
16.3.1	Securities and derivatives broking and dealing	429
16.3.2	Energy and oil markets	429
16.3.3	Stocklending	430
17	Asset managers	432
17.1	Portfolio managers	432
17.1.1	Regulatory status	432
17.1.2	Infrastructure rules	432
17.1.3	Conduct rules	432
17.2	Collective investment schemes	432
18	Trustees	434
18.1	Trustees of collective investment schemes	434
18.2	Custodians	434
18.2.1	Regulatory status	434
18.2.2	Infrastructure rules	434
18.2.3	Conduct rules	434
18.3	Other trustees	434
18.3.1	Regulatory status	434
18.3.2	Infrastructure rules	435
18.3.3	Pre-MiFID conduct rules	435
19	Retail intermediaries	438
19.1	Stockbrokers	438
19.1.1	Regulatory status	438
19.1.2	Infrastructure rules	438
19.1.3	Conduct rules	438
19.2	Packaged product intermediaries	438
19.2.1	Regulatory status	438
19.2.2	Infrastructure rules	438
19.2.3	Conduct rules	439
	Bibliography	440
	Index	441

Preface

This book, like all books, is a product of time, place, circumstances and personality. My aims in writing it are explained in Chapter 1; why I did it is, ultimately, a psychological question which I will not answer here. Instead, I want to acknowledge a number of debts which are important to me in its creation, although most will not recognise it and none have read the result in advance: Robert Orme, Head of History of Art at Latymer Upper School, Hammersmith, who taught me that history is the foundation of explanation; Graham Routledge, late Fellow of Corpus Christi College Cambridge, who taught me law as an analytic discipline; Iain Murray, late Partner of Linklaters, who showed me not only that all aspects of law are interconnected, but also that the socio-economic consequences are profound; Charles Allen-Jones, retired Senior Partner of Linklaters, who showed me law as a creative tool in solving commercial problems; Professor John Board, Director ICMA Centre, University of Reading, who has shown me not only great understanding but also how an economist's view of the Capital Markets can immeasurably enhance a lawyer's view; and my friend Dora Lawson who continues to teach me that in a world of relative, ever-shifting and, ultimately, futile values it is possible to live according to the highest standards of integrity. In the production of this book I have had the privilege of working with Andrea Philo, whose support over many years I cannot repay.

The law, or at least the regulation, is stated as at 20 September 2007.

Paul Nelson
West Hampstead

List of acronyms

APER	FSA's Statements of Principle and Code of Practice for Approved Persons
ATS	Alternative Trading System
AUTH	FSA's Authorisation Manual, part of its Handbook of Rules, in force on and after 1 November 2007
BCD	The Banking Consolidation Directive, 2000/12/EC
BN	Board Notice
CA	Companies Act
CCA	Consumer Credit Act 1974
CASS	FSA's Client Asset Rules, part of its Handbook of Rules, in force on and after 1 November 2007
CEBS	The Committee of European Banking Supervisors
CESR	The Committee of European Securities Regulators
CIS FPO	The FSMA (Promotion of Collective Investment Schemes) (Exemptions) Order 2001, SI 2001/1060
CJA	Criminal Justice Act 1993
COAF	FSA's Complaints against the FSA Rules, part of its Handbook of Rules, in force on and after 1 November 2007
COBS	FSA's Conduct of Business Rules, part of its Handbook of Rules, in force on and after 1 November 2007
COLL	FSA's Collective Investment Scheme Sourcebook, part of its Handbook of Rules, in force on and after 1 November 2007
COMP	FSA's Compensation Rules, part of its Handbook of Rules, in force on and after 1 November 2007

List of acronyms

COND	FSA's Threshold Conditions, part of its Handbook of Rules, in force on and after 1 November 2007
CP	Consultation Paper
DEPP	FSA's Decision Procedure and Penalties Manual, part of its Handbook of Rules, in force on and after 28 August 2007.
DISP	FSA's Dispute Resolution, Complaints Rules, part of its Handbook of Rules, in force on and after 1 November 2007
DP	Discussion Paper
DTR	FSA's Disclosure and Transparency Rules, part of its Handbook of Rules, in force on and after 1 November 2007
EC	The European Commission
EG	FSA's Enforcement Guide, part of its Handbook of Rules, in force on and after 28 August 2007
ENF	FSA's Enforcement Manual, part of its Handbook of Rules, in force up to 27 August 2007
FIT	The FSA's Fit and Proper Test for Approved Persons, part of its Handbook of Rules, in force on and after 1 November 2007
FS	Feedback Statement
FSA	The Financial Services Authority
FSA CP 06/9	Organisational systems and controls, FSA Consultation Paper 06/9, May 2006
FSA CP 06/14	Implementing MiFID for Firms and Markets, FSA Consultation Paper 06/14, July 2006
FSA CP 06/15	Reforming the Approved Persons Regime, FSA Consultation Paper 06/15, August 2006
FSA CP 06/19	Reforming Conduct of Business Regulation, FSA Consultation Paper 06/19, October 2006
FSA CP 06/20	Financial Promotion and Other Communications, FSA Consultation Paper 06/20, October 2006
FSA CP 07/2	Review of the Enforcement and Decision making manuals, FSA Consultation Paper 07/2, January 2007
FSA CP 07/4	The Training and Competence Sourcebook Review, FSA Consultation Paper 07/4, February 2007

FSA CP 07/8	Quarterly Consultation No. 12, FSA Consultation Paper 07/8, April 2007
FSA CP 07/9	Conduct of Business Regime: Non-MiFID Deferred Matters, FSA Consultation Paper 07/9, May 2007
FSA CP 07/16	Consequential Handbook Amendments, FSA Consultation Paper 07/16, July 2007
FSA DP 07/1	A Review of Retail Distribution, FSA Discussion Paper 07/1, June 2007
FSA FS 06/1	Reviewing our Training and Competence Regime, FSA Feedback Statement 06/1, March 2006
FSA PM CASS	FSA's Client Assets Rules, part of its Handbook of Rules, in force up to 31 October 2007
FSA PM COB	FSA's Conduct of Business Rules, part of its Handbook of Rules, in force up to 31 October 2007
FSA PM ECO	FSA's Electronic Commerce Directive Rules, part of its Handbook of Rules, in force up to 31 October 2007
FSA PM GLOSSARY	FSA's Glossary of Definitions, part of its Handbook of Rules, in force up to 31 October 2007
FSA PM MAR	FSA's Market Conduct Rules, part of its Handbook of Rules, in force up to 31 October 2007
FSA PM SUP	FSA's Supervision Manual, part of its Handbook of Rules, in force up to 31 October 2007
FSA PM SYSC	FSA's Senior Management Arrangements, Systems and Controls, part of its Handbook of Rules, in force up to 31 October 2007
FSA PM TC	FSA's Training and Competence Rules, part of its Handbook of Rules, in force up to 31 October 2007
FSA PS 06/13	Organisational Systems and Controls: Common Platform for Firms, FSA Policy Statement 06/13, November 2006
FSA PS 07/2	Implementing the Markets in Financial Instruments Directive, FSA Policy Statement 07/2, January 2007
FSA PS 07/3	Reforming the Approved Persons regime, FSA Policy Statement 07/3, January 2007

List of acronyms

FSA PS 07/6	Reforming Conduct of Business Regulation, FSA Policy Statement 07/6, May 2007
FSA PS 07/14	Reforming Conduct of Business Regulation, FSA CP 07/14, July 2007
FSA PS 07/15	Best Execution, FSA Policy Statement 07/15, August 2007
FSMA or 2000 FSMA	The Financial Services and Markets Act 2000
GEN	FSA's General Provisions, part of its Handbook of Rules, in force on and after 1 November 2007
GLOSS	FSA's Glossary of Definitions, part of its Handbook of Rules, in force on and after 1 November 2007
GN	Guidance Note
GR	Guidance Release
IOSCO	The International Organisation of Securities Commissions
ISD	The Investment Services Directive 1993, 93/22/EEC
JMLSG Guidance Notes	The Guidance Notes issued by the Joint Money Laundering Steering Group, January 2006
LC	The Law Commission
Level 1 Directive	MiFID
Level 2 Directive	Commission Directive 2006/73/EC of 10 August 2006 implementing MiFID
Level 2 Regulation	Commission Regulation (EC) 1287/2006 of 10 August 2006 implementing MiFID
LIBA	The London Investment Banking Association
LIFFE	The London International Financial Futures Exchange
LME	The London Metal Exchange
LSE	The London Stock Exchange
MAR	FSA's Market Conduct Rules, part of its Handbook of Rules, in force on and after 1 November 2007
MiFID	The Markets in Financial Instruments Directive of 21 April 2004, 2004/39/EC
MLRO	Money Laundering Reporting Officer
MTF	Multi-lateral Trading Facility
1939 LDRs	The Licensed Dealers Conduct of Business Rules, 26 July 1939, SI 1939/787
1960 LDRs	The Licensed Dealers (Conduct of Business) Rules 1960, SI 1960/1216

1983 LDRs	The Licensed Dealers (Conduct of Business) Rules 1983, SI 1983/585
1986 FSAct	The Financial Services Act 1986
OEIC	An open-ended investment company
PERG	FSA's Perimeter Guidance Manual, part of its Handbook of Rules, in force on and after 1 November 2007
PFI	The Prevention of Fraud (Investments) Act 1939, re-enacted in 1958
PN	Press Notice
PR	Press Release
PRIN	FSA's Principles for Businesses, part of its Handbook of Rules, in force on and after 1 November 2007
Prospectus Rules	FSA's Prospectus Rules, part of its Handbook of Rules, in force on and after 1 November 2007
PS	Policy Statement
RAO	The Financial Services and Markets Act 2000 (Regulated Activities) Order 2001, SI 2001/544, as amended, including by the FSMA 2000 (Regulated Activities) (Amendment No. 3) Order 2006, SI 2006/3384
Reader's Guide	FSA's Reader's Guide: an introduction to its Handbook of Rules, August 2007
REC	FSA's Recognised Investment Exchanges and Recognised Clearing House Rules, part of its Handbook of Rules, in force on and after 1 November 2007
SIB	The Securities and Investments Board
SUP	FSA's Supervision Manual, part of its Handbook of Rules, in force on and after 1 November 2007
SYSC	FSA's Senior Management Arrangements, Systems and Controls, part of its Handbook of Rules, in force on and after 1 November 2007
TC	FSA's Training and Competence Sourcebook, part of its Handbook of Rules, in force on and after 1 November 2007
2005 FPO	The FSMA (Financial Promotion) Order 2005, 2005/1529
TRUP	Transaction Reporting User Pack, Version 1, FSA, July 2007
UCIT/UCITs/UCITS	Undertakings for Collective Investment in Transferable Securities

PART I
Evolution of capital markets regulation, FSA and the European single market

I
Introduction

> It is not the purpose of this Treatise to make its totality understandable to . . . those who have not engaged in any study other than the science of the Law – I mean the legalistic study of the Law. For the purpose of this Treatise . . . is the science of Law in its true sense . . . But . . . nor should he hasten to refute me, for that which he understands me to say might be contrary to my intention. He thus would harm me in return for my having wanted to benefit him and would repay evil for good.[1]

That is the sentiment. Now, the insight. Law is applied sociology, the rules constructed by people in order that they might regulate their behaviour for the benefit of all within their particular social grouping. The sociological fact of acceptance, by-and-large, within that grouping is, notwithstanding any lack of definition of a 'formal' process, sufficient for those rules to be called 'law' and, to that extent, the psychological reason for that acceptance (and the answer to the question: Why is law binding?) does not have to be answered. Regulation, including the regulation of the Capital Markets, is law. It has legal consequences in that it affects the rights and obligations of the citizen (the regulated) and the Government (the regulator), which rights and obligations are enforceable through 'legal' process, notwithstanding any attempt by the regulator to circumvent or, at least, be creative with that process (2.5.5, 2.5.8). It follows that you can understand the content of a particular regulation or set of regulations only if you understand five extraneous facts.

First, you must understand the social context in which the rules were formulated. Regulation, by definition, regulates something and in the Capital Markets that 'thing' is an economic operation (2.4.4). Unless you understand that operation, the working of the rule is unintelligible. Second, you must understand the reason why the rule was considered necessary in the first place, in other words the policy on which it was based. But that policy is never dreamt up by the regulator in a vacuum. It is always a reaction to an historical event or series of events (see, for example 2.5, 5.1 and 12.4). You, therefore, need to understand the regulator's perception of both those events and their consequent requirements. Third,

---

[1] *The Guide to the Perplexed*, Moses Maimonides, Vol. I, pp. 5, 15, Chicago, 1983. Original, 12th century.

that policy, having been so formulated, requires articulation in a written rule. The draftsperson, usually a lawyer, will represent the rule through analogues to the general civil and criminal law in which he or she was trained. You need to understand that resemblance to properly construe the rule (see, for example 6.3.1.2, 7.1.1, 7.2.1, 8.4.1 and 10.5.1.1). Moreover, fourth, and in a sense this is an aspect of the third point, the rules so drafted will be part of the contemporaneous legal and regulatory infrastructure, perhaps modifying and/or extending other rules, although in all cases building upon that infrastructure and requiring you to have a broader understanding of those connected areas of law (see, for example, 11.1, 11.2 and 12.5). All legal rules are, of course, of two types: 'facilitative', allowing people to do that which, without the rule, they could not have done (in the form: 'If Y, then X'. See, for example, Figure 4 in 3.2.1, and 3.2.1.1); and 'regulatory', directing behaviour under certain conditions (always in one of the forms: 'Do X'. 'Do not do X', 'Do X unless Y', 'Do not do X unless Y', 'If Z do X unless Y', 'If Z do not do X unless Y'. For a schematic example, see 4.1). And, fifth, the rule does not remain static but, over time, evolves in relation to the social evolution of the behaviour so facilitated or regulated (see, for example, 6.3, 13.2). The historical development of the 'living' rule must, therefore, be understood in order to understand its current formulation and its effect upon the Capital Markets.

Stating all of this another way, the challenge with law, and the regulation of the capital markets is no exception, is to understand what it means in any particular context (fact pattern). Obviously, you can understand a rule only if you understand its meaning, but the rules for the meaningful construction of law themselves form a subject in their own right[2] and, like any set of rules, need to be understood in the same way (even though this rule set is largely judge-made law). These rules, which are applied to primary and secondary legislation indiscriminately[3] (always remembering that the regulators' rules in the capital markets are, in effect, secondary legislation), are based on an innate legal conservatism:

> the British constitution ... is firmly based upon the separation of powers: Parliament makes the laws, the judiciary interprets them. When Parliament legislates ... the role of the judiciary is confined to ascertaining from the words that Parliament has approved as expressing its intention what that intention was, and giving effect to it. Where the meaning of the statutory words is plain and unambiguous it is not for the judges to invent fancied ambiguities as an excuse for failing to give effect to its plain meaning because they themselves consider that the consequences of doing so would be inexpedient, or even unjust or immoral.[4]

---

[2] See Bennion *Statutory Interpretation*, 4th edn., LexisNexis, 2005.
[3] Bennion, section 60.   [4] *Duport Steels Ltd.* v. *Sirs* [1980] 1 AER 529 at 541.

Thus:

> in a society living under the rule of law[5] citizens are entitled to regulate their conduct according to what a statute has said, rather than by what it was meant to say or by what it would otherwise have said if a newly considered situation had been envisaged.[6]

As a result, '[w]e often say that we are looking for the intention of Parliament but that is not quite accurate. We are seeking the meaning of the words which Parliament used. We are seeking not what Parliament meant but the true meaning of what they said.'[7] 'The question of legislative intention is not about the historical or hypothetical views of legislators, but rather concerns the meaning of words used in a particular context.'[8] It is in this context that *Pepper* v. *Hart*[9] must be understood. The House of Lords stated that '[t]he days have long passed when the Courts adopted a strict constructionist view of interpretation which required them to adopt the literal meaning of the language. The courts now adopt a purposive approach which seeks to give effect to the true purpose of legislation and are prepared to look at much extraneous material that bears upon the background against which the legislation was enacted.'[10] But this is not a general purposive approach such that in all cases 'a construction which would promote the general legislative purpose underlying the provision . . . is to be preferred to a construction which would not'.[11] Rather, if 'there was an ambiguity in the meaning of the provision . . . the purpose of the provision as revealed by the legislative history could resolve that ambiguity' and, in such circumstances, 'the judge may look beyond the four corners of the statute to find a reason for giving a particular interpretation to its words'.[12] There are four, somewhat limiting, conditions for applying this: '[1] [T]he enactment . . . is ambiguous or obscure, or the literal meaning leads to an absurdity. [2] The statement must be made by or on behalf of the Minister . . . who is the promoter of the Bill [i.e. is contained in *Hansard*]. [3] The statement must disclose the mischief aimed at by the enactment, or the legislative intention underlying its words. [4] The statement must be clear.'[13] Thus, '[e]nacting history is never of binding or compelling authority'.[14]

There are a number of reasons why, certainly in the context of the regulation of the Capital Markets, such a limited approach cannot continue. First, the law is increasingly based on European Directives and Regulations and here the national Court must interpret national law 'in the light of the

---

[5] A further question in such a society is how the rules should be made and this relates to the democratic delegation of authority to the regulator without further express acceptance by the regulated (2.5.4).   [6] *Stock* v. *Frank Jones (Tipton) Ltd.* [1978] ICR 347 at 354.
[7] *Black-Clawson* v. *Papierwerke* [1975] AC 591 at 613.   [8] *Cross*, p. 26.
[9] [1993] 1 AER 42.   [10] *Ibid* at 50.
[11] The Interpretation of Statutes, LC No. 21, 1969, App. A, Clause 2 (a).   [12] *Cross*, p. 19.
[13] Bennion, section 217.   [14] *Ibid*, section 230.

wording and the purpose of the directive in order to achieve the result pursued by the latter'.[15] Accordingly, '[i]n construing Community law operating . . . in the United Kingdom the system of interpretation to be used by our courts is that practiced by the [Court of Justice of the European Community] and not our own system based in the common law'.[16] This system 'applies teleological . . . methods to . . . interpretation . . . It seeks to give effect to what it perceives to be the spirit rather than the letter of the [rule].'[17] The spirit is necessary to give effect to the underlying purpose of the Community as a Single Market (2.6) and, hence, '[t]he CJEC method may be called Developmental construction because in achieving the "spirit" it is always ready to depart from the text . . . It uses the text merely as a starting point, with the aim of developing the particular piece of Community law . . . within the context of the grand design',[18] 'the . . . purpose . . . behind it'.[19] Second, the rules operate on a day-to-day basis in a prudential supervisory context where the relationship between the regulated (the firm) and the regulator (the FSA) is subject to no further legal process. In this environment the intentions, interpretations and policies of the regulator are paramount. Third, this is re-enforced by the current, evolving, environment of 'principles-based regulation' which is characterised by the FSA as 'a shift . . . from managing a legally driven process of compliance with detailed rules to managing the delivery of defined outcomes in a more flexible regulatory environment'.[20] The FSA's views on the meaning of these vague, high level, principles is articulated, if at all, only in material extraneous to the rules (2.5.8). Fourth, when the Courts decide upon the standards required by such rules expressed as 'outcomes' it seems only natural that they would at least have regard to the views of FSA (however expressed). Even if the Court is unable to find an 'ambiguity' within the *Pepper* v. *Hart* doctrine, it ought to operate in this manner because as regulator, and self-styled standard setter for fast-moving commercially innovative Capital Markets, the intentions, interpretations and policies of FSA are the natural benchmark against which the industry seeks to operate and comply. Any other standard is even more difficult to discern, albeit that FSA's can be understood only through its historical articulation and not always in the most transparent manner.

It is for these reasons that this Book explains each rule or rule set (1) in its functional social context and by reference to (2) its original policy formulation and (3) its drafting within the then (a) legal infrastructure and (b) regulatory system and environment, (4) all as developed up to the

---

[15] *Marleasing*, Case C-108/89, [1990] ECR 1–4135, para. 8.
[16] *Understanding Common Law Legislation*, F. Bennion, Oxford, 2001, p. 153.
[17] *Henn and Darby* v. *DPP* [1981] AC 850 at 905.
[18] *Understanding Common Law Legislation*, Bennion, p. 155.
[19] *James Buchanon & Co. Ltd.* v. *Babco* [1977] 2 WLR 107 at 112.
[20] Principles based regulation, FSA, April 2007, p. 17.

present. It does this using the rule itself, such other formal material as may appear within the rulebook, and any extraneous material (discussion documents, consultation documents, policy documents, regulator comments and speeches, previous rules etc. etc.), whether or not contemporaneous with the original rule or the present rule, as may be considered relevant to the understanding of that present rule. (For this reason the reader should use this Book together with an up-to-date version of the rules.) It is necessary to construct such a patchwork because the regulator often does not provide an up-to-date articulation of the meaning and to the extent that this Book is incorrect on any particular point and that stimulates FSA to issue a different view then its purpose has been achieved.

As a matter of style, where possible the Book quotes the original source, rather than the author's summary or restatement, 'as a basis for comment, criticism or review'.[21] Further, because of their sociological/economic roots, the rules tend to have a large number of interconnections so that cross-references to other Chapters are contained in brackets at the end of a sentence, for example, '(4.2(g), 12.5, 13.2.1)'. This avoids having to restate a particular point or argument and the reader should always consider the referenced Chapter/paragraph in relation to the current point. The logic of the rule (or lack of logic) is also expressed through matrices and flowcharts in the Figures, with a textural explanation following the 'picture'.

Having said all of this, it will be clear that, for the author, law is not a search for the truth. That is the province of the physical sciences. Law, as a social science, is all about understanding and assisting people in their social relations. It may also be, in a book such as this, about challenging and stimulating the reader's understanding and, to that extent, a dose of theatre.

> People nowadays think that scientists exist to instruct them, poets, musicians etc. to give them pleasure. The idea that these have something to teach them – that does not occur to them.[22]

Accordingly, the views expressed remain solely the author's and are not be attributed to any organisation with which he is associated except to the extent that it agrees with them.

---

[21] *Hubbard* v. *Vosper* [1972] 2 QB 84 at 95.
[22] *Culture and Value*, Ludwig Wittgenstein, Blackwell, 1977, p. 36c.

2
FSMA and the single market

2.1 Evolution

When analysed historically, any area of UK financial services regulation resolves itself into seven phases of development, each of which needs to be understood for a complete understanding of contemporary regulation and, in this Chapter, is illustrated by reference to the capital markets:[1]

I. A series of ad hoc and, at first sight, random and unconnected rules formulated as a response to individual and particular social and economic problems. In the regulation of the capital markets this phase lasted up to the 1930s. See 2.2.

II. 'Institutional regulation' of a particular type of firm, conducting a particular type of business, in the form of required registration of that firm with a government body, supported by limited conduct and/or prudential rules of the type found in Phase I. Complete institutional regulation subjects the firm to regulation of all its activities, whether or not within the description that requires registration in the first place, although in this Phase, which lasted up to the 1980s in the Capital Markets, the imposed regulation was piecemeal and, once registered, the firm was regulated in only limited aspects of its activities. See 2.3.

III. 'Functional regulation' of a particular type of activity, irrespective of the nature of the firm carrying it on, through licensing by a Government Department and/or self-regulatory body (itself under statutory supervision), supported by rules governing the activities as a whole of the firm. This Phase, represented by the 1986 FSAct, lasted for 15 years up to the early 2000s. See 2.4.

---

[1] These Phases, it must be reemphasised, are not stages in regulatory development towards some form of perfection. They are merely convenient categories for analysis and explanation. The reality is that 'We cannot predict, by rational or scientific methods, the future growth of our scientific knowledge . . . We cannot, therefore, predict the future course of human history. This means that we must reject the possibility of . . . a historical social science that would correspond to theoretical physics. There can be no scientific theory of historical development serving as a basis for historical predictions' (*The Poverty of Historicism*, Karl Popper, Routledge, 1989, pp. (vi)–(vii). See also, Theses on the Philosophy of History, in *Illuminations*, Walter Benjamin, Pimlico, 1999, pp. 245–255).

IV. Licensing of particular types of activity, i.e. 'functional regulation', by a single Government regulator, supported by rules governing the activities as a whole of the firm. This is the FSMA regime. See 2.5.

V. Parallel to Phases III and IV, at a supra-national level, groups of domestic regulators, including UK regulators, set, initially, basic standards and, subsequently, detailed standards for particular activities to be adopted by domestic regulators. Such standards, set by the Bank for International Settlements (BIS)/Basel, for banks and, more recently, regulatory capital standards generally for banks and investment firms, and the International Organisation of Securities Commissions (IOSCO), for investment firms, have by-and-large found their way into, and influenced to some extent, the content of the UK regulation of the Capital Markets, although their separate content is beyond the scope of this book.

VI. From the 1970s (for the UK) the European Union trading block of sovereign States has increasingly moved towards a Single Market in financial services by adopting standards to be implemented by the sovereign States, including the UK. See 2.6.

VII. The future? The Lamfalussy methodology (2.6) seems relatively unlikely to achieve harmonisation of rules and operating procedures across the EEA[2] and, if it fails, the only long term solution will be a single central EU regulator for financial services, with local Member State regulators implementing and enforcing the rules and policies made by the central regulator. This will be something like the European Central Bank model. The question is whether the FSA will be that central regulator?

2.2 Up to the 1930s

2.2.1 The Secondary Market and The London Stock Exchange

The absence of coherent securities regulation is illustrated by the way that in 1909 the London Stock Exchange, being the only real place where company and government securities were dealt in, made a rule forcing members to choose to be either a broker (acting as agent on behalf of its client) or a 'jobber' (acting as market maker, having no direct contact with clients and dealing only with brokers). This 'single capacity', however, was introduced purely to preserve the business interests of Stock Exchange members,[3] albeit that it had the legal effect of managing conflicts of interest

---

[2] For the sheer complexity of the operation of the methodology, see Second Interim Report Monitoring the Lamfalussy Process, Inter-Institutional Monitoring Group, Brussels, 26 January 2007.

[3] *The London Stock Exchange: A History*, R. Michie, Oxford, 1999, p. 113.

in that the broker, acting as agent, owed its client fiduciary duties and could not deal with him as principal, selling his own property and making a secret profit; whereas the jobber, acting as a principal, had no direct contact with the client and, thus, owed no fiduciary duties which prevented such profit.[4]

2.2.2 Primary market new issues

As regards the Primary Markets, being new issues of securities, promoters of companies emerged and were sustained in the late 19th and early 20th centuries because of the unwillingness of merchant banks to sponsor corporate securities issues. Their worst excesses, being the promotion of fraudulent or over-optimistic schemes and the taking of enormous profits out of the monies raised, always without complete disclosure to investors, were stopped by a series of Companies Acts enforcing disclosure in the prospectus. First, in the mid 1840s, the practice of appointing stooge aristocratic directors to the board of the company was stopped by imposing a statutory penalty if the prospectus 'falsely pretend[ed the company] to be . . . directed . . . by eminent or opulent Persons' (1844 CA LXV). Then, a decade later, it was made a criminal offence to 'make, circulate or publish . . . any written statement . . . which he shall know to be false in any material Particular with intent to . . . induce any Person to become a Shareholder' (1857 Fraud Act VIII). At common law a damages claim lay for a fraudulent prospectus[5] and rescission for innocent misrepresentation,[6] but a negligence claim was introduced only in 1890:

> When . . . a prospectus . . . invites persons to subscribe for shares . . . or debentures . . . every . . . director . . . and every promoter of the company . . . shall be liable to pay compensation to all persons who shall subscribe . . . on the faith of such prospectus . . . for the loss . . . they may have sustained by reason of any untrue statement in the prospectus . . . unless . . . he had reasonable grounds to believe . . . that a statement was true. (1890 Act to amend the law relating to the Liability of Directors and Others for Statements in Prospectuses 3(1)).[7]

A claim for negligent misstatements in the prospectus against the company was possible after *Donohue* v. *Stevenson*[8] but (and this neatly illustrates the limits of investor protection in Phase I), given the partnership origins of the joint stock company, legal logic allowed the claim only if

---

[4] *Bentley* v. *Craven* (1853) 18 Beav. 74 at 76–77; *Aberdeen Rail Co.* v. *Blaikie Brothers* 1854 in [1843–60] AER 249 at 252 (6.2.2.3).   [5] *Derry* v. *Peek* (1889) 14 App. Cas 237.
[6] *Oakes* v. *Turquand* (1867) LR 2 HL 325.
[7] This provision was substantially re-enacted in 1908 CA 84(1), 1929 CA 37 (1), 1948 CA 43 (1) and 1985 CA 67.   [8] [1932] AC 562.

the shareholder rescinded the contract of allotment and ceased to be a shareholder:

> A man buys from a . . . company shares . . . [and] becomes . . . [a co-]proprietor . . . His contract, as between himself and those with whom he becomes a partner is that he will be entitled to . . . [a proportionate] part of all the property of the company, and that the assets of the company shall be applied in meeting the liabilities of the company . . . and that if those assets are deficient the deficiency shall be made good by the shareholders rateably in proportion to their shares in the capital of the company. This is the contract . . . and it is only through this contract, and through the correlative contract of his partners with him, that any liability of his or them can be enforced.
>
> It is clear that among the debts and liabilities of the company to which the assets of the company and the contributions of the shareholders are thus dedicated by the contract of the partners, a demand that the company, that is to say, those same assets and contributions, shall pay the new partner damages for a fraud committed on himself by the company, that is to say, by himself and his co-partners, in inducing him to enter into the contract . . . cannot be intended to be included . . . H[e] is making a claim which is inconsistent with the contract into which he has entered, and by which he wishes to abide [by not rescinding it].[9]

The rules of negligence liability attached to what was actually said in a prospectus, but since subscribers cannot themselves enquire as to the company's affairs, the principle of caveat emptor, which did not force any particular disclosure, could not last. '[T]he prospectus upon which the public are invited to subscribe [should] not only not contain any misrepresentation but . . . satisfy a high standard of good faith . . . [i.e.] disclose everything which would reasonably influence the mind of any investor of average prudence.'[10] Thus, for example, in 1900 CA and 1928 CA substantive disclosures to stop the practices of company promoters required: disclosure of the property to be purchased by the company from them and of any property to be contributed by them in return for shares; disclosure of the company's working capital to ensure proper financing; disclosure of commission and expenses payable out of the proceeds of the issue; and a statement of the minimum subscriptions to be raised, to stop the practice of allotting unpaid shares. The contents of mandatory disclosures increased throughout the 20th century; these were initially limited to offers of subscription (1900 CA 30) and subsequently extended to offers for sale (1928 CA 35(1)(iv)) (10.2, 10.5.1.1).

---

[9] *Houldsworth* v. *City of Glasgow Bank* (1880) 5 App Cas 317 at 324–5. This rule was not reversed until 1989 CA 131, although 1986 FSAct 150 and 152(1)(a), by imposing liability on the issuer to pay compensation, had already, in effect, repealed it.

[10] Davey Report, para. 6.

2.3 The Prevention of Fraud Acts

Although ossified by the 1980s, the Prevention of Fraud (Investments) Act 1939, re-enacted almost without change in 1958, was based on the recommendations of the 1937 Bodkin Committee, appointed 'to consider . . . share-pushing and share-hawking and similar activities':[11]

> The practices which have been described . . . all involved one or both of two distinct kinds of fraud.
>
> In the first . . . the victim is persuaded to part with money or valuable securities in exchange for shares which prove to be worthless. In the second . . . the victim is persuaded to speculate in shares and to deposit cash or his own securities with the dealer on security for the 'margin'. The victim believes that his deposit . . . except so far as it may be required for paying any differences will be returned to him when the transaction has been closed. In fact the dealer . . . has [not] bought . . . the shares which he has persuaded the victim to order . . . [The dealer] operate[s] the account . . . to show at first such results as will induce the victim to increase the extent of his dealings and so to put up more securities and ultimately to show enough loss to extinguish the whole of the 'margin'. Since the dealer has not 'covered' any of the purported transactions the forfeiture of the 'margin' represents pure profit to the dealer . . . [and] the client's loss. If the dealer should find it impossible to manipulate these paper transactions . . . to show an ultimate loss to the client, he may plead the Gaming Act [3.2.1.8].[12]

The Committee recommended a system of registration 'and until registered [the dealer] should be prohibited from describing himself in any manner indicating that he carries on the business of dealing in stocks and shares whether as principal or agent',[13] but rejected a licensing system for reasons that precisely illustrate its benefits to contemporary thinking:

> We were clearly of opinion that no system of licensing . . . by some public department . . . was either desirable or likely to be acceptable to the public department . . .
>
> We considered two different methods . . . of registration:-
>
> > (1) A scheme in which the Registering Authority would have wide powers of investigation into the qualification of applicants for registration including their reputation and experience, of granting and refusing registration after due enquiry and of disciplinary control.
> > (2) A scheme in which, certain specified conditions being complied with, an applicant would be entitled to be placed on the register . . .

---

[11] Bodkin Report, p. 5.   [12] Ibid, para. 4.   [13] Ibid, para. 76.

> We came to the conclusion that . . . scheme [1] . . . was not one which we could recommend.
>
> The two principal reasons . . . were, first, the difficulty of obtaining the services of suitable personnel for the Registration Authority and, secondly, the practical impossibility of the Authority carrying out the duties to be assigned to them . . .
>
> The Committee of Authority which exist in various professions and occupations . . . are . . . the outcome of some pre-existing voluntary association and consist of persons representative of those who are carrying on a well-recognised activity in which there has evolved a code of conduct and practice, but a Registration Authority of [this type] . . . would be a body imposed by statute upon persons of diverse kinds and carrying on diverse activities and would include among its members . . . some who would not be recognised as colleagues by those over whom . . . its control should be exercised. Furthermore, by the mere act of refusing registration, such an Authority would, in effect, be in a position to prohibit persons from carrying on a legitimate occupation on suspicion that they might, if allowed to practice, act dishonourably in the future. We do not know of any parallel to this at present existing in English law . . .
>
> As to control over those admitted to the list of registered persons, there is . . . such diversity of practice and variety of business conducted . . . that it would be impracticable to frame any workable code of regulation with which their business was to conform.[14]

Thus, registration system (2) was adopted in the Prevention of Fraud (Investments) Act. It was a criminal offence to 'carry on or purport to carry on the business of dealing in securities except under the authority of a[n annual] . . . licence' (1939 PFI 1(1)) granted by the Board of Trade on satisfaction of five conditions: completion of the prescribed form; a statutory declaration of the answers; three references, one from a bank manager, one from a member of a recognised stock exchange, and one from a solicitor or barrister; payment of the prescribed fee; and a deposit with the court of £500.[15] The Board could only refuse an application or revoke a licence if there was a failure to supply the prescribed information or if the firm or an employee was convicted of an offence or 'by reason of any other circumstances whatsoever which either are likely to lead to the improper conduct of business by, or reflect discredit upon the method of conducting business of, the applicant or holder [of the licence]' (1939 PFI 5).

'Dealing in securities' was closely defined in accordance with the original policy of prohibiting share-pushing. 'Securities' comprised (1) shares in a company, (2) bonds issued by a company, (3) 'rights or interests in any

---

[14] Ibid, paras. 72–74.
[15] The Prevention of Fraud (Investments) Act Licensing Regulations 1944, SI 1944/119.

share or [bond]' and (4) rights in a unit trust (3.2.1.9) itself investing in (1)–(3) (1939 PFI 26 (1)). By the 1970s, however, although (3) included depositary receipts, the definition was insufficient in not covering financial futures or options over securities (since they were not 'rights or interests in any share or [bond]') or other assets, nor unit trusts which held such instruments. Physically settled and cash settled derivatives over securities were within the definition of 'dealing in securities': 'whether as principal or as agent ... making or offering to make with any person, or inducing or attempting to induce any person to enter into or offer to enter into ... (a) any agreement for, or with a view to acquiring, disposing of, subscribing for or underwriting securities ... or (b) any agreement the purpose or pretended purpose of which is to secure a profit to any of the parties from the yield of securities or by reference to fluctuations in the value of securities' (1939 PFI 26(1)). However, that definition did not include all other derivatives. Similarly, while it included Primary Market new issues of securities, and Secondary Market activities of brokers and jobbers, it did not include investment advice or asset management.[16] Moreover, since 'the [Act shall be] as effective as possible in dealing with the rogue and ... as little hampering as possible in dealing with the honest man',[17] there were a large number of exemptions from registration. First, if the firm only 'effected transactions, with a person whose business involves the acquisition and disposal or the holding of securities (whether as principal or as agent)' (1939 PFI 2(2)) because professionals 'do not need protection against fraudulent dealings. Share pushing and similar activities are aimed at the inexperienced public.'[18] Nonetheless, in later years of the PFI, when the Department of Trade tried to operate it as a more all-encompassing regulatory regime, it construed this exemption as narrowly applying 'only to [firms] who may occasionally deal in securities during the pursuit of some other profession, such as solicitors acting in the capacity of trustee or executor'.[19] The second exemption was for an intermediary 'effecting transactions with, or through the agency of' a Stock Exchange member (1939 PFI 2(2)(a)) which had the result that 'a licence ... [was] not needed ... even though [the intermediary] may provide investment advice and hold clients' money'.[20] Third, to 'avoid ... any undue interference with the smooth running of the delicate machinery of legitimate "finance" in the City of London',[21] there was an exemption for the distribution of a

---

[16] Jenkins Report, para. 263; Cmnd. 6893, July 1977, para. 6; 1982 Gower, para. 5.09.
[17] President of the Board of Trade when introducing the Bill into Parliament in 1939, quoted in the Scott Report, para. 209.   [18] Bodkin Report, para. 75.
[19] Licensed Dealers in Securities: Draft Rules, September 1982, Department of Trade, para. 11(ii). The reason the Department was able to do this was that the PFI stated that the exemption did not 'authoris[e] any person to hold himself out as carrying on the business of dealing in securities' (1939 PFI 2(2), tailpiece) and 'dealing in securities' included 'offering' and 'inducing'.   [20] 1982 Gower, para. 3.04.   [21] Bodkin Report, para. 45.

registered prospectus under the CA (1939 PFI 2(2)(b), (d)) and since a merchant bank also made private placements and dealt in the Secondary Market, the Board of Trade could declare it an 'exempted dealer' for such activities (1939 PFI 15). This became, in effect, an exemption for 'wholesale dealing . . . [where the bank was] not dealing with individual members of the public'[22] such 'that the status of exempted dealer is prized beyond its practical worth as an indication of the high reputation of the holder',[23] a 'prized status symbol'.[24] And there were also exemptions for members of the London Stock Exchange and of 'any . . . recognised association of dealers in securities' (1939 PFI 2(1)(a)).[25] As a result, by 1962 there were only 35 licensed dealers, although 20 years later the number had grown to 350.[26]

Once licensed, the dealer had to comply with a very small set of Licensed Dealers Rules relating to advertising, cold calling, takeovers, record keeping, custody, contract notes, option transactions, instalment transactions and gaming transactions.[27] 'Exempted dealers' were expected to comply with the 'spirit' of the Rules, although the Department of Trade accepted that they 'may find that the texts do not accommodate every particular difficulty that this expectation may present . . . Those "expected" but unable to comply may "show cause", on the basis that their own arrangements afford at least equivalent protection to the investor.'[28]

2.4 The Financial Services Act 1986

2.4.1 Reform of securities regulation

By the mid 1970s the defects in the PFI as a regulatory regime were only too apparent and the Department of Trade's inability to properly accommodate changes in the markets resulted in the appointment in the early 1980s of Professor LCB Gower '(a) to consider the statutory protections . . . required by (i) private and (ii) business investors . . . (b) to consider the need for statutory control of dealers in securities, investment consultants and investment managers'.[29] Gower found a patchwork of regulators, ranging from the Department of Trade, a government regulator, to the London Stock Exchange and associations of dealers in securities which were, in effect, self-regulatory organisations recognised by the statute, such that '[i]t is not easy to detect any rationale for the choice of one method of regulation rather than another'.[30] There was a lack of enforcement given that the

---

[22] Jenkins Report, para. 258.   [23] Ibid, para. 259.   [24] 1982 Gower, para. 3.05.
[25] For example, the UK Association of New York Stock Exchange Members.
[26] Jenkins Report, para. 261; 1982 Gower, p. 13, FN 14.
[27] 1939 LDRs; 1960 LDRs; 1983 LDRs.
[28] Licensed Dealers in Securities: Draft Rules, Department of Trade, September 1982, para. 7.
[29] 1984 Gower, para. 1.01.   [30] 1982 Gower, para. 3.44(d).

DTI had to operate under the inflexible criminal law, and for the self-regulatory organisations:

> one of their main difficulties is that of enforcing observance [of their rules] by those who are not members . . . Self-regulatory rules . . . have to be supplemented by statutory rules if enforcement is to be effective.[31]

Moreover, a Government regulator was too inflexible, operating 'at a relatively low level by staff necessarily remote from the scene of action', the DTI did not 'identify areas of concern to which resources should be directed' and, in any event, 'the resources available to administrators, investigators and prosecutors are less than adequate' and the PFI 'is in some respects . . . extremely lax in that it fails to regulate activities where the public need protection'. Moreover, there was an unhelpful distinction between the fringe and the elite, 'between licensed dealers who are subjected to tight regulation and the various exemptive classes of dealers who are subject to hardly any'.[32]

There was, in any event, a commercial need for reform. The Conservative Government's massive privatisation programme depended upon the City merchant banks and brokers to structure, price and sell such issues to both institutions and the public. The Government, as a consumer of financial services, thus had a keen interest not only in those firms being competitive and therefore offering their services at finer rates, but also in there being an open system of licensing for such providers operating against objective, rather than club, criteria. The privatisation programme was linked to the Government's aspirations for wider share ownership: having given 'Sid', as he was referred to in the marketing of one privatisation issue, a taste for investments, the Government had to ensure investor protection by all other operators who might sell them to him. Similar drivers were present in the Secondary Markets where Government issues of Gilts needed to be sold in a more efficient way than simply through the traditional two firms of jobbers and to wider groups of purchasers, thus necessitating dual capacity firms which would lead to conflicts of interest that needed to be regulated. A case under the Restrictive Trade Practices Act against the LSE was settled in the early 1980s. This set in train an inexorable series of events: an end to the requirement to charge investors mandatory fixed commissions meant a decrease in brokers' incomes and a consequent search for other sources of income and, so, an end to single capacity (2.2.1) as they acted as broker–dealers, both principals and agents; this led to not only corporate, rather than individual, membership of the LSE, so as to limit liability, but also to the need for more capital so that they could take positions as principal, which led to the LSE allowing corporate members to be owned by outside interests; and both dual capacity, leading to conflicts

---

[31] Ibid, para. 3.43.   [32] Ibid, paras. 5.07, 5.08. 5.10, 10.12–10.13.

of interest, and outside ownership, leading to a concern that the old club rules would not be complied with, resulted in a need for detailed regulatory conduct rules. So did the ability of such firms of broker–dealers to be part of a multi-service financial conglomerate, with other products to cross-sell, always acting as both principal or agent and thus increasing conflicts of interest. The City had and was changing:

> in 1957 . . . self-regulation was very well summed up by . . . Lord Kindersley . . . when he said that when things were getting difficult in the City he would put his hat on, walk up Old Broad Street to see his friend Lord Bicester, and would say to him: 'Rufie, I think things ought to stop, don't you?' and Rufie would reply: 'Hugh, I quite agree with you', and things stopped. We have come a long way since those days 30 years ago.[33]

2.4.2 Self-regulation?

However, the City was vital to the success of the financial markets and, thus, the form of regulation imposed had to be the least unpalatable to City interests. Hence, it was promoted by Government as 'self-regulation within a statutory framework . . . self-regulation with significant practitioner input'.[34] Gower's original insight, to deal with the shortcoming of the PFI, was that:

> The main advantages [of self-regulation are] flexibility, the ability to deal with infringements of the spirit as well as the letter and thus to ensure high standards, personal expertise in the operations to be regulated, the ability to give decisions speedily . . . The main disadvantages . . . [are] the risk of imprecise and vague rules, difficulties of effective enforcement over non-members, possible insulation from public, as opposed to professional, opinion and . . . the danger that self-interest will outweigh public interest . . . The advantages and disadvantages of Governmental regulation . . . [are] largely the converse . . .

> [T]he disadvantages of self-regulation can best be minimised if it operates within a statutory framework . . . alleviat[ing] the disadvantages . . . in respect of sanctions . . . and the limitations on its authority when that extends only over members of a voluntary organisation . . . Governmental regulation . . . works best if . . . it is residuary and supervisory. The ideal [is] to weld self-regulation and Governmental regulation into a coherent statutory framework . . . in which each . . . perform[s] the role which it does best, working harmoniously together.[35]

The Government presented the structure that it favoured as in accordance with this, but in fact changed the balance. '[The regime should]

---

[33] Parl. Deb., House of Lords, 11 July 1986, Viscount Hampden, col. 637.
[34] Report of the Securities and Investment Board for 1990/91, p. 4.
[35] 1982 Gower, paras. 6.01, 6.04, 8.27.

be administered largely by the financial sector itself, but with statutory backing . . . The . . . [self-regulatory agencies] should be bodies underpinned by statute, with their fundamental rules of conduct set by Government.'[36] Thus, 'self-regulation . . . means commitment by practitioners to the maintenance of high standards as a matter of integrity and principle, not because they are imposed from outside . . . [T]he legislation . . . [gives] regulatory powers . . . to the [DTI which is] . . . enabled to delegate these powers to any body which appeared . . . to meet criteria set out in the legislation. In this way the [self-regulatory agencies] would be given their statutory backing.'[37] Thus, the DTI received the statutory powers of regulation under the 1986 FSAct which named the Securities and Investments Board as the first transferee of these powers from the DTI (1986 FSAct 114(2)). Although a company limited by guarantee and described by the Government as self-regulatory,[38] '[t]he substance is that [the SIB] will be exercising public functions conferred by statute and be subject to the statutory and public law constraints just as if it was a public body'.[39] The SIB itself had residual power to licence firms, but in the main they were licensed by Self-Regulatory Organisations (SROs), themselves approved by SIB. The SROs were organised functionally, for securities broker–dealers (TSA and later SFA), derivatives dealers (AFBD which, in 1991, merged into SFA), investment management (IMRO), life insurance and collective investment scheme (packaged) product providers (LAUTRO) and packaged product intermediaries (FIMBRA and later PIA, which was a merger of LAUTRO and FIMBRA). To obtain SIB's approval the SRO had to have in place 'rules . . . [which] afford investors protection at least equivalent to that afforded . . . by the rules and regulations [of SIB]' (1986 FSAct, Sched. 2, para. 3). This was originally introduced 'to ensure that there is maximum equivalence of treatment across the industry and that the self-regulatory organisations maintain their regulatory standards'.[40] Although publicly the Government maintained that 'the test . . . is that of equivalence, not identity, so there will be no duty on SROs to adopt the same rules, although [SIB's] rules may be a useful guide and, indeed, a model to follow',[41] the SIB Board did not have a clear policy:

> the task of SIB and its rulebook, is to set the standards which the [SROs] would have to match . . . rather than 'adopt' . . . Their rulebooks do not have to follow SIB's slavishly . . . [A]lthough it would clearly be wrong to require [SROs] . . . to have rules identical in all respects to ours . . . it would equally be inappropriate to take too much

[36] Parl. Deb., House of Commons, 16 July 1984, Minister, col. 111.
[37] 1985 White Paper, paras. 3.2(v), 5.5.
[38] DTI PR/584, 17 October 1984; 1985 White Paper, para. 5.7; Parl. Deb., House of Commons, Standing Committee E, 6 March 1986, col. 537.
[39] 1985 Gower, para. 2.09.   [40] 1985 White Paper, para. 7.1.
[41] Parl. Deb., House of Commons, Standing Committee E, 6 February 1986, Minister, col. 149.

of a 'swings and roundabouts' approach, i.e. enabling an [SRO] to have relatively weak rules in one respect because it has stronger rules in another.[42]

This enabled the SIB staff, when approving SRO rulebooks, to apply 'a detailed rule-by-rule comparison' which was 'time-consuming and detailed ... [and] has inevitably given the ... impression of near-paralysis'.[43] It resulted in SRO rules such as the following:

> These rules ... in the case of any ambiguity, are to be interpreted in the light of the rules and regulations of the [SIB].[44]

The resultant structure:

> was ... ingenious ... and presented in a way so ingenious as to amount almost to a confidence trick. The White Paper described its proposals as 'self-regulation within a statutory framework' but in fact the more accurate description of what has emerged is 'statutory regulation monitored by self-regulatory organisations recognised by, and under the surveillance of, a self-standing [Government] Commission ...
>
> The Securities and Investments Board is in reality a self-standing Commission and a quango ... [I]t exercises statutory powers ... and ... differs from the normal limited company, since its [shareholders] and directors are the same people and are appointed by the [DTI] and the Governor of the Bank of England.[45]

Such so-called self-regulation, though, had two welcome by-products for a Conservative Government. It reduced central Government spending by placing the cost of regulation on the industry and, ultimately, consumers;[46] and it distanced day-to-day regulation from Government, enabling it to deflect responsibility in relation to the inevitable firm defaults and scandals.

2.4.3 Rules and principles

The SRO rulebooks, although tested against the straightjacket of 'equivalence', were extremely long and complex and in detail often diverse, partly because of the SIB 'equivalence' precedent and partly because they were individually drafted. They contained masses of unnecessary detail. A good example is TSA's 1988 Rules which defined a Chinese Wall as:

> exist[ing] between ... employee A ... and ... employee B ... if ... the firm has ... rules ... which are ... likely to ensure that employee

---

[42] The FSAct – necessary protection or over-regulation?, Sir Kenneth Berrill, SIB Chairman, speech at the 1987 Banking Centre Lecture, Loughborough University, 18 November 1987, pp. 17–18.   [43] IMRO Bulletin No. 3, 5 August 1987, paras. 7, 12.
[44] AFBD Rulebook, November 1987, Rule 1.18.
[45] Big Bang and City Regulation, LCB Gower, 1988 MLR, p. 1 at pp. 11–12.
[46] 1982 Gower, para. 7.01(h); 1984 Gower, para. 1.18.

> A will not be ... allowed access to ... information ... which employee B acquires ... until the information becomes generally known in the city in which employee B is based.

And:

> 'city' includes any other location.[47]

Covering the whole of the Primary and Secondary Markets, '[i]n light of the statutory background and legal consequences these rules will have for [firms] and investors, it has been necessary to draft them in a style which is capable of legal application. This is particularly necessary for the Conduct of Business Rules, breach of which attracts statutory liability in damages. [TSA] has therefore attempted to be clear and precise but also to give answers within the rules to some of the questions of detail which ... could be asked about the application of a rule and how it can be complied with in certain circumstances. It is recognised that the effect is to make the rules appear to be lengthy and complicated.'[48] In consequence it was often said that the system was too detailed and too complicated and firms had little grasp of the content of the rules, leading to their widespread disregard:

> I do not regard rulebooks running to 900 or 1,000 or more pages as rational regulation. Since the rulebooks become completely uninterpretable ... I do not regard them as a way of protecting investors.[49]

The solution was perceived to lie in 'an alternative and more flexible approach. The intention is that SIB should be able to approve an SRO's rules if they provided an adequate level of investor protection taking account of the circumstances of the investors concerned in the markets where the SRO's members operate.'[50] But this had no real effect since, to 'encourage conformity between the rules applying to members of different ... SROs',[51] SIB was at the same time given power to make Principles and detailed Core Rules which directly applied to SRO members.[52] The Principles were not subject to the statutory private right of action (1986 FSAct 47A(3)), a breach having only disciplinary consequences:

> It is ... important not to have a system which allows [firms] to hide behind the letter of regulation ... [T]he more that one tries by detailed regulation to ... cover every eventuality, there is a tendency for more loopholes to emerge ... It is of great importance to investor protection

---

[47] Conduct of Business Rules, TSA, January 1988, Rules 64, 71.
[48] The Securities Association's Approach to its Regulatory Responsibilities, July 1987, para. I.7.   [49] Parl. Deb., House of Lords, 16 January 1989, Lord Peston, col. 69.
[50] Possible Changes to the FSAct 1986, DTI, 1 March 1989, para. 12. For the 'adequacy' test, see 1989 CA 203(1) substituting a new 1986 FSAct, Sched. 2, para. 3.
[51] Parl. Deb., House of Commons, Standing Committee D, 29 June 1989, col. 597.
[52] 1989 CA 192 and 193 inserting 1986 FSAct 47A and 63A.

for there to be powers backed by broad principles that encapsulate the spirit, which . . . should . . . cover those circumstances where a [firm] has managed to evade the strict letter of regulation.[53]

This enabled SIB to make 'a three part structure . . . This would comprise, at the highest level . . . [10] general principles . . . universal for all involved in investment business . . . [N]ext a layer of . . . [40] "core rules" . . . introduced by all [self-] regulatory bodies . . . Having introduced such rules, it would be for the [SROs] to determine whether and where further detailed rules were needed . . . or whether notes of guidance on the core rules . . . would suffice.'[54] Although '[t]he . . . purpose . . . is to enable a "single common core" of generally applicable provisions to act as the general standard for investor protection, so that the elaboration, adaptation and individual tailoring of the detail below that can proceed without any risk of undue interference from SIB, in the confident expectation that the essential elements of investor protection can be fully safeguarded in the overall result',[55] the reality was that the SIB stranglehold over the shape and content of regulation was merely repackaged. 'There is . . . little overall change of substance in the coverage of the two tiers taken together . . . the Core Rules and the IMRO third tier.'[56] Take for example, the suitability rule (11.2). The original SIB Conduct Rule:

> A firm shall not make a recommendation to a [private customer] . . . to purchase, sell or exchange any investment . . . unless it has reasonable grounds for believing that the transaction is suitable for that [customer] having regard to the facts known, or which reasonably ought to be known, to the firm about the investment and as to that [customer]'s other investments and his personal and financial situation.[57]

This became two Principles:

> A firm should act with due skill, care and diligence . . .
>
> A firm should seek from customers it advises . . . any information about their circumstances and investment objectives which might reasonably be expected to be relevant in enabling it to fulfil its responsibilities to them.[58]

And a Core Rule:

> A firm must take reasonable steps to ensure that it does not . . . make any personal recommendation to a private customer . . . unless the

---

[53] Parl. Deb., House of Commons, Standing Committee D, 29 June 1989, cols. 606–607.
[54] Financial Services Regulation one year after 'A' Day, David Walker, Chairman SIB, at BIIDA Conference, 14 April 1989, paras. 7–9.
[55] Regulation of the Conduct of Investment Business: a proposal, SIB, August 1989, para. 13.   [56] IMRO Bulletin 13, 14 February 1991, para. 11.
[57] SIB Conduct Rules, 7 October 1989, 5.01(1).
[58] Statement of Principle 2 and 4, SIB, 1990.

recommendation . . . is suitable for him having regard to the facts disclosed by that customer and any other relevant facts about the customer of which the firm is, or reasonably should be, aware.[59]

Nor did the SRO rulebooks become any simpler or shorter since '[t]he Core Rules . . . require substantial amplification [in third tier rules] if they are to be made applicable, in a clear and precise way, to the particular circumstances of [firms] . . . to allow [firms] a degree of certainty in the organisation of their day-to-day activities'.[60] Most of the Core Rules were, in reality, redundant either because they merely repeated the third tier rule at a higher level of generality or because they only had meaning when amplified in the third tier rule. Three levels of overlapping obligation just did not make good regulatory sense. And the first two levels often prevented the SROs introducing the much needed diversity into their rulebooks to properly accommodate the different types of business they regulated.

2.4.4 A complete (functional) regulatory regime

Nonetheless, by this stage, one way or the other, it was a complete regulatory regime requiring firms within its (functional) investment business scope to obtain a licence to do business and, once licensed, to comply with prudential and regulatory capital rules and advertising and conduct rules. Moreover, it included rules governing market conduct. Separate regimes had, in parallel, emerged for banking and insurance business, the evolution of which can also be fitted into the 7-fold analysis in 2.1, but are beyond the scope of this Book. Overall, though, the three regimes, covering investment, banking and insurance business, both reflected and encompassed the scope of the markets and the institutions within them, as explained in Figure 1.

Each of the numbered arrows in Figure 1 is explained in the following paragraphs which use the same numbering:

(1) Individuals
Individual citizens are the ultimate owners of wealth in society (+$), either through their employment salaries and/or through their savings and investments made in the various forms of investment vehicle. The Capital Markets exist as the intermediated structures to get that wealth from its ultimate source of ownership, through the investment vehicles, to the users of that wealth, i.e. the industrial and commercial companies and public authorities in (2) below who generate further wealth creation.

---

[59] Core Conduct of Business Rule 16, SIB, 30 January 1991.
[60] IMRO Special Bulletin, Rules Review, 9 October 1989, para. 3.

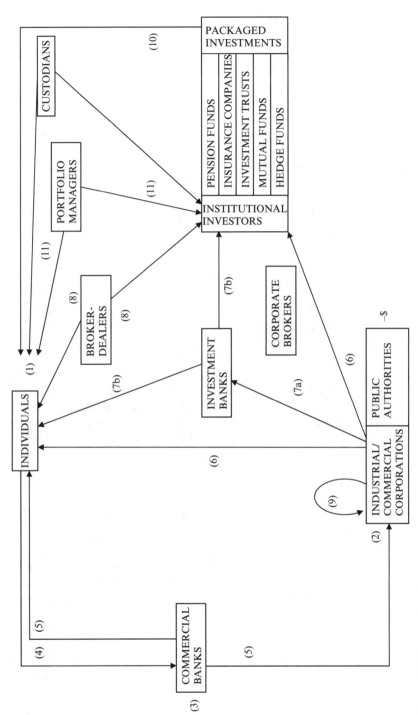

Figure 1 *The capital markets*

(2) Industrial/commercial corporations and public authorities
These bodies (–$) raise money through the Capital Markets, via various forms of intermediated structure, which they use for further wealth creation. In this context, public authorities are not raising taxes but, for example, issuing notes or Gilts to investors.

(3)–(5) Commercial banks
Commercial banks can act in the capacity of investment banks ((6), (7), (9)), portfolio managers or custodians (11) and/or broker dealers (8), but in this context they are performing their traditional role of taking deposits (4) and making loans (5) which, in this Phase III of development of the regulation of the market (2.1), was regulated under the Banking Acts 1979 and 1987 and, in respect of lending to retail customers, the Consumer Credit Act 1974.

(6) Primary Markets: the Offer for Subscription
The offer for subscription is the traditional 19th and early 20th century method of corporations (2) raising finance in either a 'primary issue' or initial public offer, or in a secondary offer thereafter. The merchant bank (now the investment bank) acts as agent/arranger and facilitator of the direct offer to investors made by the company. The prospectus, containing an application form (incorporating the terms and conditions of the offer), constitutes an invitation to treat, while the applicant's completed application form is an offer which is accepted by the company upon the allotment of the securities. In its modern form, the offer may be at a fixed price or a tender where applicants are invited to tender for shares at or above a minimum tender price and the shares are allocated either to the highest bidder (maximum price tender) or at an average price (common price tender). If the issue is over-subscribed then applicants are scaled down either on a predetermined basis of allocation or by balloting, the latter being used to avoid small holdings which are unpopular with investors and administratively inconvenient for the company's registrar.

The offer will inevitably be underwritten, whereby the investment bank (or more than one for a large issue) agrees in the underwriting agreement to procure investors and, in default, to take the shares. These underwriters' commitments are 'laid off' to institutional investors which act as sub-underwriters. The sub-underwriters are found by the corporate broker, usually a division of the investment bank or broker–dealer, which acts for listed corporates in relation to its Stock Exchange listing, and which contacts the institutional investor and gives it a draft prospectus and confirms in writing the oral agreement to sub-underwrite. As a result, the sub-underwriters take the 'stick', i.e. any amount of the issue not bought by the public less (a) any amount not sub-underwritten and agreed to be taken by the underwriters and (b) any firm commitments made by institutional investors other than in the capacity of sub-underwriters. In current practice such institutional commitments are usually found using a 'bookbuilding' procedure: based on a draft prospectus, the investment bank contacts potential institutional investors and obtains firm indications ('circling') of the price at which they are prepared to buy shares ('price talk'); then, based on all such indications, the Bookrunner or Global Coordinator will agree the price of the offer with the company; then the underwriting agreement is entered into and sales to investors 'circled' are confirmed.

The issue will be sold in a series of activities and through a series of documents. First, there may be company image advertising with the public to raise the company's profile without expressly referring to the issue. This can occur both before and during the issue. Then there will be warm-up advertising for the issue (in the press, on TV and/or on the radio) to raise public awareness that it is coming, in the form of general advertisements with a helpline which will allow potential investors to register for a prospectus. A few days before the issue is launched, the draft prospectus ('pathfinder' or 'red herring') will be issued to institutional investors for the Bookbuilding and underwriting process, together with written and oral ('roadshow') presentations to such investors to gauge their reaction. This may be preceded (if the broker–dealer is connected with the investment bank) or accompanied by brokers' circulars, being a research report on the company analysing both its prospects and the potential issue. Finally, the prospectus and application form will be issued.

By the mid 1980s, prospectus law (2.2.2, 10.5.1.1) was contained in the 1986 FSAct, for offers of listed securities, and in the 1985 Companies Act and then the 1995 Public Offers of Securities Regulations, SI 1995/1537, for offers of unlisted securities. All of these were brought together in one regime under the Prospectus Directive and FSMA (2.6(6), (7), 10.2).

(7) Primary Markets: the Offer for Sale

In an offer for sale, the investment bank agrees as principal to subscribe shares to be issued by the company (and/or a block to be sold by existing shareholders) (7a) and to itself offer them for sale to the public (7b). There is no underwriting since it is, effectively, a 'bought deal' or a 'block trade', but there will be sub-underwriting as in an offer for subscription and, otherwise, all procedures are identical.

(8) Secondary Markets: broker–dealers

The activities of broker–dealers grew from their traditional, pre-Big Bang (2.2), roles of LSE broker, acting as agent for clients, and jobber, acting as market maker and principal. The distinction had already started to break down in the late 1960s and 1970s with the growth of the Eurobond market; but the dual capacity of broker–dealers became necessary with unrestricted access to securities exchanges in other countries, the rise of derivatives exchanges in the UK (such as LIFFE) and abroad, the proliferation of over-the-counter or

OTC (off-exchange) securities and derivatives markets and, with the electronic age, the use of ATSs and MTFs (14.2). The broker–dealer, acting as principal or agent depending on the market and/or transaction, may also extend credit to the client in its purchase of securities ('margin lending'), deal in FX and/or give investment advice on markets, sectors, industries, particular investments and companies and investor strategies. Such advice is given orally by Sales and Trading Department personnel who may even come up with daily or short term standard recommendations. More formal research, though, will be published by the broker–dealer's research department in written and closely-argued reports expressing the 'house' recommendation to buy, sell or hold a particular investment.

Linked to its buying and selling activities, the broker–dealer (and the portfolio manager or custodian (11)) may run a securities lending/stocklending/repo service under which the client agrees to 'lend' (in reality transfer, with an obligation of the 'borrower' to retransfer) securities short term. The client will do this if, for example, it is a long term institutional investor and wants to earn extra income on the securities, beyond their dividends or interest payments, or if it wishes to finance their initial acquisition. On the other side, the 'borrower' may be 'short', i.e. does not own, particular securities which it has contracted elsewhere to sell, and therefore needs to 'borrow' them to settle its obligations pending their actual acquisition. The broker–dealer may act as principal or agent in these transactions.

The activities of broker–dealers were regulated on a 'functional' basis, in Phase III, under the 1986 FSAct.

(9) Takeovers

One industrial/commercial corporation (the bidder) makes a takeover offer for another (target). Here, each will employ an investment bank to help it to make the case to the target's shareholders as to why the bid should or should not proceed and, generally, to run the offer/defence and advise on its tactics. This was a true self-regulatory system, outside the 1986 FSAct and, initially, FSMA, until the Takeover Directive was implemented (2.6(9)).

(10) Packaged products

Packaged products comprise any investment vehicle which takes investors' money and uses it to buy and manage investments, the ultimate return to investors being linked, one way or another, to the return the vehicle earns on its investments. The legal form of each of these packaged products is quite different, but they all have a common purpose and, thus, are both investments (issuing their own investment entitlements to their investors) and investors (buying Capital Markets products). Insurance companies (issuing savings insurance products rather than risk products such as life and fire insurance), investment trusts, mutual funds and hedge funds or collective investment schemes all have both characteristics and while company pension funds do as well, they are part of the company's employment arrangements and open only to employees. Since they are not the type of investments which can be freely bought in the markets, they are not considered in this book.

By the late 1980s, the advertising and distribution of packaged products, both mutual funds and insurance, was regulated under the 1986 FSAct.

(11) Portfolio managers and custodians
Portfolio managers take the cash and investments of both individual and institutional investors and manage them, on a discretionary basis, without the need to refer to the investor when investment decisions are taken, or on an advisory basis seeking consent to each transaction. Invariably, in such arrangements, the custody of the portfolio is given to an independent or affiliated custodian whose only function is safe custody of the assets, although it may get involved in ancillary activities such as stocklending (8).

Portfolio management was regulated from the beginning of the 1986 FSAct, although custody only came in following the Maxwell scandal in the early 1990s (2.5).

2.5 FSMA

The so-called New Settlement (2.4.3), with its three-tier rulebooks, did not solve the structural problems with the 1986 FSAct regime. To the Labour Party Opposition 'the current system of regulation . . . is not sufficient. It has failed the consumer miserably, it has been cumbersome and inefficient for the industry and it is ineffective.'[61] Even the Minister agreed that '[t]he issue is not the amount of regulation and the need for more but the style and effectiveness of regulation'.[62] In an attempt to increase the regime's effectiveness the Government transferred control of financial services regulation from the DTI to the Treasury[63] and to produce a robust regulator of retail financial services 'encouraged' the merger of FIMBRA and LAUTRO into one retail SRO called PIA, the Personal Investment Authority, covering both packaged product providers and intermediaries.

But then the Maxwell scandal hit. Robert Maxwell, a high profile and extremely successful businessman, had been criticised by two DTI inspectors in 1971 as 'not in our opinion a person who can be relied on to exercise proper stewardship of a publicly quoted company',[64] although over the following 20 years 'banks and other professionals of the highest reputation

---

[61] Marjorie Mowlam MP, Labour Opposition spokesperson on the City, Securities Industry Update, Touche Ross, May 1991.   [62] DTI PR 92/39, 22 January 1992.
[63] SI 1992/1315.
[64] Quoted in Mirror Group Newspapers plc Investigation under the 1985 CA, Vol. 1, para. 1.1.

dealt with RM, leading politicians were entertained by him and entertained him'.[65] He controlled Mirror Group Newspapers plc and over a number of years used its pension fund assets as loans to, and collateral for bank loans to, other of his controlled companies,[66] resulting in a loss of over £400 million to the pension funds when his empire went into liquidation. The banks were generally unaware of the origin of the assets and he used in these dealings two controlled IMRO-licensed asset managers to the pension schemes.[67] In its supervision of these Maxwell-controlled companies, his 'character was not sufficiently taken into account'[68] and 'there were lapses of judgement, characterised by failure of alertness to pick up signals of possible trouble'[69] because, for IMRO, there was a somewhat old-fashioned 'point of fundamental importance to all systems of regulation . . . All regulation, whatever the powers and competencies of the regulator, depends to an extent on the respect of the law-abiding citizen. No regulator can watch everyone . . . not even every possibly suspicious character . . . all the time . . . [A]gainst deliberate, calculated theft, only general vigilance by all offers protection . . . [and s]uch vigilance was noticeably absent: not one of those with a professional or personal interest . . . or duty . . . made any effort to alert the regulator.'[70] Nonetheless, the public conclusion was of:

> IMRO's powerlessness to act as a regulatory . . . body . . . [T]he way IMRO has gone about carrying out its duties suggests . . . that this aspect of the system of self-regulation is . . . little short of a tragic comedy. IMRO . . . [say] that their part of the self-regulatory system works well providing all of the participants are honest . . . [T]he present system . . . shows itself to be completely inadequate when faced by a . . . fraudster.[71]

The whole episode 'did teach . . . that unless you could produce a regulatory system . . . that would detect the culture of the people you were dealing with . . . you were never going to get anywhere'[72] and, thus, the SROs' surveillance resources were increased 'to stimulate a further measure of enquiry, and no doubt in some cases suspicion'.[73]

Overall, as regards the 1986 FSAct regime, while the Government concluded that 'there is much that is wrong, there is much that can be done within the existing structure to redress that'[74] and it appointed the SIB

---

[65] Ibid, para. 22.4.   [66] Ibid, paras. 2.45, 2.46, 5.18–5.31.   [67] Ibid, paras. 5.5, 5.34.
[68] Ibid, para. 22.10.   [69] SIB PN/026/92, Ann. A, IMRO Report.
[70] Note to Members on the Report of the Social Security Committee, IMRO, March 1992, p. 3.
[71] The Operation of Pension Funds, House of Commons Social Security Committee, 2nd Report, 4 March 1992, paras. 228, 243.
[72] House of Commons, Treasury and Civil Service Committee, Minutes of Evidence, 15 June 1994, para. 1781.   [73] The IMRO Reporter, Issue 3, June 1992, p. 6.
[74] Minister quoted in I'm a believer in the power of fear, FT, 4 December 1992.

Chairman '[t]o review how SIB carries out its regulatory responsibilities . . . with particular reference to the way it exercises oversight of the regulatory bodies . . . as well as the general need to strengthen the implementation in practice of regulatory standards'.[75] The public perception was that the regime failed to adequately protect retail investors,[76] 'that the regulators had not yet found a satisfactory approach to enforcement . . . and . . . punishment of offenders' and that the rulebooks still suffered from 'undue complexity',[77] 'something akin to wandering through a lake of blancmange',[78] all due to the fact 'that the regulators lacked the quality of staff needed to ensure that a more effective style of regulation is produced'.[79] In short, it was a failure of the supposedly self-regulatory system. Although there were calls for a single statutory regulator, 'in the Last-Chance Saloon for self-regulation'[80] the SIB Chairman's recommendations were for 'changes . . . of style, approach and attitude, of relationships; and of regulatory method . . . But they are evolutionary. They are necessary not to move to a different system of regulation but to make the present two tier regulatory system work better.' This was to occur through 'radical changes in SIB's relationship with [SROs]'. SIB would get rid of the core rules and, instead, 'set . . . the standards for [SROs]' together with performance and cost benefit measures, leaving the SROs to draw up appropriate rules. Having 'switch[ed] emphasis . . . from rules and policy to supervision [of SROs]', SIB would take 'enforcement leadership . . . to ensure that the required standards of investor protection are delivered'.[81] The industry reaction was that while 'it was not necessarily praiseworthy to kowtow to the government's desire to avoid legislation',[82] 'what is the alternative? No one wants . . . the 'single-tier' option (in which the SIB would subsume the SROs).'[83]

This only resulted in placing the SROs into the further straightjacket of SIB's performance measures and Statement of Objectives articulated at such a high level of generality that SIB could impose whatever it liked on the SROs. The quality of SIB and SRO staff did not generally improve,[84] PIA's success in raising standards for retail investors was not conspicuous and the overall enforcement record of the regime remained patchy. Thus, for example, the mis-selling of both home income release plans and pension

---

[75] Financial Services Regulation: Making the Two Tier System Work, Andrew Large, SIB Chairman, May 1993, Foreword, p. 1 (the 'Large Report').
[76] City Regulation Tracking Survey, Accois Opinions Ltd., August 1992, p. 5.
[77] Large Report, para. 1.3(iv), (vi).
[78] The Protection of Small Investors, Justice, 1992, para. 1.11.
[79] Large Report, para. 1.3(xii). [80] City Told to Tighten Regulation, FT 3 July 1992.
[81] Large Report, paras. 1.61, 1.64, 3.13–3.20, 4.4, 4.5, 7.1–7.9.
[82] London's Regulatory Mess, *The Economist*, 29 May 1993.
[83] Big Test for Large Ambitions, FT, 26 May 1993.
[84] Speech by Andrew Large, Chairman SIB, at FT European Life Insurance Conference, 30 October 1996, para. 30.

transfers from occupational to personal pension schemes was neither prevented nor speedily redressed.[85] Moreover, as always, cost–benefit analysis in rulemaking proved to be a chimera[86] and no attempt was made to simplify the rulebooks so that when 'SIB "de-designated" the [core] rules . . . the practical effect . . . will not . . . change . . . the rules' since they stayed in place in the SRO rulebooks.[87] And the lack of effectiveness of the regime was confirmed in the mid 1990s with the Barings collapse (5.1) and Sumitomo LME Copper squeeze (12.5.5.1). From the industry's perspective:

> the structure . . . does not provide a sound basis for delivering effecting regulation . . .
>
> (i) the three tier structure of regulation by SROs reporting through the SIB to the Treasury is unnecessary and leads to an undesirable loss of accountability.
> (ii) the principal advantage of self-regulation, that of rapid, flexible and unbureaucratic judgement by peers, has now been totally lost.[88]

Moreover, for the SROs:

> [SIB] has got to acquire sufficient knowledge or the experienced staff to convince [SROs] . . . that anything of substance is being gained by SIB . . . vetting [of SROs] . . . SIB has . . . develop[ed] policy and . . . detailed [rules and] guidance. This contradicts its earlier promise to draw back from these tasks . . . SIB . . . tends to duplicate the . . . [SROs'] own efforts.[89]

The 1986 FSAct regime was doomed. Depending on your point of view, either the SROs were redundant because SIB controlled everything, or SIB was redundant because the SROs exclusively conducted day-to-day regulation. The reality was that SIB had sufficient control to prevent freedom of SRO action, yet not enough to prevent problems like Barings, Sumitomo and pensions mis-selling. And, so, to avoid criticism both the Government and SIB presented such problems as a 'failure of self-regulation', and the Labour Party Opposition was in no doubt what it would do when it gained power:

> We don't believe that self-regulation works . . . [R]egulation is a matter of public interest and for that reason we propose to end self-regulation.

---

[85] House of Commons, Treasury and Civil Service Committee, 6th Report, 23 October 1995, Vol. I, paras. 51–52.
[86] Memorandum submitted by Halifax Building Society, para. 4, House of Commons Treasury and Civil Service Committee, Minutes of Evidence, 20 April 1994.
[87] SFA Briefing 10, May 1995, p. 10.
[88] House of Commons, Treasury and Civil Service Committee, 9 March 1994, Minutes of Evidence, memo by Standard Life Assurance Company.
[89] Ibid, memo submitted by IMRO, 28 June 1995, paras. 7, 8, 13, 15.

> In any event, self-regulation is a fiction . . . [W]e will make the SIB responsible for the direct regulation of the industry.[90]

Five days after it won the general election, on 20 May 1997, the Labour Government announced the structure which three years later became FSMA:

> the regulatory structure introduced by the FSAct 1986 . . . is not delivering the [required] standard of supervision and investor protection . . . The current two tier system . . . is inefficient, confusing for investors and lacks accountability and a clear allocation of responsibilities . . .
>
> [T]he distinctions between different types of financial institution . . . banks, securities firms and insurance companies . . . are becoming increasingly blurred. Many . . . financial institutions are regulated by a plethora of different supervisors . . .
>
> So there is a strong case . . . for bringing the regulation of banking, securities and insurance together under one roof. Firms organise and manage their business on a group-wide basis. Regulators need to look at them in a consistent way . . .
>
> Responsibility for banking supervision will be transferred . . . from the Bank of England to . . . [SIB], which will also take direct responsibility for the regulatory regimes covered by the FSAct . . . The current system of self-regulation will be replaced by a . . . fully statutory regime.[91]

Acceptance by the industry, consumers, regulators and the public was to be achieved through publication on 31 July 1998, with a three month comment period, of a draft Bill in three volumes. These did not contain any clear statements of intended policy except at the most extreme level of generality. There was a Bill, a bland clause-by-clause summary and an overview summary of that summary. Moreover, crucial Statutory Instruments, such as those defining and providing exemptions from 'regulated business' and 'financial promotions' were not published until over a year later and SIB (which changed its name to the FSA) policy, let alone its rules, on all issues had not evolved. In response to the 220 sets of comments received, the Government published in March 1999 a 'Financial Services and Markets Bill: progress report' and a Joint Committee of both Houses of Parliament conducted hearings 'to scrutinise the Bill before it begins the usual Parliamentary steps'.[92] The Committee could

---

[90] Alistair Darling, Labour Party City spokesman, Fabian City Seminar, 28 February 1995, pp. 6–8.

[91] The Chancellor's Statement to the House of Commons on the Bank of England, HMT PR 49/97, 20 May 1997, paras. 12, 16–19, 22. Very soon SIB was also to regulate building societies, friendly societies and industrial and provident societies.

[92] HMT PR 199/98, 24 November 1998. The two Joint Committee reports were published on 27 April and 27 May 1999.

only look at issues at the level of the Bill as drafted and concluded 'that the structure [of FSA] provides . . . scope for an appropriate system of accountability'.[93] Although this enabled the Government to present the next version of the Bill as the result of 'consult[ation of] all those affected by the Bill . . . consumers, practitioners, professionals and regulators',[94] there were still around 1,500, mainly Government-inspired, amendments during the Parliamentary process such that, at times, '[r]ational debate is . . . difficult because the constant amendments make it hard . . . to keep track of what is in and what is out . . . and [there is] . . . precious little time to offer reasoned comment on the proposed changes'.[95] And during and after this period up to 1 December 2001, when FSMA came into force, the industry had to also deal with over 100 Consultation Papers from FSA.

Only some of this addressed '[t]he . . . serious reservations about a mega-regulator with potentially excessive powers',[96] 'the inherent tensions between flexible financial markets and rigid statutory regulation',[97] and the need to avoid 'the likely threat . . . that a unified authority will be too bureaucratic and stifle innovation'.[98] From a public interest perspective, '[i]t must . . . be open and accountable if it is to secure the confidence of investors and those who it regulates'.[99] The 1986 FSAct's structural control of SIB by the Treasury, in that the statutory powers were actually given to the Treasury which then delegated them to SIB, was not adopted in FSMA because 'we should really ask ourselves whether it would be in anybody's interests were the Treasury in a position where it was constantly being asked to second guess decisions which the FSA was making'.[100] Instead, the Treasury concluded that 'there will be a new, strong, framework to hold the FSA . . . to account',[101] which FSA itself summed up as being 'accountable in the public interest . . . in seven distinct ways:

- a clear mandate through statutory objectives . . . which provide both political accountability, and legal accountability through the scope for judicial review;
- clear governance structure: the Chairman and the Board are . . . appointed by HMT, with a majority of non-executive directors; there is also a committee of non-executive[s] . . . with clearly defined responsibilities . . .

---

[93] Joint Committee Report, Vol. I, para. 105.   [94] HMT PN 98/99, 17 June 1999.
[95] City regulation farce threatens to turn into tragedy, FT, 2 April 2000.
[96] A Blurred Outlook, FT, 30 May 1997.   [97] Act in Haste, The Times, 21 May 1997.
[98] Regulation back in the melting pot, The Times, 21 May 1997.
[99] Philip Thorpe, CEO IMRO, quoted in Super-SIB will face problems warns IMRO, The Independent, 2 July 1997.   [100] Joint Committee Report, Vol. II, App. 13, para. 425.
[101] HMT PR/144/01.

- an annual report to the Treasury on how we have carried out our functions and met our . . . objectives, which is laid before Parliament; and an open public meeting to discuss our annual report;
- direct input by the industry and consumers: Consumer and Practitioner Panels . . . enshrined in the [Act], together with a requirement to consult publicly on our rules . . .
- independent review of the FSA's rules and decisions; our rules . . . will be subject to competitive vetting . . . [and] a Tribunal run by the Lord Chancellor's department will consider afresh enforcement cases . . . where there is no agreement on the outcome;
- independent investigation of complaints against the FSA. The FSA has . . . appointed a complaints commissioner . . .
- accountability through Treasury to Parliament. Treasury will have power to commission and publish value for money audits of the FSA and to commission official enquiries into serious failure in the system of regulation established by the Act.[102]

And yet, each of these checks and balances were, in fact, weighted in favour of the 'Leviathan'.

2.5.1 The statutory objectives

The original, publicly presented, aim of the Objectives was to control FSA in the exercise of its powers because '[a] balance has to be struck between the need to protect the public interest and guarding against over-regulation'[103] and they are, thus, 'a major improvement in transparency and accountability',[104] 'a yard stick for accountability'.[105] But their statutory formulation is extremely weak:

> In discharging its . . . functions [FSA] must, so far as is reasonably possible, act in a way–
>
> (a) which is compatible with the regulatory objectives; and
> (b) which [FSA] considers most appropriate for the purpose of meeting those objectives . . .
>
> In discharging its . . . functions [FSA] must have regard to [the so-called 'principles of good regulation']. (FSMA 2(1), (3))

They form only a backdrop against which FSA needs to test any particular proposal under a substantive statutory power, inevitably satisfying the tests. Moreover, judicial review is well-nigh impossible against such statutory discretions that do not in themselves impose specific statutory duties on FSA.

---

[102] The FSA – A short guide to our preparations for the new regulatory regime, FSA, July 1999, pp. 3–4.
[103] Helen Liddell, Treasury Minister, City and Financial Conference, 17 September 1997.
[104] FSMB: A Consultation Document, HMT, July 1998, Pt. 1, para. 1.10.
[105] Joint Committee Report, Vol. I, para. 24.

There are four Objectives, all geared towards consumer protection:

> market confidence is related to consumer protection because consumers need in order to be protected the confidence that the institution with which they are dealing is properly capitalised and ... supervised ... [T]he financial crime objective relates to that as well since consumers want to know that their money is not going to be siphoned off for some fraudulent purpose. Furthermore, if they are to have that confidence, they need to understand something about the nature of the products and services that are being offered to them.[106]

Although not presented as such in FSMA, the primary objective is 'The protection of consumers ... securing the appropriate degree of protection for consumers', being 'persons ... who use ... any of the services provided by ... authorised persons' directly, indirectly through agents or fiduciaries and remotely through corporate users of such services, such as insurance companies, mutual funds or pension schemes (FSMA 5, 138(7)). This very wide definition of consumer recognised the difficulty which a Labour Government faces in achieving its intention 'to preserve ... the regulatory differential between wholesale and retail business issues'[107] since every institution acting in the wholesale market is ultimately using the assets of retail investors. That said, it enables FSA, the self-styled 'consumers' champion',[108] to maintain a wholesale–retail distinction in the content of its conduct rules:

> rooted ... in ... the nature of the market for retail financial services. It is a market characterised by asymmetric information which makes it difficult for buyers to assess the risks and returns of the transactions they undertake ... Without regulation to give consumers some independent assurance about the terms on which contracts are offered, the safety of the assets which underpin them, and the quality of advice received, savings and investment is discouraged ... This rationale underpins the case for both prudential and conduct of business regulation and for the supervision of markets and exchanges ... The ... protection of consumers ... lies at the heart of the work of the [FSA].[109]

However, 'consumers, although they have to be protected, also have a role to play in protecting themselves'[110] so that 'In considering what degree of protection [for consumers] may be appropriate, [FSA] must have regard to ... the general principle that consumers should take responsibility for

---

[106] House of Commons, Treasury Committee, Minutes of Evidence, Howard Davies, Chairman FSA, 8 December 1998, para. 221.

[107] Letter from Gordon Brown, Chancellor of the Exchequer, to Andrew Large, Chairman SIB, 20 May 1997, HMT PR 49/97, 20 May 1997.

[108] FSA PN/159/01, 29 November 2001.

[109] FSA's strategy in applying its powers under the new regime, Howard Davies, Chairman FSA, FSA Conference, 29 September 1998.

[110] Joint Committee Report, Vol. II, para. 101, Patricia Hewitt, Economic Secretary to the Treasury.

their decisions' (FSMA 5(2)(d)). The aim 'is . . . to ensure consumers are better able to make decisions in their own interests . . . [and] to ensure that consumers go into transactions with their eyes open'.[111]

Thus, intimately connected to the social protection of consumers is the second Objective of 'public awareness . . . promoting public understanding of the financial system' (FSMA 4). No matter how good conduct rules are in generating meaningful product and risk disclosure, 'the best form of protection is to make sure that consumers know to ask the right questions when they receive financial advice, or better still can make basic planning decisions without the need for advice at all'.[112] FSA has accordingly launched various campaigns over the years but, given the general low levels of financial literacy, and the modest budgets committed, the achievement is unclear.

The third Objective is 'market confidence . . . maintaining confidence in the financial system' (FSMA 3) under which '[t]he Bank [of England] will be responsible for the overall stability of the financial system . . . The . . . [FSA] will be responsible for . . . the authorisation and prudential supervision of banks, building societies, investment firms, insurance companies and friendly societies . . . [and] the supervision of financial markets and of clearing and settlement systems',[113] thus justifying FSA rules relating to 'high standards of business conduct . . . [and] market abuse' (12.5, 12.6).[114] This objective 'does not . . . imply aiming to prevent all collapses, or lapses in conduct . . . [A]chieving a "zero failure" regime is impossible and would . . . be excessively burdensome for . . . firms.'[115] Hence, FSA's risk assessment methodology (5.6). One aspect of this was covered by the fourth Objective, '[t]he reduction of financial crime . . . reducing the extent to which it is possible for a business carried on . . . by a regulated person . . . to be used for purposes connected with . . . fraud or dishonesty; . . . misconduct in . . . a financial market; or . . . handling the proceeds of crime' (FSMA 6), thus leading to FSA rules on market abuse and money laundering (11.2.2.1, 12.5, 12.6).

Government refused to make the economic effect of regulation into an Objective which would have been sensible because 'regulators do not always immediately recognise market forces. And because they are so sensitive to the constant question at the back of their mind "What if this all goes wrong?", they tend to be conservative in their approach to innovation.'[116]

---

[111] Parl. Deb., House of Commons, Standing Committee A, 6th sitting, 15 July 1999, Minister, col. 216.

[112] Change in the Economy and Financial Institutions, Annual Securities Institute Lecture, Helen Liddell, Economic Secretary to the Treasury, 4 November 1997.

[113] The FSA: An Outline, 28 October 1997, App. 2, MoU between HMT, BofE and FSA.

[114] The FSA – A short guide to our preparations for the new regulatory regime, FSA, July 1999, p. 6.   [115] A new regulator for the new millennium, FSA, January 2000, para. 6.

[116] London's pre-eminence as a financial centre depends on competition, Sir Brian Williamson, Chairman LIFFE, at the APCIMS National Conference, 18 October 2002.

The consumer protection Objective was paramount and FSA thought that 'a positive duty to promote the competitiveness of the UK's financial services . . . sits uneasily with the other responsibilities of a regulator'[117] and 'could drag us into commercial issues . . . and . . . bias our regulation in order to promote the interests of . . . [a] particular market'.[118] All that the Government would accept was more remote 'principles of good regulation' under which 'In discharging its . . . functions [FSA] must have regard to . . . the desirability of facilitating innovation; . . . the desirability of maintaining the competitive position of the United Kingdom; the need to minimise the adverse effects on competition . . . [and] the desirability of facilitating competition' (FSMA 2(3)(d)–(g)). The other of 'th[e]se criteria which [FSA] must take into consideration in setting our priorities'[119] were: 'the need to use its resources in the most efficient and economic way' (FSMA 2(3)(a)), which led to all of the need to control 'the costs of regulation . . . met by . . . firms' because 'they are ultimately passed on to consumers in the form of higher charges'[120] (although to firms it amounted to 'taxation without representation'),[121] the chimera of meaningful cost–benefit analysis in rule making (2.5.4) and risk-based supervision (5.6); 'the responsibilities of those who manage the affairs of authorised persons' (FSMA 2(3)(b)), which enables FSA to both make detailed rules for firms' governance and to absent itself from responsibility for firms' defaults (5.1); and 'the principle that a burden or restriction . . . should be proportionate to the benefits . . . expected to result' (FSMA 2(3)(c)), which again led FSA to cost–benefit analysis.

2.5.2 Governance structure

FSA, the re-named SIB, is a private company limited by guarantee exercising statutory functions. This distances Government responsibility for regulatory failures and ensures that 'it will not . . . be funded through a vote

---

[117] Financial Regulation and the Law, Howard Davies, Chairman FSA, Chancery Bar Association Spring Lecture, 3 March 1999, p 3.

[118] Joint Committee Report, Vol. II, para. 34. The FSA's view on this has not changed: 'I would favour the FSA having a fifth statutory objective to promote competition . . . I would see this as a responsibility to create better, cleaner, fairer markets and not to promote the attractiveness of London as a financial centre. We will do our bit for that agenda if we regulate sensibly and effectively and we should leave others to do the marketing' (Reflections of a soon to be former regulator, John Tiner, FSA CEO, 2 July 2007, ABI Annual Conference, p. 2). See also: Delivering better regulatory outcomes – July 2007 update, OFT and FSA; The roles and responsibilities of the FSA and the OFT, FSA/OFT, July 2007.

[119] FSA's strategy in applying its powers under the new regime, Howard Davies, FSA Chairman, FSA Conference, 24 September 1998.

[120] Helen Liddell, Economic Secretary to the Treasury, quoted in SFA Faces Tough Curbs on Costs, FT, 15 January 1998.

[121] Helen Liddell, City and Financial Conference, 17 July 1997.

of Parliament . . . [but] through the fees that it raises from the bodies that it is regulating'.[122] Although Government rationalised it as 'giv[ing] . . . a corporate structure where the lines of responsibility and the lines of accountability are clear',[123] the reality is that 'whatever the personal strengths of the Board's members, they are not responsible for their actions in the way a company director is to shareholders',[124] appointments to the Board being by the Treasury (FSMA, Sched. 1, para. 2(3)) 'on the basis of people's experience and qualities . . . not as representatives of particular interest groups'.[125] The split of the Board, over the years, is about one third executive and, of the non-executives, half are from an industry background. 'The non-executives . . . report on the performance of their function within the FSA's annual report'[126] and although there is 'a committee of [the Board], consisting solely of the non-executive[s] . . . [to] keep under review . . . whether the [FSA] is . . . using its resources in the most efficient and economic way . . . [and] whether the [FSA]'s internal financial controls secure the proper conduct of its financial affairs' (FSMA, Sched. 1, paras. 3(1)(b), 4(3)), this is, in effect, an audit committee. Thus, for example, in the 2006/07 Annual Report, the 'Report of the Non-executive Directors' is one paragraph long since '[t]he extent of the Board's role and the provision of timely and relevant information to the Board, its committees and NedCo, allows NedCo to rely largely on the Board's work'.[127] The Government would not accept 'the appointment of an oversight board . . . without decision-making responsibilities, to report on the operations of the FSA'[128] because 'it would be anomalous for the non-executive membership of the Board to monitor the performance of a Board of which they are the larger part'.[129] As a result, '[a]ll Directors are equally accountable . . . for the proper stewardship of the FSA's affairs'[130] and the governance control of FSA amounts to little more than that:

> The Chancellor will . . . have the power to remove the . . . Board . . . , but this [i]s a nuclear option, which could have a destabilising effect . . . and would not necessarily resolve regulatory problems.[131]

2.5.3 Annual report

The FSA has to produce an annual report (FSMA, Sched. 1, para. 10) and while it usually runs to a couple of hundred pages, it could be viewed as a carefully crafted, self-serving, document containing virtually no self-criticism. The 'public meetings . . . for the purposes of enabling that report

---

[122] House of Commons, Treasury Committee, Minutes of Evidence, 15 December 1998, Minister, para. 301. [123] Ibid. [124] Frankenstein's Watchdog?, FT, 3 August 1998.
[125] The FSMB: A Consultation Document, HMT, Part 1, para. 1.6. [126] Ibid.
[127] Annual Report 2006/07, FSA, p. 62. [128] Joint Committee Report, Vol. II, App. 38.
[129] Ibid, Vol. I, para. 117. [130] Annual Report 1998/99, FSA, p. 107.
[131] New regulator's powers worry unit trust body, FT, 19 October 1998.

to be considered' (FSMA, Sched. 1, para. 11) are stage managed, with the rare probing question being deflected and neutralised, and Parliamentary scrutiny is always interesting. It is difficult to see how, in practice, the Government's conclusion that 'that is a full line of public accountability'[132] is borne out.

2.5.4 Practitioner input and consultation

If self-regulation under the 1986 FSAct meant anything, it was input into regulatory standards, procedures and processes by the industry. The industry was desperate to preserve this under FSMA, notwithstanding a statutory regulator, while '[t]he Government . . . intends to create a regulator which acts . . . in the broader public interest'.[133] FSA was 'seeking to achieve an appropriate level of practitioner involvement',[134] but since consumer protection was the paramount aim of FSMA (2.5.1), as at least a counterbalance to practitioner involvement FSA 'need to involve consumers directly in our activities in order to achieve our aim'.[135] In both cases 'it is not our intention to create a supervisory body . . . to which the FSA . . . is in some way subservient'[136] and, hence, the statutory obligation was relatively bland:

> [FSA] must . . . maintain effective arrangements for consulting practitioners and consumers on the extent to which its general policies and practices are consistent with its general duties . . . [These] arrangements . . . must include . . . a panel of persons . . . to represent the interests of practitioners . . . [and] a panel of persons . . . to represent the interests of consumers. (FSMA 7, 8(1), 9(1))

In practice, the influence of the Practitioner Panel depends on the personalities in its membership and the FSA because, in formal terms, '[w]hat powers do we have to enforce accountability . . . ? The answer . . . is none except the threat of public dissent . . . [T]here will be adequate accountability of the FSA . . . if the FSA wants there to be and, if not, not.'[137] Indeed, lacking extensive resources, and given that '[t]he purpose of the panel is not to create a super-trade association . . . [but] to enable [FSA] to have access to . . . expertise to improve its ability to perform the functions conferred on it',[138] the Panel 'make our contributions at a much more strategic and conceptual level, rather than getting involved in detailed technical discussions'.[139]

---

[132] Joint Committee Report, Vol. II, Economic Secretary to the Treasury, para. 84.
[133] FSMB: Progress Report, HMT, November 1999, para. 3.6.
[134] FSA CP 2, October 1997, para. 13.   [135] FSA CP 1, October 1997, para. 16.
[136] Parl. Deb., House of Commons, Standing Committee A, 8th Sitting, 20 July 1999, Minister, col. 272.   [137] Joint Committee Report, Vol. II, para. 377.
[138] Parl. Deb., House of Lords, FSMB, 20 March 2000, Lord McIntosh, col. 50.
[139] Speech by Jonathan Bloomer, Chairman FSA Practitioner Panel, at FSA Annual Public Meeting, 21 July 2005.

Transparency in rule making was not always present under the 1986 FSAct, but FSMA contains explicit requirements:

> If [FSA] proposes to make any rules, it must publish a draft . . . accompanied by . . . a cost–benefit analysis . . . [and] an explanation of the purpose of the proposed rules . . .
>
> Before making the proposed rules, [FSA] must have regard to any representations made to it . . .
>
> If [FSA] makes the proposed rules, it must publish an account, in general terms, of . . . the representations made to it . . . and its response to them. (FSMA 155)

Given the impossibility of scientific rigour in what is, ultimately, crystal ball-gazing, FSMA did not attempt to define cost–benefit analysis as anything beyond 'an estimate of the costs together with an analysis of the benefits that will arise . . . if the proposed rules are made' (FSMA 155(10)). At least, though, it resulted in a situation where, expressly, 'regulatory options are compared . . . to determine which of them is most likely to yield the greatest excess of benefits over costs . . . The essential problem of CBA is to identify extremely complex (and to an extent unknowable) interactions within an economy and reduce them to a set of propositions that are . . . realistic . . . Thus a successful CBA might be rather like an impressionist painting . . . much less detailed than a photograph but much more recognisable than an abstract image.'[140] Every FSA Consultation Paper contains a cost–benefit analysis which should be approached by the reader as, at best, 'common sense. This is fine, as long as one does not claim any theoretical basis for one's subsequent conclusions.'[141]

2.5.5 Enforcement

FSA has always insisted that while 'effective and proportionate use of its enforcement powers plays an important role in the pursuit of its regulatory objectives', '[t]he effectiveness of the regulatory regime depends to a significant extent on maintaining an open and co-operative relationship between the FSA and those it regulates'. Thus, '[t]he FSA will seek to exercise its enforcement powers in a manner that is transparent, proportionate, responsive to the issue, and consistent with its publicly stated policies' (EG 2.1, 2.2). It may not be an enforcement-led regulator but, at times, its approach to enforcement can appear somewhat random. One of the few truly self-regulatory aspects of the 1986 FSAct regime had been the fact that practitioners sat on the Enforcement Committees of the SROs and tempered the zeal of their enforcement staff. The move to a single statutory

---

[140] FSA Occasional Paper 3, September 1999, pp. 9, 25.
[141] FSA Occasional Paper 12, October 2000, p. 25.

regulator was therefore, in this respect, viewed with alarm by the industry and, as the Government stated it, '[a] single regulator with comprehensive powers to authorise, supervise, intervene in and discipline [firms] . . . will be a powerful body . . . [W]ith power must come safeguards',[142] or, rather, as it was stated at the time, it is unfair and wrong in principle that FSA can act as investigator, prosecutor, judge and jury. There needed to be a judicial process and, yet, within FSA, the Government insisted on an administrative process, albeit with a right for the firm to appeal to an independent Tribunal[143] in order to satisfy, as a minimum, Article 6 of the European Convention on Human Rights. Moreover, FSA itself 'do not consider that the FSA should rely solely on the judgement of . . . staff . . . [but] cases should also be considered by persons who are sufficiently distanced from the investigators . . . [to] take a detached and impartial view' and, thus, FSA established the Regulatory Decisions Committee (RDC). This is chaired by a senior FSA employee with legal training and includes practitioners and was 'to consider cases in which FSA's . . . staff believe that the exercise of FSA's powers . . . is appropriate'.[144] The RDC 'would take formal enforcement decisions . . . on the [FSA] Board's behalf . . . apply[ing] the general policies . . . set by the Board',[145] without operating a judicial proceeding. It was an 'administrative process . . . to handle regulatory breaches in an expeditious way'[146] so that 'an expensive and protracted hearing . . . involving witness evidence . . . would be avoided'.[147] It was all about 'FSA having an effective capacity to investigate . . . to require corrective action [by firms], and where appropriate, to discipline'.[148]

Taking enforcement action is one thing. But discovering the breach in the first place is difficult for regulators. Hence, 'to encourage senior management to take appropriate practical responsibility for their firm's [compliance] arrangements'[149] FSA made separate Principles binding on the firm and its Approved Persons to 'deal with [FSA] . . . in an open and cooperative way, and . . . disclose to the FSA appropriately anything . . . of which the FSA would reasonably expect notice' (9.1.1) (PRIN 2.1.1, Principle 11; APER 2.1.2, Statement of Principle 4). And FSA gives 'credit to a firm which disclosed an issue . . . in a timely way . . . giving the full facts together with a proposed course of remedial action'.[150] The difficulty is how the firm convinces FSA that it is cooperating, whilst still defending itself and although

---

[142] FSMB: A Consultation Document, HMT, July 1999, Pt 1, para. 11.1.
[143] Ibid, Pt 2, Clauses 50, 58, 136.   [144] FSA CP 17, December 1998, para. 175.
[145] Joint Committee Report, Vol. II, App. 9, memo from FSA, para. 9. It maintains the same status (FSA PS 07/12, July 2007, para. 2.26).
[146] Joint Committee Report, Vol. II, para. 55, Howard Davies, Chairman FSA.
[147] Ibid, Vol. II, App 9, FSA Memorandum, para. 20.
[148] FSA Annual Report 1998/99, p. 14.   [149] FSA CP 64, August 2000, para. 4.120.
[150] Credit Suisse First Boston International, Final Notice, 11 December 2002, para. 33. See also: EG 2.33, 2.34; FSA PS 07/12, July 2007, para. 2.5.8.

'cooperation does not necessarily mean acceptance of the FSA's view of there having been a breach . . . nor acceptance of any proposed penalty . . . a firm . . . [must] still have cooperated in other ways'.[151] Even then, 'there may be circumstances where the misconduct is so serious that no amount of cooperation . . . can justify a decision not to bring any enforcement action at all'[152] and since the amount of the penalty in the first place is set by FSA, it is impossible to know how meaningful any purported discount really is.

Notwithstanding such a system, in the first three years of its existence FSA's enforcement record was not very impressive from the perspective of fairness, rationality and consistency, let alone speed and effectiveness: 'the FSA . . . will chase after technical breaches and accidental mistakes, but when it comes to real abuse it can be the case that they do not understand the detail'.[153] An example was the split capital investment trust investigation where almost thirty firms were involved in mis-selling highly geared equity investments in a falling stock market, causing between them losses to retail investors of £650 million. It would appear that FSA knew of the issue as early as January 2001; launched its investigation in April 2002; proceeded so slowly that by November 2002 it was 'accused by MPs of being asleep on the job'; was regarding it as 'a complex investigation' in February 2003 'proceeding as rapidly as possible'; and, a year later, given the inconclusiveness of the evidence, assembled 'the Chairman or Chief Executive of 21 firms . . . [and] suggested that the firms . . . consider taking part in collective settlement negotiations aimed at ensuring that . . . firms pay compensation to investors'; and finally in December 2004:

> The FSA and . . . [18] Firms have agreed a package of £194 million for investors . . . The FSA has made no determination of regulatory breaches or imposed any penalties. The FSA considers that this agreement is in the best interests of investors, for the following reasons:
>
> - The complexity . . . of this . . . investigation makes the outcome for many investors uncertain (even in the event of successful enforcement action) . . .
> - In the event of enforcement proceedings the decision making process could take a number of years.[154]

---

[151] Enforcement Process Review, FSA, July 2005, para. 7.13.
[152] Enforcement – the benefits for firms and individuals of co-operating with the FSA, 5 July 2004, para. 1.8.
[153] We'll focus on the worst cases, says regulator, Guardian, 7 November 2002.
[154] Split Capital Investment Trusts, House of Commons Treasury Committee, 5 February 2003, paras. 84–86; Review of the implications of the IFD regulatory approach to the supervision of investment firms, John Tiner, MD FSA, at FSA Regulation Conference, 16 May 2002; Speech by John Tiner to the AITC Conference, 5 February 2002; MPs round on FSA chief over split trust scandal, FT, 15 November 2002; Speech by John Tiner to the AITC Conference, 4 February 2003; FSA PN/076/2003, 17 July 2003; FSA PN/021/2004, 2 March 2004; FSA PN/114/2004, 24 December 2004.

FSA blamed the whole saga on 'concern . . . that the legal processes established by the Financial Services and Markets Act 2000 . . . takes some time to reach a conclusion'.[155] 'We would like to do it quicker but there are genuine problems established by the rules and constraints which are being placed upon us [b]y Parliament in terms of the Regulatory Decisions Committee, the Tribunal Appeal and Human Rights.'[156] Or, as the then FSA Director of Enforcement stated it:

> [Some] lawyers [representing firms] behave . . . as though they were engaged . . . in commercial litigation.
>
> It is an approach which . . . ensure[s] that there is no credit given for cooperation when we come to fix a financial penalty. Th[is] kind of lawyer . . . finds it difficult to adjust to a decision-making process that is administrative rather than judicial . . . [A]n FSA investigation is not necessarily and inevitably an inexorable and slow process from information gathering through procedural fairness to a decision.[157]

As a result, FSA tried to 'improve the speed and efficiency of our investigations . . . [and] promote the message that the RDC is an administrative decision-making body that is . . . part of the FSA and not a quasi-judicial tribunal'.[158]

FSA's enforcement process was severely criticised in two Tribunal decisions. In one 'the allegations made in the [Enforcement] Decision . . . went substantially beyond what was justified by the evidence'[159] and in the other, a case of mis-selling:

> The . . . [Enforcement] Decision . . . [stated that] 'FSA has concluded that these customers *were* . . . sold policies that were unsuitable for them . . . ' [The PriceWaterhouse Cooper (PwC)] . . . Report . . . said 'there exists persuasive evidence . . . that . . . policyholders . . . *may* . . . have been sold a policy that was unsuitable for them' . . . [T]here is no indication . . . that . . . the RDC relied on anything other than PwC's Report . . . The RDC appears to have found [the firm] guilty of mis-selling by adopting the PwC Report which PwC readily accepts (in evidence before the Tribunal) did not of itself establish guilt . . . This appears to have been a significant error.[160]

The RDC relied only on the information put before it by the Enforcement Division. As a result of these cases, FSA appointed an internal 'review

---

[155] FSA Annual Report 2003/04, p. 8.
[156] House of Commons, Treasury Committee, Minutes of Evidence, 21 October 2003, Callum McCarthy, Chairman FSA, paras. 48–49.
[157] Director of Enforcement FSA, at FSA Enforcement Law Conference, 6 November 2003.
[158] FSA PN/65/2004, 15 July 2004.
[159] *GA Hoodless* v. *FSA*, Financial Services Tribunal, 3 October 2003.
[160] *Legal & General Assurance Society Ltd.* v. *FSA*, Financial Services Tribunal, 13 January 2005, para. 208.

[of] the use of, approach to and decision making processes for ... enforcement decisions ... [to] consider ... options for making regulatory decisions based on fair procedures by persons separate from the investigation',[161] although it was still 'not intended to provide a judicial hearing of the case'[162] and, accordingly, FSA further developed its administrative stranglehold on the enforcement process in two ways. First, it removed settlement negotiations from the RDC into Enforcement Division with a 'decision ... be[ing] taken by the [FSA] Executive by ... two ... director[s] ... (one of whom would usually be the Director of Enforcement)' for the debatable reason, in this context, that there should be 'increased separation ... between the Enforcement Division and the RDC. That separation would ... be breached if the RDC were to become involved in settlement decisions where the case does not ultimately settle [and therefore comes to the RDC later for adjudication] ... Executive decision-making ... will also allow the [firm] ... to have direct access to the decision-makers during negotiations.'[163] For the procedures operated by the RDC, see DEPP 3; and for 'executive decision making' by FSA staff, see DEPP 4 and 5. And, second, FSA formalised a penalty discount for early settlement by the firm, on a scale of up to 30% depending on the timing of settlement, (DEPP 6.7; EG 5) which might challenge the firm's objectivity in settlement discussions irrespective of the merits of FSA's case, since it appeared that for FSA justice could be overridden by 'the public interest for matters to settle (and settle early)'[164] or, at least, '[w]e believe strongly that early settlement is advantageous'.[165] Overall, one may agree that:

> In the world of regulation, there is always the danger of the regulator suffering from a collective certainty of always being right, which we call the 'infallibility syndrome'. That tendency may be accentuated when the regulator has as many broad powers as the FSA enjoys.
>
> There are two problems with knowing that you are always right. The first is that you might not be; the second is that even when you are, you still need to convince people that this is the case. The FSA is a political creature and, God knows, that process is highly fallible.[166]

2.5.6 Complaints commissioner

FSMA provides that 'Neither [FSA] nor any ... member of staff ... is to be liable in damages for anything done or omitted in the discharge, or

---

[161] Review of Enforcement Processes – Terms of Reference, FSA, 2 February 2005.
[162] FSA PN/028/2005.
[163] Enforcement Process Review: Report and Recommendations, FSA, July 2005, para. 7.5.
[164] Ibid, para. 7.1.   [165] FSA PS 07/12, July 2007, para. 2.32.
[166] Where FSA enforcement is now, City Editor FT, at FSA Enforcement Conference, 6 September 2004.

purported discharge, of [FSA]'s functions' (FSMA, Sched. 1, para. 19(1)) because, otherwise, '[t]he Government considers that . . . the regulator's staff would be unable to go about their business without being unduly hampered by concerns about legal action'.[167] It followed that the Complaints Commissioner, having power to investigate FSA maladministration other than in rule making (COAF 1.4.2(3)) and while 'free at all times to act independently of [FSA]' and having the power to investigate complaints without reference from the FSA and, in all cases, 'to publish his report if he considers that it . . . ought to be brought to the attention of the public' (FSMA, Sched. 1, paras. 7, 8), was not given power to award compensation. The Government viewed this as unnecessary:

> Consumers will have access to the Ombudsman or . . . the Compensation Scheme . . . [Firms] will be able to refer any enforcement decisions . . . to the independent Tribunal . . . The Government sees the role of the Complaints Investigator as being . . . to ensure that any alleged shortcomings [in FSA] can be investigated in a transparent way, not as a route to additional recompense for firms and consumers.[168]

The real reason, perhaps, was that 'we cannot create an open season through the complaints system, allowing [firms] to seek unlimited compensation via the complaints mechanism in circumstances in which they would not be able to get damages as result of statutory immunity'.[169] All that was left was for the Complaints Commissioner 'to recommend . . . that [FSA] . . . makes a compensatory payment to the complainant' (FSMA, Sched. 1, para. 8(5)) and it is then 'for the FSA to decide whether . . . to make a compensatory payment and, if so, how much',[170] although 'mindful of our statutory obligation to use our resources economically and efficiently, the FSA . . . should retain a wide discretion as to when it will make a . . . payment'.[171]

2.5.7 Accountability to Treasury

Under FSMA the Treasury can conduct two types of review. The first enables the Treasury to set up a public enquiry (FSMA 14–18) in the context of 'serious regulatory failures'[172] 'where . . . events have occurred . . . which posed . . . a grave risk to the financial system or caused . . .

---

[167] FSMB: Progress Report, HMT, March 1999, para. 3.10.
[168] Government Response to the Reports of the Joint Committee, HMT, 17 June 1999, Pt. 1, para. 4.
[169] Parl. Deb., House of Commons, Standing Committee A, FSMB, 13 July 1999, Economic Secretary to the Treasury, col. 145.   [170] FSA CP 73, November 2000, para. 24.
[171] FSA CP 93, May 2001, para. 13.3. For the Scheme see COAF and for the limited nature of the matters investigated, see the Commissioner's Annual Report set out in FSA's Annual Report.
[172] Parl. Deb., House of Commons, Standing Committee A, 20 July 1999, col. 297.

significant damage to the interest of consumers . . . and . . . those events might not have occurred . . . but for a serious failure in . . . the system established by [FSMA] . . . or . . . the operation of that system'. The other is to appoint an independent person to conduct a 'review of the economy, efficiency and effectiveness with which [FSA] has used its resources in discharging its functions' (FSMA 12–13), a value-for-money audit, rather than an ability to look overall at how FSA is discharging its responsibilities.[173] That limitation indicated a general unwillingness of the Treasury to conduct supervisory reviews of FSA although in 2001 it was forced by public criticism to undertake that two years later it would review how FSA was working, although the extent of the review was left vague. Two years later the scope of the review was extraordinarily limited because 'the regulatory framework established by FSMA has been a resounding success'[174] so that '[t]he review will consider particular components of the existing framework'.[175] These were: first 'an assessment of the impact of FSMA on competition in financial services'[176] where the OFT only reviewed the statute and not the FSA rules and since 'FSMA largely constitutes a general legislative framework, any direct impact of the FSMA on competition is relatively limited and difficult to observe', it not surprisingly 'has not found any indication that the FSMA has had a potential adverse effect on . . . competition';[177] second, 'possible changes to the financial Ombudsman Service',[178] where the conclusion was mixed; and, third, a review of the scope of regulated activities and financial promotions, which was extremely limited and did nothing to ease the complexity of regulation (3.2, 10.4). Nonetheless, the Treasury conclusion was that 'the range of reforms and improvements . . . will ensure that the UK's regulatory environment remains . . . a model of best practice'.[179]

2.5.8 The rulebook

The Treasury's conclusion in 2.5.7 was interesting in that by this stage, 2004, notwithstanding that it was one of the main criticisms of the 1986 FSAct regime, no simplification had been made to the FSA's rulebook. As an amalgam of the SRO rulebooks, '[t]he FSA Handbook . . . may vie in length with War and Peace, but even so it will amount to a substantial

---

[173] For the first review under FSMA 12, see National Audit Office Review, 27 April 2001; HMT PN/50/07, 30 April 2007; and FSA response PN of 30 April 2007.
[174] FSMA: A Two Year Review, HMT, February 2004, para. 2.3.
[175] Statement on the Two Year Review of the FSMA, Financial Secretary to the Treasury, Statement to Parliament, 4 November 2003.
[176] HMT FSMA Bulletin 38, 27 February 2004.
[177] Competition Review of the FSMA, OFT, November 2004, paras 1.2, 1.6.
[178] HMT FSMA Bulletin 38.
[179] Two Year Review of the FSMA, Statement by the Financial Secretary to the Treasury, 2 December 2004, para. 33.

reduction in the immense volume of current materials',[180] although this was not in practice apparent to the industry: 'the usability, the navigability, the comprehensibility, the out of datedness of the rulebooks . . . is provoking a great deal of irritation and concern'.[181] Eventually, FSA accepted this and that 'we will be looking to remove rules which do not add value to achieving our statutory objectives . . . This will mean looking more to our principles and so more explicitly placing the emphasis on management to run their firms in accordance with those principles.'[182] In SIB's New Settlement, the Principles were intended as merely a high level summary of the detailed rules (2.4.3). FSA made them into self-standing and enforceable (DEPP 6.2.14) rules, 'even if the conduct is widespread within the industry or the Principle is expressed in general terms' (EG 2.21), 'a general statement of the fundamental obligations of firms' (PRIN 1.1.2), part almost of a moral crusade:

> we believe that one should for the most part proceed on the assumption that . . . [firms] wish generally, if they are sensible, to more than purely comply; wish to do good business in an ethical way.[183]

> [The Principles] set . . . out our 11 'commandments' (one more than you know who). Akin to the actual commandments they set out the cornerstone with which the community . . . should operate.[184]

> Our overall regulatory approach . . . is values-based. We feel that we have a role to play to stimulate a wide-ranging discussion on how to raise standards generally, and ethical standards of behaviour in particular . . . Poor ethical standards clearly have detrimental effects. They pose risks to market confidence and consumer protection. They can increase the scope for financial crime and have a negative impact on public awareness and confidence . . . FSA's principles . . . embody a framework of core values.[185]

In this context FSA viewed its move towards 'principles-based regulation as having a series of advantages. First, since '[f]inancial markets are constantly changing . . . [i]t is important that regulation can respond rapidly . . . [so that] regulation that focuses on outcomes rather than prescription is more likely to support . . . [market] development and innovation' and, accordingly, 'an increased emphasis on principles and outcomes is . . . right'.[186] At this level the 'outcome' is reminiscent of the parent who warns the child to be 'good' and when 20 minutes later the child does

---

[180] FSA PN 17/98, 7 April 1998.
[181] Director General LIBA, at FSA Conference, 16 May 2002.
[182] John Tiner, CEO FSA, at Corporation of London Dinner, 23 September 2003.
[183] Howard Davies, Chairman FSA, at BBA Conference, 28 November 1997.
[184] FSA Handbook Development, December 1999.
[185] An Ethical Framework for Financial Services, FSA DP, October 2002.
[186] Principles-based regulation, FSA, April 2007, p. 6.

something which the parent does not like and is therefore smacked, all the parent can answer to the question: Why did you hit me, is: I told you to be good.[187] 'Outcomes' at this degree of generality are just too difficult. For a detailed example, see 9.2. Accordingly, the Principles are sometimes said to represent a shared ethical value, but the reality is that, in practice, they are about as much of a shared value as the Mosaic Commandments: you cannot disagree with them as a policy objective or outcome but they mean many different things to many different people. There are no absolute incontrovertible values on which on all right-thinking (or, at least, regulatory-thinking) people agree. As a result, the second perceived advantage evaporates:

> we . . . take Enforcement action on the basis of principles alone. The key thing to note here is predictability. In order for consequences legitimately to be attached to the breach of a principle it must be possible to predict at the time of the action concerned, whether or not it would be in breach of a principle.[188]

The test here is somewhat unclear:

> we . . . recognise the importance of an environment in which firms understand what is expected of them. So we have indicated that firms must be able reasonably to predict, at the time of the action concerned, whether the conduct would breach the Principles. This has sometimes been described as the 'reasonable predictability test' or 'condition of predictability', but it would be wrong to think of this as a legal test to be met in deciding whether there are has been a breach of FSA rules. Rather, our intention has been to acknowledge that firms may comply with the Principles in different ways; and to indicate that the FSA will not take enforcement action unless it was possible to determine at the time that the relevant conduct fell short of our requirements. (EG 2.20)

In other words, '[w]e have clarified that "reasonable predictability" should not be seen as a legal test, but is a reaffirmation by the FSA that we will not take action on the basis of later, higher standards. We have confirmed that we will not take enforcement action unless it was possible to predict at the time that the relevant conduct took place that the conduct would fall short of what the Principles require'.[189] However, 'the use of the word "precedent" in the context of decisions by an administrative decision

---

[187] 'where firms can demonstrate their own performance (and it is good), there will be less scrutiny and therefore a regulatory dividend' (Treating Customers Fairly initiative: progress report, FSA, May 2007, p. 1). For an example of this in practice, see FSA's July 2007 requirements in respect of 'compliance risk' (5.2.1).
[188] Enforcement: Priorities and Issues for 2006, Speech by Margaret Cole, FSA Director of Enforcement at AIG Financial Institution Seminar, 11 April 2006.
[189] FSA PS 07/12, July 2007, para. 2.51.

maker [2.5.5] is unhelpful; it is wrong to think in terms of the FSA "binding itself" when it reaches a decision in an enforcement case'.[190]

On their own, the Principles are devoid of content, in the absence of an enforcement situation with 20:20 hindsight, and therefore predictability in advance, as a fair criterion against which a firm can regulate its conduct, is a mirage. The firm's value judgement can be quite different from FSA's as it emerges after the event. The third advantage perceived by FSA is that 'firms . . . will have greater flexibility . . . about how to meet their regulatory responsibilities, using their understanding of our high-level principles and desired outcome . . . [T]his approach will provide better quality regulation than would be achieved simply by imposing a mass of detailed rules'[191] because 'the economic and business interests of firms . . . can be aligned more effectively with our regulatory goals through a principles-based approach . . . giving firms increased flexibility to decide more often for themselves what business processes and controls should operate'.[192] It is, though, hard to see the advantage of uncertainty over well thought out and well drafted detailed rules which would not, on that basis, need to be voluminous. A clear regulatory policy to deal with a clearly perceived mischief and resulting in a clear rule cannot be beyond reality. In the absence of that, 'principle-based regulation' would work on a fair basis only if FSA operated it in the following manner. First, FSA must truly embrace risk-based regulation (5.6) so that it is not simply a criterion for the proper discharge of FSA's own responsibilities, but can safely be used by the firm itself. This would require a rule holding the firm liable for breach of a Principle only if failed to exercise reasonable care in complying with it, and the current rule requiring that 'Every provision . . . must be interpreted in the light of its purpose' (GEN 2.2.1) does not achieve this. Second, FSA would need to publish detailed practical guidance on the meaning of each of the Principles, which it avoids doing (9.1.1), although it is now promising 'a new regulatory architecture . . . that helps firms to understand the outcomes we want to achieve . . . [through] practical examples and guidance . . . [s]ome of [which] . . . will . . . come through . . . industry solutions and guidance materials'.[193] And, third, any resulting lack of clarity could be avoided if the firm had a right to obtain a no-action letter upon satisfaction of routine procedural formalities. FSA has always refused to countenance '[a]

---

[190] Ibid, para. 2.5.3.
[191] Enforcement: Priorities and issues for 2006, FSA Director of Enforcement, 11 April 2006. 'Detailed rules . . . tend to address processes and not outcomes. This can encourage a narrow approach to compliance with a focus on the letter of the rule and not the spirit' (Katherine Webster, Manager FSA, at the Council of Mortgage Lenders, 18 July 2007).
[192] Principles-based regulation, FSA, April 2007, p. 7.
[193] Ibid, p. 8. See also in relation to an easier route for FSA to make Guidance: The Regulatory Reform (FSMA 2000) Order 2007, SI 2007/1973; Implementing the Regulatory Reform Order in relation to guidance, FSA PS 07/10, July 2007.

"no-action" procedure [which] would involve the FSA issuing a letter which states that, in the particular circumstances described, the FSA would not take enforcement action'[194] because institutionally, 'US-style "no-action letters" . . . are perhaps more applicable to . . . a generally more legalistic environment'.[195] Equally unconvincingly, '[y]ou have to . . . address the question of whether it is right for . . . [all firms] to pay for that [through the general fees] or whether the firm . . . asking for this . . . should . . . pay for it'[196] although now FSA has bolstered the argument with the inability to waive Directive obligations.[197] Under FSMA, FSA has power to waive a rule only if 'compliance . . . with the rule . . . would be unduly burdensome or would not achieve the purpose for which the rules were made; and . . . would not result in undue risk to persons whose interests the rules are intended to protect' (FSMA 148(4)), but not if 'the purpose for which the rules were made can be achieved in a different manner'.[198] Beyond this, the firm can obtain 'oral or written . . . guidance' from its supervisor if it has made 'a . . . reasonable request' and 'If a [firm] acts in accordance with . . . written guidance . . . then the FSA will proceed on the footing that the [firm] has complied with the aspects of the rule . . . to which the guidance relates' (SUP 9.1.2, 9.2.5, 9.4.1). 'This leaves open the question of reliance on oral guidance . . . [S]imple questions can be handled orally . . . More substantive questions should always be put in writing if only to avoid . . . misunderstandings.'[199]

The end result of Principles-based regulation, and FSA acknowledges in 2007 that it is still on the journey toward it, is reminiscent of SIB's New Settlement (2.4.3):

> Whilst the Principles set out the highest level outcomes we are seeking to achieve, they still need to be underpinned with further rules. In essence this is the framework of the current regulatory regime. We intend to have fewer rules underneath the Principles and, where we decide rules are necessary to clarify or amplify, to express them in an as outcome-focused a way as possible . . .
>
> This will mean a shift in focus from managing a legally driven process of compliance with detailed rules to managing the delivery of defined outcomes in a more flexible regulatory environment.[200]

In the absence of detailed formal guidance, 'principle-based regulation' leads FSA to make increasing use of informal regulatory pronouncements such as 'Dear CEO letters' and senior executive speeches, leaving

---

[194] Joint Committee Report, Vol. II, App. 25, para. 8.
[195] Clive Briault, FSA Director, Speech at FSA Conference, 24 September 1998.
[196] Joint Committee Report, Vol. II, para. 79, Howard Davies, Chairman FSA.
[197] See, for example, SYSC, Sched. 6.
[198] Parl. Deb., House of Lords, 27 March 2000, cols. 555–8. See also SUP 8.
[199] FSA CP 64, para. 4.72.   [200] Principles-based regulation, FSA, April 2007, pp. 9, 17.

firms to attempt to read the runes. But the FSA rulebook was conceptually confused from the beginning by the inclusion of rules themselves setting out a legal hierarchy of types of provision to be found in the Rulebook. This represented a failed attempt to avoid the 'danger that ascribing a more formal status to . . . individual guidance . . . could create an overly legalistic and formal approach'.[201] Each type is designated by a different letter:

> **UK**: 'directly applicable . . . UK legislative material, such as Acts of Parliament and Statutory Instruments' (Reader's Guide, p. 25).
>
> **EU**: 'EU legislative material, such as EU Directives and directly applicable EU Regulation' (Reader's Guide, p. 25).
>
> **R**: 'Rules applying to authorised persons' (FSMA 138(1)) which 'create binding obligations on firms. If a firm contravenes such a rule, it may be subject to enforcement action . . . and . . . to an action for damages [by an investor]' (Reader's Guide, p. 23).
>
> **E**: This is 'a . . . rule' (FSMA 149) which is '[a]n evidential provision . . . not binding in its own right. It always relates to some other binding rule. When it says so, compliance with an evidential provision may be relied on as "tending to establish compliance" with the rule to which it relates. And, when it says so, contravention of an evidential provision may be relied on as "tending to establish contravention" of the rule to which it relates . . . Such evidential provisions are thus indicative in nature: they create rebuttable presumptions of compliance with or contravention of the binding rules to which they refer' (Reader's Guide, p. 23). But E is also used in two other senses in the rule book. The first is to denote all provisions in the Code of Practice for Approved Persons (5.3.2, 5.4.2) (GEN 2.2.4(2)) since '[t]hat code may be relied on so far as it tends to establish whether or not the conduct of an approved person complies with the Statements of Principle for approved persons' (Reader's Guide p. 23). And, second, in the Code of Market Conduct (12.5) (GEN 2.2.4(2)) for those paragraphs which 'specify: (1) descriptions of behaviour that . . . amount to market abuse; and (2) factors that . . . are to be taken into account in determining whether or not behaviour amounts to market abuse' (Reader's Guide, p. 23).
>
> **G**: '[FSA] may give guidance consisting of such information and advice as it considers appropriate . . . with respect to the operation of [FSMA] and of any rules made under it . . . [and] with respect to any other matters' (FSMA 157(1)). Thus, 'Guidance may be used to explain the implications of other provisions, to indicate possible means of compliance, to recommend a particular course of action . . . and for

---

[201] Parl. Deb., House of Commons, Standing Committee A, 9 November 1999, Economic Secretary to the Treasury, col. 809.

other purposes . . . [G]uidance is . . . not binding . . . nor does it have "evidential" effect. It need not be followed in order to achieve compliance with the relevant rule . . . So a firm cannot incur disciplinary liability merely because it has not followed guidance. Nor is there any presumption that departing from guidance is indicative of a breach of the relevant rule . . . If a person acts in accordance with . . . guidance . . . then the FSA will proceed as if that person has complied with the . . . rule . . . Guidance . . . represents the FSA's view, and does not bind the courts, for example in relation to an action for damages' (Reader's Guide, p. 22).

D: 'Directions and requirements given under . . . the Act . . . [which] are binding upon the person . . . to whom they are addressed' (Reader's Guide, p. 24).

P: The Statements of Principle for Approved Persons (5.3.2, 5.4.2) (Reader's Guide, p. 25).

C: In the Market Abuse Code, 'descriptions of behaviour that . . . do not amount to market abuse' (Reader's Guide, p. 25).

Short of an enforcement action when it may be necessary to plead the different legal effect of such provisions, this is too difficult a scheme to operate if only because, in fact, all Rulebook material is drafted identically, and simply given a different designation.[202] Accordingly, in this Book explanations of rules etc. are given, and citations noted, without such distinctions: all such material represents the regulator's policy and expectation. Moreover, this hierarchy makes no mention at all of two further types of material. First, FSA statements in Discussion Papers, Consultation Papers, Policy Statements, Market Watch ('This is not FSA guidance'), LIST! ('This is not FSA guidance'), enforcement cases or senior executive speeches all of which often (particularly as a result of MiFID and the need for CESR agreement before FSA will make any formal statements (2.6)) contain the real FSA 'guidance'. '[S]uch materials are intended to illustrate ways . . . in which a person can comply with the . . . rules . . . and . . . are . . . potentially relevant to an enforcement case . . .

(1) To help assess whether it could reasonably have been understood or predicted at the time that the conduct in question fell below the standards required by the Principles.

---

[202] That said, sometimes nuances are drawn. For example, in Providers and Distributors Regulatory Guide Instrument 2007, which consists entirely of Guidance, FSA provides the following 'Interpretation: In this Guide we use "must" where an action is required by a Principle or detailed Rule. We use "should" where we think a firm ought to consider a particular action (not specified in a Principle or Rule) at a reasonably high level to comply with a Principle (not that they should follow a detailed a prescribed [sic] course of action). We use "may" where an action is only one of a number of ways of complying with a Principle' (para. 1.10).

(2) To explain the regulatory context.
(3) To inform a view of the overall seriousness of the breaches . . .
(4) To inform the consideration of a firm's defence that the FSA was judging the firm on the basis of retrospective standards.
(5) To be considered as part of the expert or supervisory statements in relation to the relevant standards at the time. (EG 2.23, 2.25)

As a result, 'The FSA will not take action against a person for behaviour that is considers to be in line with guidance, other materials published by the FSA in support of the Handbook or FSA-confirmed Industry Guidance, which were current at the time of the behaviour in question' (DEPP 6.2.1(4)). This is the formal statement of 'reliance' in FSA's Rulebook; but it has also stated publicly that 'firms can rely on all the material we publish. This is fundamental to our approach. So if a firm takes a reasonable course of action which we have indicated, in the general public material or in a specific individual exchange (such as a supervisory letter), as being in compliance with a rule, then we will not take action against the firm for not having complied with the rule.'[203] Hence, the reliance placed in this Book upon such statements. In practice, though, the need to interpret rules in the context of business activities has been (partially) replaced with the need to discover 'other materials published . . . in support of the Handbook' and then interpret their relevance. For this reason alone, classic methods of statutory interpretation cannot be used (Chapter 1), although it hardly increases legal certainty.

Second, also connected with FSA's self-imposed inability to make guidance in the absence of CESR, as part of 'our intention to move towards a more principles-based approach to regulation . . . [w]e acknowledge that the industry may wish to create its own guidance to assist firms that want more information on our principles and high level rules'.[204] FSA is then faced with 'three conceptual ways that we can recognise guidance, codes or standards developed by the industry', each 'hav[ing] different legal effects . . . Safe harbour . . . [which] has an effect on the FSA and potentially third parties . . . [such that w]e would need to create rules . . . to give Industry Guidance this effect . . . . Sturdy breakwater . . . prevent[s] us from taking action but does not affect the rights of third parties . . . Our . . . guidance has this effect . . . [and] to create a sturdy breakwater we . . . need to . . . make a public statement . . . of recognition . . . Implicit recognition . . . has no legal effect on the FSA or anyone else . . . [and] is implicit in our

---

[203] Principles-based regulation, FSA, April 2007, p. 10.
[204] FSA DP 06/5, November 2006, paras. 1.1, 1.3. The example in the context of MiFID is 'MiFID Connect' (FSA/PN/062/2007), whose publications are a 'sturdy breakwater'. A number of other trade associations have provided guidance to their members which in the absence of any recognition from FSA has no legal effect. See, for example, MiFID guidance produced by the Investment Management Association (IMA) and the Alternative Investment Management Association (AIMA).

inaction.' However, 'we ... [will] limit the endorsement of Industry Guidance to FSA confirmation only', i.e. the sturdy breakwater.[205]

2.6 European Union Directives

The Treaty of Rome, establishing the European Economic Community, provided that:

> The Community shall have as its task, by establishing a common market and progressively approximating the economic policies of Member States, to promote throughout the community a harmonious development of economic activities, a continuous and balanced expansion, an increase in stability, an accelerated raising of the standard of living and closer relations between the States belonging to it.

This required 'the approximation of the laws of Member States ... for the proper functioning of the common market' so that 'restrictions on the freedom of establishment of nationals of a Member State ... [and] restrictions on freedom to provide services within the Community shall be progressively abolished',[206] the conditions upon which such freedoms were granted, and the rules to which firms exercising them were subject, being merely the harmonised pan-EU 'comfort' for the individual sovereign Member States giving up their individual rules. In the 1960s and 1970s progress was slow because each Member State had a veto and the European Commission tried to obtain complete and detailed harmonisation of Member States' laws. In the 1980s a resurgence of enthusiasm for a Single Market resulted in its June 1985 White Paper which specified nearly 300 measures to be completed by the end of 1992, the 1986 Single European Act which provided for their adoption by qualified majority voting of Member States and a principle of Home Member State supervision of firms based on 'mutual recognition. The directives would lay down ... basic minimum requirements which would be obligatory in all Member States.'[207] Capital movements had already been liberalised as a necessary precursor to opening up domestic markets to outside service providers[208] and the 1992 Programme resulted in Directives relating to securities offerings,[209] banking services,[210] investment firms' services[211] and markets.[212] However, '[r]eality has not been fully aligned with expectations ... [and] mutual recognition of national rules has

---

[205] FSA DP 06/5, November 2006, paras. 2.3–2.5, 2.7, 2.18; FSA PS 07/16, September 2007, para 2.12; DEPP 6.2.1(4); EG 2.28–2.30. CESR guidance is, in effect, a 'sturdy breakwater' (COBS 2.3.1 (3), Note; FSA PS 07/15, paras. 1.3, 2.1).

[206] Treaty of Rome, Arts 2, 3(h), 52, 59.   [207] SD, TSA, March 1989, p. 8.

[208] Directives 1960/07/12, 1963/21/EEC, 1986/566/EEC, 1988/361/EEC.

[209] The Unlisted Securities and Mutual Recognition of Listing Particulars Directives, supplementing the late 1970s/early 1980s Listing Particulars, Admission and Interim Reports Directives.   [210] The Second Banking Coordination Directive.   [211] ISD.

[212] The Insider Dealing Directive (12.2).

had a limited effect in stimulating . . . regulatory . . . convergence[213] such that '[d]ivergent approaches in implementing common rules need to be . . . eliminate[d]',[214] the Commission's initial, failed, attempt being through the issue of guidance on when Member States could deviate from Directive standards in the 'general good'.[215] The Commission then adopted a Financial Services Action Plan for over 40 Directives including a revised ISD which 'reconsider[ed] the extent to which Host country application of business conduct rules . . . which is the basic premise of the ISD . . . is in keeping with the needs of an integrated securities market', a new Prospectus Directive because '[t]he application of additional national requirements has thwarted the mutual recognition of prospectuses', a Collateral Directive for '[t]he mutual . . . enforceability of cross-border collateral [which] is indispensable for the stability of the EU financial system for a[n] . . . integrated securities settlement structure', a Takeover Directive to 'provide . . . legal underpinning for protection of minority shareholdings' and, overlaying all the detailed measures, '[t]here is . . . a pressing need for increased collaboration, monitoring and better understanding . . . between front-line authorities'.[216] Accordingly, the Commission appointed a Committee of Wise Men chaired by Baron Lamfalussy to 'propose . . . adapting current practices . . . to ensure greater convergence and co-operation in day-to-day implementation'[217] and they produced the current four stage process: at Level 1, a Framework Directive is made under the usual procedure representing '[a] . . . political level . . . text . . . [which] should not be detailed, but concentrate on the key principles'; at Level 2, based on advice from CESR, the Commission makes a further Directive and/or Regulation 'on the technical implementing details . . . [which] provide the basis for the practical implementation . . . of mutual recognition . . . binding on all Member States' which then formally implement it into their domestic laws; at Level 3 CESR adopt common guidance on the Level 1 and 2 measures 'with a view to ensuring consistent and equivalent transposition of the[m]' with the aim, ultimately, of '[s]upervisory convergence . . . in response to supervision and enforcement action';[218] and, at Level 4, there is a common Commission approach to enforcement of the rules.[219]

To achieve pan-EU uniformity and consistency, the Level 1 and 2 measures 'typically contain a high level of prescription . . . inevitably

---

[213] Challenges of financial integration in the post-FSA period, Tommasu Padoa-Schioppa, EC Conference on Financial Integration, Brussels, 23 June 2004, pp. 2–3.
[214] Financial Services: Building a Framework for Action, EC, 1998, para. 13.
[215] See, for example, the EC's Interpretative Communication on the Second Banking Directive, OJ 1997, C 209/6.
[216] EC, COM (1999) 232, 11 May 1999, pp. 1, 5, 6, 8, 9, 13, 14.
[217] Initial Report of the Committee of Wise Men, 9 November 2000, Ann. 1, para. 3.
[218] CESR/04–104b, April 2004.
[219] Initial Report of the Committee of Wise Men, pp 23–26; Final Report 15 February 2001.

leav[ing] less room for national legislative discretion'[220] and, as a result, they 'should be copied out [in domestic rules] . . . whether or not the provisions are clear . . . [I]t risks a breach of Treaty obligations to seek to give such provisions greater precision (to elaborate) because that undermines that uniformity and . . . defeats the aim . . . of the Directive . . . [and] give[s] false comfort because . . . the [European] Court [of Justice] is not bound by such words.'[221] In addition, this makes sense because 'a national court hearing a case which falls within the scope of [a] Directive . . . is required to interpret its national law in the light of the wording and the purpose of that directive',[222] although no particular language version of the Directive has precedence and they can, on occasion, differ in the meaning of particular provisions.[223] Accordingly, FSA's approach 'is . . . to . . . use "intelligent copy-out" for financial services directives; that is, our rules will generally be based on copied-out directive text to avoid placing any unintended additional obligations on firms [and to] . . . propose measures that go beyond directive requirements [i.e. are 'super-equivalent] only when these are consistent with directive requirements and are justified in their own right, by using market failure and cost–benefit analysis'.[224]

On the one hand, 'copy out' with a reluctance to add any guidance unless it is CESR guidance at Level 3, given the usual form of drafting of these EU measures at a relatively high level of generality, supports FSA's drive towards 'principle-based regulation' and suffers from all of its defects (2.5.8). That said, the interpretation of EU-derived rules has to achieve the purposes of the Single Market and EU integration. And yet, on the other hand, FSA can retain super-equivalent/gold plating provisions when it suits it to have more rules, notwithstanding that, in contrast to the traditional Directive approach of minimum standards which can be elaborated by Member States in the 'general good', under the FSAP there started to emerge maximal Directives prohibiting Member States imposing further rules. Thus, under MiFID, 'Member States . . . should not add supplementary . . . rules when transposing . . . this Directive, save where this Directive makes express provision to this effect' and, even then, 'Any [such] decision . . . should be made with proper regard to the objectives of th[is] Directive to remove barriers to the cross-border provision of investment services by harmonising the . . . requirements for investment firms', the specific

---

[220] John Tiner, FSA CEO, at BBA's Annual Supervision Conference, 8 October 2004. For costs, see The overall impact of MIFID, FSA, November 2006.
[221] Implementation of EU Legislation, a Study for the Foreign & Commonwealth Office, Robin Bellis, November 2003, pp. 28–29. See also, Transposition Guide, Department for Business, September 2007, pp. 24, 26, 28.
[222] *Marleasing SA* v. *Alimientacion SA*, Case C-106/89 [1990] ECR 1–4135. See, further, Chapter 1.   [223] See, for example, *Koschniske*, Case C-9/79.
[224] FSA CP 06/19, para. 2.11.

power being that 'Member States may . . . impose requirements additional to those in this Directive only in those exceptional cases where such requirements are objectively justified and proportionate so as to address specific risks to investor protection or to market integrity that are not adequately addressed by this Directive' (Level 2 Directive, Recitals 7 and 10, Art. 4(1)).[225] There are many examples of such super-equivalent FSA rules which are referred to in this Book.

The essential methodology now used to achieve the Single Market, or trading block, is illustrated by Figure 2.

The lettered references in Figure 2 are explained in the following paragraphs which use the same lettering:

(A) Directive/Regulation
One or more Directives and/or Regulations, whether or not under the Lamfalussy procedure, set out the common standards and, under that procedure, detailed implementation to be achieved by all Member States.

(B) Home and Host State implementation
The Directive(s)/Regulation(s) are then implemented by each Member State, in its capacity as both Home Member State (licensing firms within the Directive and up to the prudential standards required by it) and Host Member State (being the place where firms licensed in other (Home) Member States provide services either on a cross-border services basis and/or through a branch established in the Host State).

(C) Services passport
The firm licensed in its Home State can freely do business in or into any other (Host) State, either cross-border from its Home State (Ca) or through a branch established in the Host State (Cb). In neither case can the Host State itself impose a licensing requirement on the firm and the split of responsibilities, as regards the supervision of the firm, between Home and Host State depends on the particular Directive. Usually the Home State, as licensing authority, has responsibility for the infrastructure, prudential, systems and controls and regulatory capital rules binding upon the firm and, whereas under the ISD the Host State of the branch made the conduct rules binding the firm, under MiFID these are made by the Host State.

(D) Product passport
In a similar way to the Services Passport, Products (Securities and Mutual Funds) complying with the Home State implementation of the relevant Directive, when issued by a product provider located in that Home State, can be freely sold into any other (Host) State (Da).

---

[225] For the intended limited effect, see, for example: European Commission ESC Working Document 64/2006, 8 November 2006; FSA PS 07/14, Chapter 1.

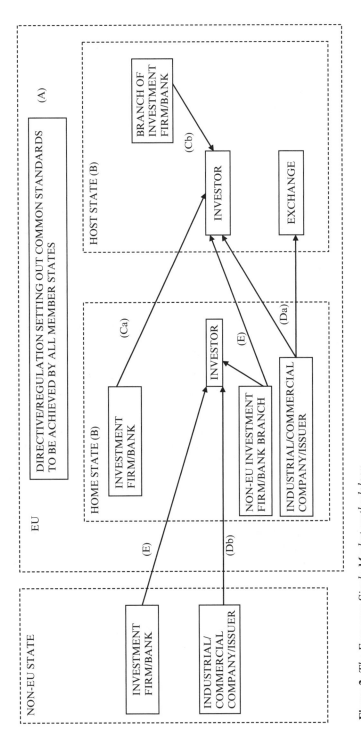

Figure 2. *The European Single Market methodology*

(E) Position of non-EU firms and banks
The Treaty of Rome contains rights only for EU persons, both individuals and EU formed/organised partnerships and corporations. Firms formed/organised elsewhere obtain no passporting rights under EU Directives, even through licensed branches established in a Member State (E). The only exception to this is the issue of securities and the Product Passport (Db).

(F) Market hygiene
Overlying the activities of firms and issuers are a series of Directives aimed at achieving so-called market hygiene and relating to matters such as anti-money laundering (11.2.2.1) and market abuse (12.5).

This methodology has been adopted for each of the commercial activities in the markets referred to in Figure 1 in 2.4.4. Thus, using the same numbering as in Figure 1:

(3)–(5) Commercial banks
The activities of commercial banks in deposit-taking, lending and (in terms of licensing) investment business are subject to the BCD.

(6), (7) Primary Markets: the Offer for Subscription and the Offer for Sale
Following the patchwork of earlier, failed, attempts at mutual recognition of prospectuses in the 1980 Listing Particulars Directive and its amending Directives[226] and the 1989 Public Offers Directive and its amendment,[227] the 2003 Prospectus Directive, applying to both listed and unlisted offers, was clear:

> Where an offer to the public [10.2] or admission to trading . . . is provided for in one or more Member States . . . the Prospectus approved by the home Member State . . . shall be valid for the public offer or the admission to trading in any number of host Member States, provided that the competent authority of each Member State is notified . . . [H]ost Members States shall not undertake any approval or administrative procedure relating to prospectuses . . . [T]he Prospectus shall be drawn up either in a language accepted by . . . [the host] Member State . . . or in a language customary in the sphere of international finance [i.e. English], at the choice of the issuer . . . The . . . host Member State may only require that the summary [at the beginning of the Prospectus] be translated into its official language. (2003 Prospectus Directive, Arts. 17(1), 19(2))

And, unlike earlier Directives where it was unclear whether non-EU issuers could benefit from mutual recognition, it was clearly stated that such an issuer can elect for a Home Member State, being 'the . . . [place of] first

---

[226] Directives 1987/345/EEC; 1994/18/EC; 2001/34/EC.
[227] Directive 1990/211/EEC.

public offer after . . . the Directive comes into force (31 December 2003)'[228] and, having complied with that State's implementation of the Directive, rely on the passporting provisions ((Db) in Figure 2) (2003 Prospectus Directive, Art. 20; Prospectus Rules 4.1, 4.2).

(8), (11) Secondary Markets: broker–dealers, portfolio managers and custodians
Initially subject to the ISD, these firms are, together with the investment activities of commercial banks, subject to MiFID and the methodology in (B), (C) and (E) in Figure 2.

(9) Takeovers
The old self-regulatory regime of the Takeover Panel remains in place albeit subject to a statutory underpinning as a result of the Takeover Directive.[229]

(10) Packaged products
European regulation distinguishes between UCITS (Undertakings for Collective Investment in Transferable Securities) which, upon satisfaction of the Home State's implementation of rules governing the corporate governance and investment powers of the scheme, can be publicly marketed throughout the EEA[230] under the methodology in (D) in Figure 2, and other collective investment schemes, which do not satisfy these conditions and can be subjected to any degree of regulation by the State in or into which they are marketed (10.5.6.1).

---

[228] LIST!, Issue 10, FSA, June 2005. For passporting of prospectuses generally, see UKLA publications Factsheet No. 4, FSA, October 2006.

[229] See Takeover Directive of 21 April 2004; Company Law Implementation of the European Directive on Takeover Bids, DTI CD, January 2005; Implementation of the Takeover Directive, Takeover Panel, CP, 18 November 2005; Panel Statement 21 April 2006; Panel Statement 2005/10; SI 2006/1183; DTI Information Note P/2006/77, 5 April 2007.   [230] See Directives of 20 December 1985 and two of 21 January 2002.

PART II
Licensing and rule application

3
Licensing

3.1 Analysing the application of regulations

The Anglo-Saxon approach to the embodiment of policy into Capital Markets 'functional' regulation follows a uniform pattern: first, define the area to be regulated in terms of products and market activities in a wide-ranging, rather catch-all, manner; second, graft on a series, and often a large series, of relatively narrow and closely defined exceptions to be removed from the area to be regulated; third, define the territorial application of the regulations as any activity that touches the UK, subject to the overwhelming economic imperative of maintaining London as a global centre for financial markets; fourth, overlay the EU Single Market methodology (2.6); and, fifth, specify the consequences of non-compliance with the applicable regulation as, where considered appropriate, criminal, administrative and/or civil sanctions. This pattern was established in the 1986 FSAct (2.4) and continued with the implementation of the ISD. However, that Directive had a much narrower scope to regulation, and used completely different language, from the 1986 FSAct. Nonetheless, the UK Government refused to redraft the scope provisions of the 1986 FSAct or to narrow its scope, initially using a 'general good' argument,[1] but in the end the debatable justification that '[t]he terminology and scope of ... services [under the ISD] is not identical to those ... covered by the FS [Act], although they do not represent a significant widening. It is not the Government's intention to align the definitions fully.'[2] Similarly, although MiFID has a wider scope than the ISD and is much nearer to the scope of the RAO, while 'a more radical revision of the RAO ... would have incorporated language from the Directive more clearly into the ... RAO [, the Treasury did] ... not ... go down this route in implementing MiFID as without changing firms' obligations it would impose an additional one-off burden as part of MiFID implementation'.[3] Thus, in effect the ISD, and now MiFID, definitions of scope are used to justify the existing scope of the RAO with limited amendments.

---

[1] EC ISD, DTI CD, 16 July 1990, para. 14.
[2] Implementation of the ISD and Capital Adequacy Directive, HMT CD, July 1994, para. 14.
[3] UK Implementation of MiFID, HMT CD, December 2005, Ann. A, para. A1.

3.2 Regulated activities

The test for the requirement to obtain a licence under FSMA 19 is best illustrated and explained as in Figure 3.

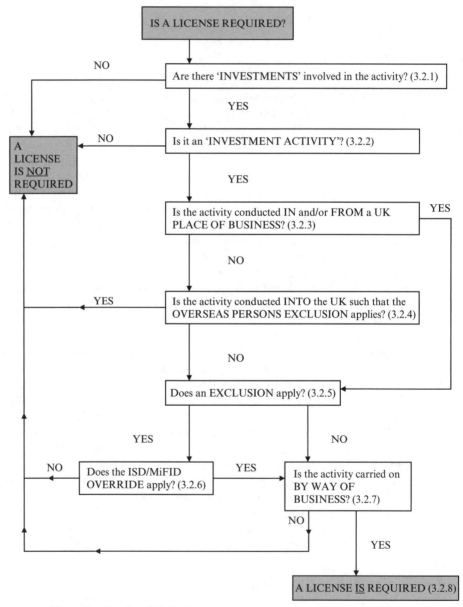

Figure 3 *Regulated Activities*

Each of the boxes in Figure 3 is explained in the following paragraphs.

3.2.1 'Investments'

To an economist an 'investment' derives its nature from the process of 'Buying and holding assets to earn income or capital gain. Investment may be in physical property, such as real estate or collectables, or in financial instruments.'[4] In the Capital Markets, from a regulatory perspective, an 'investment' is a bundle of rights and obligations capable of being created at, and recognised and enforced by, law. There are three types of legal rule that enable such creation: the law of corporations, the law of contract and the law of trust, as explained in Figure 4.[5]

Each of the 'investments' referred to in Figure 4 is explained in the following paragraphs.

3.2.1.1 Shares

The Statutory procedure for the formation of a company has the result, under the Statute, that 'On the registration of a company, the registrar of companies shall give a certificate that the company is incorporated' which 'is conclusive evidence that . . . the company is duly registered' with 'the . . . effect' that 'The . . . [shareholders] from time to time . . . are a body corporate . . . capable of exercising all the functions of an incorporated company' including that it 'is a "limited company" if the liability of its [shareholders] is limited by its constitution' (2006 CA 15(1), (4), 16(1)–(3), 3(1)). The company is, thus, given by the Statute separate legal personality from its shareholders, they being identified by the issue to them, by the separate corporate entity, of 'shares' or ownerships rights in the company, those rights being defined by the company's constitution: 'a share . . . is a fraction of the capital denoting the holder's proportionate financial stake in the company . . . and the basis of his right to . . . enjoy the rights of voting etc as conferred . . . [I]t is a species of property in its own right, a . . . chose in action, which the holder can buy, sell, charge etc.'[6] It follows that the statement in the Companies Act that 'the provisions of a company's constitution bind the company and its [shareholders] to the same extent as if there were covenants on the part of the company and of each [shareholder] to observe those provisions' (2006 CA 33(1)) is merely a Statutory provision imposing liability on shareholders and not a true contract on which the company is based, as is demonstrated by the fact that its provisions can be varied only to the extent

---

[4] *The Handbook of International Financial Terms*, Moles and Terry, Oxford, 1997, p. 302.
[5] Figure 4 does not represent partnerships (explained in 3.2.1.9), being 1890 Partnership Act partnerships (contractual arrangements), 1907 Limited Partnership Act partnerships (contractual arrangements) and 2000 Limited Liability Partnership Act partnerships (corporate form), although the latter are 'ownership rights in a company'.
[6] *Cases and Materials in Company Law*, 6th edn., LS Sealey, Butterworths, 1996, p. 459.

OWNERSHIP RIGHTS IN A COMPANY:

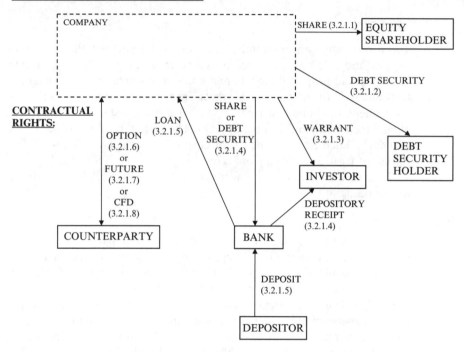

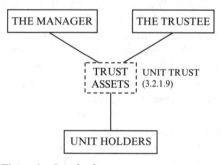

Figure 4 *Legal rules creating investments*

permitted by the statute[7] and that terms will not be implied to give the so-called contract business efficacy.[8] On this basis, the regulatory investment is 'Shares or stock in the share capital of . . . any body corporate (wherever incorporated)' except '(a) an open-ended investment company [3.2.1.9]; (b) a

---

[7] Modern Company Law for a Competitive Economy 5, DTI, March 2000, para. 4.79.
[8] *Bratton Seymour Services* v. *Oxborough* [1992] BCLC 693.

building society ... [or] (c) ... industrial and provident societies or credit unions' (RAO 76). Whether a body formed outside the UK, for example a limited partnership, has the attributes of a 'body corporate' is determined by ascertaining whether, under the relevant legal system, the body possesses the indicia of a corporation, i.e.: separate legal personality from its owners; limited liability of its shareholders; the ability to incur rights and obligations, and to sue and be sued, in its own name; and perpetual succession irrespective of the particular individual shareholders.

The ISD allowed this definition to continue since it covered 'shares in companies and other securities equivalent to shares in companies' (ISD Art. 1(4) and Ann., Sched. B, para. 1(a)) and while MiFID also applies to 'partnerships or other entities' (MiFID Art. 4.1(18)(a) and Ann. 1, Section C, para. (1)), this has not resulted in any change to the RAO since a limited liability partnership is a 'company' in any event (3.2.1.9).

3.2.1.2 Debt securities

Debt securities, representing a loan made to the issuer of the security by the holder, are negotiable by market practice and come in a number of forms. There are Promissory Notes:

> We promise to pay on 30 September 2010 against presentation of this promissory note to the order of XYZ Company plc the sum of US $500 million and to pay interest on that amount at the rate of 5.15% per annum

and Certificates of Deposit with a bank:

> Issue Date: 1 November 2007
>
> Maturity Date: 30 September 2010
>
> Principal Amount: US $500 million
>
> Interest Rate: 5.15% per annum
>
> For value received, ABC Bank plc hereby certifies that a sum has been deposited which will, on the Maturity Date, equal the above Principal Amount and to pay interest thereon at the rate specified hereon

and Debentures:

> This is to certify that ____ of ____ is the registered holder of £____ of 5.15% Debenture Stock 2010 which is secured by a Trust Deed dated 1 November 2007 and made between XYZ Company plc and ABC Bank plc as trustee. Interest at the rate of 5.15% per annum is payable on the Stock comprised in this Certificate half yearly on 1 May and 1 November in each year

Debentures were the traditional form of debt securities issued by English companies, although 'a debenture means a document which either creates the debt or acknowledges it'[9] and 'there are various kinds of instruments commonly called debentures. You may have mortgage debentures which are charges . . . on property. You may have debentures which are bonds . . . You may have a debenture which is nothing more than an acknowledgement of indebtedness.'[10] Debentures, so-called, are rarely seen now in the Capital Markets; instead there are Bonds and Notes, usually in bearer form:

> This bearer Note forms one of an issue of 5.15% Notes due 30 September 2010 in aggregate principal amount of US $500 million and constituted by a Trust Deed dated 1 November 2007 made between XYZ Company plc, the Issuer, and ABC Company plc as Trustee. The Issuer for value received hereby promises to pay the bearer of this Note on the Maturity Date the principal sum of US $5 million together with interest on such principal amount from 1 November 2007.

All these types of debt securities[11] are reflected in the definition of the regulatory investment: '(a) debentures; (b) debenture stock; (c) loan stock; (d) bonds; (e) certificates of deposit; (f) any other instrument creating or acknowledging indebtedness' other than 'a cheque or other bill of exchange, a banker's draft or a letter of credit (but not a bill of exchange accepted by a banker) [or] a bank note [or] a statement showing a balance on a current, deposit or savings account' (RAO 77). Thus, it is limited to tradeable obligations. Moreover, all forms have to 'create or acknowledge indebtedness' which refers to present and not solely future indebtedness.[12] Accordingly, instruments that create contingent debts such as tradeable loan agreements are not 'investments' since they do not acknowledge current indebtedness but merely undertake to make payment in the future.

Debt securities issued by Government and public authorities are also 'investments' (RAO 78).

Both these definitions were allowed to continue by the ISD which covered both 'bonds and other forms of securitised debt which are negotiable on the capital market . . . excluding instruments of payment' and 'instruments . . . normally dealt in on the money market' (ISD, Art. 1(4), (5) and Ann., Sched. B, paras. 1(a) and 2). While MiFID continues with both classes of instrument and gives examples of money market instruments 'such as treasury bills, certificates of deposit and commercial paper'

---

[9] *Levy v. Abercorris Slate and Slab Co.* (1887) 37 Ch. D 260.
[10] *British Land Steam Navigation Co. v. IRC* (1881) 7 QBD 165. It might be, for example, a '[c]overed bond . . . issued by [a] bank . . . and backed by certain assets, generally mortgages or public sector loans' (Proposals for a UK Recognised Covered Bonds legislative framework, HMT and FSA, July 2007, para. 1.1).
[11] However, commercial paper of under 12 months is also within 3.2.1.5 unless it is issued in denominations of at least £100,000 'to persons . . . whose ordinary activities involve them in acquiring, holding, managing or disposing of investments (as principal or agent)' (RAO 9).
[12] FSMA two year review: Changes to secondary legislation, HMT, February 2004, paras. 8.4–8.7.

(MiFID, Art. 4.1(18)(b), (19) and Ann. I, Section C, paras. (1), (2)), no change has been made to the RAO.

3.2.1.3 Warrants

A warrant over a share or a bond is a 'right . . . to "subscribe" . . . to acquire the investment directly from the issuer . . . by way of the issue of new investments (rather than by purchasing investments that have already been issued)' (PERG 2.6.13) and since the underlying instrument is itself an 'investment', the warrant is also regulated and 'it is immaterial whether the [underlying] investment . . . is in existence or identifiable' (RAO 79). Both the ISD and MiFID, which covers 'securities giving the right to acquire or sell [shares or bonds]', allow this definition to continue without amendment (ISD Art. 1(4) and Ann., Sched. B, para. 1(a); MiFID, Art. 4.1(18)(c) and Ann. I, Section C, para. (1)).

3.2.1.4 Depository receipts

A depository receipt is an instrument issued by a bank or a fiduciary custodian, backed by existing shares or bonds held by the issuer, in circumstances where by law or market practice investors cannot or do not hold the underlying instruments direct. Thus, the definition of 'investments' includes 'certificates or other instruments which confer contractual or property rights . . . in respect of any investment [within 3.2.1.1–3.2.1.3] . . . held by a person other than the person on whom the rights are conferred by the certificate . . . and . . . the transfer of which may be effected without the consent of that person' (RAO 80). Both the ISD and MiFID, which covers 'depository receipts in respect of shares . . . [or] bonds', allow this definition to continue without amendment (ISD, Art. 1(4) and Ann., Sched. B, para. 1(a); MiFID, Art. 4.1(18)(a) and Ann. I, Section C, para. (1)).

3.2.1.5 Deposits and loans

A loan is a 'debt obligation', but not a 'security' because, while it results in a debt being owed by the borrower to the lender/creditor, it is not in the form of a negotiable security, even though it will be transferable by some means (whether by novation or legal or equitable assignment) and may even include a transferable loan certificate which is a pre-agreed mechanism for novation. The loan, in the hands of the lender, is not an 'investment' unless its receipt constitutes a 'deposit' accepted in the course of a 'deposit taking business'. A 'deposit' is 'a sum of money paid on terms –

(a) under which it will be repaid, with or without interest or a premium, and either on demand or at a time on its circumstances agreed by . . . the person making the payment and the person receiving it;[13] and

---

[13] This includes certain commercial paper: see FN 11.

(b) which are not . . .
    [i] . . . paid by way of advance or part payment . . . for the sale, hire or other provision of property or services, and is repayable only in the event that the property or services . . . are not in fact sold, hired or otherwise provided; or
    [ii] . . . paid by way of security for the performance of a contract . . . or
    [iii] . . . paid by way of security for the delivery up or return of any property. (RAO 5(2), (3))

Under an earlier version of this provision, which did not include paragraph (b)[ii] in its current form, the Bank of England, when it supervised the industry under the 1979 and 1987 Banking Acts, considered that 'the definition . . . is very wide . . . [and] include[s] . . . money raised by the issue of loan stocks . . . and certain margin payments accepted by . . . brokers and dealers in financial futures . . . [and] money received by [broker-]dealers . . . from clients to be held pending its investment'.[14] This was correct as regards industrial and commercial companies issuing bonds (2.4.4(6), (7)). Indeed, the First Banking Directive stated that it 'cover[s] all institutions whose business is to receive repayable funds from the public whether in the form of deposits or . . . bonds and other comparable securities'[15] and, hence, an exemption was granted for such ordinary commercial borrowing by an industrial or commercial company (RAO 9). Similarly, an exemption is granted for broker–dealers (RAO 8), although this is unnecessary for two reasons. First, the acceptance of margin payments on derivatives dealing (2.4.4(8)) is exempt within (b)[ii] above since they are to 'be used by way of security to protect the [broker–dealer] against the risk that the [client] . . . might default'.[16] And, in any event, monies are not accepted by broker–dealers in the course of a 'deposit-taking business', which is a business where either:

(a) . . . money received by way of deposit is lent to others, or
(b) any . . . activity . . . is financed . . . out of the capital of or the interest on money received by way of deposit.

However, it is not a deposit-taking business 'if . . . he does not hold himself out as accepting deposits on day-to-day basis . . . and . . . any deposits . . . are accepted only on particular occasions' (RAO 5(1); FSMA 2000 (Carrying on Regulated Activities By Way of Business) Order 2001, SI 2001/1177, Art. 2).

Lending to others under (a) is satisfied by the recipient merely banking the deposit, since the relationship of depositor and bank is creditor-debtor,

---

[14] The Implications of Section 1 of the Banking Act 1979 for Dealers in Securities, Bank of England Aide Memoire, May 1983, p. 2.
[15] First Banking Directive, 77/780/EEC, 5th Recital.
[16] *SCF Finance* v. *Masri* [1987] 1 QB 1002 at 1020–1021.

unless placed in a segregated client account, whether or not pursuant to the Client Money Rules (7.2), since then a trust is created[17] and, thus, the broker–dealer 'was not utilising money accepted by way of deposit in the manner described in . . . (a) or . . . (b)'.[18] In any event, a broker–dealer only accepts money on 'particular occasions [within the exemption from deposit-taking business] . . . having regard to the course of the trading'.[19] Similarly, an industrial or commercial company borrowing money in the course of its usual financings, while it is accepting deposits, is not carrying on a 'deposit-taking business' within (a) and (b).

As regards territorial ambit, 'No person may carry on a regulated activity in the United Kingdom' (FSMA 19(1)). The acceptance of a 'deposit' in the course of a 'deposit-taking business' is a regulated activity. As a matter of general law, a deposit must be accepted at the place where the obligation to repay arises. It follows that if a bank, without a UK place of business, accepts a deposit (from a UK depositor) outside the UK, then there is no requirement to obtain a license. This was certainly the case under the 1987 Banking Act which provided that 'no person shall in the United Kingdom accept a deposit in the course of carrying on (whether there or elsewhere) . . . a deposit-taking business' and no change of policy is understood to have been intended.

Deposit taking and loan business is licensable under the BCD, rather than the ISD and MiFID, and has required no change in the scope of the RAO.

3.2.1.6 Options

Contractually, options are of two types: a Call Option where the holder has the right (option) during a defined period or on defined dates to call on the writer, who may not hold the underlying property when the option is entered into and thus may not be 'covered', to deliver the underlying property at a price agreed when the option contract is entered into; and a Put Option where the holder has the right (option), also during a defined period or on a defined date, to require the writer to purchase the underlying property at a price agreed when the option is entered into. Each option arrangement, therefore, involves two contracts: the option contract which grants the rights and obligations, and the purchase/sale contract resulting from the exercise of the option. The 'investment' under the original RAO was defined, in relation to the option contract, as 'options to acquire or dispose of (a) [any] other . . . investment . . . (b) currency . . . (c) palladium, platinum, gold or silver; (d) an option to acquire or dispose of an [option within] . . . (a), (b) or (c)' (RAO 83).

---

[17] *Re Kayford* [1975] 1 WLR 279; CASS 7.7.
[18] The Implications of Section 1 of the Banking Act 1979 for Dealers in Securities, Bank of England Aide Memoire, May 1983, p. 3. [19] *Masri*, at 1023.

The ISD had a more limited scope applying only to 'options to acquire or dispose of any instruments falling within [the ISD], including equivalent cash settled instruments . . . in particular options on currency and on interest rates' (ISD, Ann., Sched. B, para. 6). MiFID is much wider in that 'only a limited range of physically settled options fall within . . . the RAO, in particular the only commodity options are those relating to precious metals'[20] whereas 'MiFID requires an extension to options on all commodities and various other non-financial products'.[21] In amending the scope of the RAO, the Treasury failed to precisely define the instruments within the extension and the incomprehensible drafting in the RAO is best explained (with a relative lack of confidence) as including the following additional instruments if traded by 'an investment firm or credit institution . . . providing . . . investment services and activities on a professional basis' (3.2.6):

- A cash settled option over 'commodities', being 'any goods of a fungible nature that are capable of being delivered, including metals and their ores and alloys, agricultural products, and energy such as electricity' (Level 2 Directive, Art. 2(1)). '[E]nergy products . . . may be "delivered" by way of . . . an energy network . . . If a good is freely replaceable by another of a similar nature . . . the two . . . will be fungible . . . [T]he concept of commodity does not include services or other items that are not goods, such as currencies or . . . real estate, or that are entirely intangible' (PERG 13.4, Q.33).
- A physically settled option over 'commodities' traded on a regulated market (14.1) or MTF (14.2).
- A physically settled option over 'commodities' which 'is not . . . for commercial purposes' (3.2.1.7).
- An option which may be physically settled over climatic variables, freight rates, emission allowances, inflation rates or other economic statistics and other exotic options and is 'not for commercial purposes' (3.2.1.7). (RAO 83(2)–(5); PERG 13.4, Q.32).
- A cash-settled option to acquire any such option as is referred to above (RAO 83(1)(e)).

3.2.1.7 Futures

A future is a 'contract to buy or sell a specific amount of underlying for a specific price or rate on a specific future date',[22] the purchase of property forward applying to a vast range of what are economically non-investment situations, for example a standard house purchase, a manufacturer of tin cans purchasing its metal supplies forward for the next two years or an oil

---

[20] UK Implementation of MiFID, HMT CD, December 2005, para. 3.19.
[21] Explanatory Memorandum to the 2006 RAO, para. 7.10.
[22] *The Handbook of International Financial Terms*, Moles and Terry, p. 247.

company selling its next six months' production. Accordingly, there need to be 'pointers as to which side of the line a contract might ultimately be held to lie' 'because of the problems in defining . . . the difference between a futures contract . . . for the purpose of supplying or obtaining the commodity . . . at some later date and one which . . . is essentially a pricing, hedging or speculative mechanism'.[23] Thus, 'rights under a contract for the sale of . . . property . . . under which delivery is to be made at a future date and at a price agreed on when the contract is made' is an investment unless 'made for commercial and not investment purposes' (RAO 84 (1), (2)). The RAO contains a series of conclusive and indicative factors 'which are to be taken into account in deciding . . . [and] may carry different weights in different contexts'.[24] The contract is conclusively for investment purposes if 'traded on a recognised investment exchange . . . or on the same terms as . . . [such] a . . . contract'; and conclusively for commercial purposes 'if under the terms of the contract delivery is to be made within seven days, unless there existed an understanding [between the parties] that . . . delivery would not be made within seven days' (RAO 84(3), (4)) in which case 'in reality . . . the contract is entered into for investment purposes . . . [because] the effect . . . [is] to delay the ultimate closing out of the original open position'.[25] Otherwise, it is an indication of investment purpose if the contract is guaranteed by a clearing house or margin; an indication of commercial purposes, if 'prices, the lot, the delivery date or other terms are determined . . . for the purposes of the particular contract and not by reference . . . to regularly published prices, to standard lots or delivery dates or to standard terms'; and a further indication of commercial purposes if 'one . . . part[y] is a producer of the . . . property, or uses it in its business' or 'the seller . . . intends to deliver . . . or the purchaser . . . intends to take delivery' and the absence of any such factor 'is an indication that it is made for investment purposes' (RAO 84(5)–(7)). These indications result, for example, in a bank's forward FX activities not being an 'investment' because the price tends to be determined for each contract and the parties intend delivery to be made, notwithstanding that the bank cannot really be regarded as 'a producer of [FX] . . . or uses it in its business'.[26]

Under the ISD futures contracts were confined to 'financial futures contracts, including equivalent cash-settled instruments' and 'forward interest rate agreements (FRAs)' (ISD, Ann., Sched. B, paras 3, 4) and this allowed the Treasury to continue with the wider scope of the RAO. However, '[f]or commodity futures and certain other non-financial futures, MiFID has its own determinative criteria for identifying when a contract falls within

---

[23] Parl. Deb., House of Commons, Standing Committee E, 30 January 1986, col. 63.
[24] SIB GR 3/88, March 1988, para. 7.   [25] SIB GR 1/96, February 1996, pp. 4, 8.
[26] Ibid, p. 6.

regulation. It is necessary to ensure that these take precedence over the current criteria in the RAO'[27] and, thus, while maintaining the above definition of 'future' because it covered the rest of the scope of MiFID (RAO 84(1)), the following additional instruments are within the scope of regulation if traded by 'an investment firm or credit institution . . . providing . . . investment services and activities on a professional basis' (3.2.6) (RAO 84(1A)–(1D)):

- A future over a 'commodity' (as explained in the first bullet point in 3.2.1.6) which may be physically settled and is either traded on a regulated market (14.1) or MTF (14.2) or may be cash settled.
- A future over a 'commodity' not traded on a regulated market or MTF and which may be physically settled and is 'not . . . for commercial purposes', i.e. effectively is for investment purposes. Here MiFID provides different indicia from those used in the basic RAO definition of a 'future'. The contract is conclusively for 'investment purposes' if 'traded on . . . a regulated market, MTF or . . . third country trading facility', 'cleared by a clearing house . . . or there are arrangements for the payment of margin' and 'it is standardised so that, in particular, the price, the lot, the delivery date or other terms are determined principally by reference to regularly published prices, standard lots or standard delivery dates'; and conclusively for commercial purposes if 'delivery is . . . to be made within the longer of . . . two trading days . . . [and] the period generally accepted in the market . . . as the standard delivery period' unless 'there is an understanding between the parties . . . that delivery is to be postponed'. This does not cover 'what have hitherto been regarded . . . as commercial foreign exchange forward contracts'.[28] The reason is as follows. FX is not a 'commodity' (3.2.1.6, 1st bullet point) within MiFID, Ann. I, Section C, paras. (5)–(7) (RAO 84 (1A), (1B)) and, hence, MiFID, Ann. 1, Section C, para. (4) applies, and no specific amendment to the RAO has been made for this, reliance being placed instead on the pre-existing RAO definition of 'future' (RAO 84(1)).
- A future which may be physically settled over climatic variables, freight rates, emission allowances, inflation rates or other economic statistics and other exotic futures, if traded on a regulated market or MTF and 'not . . . for commercial purposes' (RAO 84(1A)–(1E); PERG 13.4, Q.32; FSA PS 07/5, para. 3.6).

[27] Explanatory Memorandum to the 2006 RAO, HMT, para. 7.10.
[28] UK Implementation of MiFID, HMT CD, December 2005, para. 3.21. See also PERG, 13.4, Q.30. If the FX transaction is not a 'future' within MiFID, Ann. I, Section C, para. (4), then it may be an Ancillary Service within Section B, para. (4) (4.2.I(2)), in which case best execution is an issue (13.2.2.1).

3.2.1.8   Contracts for differences (CFDs)

A CFD is a swap contract whereby money differences are paid by reference to an external event, such as a credit failure or index price change. Hence, the investment is defined as '(a) a contract for differences; or (b) any other contract the purpose . . . of which is to secure a profit or avoid a loss by reference to fluctuations in . . . the value or price of property of any description . . . or . . . an index or other factor designated for that purpose' although this 'exclude[s] . . . a contract if the parties intend . . . taking delivery' (RAO 85). For this purpose, '[c]urrency may . . . be delivered . . . [and] the operation of netting arrangements . . . may constitute delivery'[29] except where it is netting of the actual differences rather than of gross sums intended to be delivered.[30] Paragraph (b) includes a spread bet where, on a share or commodity or sporting or other index, a range is quoted and if on a certain day the index is above the range the client wins a specified sum per point of the index, and if it is below the range he pays,[31] with the result that 'an index-linked deposit . . . is . . . an "investment" [in this category] . . . if the index . . . element . . . affects . . . the capital amount'[32] so that a specific exemption is provided for 'a . . . deposit on terms that any . . . return . . . will be calculated by reference to fluctuations in an index or other factor' (RAO 85(2)(b)) which is, accordingly, within 3.2.1.5. The market operates on the basis that if the index linked deposit guarantees 100% repayment, with index fluctuations representing only an upside benefit to the investor, then it is within 3.2.1.5 and is an 'investment' within the CFD heading only if it is not. It is, however, unclear whether RAO 85(2)(b) has this effect rather than resulting in all 'deposits' being within 3.2.1.5.

Under the ISD, CFDs were limited to 'interest rates, currency and equity swaps' (ISD, Ann., Sched. B, para. 5) which resulted in no change to the wider scope of the RAO. MiFID is much wider but the existing definition of CFD covers it except for '[c]redit derivatives . . . They are covered by the . . . [existing] RAO to the extent that they take the form of agreements where the parties can make a profit or loss depending on fluctuations in the value of a product. However, some credit derivatives are more in the nature of a bet whereby a payment is made when for example, an event such as a default occurs.'[33] Similarly, other 'non-MiFID products . . . [include] sports and political spread betting'.[34] Thus, the existing definition continues and is now extended, if traded by 'an investment firm or credit institution . . . providing . . . investment services and

---

[29] Foreign Exchange and the FSAct 1986, SIB GR 1/96, February 1996, pp. 10–11.
[30] *Chigi* v. *CS First Boston Limited* [1998] CLC 227.
[31] *City Index* v. *Leslie* [1991] 3 WLR 207.
[32] Guaranteed Products, SFA Update 16, August 1997, p. 3.
[33] Explanatory Memorandum to the 2006 RAO, HMT, para. 7.10.
[34] FSA CP 06/19, para. 15.8.

activities on a professional basis' (3.2.6), to 'Derivative instruments for the transfer of credit risk' (RAO 85(3)), 'includ[ing] . . . credit default products, synthetic collateralised debt obligations, total rate of return swaps, downgrade options and credit spread products'; however this 'does not extend to . . . sports spread bets' (PERG, 13.4, Q.30, 31).

An issue with some forms of credit derivative is whether they fall within the separate regulated activity of 'Effecting a contract of insurance as principal' (RAO 10) because, if they do, the consequences for a bank or broker–dealer being regulated as an insurance company are unpalatable. However, a standard definition of insurance as '[a] contract . . . whereby one party (the "insurer") promises in return for a money consideration (the "premium") to pay to the other party (the "assured") a sum of money or provide him with some corresponding benefit, upon the occurrence of one or more specified events'[35] shows that only rarely will such a derivative be caught.

With CFDs and other derivatives in the Capital Markets the concern has always been whether they are 'wagering contracts', i.e. 'one by which two persons professing to hold opposite views touching the issue of a future uncertain event, mutually agree that, dependent upon the determination of that event, one shall win from the other . . . neither of the . . . parties having any other interest in that contract than the sum . . . he will win or lose',[36] in which case it 'shall be null and void'.[37] Although a hedging purpose prevents it being gaming,[38] the market cannot operate with such uncertainty surrounding speculation and the legislator 'must find a way of clearly distinguishing legitimate investments from illegitimate wagers'.[39] The solution is simply to provide that any 'investment' entered into in the course of the 'investment activity' of dealing (3.2.2.1) is exempt from the Gaming Act (FSMA 412; FSMA 2000 (Gaming Contracts) Order 2001, SI 2001/2510).

3.2.1.9 Collective investment schemes

Open-ended investment companies, which can issue and redeem shares in accordance with investor demand, on the Continental European model, were not possible before specific legislation in the 1990s as a result of the strict company law rules on reduction of share capital.[40] Hence, the development in the 19th and 20th Centuries of the unit trust, using trust law, under which assets were held by a (custodian) trustee for the benefit of unit holders, who each had a proportionate economic share through their

---

[35] *MacGillivray on Insurance Law*, 7th edn., Sweet & Maxwell, 1981, para. 1.
[36] *Carhill* v. *Carbolic Smoke Ball Co.* [1892] 2 QB 484 at 490–491.
[37] 1845 Gaming and Wagers Act 18.
[38] Contrast, *Thacker* v. *Hardy* 1878 QBD 685, *Morgan Grenfell and Co Ltd.* v. *Wellwyn Hatfield General Council*, TLR, 1 June 1993 and *Cobbold Roach Ltd.* v. *Onwudiwe*, Unreported, 17 April 1989.   [39] 1984 Gower, para. 4.04.
[40] *Trevor* v. *Whitworth* (1887) 12 App. Cas. 409.

equitable or beneficial interest in the assets which were discretionarily invested by the manager. Both forms are defined as an 'investment', being 'units in a collective investment scheme' (RAO 81), i.e.:

> any arrangements with respect to property of any description, including money, the purpose or effect of which is to enable persons taking part in the arrangements (whether by becoming owners of the property or any part of it or otherwise) to participate in or receive profits or income arising from the acquisition, holding, management or disposal of the property or sums paid out of such profits or income.
>
> The arrangements must be such that the persons who are to participate . . . do not have day-to-day control over the management of the property, whether or not they have the right to be consulted or to give directions.
>
> The arrangements must also have either or both of the following characteristics –
>
> (a) the contributions of the participants in the profits or income out of which payments are to be made to them are pooled; [and/or]
> (b) the property is managed as a whole by or on behalf of the operator of the scheme. (FSMA 235 (1)–(3))

This definition is of such extreme width that it is necessary to specifically exempt: parallel investment management, where the investment manager is managing separate portfolios for different investors but investing each of them in an identical proportion of the same investments; bank deposit accounts; client money accounts held for a number of clients (7.2.1); Christmas clubs, charities and other '[a]rrangements . . . operated otherwise than by way of business'; asset repackagings where the issuer buys investments or other assets and issues bonds the return on which is linked to the income and capital return on the underlying and where there may also be linked swap arrangements; depository receipts (3.2.1.4); exchange clearing houses (14.3); and even an ordinary limited liability company (FSMA 2000 (Collective Investment Schemes) Order 2001, SI 2001/1062, Arts. 1, 3–6, 15, 16, 21).

'Partnership is the relation which subsists between persons carrying on a business in common with a view to profit'[41] being 'a relationship resulting from a contract',[42] although 'while . . . a consensual arrangement based on agreement, it is more than a simple contract . . . it is a continuing personal as well as commercial relationship'.[43] If satisfying the conditions set out above it will be a collective investment scheme, except that a partnership carrying on a commercial business (for example, a firm of solicitors) where

---

[41] 1890 Partnership Act 1(I).
[42] *Lindley & Banks on Partnership*, Sweet & Maxwell, 18th edn., 2002, p. 15.
[43] *Hurst v. Bryk* [2000] 2 WLR 740 at 747–748.

each partner works in that business will not be caught because each of them does have 'day-to-day control over the management of the property'. In any event, the definition is clearly aimed at an arrangement where investors pool their resources, not where a business does so even though it has a managing partner, as is shown by the fact that, for the purposes of condition (b), 'operator' is defined as 'in relation to a unit trust scheme with a separate trustee, . . . the manager and in relation to an open-ended investment company, . . . that company', neither designation fitting an 'ordinary' partnership.[44] However, a limited partnership under the 1907 Limited Partnerships Act is a collective investment scheme because its 'essence . . . is the combination . . . of (1) one or more partners whose liability for the debts and obligations of the firm is unlimited and who alone are entitled to manage the firm's affairs, and (2) one or more partners whose liability . . . is limited in amount and who are excluded from all management functions'.[45] Here, the limited partner is an investor. A limited liability partnership formed under the 2000 Limited Liability Partnerships Act, notwithstanding that 'two or more persons associated for carrying on a lawful business with a view to profit must have subscribed . . . to an incorporation document',[46] 'is a body corporate (with limited personality separate from that of its members)'.[47] Interests in it are, thereby shares (3.2.1.1), but it cannot rely on the exemption from the definition of collective investment scheme for limited companies (FSMA 2000 (Collective Investment Schemes) Order 2001, SI 2001/1062, Art. 21(2)). However, it must still satisfy the conditions for being a collective investment scheme in the first place, and thus will not be caught where used by individuals carrying on a commercial business, but will be caught where used as an investment vehicle.

A corporate form of mutual fund is, however, only within this, rather than 'shares' within 3.2.1.1, if 'the [underlying] property belongs beneficially to, and is managed by or on behalf of, [the company] having as its [corporate] purpose the investment of its funds with the aim of . . . spreading investment risk' and 'a[n] . . . investor . . . [is] able to realise . . . within a reasonable [period], his investment in the scheme . . . on a basis calculated by reference to the value of [the company's] property' (FSMA 236; PERG 9). That said, for the purpose of the MiFID term 'collective investment undertakings', 'shares in close-ended corporate schemes, such as . . . investment trust companies, are also units in collective investment undertakings . . . (as well as being [shares within 3.2.1.1] . . .)' (PERG 13.4, Q.29). Whether or not treated as a 'share' for regulatory purposes, the open-ended investment company is in corporate form and thus subject to the same legal

---

[44] A 'unit trust scheme . . . [is] a . . . scheme under which the property is held on trust for the participants' (FSMA 237(1)) and the leading work on partnership law 'would . . . question whether . . . the interest of any partner . . . could . . . properly be characterised as held under a trust' (*Lindley*, p. 859). [45] *Lindley*, p. 841.
[46] 2000 Limited Liability Partnerships Act 2(1)(a). [47] Ibid, 1(2).

rules for its creation, albeit under the Open-Ended Investment Company Regulations 2001, SI 2001/1228, rather than the 2006 CA.

The European focus on collective investment schemes was through UCITS funds that can be sold to the public (2.6(10), 10.5.6.1), although both the ISD and MiFID, covering 'units in collective investment undertakings', allow the maintenance of the RAO definition (ISD, Art. 1(4) and Ann., Sched. B, para. (1); MiFID, Art. 4.1(18)(a) and Ann. I, Section C, paras. (1), (3)).

3.2.1.10 Rights and interests in investments

A contractual right or equitable interest in an 'investment' is itself defined as an 'investment' (RAO 89).

3.2.2 'Investment activities'

The difficulty with functional regulation is that '[f]or every firm engaged wholly in business involving investments . . . there are probably at least 10 which engage in it either in other ways . . . or only incidentally as part of another business'[48] which results in extremely wide definitions of 'investment activity' with a large series of relatively narrow excluded activities (3.2.5).

3.2.2.1 Dealing

As a matter of general law, investments are bought and sold as principal, for the legal and beneficial ownership of the purchaser, or as agent on behalf of, and with power to commit to the contract, another and for that other's legal and/or beneficial ownership (2.4.4(6)–(8), (11)). This distinction is recognised in the categorisation of the dealing activity as both 'buying, selling, subscribing for or underwriting securities or [derivatives] . . . as principal' and 'as agent' (RAO 14, 21). Both the ISD categorisation of 'Dealing . . . for own account' and 'Execution of . . . orders other than for own account', and the MiFID categorisation of Secondary Market 'Dealing on own account' and 'Execution of orders on behalf of clients' and Primary Market 'Underwriting . . . and/or placing of financial instruments' (ISD, Ann., Sched. A, paras. 1(b), 2; MiFID, Art. 4.1(5) and Ann. I, Section A, paras. (2), (3), (6), (7)) allow this terminology to continue since 'executing orders on behalf of clients' is 'either . . . dealing . . . as agent . . . or, in some cases, . . . as principal (for example by back-to-back or riskless principal trading) . . . [and] dealing on own account . . . is trading against proprietary capital . . . involv[ing] position taking . . . We do not think that this activity is likely to be relevant . . . where a person acquires a long term stake in a company for strategic purposes' (PERG 13.3, Q.15, Q.16).

[48] 1985 White Paper, para. 4.8.

Stocklending, being a sale and repurchase (2.4.4(8)), as principal or agent, is within these categories. So is booking (principal) (13.2.2.2).

3.2.2.2 Arranging deals

Although intended initially to introduce '[r]estrictions on operating exchanges',[49] the 'investment activity' of 'Making arrangements with a view to a person who participates in the arrangements buying, selling, subscribing for or underwriting investments' (RAO 25(2)) has a wider ambit and catches, for example, inter-dealer brokers[50] and even network communications which, as a result, need an express exemption (RAO 27), as do margin lending 'arrangements [11.5] having as their sole purpose the provision of finance to enable a person to buy, sell, subscribe for or underwrite investments' (RAO 32) and 'arrangements . . . under which . . . clients . . . will be introduced to another person . . . with a view to the provision of independent advice [3.2.2.3] or the independent exercise of discretion [3.2.2.4]' (RAO 33).

A further 'investment activity' is 'making arrangements for another person (whether as principal or agent) to buy, sell, subscribe for or underwrite a particular investment' (RAO 25(1)). This excludes 'arrangements for a transaction into which the person making the arrangement enters . . . as principal or as agent for some other person' (RAO 28(1)) which will, as a result, fall within 3.2.2.1, for example the investment bank on an offer for subscription (2.4.4(6)) or the company issuer itself (RAO 34). Also excluded are 'arrangements which do not . . . bring about the transaction to which the arrangements relate' (RAO 26), although 'a person is only likely to bring about an investment transaction if their involvement in a chain of events leading to a transaction is of sufficient importance that without that involvement the transaction would not take place . . . [T]his requires something more than the mere giving of advice' and, in the corporate finance context:

> activities . . . unlikely to bring about a particular transaction . . . include:
> - appointing professional advisors;
> - preparing a prospectus/business plan;
> - identifying potential sources of funding.
>
> Examples of arrangements . . . likely to 'bring about' particular . . . transactions . . . include:
> - assisting investors/subscribers to complete and submit application forms;
> - receiving application forms . . . for processing/checking and/or onward transmission . . . to the company or its registrars . . .

---

[49] 1984 Gower, para. 6.03. See 14.1.   [50] Cf. SFA BN 176, 31 March 1994, Sched., para. 2.

- negotiating terms for an investment (including an underwriting agreement) between the corporate client and a potential source of funding . . .
- acting as an intermediary between a corporate client and a potential source of funding . . . ; and
- effecting a placing of securities with investors/institutions.[51]

It follows that a mere introduction is not 'making arrangements' where a firm refers someone who has expressed an interest in an investment/transaction/service to either a product provider or an intermediary and does nothing more, even though the firm may receive commission for the introduction,[52] although there is a specific exclusion that would need to be relied upon for introductions to licensed firms (3.2.5.5). More generally, though, '[t]he word "arrangement" is . . . capable of having an extremely wide meaning, embracing matters which do not give rise to legally enforceable rights . . . A . . . person may make "arrangements" . . . even if his actions do not involve or facilitate the execution of each step necessary for entering into and completing the transaction.'[53]

The ISD and MiFID categorisation of the arranging activity/service as 'Reception and transmission of orders' (ISD, Ann, Sched. A, para.1(a); MiFID, Recital 20 and Ann. I, Section A, para. (1)) allows the RAO terminology to continue without amendment even though 'you only provide the service if you are both receiving and transmitting orders . . . This service though is also extended to include arrangements that bring together two or more investors, thereby bringing about a transaction between those investors . . . even though, having brought the investors together, the actual offer or acceptance is not communicated through you. The . . . service only applies if the firm brings together two or more investors and a person issuing new securities . . . [is] not . . . an "investor" for this purpose . . . [I]ntroducers who merely put clients in touch with other . . . firms . . . do . . . not bring about a transaction and so will not amount to receiving and transmitting orders' (PERG 13.3, Q.13, Q.14. See also: SUP, App. 3.9.5, Table 2, Note 1).

3.2.2.3 Investment advice

In practice, there is a spectrum in the types of conversations that firms have with, and documents they distribute to, investors, from 'information' (setting out in a neutral manner the facts relating to investments, transactions and services with no spin), through 'product related advice' (setting out in a selective and judgemental manner the advantages and disadvantages of a particular investment, transaction or service and expressly or impliedly advising on the type of investor for whom it is suitable), to 'personal recommendations' (based on the particular needs and circumstances

---

[51] SIB GR 3/98, paras. 16–18.   [52] SIB GR 2/88, March 1988, paras. 26–28.
[53] *In Re Inertia Partnership LLP* [2007] EWHC 539 at para. 39.

of the investor). 'Advising a person is a[n investment] activity ... if (a) given to the person in his capacity as an investor ... and (b) advice on the merits of his ... (whether as principal or agent) buying, selling, subscribing for or underwriting a particular investment' (RAO 53). Thus, 'generic advice does not constitute investment advice'[54] but both 'product related advice,' for example in a broker's circular, a research report or a Sales and Trading Department note, and a 'personal recommendation' do. The distinction is between generic statements (for example, 'buy shares because the stock market will rise' and 'sell technology shares'), which are not within the Regulated Activity, and 'advice on ... a particular investment' (for example, 'buy Microsoft shares'), whether express or in writing or through a software programme into which the investor enters personal details and the system generates an investment recommendation.[55] Nor does it 'include advice given to an issuer to issue securities [or takeover target], as ... [it] is not an investor' (PERG 13.3, Q.19).

While the ISD non-core service of 'Investment advice concerning one or more ... instruments' (ISD, Ann. Sched. C, para. 6) required no change to the RAO, the MiFID activity of 'Investment advice' is defined as 'the provision of personal recommendations to a client, either upon request or at the initiative of the ... firm, in respect of one of more transactions relating to financial instruments' (MiFID, Art. 4.1(4) and Ann. I, Section A, para. (5)), 'a personal recommendation [being] a recommendation ... made to a person in his capacity as an investor or potential investor ... presented as suitable for that person, or ... based on a consideration of the circumstances of that person, and ... constitut[ing] a recommendation to ... buy, sell, subscribe for, exchange, redeem, hold or underwrite a particular financial instrument' (Level 2 Directive, Art. 52). This is 'narrower [than the RAO definition] ... insofar as it requires the recommendation to be of a personal nature' (PERG 13.3, Q.19). Nonetheless, it is viewed as enabling the wider definition to continue as are the MiFID ancillary services of 'investment research' (which although 'investment advice' is not a 'personal recommendation')[56] and corporate finance advice (MiFID, Ann. I, Section B, paras. (3), (5)) which are subsumed in that regulated activity.

3.2.2.4 Managing investments

'Managing assets belonging to another person, in circumstances involving the exercise of discretion, is a[n investment] ... activity if ... the assets consist of or include any investment' (RAO 37), non-discretionary management being within 3.2.2.3. '[T]he property that is managed must belong

---

[54] Regulated Activities – a Consultation Document, HMT, February 1999, para. 3.6.
[55] *In Re Market Wizard Systems (UK) Ltd.* [1998] 2 BCLC 282.
[56] As a result, research reports are not subject to the suitability obligation in 11.2.2, but are marketing communications within 10.5.

beneficially to another person. This excludes ... the management by a person of his own property. But discretionary management ... by a person acting in his capacity as trustee will be caught even though he is the legal owner of the assets' (PERG 2.7.8(2)). 'The discretion must be exercised in relation to the composition of the portfolio ... and not in relation to some other function (such as proxy voting)' (PERG 2.7.8(1)), which would include operating a securities lending programme (2.4.4(8), 16.3.3), being the disposal and re-acquisition of investments (3.2.2.1).

'To most people the investment made by or for them in a pension fund is, apart from their home, the only substantial investment that they will have'[57] and, as a result, although a pensioner's interest in the scheme is not itself an 'investment' (RAO 89(2)), since [before the 1995 and 2004 Pensions Acts] 'the trustees ... need not be [professionally skilled] ... and generally are not' it was considered that '[r]eliance on the law of trusts must be supplemented'.[58] The policy is that '[a] ... [pension fund] trustee ... will not be required to be [licensed] if he delegates day-to-day management ... to a ... [licensed firm] ... He would still be able to take ... strategic decisions, for example about the proportion of the assets that should constitute investments of particular kinds or ... [where] the person managing the scheme's assets was required to consult him ... where perhaps there was a takeover bid.'[59] This is achieved by disapplying the trustee exemption for investment management (3.2.5.3) (RAO 66(3)(b)) and providing that, except in relation to pooled investments and private equity-type investments where 'many advisors ... are unwilling to consider alternative investments'[60] and thus it is sufficient if the trustees take 'the decision ... after advice has been obtained and considered from' a licensed or overseas firm, the trustees require a licence unless 'all day to day decisions ... are taken on [their] behalf by' a licensed or overseas firm (FSMA (Carrying on Regulated Activities By Way of Business) Order 2001, SI 2001/1177, Art. 4, amended by SI 2005/922).

Neither the ISD nor MiFID activity of 'Managing portfolios of investments ... on a discretionary ... basis' (ISD, Ann., Sched. A, para. 3; MiFID, Art. 4.1(9) and Ann. I, Section A, para. (4)) require any change to the RAO definition and is considered, in practice, to have the same scope except that it applies to the narrower list of MiFID 'financial instruments' (PERG 13.3, Q.17).

3.2.2.5 Operating collective investment schemes

The manager and trustee of a unit trust scheme and the depository and sole director of a UK open-ended investment company, and the general partner

---

[57] 1982 Gower, para. 9.13.   [58] 1982 Gower, para. 9.13; 1984 Gower, para.11.03.
[59] Parl. Deb., House of Lords, 29 July 1986, Minister, cols. 781–782.
[60] FSMA two year review: Changes to secondary legislation, HMT, February 2004, paras. 7.4–7.7.

of a limited partnership, are all conducting an 'investment activity' (RAO 51). This is not an activity within either the ISD or MiFID and, therefore, continues unamended.

3.2.2.6 Custody

As a result of the Maxwell scandal (2.5), both conducting and arranging custody of investments became an 'investment activity' (RAO 40) under which '[c]ustody . . . comprises . . . [both of] two elements:

- Safe-keeping, i.e. the protection of the investments themselves, including . . . physical custody . . . , registration, and/or the maintenance of accounts with clearing houses, and central depositories and other third party custodians, and ensuring that delivery of investments takes place only in accordance with properly authorised instructions.
- Administration, including accounting for individual customer entitlements to investments, settlement and cash processing, collecting and accounting for dividends and other benefits, . . . reporting to the customer and communicating and acting on corporate events.[61]

Safekeeping does not include 'a depository safeguarding locked boxes or sealed packets',[62] but requires 'the firm [to] ha[ve] physical possession of the assets . . . [or] where they are in the possession of a third party under the control of the firm'[63] for the benefit of the client so that 'holding investments as security against loans will not rank as custody . . . [since] the lender is looking after the assets for his own reason'.[64] Exclusions are provided for introductions to licensed custodians, sub-custodians/nominees for licensed UK custodians, valuation and currency services and the transmission of documents of title (RAO 41–43).

Neither the ISD non-core activities of 'Safekeeping and administration in relation to . . . instruments' and 'Safe custody services' (ISD, Ann., Sched. C, paras. 1, 2) nor the MiFID ancillary service of 'Safekeeping and administration of financial instruments for the account of clients, including custodianship and related services such as cash/collateral management' (MiFID Ann. I, Section B, para. (1)) require any change to the RAO, the only distinction in practice being that MiFID applies only to the narrower category of 'financial instruments'.

3.2.2.7 MTFs and ATSs

Before MiFID there was no separate regulated activity of operating such a system since that fell under 3.2.2.1 and 3.2.2.2. However, because of the perceived risks of such systems to the financial markets, FSA required such firms, whether or not licensed for other business as well, to obtain a FSMA

---

[61] SIB CP 90, August 1995, App. 1, p. 29.   [62] Custody, HMT CD, June 1996, para. 16.
[63] SIB CP 107, March 1997, paras. 10–11.   [64] Custody, HMT CD, June 1996, para. 49.

Part IV Permission in respect of operating an 'alternative trading system (ATS)' (FSA PM MAR 5.3). This was defined as 'a system that brings together multiple buying and selling interests . . . according to non-discretionary rules . . . in a way that results in a contract but does not include . . . . a bilateral system', itself being 'a system that brings together buying and selling interests . . . where a single person enters into one side of every transaction . . . on his own account and not merely as a central counterparty interposed between a buyer and a seller' because '[a] central counterparty will have a flat book unless there is a default . . . while the counterparty in a bilateral system will take principal positions' (FSA PM MAR 5.2.8). For this purpose, '[t]he concept of bringing together is intended to cover any process under which interests interact; this may be automatic matching, by way of selection of interest by users themselves or otherwise' and, so, 'order routing systems where interests are transmitted but do not interact are not . . . covered'. Moreover, 'The reference to non-discretionary rules . . . exclude[s] systems where the operator exercises discretion as to how the interests interact . . . [but not where] the operator has discretion as to whether or not to enter an interest into the system . . . [or] users have discretion about whether or not to . . . accept any expression of interest' (FSA PM MAR 5.2.5, 5.2.6). Thus, the following were ATSs: limit order matching books; electronic periodic auction systems; price-taking systems and crossing networks, even though not themselves forming the trading prices; quote screens and bulletin boards 'if execution takes place inside the system, i.e. under the rules of the system' but not if 'the system is a mere passive bulletin board or other advertising system whereby participants can conclude the trade outside the system'; and market maker systems 'where multiple participants act as counterparties to the order entered through the system'.[65]

MiFID contains a new heading of 'investment activity' for 'Operation of Multilateral Trading Facilities', being 'a multi-lateral system . . . which brings together multiple third party buying and selling interests in financial instruments – in the system and in accordance with non-discretionary rules – in a way that results in a contract' (MiFID Art. 4.1(15) and Ann. I, Section A, para. (8)). This has exactly the same meaning as an ATS, except that it can relate only to MiFID 'financial instruments' (PERG 13.3, Q.24). Thus, '[w]e do not intend to capture firms' order management systems, even where the[y] . . . allow occasional crossing of orders . . . [or] systems where the operator . . . applies discretion to the way that trading interests interact . . . It is not the case, however, that crossing systems generally, fall outside the MTF definition. Those that bring together third party buying and selling interests according to non-discretionary rules are caught even if they are

[65] CESR/02–086b, July 2002, Ann. B; FSA CP 153, October 2002, paras. 3.13–3.15; FSA PM MAR 5.2.3.

price-taking systems.'[66] Although the Treasury's initial view was that '[f]irms ... operating MTFs ... are [already] within the scope of ... regulation by virtue of ... [3.2.2.1 and 3.2.2.2] which relate to dealings in investments as principal ... [or] agent and arranging deals',[67] 'the language in the RAO ... is not very close to that in MiFID, and part of the Commission's purpose in creating this new activity was to provide clarity around its regulatory status ... It was therefore decided ... to create a new activity in the RAO'[68] using the MiFID wording (RAO 25D). As a result of it being an express type of MiFID Business, the activity is 'passportable' and, as with ATSs, FSA will include this heading, but no others in respect of the activity, in the firm's Part IV Permission (SUP 13.4.20 and App. 3.9.5, Table 2, Note 2; PERG 13, Ann. 1, A.8).[69] The passporting rights exist 'where the platform is providing direct access to users ... in the [Host] Member State ... for example the placing of trading screens ... in [that] ... State ... or the delivery ... of software so as to facilitate access to the platform, or the physical presence of IT infrastructure' or, where there is no electronic platform, 'when the MTF facilitates the conclusion of transactions by users ... established in another Member State under the rulebook of the MTF'.[70]

3.2.3 Activities in and/or from a UK place of business

3.2.4 Activities into the UK and the overseas persons exclusion

Under the PFI (2.3), the Board of Trade and later the Department of Trade took the traditional approach to the criminal offence of carrying on unlicensed 'dealing in securities' that, while it applied to activities in or from the UK, it did not apply to activities cross-border into the UK.[71] However, the offence of distributing misleading circulars with the intention of providing facilities for investors to participate in unauthorised collective investment schemes (10.5.6.1) was held to have been committed where, although the investor received the misleading prospectus in Germany, the application form was processed in the UK since with 'result crimes ... the offence is committed in England ... if any part of the prescribed result takes place in England'.[72] FSMA, building on a similar approach of the 1986 FSAct, takes a wide territorial approach. For UK incorporated companies, it applies to activities carried on:

- in or from the UK (FSMA 19(1), 418(2), (3)); or
- from a non-UK branch:

---

[66] FSA PS 07/2, para. 11.2.
[67] UK Implementation of MiFID, HMT CD, December 2005, para. 3.14.
[68] Explanatory Memorandum to the 2006 RAO, HMT, para. 7A.
[69] MiFID Permissions and Notices Guide, FSA, May 2007, p. 23.
[70] CESR/07-337, May 2007, paras. 51–53. [71] Cf. *Bennion*, sections 128, 130. See 12.2.2.
[72] *R v. Marcus* [1974] 3 AER 705.

- into the UK if either day-to-day management of the activity, as opposed to strategic direction of the business, is directed from a UK office (FSMA 418(4))[73] or, if not, the overseas persons exclusion does not apply (FSMA 19(1), 22(1)); or
- in the EU (FSMA 418(2)); or
- outside the EU if day-to-day management of the activity is directed from a UK office (FSMA 418(4)).

For other firms, it applies to activities carried on:

- in or from the UK (FSMA 418(5), (5A); PERG 2.4.3(4)); or
- into the UK, if the overseas persons exclusion does not apply, with the activities in 3.2.2.1–3.2.2.6; but there is a separate test for 'deposit-taking business' (3.2.1.5) (FSMA 19(1), 22(1)).

The overseas persons exclusion (RAO 72) was included because 'if overseas businesses . . . were required to be [licensed] it could divert valuable business from this country'[74] and, accordingly, applies to 'a person who . . . carries on [investment] activities . . . but . . . does not carry on any such activities, or offer to do so, from a permanent place of business maintained by him in the United Kingdom' (RAO 3(1), def. of 'overseas person') which, interpreted in the light of an analogous provision in the CA, requires 'a degree of permanence or recognisability as being a location of the company's business'[75] not operating out of a hotel room or an affiliate's UK premises unless clients know that the firm's representative can be reached there otherwise than on a short term temporary basis. However, the exclusion cannot be relied upon by a UK incorporated firm operating from outside the UK (RAO 72(8)). As a result of the exclusion:

- The dealing activity (3.2.2.1) is conducted in the UK if the client/counterparty is located there, but excluded if the transaction is conducted:
  - as principal or agent with a licensed person or in which a licensed person acts as agent or arranger (RAO 3(2), 72(1)(a), (2)(a)); or
  - as principal or agent for a non-UK client and is solicited in accordance with the financial promotion rules explained in 10.4.2 (RAO 72(1)(b), (2)(b)); or
  - as agent for a UK client and solicited in accordance with the financial promotion rules explained in 10.4.2 and either the counterparty is outside the UK or, if it is in the UK, it solicited the transaction in accordance with those rules (RAO 72(2)(b)).

---

[73] FSMA Explanatory Notes, HMT, 2000, para. 738.
[74] Parl. Deb., House of Commons, Standing Committee E, 30 January 1986, Minister, col. 55.
[75] *Re Oriel Ltd.* [1986] 1 WLR 180 at 184.

- The arranging activity (3.2.2.2) is conducted in the UK if the client/counterparty for whom the transaction is arranged is located in the UK, but excluded if:
  - the arrangements are made with a licensed person (RAO 72(3)); or
  - the arrangements are made with a view to a transaction by licensed persons (RAO 72(4)); or
  - the arrangements are solicited in accordance with the financial promotion rules explained in 10.4.2 (RAO 72(6)).
- The advice activity (3.2.2.3) is conducted in the UK if the recipient of the advice is located there, but excluded if given in compliance with the financial promotion rules explained in 10.4.2 (RAO 72(5)).
- The management activity (3.2.2.4) and the custody activity (3.2.2.6) are conducted in the location of the manager/custodian notwithstanding that the client for whom it is conducted is located in the UK and, thus, no express exclusion is necessary.
- The operation etc of a collective investment scheme (3.2.2.5) is conducted where the operator is located and if outside the UK, again, no express exclusion is necessary.

MiFID has no effect on the operation of this exclusion except that as a result of an obscure and questionable debate over the supposed application of the ISD/MiFID override (3.2.6) to the overseas persons exclusion,[76] the exclusion 'do[es] not apply where the overseas person is a [UK formed] investment firm or credit institution ... who is providing or performing investment services and activities on a professional basis' within 3.2.6 (RAO 72(8)); and the exclusion in relation to dealing and arranging is partly extended to the operation of MTFs from abroad (RAO 72(1)–(4)).

3.2.5 Excluded activities

As noted in 3.2.2, there are a series of particular exclusions linked to specific investment activities. In addition, there are five more general exclusions relevant in the Capital Markets.

3.2.5.1 Group activities

Activities with group companies are excluded (FSMA 421; RAO 69) because there is no external third party relying on the service which needs any form of investor protection.

3.2.5.2 Sale of a company

Acquisition of over 50% of the voting shares in a company is an excluded activity or of less if 'the object of the transaction may nevertheless

---

[76] UK Implementation of MiFID, HMT CD, December 2005, paras. 3.2, 3.27–3.35.

reasonably be regarded as being the acquisition of day to day control of . . . the body corporate' (RAO 70(1)) because 'such activities are carried out more often for commercial, rather than investment, purposes' by industrial and commercial conglomerates rather than by investment banks and specialist buy out funds.[77]

3.2.5.3 Trustees

The Capital Markets use a variety of trust structures, including trustees of securities issues who, while holding the covenant to repay and perhaps also any collateral securities, may on occasion advise the Note holders about, or themselves take a decision on, a company resolution relating to the Notes or any underlying shares on a convertible issue, which could amount to investment management within 3.2.2.4. Moreover, trustees of ordinary settlements, as legal owner of the underlying property, have duties of investment management and buy and sell investments. All such activities are clearly not in themselves mainstream financial services to be regulated and, therefore, exclusions are provided for a 'bare trustee' or nominee from dealing within 3.2.2.1, and an 'active trustee' is in any event excluded within 3.2.5.4 since it does not hold itself out. Moreover, a trustee is excluded from all other investment activities unless either it 'holds [it]self out as providing [such] a service' or it 'is remunerated for what [it] does in addition to any remuneration . . . receive[d] as trustee' (although 'for these purposes a person is not to be regarded as receiving additional remuneration merely because his remuneration is calculated by reference to time spent') (RAO 66(2)–(7)),[78] in which case it is providing mainstream financial services, albeit in trust form.

3.2.5.4 Buying and selling

Whether 'buying, selling, subscribing for or underwriting . . . investments . . . as principal' (3.2.2.1) requires a licence differs between securities (3.2.1.1–3.2.1.5, 3.2.1.9, 3.2.1.10) and derivatives (3.2.1.6–3.2.1.8, 3.2.1.10) (RAO 14–16). With securities, buying, selling, etc is caught only if either it is done as a market maker or as a result of 'regularly solicit[ing] members of the public', directly or through agents, or the 'person . . . holds himself out as engaging in the business of buying investments . . . with a view to selling them' (RAO 15) which, given the wide definition of dealing, is intended to distinguish a professional dealer offering services to the market from an investor acting for its own account 'which does not deal with or for customers and which may properly be regarded as itself a customer of the market' such 'that a firm which merely engages in a business of buying investments with a view to selling them, albeit on a large scale, will [not

---

[77] FSMA two year review: Changes to secondary legislation, HMT, February 2004, para. 6.3.
[78] For a disapplication of this disapplication to pension fund trustees, see 3.2.2.4.

necessarily] be regarded as holding himself out as doing so'.[79] As a result, there is principal dealing by broker–dealers throughout their activities and by an investment bank in an offer for sale and when it underwrites an offer for subscription, stabilises or engages in a bought deal, but not by sub-underwriters, and there is a specific exclusion for 'the issue by a company of its own shares or share warrants . . . [or] debentures' (RAO 18). 'Buying [or] selling' derivatives as principal is licensable unless it is done exclusively with UK licensed or EEA passported firms or non-UK dealers acting abroad or it is hedging in the course of non-investment business for 'the . . . purpose . . . of limiting the extent to which . . . [the] business will be affected by any identifiable risk' (RAO 16, 19).

'Buying, selling, subscribing for or underwriting . . . investments . . . as agent' (3.2.2.1) requires a licence except where it is hedging or the agent, dealing through a licensed firm, does not advise on the transaction (RAO 21–23). This category of investment activity applies to the broker–dealer's agency broking function and to the investment bank's function in an offer of subscription and, in all public offers, to the corporate broker seeking sub-underwriters.

3.2.5.5 Introductions to licensed firms

There is an exclusion from the investment activity of arranging deals (3.2.2.2) for an introduction to a licensed firm 'if (a) the transaction is entered into on advice to the client by [the licensed firm]; or (b) it is clear . . . that the client . . . is not seeking . . . advice from [the introducer] as to the merits of . . . the transaction' and (c) '[the introducer] does not . . . receive from any person other than the client any pecuniary reward . . . for which he does not account to the client' (RAO 29).

3.2.6 The ISD/MiFID override

The ISD, as a Single Market Directive, granted passporting freedoms to firms not as an optional facility that firms within its scope could choose whether or not to accept, but as a compulsory right whether or not they in practice chose to exercise it. It followed that 'the purpose of this Directive is to cover undertakings the normal business of which is to provide third parties with investment services on a professional basis' (ISD, 17th Recital) such that 'investment firms' within its scope were 'any legal person the regular occupation or business of which is the provision of investment services for third parties on a professional basis' (ISD, Art.1(2)) subject only to '[t]he exclusion[s] in . . . [the ISD itself which were] narrower in . . . effect than the existing . . . [RAO] exclusions'.[80]

---

[79] SIB GR 1/88, March 1988, para. 5.
[80] Implementation of the ISD and Capital Adequacy Directive, HMT CD, July 1994, para. 13.

Thus, to 'ensure . . . that the various [exclusions] from the need for authorisation contained in the [RAO] are not available to any firm which falls within the ISD's definition of an investment firm',[81] the RAO provided that:

> Where an investment firm –
>
> (a) provides core investment services to third parties on a professional basis, and
> (b) in doing so would be treated as carrying on an [investment] activity . . . but for an exclusion in any of [3.2.5.1, 3.2.5.2, 3.2.5.4 or 3.2.5.5] . . .
>
> that exclusion is to be disregarded. (RAO 4(4), (5))

The test for 'providing services to third parties on a professional basis' is equivalent to the test for 'holding out' in the dealing as principal exclusion (3.2.5.4) if only because the provision of services on a professional basis must be providing a customer function and, in practice, there is no other ready way of determining when this is occurring.[82]

MiFID has exactly the same effect as the ISD and, in particular, 'What amounts to a "professional basis" depends on . . . factors . . . indicat[ing] the existence or otherwise of a commercial element' (PERG 13.2, Q.7), except that the override applies not only to an 'investment firm' but also to a credit institution within BCD and to a non-EEA 'investment firm' (RAO 4(4), 15(4), 16(2), 19(3), 21(2), 22(3), 23(3), 25(3), 29(3)). That said, in FSA's view, 'if you are trading . . . for your own account . . . as a regular occupation or business on a "professional basis" . . . [y]ou can be an investment firm even if you are not providing investment services to others' (PERG 13.2, Q.8). This may be doubted because it leaves no clear indicia of when an active investor is caught. In any event, if the firm is 'providing services . . . on a professional basis', then instead of the exclusions in 3.2.5.1, 3.2.5.2, 3.2.5.4 and 3.2.5.5, the firm can rely only on the narrower exclusions in MiFID itself. These include: '(b) persons which provide investment services exclusively for' group companies within the narrower MiFID definition; '(d) persons who do not provide any investment service or activities other than dealing on own account unless they are market makers' or systematic internalisers (13.3), which requires that 'buying and selling . . . is . . . your main business' (PERG 13.5, Q.40); (k) commodity dealers not part of a wider financial services group; and (l) Exchange 'locals' (RAO Sched. 3). Insurers are also exempt from MiFID in respect of both their insurance business and MiFID Business (RAO, Sched. 3, para. 1(a); PERG 3.5, Q.36).

---

[81] Draft regulations to implement the ISD and CAD, HMT CD, November 1995, p. 11.
[82] SIB CP 99, August 1996, para. 3. 'Investment services' are limited to MiFID Business (4.2.I(2)), not other Regulated Activities (4.2.I(1)).

3.2.7 By way of business

A licence is required only if the non-excluded investment activity 'is carried on by way of business' (FSMA 22(1)) to distinguish those who provide such services to customers from users, albeit frequent, of such service providers. Given the different nature of the activities, a separate test is provided for 'deposit-taking business' (3.2.1.5) and 'investment business' which is 'carrying on . . . the business of engaging in one or more . . . [investment] activities' (FSMA (Carrying on Regulated Activities By Way of Business) Order 2001, SI 2001/1177). Arguably, this catches a one-off activity because the drafting of the excluded activities, themselves referring to one-off activities, seems to pre-suppose this and case law under closely analogous statutes is to that effect.[83] Nonetheless, the Government has always been clear that '[t]hat is not the intended effect . . . nor do we think that it is the actual effect'[84] and, for FSA, it is 'a question of judgement that takes account of several factors . . . include[ing] the degree of continuity' (PERG 2.3.3).

3.2.8 A licence is required

Without an exemption applying,[85] a licence is required (FSMA 19(1)). An important exemption relates to the status of appointed representative, being 'a person . . . [who] is a party to a contract with an authorised person ("his principal") . . . [for] whose activities . . . his principal has accepted responsibility'. As a result, 'The principal . . . is responsible . . . for anything done or omitted by the representative', although 'Nothing . . . is to cause the knowledge or intentions of a . . . representative to be attributed to his principal for the purpose of determining whether the principal has committed an offence, unless . . . it is reasonable for them to be attributed' (FSMA 34). The activities covered by the exemption must, in a Capital Markets context, fall within 3.2.2.2 or 3.2.2.3, although the transaction arranged does not have to be with the principal (FSMA 2000 (Appointed Representatives) Regulations 2001, SI 2001/1217), and the appointment must comply with SUP 12. MiFID has a similar category of 'tied agent', being 'a person who, under the full and unconditional responsibility of only one . . . firm on whose behalf it acts, promotes investment services

---

[83] See, under the 1900 Money Lenders Act, *Cornelius* v. *Phillips* [1918] AC 199 where the House of Lords held at 217 that 'it is immaterial whether a single transaction or a number of transactions, was involved'; and, under the 1974 Insurance Companies Act, *Bedford Insurance* [1984] 3 WLR 726 where at 735–6 'it would be sufficient to constitute a contravention . . . to enter into a single contract' and, while contradicted by *Stewart* v. *Oriental Fire* [1984] 3 WLR 741, was agreed with by the Court of Appeal in *Phoenix General Insurance* [1986] 2 LLR 552 at 571. Contrast under the PFI, *Rolls* v. *Miller* 27 Ch. D 71 at 88 ('anything which is an occupation, as distinguished from a pleasure').

[84] Parl. Deb., House of Lords, 21 July 1986, Minister, col. 52.

[85] See SI 2001/1201 as amended.

[within 3.2.2.1–3.2.2.4 and 3.2.2.6]' (GLOSS, def. of 'tied agent') or, rather, 'carr[ies] on investment services and activities or ancillary services on its behalf' (SUP 12.2.16(4)). A tied agent 'do[es] not [itself] have passporting rights . . . [but] may . . . provide cross-border services or establish a branch in another EEA State by availing itself of the appointing firm's passport . . . [F]irms may also appoint tied agents established in different EEA States' and, in each case, the tied agent must be registered with the regulator of the State in which the agent is established (SUP 12.2.16(4), 12.4.12).[86] 'A tied agent can only act . . . for one . . . firm' (SUP 12.4.12(6)) and the appointment must comply with SUP 12. Because the firm has responsibility for the activities of the tied agent, it will need to impose on the agent all MiFID obligations that it has to itself comply with.

Contravention of the licensing requirement results in a criminal offence unless 'the accused [can] show that he took all reasonable precautions and exercised all due diligence to avoid committing the offence' (FSMA 23) and 'an agreement made' by the unauthorised person or by 'an authorised person . . . in consequence of something said or done by an' unauthorised person 'is unenforceable against the other party' who 'is entitled to recover . . . any money or other property . . . transferred and . . . compensation for any loss sustained' (FSMA 26, 27) unless 'the Court is satisfied that it is just and equitable . . . [to] allow . . . the agreement to be enforced . . . or . . . money and property . . . transferred . . . to be retained' (FSMA 28(3)).[87] This requires the unlicensed person to have 'reasonably believed that he was not contravening the . . . prohibition' and the licensed person not to have 'kn[own] that . . . he . . . was . . . contravening the . . . prohibition' (FSMA 28(4)–(6)). However, the 'requirement of reasonable belief is not easily satisfied. Someone who is merely negligent and . . . fails to check whether he should be [licensed] . . . will not have a defence'[88] unless 'the . . . ignorance was reasonable. The defence would . . . be available if he had not considered the point, provided it was reasonable . . . not to have done so, say, because the particular activity was not usually considered to be investment business.'[89] Such sanctions had to be expressly provided in the Statute since at general law contracts entered into by unlicensed firms were not void because that would 'affect . . . both the guilty and the innocent parties . . . [T]his could . . . produce very great hardship and injustice on wholly innocent parties; for example, where the dealer fails to perform a bargain which would have resulted in a profit . . . [to] the investor.'[90]

---

[86] MiFID Permissions and Notifications Guide – Update, FSA, September 2007, pp. 20–22.
[87] For deposits, see also FSMA 29.
[88] Parl. Deb., House of Commons, Standing Committee E, 6 February 1986, Minister, col. 136.
[89] Parl. Deb., House of Lords, 14 October 1986, col. 775.
[90] *Hughes* v. *Asset Managers plc* [1995] 3 AER 668 at 672–3. Similarly, for banking business, see *SCF Finance* v. *Masri* [1987] 1 QB 1002 at 1020–1021.

3.3 Process and criteria

If the firm 'provide[s] . . . investment services and/or . . . activities covered by [MiFID it is] subject to authorisation by their Home Member State' under MiFID, if it is an investment firm, or under BCD, if it is a credit institution (MiFID, Recitals 17, 18; Art. 5(1)). Authorisation, or licensing, is only granted if 'the applicant complies with all requirements under the provisions adopted [by the Home Member State] pursuant to [MiFID]', being: first, that the firm 'ha[s] its head office in the same Member State as its registered office' because 'The principles of mutual recognition and of Home Member State supervision require that the Member State . . . should not grant . . . authorisation where factors such as the content of programmes of operations [and/or] the geographical distribution or the activities actually carried on indicate clearly that the investment firm has opted for the legal system of one Member State for the purpose of evading the stricter standards enforced in another Member State within the territory of which it . . . carr[ies] on the greater part of its activities' (MiFID, Recital 22, Arts 5(4), 7(1)); second, it 'has sufficient initial capital in accordance with the . . . [Capital Requirements] Directive' (MiFID, Art. 12; COND 2.4; PRU and IPRU; SUP, App. 1); third, 'the persons who effectively direct the business of . . . [the] firm . . . [are] of sufficiently good repute and sufficiently experienced so as to ensure the sound and prudent management of the . . . firm' and, as regards 10% or larger shareholders ('qualifying holdings'), 'The competent authorit[y] . . . , taking into account the need to ensure the sound and prudent management of . . . [the] firm . . . [is] satisfied as to the suitability of the shareholders' and a 20% or larger shareholding ('close link') 'doe[s] not prevent the effective exercise of the supervisory functions of the competent authority', particularly where the shareholder is from a non-EU State (MiFID, Arts. 9(1), 10; COND 2.3, 2.5; SUP 10, 11); fourth, the firm 'meets its obligations under [the Compensation Scheme] Directive' (MiFID, Art. 11), which was itself limited to a failure to repay investors' money and investments if the firm was 'for reasons directly related to its financial circumstances . . . unable to meet . . . [the] claim'[91] rather than 'negligence, such as wrong advice',[92] leaving funding solely to the Member States;[93] and, fifth, it complies with the systems and controls requirements of MiFID explained in 5.2 (MiFID, Art. 13).

3.4 Passporting

In accordance with the fundamental methodology of the European Single Market for services explained in 2.6, under MiFID:

---

[91] Directive 97/9/EEC of 3 March 1997, Art. 2(2).
[92] Commission Working Paper, 15 October 1992, XV/3039/92-EN, p. 8.
[93] Directive 97/9/EEC, Recital 23. For the UK scheme, see COMP.

> An investment firm[94] authorised in its Home Member State should be entitled to provide investment services or perform investment activities throughout the Community without the need to seek a separate authorisation from the . . . Member State in which it wishes to provide such services or perform such activities. (MiFID, Recital 23)

The passport is available on a cross-border services basis or by establishing a branch in the Host State, merely upon the firm going through a procedure notifying both the Home and Host States (MiFID, Arts. 31, 32; FSMA 31(1)(b), 37, Sched. 3; FSMA 2000 (EEA Passport Rights) Regulations 2001, SI 2001/2511, amended by SI 2006/3385; SUP 13, 13A, 14).[95] Thus, a UK firm can freely passport into any other Member State and a firm formed and licensed in another Member State which exercises its passport rights is deemed to be an FSMA authorised firm (FSMA 31(1)(b); SUP 13A.3), although the FSA rules do not always apply (SUP 13A), as explained in 4.2. In any such case, the passporting rights apply to the MiFID 'investment services and activities' and 'ancillary services' explained in 4.2. Some of these MiFID services and activities are narrower than the scope of the regulated activities under FSMA (3.2.1, 3.2.2) such that an incoming EEA firm establishing a UK branch may require a 'top up licence' (SUP 13A.7), although if passporting on a cross-border services basis it can rely on the overseas person exemption explained in 3.2.4.

A passporting notification is required only if the firm is to 'perform investment services . . . within the . . . [Host State] territor[y]' (MiFID, Art. 31(1)), which is obvious where it establishes a branch but less clear where 'the provision and receipt of the service may take place by post, telephone or fax, through computer terminals or by other means of remote control' (SUP App. 3, para. 3.6.2(2)) although here FSA, following the European Commission, applies a characteristic performance test 'to determine where the activity was carried on . . . In the case of . . . portfolio management, for example, this would mean looking at where the investment decisions and management are actually carried on in order to determine where the service is undertaken. Similarly, a UK stockbroker that receives orders by telephone from a customer in France for execution on a UK Exchange may be deemed to be dealing or receiving and transmitting orders within the . . . UK . . . Where, however, a . . . firm . . . provides advice . . . to customers in another EEA State . . . the firm should make a prior notification [because

---

[94] An equivalent passport in respect of MiFID services and activities is provided to credit institutions under the BCD.

[95] See also: MiFID Permissions and Notifications Guide, FSA, May 2007, Chapter 4 and Partial Regulatory Impact Assessment for Client Classification transitionals, HMT, 13 June 2007, the proposed FSMA (Markets in Financial Instruments) (Amendment No. 2) Regulations 2007 and the September Notifications Guide, Chapter 2 (EEA passporting firms), for transitionals as at 1 November 2007; and CESR/07-317, CESR/07-318 and CESR/07-337, May 2007, for guidance on passporting procedures.

the advice is received in that other State].' This is, in effect, the same test as is applied for the purposes of location of provision of services under the overseas person exclusion explained in 3.2.4. Nonetheless, 'other EEA States may take a different view . . . apply[ing] a solicitation test . . . as to whether it is the consumer or the provider that initiates the business relationship' (SUP App. 3, paras. 3.6.7–3.6.10). A further issue is whether the firm can exercise its passporting rights cross-border into a Host State from a branch location itself outside the EEA, for example Switzerland, which the Commission thought was possible under the ISD[96] and, on similar reasoning, should be possible under MiFID, since 'Member States shall ensure that any . . . firm authorised and supervised by the competent authorities of another Member State . . . may freely perform investment services . . . within their territories, provided that such services . . . are covered by its authorisation' (MiFID, Art. 31(1)), i.e. provided that supervision of the passporting branch is actually exercised by the Home State, a view with which the UK passporting provisions seem to agree (FSMA, Sched. 3, para. 20(1); SUP 13.4.2) although in practice such supervision, at least in terms of detailed rule application, does not occur, as is shown in 4.2.

3.5 Non-EEA firms

A non-EEA firm, for example from the US or Switzerland, can conduct business in the UK in one of three ways. It could do so cross-border into the UK either from a non-EEA location or from a branch in another EEA State, but in either case it would need to rely on the overseas persons exemption (3.2.4). Or it could set up a UK company which is licensed by FSA and operates from a UK place of business, thus being subject to the same licensing and passporting requirements as any other UK firm. Alternatively, it could set up a UK branch of the non-EEA company although under the Treaty of Rome, and consequently the implementing Directives including MiFID, the Single Market freedoms of establishment and provision of cross-border services apply only to 'nationals of the Member State',[97] i.e. a company formed in a Member State. Moreover, the Commission reasoned in relation to the ISD, 'the aim . . . is not to close the Community's financial markets but rather . . . to improve the liberalisation of the global financial markets in [non-EEA] countries' (ISD, 31st Recital). Thus the ISD included a provision, replicated to an extent in MiFID, enabling the Commission to negotiate with non-EEA countries that did not grant equivalent access to EEA firms to that afforded to non-EEA firms within the EEA (ISD, Art. 7; MiFID, Art. 15) 'intended to ensure that Community . . . firms receive

---

[96] Freedom to provide services in the interests of the general good in the Second Banking Directive, Commission Interpretative Communication, 20 June 1997, para. B.5.
[97] European Community Treaty, Arts. 43, 49.

reciprocal treatment' (MiFID, Recital 28). However, under the ISD, 'in the case of branches of [non-EEA] investment firms . . . Member States shall not apply provisions that result in treatment more favourable than that accorded to branches of . . . [EEA] firms' (ISD 5) which '[i]n practice . . . is likely to mean that a Member State would require the branch . . . to be authorised' to the same requirements as under the Directive.[98] MiFID has the same result since 'the procedures for the authorisation . . . of branches of . . . [non-EEA] firms . . . should continue to apply' (MiFID, Recital 28) and, hence, the MiFID override in 3.2.6 applies to non-EEA firms.

[98] Investment Services in the Securities Field, European Commission, XV/138/88-EN, 27 September 1988, Explanatory Memorandum, p. 5.

4
The application of FSA MiFID rules

4.1 Methodology

Like any rule set, and this includes the application of the licensing requirement under FSMA itself (3.2), particular FSA rules or sets of FSA rules apply in accordance with the answers to three questions. First, to which activities, and in relation to which instruments, after applying the exclusions, does the rule/rule set apply? Second, to which institutions? And, third, in which (territorial) locations? As always with rules, which direct behavioural consequences as a result of conditions of application, this can be represented in four different ways: through words, in a descriptive manner albeit somewhat re-ordered from the regulator's original given the ways in which the rules are often expressed; through the use of flowcharts with yes/no directions to reach a conclusion; through a matrix; or through an even more radically schematic representation using formulae, all rules being ultimately reducible to the pattern $X = Z - Y$, i.e. X (rule consequence/application) if Z (conditions of application) unless Y (exemptions). The challenges in all forms of representation are the drafting style used in the original rule, the ordering of the rules and the defined terms so beloved of regulators. This Chapter, for ease of reference, uses the matrix approach although the application rule can be visualised in a formula, with the headings in Figure 5 understood as follows:

$$X = (Z(1) + Z(2) + Z(3)) - Y$$

$$\begin{matrix} \text{rule} \\ \text{consequence} / \\ \text{application} \end{matrix} = \begin{bmatrix} \text{activities} \\ + \\ \text{instruments} \end{bmatrix} + \text{institutions} + \begin{matrix} \text{territorial} \\ \text{location} \end{matrix} - \text{exemptions}$$

4.2 Rules of application

Each of the numbered headings in Figure 5 is explained in the correspondingly numbered paragraphs that follow the Figure. Figure 5 is explained as follows in terms of the headings in the horizontal axis.

Rule / Rule Set		I. Business Covered		II. UK Firm/Bank							III. Non-EEA Firm/ Bank UK Branch	IV. EEA Firm/Bank		
		MiFID Business	Other Regulated Activities	In UK	From UK	EEA Branch			Non-EEA Branch			Into UK	UK Branch	
						Into UK	In Branch State	From Branch State	Into UK	Otherwise in or from branch			In UK	From UK
		(1)	(2)	(1)	(2)	(3)	(4)	(5)	(6)	(7)		(1)	(2)	(3)
(a)	SYSTEMS AND CONTROLS (5.2)	•	•	•	•	•	•	•	•	•	•			
(b)	TRAINING AND COMPETENCE (5.3.1)	•	•	•	•	•	•	•			•			
(c)	APPROVED PERSONS													
(c)(i)	REGISTRATION (5.3.1, 5.4.1)	•	•	•	•						•		•	•
(c)(ii)	CONDUCT (5.3.2, 5.4.2)	•	•	•	•	•	•	•	•	•	•	•	•	•
(d)	CONFLICTS OF INTEREST (6.3.1, 6.3.5)	•	•	•	•	•	•	•	•	•			•	•
(e)	CONDUCT OF BUSINESS – GENERAL													
(e)(i)	MiFID BUSINESS	•		•	•	•		•			•		•	?
(e)(ii)	DESIGNATED INVESTMENT BUSINESS		•	•	•						•		•	•
(f)	INDUCEMENTS (6.3.2)	•	•	•	•	•		•			•		•	•
(g)	SOFT COMMISSION (6.3.3)	•	•	•	•						•		•	•
(h)	RESEARCH (6.3.4)	•	•	•	•	•		•			•		•	•

Figure 5 *The Application of FSA MiFID Rules*

cont. overleaf

RULE / RULE SET		I. BUSINESS COVERED		II. UK FIRM/BANK							III. NON EEA FIRM/BANK UK BRANCH	IV. EEA FIRM/BANK UK BRANCH	
		OTHER REGULATED ACTIVITIES	MiFID BUSINESS	IN UK	FROM UK	EEA BRANCH			NON-EEA BRANCH				
						INTO UK	IN BRANCH STATE	FROM BRANCH STATE	INTO UK	OTHERWISE IN OR FROM BRANCH		IN UK	FROM UK
(i)	CHURNING (6.3.6)	•	•	•	•	•					•	•	
(j)	PERSONAL ACCOUNT DEALING (6.3.7)	•		•	•	•	•	•			•		
(k)	CLIENT PROPERTY												
(k)(i)	CLIENT ASSETS AND CUSTODY (7.1)	•	•	•	•	•	•	•			•		
(k)(ii)	CLIENT MONEY (7.2)	•	•	•	•	•	•	•			•	•	
(l)	CUSTOMER CATEGORISATION AND TERMS OF BUSINESS (8)	•	•	•	•	•		•			•		
(m)	PROMOTIONS (10)	•	•	•	•	•		•			•	•	
(n)	ADVISING CLIENTS												
(n)(i)	SUITABILITY (11.2)	•	•	•	•	•		•			•	•	
(n)(ii)	APPROPRIATENESS (11.3, 11.4)	•	•	•	•	•		•			•	•	
(o)	TRANSACTIONS / DEALING (13.1.1-13.1.3, 13.1.4.1-13.1.4.5, 13.1.4.7, 13.2)		•	•	•	•		•			•	•	
(p)	CONFIRMS (13.1.4.6)	•		•	•						•	•	•
(q)	SYSTEMATIC INTERNALISING (13.3)		•	•	•						•	•	•
(r)	THE PRINCIPLES (9.1, 9.2)	•	•	•	•	•	•	•	•		•	•	•
(s)	MTFs (14.2)		•	•	•	•	•	•	•	•	•	•	•

Figure 5 *(continued)*

I. Business covered

This is answering the very first question: To which activities, and in relation to which instruments, does the rule/rule set apply? There are only two possibilities:

(1) 'Regulated Activity' or 'Designated Investment Business'
A 'Regulated Activity' is any investment activity in 3.2.2.1–3.2.2.6 in relation to a 'designated investment' within 3.2.1.1–3.2.1.10 'carried on by way of business' within 3.2.7. 'Designated Investment Business' covers the same activities except deposit taking within 3.2.1.5 (GLOSS, defs. of 'regulated activity', 'designated investment business'). Both definitions are expressed by reference to 'the . . . activities specified in Part II of the regulated activities order' and this together with the bringing back in of one of the excluded activities in SYSC 1.1.3(2) shows that the activities are not regulated if subject to the exclusions in 3.2.5.1–3.2.5.3 or 3.2.5.5. The Rules usually conjoin 'Regulated Activities' with 'Ancillary Activity', being 'an activity which is not a regulated activity but which is: (a) carried on in connection with a regulated activity; or (b) held out for the purpose of a regulated activity' (GLOSS, def. of 'ancillary activity'), which in practice should be regarded as any other business activity.

(2) 'MiFID Business'
'MiFID Business' is a sub-set of 'Regulated Activity'/'Designated Investment Business', comprising both the so-called core 'investment services and activities' and the non-core 'ancillary services', explained in 3.2.2, in both cases in relation to the 'financial instruments' explained in 3.2.1 (GLOSS, defs. of 'investment services and activities', 'ancillary service'):

Investment services and activities

(1) Reception and transmission of orders . . .
(2) Execution of orders on behalf of clients.
(3) Dealing on own account.
(4) Portfolio management.
(5) Investment advice.
(6) Underwriting . . . and/or placing on a firm commitment basis.
(7) Placing . . . without a firm commitment basis.
(8) Operation of Multi-lateral Trading Facilities.

Ancillary services

(1) Safekeeping and administration . . . including custodianship . . .
(2) Granting credit or loans to an investor to allow him to carry out a transaction . . .
(3) Advice to undertakings on capital structure . . . and advice and services relating to mergers and the purchase of undertakings.
(4) Foreign exchange services . . . connected to the provision of investment services.

(5) Investment research.
(6) Services related to underwriting. (MiFID, Ann. 1, Sections A, B)

While 'ancillary service' (1) amounts to the Regulated Activity within 3.2.2.6, 'ancillary services' (3) and (5) are most unlikely to amount to investment advice within 3.2.2.3 and these, as well as (2), (4) and (6), are not activities requiring a licence (authorisation), although they do obtain the benefit of the passport and are often subject to Conduct of Business Rules. Thus, for example, (2) comprises margin lending, (3) corporate finance advice, (4) FX spot conversion for investment transactions (that is not itself a futures contract within 3.2.1.7), (5) research reports and (6) any corporate finance services in a Capital Markets transaction which is underwritten and not within 'investment services and activities' (6) and (7).

II. UK firm/bank

A UK firm/bank refers to a corporation or partnership formed in the UK and authorised (licensed) by FSA which may operate from a number of locations:

- a UK head office or branch, doing business:
    (1) in the UK, i.e. with UK-based clients; and/or
    (2) from the UK, i.e. with clients based overseas; and/or
- a branch in the EEA, doing business:
    (3) into the UK, i.e. from the branch with UK-based clients; and/or
    (4) in the Host Member State of the branch, i.e. with clients based in that State; and/or
    (5) from the Host State with clients based elsewhere; and/or
- a non-EEA branch, doing business:
    (6) into the UK, i.e. from the branch with UK-based clients; and/or
    (7) otherwise in or from the branch, i.e. with clients based either in the State of the branch or elsewhere other than in the UK. As explained in 3.4, the FSA is understood to take the view that such a branch cannot use its passporting right to do business from such a branch into other EEA States than the UK because the branch is not regulated to EU standards.

MiFID does not apply all of its provisions to banks (credit institutions) (MiFID, Art. 1(2)), but since FSA appears to have chosen to ignore this in relation to both UK banks and EEA banks,[1] the following analysis accepts the FSA rules as drafted.

---

[1] Even though the definition of 'MiFID investment firm' in GLOSS is similarly limited. See also FSA PS 07/2, paras. 8.28–8.30; PERG 13.2, Q.5. The Pre-MiFID limited application of the conduct rules to deposit-taking business (FSA PM COB 1.11.1) appears to have been substantially continued through the application of the particular rules themselves (COBS 1.1.1(1)).

III.   Non-EEA firm/bank UK branch

As explained in 3.5, this is a corporation or partnership formed outside the EEA, for example in the US or Switzerland, which has established a UK branch and been authorised (licensed) by FSA. It is doing business from the branch with clients located in the UK and/or elsewhere in the EEA and/or elsewhere in the World. A non-EEA firm/bank is not an EU organised corporation and, hence, has no rights under the Treaty of Rome or MiFID. As a result, technically, it cannot be carrying on 'MiFID Business', although FSA applies all of the MiFID obligations to such a firm.[2] Hence, FSA uses the term, in relation to such firms/banks, 'equivalent third country business' which, in fact, is identical to MiFID Business within I.(2) above (GLOSS, def. of 'equivalent third country business') and is therefore used inter-changeably in this Book.

IV.   EEA firm/bank

An EEA firm/bank is a corporation or partnership formed in an EEA Member State other than the UK and, as a result, with passport rights to do business:

- cross-border into the UK with UK-based clients;
- by establishing a UK branch:
  in the UK, i.e. with UK-based clients; and/or
  from the UK with clients based in other EEA or non-EEA States.

As regards the headings in the vertical axis of Figure 5 ((a), (b), (c) . . . etc.) and by reference to the types of business (I.(1), (2)) and institutions (II(1), (2) . . . etc.; III; IV(1), (2), (3)):

(a)   Systems and controls

The MiFID rules in 5.2 apply as follows:

- **I.(1), (2):** to all Regulated Activities, including MiFID Business, extending to where the firm deals as principal and to the Ancillary Activity of issuing and approving financial promotions. In addition, the rules 'apply with respect of the carrying on of unregulated activities in a prudential context . . . and . . . take into account any activity of other members of . . . [the] group . . . in determining the appropriateness of the firm's own systems and controls' (SYSC 1.1.3, 1.1.3A, 1.1.4–1.1.6, 1.3.2–1.3.8), a 'prudential context' being the context in which 'the activities have, or might reasonably be regarded as likely to have, a negative effect on . . . confidence in the financial system . . .

[2] For the policy, see FSA CP 06/19, paras. 1.15, 2.15, Ann. 5.

or . . . the ability of the firm to meet . . . the "fit and proper" test . . . or . . . the applicable requirements and standards . . . relating to the firm's financial resources' (GLOSS, def. of 'prudential context').
- **II.(1), (2):** to a UK firm/bank UK head office or branch or EEA branch and, elsewhere **(II(3)–(7))**, 'in a prudential context' (SYSC 1.1.7–1.1.9, 1.3.9–1.3.12). Insofar as the MiFID rules are new, they apply to a 'common platform firm', the following being such firms (the 'common platform' meaning, in FSA-speak, that they are each subject to both MiFID and the Capital Requirements Directive): a UK bank regulated for deposit taking; a building society; a UK investment firm (GLOSS, defs. of 'BIPRU firm', 'bank', 'BCD credit institution', 'CAD full scope firm', 'CAD investment firm', 'common platform firm', 'credit institution', 'EEA bank', full credit institution', 'full scope BIPRU investment firm').
- **III:** to a non-EEA firm/bank 'with respect to activities carried on from an establishment maintained . . . in the United Kingdom' and 'in a prudential context . . . with respect of activities wherever they are carried on' (SYSC 1.1.7, 1.1.10). Since such a firm is not a 'common platform firm', not all of the MiFID systems and controls rules apply (SYSC 1.3.1) and, thus, it must continue to comply with the Pre-MiFID Rules explained in 5.2.1–5.2.3 and 5.2.5 and with the MiFID rules in 5.2.4.

The rules do not apply to a passported EEA firm/bank **(IV)** (SYSC 1.1.1)[3] which must comply with its Home State version of the MiFID rules referred to in 5.2.1–5.2.5. That said, given the FSA's responsibility for the branch's compliance with its own (Host State) implementation of the MiFID conduct rules ((e) below) and the senior Approved Persons' requirement to comply with the Statements of Principle which, in the APER Code of Conduct, are referenced to SYSC standards (in an appropriate case), FSA could require the branch to comply with its systems and controls rules for the purpose of ensuring proper implementation and compliance with the conduct rules (SYSC, App. 1.1.8(2)). This is certainly the case in relation to record keeping and whistleblowing.[4] In any event, the rules apply if the branch carries on Regulated Activities beyond MiFID Business (SYSC 1.1.1, 1.3.1B, 1.3.2, 1.3.10A).

---

[3] Because of the definitions of 'BIPRU firm' and 'bank' in GLOSS, SYSC 1.1.1(6) and 1.3.1 appear to apply all of the systems and controls rules to a UK branch of an EEA bank but, given the Home/Host State split of responsibilities under MiFID recognised in SYSC 1.1.1(1) and 1.3.1B, the rules should not be read this way. Thus, for example, in FSA CP 07/16, Ann. D, a proposed amendment to SYSC, App. 1, para. 1.1.4 makes it clear that the requirement to apportion functions in SYSC 2.1.3 is disapplied. See, generally: SUP 13A, Ann. 1.

[4] FSA CP 07/16, Ann. AB, draft PERG, Q71; SYSC 1.3.1B; SUP 13A, Ann. 1.

(b) Training and competence requirements

Training and competence must be ensured:

- **I.(1), (2):** in respect of all Regulated Activities, and
- **II.(1)–(5):** by a UK firm/bank in respect of its UK and (in respect of MiFID Business) EEA activities,[5] and
- **III:** by a UK branch of a non-EEA firm/bank (TC 1.1.1, 1.1.2).
- **IV.(2), (3):** by a UK branch of an EEA firm/bank in respect of Regulated Activities which are not MiFID Business.

(c) Approved persons

(i) Registration

The rules requiring the registration of Approved Persons explained in 5.3.1 and 5.4.1 apply:

- **I.(1), (2):** to all Regulated Activities (SUP 10.1.1), and
- **II.(1), (2):** to a UK firm/bank's UK establishment (SUP 10.1.1), and
- **III., IV.(2), (3):** to a UK branch of a non-EEA or an EEA firm/bank, but only to the extent explained in 5.3.1 and 5.4.1.

(ii) Conduct rules

Once approved, the individual must comply with the Statements of Principle and Code of Practice for Approved Persons in all his/her activities wherever conducted (APER 1.1.1–1.1.5).

(d) Conflicts of interest

The MiFID rules on conflicts (6.3.1, 6.3.5) apply to:

- **I.(1), (2):** all Regulated Activities, and
- **II.(1)–(7):** a UK firm/bank in respect of its Worldwide operations (SYSC 1.3.3, 10.1.1, 10.1.2, 10.2.1), and
- **III:** a UK branch of a non-EEA firm/bank. Although no specific FSA MiFID conflict rules appear to have been applied to a UK branch of a non-EEA firm/bank and it is not a 'common platform firm', and hence SYSC 10 does not apply, and the Pre-MiFID Rules on conflicts of interest (in FSA PM COB 7.1) have been deleted,[6] the FSA Principle continues (6.3.1, 9.1) and, on a broad view, will import all of the MiFID requirements.
- **IV:** The rules do not apply to an EEA firm/bank: conflicts of interest are a Home State responsibility (MiFID, Arts. 13(2), 18) and, therefore, a UK branch of an EEA firm/bank must comply with its Home State rules.

---

[5] As a result, branch employees need to pass exams to FSA standards (FSA PS 07/13, July 2007, para. 2.24). [6] Cf. FSA CP 06/9, para. 9.20.

(e) Conduct of business rules – general

Before examining the application of specific conduct rules, it is necessary to consider their general, overall, application which may be used in relation to specific conduct rules or modified in their particular context. The general application differs between MiFID Business and Designated Investment Business:

(i) MiFID Business (**I.(2)**)

The conduct rules apply to MiFID Business conducted by:

- **II.(1), (2), (5):** a UK firm/bank in or from the UK and from an EEA branch, except into the UK **(3)** if, were that Host State branch a separate legal person, it would comply with the overseas persons exclusion explained in 3.2.4[7] or, as seems a likely solution to the Article 32(7) issue explained below, the Host State conduct rules apply. Similarly, a non-EEA branch doing business into the UK **(6)** can rely on the overseas persons exemption, in all such cases the application of the exemption being 'compatible with European Law' since there is no Single Market issue in those contexts (1, 2.6) (COBS 1, Ann. 1, Part 2, paras. 1.1(1), 2.1; Part 3, paras. 3.3), and
- **III:** a non-EEA firm/bank in or from the UK, and
- **IV:** an EEA firm/bank branch in the UK if the business is conducted in the UK (COBS 1.1 and Ann. 1, Parts 2, 3).

The disapplication of the FSA conduct rules to the UK branch of an EEA firm/bank doing business from the UK and into the Home State or another EEA State, and the application of FSA conduct rules to the EEA branch of the UK firm/bank doing business from that location, is a result of Article 32(1) and (7) of MiFID:

> [Host] Member States shall ensure that investment services and/or activities . . . may be provided within their territories . . . through the establishment of a branch . . . Member states shall not impose any additional requirements save those allowed under [the next] paragraph . . . in respect of the matters covered by this Directive . . .
>
> The competent authorities of the Member State in which the branch is located shall assume responsibility for ensuring that the services provided by the branch **within its territory** comply with the [conduct of business] obligations laid down in . . . [the Directive] and in measures adopted pursuant thereto. (emphasis added)

On a literal reading this means that Host State conduct rules apply to branch activities with clients located in the Host State (i.e. II.(4) and

---

[7] As a result of MiFID, the exclusion does not apply to a UK formed firm (RAO 72(8)), but this rule is intended to disapply the exemption from COBS.

IV.(2)), being 'within its territory', but not to activities with clients located elsewhere (i.e. II.(3), (5) and IV.(3)) unless the 'characteristic performance' is in the branch (3.2.4). That has the impractical result that in II.(4) and IV.(2) the branch complies with Host State conduct rules and in II.(3), (5) and IV.(3) with Home State conduct rules and so the Commission stated that 'Article 32(7) does not deal with the issue of applicable law with respect to the activity of branches, for instance it does not specify which conduct of business rules should apply, whether a branch operates within the territory of the [Host] Member State . . . or in another Member State' but, rather, it deals with 'supervision of branches'.[8] '[W]here Article 32(7) allocates responsibility for supervision to the host Member State (e.g. conduct of business rules), it is logical that supervision should take place on the basis of the host Member State's regulatory provisions . . . Conversely, in all other cases supervision should take place on the basis of the home Member State's regulatory provisions. The issue of allocation of responsibilities between the . . . home and the host Member State is, to a large extent, not relevant with respect to supervision of a large portion of wholesale business . . . in relation to eligible counterparties.'[9] Thus, 'the following situation can be envisaged concerning allocation of responsibilities [for supervision] between competent authorities:

(a) When the branch through which the service is provided and the client [are] located in the host Member State, responsibility for supervising . . . should be allocated to the host competent authority.
(b) When the client is in the . . . home Member State . . . responsib[ility] for supervising . . . should be [on] the home Member State.
(c) . . . there is a 'grey area' . . . where the client is not either in the Member State of the branch or . . . of the head office.[10]

All the Commission can suggest is that 'Competent authorities should establish Memoranda of Understanding . . . to determine the practical arrangements for their cooperation in the supervision of branches . . . indicat[ing] how supervision would be shared . . . and determine the applicable . . . conduct of business rules',[11] the implication being that this will result in an agreement that Host State rules should apply to all branch activities. This is certainly one reading of FSA's implementation of Article 32(7) for EEA firms' UK branches: 'For an EEA . . . firm, [FSA conduct] rules . . . apply only to its MiFID business carried on from an establishment in, and within the territory of, the United Kingdom.' However, its scope rule for EEA branches of UK firms seems to reach the opposite conclusion: 'For a UK . . . firm, [FSA conduct] rules . . . apply to its MiFID business carried on from an establishment in another EEA State . . . where that

---

[8] Commission Working Document ESC/21/2007, 14 May 2007, para. 6.
[9] Commission Document MARKT/G/3/MVD 2386, 18 June 2007, paras. 6, 7.
[10] Ibid, para. 8.   [11] Ibid, para. 10(3).

business is not carried on within the territory of that State' (COBS 1, Ann. 1, Part 3, paras. 3.3, 3.4).

(ii) Designated Investment Business **(I.(1))**

The conduct rules apply to Designated Investment Business which goes beyond MiFID Business conducted by:

- **II.(1), (2):** a UK firm/bank in or from the UK, and
- **III:** a non-EEA firm/bank in or from the UK, and
- **IV:** an EEA firm/bank UK branch in the UK or from the UK.

(f) Inducements

The inducements rule explained in 6.3.2 applies to both MiFID Business and Designated Investment Business and, thus, the scope rule for both in (e) above applies (COBS 2.3.1).

(g) Soft commission

This rule (6.3.3) applies to Designated Investment Business within (e)(ii) above (COBS 11.1.1, 11.1.3 and 11.6.2).

(h) Research

The systems and controls rules in 6.3.4.1 and 6.3.4.2 apply only to the MiFID Business of a UK firm/bank carried on in or from the UK or an EEA branch, although the disclosure rules in 6.3.4.3 apply to all firms' Designated Investment Business in or from their UK establishment (COBS 1.1.1, 12.1.2, 12.1.3).

(i) Churning

This rule, explained in 6.3.6, applies to discretionary management or investment advice given in the course of Designated Investment Business (COBS 9.1).

(j) Personal account dealing

The following must have personal account dealing rules (6.3.7) in place in the conduct of Designated Investment Business:

- **II.(1)–(5):** a UK firm/bank operating in or from the UK or an EEA branch and
- **III:** a UK branch of a non-EEA firm/bank,

but they do not apply to a UK branch of an EEA firm/bank **(IV)** (COBS 11.1.1, 11.1.4, 11.1.5, 11.7).

(k) Client property

The client property rules divide into:

(i) Client assets and custody
These rules apply to all MiFID Business and, on an opt-in basis, to all other Regulated Activities carried on by:

- **II.(1)–(5):** a UK firm/bank operating in or from the UK or an EEA branch, and
- **III:** a UK branch of a non-EEA firm/bank,

but not to an EEA firm/bank's UK branch **(IV)** (CASS 1.2.2, 1.2.3, 1.2.7, 2.1.2A, 2.1.9(4), 3.1.1, 6.1.1).

(ii) Client money
The client money rules have exactly the same application as in (i) above (CASS 1.2.2, 1.2.3, 1.2.7, 2.1.2A, 2.1.9(4), 4.1.1, 4.1.2(6), 7.1.1–7.1.6).

(l) Customer categorisation

The need to categorise customers applies to MiFID Business and to other Regulated Activities, with some minor differences between them in terms of the categorisation criteria (8.3), in line with the general application in (e) above (COBS 3.1.1–3.1.5, 8.1.1).

(m) Financial promotions and marketing communications

See 10.5.2.1.

(n) Advising clients

The advisory obligations divide into:

(i) Suitability
This (11.2) applies, in relation to discretionary management and investment advice (3.2.2.3, 3.2.2.4) given in the course of MiFID business or, where the client is a Retail Client or a pension scheme, Designated Investment Business as in (e)(i) and (ii) above, respectively (COBS 9.1.1, 9.1.3, 9.1.4).

(ii) Appropriateness
This obligation (11.3, 11.4) is limited to MiFID Business, in accordance with (e)(i) above, and direct offer financial promotions for derivatives (10.5.2.4) (COBS 10.1).

(o) Transactions/dealing

The rules on executing client orders/transactions (13.1.1–13.1.3, 13.1.4.1–13.1.4.5, 13.1.4.7) apply to MiFID Business as in (e)(i) above (COBS 11.1.1, 11.1.2).

For the application of the trade and transaction reporting requirements, see 13.4.

(p) Confirms

Confirms must be issued in the course of Designated Investment Business (13.1.4.6) (COBS 16.2.1).

(q) Systematic internalising

This market making type obligation (13.3) applies to MiFID Business when conducted by the following in or from the UK:

- **II.(1), (2):** a UK firm/bank, and
- **III:** a non-EEA firm/bank, and
- **IV.(2), (3):** an EEA firm/bank (MAR 6.1.1, 6.1.2).

(r) The Principles

The Principles (9.1) apply to MiFID Business and other Regulated Activities on a differential application basis in relation to the UK and Worldwide activities of:

- **II. (1)–(7):** a UK firm/bank, and
- **III:** a non-EEA firm/bank which has a UK branch, and
- **IV (2), (3):** an EEA firm/bank which has a UK branch.

For a detailed explanation, see 9.1.2.

(s) MTFs

The specific MTF rules (14.2) apply to the MiFID Business activity of operating an MTF (3.2.2.7) and, accordingly, apply to such operations of:

- **II.(1)–(7):** a UK firm/bank anywhere, and
- **III:** a non-EEA firm/bank operating an MTF in or from the UK, and
- **IV.(2), (3):** an EEA firm/bank operating an MTF in or from the UK (MAR 5.1.1).[12]

---

[12] Although such activity is passported (3.2.2.7), FSA applies its rules as a result of MAR 5.1.1(2) and the definition of 'overseas firm'.

PART III
The firm's infrastructure

5
Systems and controls

5.1 Evolution of FSA's approach

FSA's current approach to firms' infrastructure is a hybrid development from both banking and securities regulation. The former started with the 1987 Banking Act under which the licensed bank had to 'conduct its business in a prudent manner' and, for this purpose, 'maintain . . . adequate systems of control . . . to enable the business to be prudently managed and comply with the duties imposed . . . under this Act' and the Bank of England, as supervisor, had to 'publish . . . a statement of the principles in accordance with which it is acting . . . in interpreting the[se] criteria'.[1] Initially the Bank stated that 'considerations include . . . management arrangements; . . . general strategy and objectives; planning arrangements; policies on accounting, lending and other exposures . . . and recruitment arrangements and training to ensure that the institution has . . . experienced and skilled staff . . . to carry out its . . . activities in a prudent manner'.[2] However, by the mid-1990's, 'internal control systems should provide reasonable assurance that:

(a) the business is planned and conducted in an orderly and prudent manner in adherence to established policies;
(b) transactions and commitments are entered into in accordance with management's . . . authority;
(c) management is able to safeguard the assets and control the liabilities of the business . . .
(d) the . . . records of the business provide complete, adequate and timely information;
(e) management is able to monitor on a regular and timely basis . . . the adequacy of . . . capital, liquidity [and] profitability . . .
(f) management is able to identify, regularly assess and . . . quantify . . . risks.[3]

Accordingly, when FSA took over bank supervision '[t]he nature and the scope of the . . . systems . . . should be commensurate with [the bank's] . . . particular circumstances, . . . size, the nature of its business, the manner in

---
[1] 1987 Banking Act, Sched. 3, para. 4 and Section 16.
[2] Section 16: Statements of Principles, Bank of England, May 1988, para. 2.23.
[3] Bank of England BSD/1994/2, March 1994, para. 15.

which the business is structured, organised and managed [and] the nature, volume and complexity of its transactions'.[4]

At the same time, under the 1986 FSAct, the SROs, in the context of the accurate calculation of regulatory capital, required 'An adequate internal control system'[5] 'to demonstrate . . . the Firm's systems of recording and processing transactions to enable their adequacy to be assessed as a basis for the preparation of the financial statements and other regulatory returns',[6] which in the New Settlement (2.4.3) became a Core Rule ('A firm must, for the purpose of its compliance with rules of financial supervision, ensure that its internal controls and systems are adequate for the size, nature and complexity of its activities')[7] and a Principle ('A firm should organise and control its internal affairs in a responsible manner').[8] In the Maxwell scandal (2.5) these were used to conclude that 'Compliance with . . . internal control[s], and their effectiveness in practice, needs to be monitored on a continuing basis. Documentation of systems and controls is essential if they are to be understood, communicated and operated effectively and consistently.'[9] They were also used to discipline Lehman Brothers in relation to certain stocklending transactions even though '[t]here is no allegation that Lehman should not have entered into any of the transactions . . . [and] Lehman did not know or have reason to know . . . that Robert Maxwell was using the arrangements [improperly]', because 'one of the Maxwell . . . . companies was repeatedly misidentified in documents . . . [and] adequate internal account opening documentation was not retained . . . [and] It failed to employ sufficiently rigorous procedures to monitor substitution of collateral'.[10]

Then, in 1995, Barings Bank crashed due to 'the unauthorised and ultimately catastrophic activities of . . . one individual . . . that went undetected as a consequence of a failure of management and other internal controls of the most basic kind',[11] which demonstrated the need to properly regulate firms' infrastructures. The Barings Group traded derivatives on the Singapore and Tokyo Exchanges through Baring Futures (Singapore) Pte Limited which booked the proprietary transactions to Baring Securities Limited, London, all margin calls being paid by Baring Brothers & Co Limited, the bank. Nick Leeson, the trader in Singapore, disguised his losses as profit, margin calls of almost £500 million were paid to the Exchanges and, in the end, with losses of over £820 million on the positions, the bank ran out of cash, could not meet the margin calls and went

---

[4] Statements of Principles, FSA, 1998 revision, para. 2.29.
[5] TSA Enforcement, TSA, July 1987, Section III.
[6] Guidance Notes on Ch. III – Financial Regulation, TSA, 15 November 1990.
[7] Core Rule C.   [8] Statement of Principle 9, SIB, 1990.
[9] Custody Review, SIB DP, August 1993, Ch. 3, App.   [10] SFA BN 308, 4 March 1996.
[11] Report of the Board of Banking Supervision Enquiry into the Circumstances of the Collapse of Barings ('BoBs Report'), 18 July 1995, para. 14.1.

bust. The failures were legion: Leeson, who started at Barings as a book-keeper and had no training as a dealer,[12] was responsible for both dealing and back office settlement such that '[t]he independent monitoring and control . . . of risk . . . was inadequate';[13] 'reporting lines were . . . not . . . clear . . . [which] resulted in confusion and a pervasive lack of management control . . . [such that] Leeson was not properly supervised';[14] 'Barings management in London believed the trading . . . to be essentially risk free and very profitable' since they had no understanding of how derivatives worked such that, as one senior manager put it, 'all of us . . . found it very puzzling. But we accepted it' and, as a result, 'Barings . . . [ignored] significant warning signals of the danger to which it was exposed';[15] and '[t]here was a failure of financial controls with regard to the . . . payments' of margin which 'Barings did not control . . . by the use of gross limits or otherwise'.[16] However, the regulators were also at fault due to the lack of coordination between the Bank of England, as supervisor of the bank and of the Group for regulatory capital purposes, and SFA, as the regulator of Barings Securities' derivatives activities (which was the most graphic example of why a single regulator was considered necessary: 2.5). Moreover, the Bank of England's supervisory approach was criticised since '[i]t should . . . seek to obtain a more comprehensive understanding of how . . . risks . . . in . . . businesses are controlled by . . . management' and it 'regarded controls in Barings as informal but effective. It had confidence in Barings' senior management . . . Accordingly it placed greater reliance on statements made to it by management than it would have done had this degree of confidence not existed.'[17] From SFA's perspective, three factors combined in its conclusion that '[w]e have got to address management and . . . make management pay attention to their responsibilities':[18] first, that SFA should consider a firm's subsidiaries in assessing risk[19] such that 'regulators cannot perform their duties effectively without a full and thorough understanding of the internal controls and relationships within a group of companies';[20] second, '[t]he collapse of Barings illustrated that any assessment of risk cannot be based solely on prudential [regulatory capital] information. Other factors, such as the quality of the group internal controls and the degree of understanding of management of . . . risks . . . will also need to be taken into account';[21] and, third, SFA's inability to demonstrate any rule breach by the chairman and chief executive

---

[12] *The City of London*, D. Kynaston, Chatto & Windus, Vol 4, 2001, p. 765.
[13] BoBs Report, paras. 1.35, 1.42, 2.73. [14] Ibid, paras. 2.23, 2.28, 13.16.
[15] Ibid, paras. 1.41, 1.68, 3.56–3.58. [16] Ibid, paras. 13.21, 13.27.
[17] Ibid, paras. 13.58, 14.37.
[18] House of Commons, Treasury Committee, First Report, Barings Bank and International Regulation, Vol I, 12 December 1996, para. 12, Nicholas Durlacher, Chairman SFA.
[19] BoBs Report, para. 14.63. [20] House of Commons Report, para. 33.
[21] Ibid, para. 58.

personally, 'to the obvious annoyance of the SFA'[22] since, although registered with SFA, the rules imposed no clear personal responsibility for the firm's systems and controls.

As a result, SFA proposed a rule under which the firm's CEO had to 'take all reasonable steps to ensure that all employees . . . act, so as to avoid serious financial damage to the firm, or . . . its reputation' but sought a form of strict liability by reversing the burden of proof. 'Where there has been serious financial damage to the firm, or . . . its reputation, and SFA has reason to believe that failure of management controls caused or contributed to the . . . damage, it shall be presumed that the [CEO] has failed to comply with th[is] duty . . . unless it can be shown that he has taken all reasonable steps to avoid such damage.'[23] SFA ultimately withdrew this as 'unnecessarily harsh'[24] against an industry outcry 'that this would give the . . . [CEO] an open-ended responsibility for everything that happens in the . . . firm, whether or not it was within their control',[25] but then two further systems and controls cases occurred. A Flemings Asset Management company, licensed by IMRO, delegated management of client portfolios to Jardine Fleming Asset Management in Hong Kong, which re-allocated transactions to client accounts in a manner that would not have been allowed under IMRO rules, resulting in a breach by Flemings Asset Management of the systems and controls Principle since it 'failed adequately to monitor business delegated' to JFAM.[26] 'A firm may delegate functions but remains responsible . . . to customers for the services that it contracts. It should therefore check that the functions are being properly carried out by the delegate . . . [and] is expected to have procedures to ensure that it does carry out this monitoring.'[27] And Morgan Grenfell International Fund Management Limited was fined when an investment manager repeatedly breached clients' investment restrictions because 'it did not have adequate procedures or monitoring . . . to ensure that the [clients] were managed in accordance with the relevant . . . investment restrictions'.[28]

For the regulators, 'the common thread that runs through many of these cases . . . is that the organisations' own knowledge and control of their business was . . . seriously lacking . . . [and] regulators need to be comfortable that top management is in reality taking responsibility for the controls which, if in place, lessen risk',[29] 'to draw adequate comfort about the management set-up, without assuming management's proper responsibilities

---

[22] Ibid, para. 39.   [23] SFA BN 358, draft rules 2–28(2), 7–23(5).
[24] SFA BN 439, 17 September 1997, p. 4.
[25] City Regulator Targets Executives, FT, 4 September 1996.
[26] IMRO PR 21/96, 29 August 1996.   [27] IMRO Reporter 15, August 1996, p. 11.
[28] IMRO PR 05/97, 16 May 1997.
[29] Regulation and Management, Andrew Large, Chairman SIB, speech to the FT Life Insurance Conference, 30 October 1996, paras. 13–16.

for determining how their business should be run'.[30] The search was for a set of rules '[t]he purpose of [which] . . . is not retribution, . . . [but] to prevent things going wrong in the first place. But perhaps the possibility of retribution will concentrate the mind',[31] or at least lessen the regulator's public responsibility for the inevitability of such failures.

Accordingly, under FSMA, 'In discharging its general functions [FSA] must have regard to . . . the responsibilities of those who manage the affairs of authorised persons' (FSMA 2(3)(b)) which, on the one hand, enables FSA to make intrusive rules which 'look to senior management . . . to ensure that businesses are run in a sound and prudent manner, and in compliance with statutory and regulatory requirements'[32] so that 'senior management . . . [cannot] walk away from major breaches . . . without any adverse consequences for themselves'[33] and yet, on the other hand, enables FSA to back off from any responsibility of its own for firms' breaches on the basis that it 'will not seek to second guess management or . . . impose detailed requirements on the day-to-day running of firms'.[34] Of course, '[r]egulators are not in a position to engage constantly in the detailed monitoring of the affairs of all . . . firms and . . . detect . . . non-compliant acts',[35] but the key question is whether FSA is correct that 'this is not an attempt by us to run your business, neither is it an attempt to create a scapegoat if things go wrong',[36] a statement that might be questioned in the light of FSA's penchant for enforcement actions, against both firms and senior managers, based solely on the Principle of systems and controls,[37] particularly in the light of the mantra relating to principles-based regulation (2.5.8).

FSA's overall approach can be seen through three sets of rules: (Systems and Controls Rules applying to the firm (5.2); Senior Management Responsibility Rules (5.3); and Approved Person Rules (5.4)) and a risk methodology operated by FSA in monitoring firms (5.6).

5.2 Systems and controls rules

FSA's systems and controls rules are grounded in an over-arching Principle that 'A firm must take reasonable care to organise and control its affairs

---

[30] SIB CP 109, July 1997, para. 8.
[31] Andrew Large, Chairman SIB, quoted in 'Call for City Firms to Define Directors' Duties', FT, 25 July 1997.
[32] Meeting our Responsibilities, FSA, August 1998, para. 124.
[33] N2-A starting point, not a destination, Howard Davies, Chairman FSA, speech at the Foreign Banks and Securities Houses Association Conference, 29 November 2001.
[34] FSA PN/046/2001, 26 April 2001.   [35] FSA CP 35, December 1999, paras. 2–4.
[36] FSA Handbook Development, FSA, 2000.
[37] See, for example: Charterhouse Consulting, Final Notice, 11 May 2007 and BNP Paribas, Final Notice, 10 May 2007 (firms); Steven Leslie Davis, Final Notice, 21 July 2006, Paul Harrison, Final Notice, 18 September 2006 and Idris Nagaty, Final Notice, 14 September 2005 (senior managers).

responsibly and effectively, with adequate risk management systems' (PRIN 2.1.1, Principle 3) which 'include[s]:

(a) having . . . senior managers who are fit and proper for their roles, and operate adequate arrangements for securing the suitability of persons who carry out functions on its behalf;
(b) apportioning responsibilities among senior managers . . . in such a way that:
   - their individual responsibilities are clear; and
   - the business . . . [is] adequately monitored and controlled . . .
(c) operating robust arrangements for meeting the standards and requirements of the regulatory system . . .
(d) keeping adequate . . . records.

Paragraph (a) 'extends to competence as well as honesty'.[38] The Principle continues under MiFID and, as before, it is expanded upon in a number of detailed requirements which change in detail, but not overall substance. The new FSA MiFID-inspired rules implement not only MiFID but also the Capital Requirements Directive since 'both CRD and MiFID have management oversight, internal governance and systems and controls requirements. Though their approaches and the wording of their requirements are not identical, the Directives cover broadly the same ground' and, thus, FSA 'creat[ed] a unified set of requirements applying to all common platform [4.2(a)] firms based on the Directives' requirements' because even though 'setting a single unified standard can involve a substantive levelling-up of standards beyond what a particular Directive may require' and, so, 'super-equivalence',[39] 'our approach [i]s sensible and practical' resulting in 'one set of rules . . . [rather than] two parallel sets'.[40] These detailed rules are best explained under the headings set out in 5.2.1–5.2.5 and they apply as explained in 4.2(a).

5.2.1 Overall requirement

Pre-MiFID: The rule required the firm to 'take reasonable care to establish and maintain such systems and controls as are appropriate to its business' (FSA PM SYSC 3.1.1) which, since one of the recommendations in Barings was that '[a]ll institutions should maintain an up-to-date organisational chart which shows clearly all reporting lines and who is accountable to whom and for what',[41] included the requirement that 'A firm's reporting lines should be clear . . . [and], together with clear management responsibilities, should be communicated . . . within the firm' (FSA PM SYSC 3.2.2). Similarly, another conclusion in Barings was that 'clear segregation of duties is a fundamental principle of internal control . . . and . . . the first

---

[38] FSA CP 13, September 1998, p. 13 and para. 29.   [39] FSA CP 06/9, paras. 1.7, 2.13.
[40] FSA CP 06/13, para. 1.7.   [41] BoBs Report, para. 14.13.

line of protection against the risk of fraudulent or unauthorised activities'.[42] Hence, 'a firm should segregate the responsibilities of individuals and departments in such a way as to reduce opportunities for financial crime or contravention of . . . the regulatory system. For example, the duties of front office and back office staff should be segregated so as to prevent a single individual initiating, processing and controlling transactions' (FSA PM SYSC 3.2.5).

Traditionally, the firm's systems and controls were related to its financial affairs, that is market, credit and liquidity risk, but post-Barings, and certainly post-Basel II, they have to relate to every other kind of risk the firm faces, i.e. 'operational risk', being 'the risk of loss, resulting from inadequate or failed internal processes, people and systems, or from external events'. Processes and systems are in all of Front, Middle and Back Office, external events are any 'significant change to [the firm's] organisation, infrastructure and business operating environment', whether of the magnitude of a September 11 or a temporary power failure, and links into business continuity, and people risk originating in anyone within the organisation (FSA PM SYSC 3A.2.1, 3A.7, 3A.8, 3A.6).

MiFID: Systems and controls implemented within the firm to comply with the Pre-MiFID Rules[43] would continue to comply with the MiFID rules which are to the same effect albeit phrased differently.[44] For the application of these rules see 4.2(a) and 8.2.1. Thus, the firm 'must have robust governance arrangements, which include a clear organisational structure with well defined, transparent and consistent lines of responsibility, effective processes to identify, manage, monitor and report the risks it is, or might be, exposed to, internal control mechanisms, including sound administrative and accounting procedures and effective control and safeguard arrangements for information processing systems'. As part of this, the firm must 'establish, implement and maintain systems and processes . . . adequate to safeguard the security, integrity and confidentiality of information', 'segregat[e] . . . duties within the firm . . . to ensure that no one individual is completely free to commit a firm's assets or incur liabilities on its behalf' (which 'do[es] not prohibit employees from performing more than one function . . . [but requires] appropriate systems and controls . . . to prevent that person from discharging any functions dishonestly, incompetently or unprofessionally'),[45] 'ensure that . . . personn[el] are aware of the procedures that must be followed for the proper discharge of their responsibilities' (which 'cover[s] the firm's business as a whole, not just . . . MiFID [Business]')[46] and 'monitor and, on a regular basis, evaluate the adequacy

---

[42] Ibid, para. 4.17.   [43] Some of which continue to apply: SYSC 3.1.1A.
[44] For the transitional period between 1 January 2007 and 1 November 2007, and the carrying into effect generally of the rules on the latter date, see SYSC TP1.
[45] FSA PS 06/13, para. 3.8.   [46] Ibid, para. 3.4.

and effectiveness of its systems, internal control mechanisms and arrangements' 'depend[ing] on the circumstances particular to that firm' (SYSC 4.1.1, 4.1.5, 4.1.10, 5.1.7, 5.1.8, 5.1.12).[47] These 'requirements are not substantially different from . . . [the Pre-MiFID] material which [wa]s primarily detailed guidance . . . [although the new requirements] extend . . . to all employees . . . whether or not they are involved in MiFID or non-MiFID business'[48] and 'should be applied proportionately and flexibly . . . to the nature, scale and complexity of the individual firm and its business'.[49]

Risks are again widely defined to include credit, counterparty, market, liquidity, interest rate and operational risks (SYSC 7.1, 11–16) and the firm must have 'risk management policies and procedures . . . which identify the risks relating to the firm's activities, processes and systems' 'including those posed by the macro economic environment in which it operates in relation to the status of the business cycle' and 'set the level of risk tolerated by the firm . . . [and] manage the risks in light of that level of risk tolerance', including 'monitor[ing] . . . the adequacy and effectiveness of the firm's risk management policies and procedures' (SYSC 7.1.2–7.1.5). The sheer scale of the risks to which the firm is required to have regard is indicated by the continuing width of the definition of 'operational risk' (see above) and the need to:

> implement policies and processes to evaluate and manage the exposure to operational risk, including to low frequency high severity events . . . [F]irms must articulate what constitutes operational risk for the purposes of those policies and procedures. (SYSC 7.1.16)

In addition, the firm must 'have . . . risk management processes and internal control mechanisms for the purpose of assessing and managing its own exposure to group risk . . . and . . . ensure that its group has adequate, sound and appropriate risk management processes and internal control mechanisms at the level of the group' (SYSC 12.1.8, 13, 14.1.14, 14.1.65). As a consequence, 'Business planning and risk management are closely related activities . . . [and] the forward-looking assessment of a firm's financial resources needs, and of how the business plans may affect the risks that it faces, are important elements of prudential risk management' such that 'A firm must . . . maint[ain] . . . a business plan and appropriate systems for the management of prudential risk' (SYSC 14.1.17, 14.1.18).

All of this is relatively easy to comprehend. However, in the light of its increased emphasis on principles-based regulation (2.5.8), FSA is now saying that 'managing compliance risk is a complex and demanding task for firms, but one which we attach the highest importance to'.[50] It has not

---

[47] Ibid, para. 2.12. See also: SYSC 14.1.30–14.1.33 (Segregation of Duties) and 14.1.46–14.1.50 (Management Information).   [48] FSA CP 06/9, paras. 6.3, 6.4.
[49] FSA PS 06/13, para. 5.5.
[50] 'Managing Compliance Risk in Major Investment Banks – Good Practices, FSA Dear CEO Letter, 19 July 2007.

defined 'compliance risk', although it presumably means the risk of any rule breach, and the 'good practices observed' by FSA in the industry include:

> . . . a clear definition of compliance risk [formulated by the firm] that is accessible to all staff . . .
>
> . . . a clear message within the firm that compliance risk is owned by the business . . .
>
> The firm articulates the characteristics of the desired culture and behaviours that it expects . . . An example . . . is . . . a values statement and providing training around this.
>
> Senior management provide leadership in defining and embedding desired behaviours and culture.[51]

As with so much in principles-based regulation one must agree, but in practice the direction to 'be good' tends to be opaque at best (2.5.8).

5.2.2 Apportionment of responsibility

Pre-MiFID: To ensure that management at all levels was held to account and because one of the key recommendations in Barings was that 'clearly defined lines of responsibility and accountability covering all activities must be established and all managers and employees informed of the reporting structure . . . beyond profit performance to encompass risks, clients, support operations and personnel issues',[52] FSA required the firm to 'take reasonable care to maintain a clear and appropriate apportionment of significant responsibilities among its directors and senior managers in such a way that:

(1) it is clear who has which of those responsibilities; and
(2) the business and affairs of the firm can be adequately monitored and controlled by the directors, relevant senior managers and governing body of the firm. (FSA PM SYSC 2.1.1)

Moreover, to ensure clear accountability, the firm had to appoint at the top of the firm 'one or more individuals . . . [with] the functions of . . . dealing with the [above] apportionment of responsibilities . . . and . . . overseeing the establishment and maintenance of systems and controls [under 5.2.1]', this function usually going to the CEO, 'a record of the [apportionment] arrangements' throughout the firm being kept, which usually 'include organisational charts . . . , job descriptions, committee constitutions and terms of reference' (FSA PM SYSC 2.1.3, 2.1.4–2.1.6, 2.2.1(1), 2.2.2(1)). And, as part of this, the 'arrangements should . . . furnish [the firm's] governing body with the information it needs to play its part in identifying,

---

[51] Ibid, App.   [52] BoBs Report, para. 4.12.

measuring, managing and controlling risks of regulatory concern', such risks being defined identically with the FSA's four Objectives explained in 2.5.1 (FSA PM SYSC 3.2.11).

These requirements were reflected in the rules for the appointment of senior management as Approved Persons (5.3.1).

MiFID: The requirement to apportion responsibility will not continue expressly (SYSC 1.1.1), but only implicitly as a result of rules requiring a firm to have:

> robust governance arrangements, which include a clear organisational structure with well defined, transparent and consistent lines of responsibility . . . and internal control mechanisms . . . [and]
>
> (1) . . . decision-making procedures and an organisational structure which clearly and in a documented manner specifies reporting lines and allocates functions and responsibilities;
> (2) . . . adequate internal control mechanisms designed to secure compliance with decisions and procedures at all levels of the firm; and
> (3) . . . effective internal reporting and communication of information at all relevant levels of the firm. (SYSC 4.1.1, 4.1.4)

Moreover, the 'firm, when allocating functions internally, must ensure that senior personnel . . . are responsible for ensuring that the firm complies with its obligations under MiFID' (SYSC 4.3.1). Originally, FSA intended to maintain the express apportionment rule, but this required (in relation to UK incorporated firms and UK branches of EEA firms) a notification under Article 4 of the Level 2 Directive as 'super-equivalent' which it withdrew when it 'concluded that, given the similarities between [Pre-MiFID] SYSC 2 and the MiFID requirements, we can rely on copy-out of the MiFID provisions . . . So, the impact of dis-applying SYSC 2 . . . is not likely to be significant. We asked a sample of . . . firms if the difference between SYSC 2 and MiFID . . . would affect their behaviour. Ninety-seven percent . . . said this would not lead to any change.'[53] Thus, the FSA expectation is identical, and the express requirement will be retained for UK branches of non-EEA firms and firms carrying on solely Regulated Activities which are not MiFID Business (4.2.I(1), 4.2.I(2)).

Part of complying with (3) includes 'that its senior personnel receive on a frequent basis, and at least annually [which in practice, will not be frequent enough given senior management's overall responsibility for compliance explained in 5.3.1], written reports on [compliance, internal audit and risk]' (SYSC 4.1.4, 4.3.2(1). See also: SYSC 4.3). Hence, the requirements for registration of senior managers as Approved Persons also continue (5.3.1).

---

[53] FSA CP 07/16, paras. 3.6, 3.8. See also: Ibid, Ann. D.

Systems and controls

For the application of these rules, see 4.2(a) and (c)(i). Where an EEA firm provides services into the UK on a cross-border basis the rules do not apply at all and if it establishes a UK branch then it is required only to 'allocate to one or more individuals . . . the function . . . of . . . overseeing the establishment and maintenance of systems and controls' 'relating to the conduct of the firm's activities [with clients] carried on from its UK branch' (SYSC 1.1.1, 2.1.3(2), 2.1.6, Q12).

5.2.3 Control functions

Pre-MiFID: In Barings there had been '[a] breakdown in, or absence of, internal controls at a basic and fundamental level . . . Each institution must determine . . . the controls most relevant and applicable to its business . . . A . . . financial institution [should establish] . . . an independent risk management function overseeing all activities . . . and covering all aspects of risk.'[54] As a result, against the background of 'plann[ing] its business appropriately so that it is able to identify, measure, manage and control risks of regulatory concern', including business continuity planning, 'A firm must take reasonable care to establish and maintain effective systems and controls for compliance with applicable requirements and standards under the regulatory system' and, as part of this, it had to have: 'systems and controls . . . to identify, assess, monitor and manage money laundering risk'; 'a separate compliance function . . . staffed by an appropriate number of competent staff who are sufficiently independent to perform their duties objectively . . . [with] ultimate recourse to its governing body', and which is 'sufficiently focused on the setting and monitoring of compliance standards';[55] 'a separate risk assessment function responsible for assessing the risks that the firm faces and advising the governing body and senior managers on them'; an internal audit function with 'the task of monitoring the appropriateness and effectiveness of . . . . systems and controls'; and 'an audit committee . . . [which] examine[s] management's processes for ensuring the appropriateness and effectiveness of systems and controls . . . [and] the arrangements made by management to ensure compliance with . . . the regulatory system' (FSA PM SYSC 3.2.6, 3.2.6A, 3.2.7, 3.2.10(1), 3.2.15, 3.2.16, 3.2.17, 3.2.19).

MiFID: Very similar requirements continue, although phrased differently and usually in more detail, including the need for business continuity planning and 'systems and controls that . . . enable [the firm] to identify, assess, monitor and manage money laundering risk' (11.2.2.1) (SYSC 4.1.6–4.1.8, 6.3). Overall, obligations are placed upon the firm to have 'adequate policies and procedures sufficient to ensure compliance . . . with its obligations under the regulatory system' and 'to detect any risk of failure by the firm to

---

[54] BoBs Report, paras. 14.20, 14.24.
[55] Carr Sheppards Crosthwaite, Final Notice, FSA, 19 May 2004, para. 3.1.

comply' (SYSC 6.1.1, 6.1.2). Here, FSA noted the 'concern ... that the requirement ... [to] "ensure compliance" ... might be ... more ... onerous ... than the ... [Pre-MiFID] requirement ... "to take reasonable care"', but its only comment was that this 'is a direct copy out of MiFID'.[56] The definition of 'regulatory system', with which the controls need to ensure compliance, is extended to any directly applicable European Regulation, although FSA 'confirm that the requirements of the regulatory system are those that are derived from ... FSMA, and EU Directives and Regulations. Guidelines, standards and advice issued by CESR and CEBS fall outside the regulatory system and do not therefore set binding obligations on firms.'[57] To this end, the 'firm must maintain a permanent and effective compliance function which operates independently and which has the following responsibilities:

(1) to monitor and, on a regular basis, to assess the adequacy and effectiveness of the measures and procedures put in place ... and the actions taken to address any deficiencies ... ; [and]
(2) to advise and assist ... person[nel] ... to comply.

Moreover:

(1) the compliance function must have the necessary authority, resources, expertise and access to all relevant information; [and]
(2) a compliance officer must be appointed and must be responsible for the compliance function ... ; [and]
(3) ... persons involved in the compliance function must not be involved in the performance of services or activities they monitor; [and]
(4) the method of determining the remuneration of the ... persons involved in the compliance function must not compromise their objectivity. (SYSC 6.1.3, 6.1.4)[58]

Although the express articulation of the monitoring requirement is new, FSA 'do not believe this adds materially to our existing requirements as we believe this obligation is implicit in [the Pre-MiFID Rules]'.[59] As regards the independence of Compliance, 'a firm may give additional responsibilities [beyond those referred to above] to the compliance officer ... [T]hose working in ... the compliance function may receive bonuses calculated according to the performance of the firm as a whole. This would not compromise their objectivity. However, objectivity is more likely to be compromised where bonuses for compliance staff are calculated according to the performance of specific areas or business lines they

---

[56] FSA PS 06/13, para. 4.5.   [57] Ibid, para. 4.7.
[58] For the supra-national standards on which the MiFID standards are based, see Compliance Functions at Market Intermediaries, IOSCO, March 2006; Compliance and the compliance function in banks, Basel Committee, April 2005; and CESR/05-024c, March 2005.   [59] FSA CP 06/9, para. 3.7.

monitor . . . Where a firm has an internal audit function, it must be separate and independent from the firm's compliance function. For example . . . internal audit [may] . . . review the effectiveness of the compliance function.'[60]

The 'firm must maintain a risk management function that [also] operates independently' (SYSC 7.1.6, 14.1.38–14.1.41), and it may be 'appropriate to use a head office internal audit function'[61] and also maintain an internal audit function and an audit committee (SYSC 14.1.42–14.1.45, 4.1.11) which is, loosely, connected with the requirements to 'maintain accounting policies and procedures that enable it, at the request of the FSA, to deliver in a timely manner to the FSA financial reports which reflect a true and fair view of its financial position' (SYSC 4.1.9), '[t]rue and fair view' bear[ing] its usual corporate law meaning and 'timely manner' 'depend[ing] on the circumstances of [FSA's] request'.[62] Moreover, the firm must 'ensure that its internal control mechanisms and administrative and accounting procedures permit the verification of its compliance with [capital adequacy] rules'.[63] This:

> requires firms to have systems in place that can record compliance . . . at any time. It does not require the firm to address a breach . . . at the moment it occurs (i.e. it does not mandate a 'real time' monitoring system), but the system must be capable of generating records at any time that will permit verification of compliance with [capital requirements] . . . Nor does . . . [it] require firms . . . to operate a 'zero failure' approach to [such] compliance.[64]

5.2.4 Employees

Pre-MiFID: Nick Leeson had no training as a derivatives dealer and, due to confused reporting lines, was effectively unsupervised. Under FSA rules, though, delegation to an employee down the chain of apportioned responsibilities could occur only if 'appropriate safeguards [are] put in place . . . [and] the [employee] is suitable to carry out the . . . function . . . [and t]he extent and limits of . . . delegation . . . [are] clear to those concerned . . . [and t]here [are] arrangements to supervise . . . and . . . monitor . . . [and i]f cause for concern arises . . . there should be appropriate follow-up action at an appropriate level of seniority within the firm' (FSA PM SYSC 3.2.3). The firm had 'to satisfy itself as to the suitability of anyone who acts for it' which 'includes assessing an individual's honesty and competence' (FSA PM SYSC 3.2.13, 3.2.14(1)) and, to that end, 'mak[e] proper arrangement for any employee . . . to achieve, maintain and enhance competence' (FSA PM TC 1.1.3). This meant that there was an overall requirement on the firm, under the so-called 'Commitments', to ensure 'that: (1) its employees are competent; (2) its employees remain

---

[60] FSA PS 06/13, paras. 4.8, 4.11.   [61] Ibid, para. 4.16.   [62] Ibid, para. 2.10.
[63] Ibid, para. 4.12.   [64] Ibid, para. 2.16.

competent for the work they do; (3) its employees are appropriately supervised; (4) its employees' competence is regularly reviewed; [and] (5) the level of competence is appropriate to the nature of the business', more detailed requirements being imposed in relation to advising, portfolio management and custody functions (FSA PM TC 1.2.1, 2). The crucial need for a proper training regime was emphasised in Barings all the way up to senior management: '[i]t . . . [is] absolutely essential that top management understand the broad nature of all the material activities of the institution . . . and that product management have a detailed understanding of all aspects of the activities they manage'.[65]

Overlaying the employee function was regulator concern about 'the very high earnings possible in the . . . sector . . . I . . . would not wish to . . . tell firms . . . how much they should pay their executives . . . [However, w]e want to ensure that the bosses are . . . controlling their . . . businesses, even if they are lucky enough to be employing superstars.'[66] Yet, given that these bonuses not only reflected the reality of the vast sums of money being dealt with in the City but were probably crucial to the efficient economic functioning of the Capital Markets, FSA's regulatory response was half-hearted. Its initial draft rule required that 'A firm's remuneration arrangements . . . should be organised in a way which does not . . . risk any conflict with regulatory compliance'[67] but when 'firms . . . question[ed] . . . whether it is feasible . . . to set remuneration policies which are entirely free from conflicts of interest',[68] FSA backed off and merely pointed out that 'a firm should have regard to . . . whether the way employees are remunerated exposes the firm to the risk that it will not be able to meet its regulatory obligations' and 'It is possible that firms' remuneration policies . . . lead to tensions between the ability of the firm to meet the requirements and standards under the regulatory system and the personal advantage of those who act for it. Where tensions exist, these should be appropriately managed' (FSA PM SYSC 3A.6.2(2), 3.2.18).

MiFID: As a result of the MiFID obligation on a UK firm to 'employ personnel with the skills, knowledge and expertise necessary for the discharge of the responsibilities allotted to them' (SYSC 5.1.1, 3.1.6), FSA felt able to retain all of the Approved Persons regime (5.3.1 and 5.4) and 'to drop the Commitments altogether' because 'the[y] are covered . . . either explicitly or implicitly . . . by the MiFID competence requirement. The obligation to employ personnel with the relevant skills, knowledge and expertise is an ongoing one, carrying with it the expectation that employees will need to maintain as well as attain the relevant standard of competence.

---

[65] BoBs Report, para. 14.10.
[66] Nicholas Durlacher, Chairman SFA, in SFA Briefing 15, November 1997.
[67] FSA CP 35, December 1999, Ann. A, draft Rule X.13.1.
[68] High level standards for firms and individuals, FSA PS, June 2000, para. 3.3.6 (b).

This, in turn, implies the need for employees' competence to be appropriately supervised and subject to regular review.'[69] As a result, '[t]he change . . . to our T&C regime will neither raise nor lower standards'.[70] For this purpose, 'knowledge can be assessed and demonstrated by various means, but one of the most common methods is through an exam . . . However, . . . knowledge is only one strand of the competence assessment. Equally important is an individual's possession of the skills needed to do the job and their expertise in applying their knowledge and skills in practice. This generally calls for "on the job training" and close supervision by suitably qualified and experienced staff to determine when the individual has achieved the required level.'[71] Here, though, '[t]he Training and Competence Sourcebook (TC) contains additional rules and guidance [including exams] relating . . . [only] to retail activities' (SYSC 3.1.8, 5.1.4; TC 1–3), rather than 'in a principles-based environment [2.5.8] . . . remov[ing] the TC Sourcebook altogether and rely[ing] instead [solely] on the high level requirements in . . . SYSC' because 'the risks on the retail side' require 'an appropriate level of consumer protection'.[72] Thus, the Training and Competence Rules 'appl[y] to a firm where its employee carries on an activity . . . for retail clients' (TC 1.1.1) and 'MiFID allows us . . . to retain requirements (including exam requirements) as a supervisory tool for checking firms' compliance with the MiFID competence requirement'.[73] Moreover, in relation to 'activities that are not subject to TC [for example, wholesale business] firms may wish to take TC into account in complying with . . . SYSC' (SYSC 3.1.9, 5.1.4A) and 'many of these firms will want to continue to use exams as part of their T&C arrangements'.[74]

The application of these rules is explained in 4.2(b) and (c).

The guidance on remuneration no longer appears but, in practice, should continue to be complied with since 'A firm's systems and controls should enable it to satisfy itself of the suitability of anyone who acts for it . . . and a[ny] assessment of . . . suitability should take into account the level of responsibility [of] that individual' (SYSC 5.1.2, 5.1.3). Moreover, now (in a re-flowering of moralism, for which see, generally, 2.5.8), 'competence . . . includes . . . achiev[ing] a good standard of ethical behaviour' (TC 1.1.4), although this only expressly applies to retail business notwithstanding that '[a]ppropriate ethical behaviours are closely linked to the corporate culture of the firm and [is] a key responsibility of senior management'.[75] Thus, and with the usual difficulties (2.5.8), 'with a move to a principle-based T&C regime . . . it will be up to senior management to decide how best to comply with our requirements'.[76]

---

[69] FSA CP 07/4, paras. 3.17, 3.18. [70] FSA PS 07/13, July 2007, para. 2.6.
[71] Ibid, paras. 2.20, 2.21. [72] FSA CP 07/4, paras. 1.12, 1.13. [73] Ibid, para. 3.35.
[74] Ibid, para. 3.24. [75] Ibid, para. 2.22. [76] FSA PS 07/13, July 2007, para. 2.24.

5.2.5 Outsourcing

Pre-MiFID: If a firm has a regulatory responsibility to conduct its business in a certain manner, whether deriving from an infrastructure/systems and controls rule or from a client-facing rule, it cannot delegate the relevant business function to a third party, inside or outside its group, such that it fails to discharge that obligation, whether the delegation is referred to as the employment of an agent or as an outsourcing, which are interchangeable terms. The distinction is between where the firm is contractually obliged to its client to perform a service, and delegates that performance to another (for example, a broker–dealer contractually liable to its client for all execution services employs a local broker to execute client transactions on an Exchange of which it is not a member as opposed to providing a service of arranging for the local broker to itself execute in direct contractual relation with the client; or a custodian uses a sub-custodian), which is outsourcing, and where a firm accesses a service to itself perform its service to the client (for example, use of a public communications network or the services of a clearing house attached to an Exchange), which is not outsourcing. The fact that a firm cannot, by outsourcing, avoid its regulatory obligation was shown by the Morgan Grenfell case referred to in 5.1 and, hence, FSA's Pre-MiFID Rules emphasised that 'A firm cannot contract out of its regulatory obligations . . . [and] should take reasonable care to supervise the discharge of outsourced functions by its contractor . . . [and] obtain sufficient information from its contractor to enable it to assess the impact of outsourcing on its systems and controls'. Accordingly, 'Before entering into . . . an outsourcing . . . a firm should:

(1) analyse how the arrangements will fit with its organisation and reporting structure; business strategy; overall risk profile; and ability to meet its regulatory obligations; [and]
(2) consider whether the [outsourcing] agreement . . . will allow it to monitor and control its operational risk exposure relating to the outsourcing; [and]
(3) conduct appropriate due diligence of the service provider's financial stability and expertise.

The contract with the outsourcee had to contain provisions on 'reporting . . . [by] the service provider; . . . access . . . [by the firm's] auditors . . . and . . . FSA . . . ; the extent to which the service provider must comply with the firm's policies and procedures . . . [and] change [management]' and an appropriate service level agreement (FSA PM SYSC 3.2.4, 3A.9.4, 3A.9.5, 3A.9.6).

MiFID: FSA's definition of 'outsourcing' as 'an arrangement of any form between a firm and a service provider by which that service provider performs a process, a service or an activity which would otherwise be undertaken by the firm itself' (GLOSS, def. of 'outsourcing', para. (2)) should be interpreted consistently with the Pre-MiFID understanding of the term, although it appears that FSA has taken the pragmatic view that a custodian does not outsource its functions to a sub-custodian. MiFID expressly retains the outsourcing firm's regulatory responsibilities (SYSC 8.1.6) and links outsourcing to risk in providing that 'A . . . firm must:

(1) when relying on a third party [which can be in or outside its group: SYSC 8.1.10] for the performance of operational functions which are critical for the performance of regulated activities, [MiFID] activities or ancillary services [4.2.I(1), (2)] . . . ensure that it takes reasonable steps to avoid undue additional operational risk; [and]
(2) not . . . outsourc[e] . . . important operational functions in such a way as to impair materially . . . the quality of its internal control. (SYSC 8.1.1)

This applies 'to . . . regulated activities whether MiFID business or not' and 'is [arguably] super-equivalent for a MiFID firm which also does non-MiFID business'[77] such that 'MiFID does not exempt existing arrangements so firms must ensure that their [pre-1 November 2007] existing outsourcing arrangements comply . . . with effect from 1 November 2007'.[78] For this purpose, 'an operational function is . . . critical or important if a defect or failure in its performance would materially impair the continuing compliance of a firm with . . . its . . . obligations under the regulatory system, or its financial performance, or the soundness or continuity of its relevant services and activities'. This does not include 'the provision to the firm of . . . services which do not form part of . . . [its] services and activities', which are not outsourcings in the first place, such as legal advice, staff training, telecoms and clearing and settlement of transactions and custody of assets where the latter are not client-facing functions or responsibilities of the firm. Nor does it include 'the purchase of standardised services, including market information services and the provision of price feeds', although here care should be exercised since, for example, a price feed for the valuation of OTC derivatives written by the firm can, nonetheless, be critical to its financial and other risks (SYSC 8.1.4, 8.1.5). FSA 'do not intend to give guidance on what is meant by a 'critical' or 'important' function . . . because [t]hat . . . is likely to vary according to the nature and circumstances of each firm'.[79] The firm must comply with the outsourcing rules in relation to critical or important outsourcings but for all others, and this is super-equivalent to MiFID, 'should take into account, in a manner that is proportionate given the nature, scale and complexity of the outsourcing, the rules' (SYSC 8.1.3). Although this is 'not . . . rules . . . [but] guidance' and is intended to 'give a firm . . . the flexibility needed to control the risks . . . in a manner appropriate . . . to the firm's needs',[80] in practice it should be

[77] FSA CP 06/9, paras. 7.8, 7.11.   [78] FSA PS 06/13, para. 8.
[79] FSA CP 06/9, para. 7.12.   [80] Ibid, para. 7.10.

regarded as pretty much the same thing in order to minimise so-called 'regulator risk'. The only difference is that only critical or important outsourcings have to be notified to FSA (SYSC 8.1.12). The Pre-MiFID required procedures before entering into an outsourcing and contents of the outsourcing documentation are retained in relation to 'material outsourcings', defined as 'outsourcing services of such importance that weakness, or failure, of the services would cast serious doubt on the firm's continuing satisfaction of the threshold conditions or compliance with the Principles' (SYSC 13.9). In addition, for 'critical or important' outsourcings, the 'firm must exercise due skill and care and diligence when entering into, managing or terminating . . . the outsourcing', including 'ensur[ing] that . . .

(1) the service provider . . . ha[s] the ability, capacity and any authorisation required . . . to perform the . . . functions . . . reliably and professionally;
(2) the service provider . . . carr[ies] out the . . . services effectively, and . . . the firm must establish methods for assessing the standard of performance . . .
(3) the service provider must properly supervise the carrying out of the . . . functions, and adequately manage the risks associated . . .
(4) appropriate action must be taken if . . . the service provider may not be carrying out the functions effectively and in compliance with . . . regulatory requirements;
(5) the firm must retain the necessary expertise to supervise the outsourced functions . . .
(8) the firm, its auditors [and] the FSA . . . must have effective access to data . . . as well as the business premises of a service provider. (SYSC 8.1.7, 8.1.8)

Under requirement (4), '[FSA] would expect firms to have in place appropriate arrangements and procedures by which they will be able to be satisfied that a service provider complies with applicable laws and regulatory requirements' and 'such oversight function should be carried on by an employee of the firm rather than outsourced'.[81] Requirement (5) reflects the fact that '[t]he outsourcing of functions does not relieve a . . . firm of its regulatory responsibilities for these outsourced activities, services or functions. It cannot delegate those responsibilities [and] . . . therefore . . . [the] firm . . . must retain sufficient competence and expertise at a senior operational level . . . to be able to devise suitable alternative arrangements in the event of difficulties with, or the failure of, the service provider.'[82] All such requirements will need to be included in the outsourcing agreement so that they can be enforced by the firm, and although the rules on employees (5.2.4) do not apply in relation to the outsourcee's employees, 'firms should

---

[81] FSA PS 06/13, para. 6.9; FSA CP 06/15, para. 3.77.   [82] Ibid, para. 6.10.

have regard to the importance of employees at the service provider in complying with the[se] outsourcing . . . requirement[s]'.[83]

Although generally there are 'no . . . specific limitations on firms' ability to outsource to non-authorised entities . . . [because] the obligation[s] on . . . firms . . . are sufficient to achieve sound management of the . . . firm',[84] there are detailed requirements which should be included in the outsourcing documentation where the firm outsources portfolio management for retail clients to a non-EEA firm. Such outsourcing can occur only if either 'the service provider [is] authorised or registered in its home country . . . and . . . subject to prudential supervision . . . [with] a . . . cooperation agreement between the FSA and the supervisor' or 'prior notification . . . [is given] to the FSA . . . and the FSA does not object . . . within one month of receipt' (SYSC 8.2.1). This rule applies only to the outsourcing of the management activity rather than 'ancillary activities connected with portfolio management, for example IT processes or execution only services', but applies 'whether [the] firm outsources portfolio management directly or indirectly via a third party' (SYSC 8.2.3, 8.3.1). FSA will allow the outsourcing only if the firm can demonstrate that it will be properly conducted, with adequate reporting to the firm, in accordance with all legal requirements and FSA regulations (SYSC 8.3.2–8.3.7).

More problematic than the necessary systems and controls requirements within the firm, is that various MiFID obligations have, on their terms, to be complied with by the outsourcee itself. These relate to certain systems and controls with regard to notification of procedures, segregation of duties, compliance responsibilities and risk processes and systems (SYSC 5.1.2, 5.1.6, 6.1.3(2), 7.1.5(2)), personal account transactions (COBS 12.7.1), conflicts of interest (SYSC 10.1.4, 10.1.7), research reports (COBS 12.2.3, 12.2.5, 12.4.9) and associated record keeping. These requirements arise because these MiFID obligations with which the firm must comply are imposed in relation to its 'relevant persons' which includes 'a natural person who is directly involved in the provision of services to the . . . firm . . . under an outsourcing arrangement for the purpose of the provision by the firm of investment services and activities', although that limits them to the employees directly involved in the outsourced function. For such employees and requirements the firm could either impose its own procedures, which would cause difficulty where the outsourcee provides services to more than one MiFID regulated firm, or could satisfy itself that the outsourcee's procedures were, in this regard, up to MiFID standards and then require the outsourcee to covenant in the outsourcing agreement not to change those procedures unless such compliance was maintained.

---

[83] Ibid, para. 3.10. For the European standards for banks, see Guidelines on Outsourcing, CEBS, 14 December 2006.

[84] Explanatory Note, Working Doc. ESC/18/2005, Commission, 13 May 2005, p. 3.

5.3 Senior management responsibility

As a result of Barings, 'in the absence of regulation of individuals, the incentives of firms and individuals within firms are not necessarily aligned. The history of regulatory problems has demonstrated that managers have not always had sufficient incentives to focus on systems and controls . . . It is therefore appropriate for regulation to step into this gap'[85] and, thus, senior managers are required to be registered with FSA and, then, subject to detailed and enforceable conduct rules which mirror those placed upon the firm.

> FSA recognises that cases against individuals are very different in their nature from cases against corporate entities . . . However, taking action against individuals sends an important message about the FSA's regulatory objectives and priorities and the FSA considers that such cases have important deterrent values. The FSA is therefore committed to pursuing appropriate cases robustly, and will dedicate sufficient resources to them to achieve effective outcomes. (EG 2.32)

5.3.1 Registration as an Approved Person

Pre-MiFID: Under FSMA two categories of Approved Person (see also 5.4) that require registration are for 'function[s] . . . likely to exercise a significant influence on the conduct of the [firm]'s affairs' and 'dealing with property of customers' (FSMA 59(5), (6)). The controlled functions specified by FSA are divided into four groups which mirror the apportionment and control functions required by the firm's infrastructure systems and controls (5.2.2, 5.2.3): 'governing functions' (CEO; and Directors); 'required functions' (Apportionment & Oversight, responsible for the apportionment and oversight functions set out in the systems and controls rule applying to the firm explained in 5.2.2; Compliance Officer; Money Laundering Reporting Officer); 'systems and controls functions' (Finance; Risk; Internal Audit); and 'significant management functions' ('senior managers with significant responsibility' for 'a significant business unit', '[the] firm's financial resources' or the settlements function) (SUP 10.4–10.9). Registration was required in relation to a UK firm (in full), and the UK branch of a non-EEA firm (only for the CEO function; all 'required functions'; and the 'significant management functions' for 'a significant business unit'; and settlements) or EEA firm (only an 'EEA investment business oversight function' which was apportionment and oversight for UK businesses; Compliance Officer and MLRO; and the 'significant management functions' for 'a significant business unit'; and settlements), but not for firms operating cross-border into the UK (SUP 10.1.6–10.1.15).

[85] Procedural Formalities for the Handbook, FSA CP 90, May 2001, Ann. C, para. 14.

MiFID: As regards application, see 4.2(b) and 4.2(c)(i). At 1 November 2007, although this is not a change required by MiFID, the three systems and controls functions are merged into one overall 'systems and controls function' 'with responsibility for . . . (1) [the firm's] financial affairs; (2) setting and controlling its risk exposure . . . [and] (3) adherence to internal systems and controls, procedures and policies' (SUP 10.8.1) and all of the significant management functions are merged into one 'significant management function' which requires registration under the same headings as before (SUP 10.9.10). Existing Approved Persons in the old categories are grandfathered into the new categories (SUP TP 8A, 8B). FSA is expressly permitted by MiFID to maintain the Approved Person registration regime with only minor changes[86] and the same overall application (4.2(c)(i)) although the training requirements are no longer imposed (5.2.4). MiFID Art. 9 requires that 'the persons who effectively direct the business of a . . . firm [shall] be of sufficiently good repute and sufficiently experienced as to ensure the sound and prudent management of the . . . firm' (SYSC 4.2.1). For FSA, '[t]he [Systems and Controls Rules] implement the MiFID requirements regarding the sound and prudent management of the firm [5.2.2] while the Approved Persons regime focuses on how we vet "good repute and experience" . . . So, we intend to retain the Approved Persons regime and use it as a supervisory tool in relation to our obligations under MiFID and as a means to take enforcement action against approved individuals.'[87] Beyond this, the MiFID systems and controls requirements are somewhat different from the pre-existing requirements (5.2) and this is mirrored in the new scope of the controlled functions.[88] With UK branches of EEA firms, the EEA business oversight and compliance officer functions can no longer be applied to MiFID passported business, since both are Home State responsibilities, and for the remaining controlled functions 'we will no longer assess competence . . . [but] MiFID will not prevent us from continuing to approve the individual in respect of . . . probity and financial soundness'.[89]

Initially, notwithstanding that under MiFID Art. 9, 'when allocating functions internally it is the [collective] responsibility of the governing body to ensure that the firm complies with its responsibilities under MiFID',[90] FSA intended to retain the Apportionment & Oversight function as a sole, or at most joint, responsibility and, thus, as a 'super-equivalent' provision since '[t]he specific risk . . . that is not adequately addressed by the Directive is the risk of weakness in the organisation and compliance culture of a firm.

---

[86] MiFID, Recital 13.   [87] FSA CP 06/15, August 2006, paras. 3.67, 3.73.
[88] Ibid, paras 3.75–3.77; Reforming the Approved Persons Regime, FSA PS 07/3, January 2007, paras. 2.2–2.4.
[89] FSA CP 06/15, paras. 3.80–3.81; FSA PS 07/3, para. 2.7; FIT 1.2.4A and SUP 10.1.13A and 10.1.13B, Ann. D and G; FSA CP 07/16, Ann. R, draft SUP 10.1.13B, 10.1.13C.
[90] FSA CP 06/15, para. 3.85.

This would arise if each individual senior manager sought to hide behind the collective responsibility of the firm's senior management team to reduce the risk that they will be personally called to account for specific failings in the firm's systems and controls . . . If these functions were not so allocated, it is less likely in practice that a failure of the firm's systems and controls would lead to direct action against individual senior staff . . . The[se] risks . . . are of particular importance in view of past failures of . . . UK firms . . . and a specific example . . . is the collapse of Barings.'[91] Eventually, though, FSA concluded that 'MiFID allows . . . firms to choose the appropriate means for ensuring that senior management is responsible for the firm's compliance with its MiFID obligations . . . such as by the allocation of responsibility to a group of persons or to committees, rather than to an individual'. In any event, 'those persons who effectively direct the business should also be approved for the governing functions. We will still be able to look to these individuals . . . to be responsible for apportionment and oversight . . . although the task . . . could be delegated to [one person] by senior management.'[92] Hence, while the apportionment and oversight rule is removed (5.2.2), FSA is following MiFID in providing that senior personnel (defined as 'those persons who effectively direct the business', including the managing board) 'are responsible for ensuring that the firm complies with its obligations under MiFID' and, therefore, 'must assess and periodically review the effectiveness of the policies, arrangements and procedures put in place to comply with the firm's obligations under MiFID and take appropriate measures to assess any deficiencies' (SYSC 4.3.1). Thus, while there must be a compliance function (5.3.2.3), senior management cannot delegate its ultimate compliance responsibilities to it.

None of the procedures relating to the approval process are changed by MiFID. Thus: to obtain approval the applicant still has to meet the criteria in FIT; when considering making an appointment to a controlled function, if the appointing firm 'requests . . . a former employer . . . for a reference or other information . . . [the former employer] must . . . give . . . all relevant information of which it is aware' (SUP 10.13.12), which often results in careful drafting to avoid liability; and upon 'dismiss[al], . . . suspen[sion] . . . or . . . resignation . . . while under investigation', the firm must 'submit a qualified Form C' to FSA (SUP 10.13.7). Moreover, as regards the decision as to who is performing a controlled function within an international group, it may be 'a manager who is based overseas . . . especially where the

---

[91] Justification for the retention of the FSA's requirements on the apportionment of responsibilities under Article 4, 31 January 2007, paras. 4, 9, 10, attached to Article 4 Notification to the European Commission, FSA, 31 January 2007.

[92] FSA CP 07/16, paras. 4.2, 4.9, 4.10. The CF8 function is to be removed for firms that only carry on MiFID Business (4.2.I(2)), in favour of collective responsibility; thus a non-EEA firm with a UK branch will still require a CF8 (Ibid, Ann. R, draft SUP 10.7.2A).

Systems and controls

firm operates matrix management'. '[W]here an overseas manager's responsibilities in relation to the United Kingdom are strategic only, he will not need to be an approved person. However, where . . . he is responsible for implementing that strategy in the United Kingdom . . . he is likely to be performing a controlled function' (SUP 10.7.4, 10.9.5).

5.3.2 Rule responsibilities

A senior manager has the general rule responsibilities of all Approved Persons (5.4.2) but, beyond this, '[i]f the FSA is to rely on those who manage the affairs of firms exercising their responsibilities effectively . . . FSA must . . . set out its expectation of the conduct of such individuals,'[93] in part because '[t]his . . . will help to promote a strong compliance culture, since the leadership of the firm is the prime influence on its compliance culture',[94] FSA regarding the rules that it laid down as 'do[ing] no more than represent[ing] good business practice'.[95] These are a series of specific responsibilities enforceable against the Approved Person personally (ENF 11.5; EG 9; DEPP 6.2.4–6.2.13), which are both a reflection of the Systems and Controls rules binding upon the firm and FSA's way of ensuring that responsibility for any significant rule breach within the firm can always be put upon one or more senior managers on the basis that either the senior manager knew about the issue and did not properly deal with it or he/she did not know about it and therefore failed to implement sufficient systems and controls. This position, which is not affected by MiFID, results from the three Principles placed upon senior managers to:

[5] . . . take reasonable steps to ensure that the business . . . for which he is responsible . . . is organised so that it can be controlled effectively [and] . . .

[6] . . . exercise due skill, care and diligence in managing the business . . . for which he is responsible [and] . . .

[7] . . . take reasonable steps to ensure that the business . . . for which he is responsible . . . complies with the relevant requirements and standards of the regulatory system. (APER 2.1.2, Statements of Principle 5, 6, 7)

These Principles are used by FSA to justify a series of requirements of the senior manager[96] to avoid the type of problems that emerged in Barings. As regards their application, see 4.2(c)(ii).

5.3.2.1 Self-education

Never again could a senior manager, as in Barings, use the defence that he did not know or understand what was going on, since now he must 'take

---
[93] FSA CP 26, July 1999, para. 34. [94] FSA CP 35, December 1999, para. 3.2.
[95] FSA CP 90, May 2001, Ann. C, para. 6.
[96] These are provided in the APER Code of Conduct. For its status, see 2.5.8, material E.

reasonable steps to adequately inform himself about the . . . business . . . include[ing] . . . not:

(1) permitting transactions without a sufficient understanding of the risks involved;
(2) permitting expansion of the business without reasonably assessing the potential risks . . .
(3) independently monitoring highly profitable transactions . . . or unusual transactions . . .
(4) accepting implausible or unsatisfactory explanations . . .
(5) failing to obtain independent expert opinion where appropriate. (APER 4.6.3, 4.6.4)

Thus, while he 'will not always manage the business on a day-to-day basis himself' and may delegate, he must 'maintain an adequate level of understanding about a . . . business . . . delegated' because 'he cannot delegate responsibility' (APER 4.6.6, 4.6.11, 4.6.14).

5.3.2.2 Systems and controls and apportionment of responsibility

To avoid confusing reporting lines, and lack of middle management responsibility, the senior manager must 'take reasonable steps to apportion responsibilities for all areas of the business under . . . [his] control' and do so 'clearly'. 'The organisation of the business and the responsibilities of those within it shall be clearly defined . . . [in r]eporting lines' and 'staff . . . levels of authorisation . . . shall be clearly set out and communicated to staff. It may be appropriate for each member of staff to have a job description' (APER 4.5.3, 4.5.4, 4.5.12, 4.5.13).

5.3.2.3 Compliance

To ensure personal responsibility for compliance breaches all the way up the management chain, the senior manager must 'take reasonable steps to implement (either personally or through a compliance department or other departments) adequate and appropriate systems and controls to comply with the . . . regulatory system' and, similarly, 'monitor . . . compliance' and investigate, review and improve the systems as appropriate (APER 4.7.3, 4.7.4, 4.7.6, 4.7.7). These steps must include monitoring and, for that purpose, production of management information.[97]

5.3.2.4 Employees

Nick Leeson's lack of training, suitability and purported financial success should now be avoided since the senior manager must 'ensure that suitable individuals are [employed]' and, accordingly:

---

[97] For an example in relation to management's 'treat the customer fairly' obligations, see 9.2, FN 21.

(1) ... review the competence, knowledge, skills and performance of staff ... [and]
(2) [not] giv[e] undue weight to financial performance when considering suitability or continuing suitability of an individual.

Moreover, while delegation is acceptable given the size of, and necessary specialisations to be found within, firms, it can occur only if the senior manager has 'reasonable grounds for believing that the delegate had the necessary capacity, competence, knowledge, seniority [and] skill' and if the senior manager continues to 'supervise and monitor adequately the individual' (APER 4.5.8, 4.6.5, 4.6.8).

5.3.2.5 Liability

If FSA is correct that these requirements 'do no more than represent good business practice',[98] then responsibility for failure to live up to them needs to be understood in its general legal context. As an employee, the senior manager:

> undertakes to perform his work competently, using reasonable skill and care ... For a dismissal to be warranted, the act of negligence must be a serious one ... or a series of minor acts of neglect ... It is an implied term of the contract of employment that an employee will exercise skill and care in the performance of his duties, and a breach of that term entitles the employer to claim damages in respect of the negligent performance of the contract.[99]

Such liability to the company/firm is reinforced if the senior manager is a director. In 19th century corporate law the ethos of 'Gentlemanly Capitalism', of the leisured amateur director,[100] combined with the origin of the joint stock company in the (trust) deed of settlement to produce a low level of liability, such that 'so long as [directors] act honestly they cannot be made responsible in damages unless guilty of gross negligence',[101] and the negligence standard was a subjective test:

> A director need not exhibit in the performance of his duties a greater degree of skill than may reasonably be expected from a person of his knowledge and experience ... [D]irectors are not liable for mere errors of judgment ... In respect of duties that ... may properly be left to some other official, a director is, in the absence of grounds for suspicion, justified in trusting that official to perform such duties honestly ... Business cannot be carried on upon principles of distrust. Men in responsible positions must be trusted by those above them ...

---

[98] Procedural Formalities for the Handbook, FSA CP 90, May 2001, Ann. C, para. 6.
[99] *Selwyn's Law of Employment*, 13th edn., Oxford, 2004, p. 262.
[100] *The City of London*, D. Kynaston, Chatto & Windus, Vol. 2, 1995, p. 266; Vol. 3, 1999, pp. 326–7. [101] *Re Brazilian Rubber Plantation & Estates* Ltd [1911] 1 Ch. 425.

until there is reason to distrust them . . . [C]are and prudence do not involve distrust.[102]

However, as developments such as the FSA rules and, in particular, the Statements of Principle, and various corporate governance reports[103] showed, by the third quarter of the 20th century the social ethos was for professional directors and this was accepted by the Court in its reformulation of the directors' negligence standard as a base-line objective test which could be higher depending on the director's particular skills:

> the duty of care owed by a director at common law is accurately stated in Section 214(4) of the Insolvency Act 1986. It is the conduct of 'a reasonably diligent person having both (a) the general knowledge, skill and experience that may reasonably be expected of a person carrying out the same functions as are carried out by that director in relation to the company and (b) the general knowledge, skill and experience that that director has'. [This is] both [an] objective test and . . . [a] subjective test.[104]

Hence, a culture of trust having disappeared, and like FSA requirements on Approved Persons:

> each . . . director owes duties to the company to inform himself about its affairs and to join with his co-directors in supervising and controlling them . . . [A] Board of Directors may delegate specific tasks and functions . . . [b]ut . . . [this] does [not] mean that, having delegated a particular function, he is no longer under any duty in relation to the discharge of that function, notwithstanding that the person to whom the function has been delegated may appear both trustworthy and capable of discharging the function . . . Overall responsibility is not delegable . . . The degree of personal blameworthiness that may attach to the individual with the overall responsibility . . . must depend on the facts. Sometimes there may be the question of whether the delegation has been made to the appropriate person; sometimes there may be a question of whether [he] . . . should have checked how his subordinates were discharging their delegated functions. Sometimes the system itself, in which the failures have taken place, is an inadequate system for which the person with overall responsibility must take some blame.[105]

All of these cases are relevant to the interpretation of the 2006 statutory codification of the mixed objective/subjective test under which:

> A director . . . must exercise . . . the care, skill and diligence, that would be exercised by a reasonably diligent person with –

---

[102] *Re City Equitable Fire Insurance Co Ltd* [1925] Ch. 407.

[103] Report of the Committee on the Financial Aspects of Corporate Governance (Cadbury), 1992; Directors Remuneration (Greenbury), 1995; Committee on Corporate Governance (Hampel), 1998; LSE Combined Code, June 2000.

[104] *In Re D'Jan of London Limited* [1994] 1 BCLC 561.

[105] *In Re Barings plc (No. 5)* [1999] 1 BCLC 433 at 486–8.

(a) the general knowledge, skill and experience that may reasonably be expected of the person carrying out the functions carried out by the director in relation to the company; and
(b) the general knowledge, skill and experience that director has. (2006 CA 174)

The FSA's standard for the duties of all Approved Persons, however, is only the objective standard since 'An approved person will only be in breach . . . where . . . [his] conduct was deliberate or . . . below that which would be reasonable in all the circumstances' (APER 3.1.4(1), 3.1.8) and, with senior managers, 'the following . . . factors . . . are to be taken into account:

(1) whether he exercised reasonable care when considering the information available to him;
(2) whether he reached a reasonable conclusion which he acted on;
(3) the nature, scale and complexity of the firm's business;
(4) his role and responsibility . . .
(5) the knowledge he had, or should have had, of regulatory concerns, if any, arising in the business under his control. (APER 3.3.1. See also EG 9.12, 9.13)

According to FSA, although 'in some cases [his] judgment will, with the benefit of hindsight, be shown to have been wrong [h]e will not be in breach . . . unless he . . . fails to reach a reasonable conclusion' (APER 4.6.13(4)). Thus:

> The FSA will not discipline approved persons on the basis of vicarious liability (that is, holding them responsible for the acts of others), provided appropriate delegation and supervision has taken place . . . In particular, disciplinary action will not be taken . . . simply because a regulatory failure has occurred in an area of business for which he is responsible [unless] . . . his conduct was below the standard which would be reasonable in all the circumstances . . . An approved person will not be in breach if he has exercised due and reasonable care when assessing information, has reached a reasonable conclusion and has acted on it. (DEPP 6.2.7, 6.2.8)

As a result of the conditions to this 'comfort', given the web of systems and controls requirements binding upon both the firm (5.2) and him personally (5.3.2.1–5.3.2.4), in practice the senior manager is always at substantial personal risk whenever a compliance failure occurs.

5.4 Approved Persons

5.4.1 Registration as an Approved Person

Pre-MiFID: As well as regulation of senior managers (5.3.1), the statute contains a further category of registration, 'dealing with customers' (FSMA 59(7)), implemented by FSA in the customer functions of investment adviser, corporate finance adviser, customer trading and investment management (SUP 10.10). These applied to UK firms and UK branches of non-EEA and passported firms (SUP 10.1.1, 10.1.7(5), 10.1.13(6)).

MiFID: No change is made in this respect.[106] For the application of the requirements, see 4.2(c)(i).

5.4.2 Rule responsibilities

Again, unaltered by MiFID, all Approved Persons must:

[1] ... act with integrity ...
[2] act with due skill, care and diligence ...
[3] observe proper standards of market conduct ...
[4] deal with the FSA and with other regulators in an open and co-operative way and ... disclose as appropriate any information of which the FSA would reasonably expect notice. (APER 2.1.2, Statements of Principle 1–4)

Principle 1 extends beyond misleading, fraudulent and dishonest behaviour to 'failing to inform ... a customer ... of the fact that their understanding of a material issue is incorrect', 'front running client orders' (6.3.4.2) and 'recommending an investment ... unable to justify its suitability for that customer' (11.2) (APER 4.1.5, 4.1.6(1), 4.1.11(1)). Principle 2 extends beyond negligence to 'failing to explain the risks of an investment to a customer', 'failing to disclose ... details of ... charges', 'providing advice ... without a reasonable understanding of the risk exposure of the transaction to a customer' and '[f]ailing ... to disclose ... a conflict of interest' (APER 4.2.4(1), (2), 4.2.6, 4.2.10), thus showing that FSA has a wider view of intention and negligence than at common law. Principle 3 is a direct reflection of the Principle binding the firm (9.1) and gives the Approved Person the responsibility to comply with the Market Abuse Code (APER 4.3). As regards Principle 4, while the individual's direct responsibility to report to FSA is limited by the firm's own reporting procedures (APER 4.4.4),[107] it requires compliance with the firm's Whistleblowing procedures (APER 4.4; SYSC 18).

The individual's standard of liability for compliance with these requirements is explained in 5.3.2.5, and the rules of application are explained in 4.2(c)(ii).

5.5 Record-keeping

Record-keeping by regulated firms is fundamental, and even a system of registration such as the PFI (2.3) required both 'books of account' and 'a

---

[106] FSA PS 07/3, App. 1, Ann. G. See also 5.3.1.   [107] See 9.1.1.

record' of securities received and dispatched,[108] whereas under a full-scale regulatory system such as the 1986 FSAct 'enforcement of [conduct] of business [rules] will be facilitated . . . if adequate records of transactions are in existence and are kept up to date'.[109] Detailed records were necessary to support financial reporting and regulatory capital requirements and this was ultimately reflected in both a Principle that 'A firm should . . . keep proper records' and, in the New Settlement, a Core Rule that 'A firm must ensure that it maintains adequate accounting records . . . [which]:

a. must be kept up to date and . . . disclose . . . at any time, the firm's financial position . . .
b. must enable the firm to demonstrate its continuing compliance with its financial resources requirement, and
c. must provide the information . . . which the firm needs to prepare such financial statements and periodical reports as may be required by its regulator.

This approach continues under FSMA and MiFID and each Chapter of FSA's Rulebook contains its own record-keeping requirements which are a specific application of the overriding requirements to:

> take reasonable care to make adequate records of matters and dealings (including accounting records) which are the subject of requirements under the regulatory system. (SYSC 3.2.20)
>
> A firm must arrange for orderly records to be kept of its business and internal organisation, including all services and transactions undertaken . . . which must be sufficient to enable the FSA . . . to monitor the firm's compliance with the requirements under the regulatory system. (SYSC 9.1.1)[110]

Under MiFID,[111] the records have to be kept for 5 years (SYSC 9.1.2) and the FSA's requirements apply to a UK branch of an EEA firm (SYSC 1.3.10A), and include records in relation to:

- Systematic internalisers (13.3) (MAR 6.7.2(b)).
- Inducements (6.3.2) (COBS 2.3.17).
- Conflicts (6.3.1) (SYSC 10.1.7).
- Financial promotions (10.5) (COBS 4.11).
- Client agreements (8.4) (COBS 8.1.4–8.1.6).
- Suitability assessments (11.2) (COBS 9.5).
- Appropriateness assessments (11.4.2.6) (COBS 10.7).
- Best execution (13.2) (COBS 11.5).

---

[108] 1939 LDRs 9, 10(a).   [109] 1985 White Paper, para. 7.16.
[110] For policy, see FSA CP 06/9, Ch. 8; FSA PS 07/6, paras. 1.19–1.21, Ch. 25. For minimum records required, see CESR/06-552c and CESR/07–085, February 2007.
[111] See, generally, FSA CP 06/9, Ch. 8; FSA PS 06/13, para. 2.15 and Ch. 7; SYSC 14.1.51. The 5-year period applies only to records generated after 30 October 2007 (SYSC TP 1.4).

5.6 FSA's risk assessment methodology

The supervisory and regulatory practices of the Bank of England and SFA, in relation to Barings, and of IMRO, in relation to Maxwell, were, at least partly, regarded as being responsible for those regulated firm failures. Indeed, with those events having led to an emphasis being placed by the regulators on firms' systems and controls and senior management responsibilities for them, the supervisory and monitoring techniques used by the regulators inevitably moved away from 'the past tende[ncy] to focus on the measurable, concentrating on checking compliance with rules'[112] towards 'risk rating [individual] firms'[113] to 'determine . . . the level of surveillance attention we give to a firm'.[114] SFA used FIBSPAM, where '[t]he rating . . . is based on . . . Financial Stability . . . Internal control . . . quality of Business Supervisory complexity . . . quality of Personnel and Management;[115] IMRO used RRAM, the Relative Risk Assessment Model, where '[e]ach key risk is covered by . . . the factors used . . . [being] Inherent risk factors . . . [and] Control risk factors';[116] and the Bank of England used RATE, the Risk Assessment, Tools and Evaluation, under which '[a]fter each [R]isk [A]ssessment the [supervisor] will feed back [his] views on the bank's risk profile in a letter to the bank . . . contain[ing] details of any remedial action . . . the bank . . . [should] take, and of the supervisory programme comprising the [T]ools of supervision . . . which the [supervisor] intends to apply . . . [and it] will [later] undertake a formal [E]valuation to ensure that the bank has completed any agreed remedial action'.[117] FSA decided to take these 'models . . . devised and applied with different types of firm in mind and on the back of different supervisory experiences' and 'harmonise these approaches'[118] because the Treasury's fundamental idea in designing the FSMA regime that '[r]egulation should not be expected to provide an absolute guarantee that nothing can ever go wrong'[119] was reflected in the discretionary nature of FSA's Objectives and 'principles of good regulation' (2.5.1). This enabled FSA to:

> adopt a flexible and differentiated risk-based approach to setting standards and to supervision, reflecting the nature of the business activities concerned, the extent of risk within particular firms and markets, the quality of firms' management controls and the relative sophistication of the consumers involved . . . [in] wholesale and retail business . . . and their relative need of protection.[120]

---

[112] SFA Report & Accounts 1994/1995, p. 28.
[113] SFA Annual Accounts 1995/1996, p. 24. [114] SFA Briefing 15, March 1997, p. 3.
[115] Ibid. [116] IMRO Reporter 9, November 1994, pp. 11–12.
[117] Risk-based approach to supervision of banks, FSA, June 1998, paras. 16–20.
[118] Meeting our Responsibilities, FSA, August 1998, paras. 127–128.
[119] Helen Liddell, Treasury Minister, Speech to City and Financial Conference, 17 July 1997.
[120] Reform of the Financial Regulatory System, SIB, 29 July 1997, p. 2.

Thus, 'we do not aim to prevent failures of firms or all lapses of conduct. We . . . refer to this as a "non-zero failure" regime . . . [which] is implicit in the FSMA. The Act states, for example, that our consumer protection objective means 'securing the appropriate degree of protection for consumers' . . . It does not require us to protect consumers from all risks . . . We seek to meet our objectives . . . with finite resources. We need to make judgments and set priorities . . . With our risk-based approach, we have to target our resources to those tasks that pose the greatest risk to our objectives. We have therefore developed a framework for allocating resources against risks according to their probability and possible impact . . . to minimise the risks to our objectives.'[121]

There is clearly a distinction between the regulator's risk assessment of firms and the methodology it uses for this, and its own 'performance measurement and quality assurance' based on 'the risks to which it is subject in the course of its business as a regulator . . . which might lead to failures in . . . [its] regulatory processes'.[122] FSA, however, if not confusing these two aspects, at least is running them together in ARROW, the Advanced Risk-Responsive Operating FrameWork, which 'provides the link between our statutory objectives and our regulatory activities, and is designed to: identify the main risks to our objectives . . .; measure the importance of those risks; mitigate those risks . . .; and monitor . . . our risk management . . . Our objectives are clearly set out in FSMA. So, for us to consider something as a risk, it must have the potential to cause harm to . . . our statutory objectives.'[123] What has been described as 'the ultimate management consultancy tool for regulators' operates through a number of applications. There are the four Objectives (2.5.1): (1) Market Confidence, (2) Consumer Protection, (3) Financial Crime and (4) Public Awareness; and there are seven Risks to these Objectives (RTOs), each related to one or more of them: (i) Financial Failure (1, 2), (ii) Misconduct/Mismanagement (1, 2), (iii) Consumer Understanding of Products (2, 4), (iv) Market Quality (1, 2), (v) Fraud (1, 3), (vi) Market Abuse (1, 2, 3) and (vii) Money Laundering (1, 3). 'We consider risks to be the combination of impact (the potential harm that could be caused) and probability (the likelihood of the particular event occurring), i.e.:

Risk to FSA's Objectives = Impact × Probability

'We then use this measure to prioritise risks and make decisions on what, if anything, our regulatory response should be. We also use it to set out our strategic aims and outcomes and to allocate resources based on our

---

[121] Reasonable expectations: Regulation in a non-zero failure world, FSA, September 2003, paras. 1.2, 1.7, 1.13, 1.15. Part of this risk-based resource allocation relates to taking enforcement action (EG 2.7).
[122] Regulatory Plan 1996–97, IMRO, p. 12, para. 9.
[123] The FSA's risk-assessment framework, FSA, August 2006, paras. 2.6, 2.10.

regulatory priorities.'[124] The calculation of Impact 'take[s] into account not only quantitative information about the scope and severity of the potential problem (e.g. the number of consumers affected, or the monetary amounts involved) but also qualitative factors (e.g. the vulnerability of the consumers and the nature of the harm they are likely to suffer).' The pseudo-scientific credence of 'using numerical data, taken from the firm's regulatory returns' is perhaps undermined by the admission that '[o]ur impact measures are, at best, proxy measures. Supervisory overrides . . . do, therefore, take place where we do not consider the numerical answer is a fair reflection of the firm's impact.'[125] With Probability, 'we first consider . . . the level of business risk in a firm before separately assessing the quality of the controls the firm has in place to deal with those risks', there being 4 Business Risk groups (Environmental Risk, Customers, Prudential Risk, Business Process) and 6 Control Risk groups (Customers, Financial and Operations, Prudential, Management, Capital, Control), the total being sub-divided into 52 risk elements, and again the inevitable discretion creeps in since 'we . . . also take an overall view of the firm, weighing both positive and negative aspects and the importance of each risk element to the firm'. Unsurprisingly, '[t]he model contains parameters that can be set by our senior management to reflect their risk appetite', presumably as regulators operating a regulatory regime.[126] The end result for the firm is a scoring against each RTO of High, Medium/High, Medium/Low or Low, which maps into an overall scoring against each Objective and, hence, the risk to FSA's Objectives and a prioritisation of FSA's resources in terms of remedial work and monitoring of that firm.

This methodology is used for about 5.5% of all the firms FSA regulates, of which 2.5% are '[m]edium sized businesses with a high risk profile' and '[s]ignificant business[es] normally formed into groups' where, for the former, on an annual basis there will be 'an on-site assessment (usually three days to a week), reviewing all aspects of the firm's business, but paying particular regard to sector priorities' and the latter, in addition, will also be subject to 'Close and Continuous monitoring', i.e. 'regular . . . meetings and assessment work that is designed to test the key control functions of the firm/group'. Three per cent of all regulated firms are other '[m]edium-sized . . . businesses where [FSA's] supervisory remit is relatively narrow e.g. firms from . . . [the] EEA' and here FSA applies 'ARROW Light', being '[u]sually an on-site visit covering core areas (normally one day), plus any issues that are priorities for the firm's sector'. The ARROW process results in a letter to the firm setting out the key findings and a Risk Mitigation Programme (RMP) 'setting out: the issues identified . . . ; the intended outcomes [FSA] seek[s] for each issue; the action to be taken to achieve the

---

[124] Ibid, paras. 3.1, 3.2.   [125] Ibid, paras. 3.6, 3.7, 3.9.   [126] Ibid, paras. 3.11–3.14, 3.33.

intended outcome . . . by [the] firm; and the timetable for action'. For 95% of firms the '[m]ain focus is an analysis of the returns submitted,'[127] since with such 'firms . . . assess[ed] as being low impact we rarely carry out firm-specific risk assessment work, placing reliance on . . . remote monitoring of information submitted by the firm'.[128] For all firms there are 'thematic assessments' through '[r]eviews focusing on key trends and priorities determined [by FSA] from intelligence gathered by the FSA largely on site [at firms]'.[129]

This type of methodology for the assessment by the regulator of how to regulate, supervise and monitor the firm is, obviously, a risk assessment of the type that, under the Systems and Controls Rules, the firm should itself be going through. Thus, while supervisory techniques are not at this stage harmonised across CESR in respect of MiFID, the underlying rule set on systems and controls and prudential regulation is harmonised, and it would not be surprising if for that reason alone and to further maximise its own scarce resources FSA introduced for firms some form of ARROW self-assessment since '[w]e regulate around 27000 firms covering a vast range of sizes and activities, from international investment banks operating in Wholesale markets to small retail firms selling mortgages on the High Street'.[130]

---

[127] The FSA's Risk-Based Approach, November 2006, pp. 4–5, 13–14.
[128] The FSA's Risk-Assessment Framework, August 2006, para. 4.1.
[129] The FSA's Risk-Based Approach, November 2006, p. 5.
[130] Better Regulation Action Plan, FSA, December 2005, p. 5.

6
Conflicts of interest

6.1 Differences in interests and conflicts of interest

There has always been under English law, and notwithstanding MiFID will continue to be, a law of fiduciaries governing conflicts of interest as well as a regulatory regime dealing with the same issue, albeit in a different manner. Under any such law or regime there are, as with any rule, three questions: When does it apply, i.e. what type of relationship between the parties is considered sufficient for the rule to apply? What does it require, i.e., for this purpose, what is a 'conflict'? And: How can it be complied with, in other words is the conflict prohibited such that the transaction cannot proceed, or can it simply be disclosed to the other party or must it be managed in some other way? Each of these is a very difficult question to answer in practice, often involving relative degrees of uncertainty. But answering the first two questions can result in fundamental misconceptions unless you understand that a Conflict of Interest is not a Difference in Interests. Any commercial situation involves a Difference in Interests: as the seller I want the highest price and as the buyer you want to pay the lowest price, a Difference in Interests which is in practice resolved through commercial negotiations in which each party brings to bear the full force of its own interests. It does not involve a Conflict of Interests unless there is some special reason, recognised by the rule, under which one party's interest has to be subordinated, in his own conduct, to the interest of the other party. Such a reason can arise only because of the presence of particular facts recognised by the rule as meriting special treatment.

6.2 The general law of fiduciaries

6.2.1 A fiduciary relationship

The general law rules on conflicts apply only where the firm is a 'fiduciary' to the particular client and 'it is possible to divide fiduciaries into two categories, status-based fiduciaries and fact-based fiduciaries . . . [S]tatus-based fiduciaries . . . include people who by virtue of their involvement in certain relationships are considered without further enquiry to be fiduciaries. Such relationships include those between trustee–beneficiary, . . .

agent–principal, director–company'[1] and 'trust or . . . agency . . . is none the less fiduciary because it happens to arise in a commercial context'.[2] Thus, the firm will be a fiduciary when it acts as broker (even execution-only) or portfolio manager, and hence as an agent, or as trustee custodian or when it holds client money (7.2.1, 7.2.2). In all other relationships between the firm and client (whether a private or institutional client) it can be fiduciary, if at all, only under the 'fact-based' heading[3] and here '[t]he one factor . . . which is . . . indispensable to the existence of the [fiduciary] relationship . . . is that of dependency or vulnerability . . . which causes him to place reliance upon the other',[4] in other words 'a . . . relationship of trust and confidence'.[5] 'That . . . will be found . . . where the function the adviser represents himself as performing . . . is that of counselling an advised party as to how his interests will or might best be served in a matter . . . of importance to the advised's personal or financial well-being, and in which the adviser would be expected both to be disinterested (save for his remuneration . . .) and to be free of adverse responsibilities.'[6] Thus, the firm acting as broker–dealer will be a fiduciary when it gives advice that it is intended to be relied upon, even when dealing as a principal, as will an investment bank acting as corporate finance adviser.[7] Where its client in those relationships is an institution '[t]raditionally . . . the fact that the agreement between the parties was of a purely commercial kind and that they . . . dealt at arm's length and on an equal footing has consistently been regarded by th[e] Court as important, if not decisive, in indicating that no fiduciary duty arose'[8] because 'the parties themselves . . . are to be the authors of their respective rights and obligations' 'where . . . the adviser is reasonably entitled to expect that (a) the other party, because of his position, knowledge etc will make his own evaluation of the matter . . . and . . . exercise an independent judgment in his own interests . . . or (b) the other is assuming the responsibility for how his own interests are to be served . . . however incompetent in this he may in fact be'.[9] Nonetheless, '[i]t is, however, difficult to see why, if a relationship has the characteristics which, in another context, would . . . [be] fiduciary . . . it should be treated differently simply because it is "commercial" . . . In truth every . . .

---

[1] Fiduciary Duties and Regulatory Rules, LC CP No. 124, 1992, para. 2.4.3.
[2] *Meagher*, para. 504.   [3] *Varcoe* v. *Stirling* (1992) 7 DR (3d) 204.
[4] *Lac Minerals Ltd.* v. *International Corona Resources Ltd.* 1989 61 DLR 4th 14.
[5] *Hospital Products Ltd.* v. *United States Surgical Corporation* (1984) 156 CLR 41 at 96.
[6] Fiduciary Law and the Modern Commercial World, Paul Finn, in *Commercial Aspects of Trustees and Fiduciary Obligations*, Norton Rose Oxford Law Colloquium, September 1991, para. I(iv) ('Finn'). 'A fiduciary . . . has undertaken to act for or on behalf of another . . . in circumstances which give rise to a relationship of trust and confidence. The . . . principal is entitled to the single-minded loyalty of his fiduciary' (*Bristol & West Building Society* v. *Mothew* [1998] Ch. 1 at 18).
[7] *Daly* v. *Sydney Stock Exchange Ltd.* (1986) 160 CLR 371; *Estate Realities Ltd.* v. *Wignell* [1991] 3 NZLR 482.   [8] *Meagher*, para. 504.   [9] Finn, paras. I(v), II.

transaction must be examined on its merits with a view to ascertaining whether it manifests the characteristics of a fiduciary relationship.'[10] Thus, advice to an institution which is, and is reasonably known by the firm to be, relying on it will make the firm a fiduciary whether in a dealing or corporate finance context, and a broker–dealer, albeit entering into transactions as a principal with its institutional client, will be a fiduciary where the broker–dealer:

> was a 'riskless principal' [6.2.2.1(1)] . . . ; the risk of going short or long attached to the [client] . . . Secondly, for effecting the transaction [the broker–dealer] . . . received a commission. Thirdly, the [client] . . . gave [the broker–dealer] . . . a considerable measure of discretion. Fourthly, in return [the broker–dealer] . . . assured the [client, in the Terms of Business] . . . that, although it . . . excluded 'best execution' [13.2], it would 'of course always attempt to transact business with you in the best terms available at the relevant times'.[11]

6.2.2 A conflict of interest

As regards the scope of the fiduciary's duties, it 'is . . . a mistaken assumption that all fiduciaries are the same duties in all circumstances'[12] because it 'depends upon the precise nature and scope of the relationship' including the 'express . . . terms of the contract'.[13] Given the multiplicity of businesses and functions in a financial conglomerate and, indeed, in each of its operating companies and divisions, and the mass of conflicts to which these give rise (see below), it would be relatively unusual to imply into the firm's Terms of Business a term avoiding a fiduciary duty that would otherwise apply either on the ground that it 'is something so obvious that it goes without saying' (on the officious bystander test) or that it gives 'such business efficacy as the parties must have intended . . . The . . . Courts will not imply a term merely because it would be reasonable to do . . . [A]ttempts to imply terms . . . commonly fail . . . [because] it may not be clear that both parties would in fact have agreed to the alleged term. Where their interests are opposed, an implication that may be regarded as obvious to one party may well be rejected by the other.'[14] However, in really obvious cases a term will be implied, for example in *Kelly* v. *Cooper*[15] where an estate agent was, unknown to either vendor, acting for two vendors with adjoining land who each sold to the same purchaser and, had they known of the other vendor, could have obtained a much higher price. The claim of one vendor against the estate agent for the missed value failed:

---

[10] *Meagher*, para. 504.
[11] *Brandeis (Brokers) Ltd.* v. *Herbert Black* [2001] AER 342 at para. 41. See, further: SFA BN 578, 16 March 2001; SFA BN 609, 20 December 2001.
[12] *Henderson* v. *Merrett Syndicates Ltd.* [1995] 2 AC 145 at 206.
[13] *Meagher*, paras. 514–515.   [14] *Trietel*, pp. 185–7.   [15] [1993] AC 205.

where a principal instructs as selling agent for his property . . . a person who to his knowledge acts . . . for other principals selling property of the same description, the terms to be implied into such agency contract must differ from those to be implied where an agent is not carrying on such general agency business. In the case of estate agents, it is their business to act for numerous principals: where properties are of a similar description, there will be a conflict of interest between the principals each of whom will be concerned to attract potential purchasers . . . Yet, despite this conflict of interest, estate agents must be free to act for several competing principals otherwise they will be unable to perform their function . . . In the course of acting for each of their principals, estate agents will acquire information confidential to that principal. It cannot be sensibly suggested that an estate agent is . . . bound to disclose to any one of his principals information which is confidential to another of his principals. The principle as to confidentiality is even clearer in the case of stockbrokers who cannot be . . . bound to disclose to their private clients inside information disclosed to the brokers in confidence by a company for which they also act. Accordingly in such cases there must be an implied term of the contract with such an agent that he is entitled to act for other principals selling competing properties and to keep confidential the information obtained from each of his principals.[16]

Although, following this case, 'it will be clear to any customer of a broker that the broker acts for other customers, and that the broker would not be able to operate without doing so' and, therefore, 'a firm may be permitted . . . to act for customers with conflicting interests in different situations and to keep confidential the information obtained from each', 'the large range of different functions which different departments of a financial conglomerate carries out . . . may be less obvious to any one customer of a particular department, especially if he . . . is an inexperienced private customer'. Hence:

> [Kelly does not cover] three situations of conflict . . . The first is where the firm is acting for two customers in the same transaction. The second is where there is a conflict between the firm's own interests and the duty which it owes to a customer and that conflict is more acute than that which arose in *Kelly*. The conflict of interest in *Kelly* arose . . . where the plaintiff 'was well aware' that the . . . [estate agents] would be acting for vendors of competing properties. The conflict would be more acute if, for example, (i) a firm has a direct beneficial interest in a transaction with a customer, such as where it sells its own property to a customer, or (ii) the discretionary fund management arm of a firm purchases the commercial paper issued by a company for a client at a time when the corporate finance department is calling in a loan to that company which will cause it to default on the

---

[16] *Ibid* at 213–5.

commercial paper. The third situation is where there has been 'inequity'. This might arise where a sectoral analyst who has been made an insider by the corporate finance department in relation to a particular stock returns to his normal duties before the inside information . . . is in the public domain . . . If, on the basis of his last published opinion, the analyst advised a customer to purchase the stock, despite having inside knowledge that the stock was about to fall in price, although the Court will not hold that the analyst should have committed a criminal offence and disclosed the inside information to the customer, it might well consider that the firm should not have placed itself in a position of conflict which would require it deliberately to mislead a customer.[17]

It follows that, given the narrow grounds on which to imply terms, a modern financial conglomerate, post-Big Bang (2.4.1), is subject to the following 'conflicts of interest'.

6.2.2.1 Proprietary dealing

Commercial situations:

(1) The broker–dealer sells its own investments to, or buys for its own account from, the client, even though the sales desk dealing with the client is separate from the trading desk. This includes a riskless principal transaction (where the firm buys as principal from one client and immediately sells to another).

(2) Underwriting/buying a new issue of securities and selling them to the client.

(3) The portfolio manager buys securities for its clients from its affiliated broker–dealer.

Legal analysis: The general rule that 'an agent employed to purchase cannot legally buy his own goods for his principal . . . [and] neither can an agent employed to sell, himself purchase the goods of his principal'[18] is strictly applied to agency brokers.[19] 'It matters not that the broker sells at the market price', for example, achieves best execution (13.2), 'nor is it material to enquire whether the principal has or has not suffered a loss'[20] because 'this rule . . . is founded on th[e] principle . . . that an agent will not be allowed to place himself in a situation which, under ordinary circumstances, would tempt a man to do that which is not the best for his principal'.[21]

---

[17] Fiduciary Duties and Regulatory Rules, LC, No. 236, December 1995, paras. 3.30–3.32.
[18] *Bentley* v. *Craven* (1853) 18 Beav. 74 at 76.
[19] *Erskine, Oxenford & Co* v. *Sachs* [1901] 2 KB 504; *Christoforides* v. *Terry* [1924] AC 566.
[20] *Armstrong* v. *Jackson* [1917] 2 KB 822 at 824.   [21] *Bentley* v. *Craven*, at 77.

Conflicts of interest

6.2.2.2 Secret profit

Commercial situations:

(1) The firm uses client confidential information for its own benefit, for example, front running a large customer order either to acquire the securities which the client ordered or to 'piggy back' on the market impact of the client order.

(2) The firm front runs a research report to be issued by the firm to clients by buying the securities for its own account in order to ensure that the firm has the securities to meet anticipated client demand as a result of the report (6.3.4.2).

(3) A portfolio manager receives an inducement or soft commission (6.3.2, 6.3.3) to manage the client relationship in a particular manner, for example put client transactions through a particular broker–dealer.

(4) Receiving any other benefit from a third party as a result of a transaction carried out with that third party on behalf of the client.

(5) The portfolio manager 'churns' the portfolio, i.e. buys and sells investments) simply to generate commission for itself (6.3.6).

Legal analysis: '[A] "fundamental rule" . . . requires the fiduciary to account for any benefit or gain obtained or received by reason of or by use of his fiduciary position or of opportunity or knowledge resulting from it: the objective is to preclude the fiduciary from actually misusing his position for his personal advantage.'[22] '[T]he . . . [rule] oblige[s] the [fiduciary] to account, [even though] the . . . [beneficiaries] will receive a benefit which . . . it is unlikely they would have got for themselves had the [fiduciary] complied with its duty to them.'[23]

6.2.2.3 Duty of good faith

Commercial situations:

(1) The firm's corporate finance or proprietary research department has information on a company which is not disclosed to a client of the broker–dealer department who buys or sells the securities of that company.

(2) The firm holds a large unexecuted sale order in an investment (which, when executed, will have the effect of decreasing the market price of the security) at a time another client places (and the firm executes for that client) a buy order (or vice versa).

(3) The firm holds through its proprietary dealing department identical investments to a client of the sales and trading department and sells them with a market impact which affects the price to the client's detriment.

---

[22] *Chan v. Zacharia* (1984) 159 CLR at 198–9.
[23] *Industrial Development Consultants Ltd. v. Cooley* [1972] 1 WLR 443 at 452.

(4) The firm favours one client over another, for example, by releasing client research at different times or by not offering new issue subscriptions to all clients or by aggregating client orders such that not all clients aggregated benefit all of the time.

Legal analysis: The first question in situations (1) and (2) is whether knowledge held by an employee (for example, in the corporate finance department) is imputed to the whole company such that the firm (through the broker–dealer department) breaches its duty of good faith to its client by not disclosing a fact of which the actual employee in the broker–dealer department was in any event unaware. The rule is that since 'a corporation is an abstraction'[24] it 'can only act by agents'[25] and, thus, '[t]he law imputes to the principal . . . all . . . knowledge relating to the subject-matter of the agency which his agent acquires or obtains while acting as such agent'.[26] 'The . . . knowledge of an agent is imputed to the principal . . . [where] the agent has actual or ostensible authority to receive . . . information . . . on behalf of the principal.'[27] 'The rule that a principal is treated in law as having knowledge of all facts which its . . . agent acquires in circumstances where a duty exists to pass the information on is based upon three considerations: first, fairness as between the parties; secondly, public necessity and business convenience; and, thirdly, the strong probability that the presumption accords with the facts.'[28] The fact, if it be the case, that the information is held behind a Chinese Wall is irrelevant[29] since the Chinese Wall is a defence only that the firm did not use the information (6.2.3.1) and does not affect the fact that it possesses it in the first place. Moreover, as regards the duty of good faith or undivided loyalty, a firm engaged to advise is obliged to:

> put at his client's disposal . . . his knowledge, so far as is relevant; and if he is unwilling to reveal his knowledge to his client, he should not act for him. What he cannot do is to act for the client and at the same time withhold from him any relevant knowledge that he has.[30]

In situations (3) and (4), the legal analysis of the duty of undivided loyalty is as in 6.2.2.4.

6.2.2.4   Conflict of two duties

Commercial situations:

(1) The firm acquires confidential information from one client which is material to another, for example, the broker–dealer or portfolio

---

[24] *Leonard's Carrying Co Ltd.* v. *Asiatic Petroleum Co Ltd.* [1915] AC 705.
[25] *Bowstead*, p. 13.   [26] *Bowstead*, Art. 97(2).
[27] *El Ajou* v. *Dollar Land Holdings plc* [1994] 2 AER 685 at 702–6.
[28] *Equiticorp Industries Group Ltd.* v. *The Crown* [1996] 3 NZLR 586.
[29] *Marks & Spencer plc* v. *Freshfields* [2004] 3 AER 773.
[30] *Spector* v. *Ageda* [1973] Ch. 30 at 48.

management department is advising clients to buy Company X's securities at a time when the corporate finance department is trying to put together a rescue package for Company X.

(2) The broker–dealer conducts an agency cross trade matching two client orders and receiving commission from both.

Legal analysis: As regards situation (2), 'the general principle is that an agent may not act for both parties to a transaction unless he ensures that he fully discloses the material facts to both parties and obtains their informed consent to his so acting'.[31] In both situations, '[t]he law's object . . . is twofold: (a) to preserve the expectation the client is entitled to have that it is his interests alone that the fiduciary is safeguarding; and (b) to preclude the fiduciary from putting himself in a position where he may be required to choose between conflicting duties or be led to an attempt to reconcile conflicting interests'.[32]

6.2.3   Solutions

Breach of the rules against proprietary dealing and secret profits (6.2.2.1, 6.2.2.2) renders the fiduciary liable to an account of profits, tracing or constructing trust unless the rights of an innocent third party have supervened. With a breach of the duty of good faith or a conflict of two duties (6.2.2.3, 6.2.2.4), the remedies are injunction to prevent the breach or damages for loss suffered.[33] Hence, the search for a practical solution.

6.2.3.1   Separate companies, management, personnel and location

The issue of conflicts of interest did not, by and large, arise pre-Big Bang since the functions of corporate finance, broking, dealing and portfolio management were carried on in separate companies with separate management, personnel, location and ownership due to restrictive Stock Exchange membership rules (2.2.1, 2.4.1). Big Bang and the ability to form multi-service companies, particularly broker–dealers, with common ownership within financial conglomerates, gave rise to all of the conflicts of interest referred to in 6.2.2. If a conglomerate, however, separates out two of those functions, say corporate finance and portfolio management, and places them in separate companies, with separate personnel and location, this will be effective to avoid conflicts of interest if two considerations are satisfied. First, management including directors, must be totally separate. If there is some commonality, the common directors'/managers' knowledge obtained as director/manager of one company will not be imputed to the other company, such that the Chinese Walls between the two (6.2.3.2) are

[31] *James v. Canovan* [1972] 2 NSWLR 236 at 242.
[32] Finn, para. III.1. See also: *North & South Trust Co. v. Berkeley* [1971] 1 AER 980.
[33] *Meagher*, paras. 514–544, 547–555.

rendered ineffective, if the directors/managers are not involved in day-to-day business activities which require them to talk to particular clients. This is because, although 'the board of directors . . . and perhaps other superior officers of the company . . . speak and act as the company',[34] 'English law has never taken the view that the knowledge of the director [is] ipso facto imputed to the company . . . [It] depends upon the extent of the powers which . . . he has express or implied authority to exercise on behalf of the company'[35] and, in practice, his authority will be limited to each company separately. Second, the separation must be real. So, for example, if the portfolio manager, with fiduciary duties to its clients, places all transactions with the broker–dealer, acting as principal and therefore making the secret profit, such that the two companies are really operated as one commercial undertaking, the portfolio manager may have a duty to account. It would, of course, be different if the portfolio manager dealt on arm's-length terms with the broker–dealer and others in the market.

6.2.3.2 Chinese Walls in one legal entity

For the purpose of the general law, the Courts regard a Chinese Wall as effective to prevent the deliberate, negligent or inadvertent flow of information and, hence, to protect confidential information held for a client in the situation where a separate department/team is working for another client to whom there is otherwise a duty to disclose and for whom the confidential information would be useful.[36] Moreover, a Chinese Wall is a solution to the duty of undivided loyalty and to a conflict of two duties (6.2.2.3, 6.2.2.4) so as to oust the requirement to disclose confidential information to the other client if expressly or impliedly consented to by that client in the Terms of Business,[37] although implied consent is extremely difficult to establish in practice.[38] Without consent a Chinese Wall will not oust that requirement because the duty of disclosure remains and the information is held by the legal entity (6.2.2.3). An express provision in the firm's Terms of Business would be as follows:

> The Firm is not obliged to disclose to the Customer or to take into consideration information either:
>
> (a) the disclosure of which by it to the Customer would or might be a breach of duty or confidence to any other person; or
> (b) which comes to the notice of an employee, officer or agent of the Firm, but properly does not come to the actual notice of the individual acting for the Customer.

---

[34] *Tesco Supermarkets Ltd.* v. *Nattras* [1972] AC 153.   [35] El Ajou, at 705.

[36] *Rakusen* v. *Ellis, Munday & Clarke* [1912] 1 Ch. 831; *Lee* v. *Coward Chance* [1999] 3 WLR 1278; *Re a firm of solicitors* [1992] 1 AER 353; *Prince Jefri* v. *KPMG* [1999] 2 AC 222; *Mannesmann* v. *Goldman Sachs*, Ch. 1999, Unreported, 18 November 1999.

[37] *Kelly* v. *Cooper*. [1993] AC 205.   [38] LC 236, paras. 2.16, 7.11–7.18.

However, because 'such express terms may be insufficient on their own to avoid liability for breach of a firm's duty not to put itself in a position where its own interests conflict with those of a customer, or where it owes conflicting duties to another customer',[39] further terms are necessary in the contract with the customer (6.2.3.3).

As regards the constituents of a Chinese Wall, 'Courts have ... expressed extreme scepticism as to the efficacy of Chinese Walls'[40] needing, as expressed in one case, to be 'satisfied that the ... firm has demonstrated that the Chinese Walls ... will be sound-proof'.[41] 'Chinese Walls ... contemplate the existence of established organisational arrangements which preclude the passing of information in the possession of one part of the business to other parts of a business ... [I]n the financial services industry, good practice requires there to be established institutional arrangements' rather than 'established ad hoc and ... erected within a single department',[42] although this is 'saying no more than that such Chinese Walls which had become part of the fabric of the institution, were more likely to work than if erected to meet a one-off problem'.[43] Thus, a so-called Chinese Box within a department can work provided the construction of such ad hoc arrangements is itself recognised in the firm's institutional procedures. 'Chinese walls ... normally involve[e] some combination of the following organisational arrangements: (i) the physical separation of the various departments ... to insulate them from each other [which] ... often extends to such matters of detail as dining arrangements; (ii) an educational programme, normally recurring, to emphasise the importance of not improperly or inadvertently divulging confidential information; (iii) strict and carefully defined procedures for dealing with a situation where ... the Wall should be crossed and the maintaining of proper records where this occurs; (iv) monitoring by compliance officers of the effectiveness of the Wall; (v) disciplinary sanctions where there has been a breach of the Wall.'[44] However, the firm may not need to go so far as 'prevent[ing] direct or indirect contact both socially and professionally'.[45] In requirement (iii) 'the ... most common example [i]s bringing an industry or sectoral analyst over the Wall [from the broker–dealer] to advise the corporate finance department with respect to a particular transaction ... [as to] pricing or distribution. Here good practice ... take[s] the following form:

[1] The decision to bring the analyst over the Wall should only be made ... at an appropriate level of management seniority.

---

[39] LC 236, para. 3.34.
[40] *Prince Jefri* v. *KPMG* 1998 B No. 4682, 15 February 1998; *Bolkiah* v. *KPMG* [1999] CLC 175.   [41] *Lee* v. *Coward Chance*, at 1283.   [42] *Prince Jefri*.
[43] *Young* v. *Robson Rhodes* [1999] 3 AER 524.   [44] *Prince Jefri*.
[45] *Young* v. *Robson Rhodes* at para. 42.

[2] ... care must be taken at the stage of the initial request to ensure that information of a confidential nature is not unwittingly revealed ... For this reason, it would ... be appropriate to channel the initial request through the compliance officer.

[3] The analyst should only be provided with the minimum amount of information that he needs to know ... for as short a period as possible. To achieve this ... attention has to be paid to ...: (i) the timing of the analyst's move across the Wall and (ii) the type of information that is disclosed ... [Requirement] (i) ... prevents the analyst from being privy to confidential information until the last possible moment ... (ii) is ... designed to ensure that ... the analyst is provided only with information that has a relatively short 'shelf life' ...

[4] The compliance department should monitor the process ...

The most difficult problem is what happens to the analyst when he returns over the Wall ... [O]ne way of regulating the problem ... would be to take the analyst out of circulation until the confidential information is ... part of the public domain ... [without] unwittingly tip[ping] off [his] customers that something is afoot.[46]

A similar problem arises where a senior manager 'overlook[s] the Wall and ... obtain[s] ... information which is otherwise retained behind a chinese wall'[47] although in practice 'senior managers ... above Chinese Walls would usually only be involved in decisions of strategy and policy, and ... not deal with customers, make markets or take decisions affecting day to day transactions'.[48] In any event, knowledge obtained in one capacity is unlikely to be imputed to a company where he acts in a different capacity (6.2.3.1), if there is a robust Chinese Wall otherwise sectioning off the information held by the legal entity.

As part of its Chinese Wall arrangements the firm may 'use ... "stop" or "watch" (sometimes referred to as "grey" or "monitored") lists ... whereby trading in a designated share is either prohibited (a stop list) or ... monitored (a watch list) ... [With] a stop list there is the danger that this would signal that the firm has information relevant to the activity'[49] and, hence, usually, 'a security [i]s only placed on the list once the information about it had been made public'. Thus, 'stop lists and watch lists were not intended to provide a solution to ... [conflicts in themselves but are] devices for monitoring the operation and effectiveness of Chinese Walls, and for avoiding liability under the insider dealing legislation'.[50]

6.2.3.3   Disclosure and consent

'It is not enough for the agent to tell the principal that he is going to have an interest ... He must tell him all the material facts. He must make full

---

[46] LC 124, paras. 4.5.20–4.5.22.   [47] Ibid, 4.5.23.   [48] LC 236, para. 9.3.
[49] LC 124, para. 4.5.24.   [50] LC 236, para. 9.2.

disclosure'[51] such that in proprietary dealing (6.2.2.1) the firm would have to disclose the fact that it was proposing to sell its own property, the price at which it acquired it and the profit to be made on the sale to the customer. This would make it impossible to operate financial conglomerates and the question, therefore, is whether advance general disclosure of, and consent to, the nature of the conflict, without disclosure of the terms of the particular conflict, can be sufficient. There are two ways of doing this in the Terms of Business. The first is to accept a fiduciary relationship and disclose against or exclude it, for example:

> The Firm may, without prior reference to the Customer or any further disclosure, effect Transactions in which the Firm has, directly or indirectly, a material interest or a relationship of any description with another person, which may involve a conflict with the Firm's duty to the Customer, for example because:
>
> – the Firm undertakes business for or with other Customers; and/or
> – the Firm deals for its own account in securities which the Customer buys, holds or sells; and/or
> – in a Transaction with the Customer, the Firm may benefit from a commission, fee, mark-up or mark-down[52] and/or also be remunerated by the counterparty; and/or
> – the Firm may deal in investments as principal with the Customer; and/or
> – the Firm may act as agent for the Customer in a transaction where it also acts as agent for the counterparty.

The second approach (perhaps together with the first) is to define in the Terms of Business the Firm–Customer relationship in such a way that a fiduciary relationship with consequences preventing the Firm acting in conflict situations does not arise in the first place:

> None of the services to be provided hereunder nor any other matter shall give rise to any fiduciary or equitable duties which would, in Transactions with or for the Customer, prevent the Firm acting as both dealer and broker, principal or agent, dealing with Affiliates and other customers, and generally effecting Transactions as envisaged in these Terms.

Generally, 'where a relationship is created by contract . . . the Court must have regard to all the terms of the contract . . . when determining whether the relationship is fiduciary and, if so, the scope of the fiduciary's duties . . .

---

[51] *Dunne* v. *English* (1874) CR 18 Eq. 524 at 533. See also, *Phipps* v. *Boardman* [1967] 2 AC 46.

[52] The firm may act as agent and charge a commission or fee, or as principal and add a mark-up to the price at which it sells to the customer or deduct a mark-down to the price at which it buys from the customer.

The parties to a consensual relationship would be free to set out the parameters of their respective rights and duties',[53] particularly after *Kelly* v. *Cooper* (6.2.2) which 'makes it clear that where a fiduciary relationship arises out of a contract, a clearly worded duty defining or exclusion clause would circumscribe the extent of the fiduciary duties owed to the other party. It also indicates that an unambiguous general advanced disclosure . . . will be effective, provided that the contract clearly delineates the rights and duties of the parties . . . and displaces the obligation to make full disclosure of all material facts.'[54] The duty-defining clause is not within the 1977 Unfair Contract Terms Act because it is not an exemption for 'negligence' within Section 2(2) or, having defined the relationship, an exclusion of liability for breach within Section 3(2). However, it may, as against a Private Customer or Retail Client, constitute an 'unfair term' 'which contrary to the requirement of good faith causes a significant imbalance in the parties' rights and obligations . . . to the detriment of the consumer' within the Unfair Terms in Consumer Contracts Regulations 1994, always assuming that the Regulations apply in the first place to contracts relating to choses in action as opposed to 'goods' or 'services'.[55] In addition, a duty-defining clause may still contravene the FSA's own prohibition on exclusion clauses with Private Customers which relates to an exclusion of any 'duty' (8.4.5).

Consent, as with any contractual agreement, can be express or implied by a course of conduct 'if the offeree did the act with the intention (ascertained in accordance with the objective principle) of accepting the offer'.[56]

6.2.3.4 An independence policy

The use of an independence policy (6.3.1.3) is wholly ineffective at general law since the conflict still exists in the legal entity which owes the relevant duty to the client.

6.2.3.5 Declining to act

If the conflict cannot be resolved within 6.2.3.1–6.2.3.4 then the firm would have to decline to act.

6.3 Regulatory rules

6.3.1 The general rule

Compliance with regulatory rules, whether those permitting the use of Chinese Walls or requiring best execution in proprietary dealing, does not provide a safe harbour against breach of the general law on fiduciary obligations.[57] Moreover, ever since Big Bang and the introduction to London of

---

[53] LC 124, para. 3.3.10.   [54] LC 236, para. 3.29.   [55] *Trietel*, Chapter 7, Section 3(2).
[56] *Trietel*, Chapter 2, Section 2.1(2).
[57] LC 124, paras. 5.4.2, 5.4.4, 5.5.3, 6.17–6.21; LC 236, paras. 1.14, 11.7, 11.13, 14.1–14.20.

financial conglomerates with multiple, potentially conflicting, functions, the regulators have had rules requiring the firm to manage its conflicts of interest, such rules deliberately mimicking the general law because, as Professor Gower put it:

> conflicts are . . . endemic among those providing financial services . . . which cannot be wholly avoided by erecting 'Chinese Walls'. City opinion has been remarkably complacent about this, apparently believing that reputable firms can be trusted to resolve the conflict in such a way that if anyone suffers it will be they and not their clients. That will not be so, however, unless they . . . ask themselves the critical question: 'Would we mind disclosing . . . what we are doing?' And if the answer is yes, not doing it without full disclosure and . . . consent . . . Unhappily . . . they did not always ask themselves the question or, when they do, draw the right conclusion . . . This is . . . why [all] section[s] of the investment industry . . . must be under an enforceable obligation to disclose.[58]

Thus, the original SIB rule that:

> A firm shall not effect a transaction . . . or recommend the effecting of a transaction with or for a customer . . . if the firm has directly or indirectly a material interest . . . in the transaction or in the fact of its being effected . . . or has a relationship of any description with another person such as to place the firm in a position where its duty to or its interest in relation to that other person conflicts with its duty to the customer, unless . . .
> (a) the firm has disclosed to the customer the nature of the . . . interest . . . or . . . conflict . . . and . . . the customer has consented to the transaction . . . or
> (c) . . . none of the individuals involved in effecting . . . that transaction or making the recommendation knew or ought to have known of the interest or conflict.[59]

Very similar rules continued all the way up to the introduction of MiFID. Under 2000 FSMA, Pre-MiFID, FSA had two provisions. First a Principle that:

> A firm must manage a conflict of interest fairly, both between itself and its customer and between a customer and another client. (PRIN 2.1.1, Principle 8)

Second, a Rule that:

> If a firm has or may have:
> (1) a material interest in a transaction to be entered into with or for a customer; or
> (2) a relationship that gives or may give rise to a conflict of interest in relation to a transaction in (1); or

[58] 1984 Gower, para. 6.30.   [59] SIB Conduct Rules, 7 October 1987, 5.08.

(3) an interest in a transaction that is, or may be, in conflict with any of the firm's customers; or
(4) customers with conflicting interests in relation to a transaction;

the firm must not knowingly advise, or deal in the exercise of discretion . . . unless it takes reasonable steps to ensure fair treatment for the customer. (FSA PM COB 7.1.3)

The Rule does not survive MiFID, but the Principle does (9.1), alongside the MiFID provisions on conflicts, and all of these provisions are heavily reliant on the general law of conflicts of interest. The application of the MiFID rule is explained in 4.2(d) and 8.2.1.

6.3.1.1 A customer relationship

Pre-MiFID: Whereas the general law rule applies only where there is a special reason constituted by a fiduciary relationship, both the Principle and the Rule applied where, as a result of any contractual relationship, there was a 'customer' (8.2.1) (PRIN, 2.1.1, Principle 8; FSA PM COB 7.1.3). This included an Intermediate Customer with whom a fiduciary relationship would be most unlikely (6.2.1).

MiFID: Similarly, the MiFID rule applies whenever, pursuant to the contractual relationship, services are provided to a 'client' (8.2.1), which includes a Professional Client or Eligible Counterparty (SYSC 10.1.1, 10.1.2) with whom, again, a fiduciary relationship is most unlikely.

6.3.1.2 A conflict of interest

Pre-MiFID: 'Material interests' was defined as 'any interest of a material nature', which, together with a conflict of interest was stated to include 'dealing as . . . principal . . . ; dealing . . . . as agent for more than one party; a recommendation to buy or sell a[n] . . . investment in which . . . [a] customer . . . has given instructions to buy or sell . . . [or] the firm has respectively a long or short position' (FSA PM COB 7.1.5). However, the term 'conflict of interest' was not defined and took its meaning from the general law. That said, the regulators strained to broaden that meaning into a Difference in Interests (6.1). For example, in one enforcement case KEPIT, an investment trust, was liquidating a portfolio and, without disclosing its contents but only its nature, asked a number of firms for bids. SBC's bid was accepted at 12.03pm on the basis of the market price to be set at 12.15pm. In those 13 minutes SBC, having guessed the identity of the securities in the portfolio, went into the market and sold them short, thus driving down the price that it had to pay at 12.15pm. SBC was disciplined for breach of the Principle:

> SBC traded as principal with its client and accordingly there was a conflict of interest between SBC and the client in that it was in SBC's

interests for the strike price [at 12.15pm] . . . to be lower whereas it was in the client's interests for the . . . price . . . to be higher. SBC [breached the Principle] . . . in that it failed to ensure that its participation in the market would not have a material adverse impact on the share prices . . . It has been no part of SFA's case to allege that SBC deliberately set out to impact prices so as to disadvantage the client to the benefit of SBC.[60]

This is a baffling conclusion: if SBC did not act deliberately, then whenever a firm contracts to buy securities in the future, it cannot sell them short in advance which appears to deny the entire rationale of broker–dealers. If, alternatively, SBC really did act deliberately, then this was not a conflict of interest but a failure to observe 'high standards of market conduct' (9.1.1; 12.5.5.1) although in subsequent guidance on such portfolio trades SFA continued to insist that 'the . . . Principle . . . restricts a firm from knowingly taking a position for its own book . . . ahead of the strike time unless . . . with the explicit consent of [a] suitably informed customer'.[61] Such an approach led FSA, in the context of insisting that 'senior management [in firms] should be fully engaged in conflict identification and management . . . [and] ensure that effective systems and controls have been put in place',[62] to state that '[w]e define conflicts as situations in which . . . a client may be disadvantaged in favour of another client or the firm'. A Difference in Interests had become a Conflict of Interests.

MiFID: At first sight, it appears that the MiFID rules on conflicts of interest take a similarly wide view and extend to any Difference in Interests. They require the 'firm . . . to . . . identify conflicts of interest between: (1) the firm, including its managers, employees . . . , or any person directly or indirectly linked to them by control, and a client . . . or (2) one client . . . and another client' and '[f]or the purposes of identifying . . . conflicts of interest . . . a . . . firm must take into account . . . whether the firm or a relevant person [5.2.5], or a person linked directly or indirectly by control to the firm:

(1) is likely to make a financial gain, or avoid a financial loss, at the expense of a client;
(2) has an interest in the outcome of a service provided to the client or of a transaction carried out on behalf of the client, which is distinct from the client's interest in that outcome;
(3) has a financial or other incentive to favour the interest of another client or group of clients over the interests of the client;
(4) carries on the same business as the client; or

---

[60] SFA BN 436, 28 August 1997.
[61] SFA BN 500, 13 November 1998. See also FSA PM COB 7.14.
[62] Senior Management Responsibilities: Conflict of Interest and Risks arising from financing transactions, FSA Dear CEO Letter, 17 September 2004.

(5) receives . . . from a person other than the client an inducement in relation to a service provided to the client . . . other than the standard commission or fee for that service. (SYSC 10.1.3, 10.1.4)

Types (3) and (5) are classic conflicts of interest within 6.2.2. Although (1), (2) and (4) are capable of appearing as a mere Difference in Interest, in fact there is only a 'conflict of interest' within the rule if 'there is a conflict between the interests of a firm or certain persons connected to the firm . . . and the duty the firm owes to a client; or between the differing interests of two or more of its clients, to whom the firm owes in each case a duty. It is not enough that the firm may gain a benefit if there is not also a possible disadvantage to a client, or that one client to whom the firm owes a duty may make a gain or avoid a loss without there being a concomitant possible loss to another such client' (SYSC 10.1.5). 'There is . . . a difference between profits arising from a . . . firm's normal commercial activity and profits arising from its failure to manage properly conflicts of interest.'[63] But although this appears to import the classic definition of a conflict of interest in 6.2.2, particularly since 'a . . . firm should pay special attention to the activities of investment research and advice, proprietary trading, portfolio management and corporate finance business, including underwriting or selling in an offering of securities and advising on mergers and acquisitions . . . where the firm . . . performs a combination of two or more of those activities' (SYSC 10.1.12), doubtless FSA will continue in its wider Pre-MiFID views. Accordingly, the concept of 'duty' should be construed widely in the light of the firm's contractual obligations generally and 'treat the customer fairly' regulatory obligation (9.2), particularly in relation to Retail Clients. Moreover, FSA is continuing with a series of Pre-MiFID Rules on particular perceived conflicts (6.3.2–6.3.8), notwithstanding that, where they represent true conflicts of interest, they are already covered by the general MiFID Rule.

6.3.1.3 Solutions

Pre-MiFID: The rule required the firm to take 'reasonable steps to ensure fair treatment for the customer' (FSA PM COB 7.1.3) and, as with the general law in 6.2.3, this meant one of the following:

- A Chinese Wall. Like the general law, the regulator started from the position that '[a]n employee is presumed, unless the contrary is proved, to have known of a relationship, arrangement or interest if it appears probable, having regard to the protections, procedures and organisational arrangements of the firm or . . . group . . . and . . . in assessing that probability . . . regard shall be had to the presence or absence of a Chinese Wall'.[64] Thus, although the

---

[63] CESR 05-24b, January 2005, p. 42.
[64] Draft COB Rules, TSA, 19 May 1987, Rule 41(3).

regulator will never approve the firm's Chinese Wall procedures, as under the general law (6.2.3.2) a Chinese Wall was effective only to 'withhold or not use the information held ... and ... for that purpose, permit persons employed in [one] part of [the firm's] business to withhold the information held from those employed in th[e] other part of the business' (FSA PM COB 2.4.4(1)) and not for the purpose of other conflicts, although in all circumstances without the need for customer consent (FSA PM COB 7.1.4(1)(c), (3), 7.1.8). The constituents of such a Wall were the same as at general law (6.2.3.2), being 'an arrangement that requires information held by a person in the course of carrying on one part of [the firm's] business to be withheld from, or not to be used for, persons with or for whom it acts in the course of carrying on another part of the business' (FSA PM COB 2.4.4(1), (3)).

- Separate companies, management, personnel and location are effective at general law, constituting a de facto Chinese Wall (6.2.3.1). FSA recognised such a Chinese Wall (FSA PM COB 2.4.4(2)), although total separation into two licensed entities must, in any event, have constituted 'tak[ing] reasonable steps to ensure fair treatment for the customer' (9.2) (FSA PM COB 7.1.3).
- Disclosure. Whereas the general law requires disclosure and positive consent (6.2.3.3), FSA merely required that the 'firm should: (a) disclose to the customer ... any material interest or conflict of interest it has, or may have, whether generally or in relation to a specific transaction ... and (b) ... take ... reasonable steps to ensure that the customer does not object to that material interest or conflict of interest' (FSA PM COB 7.1.6(1)).
- An independence policy, while ineffective at general law (6.2.3.4), constituted 'fair treatment' under FSA rules if it '(1) require[d] the relevant employee to disregard any material interest or conflict of interest ... [and] (2) [was] recorded in writing ... [and] (3) [was] disclosed to a private customer stating that the firm may have a[n] ... interest relating to the transaction or service concerned' (FSA PM COB 7.1.4(1)(b), 7.1.7). Perhaps operable where there was a conflict of duty and interest (6.2.2.1, 6.2.2.2), it is difficult to see how it would operate where there is a conflict of two duties (6.2.2.3(1), (2), (4), 6.2.2.4). Originally, though, it could be used only if disclosure was 'not practical'.[65]
- Declining to act '[i]f [the] firm determines that it is unable to manage a conflict of interest using one of the methods described above' (FSA PM COB 7.1.9).

[65] FSA COB, 1 December 2001, 7.1.7; COB Sourcebook (Amendment No. 14) Instrument 2003.

Under the Principle 'the[se] specific techniques . . . for managing conflicts . . . can . . . be used . . . in appropriate circumstances'.[66] For the purposes of both the Rule and the Principle the solution became, in practice, the formulaic use of general disclosures in customer documentation and Chinese Walls. As a result, FSA did two things. First, it shifted the emphasis on conflict management within firms from conduct of business rule compliance and disclosure in customer documentation, to systems and controls by stating 'what the FSA believes to be . . . the characteristics of a well managed firm . . .

> The firm has an up to date view of the totality of the types of conflicts of interest involved in its business activities . . . within or across business lines . . . [and] on a global and regional basis transcending legal entities . . .
>
> The firm reviews on a regular basis the type of mitigation it considers acceptable to address conflict risks . . .
>
> The firm has a conflict architecture that is able to deliver the mitigation resulting from the review process. Best practice includes:
>
> - Having a clear, documented policy on conflicts identification and management . . .
> - Ownership of conflict risk resides with business line management . . .
> - The use of IT solutions to monitor conflicts at the transaction level both within and across business lines.
> - Conflicts clearance processes . . .
> - Having clear arrangements for dealing with significant or sensitive transactions . . . escalated for senior management consideration . . .
> - Decisions are recorded, along with specific measures taken to control or manage the conflict.
>
> Senior management involvement in the process overall . . .
>
> Use of management information on the extent and mitigation of conflicts . . .
>
> The . . . firm's approach to conflicts management to be sufficiently documented.[67]

And, second, when a 'new' conflict arose of which FSA disapproved then, notwithstanding that it was invariably already caught by the general prohibition if it was truly a 'conflict of interest', FSA made specific rules dealing with the situation (6.3.2–6.3.8).

---

[66] The FSA Principles for Business, FSA PS, October 1999, para. 38.
[67] Senior Management Responsibilities: Conflict of Interest and Non-Standard Transactions, FSA Dear CEO Letter, 10 November 2005.

Conflicts of interest

MiFID entrenches FSA's view of conflicts as a systems and controls issue[68] since it requires the firm to 'maintain and operate effective organisational and administrative arrangements with a view to taking all reasonable steps to prevent conflicts of interest . . . from constituting or giving rise to a material risk of damage to the interests of its clients' and 'keep and regularly update a record of the kinds of service or activity . . . in which a conflict of interest . . . may arise' 'in relation to the . . . various business lines and . . . group . . . activities' (SYSC 10.1.9). Moreover, the firm must 'establish, implement and maintain a . . . conflict of interests policy . . . in writing . . . [which] must . . . (a) . . . identify . . . by reference to the specific services and activities carried out by . . . the . . . firm, the circumstances which may . . . give rise to a conflict of interest entailing a material risk of damage to the interests of . . . clients; and (b) . . . specify procedures to be followed and measures to be adopted . . . to manage such conflicts' (SYSC 10.1.6, 10.1.7, 10.1.10(1), 10.1.11(1)). '[A]s the obligation . . . is only to take "reasonable steps" to identify conflicts of interest, there is an inherent limitation on the scope of th[e] obligation [in (a)]. The firm does not need to continue identifying theoretical conflicts indefinitely . . . [T]he identification process does not need to drill down to the level of each specific conflict.'[69] The procedures in (b) must include:

- 'procedures . . . designed to ensure that . . . persons engaged in different business activities involving a conflict of interest . . . carry on those activities at a level of independence appropriate to the . . . activities';
- 'effective procedures to prevent or control the exchange of information';
- 'separate supervision of . . . principal [conflicting] functions';
- 'removal of any direct link between the remuneration of . . . persons . . . engaged in . . . [conflicting] activit[ies]';
- 'measures to prevent or limit . . . inappropriate influence'; and
- 'measures to prevent or control the simultaneous or sequential involvement of a . . . person in separate . . . activities where such involvement may impair the proper management of conflicts', in other words Wall-crossing procedures. (SYSC 10.1.11(2))

This is merely a 'list of examples . . . [which] should not be considered as exhaustive'[70] and, moreover, '[t]he obligation . . . is not to prevent conflicts of interest from arising, it is for the firm to take all reasonable steps to prevent conflicts adversely affecting the interests of its clients'. Thus, the rule 'does not . . . [require] particular structures [but i]nstead . . . set[s] out flexible principles of general application across the whole range of business

---

[68] The MiFID rules on conflicts appear in the System and Controls (SYSC) part of FSA's Rulebook rather than, as Pre-MiFID, in the Conduct of Business Rules. Accordingly, there is no statutory right of action for breach (SYSC 1.3.12; SYSC, Sched. 5.4) and a client could bring a claim only if the Conflicts Policy sent to him incorporated into the contract compliance with the rules or constituted an actionable representation (8.4.2).

[69] CESR 05-025, January 2005, p. 24.   [70] CESR 04-603b, November 2004, p. 9.

models. [T]he occurrence of conflicts of interest will be inevitable . . . [and this does] not require . . . firms to disaggregate in order to prevent conflicts of interest arising.'[71] It is clear from these examples of conflicts management that the Pre-MiFID techniques of Chinese Walls, separate companies and even an independence policy can continue to be used;[72] indeed, the Pre-MiFID Rule defining the use of Chinese Walls is maintained (SYSC 10.2). The change effected by MiFID is that these techniques must now be applied to conflicts which, previously, were managed solely by disclosure.

Disclosure of 'the general nature . . . of conflicts . . . in . . . sufficient detail . . . to enable the client to take an informed decision with respect to the service in the context in which the conflict of interest arises' is required '[i]f arrangements made . . . to manage conflicts . . . are not sufficient to ensure, with reasonable confidence, that risks of damage to the interests of the client will be prevented' (SYSC 10.1.8). But this is an additional measure and the question, therefore, is whether, given that disclosure must continue to be made at general law (6.2.3.3), it is a sufficient management technique under the MiFID rules? On its own it is not since 'the disclosure of conflicts . . . should not exempt [the firm] from the obligation to maintain and operate . . . effective organisational and administrative arrangements . . . [A]n over-reliance on disclosure without adequate consideration as to how conflicts may appropriately be managed is not permitted' (SYSC 10.1.9). Thus, 'disclosure is not an equal choice to other measures . . . even for professional clients'[73] 'who might reasonably be expected to protect their own interests and who are more likely to be able to use the [disclosure] . . . to influence the . . . firm or choose another firm'.[74] 'Often the appropriate approach will be a combination of management and disclosure'[75] using the Conflicts Policy to record the management technique used and then publishing that Policy or a summary (8.4.7.2), i.e. making disclosure, not only to Private Clients as is required by the MiFID rule (COBS 6.1.4(8)), but to all clients, thus satisfying the general law as well.

6.3.2 Inducements

The criminal offence: Since 1906 it has been, and it remains, a criminal offence if 'any agent', which includes an individual employed by a firm and the firm itself acting for its client, 'accepts any gift or consideration as an inducement or reward for doing or forebearing to show favour or disfavour to any person in relation to his principal's affairs or business' or '[i]f any person corruptly gives . . . any gift or consideration to any agent as an inducement or reward for his doing or forebearing to do . . . any act in

---

[71] CESR 05-024b, January 2005, pp. 42–43.
[72] FSA CP 06/9, para. 9.11; FSA PS 06/13, para. 8.7; SYSC 10.1.11(3).
[73] FSA PS 06/13, para. 8.5.   [74] FSA CP 06/9, para. 9.12.   [75] FSA PS 06/13, para. 8.7.

relation to his principal's affairs or business, or for showing or for forebearing to show favour or disfavour to any person in relation to his principal's affairs or business' (1906 Prevention of Corruption Act 1). Territorially 'it is immaterial if (a) the principal's affairs or business have no connection with the United Kingdom . . . (b) the agent's functions have no connection with the United Kingdom and are carried out . . . outside the United Kingdom' (1906 Act 1(4), inserted by the 2001 Anti-Terrorism, Crime and Security Act 108(2)) as long as some element of the offence occurs in the UK (12.2.2). The offence is not committed if the gift is given to a third party, even with the intent of influencing the agent.[76] The key question is the meaning of 'corruptly'. Although some cases require dishonesty by the payer/recipient,[77] the better view is that it means 'deliberately doing an act which the law forbids',[78] i.e. 'deliberately offering money . . . with the intention that it should operate on the mind of the [recipient] so as to make him enter into . . . a corrupt bargain . . . [not] that the intention must be that the transaction should go right through and that the offeror should obtain the favour . . . he sought'.[79]

Pre-MiFID: From the beginning of the 1986 FSAct regime the regulators ignored the existence of the criminal law on inducements and the fact that inducements were also prohibited by the general law on fiduciaries (6.2) and, indeed, by the general regulatory rule on conflicts of interest (6.3.1) and determined that investor protection required a 'rule . . . [which] prohibit[s] firms from . . . entering into certain types of reciprocal arrangement or giving or receiving . . . inducements . . . [since s]uch arrangements . . . are likely to distort a firm's judgment and make it less likely that the client will receive independent advice . . . [S]uch arrangements cannot adequately be dealt with by disclosure [of the conflict].'[80] This resulted in two prohibitions. First, on introductions. 'A firm must take reasonable steps to ensure that it . . . does not . . . direct or refer any designated investment business to

---

[76] Legislating the Criminal Code: Corruption, LC No. 248, 3 March 1998, para. 2.23.
[77] *R.* v. *Lindley* [1957] Crim. L.R. 321; *R.* v. *Calland* [1967] Crim. L.R. 236.
[78] *R.* v. *Leslie Charles Parker* (1986) 82 Cr. App. R. 69 at 73.
[79] *R.* v. *Smith* [1960] 2 QB 415 at 428–9. This view was adopted in *R.* v. *Geoffrey Elliot Wellborn* (1979) 69 Cr. App. R. 254; *R.* v. *Harvey* [1999] Crim. L.R. 70. The Law Commission, however, considers the cases to be in disarray: LC 248, paras. 2.29–2.30, 5.65. For attempts to reform this law, see LC 248; Criminal Convention on Corruption, Council of Europe, 27 January 1999; Raising Standards and Upholding Integrity: the Prevention of Corruption, Home Office, June 2000; Corruption Draft Legislation, Home Office, Cmnd. 5777, March 2003; Draft Corruption Bill, Report of Joint Committee, HL Paper 157, 31 July 2003; Draft Corruption Bill, Government Reply to the Joint Committee Report, Cmnd. 6086, December 2003; Bribery, Reform of the Prevention of Corruption Acts, Home Office CP, December 2005; draft Corruption Bill, 29 November 2006; draft Corruption Bill, 13 June 2007.
[80] Regulation of Investment Business – The New Framework, SIB and MIBOC, December 1985, 3.33.2.

another person on its own initiative or on the instructions of an associate . . . if it is likely to conflict to a material extent with any duty that the firm owes to its customers' (FSA PM COB 2.2.3(2)). And, second, 'A firm must take reasonable steps to ensure that it . . . does not . . . offer, give, solicit or accept an inducement . . . if it is likely to conflict to a material extent with any duty that the firm owes to its customers . . . or any duty which such a recipient firm owes to its customers' (FSA PM COB 2.2.3(1)). The first prohibition prevented the second being circumvented 'by an inducement being given or received by an unregulated associate' in return for the firm 'direct[ing] business to another person on the instructions of [the] associate' (FSA PM COB 2.2.4). It also prevented volume override commissions where commission on a particular transaction paid to the intermediary by the product company is calculated by reference to the size, volume or nature of other transactions carried out by the intermediary for its clients generally. The materiality test had the result that the 'rule permits low-value Christmas presents . . . and moderate business entertaining'[81] although it depends on context: 'a Porsche would be over the limit in most places and markets, so would hotel expenses in Bali for a UK-based recipient; a crate of Chivas Regal and a Cross pen would not influence many decisions in Hong Kong but might in Exeter'.[82]

Although the recipient of the inducement would appear, on the drafting of the rule, to have to be a licensed 'firm', it was interpreted as applying to unlicensed recipients because of Principles 1 (Integrity) and 6 (Treat the Customer Fairly) (9.1, 9.2). Contravention of duty, for the purpose of both rules, required a rule-based obligation derived from elsewhere, whether the general law (for example, fiduciary duties) or regulation (for example, the duty of suitable advice (11.2.2) or best execution (13.3)). But the real difficulty was how the firm providing the 'inducement' (itself undefined, but probably to be construed as later determined for financial promotion (10.4.2.1)) could assess the recipient's conflict with its clients given that the duties there would depend on a contract, facts and (with overseas recipients) rules of which the paying firm was unaware. FSA's only response was that '[w]e have tackled this concern by requiring a firm only to take "reasonable steps" to ensure that it does not . . . give an inducement if it is likely to conflict with the duties of the recipient to its customers'.[83] Thus, the view was taken that normal market commissions for the distribution of products, whether direct payments or retrocessions (reductions) which the intermediary deducted from the purchase price received from the client and accounted for to the product provider, were acceptable as payment for the intermediary's services to the product provider and were not a 'material

---

[81] SIB Conduct Rules, February 1986 Draft, Explanatory Memorandum, 3.10.
[82] SIB Conduct Rules, Draft: September 1986, 3.16.
[83] COB Sourcebook, FSA PS, February 2001, para. 5.2.

inducement'. This, of course, left the intermediary to manage its conflict of interest towards the client within 6.2 and 6.3.1.

MiFID: The policy is to 'establish . . . a flexible general rule . . . [although that] entails the risk that it would permit the acceptance of inducements that should properly be prohibited'[84] and, hence, there is an absolute prohibition.[85] 'A firm must not pay or accept any fee or commission, or provide or receive any non-monetary benefit', and this is widely interpreted as covering not only both inducements and referrals of business as in the first Pre-MiFID Rule (COBS 2.3.1, 2.3.5) but also 'a standard commission or fee',[86] fee for distributing products, finder's fee or, even, underwriting or sub-underwriting fee, in any of these cases 'provided to or made by a legal entity within the same group as the . . . firm . . . [or] any other . . . entity',[87] but 'not . . . payments made within the . . . firm, such as internal bonus programmes, even though these could give rise to a conflict of interest'.[88] The recipient/payer can be located within or outside the EEA. 'Therefore, . . . [the rule] should not be treated as applying only to payments or receipts that are made with the purpose or intent to influence the actions of the firm.'[89] There are only three exemptions to this wide ambit:

(1) It is paid by or on behalf of the client

This covers both commissions directly paid by the client (or a mark-up: p. 401, FN 67) and indirectly through a third party, for example an instruction from the client to his executing broker to pay, out of the proceeds of a sale transaction, the fee of the introducing broker.[90] However, it does not include '[c]ircumstances in which a product provider pays a share of commission to an [intermediary] . . . firm'[91] unless the payment by the product provider is contractually structured, as between it and the client, as a payment 'on behalf of the client' (COBS 2.3.1(1)) (9.2).

(2) It is necessary for the firm to provide its services

This must be 'proper fees which enable or are necessary for the provision of [the firm's] . . . services, such as custody costs, settlement and exchange fees, regulatory levies or legal fees, and which, by their nature, cannot give rise to conflicts with the firm's duties to act honestly, fairly and professionally in accordance with the best interests of its clients' (COBS 2.3.1(3)). 'Proper fee' is not to be given a wide interpretation because 'it is clear that the possibility of a receipt of a standard commission or fee can act as an incentive

---

[84] European Commission Working Document ESC/24/2005 – Explanatory Note, p. 3.
[85] There is an exemption for 'small gifts and minor hospitality' (COBS 2.3.8, 13.2.8), although '[a] firm's conflicts of interest policy should address the issues that arise in such cases' (FSA PS 07/6, para. 6.17).   [86] CESR/06–687, para. 2.
[87] CESR/07-228b, May 2007, Box 1.   [88] Ibid, para. 2.   [89] Ibid, para. 3.
[90] CESR/06-687, paras. 13–14.   [91] Ibid, para. 15.

for a . . . firm to act other than in the best interests of its client. So . . . any items that are not of a type similar to the costs [that the rule] mentions . . . are unlikely to fall within this exception.'[92] Moreover, '[t]his . . . test . . . needs to be considered in the abstract, on the "nature" of the item; that is not on the basis of whether the result of the payment has been to give rise to such a conflict. The possibility of a receipt of a standard commission or fee is of a nature to give rise to conflicts with a duty owed to clients.'[93]

(3) It enhances the firm's services

Here four conditions must be satisfied: (a) 'the existence, nature and amount of the fee, commission or benefit or, where the amount cannot be ascertained, the method of calculating that amount, is clearly disclosed to the client', (b) it 'is designed to enhance the quality of the service to the client' and, in this context, 'the receipt . . . of a commission in connection with a personal . . . or general recommendation . . . where the advice or recommendation is not biased as a result . . . should be considered as designed to enhance the quality of the recommendation to the client', (c) it 'does not impair compliance with the firm's duty to act in the best interests of the client' and (d) a record must be kept (COBS 2.3.1(2), 2.3.6, 2.3.17). Condition (b) requires 'that a permitted item must relate to the service provided to the client, and not to some other service; and there must be benefit to the client in relation to that service, and, not just to the . . . firm or to other clients'. It follows that 'it is not the intention . . . to prohibit . . . distribution arrangements where an issuer or product provider pays a . . . firm for distribution'.[94] In other words, 'such payments may also benefit other clients . . . [I]n this case the requirement to enhance the quality of the relevant service to the client is met at the level of the service, provided that the other clients . . . are receiving such a service.'[95] Thus, capable of meeting conditions (b) and (c) are structures where the distributor may or may not advise the client and receives a commission out of the product provider's charges to the client unless, under (c), 'the commission is disproportionate to the market [so that] it is more likely [that it] . . . will impair the . . . firm's duty to act in the best interests of its client'. The fee ensures the availability of the product and, thereby, 'enhanc[es] the quality of the service to the client'[96] because 'in the absence of payment by the product provider . . . these investment services, most likely, would not be provided'.[97] Payment of a share of dealing commissions by an executing broker to an introducing broker also meets the conditions if, under (c), the share is a market rate and, under (b), the executing broker 'is . . . likely to enhance the quality of the service to the client'. Similarly, payment of underwriting and

---

[92] CESR/06-687, para. 6.   [93] CESR/07-228b, May 2007, para. 10.
[94] CESR/06-687, paras. 19, 23. See also 9.2.   [95] CESR/07-228b, May 2007, para. 15.
[96] CESR/06-687, para. 25, Examples 1, 2.   [97] CESR/07-228b, para. 21.

sub-underwriting fees in Primary Market transactions vis-à-vis the investor client of the underwriter/sub-underwriter.

But the following do not meet the conditions: payment by a broker to a portfolio manager for order flow; and volume overrides. And if the conditions are not met, 'one option . . . is for the . . . firm to repay to its client any commission received'.[98] The final form of CESR's advice permits some soft commission,[99] but these would not be allowed under FSA's super-equivalent rules (6.3.3) whereas FSA permitted soft commission is within (3)(b). As regards condition (a), client consent is not required (8.4.7.2) and '[a] generic disclosure which refers merely to the possibility that the firm might receive inducements is not . . . sufficient to enable the investor to make an informed decision . . . whether to proceed with the investment . . . and whether to ask for the full information. In particular, the investor must be able to relate the disclosure to the particular investment . . . [and] assess [its] suitability for him',[100] so that a summary disclosure is permitted if it 'contain[s] the "essential terms" . . . to enable the investor . . . to make an informed decision whether to proceed with the . . . service and whether to ask for the full information'.[101]

In addition to all this, there is specific guidance on inducements in the context of packaged products[102] and in all cases, of course, the firm must continue to comply with both the general law on conflicts (6.2) and the general regulatory rule (6.3.1) (COBS 2.3.8) because '[c]ompliance with the conflicts rule does not provide a safe harbour from the inducements rules. Compliance with the inducements rules does not provide a safe harbour from the conflicts rules.'[103] Moreover, in contrast to the general rule on conflicts which is an infrastructure rule, this is a client-facing conduct rule and its application is explained in 4.2(f) and 8.2.1.

6.3.3 Soft commission and bundling

Pre-MiFID: Soft commission represents a conflict of interest under both the general law (6.2) and the general regulatory rule (6.3.1) since the portfolio manager is 'us[ing] client assets (e.g. brokerage commissions) for their own benefit':[104]

> [With] 'soft dollar services'. . . a broker/dealer provides research, computer software, valuation services, information services, et al to a portfolio manager or investment adviser not in return for direct payment but . . . for a flow of . . . dealing business. The customers therefore pay . . . via the commission the managers incur for their account.[105]

---

[98] CESR/06-687, para. 25.   [99] CESR/07-228b, paras. 3.XI, XII.   [100] Ibid, para. 30.
[101] CESR/07-228b, Box 6. COBS 2.3.2 must be interpreted accordingly.
[102] COBS 2.3.9-2.3.16. See also FSA PS 07/14, Chapter 2.   [103] CESR/07-228b, para. 17.
[104] Soft Commissions, IOSCO Technical Committee Consultation Report, November 2006, p. 8.
[105] SIB Conduct Rules, Draft: September 1986, Explanatory Memorandum, 3.30.

Nonetheless, ever since the beginning under the 1986 FSAct the regulators have insisted on an additional rule which, over the decades, has permitted increasingly less. The policy in 1986 was that '[t]here is no mischief in this provided that the services . . . improve the performance of the manager in fulfilling his obligations to the customers, so that they benefit . . . them. Difficulties arise in drawing a line between what can clearly be of service to the customer, e.g. research . . . and what is really just nice for the manager . . . e.g. . . . a holiday because a rest would improve his performance.'[106] Thus, the rule permitted soft commission if '(a) the [firm's customer] agreement provide[s] . . . that all transactions . . . will be effected so as to secure . . . best execution, or (b) the firm has given . . . the customer a statement which . . . contains . . . particulars of each [such] arrangement . . . [and the] firm . . . give[s] . . . the customer [every] 12 months . . . a statement of particulars of each [such] arrangement [and upon] . . . request . . . particulars of the value in money . . . of those services'.[107] In the late 1980s the use of soft commission agreements grew to the point where it was estimated that up to 20% of all commission-bearing broking business was done on soft-terms[108] and although 'SIB recognises the potential for soft commission agreements to create some distortion in the market . . . [it] believes that this can be controlled . . . and . . . this threat is not so great as to justify . . . a ban' rather than 'a clearer definition of acceptable services coupled with stricter requirements for disclosure' and a ban on so-called soft for net arrangements 'under which [firms dealing as principal] . . . offer [softing] services . . . to fund managers dealing direct with them on a principal basis. In return, the fund manager agrees to provide a certain volume of turnover [and] is constrained in his ability to negotiate the best price.'[109] The rule consequently adopted by SIB in the early 1990s essentially survived into FSA's 2001 rule. This defined a 'soft commission agreement' as 'an agreement in any form under which a firm receives goods or services in return for . . . business put through or in the way of another person' and provided that 'A firm must not deal in investments as agent for a customer . . . through any broker, under a soft commission agreement, unless:

(1) the agreement is . . . for the supply of [permitted] goods or services . . . which do not . . . include cash or any other direct financial benefit;

[106] Ibid.   [107] SIB Conduct Rules, 7 October 1987, 5.09.
[108] Soft commissions lead to security house criticism, FT, 30 July 1990. '[T]otal commissions paid to UK brokers in 2002/2003 were around £2.9–3.5 billion, and around £758–905 million was used to "purchase" goods and services through soft commission or bundled brokerage arrangements . . . [Out of this] the over-consumption of bundled and softed services (and associated expenses borne by investors) was at least £50–72 million per year (Soft Commissions, IOSCO, pp. 30–32).
[109] SIB CP 29, October 1989, paras. 20, 26, 44, 46.

(2) the broker has agreed to provide best execution...
(3) the firm has taken reasonable steps to ensure that the terms of business and methods by which services will be supplied by the broker do not involve any potential for comparative price disadvantage to the customer;
(4) for transactions in which the broker acts as principal... commission paid under the agreement will be sufficient to cover the value of the goods or services...; and
(5) the firm... disclos[es:]...
    [a] [b]efore... it enters into a client agreement... the existence of the soft commission agreement... and... the firm's... policy relating to soft commission agreements... [and]
    [b] ... at least once a year... the percentage paid under soft commission agreements of the total commission paid by... the firm...; the value... of goods or services received by the firm... expressed as a percentage of the total commission paid by... the firm...; a summary of the goods or services received... a list of the brokers...; and... the total commission paid from the portfolio of that customer. (FSA COB, 1 December 2001, 2.2.8, 2.2.16, 2.2.18)

Item (4) banned 'soft for net'. In relation to Item (1), the goods and services had to be 'directly relevant to, and... used to assist in, the provision to the firm's customers of... investment management... advice... custody... or... valuation or performance measurement of portfolios' (FSA COB, 1 December 2001, 2.2.12). Hence, lists of goods and services were given which were permitted (for example, research, market data services, dealing systems, dedicated telephone lines) and prohibited (for example, travel expenses, seminar and publication fees not connected to the above-listed services, office administration and fixtures, direct money payments) (FSA COB, 1 December 2001, 2.2.13, 2.2.14).

By this time in the market there were three types of arrangement being used, soft commission subject to the above rule and '"commission recapture" and "directed commission"... not [being] covered... [unless within] the prohibition on inducements' (FSA COB, 1 December 2001, 2.2.11). These are illustrated in Figure 6. The three structures ((2), (3) and (4), respectively) are explained as follows, using the same numbering as in the Figure:

(1) Investment Management Service

    (a) Investment management agreement
    (b) Payment of management fee

(2) Soft Commission

    (a) Agreement/Terms of Business for broker–dealer services, including agreement on minimum overall commissions

Capital Markets Law and Compliance

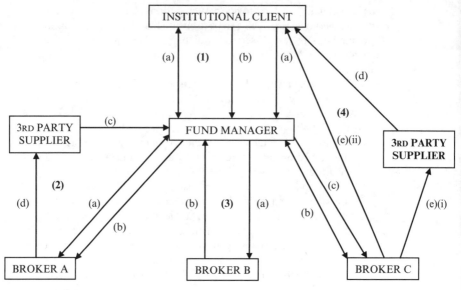

Figure 6 *Soft Commission Structures*

      (b) Payment of commission on deals executed
      (c) Supply of goods/services
      (d) Payment of price for goods/services

(3)   Bundled brokerage

      (a) Payment of commission on deals executed
      (b) Supply of research and access to analysts for no direct payment, the cost of production being in effect part of the commission received. Thus, the 'fund manager ... effectively get[s] a partial rebate on the commission he paid for the broker's transaction services'[110]

(4)   Commission recapture/directed commission

      (a) Client instructs fund manager to direct a certain proportion of transactions to Broker
      (b) Agreement to rebate
      (c) Payment of commission on deals executed
      (d) Supply of goods/services
      (e) Broker pays credit (based on amount of commission received from the Fund Manager) to:
          (i) Supplier for price of goods/services ('Directed Commission') or
          (ii) Client ('Commission Recapture')

[110] FSA CP 176, April 2003, para. 3.4.

SIB had always regarded 'the complete unbundling of broker services ... [as] a desirable long-term aim'[111] and FSA's inherited dislike of all these arrangements was fuelled by two political developments. First, a wide-ranging review of institutional investments focusing on the inefficiencies of pension funds and investment media criticised the fact that '[p]ension funds using ... managers will ... be paying ... commission to ... stockbrokers ... for ... dealing and research [(2)(b), (3)(a), (4)(c)] ... in a way which is far from transparent ... distorting competition ... Clients' interests would be better served if they required fund managers to absorb the cost of ... commission ... offset ... through higher fees ... agree[d] with their clients ... Institutional clients could see more clearly what they were actually paying ... [and] fund managers would ... purchase only those services which contributed to [their achieving superior investment returns] ... [T]his ... would mean that current inefficiencies and complexities associated with practices such as soft commission and commission recapture would be likely to cease.'[112] And, second, for the politicians, it was all about 'maximising the amount that goes into the pensions pot'.[113] Accordingly, FSA ignored a study which showed that, from an economic perspective, the distorting costs may actually 'be limited' so that 'not changing the regulation is a policy option'[114] and, using the twin mantras of Conflicts of Interest and Treat the Customer Fairly (9.2), concluded that '[t]here is ... a need to ... address the inherent conflicts of interest arising from bundling and softing and the lack of transparency in the way goods and services are paid for' since '[b]undled and soft commission arrangements ... create ... conflicts of interest ... [which] raise doubts about the ability of fund managers both to obtain value for money when spending their customer's funds on acquiring additional broker services, and to deliver best execution'.[115] Thus, to avoid any possibility of 'induc[ing] a fund manager to act in ways that are not in his customer's best interests',[116] the rule provided that he can only 'execute ... customer orders through a broker ... [and] pass ... the broker's ... charges (whether commission or otherwise) to its customer ... and ... in return for the charges ... receive ... goods or services in addition to the execution of its customer orders', i.e. Soft Commission within (2) and Bundled Brokerage within (3), if the goods or services:

---

[111] Soft Commission arrangements in the Securities Markets: a Policy Statement, SIB, July 1990, para. 5.
[112] Institutional Investment in the UK – a Review, Paul Myners, HMT, 6 March 2001, 5.102 – 5.109.
[113] Ruth Kelly, Financial Secretary to the Treasury, NAPF Conference, HMT PR 38/03, 12 March 2003.
[114] An Assessment of Soft Commission Arrangements and Bundled Brokerage Services in the UK, OXERA, April 2003, Executive Summary.
[115] FSA CP 176, April 2003, paras. 2.11, 3.44.   [116] Ibid, para. 4.4.

(a) (i) are related to the execution of trades on behalf of the . . . customer; or (ii) comprise the provision of research; and
(b) will reasonably assist the investment manager in the provision of its services to its customers . . . and . . . are not likely to, impair compliance with the duty of the investment manager to act in the best interests of its customers. (FSA PM COB 7.18.3)

These 'best interests' included the firm's 'ability to comply with the best execution obligation' (FSA PM COB 7.18.11). Since the investment manager does not itself 'receive . . . goods or services' within the rule, it follows that Directed Commission and Commission Recapture were permitted.

Under FSA's final Pre-MiFID Rules permitted Soft Commission could relate only to execution of trades or research. '[G]oods or services relat[ing] to the execution of trades' must be 'linked to the arranging and conclusion of a specific investment transaction (or series of related transactions)' and 'provided between the point at which the investment manager makes an investment or trading decision and the point at which the investment transaction (or series of related transactions) is concluded' and, accordingly, 'does not . . . [include] post-trade analytics' (FSA PM COB 7.18.4), unless 'the . . . analytical software meets . . . [the] criteria of a "research service" because it assists in the making of investment . . . decisions',[117] or 'services relating to the valuation or performance measurement of portfolios . . . [or] computer hardware . . . [or] dedicated telephone lines . . . [or] office administration computer software such as word processing or accounting programmes . . . [or] purchase or rental of standard office equipment or ancillary facilities . . . [or] custody services . . . other than those services that are incidental to the execution of trades' (FSA PM COB 7.18.6, 7.18.8). '[As regards] clearing and settlement services . . . [s]ervices such [as] netting of positions to reduce costs, corresponding with sub-custodians on specific trades, and resolving and reporting failed trades, are all relevant to execution. But . . . some settlement services are closely related to custody services . . . for example . . . charges levied by central depositaries or deposit or withdrawal of securities.'[118] More generally, though, 'execution service . . . include[s] broking and processing of orders, . . . related costs arising directly from trading . . ., active order management, carrying out programme trades and other complex trading strategies, and "working" orders in tranches to minimise market impact costs . . . [S]ales and trading advice . . . [i]s a component of execution if it can be attributed to a specific transaction . . . after the point at which the fund manager makes a specific investment decision. For example, trading advice which covers services such as advice on liquidity and market-related timing, negotiation of the terms of trade and other aspects of order handling, can be seen as part of execution.'[119] On the other

---

[117] FSA CP 05/5, March 2005, para. 2.19.   [118] FSA PS 04/23, November 2004, para. 2.20.
[119] Ibid, 2.13–2.16.

hand, 'goods or services relat[ing] to the provision of research', which permits research provided by the executing broker in Bundled Brokerage (3) and research provided by a non-executing broker as the third party Supplier in a Soft Commission Agreement (2),[120] requires research which:

(a) is capable of adding value to the investment or trading decision by providing new insights that inform the investment manager when making such decisions about its customers' portfolios; [and]
(b) . . . represents original thought in the critical and careful consideration and assessment of new and existing facts, and does not merely repeat or repackage what has been presented before; [and]
(c) has intellectual rigour and does not merely state what is commonplace or self-evident; and
(d) involves analysis or manipulation of data to reach meaningful conclusions. (FSA PM COB 7.18.5)

This 'doe[s] not . . . include price feed or historical price data that have not been analysed or manipulated to reach meaningful conclusions' or 'publicly available information', only material which is 'directly relevant to and . . . used to assist in the management of investments', classically 'a document . . . which contains . . . the results of research into a[n] . . . investment or its issuer . . . [and/or] analysis of factors likely to influence the future performance of a[n] . . . investment or its income . . . and [/or] advice or recommendations based on those results or that analysis' (FSA PM COB 7.18.5, 7.18.7–7.18.9; FSA PM GLOSS., def. of 'investment research'). Although this is 'seeking to exclude the mere repackaging of existing research . . . [it is] not seeking to exclude the use of existing material in research; . . . new insights can be drawn from existing materials. Similarly, research produced by a UK research provider's sister company in another country and then passed on to the UK research provider's customers might be regarded as researched – for example, if it was not generally available in this country already.'[121] Moreover, '[w]e would also expect discussions between the fund manager and the author of the research to be covered, and probably . . . "sales and trading advice" that is not explicitly execution-related'.[122] But neither heading included, on any basis, 'seminar fees . . . [or] subscriptions for publication . . . [or] travel, accommodation or entertainment costs . . . [or] membership fees to professional associations . . . [or] employees' salaries . . . [or] direct money payments' (FSA PM COB 7.18.8).

Anything not permitted must 'be treated like any other fund management overhead, and . . . paid for in hard cash'[123] because 'they are not sufficiently connected with particular investment management decisions or transactions to be classified as execution or research'.[124] This prohibition

[120] Ibid, paras. 2.40, 2.41.   [121] Feedback on CP 05/5, FSA, July 2005, para. 2.18.
[122] FSA PS 04/23, November 2004, para. 2.24.   [123] FSA PS 04/13, May 2004, para. 3.6.
[124] FSA PS 04/23, November 2004, para. 2.11.

related only to the receipt by the investment manager who, as a result 'must in a timely manner make adequate ... prior and ... periodic disclosures ... to its customers of the [permitted] arrangements entered into' in accordance with the FSA rules (FSA PM COB 7.18.12–7.18.14) and the Investment Management Association Pension Fund Disclosure Code, and 'make a record of each periodic disclosure' (FSA PM COB 7.18.15). Where Bundled Brokerage was involved, the broker will participate in 'discussions ... [with the manager] designed to agree a ... split between research and execution components of commission'.[125] In all arrangements the broker had to, in any event, comply with the inducements rule (6.3.2) and avoid participating in either a breach by the manager of its fiduciary duties to its client (6.2), which could result in the broker being liable for dishonest assistance in the breach of fiduciary duty,[126] and/or in a breach by the manager of the general regulatory rule on conflicts of interest (6.3.1), which would result in a breach of Principle (9.1) by the broker.

MiFID: The Pre-MiFID prohibition in relation to Soft Commission and Bundled Brokerage is carried over more or less identically under the MiFID-inspired FSA rules, although the disclosures to be made by the investment manager have been amended slightly.[127] FSA regards these 'super-equivalent' rules as necessary because 'the specific risks addressed by the requirements are of particular importance in the circumstances of the market structure of the UK' and 'reliance on [the MiFID inducements rule] would not be sufficient to address the market failures' since 'there is a wide range of services that an investment [management] firm may be able to reasonably assert it would be permitted under [the inducements rule] to receive from a broker and that could be paid for out of dealing commission charged to clients ... include[ing] seminars, external publications, and data price fees'.[128] The consequences for the broker remain unchanged and the rule applies as explained in 4.2(g).

6.3.4 Investment research

6.3.4.1 Systems and controls

Pre-MiFID: Following action by the New York Attorney-General and United States SEC against investment banks for publishing over-favourable investment research on companies whose securities issues were managed by the banks, 'given the position of US-based institutions in the UK ... [FSA] expected similar business practices and pressures to have

---

[125] Statement of Good Practice, LIBA, 24 March 2005.   [126] *Hanbury*, Chapter 12.2.B.
[127] COBS 11.6. The manager must also comply with the inducements rule (6.3.2).
[128] Article 4 Notification of FSA's Requirements on the use of dealing commissions, FSA, September 2007, paras. 13, 17. See also PS 07/14, para 5.2. For supra-national developments, see Soft Commissions, IOSCO Consultation Report, November 2006.

Conflicts of interest

emerged here'[129] and, indeed, 'analysts' recommendations in relation to companies with whom their . . . [firm] has a relationship are systematically more positive than the average'.[130] Moreover, the analysts' role had changed. 'In the past, the . . . research analyst . . . gathered all sorts of information about particular stocks . . . [and] used . . . [it] to come up with investment recommendations for brokerage clients . . . Today, analysts . . . are . . . also required to perform other functions. For example, . . . help the . . . sales force generate orders . . . [a]nd . . . play a role in helping the firms obtain underwriting and mergers . . . advisory business . . . These other functions can give the analyst diverse incentives . . . [A]nalysts' compensation depends on a variety of factors . . . include[ing] . . .

- volume of trading (i.e. brokerage commission) generated following release of their research reports;
- the evaluations they receive from their firm's brokerage sales force;
- the success of their buy/sale recommendations;
- their reputation . . . and
- their ability to help secure and retain investment banking clients.[131]

Reflecting on the conflicts of interest involved, FSA concluded that 'investors should be able to operate on the basis that the research that they see is . . . objective . . . [t]hat is, that it is not biased'.[132]

As a result, 'investment research' was defined as 'a document (other than a personal recommendation [11.2.2]), or material the substance of which is common to a number of documents although worded as if they are personal recommendations, which contains . . . (a) the results of research into a[n] . . . investment or its issuer; [and/or] (b) analysis of factors likely to influence the future performance of a[n] . . . investment or its issuer; and [/or] advice or recommendations based on those results or that analysis'. This was subject to a number of systems and controls requirements to avoid conflicts if:

[•] the firm holds it out . . . as being an impartial assessment of the value or prospects of its subject matter; or

[•] it is reasonable for those to whom the firm has published or distributed it to rely on it as [such] an impartial assessment.

It 'may be held out as impartial . . . if . . . labelled . . . independent or objective' (FSA PM COB 7.16.5(1), 7.16.6(1)). The firm subject to this rule could be on the so-called sell side (brokers, dealers, investment banks) or buy side (private client stockbrokers, private banks, investment managers).[133] While it 'do[es] not cover research that is for internal use only', the difficult issue was how to treat 'categories of report, such as [Sales & Trading

---

[129] FSA CP 205, October 2003, para. 3.14. [130] FSA PN/081/2002, 31 July 2002.
[131] FSA DP 15, July 2002, paras. 3.7, 3.8. [132] FSA CP 171, February 2003, para. 4.2.
[133] FSA CP 205, October 2003 paras. 3.33–3.35.

Department] "sell notes", that are not [commercially] considered research'.[134] The FSA accepted the industry's conclusion that:

> The use of the terms 'research' and 'analysis' in the . . . definition of 'investment research' refers to substantive analysis – i.e. the careful and critical consideration and assessment of new and existing facts . . . [M]aterial emanating from a sales and trading division . . . will be 'investment research' if it contains substantive analysis into a[n] . . . investment or its issuer. In practice, such sales and trading material, such as 'sales notes', execution ideas, market or trader commentary and other short term recommendations, will ordinarily fall outside the . . . definition . . . [It] does not cover material to the extent that it reproduces, summarises or refers to investment research already known to the market (including material contained in . . . investment research already issued).[135]

For the rest, though, it had to be 'research and analyses into factors that are likely to influence one or more . . . investments or issuers. Generic material (for example reports . . . on general political, economic or market issues, industries, asset classes, types of investments or broadly based indices and material explaining models) will not therefore be covered.'[136] With 'investment research', although the firm technically had a choice whether or not to designate it 'objective', FSA 'expect that most firms would want to present most of their research as objective'[137] and 'does not expect firms to publish material categorised as not being impartial simply in order to avoid the need to operate proper conflict management policies . . . Firms which publish such material will therefore need to conclude that the circumstances in which it is produced are such that it is not appropriate to categorise it as impartial, for example . . . research published by sales and trading personnel . . . remunerated by reference to specific transactions or the level of business or profits of his . . . desk.'[138] The designation did not have 'to use particular terminology, such as "non-objective" . . . [b]ut any terms used (and the accompanying disclosures) . . . need to be carefully chosen to avoid clients reasonably relying on the material as impartial research'.[139]

With such research the firm 'should organise the . . . research function . . . in a way which minimises the potential influence of the commercial interests of the firm, its employees, its associates, or its clients, on the impartiality of its investment research' and, for this purpose, 'establish . . . a policy . . . for managing effectively the conflicts of interest . . . [and] take reasonable steps to ensure that it and its employees comply with the policy . . .

---

[134] Ibid, paras. 3.34, 3.19.
[135] Industry Guidance on COB 7.3, LIBA, BBA, ISMA and IPMA, 9 February 2004, paras 1, 4. FSA 'agree . . . that th[is] guidance reflects the principles set out in the rule' (FSA PS 04/6, Ann. 4, para. 7).   [136] Ibid, para. 5.   [137] FSA CP 205, para. 3.20.
[138] Industry Guidance, paras. 2.3, 4.7.   [139] FSA PS 04/6, Ann. 2, para. 7.

[and] make [it] available to any person in writing, on request'. The policy had 'to manage . . . at least the following' 'conflicts of interest which might affect the impartiality of the investment research' (FSA PM COB 7.16.5(2), (3), 7.16.7). It may, however, be doubted whether in fact any of these situations were 'conflicts of interest' as classically conceived (6.2.1), the issue of a research report with a conclusion in which the analyst did not really believe being rather the tort of deceit, i.e. '(1) a false statement (2) of existing fact (3) with knowledge of its falsity and with the intention that the plaintiff should act on it, with the result (4) that the plaintiff does act on it to his detriment'.[140] The systems and controls requirements were as follows. First, as regards 'the supervision and management of investment analysts', 'an individual (such as someone involved in raising capital for a corporate client) . . . [with] responsibilities that might reasonably be considered to conflict with the interests of the clients to whom the investment research is published . . . [should] not usually be . . . responsible for: (a) the day-to-day supervision or control of an . . . analyst; (b) decisions on the subject matter or content of . . . research or the timing of its publication . . . [or] (c) determining the remuneration of an . . . analyst' (FSA PM COB 7.16.5(3)(b)(i), 7.16.9). 'This does not necessarily mean that both those supervising analysts and investment banking or sales and trading personnel cannot report to the same person at a more senior level, or that those responsible for supervision of analysts cannot report to senior sales and trading personnel . . . However, firms will need to consider whether such reporting structures could in fact prejudice the analyst's impartiality.'[141] Second, the 'analyst's remuneration should be structured so as not to create . . . an incentive which is inconsistent with . . . an impartial assessment of . . . research by the analyst' and, in particular, his/her 'remuneration should not be linked to a specific transaction, or to recommendations contained in . . . research, but it may be linked to the general profits of the firm' (FSA PM COB 7.16.10). Nonetheless, 'it seems reasonable to continue to regard as relevant . . . factors such as productivity, quality and accuracy of research, experience and individual reputation and evaluations by investor clients and employees in other parts of the firm with whom analysts interact, provided that these factors are not assessed in a way which is likely to put analysts under improper pressure'.[142]

Third, the policy had to set out 'the extent to which . . . analysts may become involved in activities other than the preparation of . . . research' and, while they 'may . . . assist . . . research[ing] corporate finance business opportunities, . . . provide ideas to sales and trading staff . . . [and] provide information and advice to the firm's investment clients', they 'should not be involved in [such other] activities . . . if . . . inconsistent with providing an

---

[140] *Markesinis*, p. 462.
[141] Policies for Managing Conflicts of Interest in connection with Investment Research, BBA, LIBA, ISMA and IPMA, 19 May 2004, para. 4.2.   [142] Industry Guidance, para. 4.6.

impartial assessment of the value or prospects of the . . . investments', in particular not act 'in a marketing capacity (for example in pitches to . . . obtain corporate finance business from the issuer . . .) . . . [or] representing the issuer . . . for example, in roadshows relating to issues' (FSA PM COB 7.16.5(3)(b)(iii), 7.16.11). However, it was still possible to 'tak[e] . . . analysts 'over the wall', and . . . tightly control this in the traditional manner [12.2, 12.5.3][143] and, to add value to investor clients . . . [by] passive participation in the audience at a roadshow in a manner which could not reasonably be perceived as an endorsement of the issuer . . . [Indeed, t]he . . . [FSA's] restrictions do not entail a general restriction on contacts between analysts and investment banking or sales and trading employees, or between analysts and investment clients . . . Accordingly, a firm may . . . permit . . .

> (a) meeting potential investment banking clients prior to award of a mandate for the purpose of assisting . . . the client's decision to involve the firm . . .
> (b) advising investment banking colleagues on pricing and structuring of a securities offering, or on market sentiment and the likely reception of an offering . . . and
> (d) participating in investor education meetings . . . not involving the presence of company management.
>
> Similarly, the FSA guidance does not preclude analysts from maintaining an active dialogue with sales and trading personnel . . . provided that they do not disclose the content or timing of forthcoming research reports.[144]

Fourth, in line with the general rule on inducements (6.3.2), the policy had to 'prohibit . . . analysts or other employees, from offering or accepting an inducement to provide favourable . . . research' (FSA PM COB 7.16.12(1)). Fifth, because of a concern that '[i]f the analyst, his friends, family or firm held shares in particular companies . . . he may be inclined to produce favourable research reports . . . in an attempt to . . . boost the value of . . . [the] holding',[145] FSA provided that:

> an . . . analyst [or close relative] may not undertake a personal account transaction in a[n] . . . investment if the . . . analyst proposes investment research . . . on that . . . investment or its issuer . . . unless . . . the transaction is:
>
> [•] not contrary to . . . [his] published . . . recommendation . . . or
> [•] . . . undertaken . . . to assist an obligation of the . . . analyst . . . and . . . the firm has given its permission in writing . . .
>
> [A] firm may decide:

---

[143] FSA CP 171, para. 4.7.
[144] Policies for managing conflicts of interest in connection with investment research, BBA, LIBA, ISMA and IPMA, 19 May 2004, paras. 5.1–5.4.   [145] FSA DP 15, para. 4.20.

(a) that an . . . analyst should be prohibited from carrying out any personal account transaction . . . or
(b) that an . . . analyst should be prohibited from undertaking a personal account transaction in a[n] investment if the . . . analyst proposes investment research . . . on that . . . investment or its issuer; or
(c) that there should be a prohibition on personal account transactions . . . before and after the intended publication date for . . . research. (FSA PM COB 7.13.7(1)(aa), 7.13.10A(1))

Sixth, the policy had to contain a procedure for 'who may comment on draft . . . research before publication', but 'the firm should not give effective editorial control to someone whose role or commercial interests might . . . conflict with the interests of the client to whom the . . . research is to be published . . . [and] accordingly, a firm should:

[•] not allow anyone other than an . . . analyst (such as a[n] . . . issuer) to approve the content of . . . research before publication; and
[•] only allow a person outside the firm (such as a[n] . . . issuer), or any employee other than the . . . analyst, to view it before its publication for verification of factual information. (FSA PM COB 7.16.5(3)(b)(v), 7.16.12(2))

And, lastly, addressing a different cause of 'the reasonable perception that its investment research may not be . . . impartial', the 'firm should consider whether its policy should contain any restriction on the timing of publication . . . [f]or example, . . . around the time of an investment offering' (FSA PM COB 7.16.14) 'or during other significant transactions in relation to which investment banking services are being provided'.[146]

MiFID:[147] The MiFID-inspired rules are to the same effect, and their application is as explained in 4.2(h), but they use different wording. Thus, they apply in relation to independent research which uses a new definition of 'research or other information recommending or suggesting an investment strategy, explicitly or implicitly, concerning one or more financial instruments or . . . issuers . . . including any opinion as to the present or future value of price of such instruments . . . and . . .

(a) . . . labelled or described as investment research . . . or is otherwise presented as an objective or independent explanation . . . [and]
(b) if the recommendation . . . were to be made . . . to a client, it would not constitute . . . a personal recommendation [11.2.2].[148]

---

[146] Policies for Managing Conflicts of Interest in connection with Investment Research, BBA, LIBA, ISMA, IPMA, 19 May 2004, para. 7.2.
[147] For an overview of EU regulation of research, see Investment Research and Financial Analysts, EC, 12 December 2006.
[148] GLOSS, def. of 'investment research'. '[I]t is clear that fixed income research is included' (FSA PS 07/6, para. 15.7).

This is to exactly the same effect as the interpretation of the Pre-MiFID definition of 'investment research', particularly since 'non-independent research must . . . [be] clearly identified as a marketing communication [and is subject to the financial promotion rules in 10.5] . . . and . . . contain a . . . statement that . . . it . . . has not been prepared in accordance with the legal requirements designed to promote the independence of investment research . . . and . . . is not subject to any prohibition on dealing ahead' (COBS 12.3.2).[149] However, although only the fifth of the specific rules (dealing on own account) is applied to financial instruments subject to non-independent research, generally '[i]n accordance with [the systems and controls rules in 5.2] a firm will be expected to take reasonable steps to identify and manage conflicts of interest which may arise in the production of non-independent research' (COBS 12.3.4). For independent research, as with the Pre-MiFID Rules, there is a need for the producer and any group (but not third party) disseminator to implement systems and controls 'measures for managing conflicts of interest in [accordance with those MiFID rules] . . . in relation to the . . . analysts involved . . . and other . . . persons whose responsibilities or business interests may conflict with the interests of the persons to whom investment research is disseminated', such other persons 'include[ing] corporate finance personnel and persons involved in sales and trading' (COBS 12.2.10, 12.2.2, 12.2.3). Thus, the first and second Pre-MiFID Rules, while not expressly contained in the MiFID rules, are implied and should be reflected in the firm's systems and controls. The third, and its Pre-MiFID interpretation, continues in a rule that an 'analyst should not become involved in activities . . . inconsistent with the maintenance of the . . . analyst's objectivity', which includes:

(1) participating in investment banking activities such as corporate finance business and underwriting;
(2) participating in 'pitches' for new business or 'roadshows' for new issues . . . or
(3) being otherwise involved in the preparation of issuer marketing. (COBS 12.2.9)

Fourth, as before MiFID, 'the firm . . . [and] analysts . . . must not accept inducements from those with a material interest in the . . . research' (COBS 12.2.5(3)); and, fifth, there is a ban on personal account transactions, which includes advising, procuring or disclosing to others, 'until the recipients of the . . . research have had a reasonable opportunity to act on it' and, even then, 'contrary to current recommendations, except in exceptional circumstances [including financial hardship] and with the prior approval of . . . the firm's legal or compliance function' (COBS 12.2.5(1), (2), 12.2.7(2),

---

[149] This statement, although copied out from MiFID Level 2, Art. 24(2), is incorrect in that FSA included 'super-equivalent' rules imposing the dealing ahead rule on non-independent research, thus maintaining the Pre-MiFID position (6.4.3.2).

11.7.2(1)). Sixth, 'the firm . . . [or the] analyst . . . must not promise issuers favourable research coverage' and, in contrast to the Pre-MiFID Rule, 'issuers . . . and any other persons must not . . . be permitted to review a draft of the . . . research for the purpose of verifying the accuracy of factual statements . . . or for any other purpose other than verifying compliance with the firm's legal obligations' (COBS 12.2.5(4), (5)), which includes for accuracy so that no misrepresentation is made. And, lastly, the guidance on distribution of research continues (COBS 12.2.12).

6.3.4.2 Dealing ahead ('front running')

Pre-MiFID: Ever since the 1986 FSAct it was considered wrong for the firm to publish research on securities which would stimulate customer demand and, before publication, buy those securities in order to make a profit, a classic conflict of interest within 6.2.1. FSA's initial 2000 FSMA rules provided that 'If a firm . . . intends to publish . . . investment research [as defined in 6.3.4.1] to clients . . . the firm must . . . not knowingly undertake an own account transaction in the . . . investment concerned or any related . . . investment . . . until the clients for whom the publication was principally intended have had . . . a reasonable opportunity to act upon it' (FSA PM COB 7.3.3). The original exceptions to the rule if '(1) the publication would not reasonably be expected to affect significantly the price of the . . . investment . . . [2] the firm has taken reasonable steps to ensure that it . . . needs to deal to fulfil a customer order that is likely to result from the publication, and . . . doing so will not cause the price of the . . . investment . . . to move against a customer's interests by a material amount [or (3)] the firm . . . discloses in the publication that the firm . . . may undertake an own account transaction' (FSA COB, 1 December 2001, 7.3.4(1), (4), (5)) were removed since they were 'too broad, and . . . effectively allowed . . . a firm to deal ahead in almost any circumstances'.[150] This left only two exceptions:

- [•] the firm . . . is a market maker . . . and . . . undertakes the transaction in good faith and in the normal course of market making; or
- [•] the firm . . . deals in order to fulfil an unsolicited customer order. (FSA PM COB 7.3.4(2), (3))

Nonetheless, 'the rule relates to exclusive knowledge [of publication] and not to . . . expectation . . . Consequently, the rule does not preclude dealing merely because relevant employees (on the basis of information available generally) expect or think it likely that the firm's analyst will publish research in accordance with a regular cycle or following the impending announcement of a company's . . . results . . . [I]ndividuals on one side of a "Chinese wall" will not be regarded as being in possession of information

---

[150] FSA CP 171, para. 4.32.

denied to them by the Chinese wall.'[151] As regards procedures, 'physical separation . . . is . . . effective. Alternatively a firm could provide desks away from the trading floor at which research would be prepared . . . and . . . robust policies and surveillance to prevent the inappropriate receipt and use of knowledge of timing and content of forthcoming research by sales and trading personnel.'[152] This rule is all about the regulator's perception of 'tak[ing] unfair advantage of . . . clients',[153] not a classic conflict of interest since the firm has not profited from an opportunity that in Equity belongs to the client where disclosure of and consent to proprietary dealing was made and obtained.

MiFID: As before, and thus subject to the same interpretations, and with the application explained in 4.2(h), 'if a[n employee] . . . has knowledge of the likely timing or content of . . . research . . . [he] must not . . . trade on behalf of . . . the firm, other than as market maker acting in good faith and in the ordinary course of market making or in the execution of an unsolicited client order . . . until the recipients of the . . . research have had a reasonable opportunity to act on it'. Thus, 'it is inappropriate . . . to prepare . . . research which is intended firstly for internal use for the firm's own advantage, and then for later publication to its clients' and 'FSA would expect a firm's conflicts of interest policy to provide for . . . research to be published . . . in an appropriate manner . . . [so that] it will be:

(1) appropriate . . . that . . . research is published . . . only through [the firm's usual distribution channels; and
(2) inappropriate for an employee . . . to communicate . . . research, except as set out in the . . . policy. (COBS 12.2.5(1), 12.2.11, 12.2.13)

As with the Pre-MiFID Rules, this prohibition applies to independent and non-independent research (COBS 12.3.4(2), (3)).[154]

6.3.4.3   Research disclosures

As a result of the structural solutions necessary for the production of research (6.3.4.1), FSA requires that 'A firm should consider what . . . disclosures should accompany the investment research it publishes' (FSA PM COB 7.16.15) and this is supplemented by detailed requirements in the Market Abuse Directive which, continuing under the MiFID-inspired FSA conduct rules, overall require a firm to 'take reasonable care to ensure that a research recommendation produced or disseminated . . . is fairly presented;

---

[151] Industry Guidance on COB 7.3, LIBA, BBA, ISMA, IPMA, 9 February 2004, paras 7, 8. For the effect of this industry guidance, see FSA PS 04/6, Ann. 4, para. 7.
[152] Policies for Managing Conflicts of Interest in connection with Investment Research, BBA, LIBA, ISMA, IPMA, 19 May 2004, para. 6.2.   [153] Ibid, para. 3.
[154] This is 'super-equivalent' to the Level 2 Directive, Art. 24(2), implemented in COBS 12.3.2(2)(b).

Conflicts of interest

and ... disclose[s] its interests or indicate[s] conflicts of interest' (COBS 12.4.4). These rules apply as explained in 4.2(h) to 'research recommendations', itself defined differently from 'investment research' in 6.3.4.1 as research or other information:

(a) concerning one or several financial instruments admitted to trading on regulated markets ... [and]
(b) intended for distribution so that it is ... likely to become, accessible by a large number of persons, or for the public, but not ...
   (i) an informal short term investment personal recommendation expressed to clients, which originates inside the sales or trading department, and which is not likely to become publicly available or available to a large number of persons; or
   (ii) advice given ... to a body corporate in ... a takeover bid ... and
(c) which:
   (i) explicitly or implicitly, recommends or suggests an investment strategy; or
   (ii) directly or indirectly, expresses a particular investment recommendation; or
   (iii) expresses an opinion as to the present or future value or price of such investments. (GLOSS. def. of 'research recommendation')

In practice, although '[w]e do not consider that the definition of investment research [in 6.3.4.1] is on all fours with the definition of a research recommendation ... we believe them to be very close'[155] and 'probably the only practical differences ... [are] that the research recommendation definition is wider in that it includes oral communications and narrower in its restriction to investments ... admitted to ... trading'.[156] Sales and trading recommendations are explained in 6.3.4.1 and 'personal recommendations' in 11.2.2. There is an extensive set of disclosures that need to be made, unless the information is held the other side of a Chinese Wall (FSA PM COB 7.17.4; COBS 12.4.3), which can be broadly summarised as follows:

- the identity of the firm, the analyst, and the regulator must be disclosed (FSA PM COB 7.17.6; COBS 12.4.5); and
- the research must be fairly presented in terms of facts, sources, projections, bases of valuation, substantiation of recommendations, explanation of the terms 'buy', 'sell' and 'hold' and disclosure of any different recommendations in the last 12 months (FSA PM COB 7.17.7, 7.17.8; COBS 12.4.6, 12.4.7); and
- the following conflicts disclosures must be made:
  - 'whether the research recommendation has been disclosed to th[e] issuer and amended ... before its dissemination' (FSA PM COB 7.17.8(1)(a); COBS 12.4.7(1)(a)); and

[155] FSA PS 05/3, March 2005, para. 4.4
[156] Market Watch, Issue 12, FSA, June 2005, Q. 28.

- 'all of the relationships and circumstances that may reasonably be expected to impair the objectivity of the research recommendation, in particular a significant financial interest in . . . [the] investment . . . or a significant conflict of interest with respect to . . . [the] issuer', including those of affiliated companies and of the analyst and 'whether his remuneration is tied to investment banking transactions' (COB 7.17.10; COBS 12.4.9); and
- shareholdings that exceed 5% (or a lesser number chosen by the firm) of the firm or its affiliate in the issuer or vice versa, for which purpose 'a firm [c]ould use the applicable company law of the top member of the group to calculate the holding, . . . of each member of the group',[157] 'any other financial interests held by the firm or any affiliate . . . in relation to the . . . issuer which are significant', which includes holding a bond or derivative or loan position with the issuer[158] and, if applicable, statements that 'the firm or any affiliate . . . is a market maker in the securities of the . . . issuer or in any related derivatives', 'the firm or any affiliate has been lead manager or co-lead manager over the previous 12 months of any . . . offer of securities of the . . . issuer' or 'is party to any other agreement with the . . . issuer relating to the provision of investment banking services' (but not commercial banking loans) or 'relating to the production of the research recommendation' (FSA PM COB 7.17.11(1), 7.17.12, 7.17.13; COBS 12.4.10(1), 12.4.11, 12.4.12); and
- 'in general terms, . . . the effective organisational and administrative arrangements set up' under 6.3.4.1 (FSA PM COB 7.17.11(2); COBS 12.4.10(2)); and
- the price and date of acquisition of any shares held by the analyst (FSA PM COB 7.17.11(3); COBS 12.4.10(3)); and
- 'the proportion of all research recommendations published during the relevant quarter that are "buy", "hold", "sell" . . . and . . . the proportion of . . . investments in each of these categories, issued by issuers to which the firm supplied material investment banking services during the previous 12 months' (FSA PM COB 7.17.11(4); COBS 12.4.10(4)). '[T]his disclosure should be meaningful to the recipients . . . [for example] according to the asset class and/or the long/short term nature of the recommendation.'[159]

These requirements apply to firms producing research recommendations, whether written or oral although where oral each of the rules provide that

---

[157] UK Implementation of the EU Market Abuse Directive, HMT and FSA Consultation Document, June 2004, para. 4.79.   [158] FSA PS 05/3, March 2005, para. 4.6.
[159] Market Watch, Issue 12, FSA, June 2005, Q. 30.

'the requirements . . . do not apply to the extent that they would be disproportionate', whatever that means in practice, and there are separate, but analogous, requirements on firms which distribute others' research (FSA PM COB 7.17.16–7.17.18; COBS 12.4.15–12.4.17).

6.3.5 Corporate finance securities issues

Pre-MiFID: Again, as a result of SEC enforcement action in the United States, 'although we do not have evidence of comparable abuses in the UK', FSA regarded two 'pricing and allocation practices' as 'contrary to the Principle . . . [on] conflicts of interest'. These were 'laddering . . . [where] the investment banks underwriting the IPOs sought to recapture profits made by investors receiving allocations [which increased in value] . . . by charging abnormally high commissions on unrelated dealings . . . [S]econd . . . shares in hot IPOs [which also increased in value] were allotted to senior executive officers of . . . corporate customers . . . [as] an incentive for the executives to place investment banking mandates from their companies with the investment bank . . . known . . . as spinning.'[160] With pricing, '[t]he . . . corporate issuer wants a high price while the investors prefer a low price. The . . . firm . . . is . . . acting for the issuer (or vendor) and not for the investors. However, the firm has a commercial interest in ensuring that its investment customers are not dissatisfied . . . and may also have a proprietary interest in receiving underpriced securities'; and, on allocation, '[t]he issuer has a legitimate commercial interest in its shareholding base . . . However, the firm will also have an interest . . . as . . . agent of investment clients.'[161] FSA required the 'firm to manage [these] conflicts of interest . . . in a way that ensures that all of its clients are treated fairly' and this meant 'hav[ing] in place systems, controls and procedures to ensure that the duties which the firm owes to its clients are identified effectively and discharged appropriately' (FSA PM COB 5.10.3, 5.10.4). Early in the transaction the firm had to 'agree . . . with its corporate finance client . . . the process the firm proposes to follow in . . . recommend[ing] . . . allocations . . . ; how the target investor group . . . will be identified; the process through which recommendations on allocation and pricing are prepared, and by whom; and . . . that it may recommend placing securities with an investment client of the firm . . . and with the firm's own proprietary book, or with an associate, and this represents a potential conflict of interest' (FSA PM COB 5.10.5(1)). Such systems and controls had to be 'designed to ensure that the firm will give unbiased . . . advice . . . about the valuation and pricing for an offering' and, in particular, 'individuals . . . provid[ing] services to . . . investment clients . . . [should] not [be] involved directly in [such] decisions' and must 'bas[e] recommendations about . . . pricing on objectives agreed with the . . . client' (FSA PM COB 5.10.5(2), (3), (4)(c)).

---

[160] FSA CP 171, paras. 5.4–5.6, 5.8.   [161] Ibid, paras. 5.31–5.33.

The 'systems, controls and procedures . . . [in relation to] the allocation process' had to ensure that such 'recommendations on allocation (names and amounts . . . to be allocated) are made . . . only by staff who do not have any responsibilities for servicing investment clients' and are 'bas[ed] . . . on objectives agreed with the . . . client' (FSA PM COB 5.10.5(4)(a), (c)). Allocation to private clients had to be made 'as a single block and not on a named basis' leaving 'senior personnel in the department . . . responsible for . . . private customers [to] make the individual allocation' (FSA PM COB 5.10.5(4)(d), (e)), in order to manage the '[c]onflict . . . [that] can arise where a private client obtaining securities in an issue could be an officer of an . . . investment banking client'.[162] More generally, 'allocation recommendations . . . [must] not [be] determined by the level of business which [the] firm does or hopes to do with any other client' (FSA PM COB 5.10.5(5)). Thus, the following were outlawed:

(a) an allocation made as an inducement for the payment of excessive compensation in respect of unrelated services provided by the firm; for example, very high rates of commission paid to the firm by an investment client, or an investment client providing very high volumes of business at abnormal levels of commission . . . and
(b) an allocation made to a senior executive . . . of a . . . corporate finance client . . . in consideration for the future or past award of corporate finance business. (FSA PM COB 5.10.7(1)(a), (b))

However, FSA 'accepts that the level of business (volume of commission) may be correlated with the size of an investment client's portfolio . . . [and] that the size of a portfolio could be a legitimate factor when determining allocations. But . . . the level of commission business should not be the determining factor . . . Allocation should depend on considerations other than the absolute level of commissions received.'[163] These other considerations were set out in industry guidance and revolve around 'the size of an investor's expressed interest . . . [its] behaviour in and following past issues . . . , past dealings in . . . other securities of the issuer . . . [and] its involvement in roadshows and other direct contacts with the issuer . . . [and] the possibility that the investor may be using the offer as a means of building a strategic stake' and a range of other objective factors.[164]

MiFID: These provisions have been substantially cut down (SYSC 10.1.13–10.1.15). However, since they are now contained in the section of the rules requiring systems and controls in relation to conflicts of interest, with the application explained in 4.2(d), and since the Pre-MiFID provisions were expressed as Guidance on the Principle concerning conflicts of

---

[162] FSA CP 171, para. 5.40(f).   [163] FSA CP 205, para. 5.29.
[164] Guidance on Policies and Procedures for Managing Conflicts of Interest in the context of allocation and pricing of securities offerings, LIBA, IPMA, ISMA, BBA, 10 May 2004, para. 4.2.

Conflicts of interest

interest, the Pre-MiFID provisions should continue to be used in interpreting the MiFID requirements.

6.3.6 Churning

Pre-MiFID: The conflict of interest involved in generating personal profit from the client relationship was viewed by SIB as particularly intense with discretionary or advisory services and, hence, it was 'concerned to prevent "churning" . . . by . . . effect[ing] . . . transactions for the sake of commission or other profit to the firm'.[165] FSA continued with a rule stating that 'A firm must not:

> (1) deal . . . in the exercise of discretion for any customer; or
> (2) make a personal recommendation [11.2.2] to a private customer to deal . . .
> unless the firm has taken reasonable steps to ensure that the deal . . . is in the customer's best interests, both when viewed in isolation and . . . in the context of earlier transactions. (FSA PM 7.2.3)

This was viewed as an aspect of 'treating the customer fairly' (9.2) rather than, which it surely was, conflicts of interest (FSA PM COB 7.2.3, 7.2.2).

MiFID: These rules are to exactly the same effect, but phrased differently in that 'A [discretionary or advisory] transaction may be unsuitable for a client because of . . . the frequency of the trading' and 'A series of transactions that are each suitable when viewed in isolation may be unsuitable if the recommendation or the decisions to trade are made with a frequency that is not in the best interests of the client' (COBS 9.3.1(1), 9.3.2(1)). The rule applies as referred to in 4.2(i).

6.3.7 Personal account dealing

Pre-MiFID: As a further detailed articulation of the Principle on conflicts of interest (6.3.1), 'to ensure that a firm's customers are not disadvantaged by the personal dealings of the firm's employees', through 'conflicts of interest, exploitation of knowledge of customer intentions and other forms of undesirable, or even . . . illegal, exploitation of privileged information',[166] FSA required the 'firm . . . [to] take reasonable steps to ensure that:

> (1) a personal account transaction . . . by an . . . employee . . . does not conflict with the firm's duties to its customers . . . and

---

[165] Regulation of Investment Business – The New Framework, SIB and MIBOC, December 1985, para. 3.33.14.
[166] The Securities and Investments Board's Application for Designated Agency Status, February 1987, Explanatory Statement, para. 15(f).

(2) when it permits an employee to undertake a personal account transaction . . . it receives prompt notification of, or is otherwise able to identify, that transaction. (FSA PM COB 7.13.3, 7.13.4)

A 'personal account transaction' was 'a transaction for the account of an employee, or' 'any other person whose business or domestic relationship with [him/her] or [any such other person] might reasonably be expected to give rise to a community of interest between them which may involve a conflict of interest in dealing with third parties' in any investment other than Government securities, life policies and regulated collective investment schemes, and other than 'a discretionary transaction if there is no prior communication with the employee'. Each employee involved in the firm's 'designated investment business' (4.2.I(1)) had to receive 'a written notice . . . [which was] a term of his contract of employment' 'stat[ing] that, if [the] employee is precluded from entering into a transaction for his own account, he must not (except in the proper course of his employment):

(i) procure any other person to enter into such a transaction; or
(ii) communicate any information or opinion to any other person if he knows, or ought to know, that the person will, as a result, enter into such a transaction, or counsel or procure some other person to do so. (FSA PM COB 7.13.6(2). 7.13.7(1)(a), (b))

MiFID: A 'personal account transaction' retains exactly the same meaning (COBS 11.7.5), with the scope explained in 4.2(j), but the rule applies to any 'relevant person', being not only a director or employee of the firm but also 'a natural person who is involved in the provision of services to the firm . . . under an outsourcing arrangement for the purpose of the provision by the firm of regulated activities [4.2.I(1)]' (5.2.5) (GLOSS, def. of 'relevant person') to the extent directly 'involved in the provision of designated investment business' (COBS 11.7.6). The firm is required to:

maintain adequate arrangements aimed at preventing the following activities . . . of any relevant person who is involved in activities that may give rise to a conflict of interest, or has access to inside information . . . or to other confidential information relating to clients or transactions with or for clients . . .

(1) entering into a personal [account] transaction . . .
  (a) . . . prohibited . . . under the Market Abuse Directive; [or]
  (b) . . . involv[ing] the misuse or improper disclosure of that confidential information; [or]
  (c) . . . conflict[ing] with an obligation of the firm to a customer . . .
(2) advising or procuring, other than in the proper course of his employment . . . , any other person to enter into a transaction . . . covered by (1) . . .

(3) disclosing, other than in the normal course of his employment
..., any information or opinion to any other person if the relevant person ... ought to know, that as a result ... that other person ... would be likely to ... enter into a transaction ... covered by (1) ... [or] advise or procure another person to enter into such a transaction. (COBS 11.7.1)

However, FSA has:

> observed the widest range of practices ... Some firms favoured a blanket PA dealing ban; others allowed dealing if permission was sought and granted and the individual attests that they do not hold inside information, others did not monitor PA dealing.
>
> ... detailed good practice points ... include ...
>
> - Maintain a formal, written procedure for any personal account dealing by members of staff and ensure that staff are aware of this (some firms included it in an individuals employment contract; some firms tested understanding from time to time) ...
> - Policy is extended to immediate families ...
> - Policy includes limiting trading in companies in a related sector to a company on which an individual holds inside information ...
> - Explicit reference to PA dealing policy covering derivatives or related products ...
> - Only allow staff members to deal (if they attest that they do not hold any inside or relevant information) after they have obtained permission to deal from their immediate manager or compliance officer.
> - All staff are subject to a blanket ban on PA dealing.
> - Control Room staff are subject to a blanket ban on PA dealing.
> - Require staff to use specified brokers when dealing.
> - Require staff to file annual declarations of their holdings.
> - Keep a written log of permission requests and their outcomes, including details of why the request was made and why (if any) permission to deal was given.
> - Carry out risk-based monitoring of staff trading activities against announcements.[167]

As before, a written notice of the firm's personal account dealing rules is required and records must be kept (COBS 11.7.4).

6.3.8 Polarisation

See 10.5.6.2.

---

[167] Market Watch, Issue 21, July 2007, pp. 10–11.

7
Client property

7.1 Client assets and custody

7.1.1 Protecting the client's assets

Pre-MiFID: Ever since the 1986 FSAct regime, '[i]nvestors have a right to the assurance that their assets are properly safeguarded while they are under the control of a [firm]'[1] and, thus, '[t]he ultimate safeguard for investors is the assurance that on the failure of the [firm] . . . their . . . investments . . . are recoverable by them . . . [T]his can be achieved only by . . . segregation of clients' . . . investments from the firm's . . . investments . . . in such a way that ownership remains with [the client].'[2] Hence, a 'safe custody investment' was 'a designated investment, which is not the property of the firm, but for which the firm or any nominee/company controlled by the firm or by its associate is accountable; which has been paid for in full by the client; and which . . . the firm has [not] disposed of . . . in accordance with a valid instruction' and in respect of which the firm was conducting the licensable activity of custody (3.2.2.6) in or from the UK or an EEA branch (but not a non-EEA branch) with Private Customers, Intermediate Customers, or Market Counterparties. The firm had to:

> segregate safe custody investments from its own . . . investments

and:

> ensure that if a safe custody investment is [1] recorded in an account with itself, the title to that account makes it clear that the . . . investment belongs to the client, and is segregated from the firm's . . . investments . . . [or 2 if] recorded in an account with a custodian, the custodian makes it clear in the title of the account that the investment belongs to . . . clients of the firm'. (FSA PM CASS 1.2.2, 1.2.8, 1.3.1, 1.3.3, 1.4, 2.1.1, 2.1.8, 2.2.5, 2.2.7)

The three limbs of the definition of 'safe custody investment' were evolved by the regulators over a decade or more. The phrase 'for which the firm is accountable' covered all forms of control, including 'holding customers' assets . . . [and] having discretion to transfer or move customers' . . . assets'

---

[1] 1985 White Paper, para. 7.8. [2] 1984 Gower, para. 6.31.

and 'the holding of . . . [title] documents by a . . . custodian acting for the [firm]'.[3] The requirement of full payment by the client excluded assets against which the firm has lent the purchase price and was holding as collateral. And the condition not to have disposed of them meant that once subject to a sale contract they could be moved out of custody and the need to hold them with specified institutions (7.1.3.1), and similarly when they were transferred on as collateral on derivatives or stocklending transactions, although where the firm itself held the assets as collateral they were subject to the custody rules unless received under absolute title transfer (7.1.2.6). In addition, though, the firm had to apply such custody rules 'in a manner appropriate to the nature and value of' 'any other asset . . . held for, or on behalf of a client' (FSA PM CASS 2.1.3) because 'a client can reasonably expect that any other asset held . . . is treated in the same way',[4] which in practice meant applying all of the rules.

Unlike with client money (7.2.1), 'FSMA does not specifically empower [FSA] to make rules providing for such assets to be held on a trust basis',[5] which '[w]ould . . . make it easier to establish valid claims against trust assets in the event of a default of a . . . custodian'[6] and, therefore, the issue was the legal effect of segregation. Custodians always speak of holding client assets in a 'custody account' or 'omnibus account' which is, in fact, a series of book entries in the custodian's books of account recording the entitlement of each client to a particular number of a total pool of investments held by the custodian and registered either in its name or in the name of its wholly-owned nominee company (so that the custodian/nominee has absolute and perfected legal title to the investments), or in the name of a sub-custodian or clearing system against which the custodian and/or the client may have beneficial/equitable and/or merely contractual rights (7.1.3.1). No particular investment in the pool is attributable to any particular client and, like cash in the client money account, the investments of a particular issue and/or type are fungible although the custodian's balance sheet will not show the investments as assets belonging to it. So: Who is entitled to the investments/contractual rights in the chain if the custodian goes into liquidation? There are three situations.

7.1.1.1   The client transfers investments to the custodian

Before the transfer, the client is absolute legal and beneficial owner of the investments but after the transfer of legal title to the custodian/nominee, the client can trace and recover his property. This would not be tracing at common law because that 'follows the nature of the thing itself, as long as it

---

[3] IMRO Bulletin No. 3, 5 August 1987, para. 44; Safe-guarding of customer investments, IMRO, February 1991, Rule 5.1(2), Note.
[4] FSA CP 45A, February 2000, para. 13.8(iv).   [5] FSA PS 06/14, para. 10.4.
[6] Custody Review, SIB, August 1993, para. 10.3.

can be ascertained to be such, and the right . . . ceases when the means of ascertainment fail, which is the case when the subject is turned into money, and mixed and confounded in a mass of the same description'.[7] By analogy this applies with fungible investments in the custody account although not, for example, with unique illiquid securities which the custodian is holding only for one client. With fungible investments tracing would be in Equity where it is necessary to prove three things. First, that there is a fiduciary relationship between the recipient custodian and the client,[8] which can be based on either an express trust in the custody contract, or an implied trust on the analogy of the *Quistclose* principle (7.2.1) since the investments are received from the client for the specific purpose of custody, or on a resulting trust on the basis that the custodian is a volunteer who gives no value for the investments,[9] or on the basis of a constructive trust having received the property with knowledge that it belongs to another.[10] Second, it is necessary to prove that the client had an equitable interest in the pool of investments to start with. This must be the case since there are established rules that an 'assignment, for consideration which is paid or executed, of part of a debt or other chose in action is . . . effective in equity'[11] and that it is possible to create an express trust of part of a holding of securities,[12] notwithstanding the impossibility of an equitable assignment of the unascertained part of goods held in bulk,[13] the distinction between these two lines of cases being 'fair . . . sensible and workable . . . [and] an example of the court's policy of preventing a clearly intended trust from failing for uncertainty'.[14] And, third, the client must retain an equitable beneficial interest in the investments since '[t]racing is the process by which the plaintiff traces what has happened to his property, identifies the person who has handled or received it, and justified his claim that the [assets] which they handled or received (and, if necessary, which they still retain) can properly be regarded as representing his property. He needs to do this because his claim is based on the retention by him of a beneficial interest in the property . . . Unless he can prove this he cannot . . . raise an equity against the defendant'[15] and this comes down to whether the client intended the investments to become the absolute property of the custodian[16] which, patently, he did not, as is borne out by the custodian's records. Since the Equitable tracing remedy is available to assert the client's beneficial ownership, it follows that if there is a shortfall in the total investments held for all clients, it is borne proportionately to their individual entitlements;[17] and if

---

[7] *Taylor* v. *Plumer* (1815) 3 M&S 562 at 575.   [8] *Goff & Jones*, pp. 103–105.
[9] *Hanbury*, pp. 69–70.   [10] Ibid, pp. 310–317.   [11] *Meagher*, p. 167.
[12] *Hunter* v. *Moss* [1994] WLR 452; *MacJordan Construction Ltd.* v. *Brookmount* [1993] BCLC 350.
[13] Re Wait [1927] 1 Ch. 606; *In Re London Wine Co. (Shippers) Ltd.* [1986] PCC 121; Re Goldcorp Exchange Ltd. [1995] 1 AC 74.   [14] *Hanbury*, p. 101.
[15] *Boscawen* v. *Bajwa* [1996] 1 WLR 328 at 334.   [16] *Hanbury*, p. 685.
[17] *Re Diplock* [1948] Ch. 465; *Fastett* v. *McKeowa* [2000] 2 WLR 1299.

the depleted total included the custodian's own investments (or those of an affiliate?), the clients have first call on the depleted pool.[18]

7.1.1.2 Sale of investments

Upon a sale of investments, the client's beneficial entitlement in the pool of investments held by the custodian diminishes proportionately and is replaced by an entitlement to, and right to trace into, the cash proceeds, including where paid into the client money account (7.2.3.2).

7.1.1.3 Purchase of investments

The client has a beneficial entitlement to the client money which will be used to purchase the investments (7.2.1). If the money is paid to the vendor, the client thereupon obtains a beneficial interest in the investments provided that the vendor owns at least the amount of investments sold to the client[19] even if the precise investments have not been ascertained out of the pool owned by the vendor.[20] Accordingly, an equitable tracing claim will lie or, stated in a different way, the custodian holds his claim against the vendor under the purchase contract in trust for the client. The Court took this approach in a case involving a futures dealer which used client money in a segregated pooled trust account to acquire on-exchange futures contracts through a broker:

> Moneys were paid out of [the segregated account] . . . to the broker . . . to pay for futures contracts and margin calls. Moneys were paid into the account . . . by the broker which represented the proceeds of those futures contracts. The only question is whether those contracts and the balance with brokers, prior to payment into the segregated account . . . were also trust assets . . . [A]s . . . between the [futures dealer] and its clients, they were . . . The [futures dealer was] . . . a trustee of the benefit of the contracts for its clients . . .
>
> The futures contracts were . . . the authorised form of investment of the trust moneys . . . As such . . . the benefit of the contracts and the balance in the hands of the [brokers], prior to payment into the segregated bank account, were assets held by the [futures dealer] . . . in trust for its clients.[21]

And when the investments are transferred to the custodian, the position is as in 7.1.1.1. There must, however, be something upon which the trust can bite, as is illustrated by so-called contractual settlement where 'the customers' accounts (both cash and assets) are debited and credited on the

---

[18] *Re Tilley's W.T.* [1967] Ch. 1179; *Fastett* v. *McKeowa*.
[19] *Holroyd* v. *Marshall* (1862) 10 HLC 191; *Tailby* v. *Official Receiver* (1886) 13 App. Cas. 523.
[20] This point is asserted on the basis of the established rules for equitable assignment of part of a debt and the ability to create an express trust of part of a holding of securities referred to above.   [21] *Re Eastern Capital Futures Ltd.* [1989] ECLC 371 at 372.

settlement due date rather than the actual settlement date. Cash is physically moved despite the fact that no [investments] ha[ve] been received. The . . . custodian can find itself exposed to a financing risk (for which it will charge a fee) . . . but in practice this risk is limited because the custodial agreement . . . will . . . allow . . . the . . . custodian to reverse accounting entries and re-credit the cash in respect of transactions which fail to settle . . . and transfer the financing costs back to the customer . . . [C]ustomers . . . risk . . . [being] "out of [investments] and out of money" . . . [since if] the securities have not actually been received . . . the customer will not have good title to the investments with which he has been credited . . . should [the] . . . custodian become insolvent.'[22]

The initial SIB and SRO custody rules under the 1986 FSAct applied only insofar as the firm was performing custody functions in the course of 'investment business' since a licence for custody was not required until after the Maxwell scandal (2.5) when a greater volume of rules was introduced. In the New Settlement (2.4.2), SIB adopted a general Principle, that 'Where a firm has control of or is otherwise responsible for assets belonging to a customer which it is required to safeguard, it shall arrange proper protection for them, by way of segregation and identification of those assets or otherwise, in accordance with the responsibility it has accepted'.[23] This 'covers custody of all types of customer assets held by a firm: investment certificates, money and any other property belonging to its customer'[24] and, under FSA, became:

> A firm must arrange adequate protection for client's assets where it is responsible for them. (PRIN 2.1.1, Principle 10)

In practice, it was extremely difficult to understand what this required beyond compliance with the detailed Custody Rules (cf. FSA PM CASS 2.1.12) and best market practice, however that is to be discovered, for example, '[p]rocedures . . . should ensure that . . . title . . . [is] released [i.e. free deliveries made] only to the customer, to a . . . custodian or in accordance with the terms of the customer agreement'.[25]

MiFID: The Principle continues to 'require . . . a firm to arrange adequate protection for client assets', although the Custody Rules are still, unhelpfully, stated to be only 'part of these protections' (CASS 6.1.22), and there are now two sets of Custody Rules, neither of which affect the general law analysis of ownership rights. The Pre-MiFID Rules, CASS 2, continue to apply to UK branches of non-EEA firms and banks, although they can elect to opt-in to the new MiFID Custody Rules, CASS 6, which apply, in any event, to UK firms and banks in respect of MiFID 'financial

---

[22] Custody Review, SIB, August 1993, paras. 5.14–5.16.
[23] Statements of Principle, 1990, SIB, Principle 7.
[24] Custody Review, SIB, August 1993, para. 2.5.   [25] Ibid, Ch. 3, App., para. B(d).

instruments' and 'MiFID Business' (4.2.I(2)). Moreover, UK firms and banks can elect to comply with CASS 6 in respect of all other custody activities (3.2.1.6) although in default of such election the Pre-MiFID Rules apply (CASS 1.2.2, 1.2.3, 1.2.7(3), (5), (6), 2.1.1, 2.1.2A, 2.1.9(4), 2.1.10A, 3.1.1, 6.1.1, 6.1.17). Such an election would be sensible because otherwise the firm will be subject to the challenging direction to operate two separate regimes:

> Where a firm is subject to both the . . . [Pre-MiFID] custody [rules] . . . and the MiFID custody [rules] . . . it must ensure segregation between . . . investments held under [each set of rules] . . . including that . . . investments held . . . with the same third party, are held in different, separately designated, accounts . . . The purpose of the rules regarding the segregation of investments . . . held under different regimes is to reduce the risk of confusion between assets held under different regimes either on a on-going basis or on the failure of a firm or third party holding those assets. (CASS 1.2.10, 1.2.12)

MiFID does not require FSA to introduce such 'confusion', in particular the rules that 'A firm (other than a [non-EEA firm or bank] . . .) that is only subject to the . . . [pre-MiFD] custody [rules] . . . may not choose to comply with th[e] [MiFID] Rules' (CASS 6.1.20), and nor can a firm 'opt-in in respect of arranging [custody or] depositary receipt business' (CASS 6.1.18). In practice this may prevent the operation by the group or firm of one custody system.

The MiFID rules contain two additional systems and controls principles, copied out from MiFID itself. 'A firm must . . . make adequate arrangements to safeguard clients' ownership rights, especially in the event of the firm's insolvency, and to prevent the use of financial instruments belonging to a client on the firm's own account except with the client's express consent.' In addition:

> A firm must introduce adequate organisational arrangements to minimise the risk of the loss or diminution of clients' financial instruments . . . as a result of the misuse of the financial instruments, fraud, poor administration, inadequate record-keeping or negligence. (CASS 6.2.1, 6.2.2)

As with the FSA Principle, it is difficult to understand what this adds to compliance with the detailed rules.

7.1.2   Application of the custody rules

Pre-MiFID: The application of FSA CASS 2 is explained in 7.1.1.

MiFID: See, generally 4.2(k)(i) and 8.2.1. The Pre-MiFID Rules, CASS 2, apply, as in 7.1.1 above, 'to a firm when it is [carrying on custody [3.2.1.6]] . . . other than . . . holding financial instruments belonging to a client in the course of conducting MiFID business [4.2.I(2)]' and the MiFID Rules apply 'to a . . . firm . . . when it holds financial instruments belonging to a client in the course of its MiFID business [4.2.I(2)]' (CASS 1.4.2–1.4.5, 2.1.1, 6.1.1). Where neither sets of rules applies then, as before MiFID (FSA PM CASS 4.5), the Mandate Rules apply if the firm has power over the clients' assets (CASS 1.2.7 (6), 8.1).

However, there are a number of exceptions.

7.1.2.1 Introducers and arrangers

Pre-MiFID: The regulated activity of custody comprises both 'safeguarding and administration of assets' and 'arranging safeguarding and administration of assets' (3.2.1.6), the latter being subject only to the rules on assessing the custodian (7.1.3.2), risk disclosure (7.1.3.4), and recordkeeping (CASS 2.1.15, 2.1.21–2.1.22). On the other hand, no rules apply to a person who 'introduces a client to another firm whose permitted activities include . . . safeguarding and administration . . . with a view to that other firm . . . [either] providing a safe custody service in the United Kingdom; or . . . arranging for the provision of a safe custody service in the United Kingdom by another person; and the other firm . . . or other person who is to provide the safe custody service is not in the same group . . . and does not remunerate [the introducer]' (CASS 2.1.5). In these circumstances the necessary investor protection is provided by the other firm.

MiFID: The position continues under both the Pre-MiFID Rules, CASS 2, and the MiFID Rules, CASS 6 (CASS 6.1.13, 6.1.14).

7.1.2.2 DvP

Pre-MiFID: '[I]nvestments need not be treated as [within the rules] . . . in respect of a delivery versus payment transaction through a commercial settlement system if it is intended that the . . . investment is meant to be:

> (1) in respect of a client's purchase, due to the client within one business day following the client's fulfilment of a payment obligation; or
> (2) in respect of a client's sale, due to the firm within one business day following the fulfilment of a payment obligation;
> unless the delivery or payment by the firm does not occur by the close of business on the third business day following the date of payment or delivery . . . by the client.

However, in such circumstances, to avoid the client being out of both its cash and securities the 'firm may segregate money (in accordance with the client money rules [7.2.2]) instead of the client's safe custody investments' (CASS 2.1.13, 2.1.14).

MiFID: This exception continues in both the Pre-MiFID Rules, CASS 2, and the MiFID Rules, CASS 6 (CASS 6.1.12).

7.1.2.3 Affiliates

Pre-MiFID: As with client money (7.2.2.4), the custody rules did not apply to affiliates' investments 'unless . . . the firm has been notified that the . . . investment belongs to a client of the affiliate . . . or . . . the affiliate . . . is a client dealt with at arm's length' (CASS 2.1.9(1)).

MiFID: This exception continues under the Pre-MiFID Rules, CASS 2, but not in the MiFID rules, CASS 6, except in respect of non-MiFID Business for which the firm has elected to comply with the MiFID Rules (CASS 6.1.10, 6.1.11). This, however, is not consistent with FSA's Policy Statement since '[i]t was our intention to maintain the status quo'[26] and, in practice, it is understood to be taking this view.

7.1.2.4 Fiduciaries

Pre-MiFID: Unlike with client money (7.2.2.6), the custody rules applied in part to collective investment scheme depositaries, but not to the operator of regulated schemes or to trustees (CASS 1.4.6–1.4.8, 2.1.9(2), 2.1.15–2.1.20, 2.2.4).

MiFID: This continues to be the position under the Pre-MiFID Rules, CASS 2, but the MiFID Rules, CASS 6, apply to depositaries and trustees (18.3.4) (CASS 1.4.7, 1.4.8).

7.1.2.5 Depositary receipts

Pre-MiFID: The custody rules applied in part to the issuer of depositary receipts since 'the underlying security is held for the benefit of the depositary receipt holder' even though he 'will not be known to the firm' (CASS 2.1.23–2.1.26).

MiFID: This continues to be the position under the Pre-MiFID Rules, CASS 2, and the MiFID Rules, CASS 6 (CASS 6.1.3).

7.1.2.6 Collateral and absolute title transfer

Pre-MiFID: If investments were transferred to the firm or to its control as collateral, for example, in respect of margin on derivatives transactions, and the firm was given some form of equitable or legal charge, i.e. 'the right to use the assets in a . . . default', being 'a bare security interest . . . [then] the firm must comply with the custody rules' (CASS 3.1.3, 3.1.4). If, however, 'the firm is given a right to use the asset', and 'the client has transferred to the firm the legal title and associated rights' 'subject only to an obligation to return equivalent assets . . . upon satisfaction of the client's obligations to the firm', then the custody rules did not apply and, instead 'a differing level or regulatory protection' required only that the 'firm . . .

---

[26] FSA PS 07/2, para. 8.21.

must ensure that it maintains adequate records to enable it to meet any future obligations including the return of equivalent assets to the client' (CASS 3.1.5, 3.1.7, 3.2.2). This rule operated in the same way in respect of client money (7.2.2.7).

MiFID: These Rules, CASS 3, continue to apply generally (CASS 1.2.7(3A)) and, in addition, the use of total title transfer is accepted under the MiFID Rules, CASS 2, so that 'The custody rules do not apply where a client transfers full ownership of a financial instrument to a firm for the purpose of securing or otherwise covering present or future, actual, contingent or prospective obligations' (CASS 6.1.6). Although this can be used with Retail Clients, in most cases it may be doubted whether the fact that, as a result, the client loses his proprietary rights in the investments would be accepted by FSA as complying with 'the client's best interests rule [9.3], which requires the . . . [firm] to act honestly, fairly and professionally in accordance with the best interests of the . . . client' (CASS 6.1.8). FSA thus concludes that, although generally 'the arrangements . . . [must be] properly documented between the firm and the client and . . . involve good faith collateral . . . such arrangements may be used for Retail Clients . . . only in very limited circumstances, for example stocklending'.[27] Under another FSA MiFID Rule, 'The custody rules do not apply where a firm carries on business in its name but on behalf of a client where that is required by the very nature of the transaction and the client is in agreement . . . [f]or example. . . . where a firm borrows financial instruments from a client as principal under a stocklending agreement' (CASS 6.1.4, 6.1.5). This provision is extremely unclear, but as with the equivalent provision for client money (7.2.2.7) would seem to also apply to repo's and on-exchange derivatives dealing carried on as a principal with the client.

7.1.2.7   Temporary holdings

Although there was no express exemption under the Pre-MiFID Rules 'if a firm temporarily handles a financial instrument belonging to a client', such an exclusion is created in the MiFID Rules (CASS 6.1.15, 6.1.16). Here, 'temporary' must mean only for so long as is strictly necessary to properly transfer the instrument elsewhere.

7.1.2.8   Passported branches

Pre-MiFID: Under the ISD, as with client money (7.2.2.8), UK branches of passported firms were subject to the custody rules of the Home State (CASS 1.2.3(2), 2.1.6).

MiFID: This continues to be the position (4.2(k)(i)).

---

[27] FSA CP 06/14, paras. 10.13, 10.15.

7.1.3 Procedures

7.1.3.1 Segregation

Pre-MiFID: A rigid segregation was required (7.1.1), which had to be reflected in, first, the title to the custody account held in the firm's and any custodian's books; and, second, the registered legal title, which had to be in the name of the client or the nominee of the firm/custodian and not in the 'firm[s] . . . own name . . . to protect customers against their instruments being seized by liquidators on the insolvency of the . . . firm'[28] except where 'appropriate to the client concerned' and 'if . . . the investment is subject to the law of a jurisdiction outside the United Kingdom and . . . it is not feasible to do otherwise, because of . . . the applicable law or market practice', in which case it could be registered in the name of the firm or custodian. The segregation had to also be reflected in the holding of documents of title by the firm/custodian in such a custody account and, if in bearer form, separate from the firm's own investments (CASS 2.2.3, 2.2.5, 2.2.7, 2.2.10–2.2.12, 2.2.15–2.2.17).

The nominee was a bare trustee and, as such, did not require a licence (3.2.5.3). It was 'a separately incorporated entity from the . . . firm, although . . . their . . . operations are . . . very closely integrated . . . It is often difficult to pinpoint where . . . [firm] employees stop acting for the . . . firm and start acting for the nominee . . . As the registered holder of the investments, the nominee will be sent dividend or interest payments and will be under a general law obligation to account for them to the beneficial owners. It has no trustee duties to perform in relation to the assets which it holds other than to deliver them to those persons entitled to them . . . A typical nominee company is . . . capitalised . . . [for] as little as £2 . . . [which] is justified on the grounds that a nominee company is not exposed to financial risk. It can act only on the instruction of . . . the . . . firm . . . and undertakes no transactions [for its own account]. Transactions entered into in the nominee's name are typically recorded in the books of the . . . firm. Furthermore, a nominee company will have no employees of its own; but will rely on the . . . firm for its staff.'[29] Thus, FSA required that:

> A firm must accept the same level of responsibility to its client for any nominee company controlled by the firm in respect of any requirement of the custody rules. (CASS 2.1.11)

Segregation requires, procedurally, different systems depending upon: the nature of the investment (registered or bearer); the manner in which it is recorded (paper-based or electronic or dematerialised); the type of holding (for an individual client or for all clients pooled together); and the type of holder (whether the firm, a custodian, a sub-custodian, a nominee, a

---

[28] Custody Review, SIB, August 1993, para. 4.2.   [29] Ibid, paras. 4.7, 4.9, 4.10.

broker–dealer, a clearing agent or clearing system) and, of course, there may be a chain of holders governed by different legal systems with, in English law terms, different beneficial/equitable and/or contractual rights against each. The method of recording the segregation in the firm's books can affect the client's eventual entitlement on a custodian default. If 'the ... firm's record indicates not only that 1,000 shares are held for each of ... A and ... B, but also ... record the [custodians f]or example:

- client A – 1,000 shares in XYZ PLC: 250 with [custodian] X and 750 with [custodian] Y; and
- client B – 1,000 shares in XYZ PLC: 750 with [custodian] X and 250 with [custodian] Y.

In the event of the insolvency of ... X ... such records would allow the clear allocation of loss between Client A (250) and Client B (750).[30]

But, in the absence of such clear allocation, which is not required by the Rules, the loss would be proportionate to the total shares held for each client.

MiFID: The Pre-MiFID Rules, CASS 2, continue in identical form, and the MiFID Rules, CASS 6, are extremely similar (CASS 6.2.1–6.2.7, 6.3.1(2), 6.5.1, 6.5.2).

7.1.3.2   Using a custodian

Pre-MiFID: Before using a custodian, the firm had to, as a result of Principle 2 (9.1), 'use due care, skill and diligence (including considering the potential effect of the custodian's insolvency) to select a suitable custodian'[31] and, thus, 'undertake an appropriate risk assessment ... and ... assess the continued appointment ... periodically as often as is reasonable in the relevant markets', including:

(1) the expertise and market reputation of its custodian ...
(2) the arrangements for holding and safeguarding an investment;
(3) an appropriate legal opinion as to the protection of custody assets in the ... insolvency of the custodian;
(4) whether the custodian is regulated ...
(5) the ... financial resources of the custodian;
(6) the credit rating of the custodian;
(7) any other activities undertaken by the custodian and ... any affiliate. (CASS 2.2.18, 2.2.20, 2.2.21)

'Not all ... firms will have the necessary resource or expertise to carry out this "quality control". Therefore such firms will need to look to the custodians themselves to provide the necessary assurances. Notwithstanding the quality and strengths of any internal audit function established by the custodian, this is unlikely to be ... sufficiently independent to provide the level

[30] CESR 04–261(b), June 2004, pp. 32–33.   [31] SIB, CP 90, August 1995, para. 1.6.

of assurance required. Firms may therefore need to look to the external auditors of the custodian to provide the necessary assurances.'[32] In addition, 'all arrangements with . . . custodians, including respective responsibilities . . . [must be] evidenced in writing'[33] and, hence, the firm had to enter into an agreement with the custodian containing a number of mandated items (CASS 2.4).

MiFID: The Pre-MiFID Rules, CASS 2, continue to be identical and the MiFID Rules, CASS 6, are to exactly the same effect except that, in addition:

> A firm may only deposit financial instruments with a third party in a jurisdiction which specifically regulates and supervises . . . safekeeping . . . with a third party who is subject to such regulation.
>
> A firm may not deposit financial instruments . . . with a third party in a country that is not an EEA State . . . and which does not regulate . . . safekeeping . . . unless:
>
> (a) the nature of the financial instruments or of the investment services . . . requires them to be deposited with a third party in that . . . country; or
> (b) the financial instruments are held on behalf of a professional client and the client requests the firm in writing [8.4.7.1] to deposit them with a third party in that country. (CASS 6.3.4)

These rules do not apply to non-MiFID custody business opted into the MiFID rules (7.1.1) and, instead, there is a special regime (CASS 6.3.4) which, given the difficulty of distinguishing MiFID and non-MiFID custody (3.2.2.6), means that in practice these rules will be complied with in all cases. The second requirement 'appl[ies] to subcustodians appointed by a third party . . . [but] not . . . to those third parties (including sub-custodians) appointed in places where the activity is not regulated in the first place . . . The rule does not prevent the use of unregulated fund registers, central securities depositaries or unregulated nominee companies appointed by regulated sub-custodians that firms appoint.'[34]

7.1.3.3 Stocklending

Pre-MiFID: Stocklending required prior consent from a Private or Intermediate Customer and, with a Private Customer, entry into of a detailed agreement and the taking of collateral at least equal to the value of the securities lent, which was to be held subject to the custody or client money rules, as relevant. In addition, for both types of Customer, there

---

[32] Custody Review, SIB, August 1993, para. 5.29.   [33] Ibid, Chapter 3, para. 6.
[34] FSA PS 07/2, para. 8.18.

had to be 'documentation with borrowing counterparties which is adequate and appropriate' (CASS 2.5.4–2.5.14). See also 16.3.3.

MiFID: The Pre-MiFID Rules, CASS 2, continue with the changed client nomenclature. Under the MiFID Rules, CASS 6, 'prior consent' (8.4.7.1, 10.5.1.3) is required from all clients to 'securities financing transactions', being 'stocklending or stockborrowing . . . repurchase or reverse repurchase . . . or . . . buy-sale back or sell-buy back transaction[s]'. Moreover, 'express prior consent' is required if the client securities in such transactions are held in an omnibus account, and the collateral rule for Retail Clients has been carried over (CASS 6.4.1, 6.4.2).

7.1.3.4 Client disclosure

Pre-MiFID: A range of disclosures had to be made to the client (8.4.7.2):

- Disclosure of the Terms and Conditions of the custody service including: fees; the mechanics of takeovers, offers, distributions, dividends, information provision; 'registration . . . [other than] in the client's name' (7.1.3.1); 'the extent of the firm's liability in the event of a default by a custodian, except that a firm must accept the same level of responsibility . . . for [its] nominee . . . as for itself and may not disclaim responsibility for losses . . . from the fraud, wilful default or negligence of the firm'; 'the circumstances in which the firm may realise [an] . . . investment held as collateral'; 'if the firm intends to pool . . . investment[s] with . . . other clients, notification of its intention to the market counterparty or intermediate customer and if . . . a private customer, an explanation . . . that . . . individual entitlements may not be identifiable . . . and . . . in the event of a . . . shortfall after the failure of a custodian, clients may share in that shortfall' (CASS 2.1.11, 2.3.2, 2.3.3).
- A statement of the arrangements for the giving and receiving of instructions by . . . the client . . . and . . . any lien or security interest . . . [of] the firm or a third party, except in respect of charges' and a risk warning if investments were to be registered in the firm's name (7.1.3.1), requiring a notification to market counterparties and intermediate customers and a written agreement by private customers, and notification to all clients was required if they were to be registered in a name provided by the client or held by a group custodian (CASS 2.3.4–2.3.6, 2.3.10, 2.3.11, 2.2.23).
- With investments 'to [be] h[e]ld . . . overseas, . . . notif[ication] . . . that there may be different settlement, legal and regulatory requirements in overseas jurisdictions from those applying in the United Kingdom' had to be made to Intermediate and Private Customers (CASS 2.3.7–2.3.9), although originally it was considered that '[t]he risk disclosure envisaged under [this] rule . . . is not easy to express

definitively. For example, . . . [with] U.S. investments . . . it would not be appropriate to advise that . . . investments would be subject to different settlement, legal and regulatory requirements to those in the U.K. The rule is expected to be applied appropriately in the circumstances.'[35]
- Use of the client's investments by the firm or another client had to be disclosed. For example, in derivatives dealing if all client investments were held in a pool, this required written consent from a Private Customer and notification to an Intermediate Customer or Market Counterparty; and the pooling of customers' securities on stocklending required consent from Private and Intermediate Customers (CASS 2.5.2, 2.5.3, 2.5.9).
- There were detailed requirements for regular dispatch of client statements with mandated contents (CASS 2.3.12–2.3.21).

MiFID: The Pre-MiFID Rule, CASS 2, continues in the same form with the new client terminology, and the MiFID Rule, CASS 6, contains a different set of disclosures, all of which have to be provided to Retail Clients, but only (d)–(f) to Professional Clients:

(a) if applicable:
  (i) that the . . . investments . . . may be held by a third party [7.1.3.1] . . .
  (ii) the responsibility of the firm under the applicable contract law for the acts or omissions of the third party; and
  (iii) the consequences for the client of the insolvency of the third party;
(b) if applicable, that the . . . investments . . . may be held in an omnibus account by a third party and a prominent warning of the resulting risks [7.1.3.1];
(c) if it is not possible under national law for . . . investments belonging to a client held with a third party to be separately identifiable from the proprietary . . . investments of that third party or of the firm, that fact and a prominent warning of the resulting risks;
(d) if applicable, that accounts . . . will be subject to the law of a jurisdiction other than that of an EEA State, an indication that the rights of the client relating to those instruments . . . may differ accordingly [7.1.3.2];
(e) . . . information about the existence and terms of any security interests or lien which the firm has . . . over the client's investments; or any right of set-off it holds in relation to the . . . investments [7.1.2.6] . . .
(f) if applicable, that a depositary may have a security interest or lien over, or right of set-off in relation to those investments . . . [and]
[g] . . . clear, full and accurate information on the obligations and responsibilities of the firm in respect to [any securities financing

---

[35] SFA BN 410, 3 April 1997, Sched. 1, para. 16.

transactions] . . . including the terms for the . . . restitution [of securities lent], and . . . the risks involved [7.1.3.3]. (COBS 6.1.7)

7.1.3.5   Reconciliation

Pre-MiFID: At least 'every 25 business days [the firm had to] perform a reconciliation of its record of . . . investments . . . which it does not physically hold, with statements obtained from custodians' and 'as often as necessary, but no less than every six months . . . carry out:

(1) an account of all . . . investments it physically holds and reconcile the result . . . with its record . . . and
(2) a reconciliation between the firm's record of client holdings, and the firm's record of the location of . . . investments.

For the reconciliation the firm had to use either:

(1) the 'total count method', which requires that all . . . investments be counted and reconciled as at the same date; or
(2) . . . the rolling stock method . . . provided that:
   (a) all of the particular . . . investments are counted and reconciled as at the same date; [and]
   (b) all . . . investments are counted and reconciled during a period of six months; and
   (c) written confirmation is given to the FSA from the firm's auditor that the firm has in place systems and controls which enable it to adequately perform the alternative method. (CASS 2.6.2, 2.6.6, 2.6.10)

For this purpose, 'the rolling basis . . . has the following positive benefits: a) the workload . . . can be spread throughout the six monthly cycle, and b) rolling reconciliations should more quickly highlight any problems, these being easier to resolve when comparatively recently discovered'.[36]

MiFID: The Pre-MiFID Rules, CASS 2, continue in identical form and the MiFID Rules, CASS 6, are extremely similar (CASS 6.5.4–6.5.12).

7.2   Client money

7.2.1   Protecting the client's money

Pre-MiFID: When the client entrusts his money to the firm, whether by direct payment to the firm or receipt by the firm in the course of transactions with or for the client, he takes two risks in respect of both the firm and any other institution to whom the money is passed: fraud and insolvency. These risks are, to an extent, minimised by the regulatory requirements of

---

[36] Reconciliation of Customers' Investments, IMRO, August 1989, p. 1.

licensing, regulatory capital and the Compensation Scheme. In addition, though, regulators have, since the 1983 Licensed Dealers Rules (2.3), sought to protect the money itself. At general law, receipt of money gives rise to merely an unsecured debt unless, under the *Quistclose* principle, it is paid for a specific articulated purpose into a segregated bank account in which case a trust over that money is created by operation of law in favour of the persons intended to benefit, such that the monies are not available to the recipient's liquidator.[37] Whether a trust is actually created is a question of the parties' intention and the way in which the money is paid over and, in the absence of express agreement, the Courts are loathe to imply a trust into a commercial agreement where money is received by an agent, much less if the recipient is acting as a principal.[38] Thus, for Professor Gower:

> The ultimate safeguard for investors is an assurance that on a failure of the [firm] . . . such of their money . . . as [has] not been disposed of . . . legitimate[ly] . . . are recoverable . . . [T]his can be achieved . . . by the segregation of clients' money . . . from the firm's money . . . effective[ly] only if . . . ownership remains with them . . . To provide for the establishment of effective trust accounts . . . is difficult . . . in the absence of specific legislation.[39]

Hence, the detailed provisions of the 1986 FSAct, carried over into FSMA, which empowered FSA to make '[r]ules relating to the handling of money held by an authorised person . . . [which] make provision which results in that clients' money being held on trust' (FSMA 139(1)(a)):

> A firm . . . receives and holds client money as trustee . . . on the following terms:
>
> (1) for the purposes of and on the terms of the client money rules;
> (2) . . . for the clients for whom the money is held, according to their respective interests in it;
> (3) on the failure of the firm, for the payment of the costs properly attributable to the distribution of the client money in accordance with (2); . . . and
> (5) after all valid claims and costs under (2) and (3) have been met, for the firm itself. (CASS 4.2.3)

This statutory trust could not be varied and there were detailed rules on the distribution of client money in the insolvency of the firm or any institution holding it (CASS 4.4). The client's proprietary interest under the trust was an asset which could be disposed of, including by the grant of a security

---

[37] *Barclays Bank Ltd.* v. *Quistclose Investments Ltd.* [1968] 3 AER 651; *Carrerras Rothmans Ltd.* v. *Freemans, Matthews Ltd.* [1984] WLR 1016; The Quistclose Trust, P J Millett QC, LQR, April 1985, Vol 101, pp. 269–291; *Re Kingford Ltd.* [1975] 1 AER 604; *Re Eastern Capital Futures Ltd.* [1989] BCLC 371.
[38] *Kirkham* v. *Peel* (1880) 43 LT 171; *New Zealand Land* v. *Watson* (1881) 7 QBD 374; *Nesté Oy* v. *Lloyd's* [1983] 2 Lloyds Rep. 658.   [39] 1984 Gower, para. 6.31.

interest over it, for example in favour of the firm in respect of transactions undertaken with or through the firm. Such an asset was available to his liquidator/trustee in bankruptcy who could terminate the trust by demanding back the client money,[40] leaving the firm as an unsecured creditor. Indeed, the firm did not seem to be a beneficiary of the trust, but rather a trustee granted specific powers over the assets; and, hence, there was no registerable charge in favour of the firm (1985 CA 395; 2006 CA 860), no proprietary interest in favour of any counterparty with whom the firm dealt on behalf of the client, and immediate vested interests such that the rule against perpetuities did not apply.[41] And since 'A firm held all client money in general client bank accounts for its clients as part of a common pool of money so those particular clients do not have a claim against a specific sum in a specific account; they only have a claim to the client money in general' (CASS 4.2.4), a specific exemption had to be granted from the definition of collective investment scheme (3.2.1.9).

The Principle relating to client assets adopted in the New Settlement and redrafted by FSA (7.1.1) extended to client money although, in practice, it was extremely difficult to understand what it required beyond compliance with the detailed Client Money Rules.[42]

MiFID: The Principle continues, although FSA unhelpfully refers to the rules as only '[a]n essential part of th[e] protection' of the Principle (CASS 7.1.16(1)), and there are now two sets of client money rules. The Pre-MiFID Rules, CASS 4, continue to apply to UK branches of non-EEA firms and banks, although they can elect to opt-in to the new MiFID Client Money Rules, CASS 7, which apply, in any event, to UK firms and banks in respect of MiFID Business (4.2.I(2)). Moreover, UK firms and banks can elect to comply with CASS 7 in respect of all other 'designated investment business' although in default of such election the Pre-MiFID Rules apply (CASS 1.2.7(3), (5), (6), 4.1.2(6), 4.1.2C, 7.1.1, 7.1.2–7.1.7). Such an election is sensible because otherwise the firm will be subject to the challenging direction to operate two separate client money regimes:

> Where a firm is subject to . . . the [Pre-MiFID] client money [rules] . . . and the MiFID client money [rules] . . . it must ensure segregation between money held under each [set of rules] . . . The purpose of the rules regarding the segregation of . . . money held under different regimes is to reduce the risk of confusion between assets held under different regimes either on an ongoing basis or on the failure of a firm or a third party holding those assets. (CASS 1.2.11, 1.2.12)

MiFID does not require FSA to introduce such 'confusion', in particular the requirement that 'A firm (other than a [non-EEA firm or bank] . . .)

---

[40] Under the principle in *Saunders* v. *Vautier* (1841) Cr & Ph. 240. See *Hanbury*, pp. 629–631.
[41] *Hanbury*, pp. 348–352, 374–8, 380–383.   [42] Cf. CASS 4.1.7.

that is only subject to the [Pre-MiFID] client money [rules] . . . may not opt to comply with [the MiFID rules]' (CASS 7.1.6), which may prevent the operation by the firm or group of one client money system. The MiFID Rules contain an additional principle, copied out from MiFID itself: 'A firm must, when holding client money, make adequate arrangements to safeguard the client's rights and prevent the use of client money for its own account' (CASS 7.3.1). This adds nothing to the detailed rules. The MiFID Rules also restate the statutory trusts in identical terms to the Pre-MiFID Rules (CASS 7.7, 7.9).

7.2.2 Defining client money

Pre-MiFID: The definition of 'client money' was wide-ranging: 'money of any currency which, in the course of carrying on designated investment business [4.2.I(1)], a firm holds in respect of any investment agreement entered into, or to be entered into, with or for a client, or which a firm treats as client money in accordance with the client money rules', i.e. 'receives or holds money from, or on behalf of, a client' (CASS 4.1.1). It applied to all types of firm acting in or from the UK or an EEA branch (but not a non-EEA branch) in respect of any type of 'designated investment business' carried on 'with' (i.e. as principal) or 'for' (i.e. as agent) any type of 'client' (8.2) itself acting as principal or agent (CASS 1.2.2, 1.2.7–1.2.9, 1.3.2, 1.3.3, 1.4.1–1.4.4). But it applied only where the firm 'held' the money, not where it merely had 'a . . . written authority from a client under which the firm may control a client's assets', i.e. a mandate over an account in the client's name (CASS 4.5.1). There were separate rules governing the firm's use of mandates (CASS 4.5). The tailpiece, 'or which a firm treats its client money in accordance with the . . . rules', was necessary because where 'the firm executes a sell order as agent . . . it will . . . receive the purchase price and hold it on [the statutory] trust . . . [but if] it buys [from the client] for its own account [as principal] . . . it will not receive or hold any money for the account of the client'[43] and, therefore, the rules required the firm to pay the purchase price into the client money account (7.2.3.2). Thus, where the firm acted as agent, on a client buy order the purchase price was client money upon receipt by the firm (with power to pay it to the counterparty upon settlement) (7.2.3.2), and on a client sell order the purchase price was client money held for the counterparty before the client's securities were delivered and held for the client thereafter. And where the firm acted as principal, on a client buy order the purchase price had to be paid into the client money account (with power to pay it to the firm when the securities had been transferred), and on a client sell order, again the purchase price had to be transferred

---

[43] The Financial Services (Clients' Money) Regulations 1987, 7 October 1987, SIB, Chapter VI, section 8, para. 8.

into the client money account when the client securities were transferred to the firm.

MiFID: For the application generally of the rules, see 4.2(k)(ii) and 8.2.1. The Pre-MiFID definition continues in relation to the Pre-MiFID Rules, CASS 4, but in relation to the MiFID Rules, CASS 7, 'client money' is defined as 'money . . . that the firm receives or holds for, or on behalf of, a client in the course of, or in connection with, its MiFID Business' (CASS 7.2.1). This is similarly wide-ranging in applying to all types of firm in respect of any type of MiFID Business (4.2.I(2)) carried on as principal 'with' or agent 'for' any type of 'client', itself acting as principal or agent, and whether a Retail Client, Professional Client or Eligible Counterparty (CASS 1.2.8, 1.4.2–1.4.8). The phrase 'receives or holds' is to be interpreted in the same way as the tailpiece to the Pre-MiFID definition because that tailpiece was and remains subject to a rule that applies the Pre-MiFID Rules to the firm where it 'receives or holds money' (CASS 4.1.1) and FSA's intention in the drafting was 'to carry forward the current approach to the definition of client money'.[44] Thus, where the firm, for example dealing as principal or having agreed to rebate commission to the client, will become liable to pay money to the client, it 'need not be treated as client money until . . . [it] become[s] due and payable to the client in accordance with the terms of the contractual arrangements' (CASS 7.2.12). Where it is not 'client money' but the firm has power over the client's account, identical mandate rules to the Pre-MiFID Rules apply whether or not it is in the course of MiFID Business (CASS 1.2.7(6), 8.1).

However, there were and remain a large number of exceptions.

7.2.2.1 Banks

Pre-MiFID: This exception was for 'money held . . . by an approved bank . . . in an account with itself', although this 'is not an absolute exception from the client money rules' (CASS 4.1.2(3), 4.1.6) and FSA recognised that the 'firm . . . should be able to account to all of its clients for amounts held on their behalf at all times. A bank account . . . in the name of the client would generally be sufficient. When money from clients . . . is held in a pooled account, this account should be clearly identified as an account for clients. The firm should also be able to demonstrate that an amount owed to a specific client . . . can be reconciled with . . . that individual's client balance . . . at any time. Similarly, where that money is reflected only in a firm's bank account with other banks (nostro accounts), the firm should be able to reconcile amounts owed to that client' (CASS 4.1.5). This exemption was necessary because:

---

[44] FSA CP 06/14, para. 10.10.

Money, when paid into a bank ceases altogether to be the money of the principal . . . [I]t is the money of the banker, who is bound to return an equivalent . . . sum . . . [I]t is the banker's money . . . [and] he makes what profit he can, which profit he retains to himself . . . ; he is guilty of no breach of trust in employing it; he is not answerable to the principal if he puts it into jeopardy, if he engages in a hazardous speculation . . . but he is . . . answerable for the amount because he has contracted . . . to repay . . . a sum equivalent.[45]

Indeed, even if it designated the money is held in a trust account, the bank is not holding it subject to an enforceable trust unless held in a segregated account with a third party bank such that the debt owed from that bank is held in trust.[46] As a result, '[w]here a bank . . . holds money . . . it does so as the clients' banker and such money is not subject to the Regulations. However, where . . . [the bank] deposits money received from clients with another . . . bank, rather than with itself, the . . . Regulations apply . . . and the money must be treated as . . . client money',[47] and, similarly, when 'passed to a third party to effect a transaction'.[48] Hence, the statement at the beginning of this paragraph that this 'is not an absolute exemption'.

MiFID: This exemption continues under the Pre-MiFID Rules, CASS 4, and the MiFID Rules, CASS 7, are identical in their effect (CASS 7.1.8–7.1.11).

7.2.2.2   Opt-out

Pre-MiFID: Here, 'money is not client money when a firm . . . holds that money on behalf of a market counterparty or intermediate customer . . . and . . . has obtained written acknowledgement . . . that . . . the money will not be subject to the protections conferred by the client money rules', although with non-ISD business (cf. 4.2.I(2)) a one-way notice from the firm was sufficient (CASS 4.1.8–4.1.14). However, 'When a firm transfers client money to another . . . the firm must not enter into an [opt-out] agreement . . . in relation to that client money' (CASS 4.1.13) because '[t]he fiduciary obligations of the firm holding client money on trust . . . would indicate that it should not contract out of segregation when passing money on'.[49]

MiFID: The Pre-MiFID Rules, CASS 4, continue to allow an opt-out but only with the written acknowledgement of the Professional Client or Eligible Counterparty (CASS 4.1.8–4.1.12). There is no permitted opt-out from the MiFID Rules, CASS 7.

---

[45] *Foley* v. *Hill* (1848) 2 HL Cas 28 at 36–7.
[46] *Space Investments* v. *Canadian Imperial Bank* [1986] WLR 1072; *In* Re *Goldcorp Exchange Ltd.* [1995] 1 AC 74; *Bishopsgate Investment Management Ltd.* [1995] Ch 211; *Fortex* v. *MacIntosh* [1998] 3 NZLR 171.
[47] The Financial Services (Client Money) Regulations 1991, SIB, 1.02(4).
[48] SFA BN 329, 20 June 1996.   [49] SIB CP 61, March 1992, para. A2.

7.2.2.3 DvP

Pre-MiFID: As an analogue to the custody rules (7.1.2.2), 'Money need not be treated as client money in respect of a delivery versus payment transaction through a commercial settlement system if it is intended that . . . money . . . will be due . . . within one business day . . . unless the delivery or payment by the firm does not occur by the close of business on the third business day following the date of payment or delivery of the investments by the client' (CASS 4.1.15). In this event there was a real risk of the client being out of both its cash and its securities.

MiFID: This exemption continues in both the Pre-MiFID Rules, CASS 4, and the MiFID Rules, CASS 7 (CASS 7.2.8).

7.2.2.4 Affiliates

Pre-MiFID: Like the custody rules (7.1.2.3), the money of affiliates was not client money 'unless . . . the firm has been notified . . . that the money belongs to a client of the affiliate' (CASS 4.1.18).

MiFID: This exemption continues in the Pre-MiFID Rules, CASS 4, but not in the MiFID Rules, CASS 7, except in respect of non-MiFID Business for which the firm has elected to comply with the MiFID Rules (CASS 7.1.12, 7.1.13). This, however, is not consistent with FSA's Policy Statement since '[i]t was our intention to maintain the status quo'[50] so that in practice FSA treats the exemption as applying to CASS 7.

7.2.2.5 Firm's money

Pre-MiFID: 'Money is not client money when it becomes properly due and payable to the firm for its own account', 'for example, because the firm acted as principal [in selling investments to the client] . . . or . . . acting as agent, has itself paid for securities in advance of receiving the purchase money from its client' or 'a client's obligation . . . that is secured by that client's asset, crystallises, and the firm realises the asset' (CASS 4.1.19, 4.1.21, 4.1.23). Moreover, 'fees and commissions payable by customers [become] "due and payable" [when] . . . (a) they have been accurately calculated and are in accordance with the formula or basis previously disclosed to the client . . . or (b) five business days have elapsed since a statement showing the amount . . . has been dispatched to the client . . . or (c) the precise amount . . . has been agreed by the client' (CASS 4.1.20). Beyond this, '[t]he regulations do not . . . lay down when money . . . become[s] "due and payable" . . . This will depend on the terms of the contract interpreted in the light of market custom.'[51]

---

[50] FSA PS 07/2, para. 8.21.
[51] The Financial Services (Client Money) Regulations 1987, SIB, 7 October 1987, 2.1(2).

MiFID: This continues to be the position under both the Pre-MiFID Rules, CASS 4, and the MiFID Rules, CASS 7 (CASS 7.2.9–7.2.11).

7.2.2.6 Fiduciaries

Pre-MiFID: The client money rules did not apply to regulated collective investment scheme depositaries, even though the custody rules applied in part (7.1.2.4), and they applied in limited respects to trustees, notwithstanding their fiduciary duties at general law (CASS 1.4.6, 1.4.8, 4.1.2(4), 4.1.27–4.1.29).

MiFID: This continues to apply under the Pre-MiFID Rules, CASS 4, but does not appear in the MiFID Rules (18.3.4).

7.2.2.7 Collateral and absolute title transfer

Pre-MiFID: If money was transferred to the firm or into its control as collateral, for example in respect of margin on derivatives transactions, and the firm was given some form of legal or equitable charge, i.e. 'the right to use the assets on a . . . default', being 'a bare security interest . . . [then] the firm must comply with the . . . client money rules' (CASS 3.1.3, 3.1.4). If, however, 'the firm is given a right to use the asset' and 'the client has transferred to the firm the legal title and associated rights' 'subject only to an obligation to return equivalent assets . . . upon satisfaction of the client's obligations to the firm', then the client money rules did not apply and, instead, 'a differing level of regulatory protection' required only that the 'firm . . . must ensure that it maintains adequate records to enable it to meet any future obligations including the return of equivalent assets to the client' (CASS 3.1.5, 3.1.7, 3.2.2). This rule operated in the same way in respect of custody of client assets (7.1.2.6).

MiFID: These rules, CASS 3, continue to apply generally (CASS 1.2.7 (3A)) and, in addition, the use of total title transfer is accepted under the MiFID Rules, CASS 7. 'Where a client transfers full ownership of money to a firm for the purpose of securing or otherwise covering present or future, actual or contingent or prospective obligations, such money should no longer be regarded as client money' (CASS 7.2.3). This can be used to replace the Pre-MiFID opt-out by Eligible Counterparties and Professional Clients (7.2.2.2) provided that 'the arrangement . . . [is] properly documented . . . and . . . involve[s] good faith collateral'[52] and is structured so as not to involve the unlicensed acceptance of deposits (3.2.1.5). As with the equivalent provision for investments (7.1.2.6), although this can be used with Retail Clients, in most cases it may be doubted whether the fact that, as a result, 'the client no longer has a proprietary claim over the money and the firm can deal with it on its own right' thus destroying any

---

[52] FSA CP 06/14, para. 10.13.

client money protection, would be accepted by FSA as 'treating the customer fairly' (9.2) (CASS 7.2.6, 7.2.7). In this respect, FSA concludes 'that such arrangements may be used for retail clients . . . only in very limited circumstances, for example stocklending . . . We would be concerned if firms tried to use th[is] . . . to avoid providing client money protection to retail clients. However, we do not propose any specific rules to counter this risk at this stage, but will be sensitive to firms seeking to push the envelope in this way.'[53]

The reference to collateral is included because another FSA MiFID rule, to the same effect as a custody rule (7.1.2.6), provides that 'Money is not client money where the firm carries on business in its own name on behalf of the client where that is required by the very nature of the transaction' (CASS 7.2.2) and Recital 26 to MiFID, from which this is copied out, concludes the sentence with the words 'for example stocklending'. The provision is extremely unclear, but if it applies to stocklending it must also apply to repo's and on-exchange derivatives dealing which is invariably structured as principal-to-principal contracts between the clearing house and the firm, and between the firm and the client. So, here, collateral given/payments made to the firm, even though not by absolute title transfer, would seem not to be 'client money', presumably on the policy rationale that, otherwise, the pooling of client money would prevent any payments being made to the clearing house since one client's money would potentially be used to fund another client's obligations (7.2.3.2, 7.2.3.5).

7.2.2.8 Passported branches

Pre-MiFID: As with the custody rules (7.1.2.8), under the ISD, UK branches of passported firms were subject to the client money rules of the Home State (CASS 1.2.3(2), 4.1.3).

MiFID: This continues to be the position.

7.2.3 Procedures

The client money rules are a series of procedures designed to support, in practice, the effectiveness of the trust (7.2.1).

7.2.3.1 Segregation

Pre-MiFID: 'A firm must . . . hold client money separate from the firm's money' and could only 'hold [other] money . . . in a client bank account . . . [if]: (1) a minimum sum required to open the account . . . or (2) money temporarily in the account in accordance with . . . [the] mixed remittance [rule] . . . or (3) interest' (CASS 4.3.3, 4.3.5).

---

[53] Ibid, paras. 10.15, 10.16.

MiFID: The Pre-MiFID Rules, CASS 4, continue identically and, similarly, under the MiFID Rules, CASS 7, 'A firm must take the necessary steps to ensure that client money . . . is held in an account . . . identified separately from any account used to hold money belonging to the firm' (CASS 7.4.11).

7.2.3.2 Payment in and out

Pre-MiFID: 'If a firm is liable to pay money to a client [for example it bought as principal securities from the client], it must as soon as possible, and no later than one business day after the money is due and payable . . . pay it into a client bank account . . . or . . . pay it to . . . the client' (CASS 4.3.24). Under the so-called 'normal approach', client money has in all cases to be '[paid] in as soon as possible, and in any event no later than the next business day after receipt'. It can only be paid out: '(1) to the client, or a duly authorised representative . . . or (2) to a third party on the instructions of the client . . . [or] transferred to the third party in the course of effecting a transaction . . . or (3) into a bank account of the client . . . or (4) to the firm itself, when it is due and payable [7.2.2.5]' (CASS 4.3.10, 4.3.99. See also 4.3.19–4.3.25). The so-called 'alternative approach', with FSA's consent, allowed 'client money [to be] received into and paid out of a firm's own bank account; consequently systems and controls that are capable of monitoring the client money flows are required so that the firm can perform the daily client money calculation accurately [7.2.3.5]. A firm that adopts the alternative approach will segregate client money into a client bank account on a daily basis, after having performed the client money calculation to determine what the client money requirement was at the close of the previous business day' (CASS 4.3.9. See also 4.3.12). In any event, client money could only be transferred to 'another person, such as an exchange, a clearing house or an intermediate broker . . . if:

(1) the firm transfers the client money . . . for the purpose of a transaction for a client . . . or . . . to meet a client's obligations to pay collateral (for example, . . . margin . . .); and
(2) . . . a private customer . . . has been notified that the client money may be transferred to the other person. (CASS 4.3.30)

The firm had to notify the recipient to segregate such monies from the firm's own and 'acknowledge in writing that . . . no . . . right of set-off [is] to be exercised. . . . in respect of any sum owed to that person on any other account' and, where the recipient was outside the UK, give a risk warning to the client (CASS 4.3.52, 4.3.61).

MiFID: The Pre-MiFID Rules, CASS 4, are identical. Under the MiFID Mules, CASS 7, 'A firm, on receiving any client money, must promptly place the money into one or more accounts' and can operate the normal or alternative approach (CASS 7.4.1, 7.4.14–7.4.31). It can pay out client money only in the same circumstances as the Pre-MiFID Rules (CASS 7.2.15, 7.5.2, 7.8.2).

7.2.3.3 Interest

Pre-MiFID: Absent agreement to the contrary, interest earned on a client money account had to be paid to a Private Client (CASS 4.3.26–4.3.28), which reflected the trust law position.

MiFID: The Pre-MiFID Rules, CASS 4, continue and the MiFID Rules, CASS 7, have the same effect (CASS 7.2.14).

7.2.3.4 Client bank accounts

Pre-MiFID: In selecting and continuing with a bank, including a group bank, the firm had to 'take reasonable steps to establish that the bank is appropriate' and, with group banks, 'disclose [to the client] in writing . . . that it . . . intends to hold client money with [such] a bank . . . and . . . the identity of the bank' (CASS 4.3.42, 4.3.46). This was because '[i]n most circumstances, clients will probably correctly assume that their money is held at a bank, separate and protected from the effects of financial difficulties at the firm'.[54] The appropriateness test had been introduced in the mid-1990s following the collapse of BCCI[55] and was intended to be 'an appropriate and continuing risk assessment . . . to ensure that the risks inherent in depositing client money . . . are minimised'[56] such that 'a firm should consider taking into account . . .

(1) the capital of the bank;
(2) the amount of client money placed, as a proportion of the bank's capital and deposits;
(3) the credit rating of the bank . . . and
(4) . . . the level of risk in the investment and loan activities undertaken by the bank and its affiliate[s].

The firm had to also 'consider diversifying placements of client money with more than one bank' (CASS 4.3.44, 4.3.47). The accounts had to be with an 'approved bank' as defined, unless outside the UK for the purpose of settlement or income distribution and 'because of the applicable law or market practice of that overseas jurisdiction, it is not possible to hold the client money . . . with an approved bank' (CASS 4.3.34, 4.3.40). The bank had to 'acknowledge . . . in writing . . . that all money standing to the credit of the account is held by the firm as trustee [7.2.1] . . . and that the bank is not entitled to combine the account with any other account or to exercise any right of set-off . . . in respect of any sum owed to it on any other account of the firm' and the client had to receive notice of the risks when money was held with a non-UK approved bank (CASS 4.3.48, 4.3.56).

---

[54] SIB CP 53, April 1991, para. 9.   [55] See *BCCI*, Truell and Gurwin, Bloomsbury, 1992.
[56] SFA BN 297, 20 December 1995, rule 4–53(1).

Having knowledge of the trust through the notice, '[t]he fact that [banks] . . . can be expected to play their part in ensuring that such money is not misused is a really important additional safeguard for investors'.[57] As a result, under the 1986 FSAct, and the provision was carried into FSMA, the Government refused to clarify whether the bank would be liable as a constructive trustee for wrongful payments by the firm notwithstanding that the law was 'in . . . a muddle'[58] and merely codified the then likely state of the law:

> An institution with which an account is kept does not incur any liability as constructive trustee if money is wrongfully paid from the account, unless the institution permits a payment
>
> (a) with knowledge that is wrongful; or
> (b) having deliberately failed to make enquiries in circumstances in which a reasonable or honest person would have done so. (FSMA 139(2))

MiFID: The Pre-MiFID Rules, CASS 4, continue identically. The MiFID Rules, CASS 7, also require 'due skill, care and diligence in the selection, appointment and periodic review of the . . . bank' and the same due diligence as the Pre-MiFID Rules (CASS 7.4.7–7.4.10) and the use of an approved bank (albeit with a different definition) which must acknowledge the trust status of the account in the same way as before. Alternatively, the firm can use a 'qualified money market fund' (CASS 7.4.1–7.4.6, 7.4.11, 7.8.1) in which case the '[f]irm will . . . be converting the assets from "money" to "financial instruments" and will need to have regard to any relevant [client asset rules (7.1)]'.[59] The Retail Client risk warnings (8.4.7.2) are, however, different:

> A firm that holds client money for a retail client must provide that client with the following information:
>
> (a) if applicable:
>   (i) that the . . . client money . . . may be held by a third party on behalf of the firm;
>   (ii) the responsibility of the firm under the applicable national law for any acts or omissions of the third party; and
>   (iii) the consequences for the firm of the insolvency of the third party . . .
> (d) if . . . accounts that contain . . . client money are . . . subject to the law of a jurisdiction other than that of an EEA State, an indication that the rights of the client . . . may differ accordingly;

---

[57] Parl. Deb., House of Lords, 23 July 1986, Minister, col. 345.
[58] Re *Montague's Settlement Trust* [1987] Ch 264. See also *Karak Rubber Co.* v. *Burden* (No. 2) [1972] 1 AER 1210; *Rowlandson* v. *National Westminster Bank Ltd.* [1978] 3 AER 370; *Baden, Delvaux* v. *Société Générale* [1983] BCLC 1.   [59] FSA CP 06/14, para. 10.25.

(e) ... information about the existence and the terms of any security interest ... which the firm has ... over the ... client money, or any right of set-off it holds in relation to the ... client money; and

(f) if applicable, that a depositary may have a security interest ... over, or right of set-off in relation to th[e] ... money ...

A firm that holds ... client money for a professional client must provide that client with the information in paragraphs ... (d), (e) and (f). (COBS 7.1.7)

7.2.3.5 Reconciliations

Pre-MiFID: On a daily basis the firm had to perform a detailed 'client money calculation', '[t]he purpose of ... [which] is ... for the normal approach [7.2.3.2] to act as a check that the amount of client money that is segregated at banks and third parties is sufficient to meet the firm's obligations to its clients on a daily basis [and] for the alternative approach, to calculate the appropriate amount of client money to be segregated at banks and third parties which is sufficient to meet a firm's obligations to its clients on a daily basis' (CASS 4.3.65. See also: 4.3.66–4.3.97). This was introduced originally because with all clients' money pooled in one or more client money bank accounts and settlement and margining of exchange-traded derivatives to the clearing house on the basis of the firm's net position, it was impossible to ensure that one client's money was not used to settle/margin another's transaction. It was also to avoid, with securities transactions, the need for the firm to monitor and ensure real-time that one client's money was only transferred in respect of the movement of particular stock. The regulators realised from the beginning of the client money regime that 'the gravest difficulties would be experienced if firms attempted to comply with the ... regulations in their pristine form and the expense and work involved in attempting to do so would be disproportionate'.[60] Hence:

> Each business day, a firm that adopts the normal approach ... must ... check whether ... the appropriate balance on the firm's client bank accounts, as at the close of business on the previous business day, was at least equal to the client money requirement ... as at the close of business on that day ...
>
> Each business day, a firm that adopts the alternative approach ... must ensure that the aggregate balance on the firm's client bank accounts, as at the close of business on that business day is at least equal to the client money requirement ... as at the close of business on the previous business day. (CASS 4.3.66(1), 4.3.67)

---

[60] The Financial Services (Client Money) Regulations 1987, SIB, Explanatory Memorandum, 49.

The 'client money requirement' reflected the overall sum due to the client, ignoring this pooling, being cash held in securities and derivatives positions (CASS 4.3.71–4.3.86).

MiFID: The Pre-MiFID Rules, CASS 4, continue to the same effect and under the MiFID Rules, CASS 7, since '[a] firm must maintain its records and accounts in a way that ensures their accuracy'; '[c]arrying out internal reconciliations of records and accounts of the entitlement of each client . . . with the records and accounts of the client money the firm holds . . . should be one of the steps a firm takes' and, for this purpose, the FSA adopted a more or less identical method to the Pre-MiFID Rules (CASS 7.6.2, 7.6.6(1), (3)). However, under the MiFID regime, the detailed 'client money requirement' provisions are 'Guidance rather than Rules [2.5.8] . . . provid[ing] . . . flexibility for firms . . . [to] perform . . . the calculations/reconciliations . . . reasonably required in all the circumstances . . . as often as is necessary to ensure the safeguarding of clients'. . . funds'.[61]

7.2.3.6   CFTC part 30 exemption order

In effect, the Pre-MiFID regime (FSA PM CASS 4.3.106A, 4.3.107–4.3.111) continues under MiFID.[62]

[61] FSA CP 06/14, paras. 10.7, 10.24.
[62] FSA PS 07/2, paras. 8.31–8.32; FSA CP 07/9, paras. 20.2–20.5.

PART IV
Conduct of business

8
Client classification and client documentation

8.1 Regulatory policy

Pre-MiFID: Regulators have always taken the view that 'the professional will be deemed capable of looking after his own interests'[1] and, so, subject to a lower level of protection, the issues being, first, how to define a professional and, second, how low that level should be in contrast to retail clients. At one end of the spectrum, the 1939 PFI (2.3) exempted from registration any firm whose 'main business . . . consists of . . . effecting any transaction with a person whose business involves the acquisition and disposal or the holding of securities . . . as a principal'[2] because, as a matter of policy, there was 'the necessity of avoiding any undue interference with . . . legitimate "finance" in the City of London . . . [by] banks, merchant bankers, discount houses, issuing and finance houses' in the Primary Market.[3] The policy under the 1986 FSAct was, however, rather different in that '[c]ertain basic safeguards . . . should apply to everyone and are essential if the UK is to be seen as a clean place to do business',[4] '[t]he . . . distin[ction being] . . . between professional and non-professional investors, for purposes of determining the level of protection to be afforded'.[5] SIB ended up with a threefold classification under which it is 'not . . . appropriate to apply Conduct of Business Rules which are designed to protect individuals and institutions in their capacity as customers of . . . firms to the relationship between market professionals acting as competitors and professional counterparties. Business customers are institutional investors and also those individuals who by virtue of their experience can be regarded as experts . . . The . . . rules . . . provide . . . protections for business customers . . . Private customer protections are not . . . extended to this category of customers. They will be fully able to determine what, if any, additional protections they require, in . . . the[ir] . . . contractual arrangements with the . . . firm . . . This approach has been adopted . . . to avoid impeding business . . . between sophisticated investors. The full range of . . . protection is

---

[1] Regulation of Investment Business – The New Framework, SIB and MIBOC, December 1985, para. 3.32.   [2] 1939 PFI 15; 1959 PFI 16.   [3] Bodkin Report, para. 45.
[4] Parl. Deb., House of Commons, Standing Committee E, 4 March 1986, Minister, col. 460.
[5] Regulation of Investment Business – The New Framework, SIB and MIBOC, December 1985, para. 3.31.

... extended to private customers.'⁶ A virtually identical approach was carried over into FSMA which recognised, in both FSA's Objectives (2.5.1) and rule-making powers, that there should be an 'appropriate degree of protection' for consumers and professional clients (FSMA 5, 138), which FSA reflected in 'a three . . . -way classification scheme identifying professional, intermediate and retail categories . . . correspond[ing] to: dealers, market-makers and arrangers; institutions; and private clients . . . with conduct of business requirements better tailored to their needs'.[7] 'The key feature distinguishing intermediate customers from private customers is that intermediate customers will generally either have appropriate expertise in-house, or will have the means to pay for professional advice where needed.'[8]

MiFID 'adopt[s] the same broad regulatory objective . . . to allow for the tailoring of regulatory requirements according to the knowledge and experience of clients through the use of client categories. MiFID introduces two main categories of clients (retail clients and professional clients), and a separate and distinct third category for a limited range of business (eligible counterparties). Different levels of regulatory protection attach to each category.'[9] There is, as explained in 8.3, substantial but not complete overlap between the categories of Market Counterparty and Eligible Counterparty, Intermediate Customer and Professional Client, and Private Customer and Retail Client; and the level of protection afforded to each is summarised in Figure 7. For the application of the client categorisation rules, see 4.2(l).

8.2 'Clients' for regulatory purposes

8.2.1 The definition of 'client'

Pre-MiFID: A 'client' was 'any person with or for whom a firm undertakes . . . any regulated activity', with exclusions in the context of corporate finance (15.3) and trustees (18.3.3), but 'includes . . . a potential customer', for example a recipient of a financial promotion (10.5) and a Market Counterparty, in each case whether located in or outside the UK. Although '[t]he concept of "customer" is not always obvious',[10] it 'means a person who wishes to buy or sell investments with or through the firm, or otherwise to have investment services performed for him by the firm, and this is so whether or not there is a customer agreement between the[m] . . . and

---

[6] The Securities Association's Approach to its Regulatory Responsibilities, TSA, July 1987, para. IX.3.
[7] Differential Regulatory Approaches: Future Regulation of Inter-Professional Business, FSA DP, October 1998, para. 2.33.   [8] FSA CP 43, February 2000, para. 2.31.
[9] Implementing MiFID's Client Categorisation Requirements, FSA, August 2006, paras. 2.4, 2.5.
[10] Comments on Proposed Changes to the Rules, AFBD, 26 April 1988, para. 37.

Client classification and client documentation

RULE AREA (with Chapter reference)	MARKET COUNTER PARTY	ELIGIBLE COUNTER PARTY[23]	INTERMEDIATE CUSTOMER	PROFESSIONAL CLIENT	PRIVATE CUSTOMER	RETAIL CLIENT
Infrastructure/ Systems and Controls (5)	Yes[1]	Yes[2]	Yes[1]	Yes[2]	Yes[1]	Yes[2]
Principles (9.1, 9.2)	In part[3]	In part[4]	Yes[3]	Yes[4]	Yes[3]	Yes[4]
Conflicts of Interest (6.3.1)	No[5]	Yes[6]	Yes[5]	Yes[6]	Yes[5]	Yes[6]
Inducements (6.3.2)	No[7]	No[8]	Yes[7]	Yes[8]	Yes[7]	Yes[8]
Client Assets/ Client Money (7.1, 7.2)	Yes[9]	Yes[9], [10]	Yes[9]	Yes[9], [10]	Yes[9]	Yes[9], [10]
Advertising Disclosures (10.5)	No[11]	No[12]	No[11]	Yes[13]	Yes[11]	Yes[13]
Suitability (11.2)	No[14]	No[15]	No[14]	Yes[15]	Yes[14]	Yes[15]
Appropriate- ness (11.4)	–	No[16]	–	Yes[16]	–	Yes[16]
Execution (13)	No[17]	No[18]	Yes[17]	Yes[18]	Yes[17]	Yes[18]
Terms of Business (8.4)	No[19]	No[20]	Yes[19]	Yes[20]	Yes[19]	Yes[20]
Reporting (13.4.2)	No[21]	No[22]	Yes[21]	Yes[22]	Yes[21]	Yes[22]

[1] FSA PM SYSC 1.1.3–1.1.6
[2] SYSC 1.3.2–1.3.8
[3] PRIN 1.2.1, 1.2.2
[4] PRIN 1.2.2, 1.2.5, 4.1.4 (see 9.1.2.1)
[5] FSA PM COB 7.1.1(1)
[6] SYSC 1.3.3, 10.1.1, 10.2.1
[7] FSA PM COB 2.2.1
[8] COBS 1, Ann. 1, Part 1, para. 1.1. But all inducements are conflicts.
[9] CASS 1.2.8(1), 2.1.1, 3.1.1, 4.1.1
[10] CASS 6.1.1(1), 7.1.1(1)
[11] FSA PM COB 3.2.5(1)
[12] COBS 1, Ann. 1, Pt. 1, para. 1.1; COBS 4.1.5 (apart from fair, clear and not misleading communications: see 10.5.1.3)
[13] COBS 4.1.1, 4.1.5. But, see 10.5.2.1.
[14] FSA PM COB 5.2.1(1), (2), 5.3.1(1), (2)
[15] The suitability requirement applies in relation to a 'personal recommendation' to any client, including an Eligible Counterparty which, in that respect, will be a Professional Client unless the recommendation is 'directly related' to a transaction, in which case Eligible Counterparty status applies (see 8.3.3) (COBS 9.2.1(1))
[16] COBS 10.1.1; COBS, Ann. 1, Pt. 1, para. 1.1
[17] FSA PM COB 7.4.1, 7.5.1, 7.6.1, 7.7.1. However, the Inter-professionals Code (FSA PM MAR 3) applied to dealings with a Market Counterparty
[18] COBS 11.1.1; COBS 1, Ann. 1, Pt. 1, para. 1.1. Only the client limit order rule in relation to equities applies to dealings with an Eligible Counterparty
[19] FSA PM COB 4.2.1
[20] COBS 8.1.1, 8.1.4(1); COBS 1, Ann. 1, Pt. 1, para, 1.1
[21] FSA PM COB 8.1.1, 8.2.1
[22] COBS 16.1.1, 16.1.2; COBS 1, Ann. 1, Pt. 1, para. 1.1
[23] The disapplication indicated by 'No' and the limited application of the Principle also apply in favour of transactions between members of regulated markets (COBS 1, Ann. 1, Pt. 1, para. 4.1 and PRIN 4.1.4), and, whereas for Eligible Counterparties, these disapplications apply to MiFID Business (see 4.2.I(2)). FSA 'propose to extend the disapplication of certain COBS rules… to cover non-MiFID business as well' (FSA CP 07/9, para. 15.25)

Figure 7 *Application of rules to different client types*

whether or not the firm is remunerated . . . by a third party; and the person remains a customer as long as there is an acknowledged contractual or other relationship between the person and the firm'.[11]

MiFID: Similarly, a 'client' is 'A person to whom a firm provides . . .

(a) a service in the course of carrying on a regulated activity [4.2.I(1)]; or
(b) in the case of MiFID business or equivalent third country business, an ancillary service [4.2.I(2)].

This 'includes a potential client' (COBS 3.2.1) and, with a trust, the trustee and not the underlying beneficiaries (COBS 3.2.3(3)). During the negotiation of the Level 1 and Level 2 Directives, it appears that FSA did not focus on the fact that, technically, they apply the best execution obligation to OTC dealer markets in fixed income securities (13.2) and, in an attempt to argue its way out of this conclusion, at one point FSA contended that the rules would not apply if the firm, in dealing, was not providing a 'service' and, hence, was not transacting with a 'client'. '[MiFID Business (4.2.I(2))] lists eight types of investment services and activities but does not indicate which are "services" and which are "activities" . . . [S]ome of these businesses may be conducted only by way of investment services . . . for example, portfolio management and investment advice . . . [A] firm could conduct other of the businesses . . . as either . . . services or . . . activities . . . [and this] will, at least in part, depend on the nature of the relationship between the parties . . . [C]entral . . . is the presence (or absence) of a "client" relationship. Criteria indicating that a . . . firm has a client relationship with another person could include:

- the nature of the obligations . . . each . . . has agreed to undertake;
- whether the relationship involves some act or work to be done for the other person, for example:
  - customisation of a particular product or transaction to meet the needs of that other party;
  - where a . . . firm 'works' a transaction . . . or
  - where a . . . firm is providing a facility to the other person such as the facilitation of transactions or providing an opportunity to trade;
- the reasonable expectations of the parties as to their relationship . . .
- whether a . . . firm has agreed to treat a person as a retail or professional client;
- whether the . . . firm holds itself out as providing services; and
- whether the relationship involves fiduciary, agency or similar obligations.

. . . '[D]ealing on own account' could be an investment service; but where there is no client relationship, dealing on own account could be a

---

[11] The Financial Services (Glossary and Interpretation) Rules and Regulations 1989, SIB, def. of 'customer'.

pure investment activity . . . [T]here is a strong presumption that a . . . firm is providing an investment service where it is conducting . . . [MiFID B]usiness . . . for a retail client.[12]

FSA then realised that this could result in, effectively, a fourth category of non-clients to whom no MiFID conduct obligations were owed, which is clearly not the intention of MiFID and, rationalising its way out of the best execution obligation on the basis of an absence of a 'client order' in fixed income markets (13.2.2), implicitly withdrew its earlier view:

> determining whether a person is in the circumstances a 'client' of the firm may require enquiry into a wider range of factual circumstances . . . We consider that a dealing firm which for example, provides ongoing access to its published quotes or request for quote service may thereby be at least providing a service which could be described as facilitation of transactions or providing an opportunity to trade. In these circumstances the firm will be required to provide a range of client facing protections to such persons who will be clients.[13]

The fact that that was not MiFID Business at all (4.2.1(2)) was ignored. Instead, the European Commission killed the argument on the basis that '[w]e do not consider it fruitful to distinguish between . . . cases where the service is being provided to a client and . . . where an activity is simply being carried on with a person who is not a client. The Level 1 Directive provides no clear criterion for distinguishing between these two situations.'[14]

8.2.2 Clients acting as agent

Pre-MiFID: At general law where a principal acts through a disclosed agent, say a fund manager, whether the principal is named or not, he can enforce the contract and, conversely an undisclosed agent is liable on the contract.[15] It follows that, at least with the disclosed agent and probably also with the undisclosed agent, the 'client' 'with or for whom [the] firm undertakes . . . regulated activity' (8.2.1), for example selling investments or giving advice, is, as well as the agent through whom the activity is conducted and with whom the firm deals directly, the principal to whom the firm provides the regulated activity indirectly. A fund manager dealing with a broker–dealer liked this result (since he wanted the broker–dealer to, for example, owe best execution to the fund manager's client), but the broker–dealer did not since he wanted to treat the manager, being a Market Counterparty, as his sole 'client' and not subject to any best execution obligation. The broker–dealers won this debate since the policy was 'that clients of [fund managers] . . . should not normally be treated as customers

---

[12] Implementing MiFID's Client Classification Requirements, FSA, August 2006, paras. 4.3–4.5, 4.7.   [13] FSA CP 06/19, paras. 16.25, 16.26.
[14] Commission Working Document ESC-07-2007, para. 1.   [15] *Treitel*, pp. 672–679.

of the firm... unless the parties have contractually agreed otherwise'[16] and thus:

(1) If a firm ('F') is aware that a person ('C1') with or for whom it is conducting designated investment business ... is acting as agent for another person ('C2')... C1, and not C2, is the client of F... if:
   (a) C1 is another firm or an overseas financial services institution; or
   (b) C1 is any other person, provided that avoidance of duties which F would otherwise owe to C2 is not the main purpose of the arrangements...
(2) Paragraph (1) does not apply if F has agreed with C1 in writing to treat C2 as its client. (FSA PM COB 4.1.5)

Using the tax law distinction between evasion and avoidance, the proviso to (b) always applied. This rule applied whether C1 was a so-called introducing broker, placing an order for a transaction with F, or an executing broker which, under exchange rules, 'gives up' the transaction to F for clearing and settlement. But even if paragraph (1) applied, the issue, then, was whether the intermediary was to be classified as a Market Counterparty or as an Intermediate Customer with higher regulatory protections.

MiFID: Although FSA has changed the wording, it has adopted a rule to identical effect (COBS 2.4.3(1), (2), 3.2.3(1)), even though MiFID itself does not contain such a provision, 'because of the strong practical benefits... [and it] is not inconsistent with... MiFID'.[17] In any event, reliance on the agent is always possible, subject to conditions (COBS 2.4.4).

8.3 Client categorisation

Clients must be categorised as well as identified for money laundering risk and any KYC enquiry conducted (11.2.2.1) by the firm or an affiliate as outsourcee (5.2.5). The Pre-MiFID categories applied to all Regulated Activities (4.2.I(1)) and the MiFID categories similarly apply although, here, 'for non-MiFID business... modif[ied definitions] apply'.[18] The Pre-MiFID and MiFID categories substantially overlap and FSA provided some very helpful transitional provisions as at 1 November 2007 (COBS TP 1),[19] although for new clients notifications are required (8.4.7.2).

---

[16] SFA BN 2, 15 April 1991, Part 2, para. 3.1(vii).
[17] Implementing MiFID Client Categorisation Requirements, FSA, August 2006, paras. 5.7, 5.8.   [18] FSA CP 06/19, para. 7.13; FSA CP 07/9, paras. 15.4, 15.5. The transitional ends on 1 July 2008 (Permissions Guide – Update, FSA, September 2007, p. 17).
[19] For the policy, see FSA CP 06/19, paras. 7.63–7.87; FSA CP 07/9, Chapter 15; MiFID Permissions and Notifications Guide, FSA, May 2007, Chapter 2; Permissions Guide – Update, Chapter 5.

8.3.1 Private customers and retail clients

Pre-MiFID: A 'private customer' was 'a client who is not a market counterparty or an intermediate customer, including . . . an individual who is not a firm', although 'A firm may classify as a private customer any client (other than a firm, unless it is an [OEIC: see 3.2.1.9], or an overseas financial services institution) who would otherwise be a market counterparty or an intermediate customer' (FSA PM COB 4.1.14), this being 'a commercial matter between the parties. It is for a firm to determine whether they want the business if a customer chooses to insist on extra regulatory protection.'[20]

MiFID: Similarly 'A retail client is a client who is not a professional client or an eligible counterparty', although:

> A firm must allow a professional client or eligible counterparty to request re-categorisation as a client that benefits from a higher degree of protection.
>
> It is the responsibility of a professional client or eligible counterparty to ask for a higher degree of protection when it deems it is unable to properly assess or manage the risks involved [i.e. vis-à-vis its underlying clients].
>
> A firm may, either on its own initiative or at the request of a client . . . treat as a . . . retail client a . . . per se eligible counterparty [8.3.3.1, 8.3.3.2] . . . [or] a per se professional client [8.3.2.1–8.3.2.7] . . . [and if this is] in relation to MiFID business or equivalent third country business [4.2.I(2), 4.2.III] . . . the client . . . [must] enter into a written agreement with the firm . . . specify[ing] the scope of the re-categorisation, such as whether it applies to one or more particular services or transactions . . . or . . . products . . . or . . . rules. (COBS 3.6.1, 3.7.1–3.7.3, 3.7.5, 3.7.7)

'A firm must . . . prior to the provision of services, inform a client . . . about . . . any right a client has to request a different categorisation' (COBS 3.3.1(2), see also 3.3.2), although it does not have to agree to it. The 'written agreement . . . is not . . . positive consent . . . [A] one-way written notice [8.4.7.2] . . . to the client would be enough.'[21]

8.3.2 Intermediate customers and professional clients

8.3.2.1 Government bodies

Pre-MiFID: This was defined as 'a local authority or public authority' the latter 'referr[ing], in England, to bodies set up to run state-owned enterprises or to administer state-controlled activities (such as the provision of public health care) . . . [and] fund holders'.[22] 'Whilst some [in both

---

[20] FSA CP 57, July 2000, para. 4.68. [21] CP 06/19, p. 37.
[22] FSA CP 57, July 2000, para. 4.37.

categories] undoubtedly have the skills and resources necessary to deal as market counterparties, this is not the case for all of them . . . However there is nothing to stop those authorities that do not . . . need the protections afforded by the intermediate customer category from negotiating an opt-up to market counterparty status [under 8.3.3.3] if they believe it is in their interest.'[23]

MiFID: Although all but a 'regional government' are, alternatively, to be categorised as an Eligible Counterparty (8.3.3.1), 'a national or regional government, a public body that manages public debt, a central bank, an international or supra-national institution (such as the World Bank, the IMF, the ECB, the EIB) or another similar international organisation' is a Professional Client (COBS 3.5.2(3)).

8.3.2.2 Corporations

Pre-MiFID: To be an Intermediate Customer, a corporation (including a limited liability partnership) either had to be 'listed or admitted to trading on any EEA Exchange . . . [or] on the primary board of any IOSCO member country official exchange' (so that it was 'unnecessary for the[m] . . . to receive extra statutory protection . . . as private customers . . . when they already use public markets to access funds and should have the resources to take advice')[24] or 'has (or any of whose holding companies or subsidiaries has) (or has had at any time during the previous two years) called up share capital or net assets of at least £5m (or its equivalent in any other currency . . .)' (FSA PM GLOSSARY, def. of 'intermediate customer'). FSA's view was that 'a size-based test is . . . reasonable . . . on the grounds that an entity with greater resources is more likely to be in a position to buy in any expertise . . . that it needs. It is preferable to an approach based on a more subjective assessment of a corporate customer's expertise',[25] while 'companies with little asset-backing are as much in need of protection as individuals with limited resources'.[26]

MiFID uses a different size-based test under which the corporation itself (and not an affiliate)[27] must 'meet . . . two of the following . . . balance sheet total of €20,000,000; net turnover of €40,000,000; own funds of €2,000,000' (COBS 3.5.2(2)). The terms 'balance sheet total' and 'net turnover' have the meaning in the 4th Company Law Directive; and with 'own funds' '[i]t is not our view that firms should have to undertake an "own funds" calculation as defined in the . . . BCD . . . [W]e . . . leave it to

---

[23] Ibid, para. 4.35. [24] FSA CP 57, July 2000, para. 4.44.
[25] FSA CP 43, February 2000, para. 2.33. [26] FSA CP 57, July 2000, para. 4.52.
[27] However, FSA 'proposes . . . that clients should be assessed on a "group basis" for all non-MiFID business' (FSA CP 07/9, para. 15.21).

firms to determine an appropriate measure analogous to "own funds" [in the BCD]'.[28] On this basis the measure becomes paid up share capital and reserves and other long term capital funding. However, for non-MiFID Business, FSA will allow the Pre-MiFID size test, on the basis of £10m, or 'a large undertaking that meets (or any of whose holding companies or subsidiaries meets) two of . . . (i) a balance sheet total of EUR 12,500,000; (ii) a net turnover of EUR 25,000,000; an average number of employees during the year of 250'[29] because, otherwise, 'more clients would need to be categorised as retail because of the higher [MiFID] quantitative thresholds'.[30]

8.3.2.3 Special purpose vehicles/institutional investors

Pre-MiFID: This was defined as 'a body corporate, explicitly established for the purpose of securitising assets, whose sole purpose . . . is to . . .

(a) issu[e] . . . investments . . . ; [or]
(b) redeem . . . or terminat[e] or repurchase[e] (whether with a view to reissue or cancellation) an issue . . . of . . . investments . . . ; [or]
(c) enter . . . into transactions or terminat[e] . . . transactions involving . . . investments in connection with the issue, redemption, termination or repurchase of . . . investments. (FSA PM GLOSSARY, def. of 'intermediate customer')

MiFID includes SPVs in a wider category of 'an . . . institutional investor whose main activity is to invest in financial instruments . . . or designated investments . . . This includes entities dedicated to the securitisation of assets or other financing transactions' (COBS 3.5.2(4)) 'and . . . UK private equity funds'.[31] MiFID includes a second category of 'any other institutional investor' which does not have to have a 'main activity' and, therefore, can invest on an ad hoc basis, as long as it is 'an entity required to be authorised or regulated to operate in the financial markets' (COBS 3.5.2(1)(i)). In relation to this second category 'firms asked [FSA] for guidance . . . and urged that it should be interpreted widely to allow certain firms who might not otherwise meet the . . . criteria for professional clients to be treated as . . . professionals', although FSA would only respond 'that where the Directive has not defined a particular term, firms should take a purposive approach'.[32] Private/personal holding companies would therefore fall within this category, together with hedge fund managers.[33]

---

[28] FSA CP 06/19, paras. 7.37, 7.38. See also Implementing MiFID Client Categorisation Requirements, FSA, August 2006, p. 34.
[29] FSA CP 07/9, Ann. B, draft COBS 3.5.2(3).   [30] FSA CP 07/9, para. 15.18.
[31] Implementing MiFID Client Categorisation Requirements, FSA, August 2006, p. 34.
[32] FSA CP 06/19, paras 7.46, 7.47.
[33] European Parliament/A5-0114/2004, 25 February 2004, p. 38.

8.3.2.4   Partnerships and unincorporated associations

Pre-MiFID: This had to be 'a partnership or unincorporated association which has (or has had at any time during the previous two years) net assets of at least £5 million (or its equivalent in any other currency . . .) and calculated in the case of a limited partnership without deducting loans owing to . . . the partners' (FSA PM GLOSSARY, def. of 'intermediate customer').

MiFID applies the size test for corporations in 8.3.2.2 to 'large undertakings' (COBS 3.5.2(2)), which include a partnership or unincorporated association, applying 'an appropriate measure analogous to "own funds" '.[34]

8.3.2.5   Trustees

Pre-MiFID: The trust had to be either an occupational pension scheme, small self-administered scheme or stakeholder pension scheme with '(or . . . at any time during the previous two years) . . . at least 50 members . . . and . . . assets . . . of at least £10 million (or its equivalent in any other currency . . .)' or any other trust which 'has (or has had at any time during the previous two years) assets of at least £10 million (or . . . equivalent . . .) before deducting . . . liabilities' (FSA PM GLOSSARY, def. of 'intermediate customer').

Under **MiFID** a trust, whether UK or overseas, is only a Professional Client if it is either 'a pension fund or [its] management company' (COBS 3.5.2(1)(f)), which includes all of the above categories and also SIPPs,[35] or an institutional investor within 8.3.2.3, which it may not always be, or it is expertised up to Professional Client within 8.3.2.8 or it is a 'large undertaking' within 8.3.2.4. Alternatively, 'a pension fund or its management company' can be categorised as an Eligible Counterparty (COBS 3.6.2(5)), although then the firm could agree to opt it down to Professional Client under the rules referred to in 8.3.2.6.

8.3.2.6   Other firms

Pre-MiFID: A firm, whether UK or overseas, usually classified as Market Counterparties (8.3.3.2), was classified as Intermediate in three situations. First, if it was 'acting for an underlying customer', i.e. as agent (8.2.2), and the firm agreed to provide services to it as an Intermediate given that the agent may have needed to use the firm to discharge its own responsibilities to the underlying client for delivering regulatory protections such as best execution although the firm was entitled to refuse to agree. Second, if in respect of any other service the firm 'has not indicated that it is acting on its own behalf' (FSA PM COB 4.1.7(2), (3), 4.1.8(2), (3)). And, third, if the firm with whom they dealt 'offers . . . protections over and above those that are owed to . . . a market counterparty . . . in contract' (FSA PM COB

---

[34] FSA CP 06/19, para, 7.38.   [35] Ibid, para. 7.52.

4.1.8(6)). The second and third cases existed because '[b]efore permitting itself to be treated as market counterparty, a firm should take into account customer protections it will lose as a result. Where a firm believes that it will be unable to fulfil the duties . . . [it] owe[s] to its private customers . . . it should not permit itself to be treated as a market counterparty.'[36] FSA regarded the rule as:

> the least interference in the commercial process . . . [and] supports the natural working of the commercial negotiation process . . . as part of agreeing terms of business . . . FSA does not . . . require that the regulatory protections . . . in the conduct of business rules should be delivered by all firms. Thus firms that opt down . . . may . . . be limiting the number of counterparties prepared to deal with them.[37]

MiFID: Similarly, banks, investment firms and insurance companies, whether UK or overseas, can be classified as Eligible Counterparties (8.3.3.2) or, together with 'any other authorised or regulated financial institutions' (which 'exclude[s] insurance and mortgage intermediaries'),[38] as Professional Clients. However, as with the Pre-MiFID Rule:

> A firm must allow . . . an eligible counterparty to request re-categorisation as a [professional] client . . .
>
> It is the responsibility of a[n] . . . eligible counterparty to ask for a higher level of protection when it deems it is unable to properly assess or manage the risks involved.
>
> A firm may, either on its own initiative or at the request of the client . . . treat as a professional client . . . a client that might otherwise be categorised as a[n] . . . eligible counterparty . . . [and if this is] in relation to MiFID business or equivalent third country business [4.2.I(2), 4.2.III] . . . the client [must] . . . enter . . . into a written agreement with the firm to the effect that it will not be treated as a[n] eligible counterparty . . . [Such] re-categorisation [may be] on:
>
> (1) a general basis;
> (2) a trade by trade basis;
> (3) in respect of one or more specified rules;
> (4) in respect of one or more specified services or transactions; or
> (5) in respect of one of more types of product or transaction.
>   (COBS 3.5.2(1)(a)–(d), 3.7.1–3.7.3, 3.7.5, 3.7.7)

'A firm must . . . prior to the provision of services, inform a client . . . about . . . any right a client has to request a different categorisation' (COBS 3.3.1(2)), although it does 'have the choice whether to . . . provide services on that basis'.[39]

---

[36] SFA Rules Release No. 1, 6 December 1991, Rule 5-4.
[37] FSA CP 57, July 2000, paras. 4.18, 4.20.   [38] FSA CP 06/19, p. 33.
[39] Implementing MiFID Client Categorisation Requirements, FSA, August 2006, p. 34.

In addition, 'a commodity or commodity derivatives dealer . . . [and] a local', whether a UK or overseas entity, are also Professional Clients if 'required to be authorised or regulated to operate' (COBS 3.5.2(1)(g), (h)). They can be an Eligible Counterparty only under 8.3.3.3 whereas, bizarrely, if exempted from regulation they are automatically an Eligible Counterparty as referred to in 8.3.3.2.

8.3.2.7 Packaged products

Pre-MiFID: 'A long-term insurer acting on behalf of its life fund' was an Intermediate Customer in respect of any service other than dealing, arranging and advice, and so was a collective investment scheme in respect of any activity (FSA PM COB 4.1.7(4), 4.1.7A(1)), unless it was an unregulated collective investment scheme which agreed to be treated as a Market Counterparty under 8.3.3.3, or the firm agreed to treat an OEIC as a Private Customer within 8.3.1. In any such case, the firm should have categorised the scheme, rather than the manager or trustee/depositary, as its 'client'.

MiFID has a much simpler categorisation in that, whether UK or overseas, an insurance company and 'a collective investment scheme or the management company of such a scheme' are Professional Clients, although an insurance company and a UCIT can be treated as an Eligible Counterparty (COBS 3.5.2(1)(d), (e), 3.6.2(3), (4)) except that even then the firm can agree to an opt-down under the rules referred to in 8.3.2.6. It follows that for MiFID Business or equivalent third country business (4.2.I(2), 4.2.III) the firm can treat either the scheme or the manager as the 'client', although for other designated investment business (4.2.I(1)) with 'a collective investment scheme that does not have separate legal personality [i.e. a unit trust], that collective investment scheme will be the firm's client' (FSA COBS 3.2.3(4)) which, in practice, makes no difference because it can be categorised as a Professional Client or, if a UCIT, as an Eligible Counterparty.

8.3.2.8 Experts

Pre-MiFID: A Private Customer could be categorised as an Intermediate if 'the firm has taken reasonable care to determine that the client has sufficient experience and understanding to be [so] classified . . . hav[ing] regard to:

(a) the client's knowledge and understanding of the relevant . . . investments and markets, and of the risks involved; [and]
(b) the length of time the client has been active in those markets, the frequency of dealings and the extent to which he has relied on the advice . . . of the firm; [and]
(c) the size and nature of transactions that have been undertaken for the client . . . [and]

(d) the client's financial standing, which may include an assessment of his net worth or of the value of his portfolio.

In addition, the firm had to give 'the client . . . a written warning . . . of the protections . . . that he will lose' and 'give . . . the client sufficient time to consider the implications of being classified as an intermediate . . . and . . . obtain . . . the client's written consent' (FSA PM COB 4.1.9–4.1.11). 'The test is a high one. The individual must "fully" understand the risks involved in the relevant transaction: a general appreciation of what is involved is insufficient. He must be able to form an adequate judgment of his own about the . . . transaction's suitability in the context of his financial position . . . [With] an individual's track record . . . of transactions . . . one needs to consider the circumstances in which the transactions were entered into, for example, was the individual trading on [his] own initiative or were the relevant transactions effectively done by him in complete reliance on advice . . . ?'[40] '[K]nowledge of the client's financial standing is relevant because it points to an ability to buy advice . . . [but] will never, taken alone, be sufficient to allow an opt-up.'[41] The firm can 'take . . . into account . . . any other relevant experience which the customer has . . . to supplement his knowledge or which, coupled with an explanation from the firm, would make it possible for him to have sufficient understanding',[42] but '[a] firm should not treat a customer as expert in options or futures on securities even though he . . . ha[s] sufficient expertise in securities. The customer would have to demonstrate experience in derivatives trading before he could be so classified',[43] although with some instruments there may be a 'rationale for regarding some experience as . . . transferable across markets'.[44] In all cases, the judgment about experience and understanding had to be 'on the basis of information known about the customer and/or any representations made by him',[45] must have been recorded and reviewed at least annually (FSA PM COB 4.1.15, 4.1.16) and the consent 'given . . . without coertion or undue pressure by the firm'.[46]

Under **MiFID** the qualitative test is 'similar'[47] in that the firm has to 'undertake . . . an adequate assessment of the expertise, experience and knowledge of the client that gives reasonable assurance, in light of the nature of the transaction or service envisaged, that the client is capable of making his own investment decisions and understanding the risks involved'. In addition, 'in relation to MiFID business or equivalent third country business [4.2.I(2), 4.2.III], at least two of the following criteria . . . [must be] satisfied:

---

[40] TSA Rules, July 1987, Chapter XII, Guide, para. 5.
[41] FSA CP 57, July 2000, para. 4.59.
[42] SFA BN 168, 1 February 1994, and BN 187, 3 June 1994, Rule 5-5.
[43] SFA BN 168, 1 February 1994.   [44] Further Amendments, SIB, August 1987, p. vii.
[45] IMRO Rules CD, 30 November 1990, Chapter II, Rule 2.1(2)(b).
[46] TSA BN 205, 30 July 1990, Rule 13.03.   [47] FSA CP 06/19, p. 35.

(a) the client has carried out transactions in significant size, on the relevant market at an average frequency of 10 per quarter over the previous four quarters;
(b) the size of the client's financial instrument portfolio . . . including cash deposits exceeds €500,000;
(c) the client works or has worked in the financial sector for at least one year in a professional position, which requires knowledge of the transactions or services envisaged. (COBS 3.5.3(1), (2))[48]

'[I]n assessing the size of a client's portfolio . . . the firm should include only . . . financial instruments . . . and cash deposits'[49] and 'significant size' depends on the market although 'carried out . . . [need not be with the firm itself and does not] include discretionary management decisions in which the client plays no part or has no knowledge'.[50] Sophistication/ expertise without wealth is insufficient. The portfolio need not be with the firm itself.

A separate signature consent is required from the client (8.4.7.1).

The test can be applied to an entity, as well as an individual, but 'the qualitative test should be performed in relation to the person authorised to carry out transactions on its behalf' (COBS 3.5.4), which can be an employee or agent. Generally, the procedure to be followed is similar to the Pre-MiFID Rule in that 'the firm must give the client a clear written warning of the protections and investor compensation rights the client may lose', but FSA requires 'evidence of a positive action (for example, signature . . .)'[51] since 'the client must state in writing . . . that it wishes to be treated as a professional client . . . [and], in a separate document from the contract [8.4], that it is aware of the consequences of losing such protections' (COBS 3.5.3(3)). Such classification must be 'treating the customer fairly' (9.2) and 'if [the firm is itself] initiating such a [client] request . . . for example in their standard terms of business . . . [complying with] the Unfair Contract Terms Act . . . Regulations [8.4.5]'.[52] It follows that the 'firm . . . should be able to demonstrate that they had the necessary information to ensure that the client meets the criteria . . . Firms will be able to rely on the information provided by clients . . . but [a] representation [by the client that it does], on its own, may not be sufficient'[53] if it ought to result in further enquiries. Since under the transitional provisions as at 1 November 2007, an expert Intermediate Customer 'that was correctly categorised' was automatically deemed to be a Professional Client (COBS TP 1, para. 1.2), it follows that procedures adopted under the Pre-MiFID

---

[48] However, since 'the quantitative test establishes a much higher threshold . . . [a]nd certain of the criteria are not relevant in certain industry sectors such as corporate finance [and] venture capital', FSA is 'proposing that the quantitative test should not . . . be applied [to non-]MiFID [regulated activities: 4.2.I(1)]' (FSA CP 07/9, paras. 15.13–15.14).
[49] FSA CP 06/19, para. 7.27.   [50] Ibid, p. 37.   [51] Ibid.   [52] Ibid, p. 35.
[53] Ibid p. 36.

Rules must, subject to also satisfying the quantitative tests ((a), (b) and/or (c) above), also satisfy the MiFID requirements. Once expertised, there is no need for an annual review and FSA 'would not expect firms to proactively monitor this information'[54] since 'clients are responsible for keeping the firm informed about any changes that could affect their current categorisation' and 'If a firm becomes aware that a client no longer fulfils the . . . conditions . . . [it] . . . must [re-categorise the client]' (COBS 3.5.8, 3.5.9).

8.3.2.9 Exchanges and clearing houses

Pre-MiFID: These could be classified as Intermediates or Market Counterparties (FSA PM COB 4.1.8A).

MiFID: This category no longer exists.

8.3.3 Market counterparties and eligible counterparties

Whereas Pre-MiFID a client could be categorised as Market Counterparty in relation to any Regulated Activity (4.2.I(1)) and under the MiFID Rules this remains the case in relation to non-MiFID Business which is Regulated Activity (4.2.I(1)), for MiFID Business[55] a client can only be an Eligible Counterparty in relation to dealing on own account, execution of orders on behalf of clients, reception and transmission of orders and 'directly related' ancillary services (COBS 3.6.1(2)) such as 'investment advice . . . directly related to a transaction with an eligible counterparty'.[56] 'The reason . . . [is] that investor protection . . . is unnecessary in some business relationships, given the . . . nature, knowledge and experience of financial markets that characterise some entities.'[57] For all other services provided by the firm, including advice not linked to a particular transaction and portfolio management, the ECP has to be categorised as a Professional Client and, accordingly, receive relevant investor protections (8.1).

8.3.3.1 Government bodies

Pre-MiFID: These comprised 'a . . . government (including a quasi-governmental body or a government agency) of any country . . .; a central bank or other national monetary authority . . .; a supra-national whose members are other countries or central banks or national monetary authorities; [and] a State investment body, or a body charged with, or intervening in, the management of the public debt' (FSA PM GLOSSARY, def. of 'market counterparty').

---

[54] Ibid, para. 7.59.
[55] This is proposed to be changed so that the categorisation applies to all Regulated Activities (FSA CP 07/9, Ann. B, draft COBS 3.6.1(2)).   [56] FSA CP 06/19, para. 2.13.
[57] CESR/05-291b, August 2005, p. 47.

MiFID: Similarly, all but a State investment body can be categorised as an Eligible Counterparty (and it can potentially be opted-up under 8.3.3.3) or, alternatively, all including such a body can be a Professional Client (8.3.2.1) (COBS 3.6.2(8)–(10)). In any event, the firm can agree to opt-down any such Eligible Counterparty to Professional Clients under the rules referred to in 8.3.2.6.

8.3.3.2 Other firms

Pre-MiFID: '[A]nother firm, or an overseas financial services institution' was a Market Counterparty, unless an Intermediate Customer within 8.3.2.6 or 8.3.2.7 and so was its 'associate . . . if the firm or institution consents' (FSA GLOSSARY, def. of 'market counterparty').

MiFID: A bank, investment firm or insurance company, whether UK or overseas, or UCITs or 'another [EEA] financial institution authorised or regulated' is an Eligible Counterparty, unless it is a Professional Client within 8.3.2.6 or 8.3.2.7 (COBS 3.6.2, 3.6.3), and, if exempt from regulation, so are commodities dealers (being 'persons whose main business consists of dealing on own account in commodities and/or commodity derivatives' who are not part of an investment firm or banking group) and 'locals' (being 'firms which . . . exclusively . . . deal on own account on markets in . . . derivatives . . . or which deal for the account of other members of those markets . . . and which are guaranteed by clearing members') (COBS 3.6.2(7)). Fund managers, themselves owing best execution to their clients, will as a result not accept being categorised as an ECP by the broker–dealers they use to execute transactions (8.1). Accordingly, the Investment Management Association has suggested that its members send to brokers a letter requiring categorisation as a Professional Client.

8.3.3.3 Large intermediates/professionals and large undertakings

Pre-MiFID: Any corporation within 8.3.2.2 with called-up share capital of £10m or 'a body corporate that meets (or any of whose holding companies or subsidiaries meets) two of . . . (i) a balance sheet total of 12.5 million euros . . . (ii) a net turnover of 25 million euros . . . [and] (iii) an average number of employees during the year of 250' or an institution within 8.3.2.1 or a partnership within 8.3.2.4 with net assets of at least £10 million or a trust within 8.3.2.5, could agree to be treated as a Market Counterparty if 'given a written warning . . . that he will loose protections under the regulatory system' and, if a corporation, the firm has 'not been notified . . . that the client objects' or otherwise has given 'written consent' (FSA PM COB 4.1.12, 4.1.13). A regulated collective investment scheme could not so consent (FSA PM COB 4.1.7A(1)), but a corporate was allowed to because '[m]any corporates have sophisticated treasury functions through which they deal for their own account . . . [and] are often well-resourced, employing experienced staff capable of dealing with authorised persons on even terms'.[58] Nonetheless, this opt-up was not available to 'expert private investors . . . [because FSA was] not persuaded that there is . . . any real need'.[59]

MiFID: A risk warning is no longer necessary, only 'in relation to MiFID Business or equivalent third country business [4.2.I(2), 4.2.III] . . . express confirmation from the . . . [client] that it agrees to be treated as an eligible counterparty [8.4.7.1], and the following can be opted-up to Eligible Counterparty: Professional Clients within 8.3.2.1, 8.3.2.2, 8.3.2.3 (only the second category of 'any other institutional investor'), 8.3.2.4, 8.3.2.5 (if either a 'pension fund or its management company' or such second category of institutional investor), 8.3.2.6, 8.3.2.7 and 8.3.2.8 (if an 'undertaking', which includes 'a . . . natural person . . . acting for purposes . . . of his trade, business or profession . . . for example, a local in the derivatives market')[60] (COBS 3.6.4–3.6.6). The ' "express confirmation" . . . mean[s] some form of acknowledgement or active demonstration of consent . . . [rather than] silence or lack of objection'.[61] Although a further rule is expressed generally in relation to Eligible Counterparties, having regard to its origin in MiFID, Article 24(3), it only applies to this category and requires that where the client is located in a Continental Member State, the firm can only opt it up under this category if permitted by the law of that State (COBS 3.6.7). Otherwise, the FSA's categorisation is to be used. Moreover, FSA requires any such classification to 'treat the customer fairly' (9.2) and 'if [the firm is itself] instituting such a [client] request . . . for example in their standard terms of business . . . [to comply with] the Unfair Contract Terms Act 1977 and the Unfair Contract Terms in Consumer Contracts Regulations 1999 [8.4.5]'.[62]

8.4 Terms of business

8.4.1 The requirement

Pre-MiFID: Under the 1939 and 1958 PFI there was no requirement for a licensed dealer or any other firm for that matter to have in place any particular form of agreement with its customer until the 1983 Licensed Dealers Rules (2.3) required a discretionary management contract to contain certain mandatory terms. Building on this the 1986 FSAct regime required the firm to 'disclose the full terms of business dealing to actual and prospective customers'[63] since 'such agreements . . . play a useful role in clarifying the relationship between the firm and the customer . . . especially as regards

---

[58] FSA CP 43, para. 3.7. [59] FSA CP 57, July 2000, paras. 4.55, 4.62.
[60] FSA CP 06/19, paras. 7.29, 7.30. [61] Ibid, p. 38. [62] Ibid, p. 35.
[63] 1985 White Paper, para. 7.15.

disclosure of fees, charges and the capacities in which the firm may act',[64] and the requirement was nuanced as between types of customer and types of service. 'In the case of a professional, business or experienced investor the agreement may be a "terms of business" letter describing the services . . . and the terms on which it is to be provided . . . In other cases, the relationship between the investor and the firm must be governed by a "full customer agreement" which sets out all the salient features of the relationship . . ., the basis for payment, arrangements for the custody of the customer's assets and the periodic information to be provided to the investor. Particular terms are also required of customer agreements governing a portfolio management service to ensure that the basis for the provision of the service is clearly and fully set out to the investor.'[65] This approach was continued by FSA under FSMA and reflected in a Principle that 'A firm must pay due regard to the information needs of its clients, and communicate information to them in a way which is clear, fair and not misleading' (PRIN 2.1.1, Principle 7). The regulatory policy was 'that both a Private and Intermediate Customer needs to know on what basis a firm intends to do business with him. Terms of business or a client agreement set this out' (FSA PM COB 4.2.4). There were two rules. First, 'a [Private] customer must, in good time before . . . business is conducted, be provided with [i.e. sent, with no requirement for customer signature] . . . terms of business, setting out the basis on which . . . business is to be conducted with or for the customer' (FSA PM COB 4.2.5) and 'an intermediate customer . . . must [be] provide[d with] terms of business within a reasonable period of the firm beginning to conduct business with or for the customer' (FSA PM COB 4, Ann. 1, para. (15)), although in both cases there was an exemption for an 'execution-only transaction', i.e. 'a transaction executed . . . upon the specific instructions of a client where the firm does not give advice . . . relating to the merits of the transaction' unless it was a derivatives transaction for a Private Customer (Ibid, para. (13)). And, second, where 'a private customer [was provided with] . . . manag[ement] . . . on a discretionary basis . . . [or derivatives transactions or] stocklending . . . or underwriting [transactions the] . . . terms of business . . . must . . . take the form of a client agreement' 'signed by the client or to which the client has consented in writing' after 'ha[ving] had a proper opportunity to consider the terms' (FSA PM COB 4.2.7).

MiFID: The effect of the rules is similar in that, for both MiFID Business and other Designated Investment Business (4.2.I(1), (2)), even 'providing investment advice',[66] as FSA euphemistically puts it 'the [Pre-MiFID] exceptions . . . are no longer required'.[67] With a Retail Client, 'the firm

---

[64] Regulation of Investment Business – the New Framework, SIB and MIBOC, December 1985, para. 3.33.5.
[65] SIB's Application for Designated Agency Status, February 1987, 15(b).
[66] FSA PS 07/6, para. 11.8.   [67] FSA CP 07/9, para. 11.6.

must enter into a written basic agreement . . . with the client setting out the essential rights and obligations of the firm and the client', the terms being provided 'in good time before a retail client is bound by any agreement' (COBS 8.1.1, 8.1.3(1)) and 'enter into' 'does not distinguish between' 'one-way' and 'two-way' agreements or require that agreements are signed'.[68] Even though the requirement to have terms of business with a Professional Client is not so clearly expressed and, indeed, FSA has stated that '[w]e . . . no longer require firms to provide Terms of Business . . . to Professional Clients',[69] such a requirement actually follows from the additional requirement to 'establish a record that includes the document . . . agreed between [the firm] and a client that sets out the rights and obligations of the parties, and the other terms on which it will provide services to the client' (COBS 8.1.4(1))[70] because without a written customer document the firm would have to agree such terms orally and then record them in a memorandum, which is patently impractical (8.2.1). There are two reasons why the firm would have to agree such terms and write them down. First, in order to manage its own legal risk it would be extraordinary if it took any other view than that it needed to write down the terms on which it is providing services and send them to the Professional Client.[71] And, from the client's perspective, given that MiFID represents generally increased protection for Professional Clients (8.1, see Figure 7), it would seem to be contrary to the Principle of 'treating the customer fairly' and the MiFID principle of 'acting honestly, fairly and professionally in . . . the best interests of the client' (9.2, 9.3) not to do so (cf. COBS 8.1.6), particularly since 'A firm must provide appropriate information in a comprehensible form to a client about . . . the firm and its services' (COBS 2.2.1(a)).

See 4.2(e) for the application of these rules.

8.4.2 Content

Pre-MiFID: Whether terms of business or a client agreement, the document had to 'set out in adequate detail the basis on which [the firm] will conduct . . . business with the customer' and FSA considered this to require 'a provision about each [of 25 mandated] item[s]' and a further five for management contracts (FSA PM COB 4.2.10, 4.2.11). These requirements can be placed into two groups. First, some of them related to the essential terms of the commercial relationship:

(1) When . . . the terms . . . are to come into force . . .
(3) The customer's investment objectives.

---

[68] FSA CP 06/19, para. 13.6. [69] Ibid, para. 13.10.
[70] CESR took the view that this provision requires an agreement with a Professional Client: CESR/05-291b, pp. 27–28.
[71] FSA effectively makes this point in FSA CP 06/19, Ann. 1, para. 6.1.

(4) (a) Any restrictions on (i) the types of . . . investment in which the customer wishes to invest; and (ii) the markets on which the customer wishes transactions to be executed; or
  (b) that there are no such restrictions.
(5) The service the firm will provide.
(6) Details of any payment for services payable by the customer . . .
(7) If the firm is to act as investment manager:
  (a) the arrangements for giving . . . and acknowledging . . . instructions;
  (b) the initial value of the . . . portfolio;
  (c) the initial composition of the . . . portfolio . . .
(8) The arrangements for accounting to the customer for any transaction . . .
(22) How the terms of business may be terminated, including a statement:
  (a) that termination will be without prejudice to the completion of transactions already initiated . . .
  (b) that the customer may terminate . . . by written notice to the firm and when this may take effect;
  (c) that if the firm has the right to terminate . . . it may do so by notice given to the customer, and specifying the minimum notice period . . .
(23) The way in which transactions in progress are to be dealt with upon termination.

And, second, others were disclosures enhancing substantive rule protections:

(2) The firm's [regulatory] status . . . [d]isclosure . . .
(6) . . . whether or not any other payment [than referred to in (6) above] is receivable by the firm (or . . . an . . . associate . . .) in connection with any transaction executed by the firm [6.3.1, 6.3.2, 6.3.3].
(7) If the firm is to act as investment manager . . .
  (d) the period of account for which statements of the portfolio are to be provided [13.4.3.2] . . .
(9) Cancellation and withdrawal [rights in respect of packaged products] [10.5.6.4].
(10) In the case of a private customer, the circumstances, if any, in which the firm . . . may communicate an unsolicited real time financial promotion [10.5.3] . . .
(11) That the firm may act as principal . . . if this is the case [6.3.1].
(12) When a material interest or conflict of interest may or does arise, the manner in which the firm will ensure fair treatment of the customer [6.3.1] . . .
(14) If the firm is to be authorised under the terms of business to undertake transactions with or through the agency of another person with whom the firm has a soft commission agreement, the prior disclosure required by [the rules referred to in 6.3.3].
(15) Where a firm chooses to fulfil its obligations under [the rules referred to in 10.5.1.3] . . . in the terms of business in relation to . . .

(a) warrants or derivatives;
(b) non-readily realisable investments;
(c) penny shares;
(d) securities which may be subject to stabilisation [12.3.7];
(e) stocklending . . .
the relevant risk warning.
(16) That the services to be provided . . . will or may include advice on . . . or executing transactions in . . . unregulated collective investment schemes, if this is the case [10.5.6.1].
(17) That the firm may enter into transactions . . . where the customer will incur obligations as an underwriter or sub-underwriter, if this is the case.
(18) In the case of a private customer, that the firm may undertake stocklending . . . (if this is the case), specifying the assets to be lent, the type and value of relevant collateral from the borrower and the method and amount of payment due to the . . . customer in respect of the lending [7.1.3.3].
(19) The information required by the [rule referred to in 8.4.6] . . . if applicable.
(20) How to complain to the firm, and a statement, if relevant, that the customer may subsequently complain directly to the Financial Ombudsman Service.
(21) Whether or not compensation may be available from the compensation scheme . . . and . . . the extent and level of cover and how further information can be obtained . . .
(24) When the obligation to provide best execution can be and is waived, a statement . . . that the firm does not owe a duty of best execution [13.2.2]. (FSA PM COB 4, Ann. 2)

The disclosure of charges under (6) 'helps to ensure that there is sufficient information in the market-place to enable investors to make informed investment decisions . . . [i.e.] to make effective cost comparisons, and thus ultimately a more informed choice'[72] and, with Private Customers, was supported by a rule requiring the firm to 'disclose in writing . . . the basis or amount of its charges . . . and the nature and amount of any other income receivable by it or . . . its associate and attributable to that [customer's] business' including 'any product-related charges that are deducted from the customer's investment' (FSA PM COB 5.7.3(1), 5.7.4). Moreover, like SIB before it, FSA sought to control the level of charges to a Private Customer by providing that the 'firm must ensure that its charges are not excessive. When determining whether a charge is excessive, a firm should consider:

[i] the amount of its charges . . . compared with charges for similar services or products in the market; [and]
[ii] the degree to which the charges are an abuse of the trust which the customer has placed in the firm. (FSA COB 5.6.3, 5.6.4)

---

[72] IMRO Reporter 11, October 1995, pp. 1–2.

As regards [i], FSA 'have considered whether a specific provision of this nature is desirable, given the FSA's duty to have regard to the need to minimise adverse effects on competition [2.5.1] . . . Our conclusion is that . . . [this] provision does set an appropriate standard for the protection of private customers.'[73] Given the required disclosure (6), the meaning of [ii] was challenging at best. In addition, 'Where . . . charges for . . . managing a private customer's assets are dependent on the value of . . . investments that are not readily realisable investments, the valuation . . . must be based upon the price likely to be agreed between a willing buyer and a willing seller dealing at arm's length who are both in possession of all freely available information concerning those investments' (FSA PM COB 5.6.5).[74]

Such extensive regulatory requirements, together with the word processor, resulted in long and complex customer documentation because 'some firms . . . have taken the view . . . that . . . the detailed nature of the Conduct of Business Rules have exposed firms to so serious a risk of legal action . . . that agreements need to be structured in such a way that in the event of a dispute the firm can use the agreement to evidence that a customer has accepted certain behaviour by [the] firm as part of the relationship',[75] with three consequences. First, some provisions could often be unintelligible and/or difficult to locate or understand in context and it was difficult to see how they complied with the Principle that 'A firm must . . . communicate information . . . in a way which is clear, fair and not misleading' (PRIN 2.1.1, Principle 7) or, as one Ombudsman put it: 'there are cases in which the documents are not clearly enough expressed; I do not adopt a legalistic approach to this question . . . [M]y test is not whether a good Chancery lawyer could divine the right message but whether a reasonably intelligent investor with limited experience in investments could do so.'[76] Second, institutional customers, dealing with a number of firms all using different documents, sometimes produced, competing or overriding terms of their own, thus resulting in a 'battle of the forms'.[77] And, third, it was always necessary to draft the Terms so as to avoid incorporating the Conduct Rules as a term of the contract on which the client could sue the firm for breach if they were not complied with in circumstances where the statutory right of action did not apply, for example because it was an Intermediate Customer.[78] In one

---

[73] FSA CP 57, July 2000, paras. 7.19–7.20.
[74] This does not appear in the MiFID rules although, given its reasonableness, must continue to be FSA's expectation under the Principles (9.1, 9.2).
[75] SIB CP 8, November 1988, para. 3.
[76] Annual Report 1994/95, The Investment Ombudsman, May 1995, p. 7.
[77] Cf. *Treitel*, pp. 19–21.
[78] The statutory right of action is contained in FSMA 150 and is, in reality, a statutory codification of the rules on tortious breach of statutory duty. It is, in effect, limited to Private Customers (FSMA 2000 (Rights of Action) Regulations 2001, SI 2001/2256). For its post-MiFID extent, see FSA CP 07/9. Accordingly, a Professional Client can sue the

case where the Terms stated that 'your transactions with us . . . will be governed by [the Rules], to which we will adhere', the Court held that:

> The[se] words . . . are amongst the clearest that could be chosen by the parties to indicate that the transactions . . . were to be governed by the [Rules].[79]

MiFID: It follows that, in a post-MiFID context, regulatory obligations will be incorporated into the contract where the Terms (1) covenant to comply with the Rules, (2) contain or refer to the Execution Policy (13.2.3.1) which itself covenants to comply with the Rules,[80] or (3) state that a particular rule does not apply (for example, Suitability (11.2) because 'we do not give advice as part of our transaction execution services') when, in fact, it does so that the representation is incorrect and the claim is for a failure to comply with the (mis-represented) FSA standard.

FSA's MiFID implementing rules no longer contain a specific list of mandatory terms to be inserted in customer documentation (and, hence, a transitional provision for Terms of Business was not required as at 1 November 2007), but the Pre-MiFID essential terms of the customer relationship are clearly still required by the need to 'set . . . out the . . . rights and obligations' (COBS 8.1.2, 8.1.4(1)). Moreover, there are a large number of analogous regulatory disclosures which can appear in the customer documentation. Using the same numbering as above:

(2) '[A] statement of the fact that the firm is authorised and the name and contact address of the competent authority' (COBS 6.1.4(4)).
(5) '[T]he firm and its services' (COBS 2.2.2(1)(a)).
(6) 'A firm must provide a retail client with information on costs and associated charges, including . . .
   [i] the total price to be paid by the client . . . including all related fees, commissions, charges and expenses . . . or, if an exact price cannot be indicated, the basis for the calculation of the total price . . . The commissions charged . . . must be itemised separately . . .
   [ii] if any part of the total price . . . is to be paid in or represents an amount of foreign currency, an indication of the currency . . . and the applicable . . . conversion rates and costs;

---

firm for failure to comply with the Conduct of Business Rules only if it can establish a contractual or tortious claim based on the standards set out in the Rules. FSA, of course, can always take enforcement action for rule breaches or seek injunctions or restitution orders (EG 10, 11). Transactions are not unenforceable for rule breaches (FSMA 151).

[79] *Chigi* v. *CS First Boston Ltd.* [1998] CLC 227. For different outcomes on different wording, see *Brandeis (Brokers) Ltd.* v. *Herbert Black* [2001] AER 342; *Clarion Ltd.* v. *National Provident Institution* [2000] 1 WLR 1888; FSA PS 07/15, para. 2.7.

[80] If compliance with the Execution Policy is a term of the contract, then a failure to comply with it will be a breach of contract. Alternatively, if compliance with the Execution Policy is, by virtue of having sent it separately to the client, a representation, then failure to comply will render the firm liable to a tortious claim.

[iii] notice of the possibility that other costs . . . may arise . . . and
[iv] the arrangements for payment or other performance' (COBS 6.1.9. See also: COBS 2.2.2(1)(b). A principal dealing 'mark-up/mark-down is a commission or charge' where the client is owed best execution (13.2),[80A] and, hence, the confirm disclosure (13.1.4.6(13)).

(7) 'If a firm proposes to manage investments for a retail client . . . information on the method and frequency of valuations of the . . . portfolio' (COBS 6.1.6(2)(a)).

(9) Cancellation rights (10.5.6.4) (COBS 15.2.5).

(10) The customer's agreement to real time solicitations (10.5.3).

(11),(12),(14) '[A] description, which may be provided in summary form, of the conflicts of interest policy' (6.3.1.2, 6.3.1.3) (COBS 6.1.4(8)).

(15)–(18) The disclosures about the risks of services and products etc referred to in 10.5.1.3.

(19) This disclosure should continue: see 8.4.6.

(20), (21) These should be retained (DISP 1.2; COBS, Ann. 1, Pt. 3, para. 8; COBS 4.2.5, 6.1.14).[81]

(24) Execution policy and venues (13.2.2.1) (COBS 2.2.1(1)(c)).

In addition, as with the Pre-MiFID Rules, there are also requirements for disclosures in relation to client assets and client money (7.1.3.4, 7.2.3.4). As referred to above, full disclosure of charges is required (COBS 2.2.1(1)(d)), although the specific rule controlling the level of charges has been abandoned because 'we have never used these rules . . . [to] take . . . enforcement action . . . [and to] take action . . . we would have to determine what constituted an excessive charge, something for which there may be no appropriate benchmarks . . . [so that] we would in effect be setting a price ceiling . . . There is a danger that we set an incorrect ceiling price, and there is a further danger that firms ratchet . . . up their prices towards a ceiling price.'[82] Nonetheless, because 'we do not expect changes in the prices firms levy'[83] and because of the overriding requirement to 'treat the customer fairly' (9.2), firms still need to be cautious in setting their prices. Moreover, although this provision 'may . . . be negatived or varied by express agreement', the 1982 Supply of Goods and Services Act provides that 'Where, under a contract for the a supply of a service, the consideration for the service is not determined by the contract [or] left to be determined in a

---

[80A] FSA PS 07/14, para. 7.3.
[81] For CESR policy, see CESR/07-317, May 2007, Ann. 5; CESR/07-337, May 2007, para. 70. For FSA's implementation of MiFID complaints handling requirements, see FSA CP 06/19, Chapter 31; Treating Complainants Fairly, FSA PS 07/9, July 2007; Dispute Resolution: Complaints (Simplification and MiFID) Instrument 2007, FSA 2007/38; Dispute Resolution: the Complaints Sourcebook, FSA CP 07/14, July 2007. The rules apply only to complaints from Retail Clients (DISP 1.1.3(2)). As the title of PS 07/9 indicates, FSA views firms' complaints handling as an aspect of 'treating the customer fairly' (9.2). [82] FSA CP 06/19, paras. 11.57, 11.58. [83] Ibid, para. 11.56.

manner agreed by the contract . . . there is an implied term that the party contracting with the supplier will pay a reasonable charge' (1982 SOGASA 15(1), 16(1). For this Act see also 11.1).

8.4.3 Form

Pre-MiFID: Customer documentation could be in any form, whether a letter or agreement or Terms of Business, and, in particular, 'may comprise more than one document . . . provided th[is] . . . does not materially diminish the significance of any information the firm is required to give . . . or the ease with which this can be understood' (FSA PM COB 4.2.12) and, generally, of course, the document(s) must be 'clear, fair and not misleading' (PRIN 2.1.1, Principle 7). It could be in electronic and/or paper form and signed electronically (2000 Electronic Communications Act; cf. FSA PM COB 2.6).

MiFID: The Principle continues and is supported by an additional rule that any 'communication . . . is fair, clear and not misleading' (COBS 4.2.1) and the agreement and information must be provided in a 'durable medium', i.e. 'paper . . . or . . . any instrument which enables the recipient to store information . . . in a way accessible for future reference . . . and . . . allows . . . unchanged reproduction'. With MiFID Business and equivalent third country business (4.2.I(2), 4.2.III) sending in electronic form has to be 'chosen by the [Retail Client] when offered the choice between [this] and paper', or via a website if:

(1) . . . there is evidence that the client has regular access to the internet . . . [and]
(2) the client . . . specifically consent[s] to . . . that form; [and]
(3) the client must be notified electronically of the address of the website . . . and the place on the website where the information may be accessed; [and]
(4) the information must be up to date; and
(5) the information must be accessible continuously. (COBS 8.1.3(2); GLOSS, def. of 'website conditions').[84]

That said, it can continue to be provided in a number of documents (COBS 8.1.5).

8.4.4 Amendments

Pre-MiFID: Contract law requires an amendment to be agreed by both parties unless the contract contains its own mechanism for unilateral

---

[84] See, further, for 'durable medium': The European Securities Markets Experts Group (ESME) Report on Durable Medium, June 2007. For information disclosure in that form, see COBS 14.3.8.

amendment by the firm. To protect investors against the latter, FSA provided that 'If the terms . . . allow a firm to amend . . . without the customer's consent, the firm must give at least 10 business days' notice . . . before conducting . . . business . . . on any amended terms, unless it is impracticable in the circumstances to do so' (FSA PM COB 4.2.13), for example, urgent legislative change.

MiFID: The FSA rule is replaced by a new rule requiring the firm to 'notify a client in good time about any material change' (COBS 8.1.3(4)(a)) which, given the requirement to 'treat the customer fairly' (9.2) must be interpreted to the same effect as the Pre-MiFID Rule.

8.4.5 Standard terms and exclusion clauses

Pre-MiFID: Because firms use customer documentation more for their own legal risk management, rather than to provide investor protection, notwithstanding the general law on exclusion clauses,[85] the FSA had 'the power [under the 1999 Unfair Terms in Consumer Contracts Regulations] to consider whether a particular term in a contract appears unfair . . . [and], if a firm disagrees with the [FSA's] . . . analysis of the fairness of the term and declines to change it, the [FSA] . . . may . . . go to court to try to enforce the change'.[86] Since, under the Regulations, 'A contract term may be unfair if . . . it gives significant advantage to the firm against the consumer . . . and . . . it breaches the general requirement that the firm must act in 'good faith',[87] 'firms may consider issues arising under the Regulations along with their wider obligation to treat the customer fairly [9.2]. We expect firms not to rely on narrow and technical interpretations of the Regulations to seek to justify a contract term that may be, in the wider context, unfair and in which context it may be open to challenge.'[88] A legal test for a 'principles-based approach' (2.5.8) to 'good faith' has yet to be devised. A 'consumer' is 'any natural person who . . . is acting for purposes which are outside his trade, business or profession' (1999 UTCCR 2(1)).

Beyond this, FSA built on SIB's policy that 'the agreement must . . . be broadly even-handed as between the parties (and in particular must not remove rights from the customer unreasonably or by stealth)'.[89] Hence, the following rules:

---

[85] *Treitel*, Chapter 7.
[86] FSA CP 148, July 2002, para. 3.3. See also: Fairness of terms in consumer contracts: Statement of Good Practice, FSA, May 2005. FSA is also a UK competent authority for the purpose of EU-wide information sharing under the EC Consumer Protection Co-operation Regulation (FSA appointed as competent authority, FSA PN 23, January 2007).
[87] Unfair Contract Terms, FSA Fact Sheet, June 2001, p. 3.
[88] Fairness of Terms in Consumer Contracts: Statement of Good Practice, FSA, May 2005, para. 1.10.   [89] Principles and Core Rules, Draft, 10 May 1989, SIB, Core Rule 22.

> A firm must not . . . seek to exclude or restrict . . . any duty or liability it may have to [an Intermediate or Private] customer . . . under the regulatory system.
>
> A firm must not . . . [with] a private customer . . . seek to exclude or restrict any [other] duty or liability . . . unless it is reasonable for it to do so. (FSA PM COB 2.5.3, 2.5.4)

The second rule merely summarised the effect of the general law. Because both rules covered exclusions and indemnities, it was common to see a provision in customer documentation stating that no term has effect insofar as it contravened a rule.

MiFID: FSA's Unfair Terms in Consumer Contracts Regulations powers remain,[90] as do the express rules on exclusion clauses (COBS 2.1.2, 2.1.3). The second rule on exclusion clauses has been explicitly linked to the overriding MiFID requirement to 'act honestly, fairly and professionally in accordance with the best interests of the client' (9.3) so that the exclusion is only permitted if 'it is honest, fair and professional' (COBS 2.1.3(1)), which is devoid of meaning in this context. It has also been linked by FSA to the 'treat the customer fairly' requirement (9.2),[91] with similar difficulties.

8.4.6 Enforcement

Pre-MiFID: The actions which the firm may take upon a customer default are governed by the express and implied terms of the documentation but, in addition, FSA provided that the firm cannot 'realise a private customer's assets . . . to discharge an obligation . . . unless it is legally entitled to do so [i.e. the document permitted], and it has . . . set out in the . . . agreement . . . the action it may take . . . [and] the circumstances in which it may do so' (FSA PM COB 7.8.3).

MiFID: Although the express rule has not been retained, such notice should continue to be included in the customer documentation as a result of the overriding requirement to 'treat the customer fairly' (9.2).

8.4.7 One-way and two-way notifications

As referred to in 8.4.2, although the FSA rules no longer mandate any particular content in the customer documentation, other rules require disclosure and terms which can appear together in the customer agreement/ Terms of Business. These provisions are, however, subject to different requirements:

---

[90] See FSA's Unfair Contract Terms Regulatory Guide in its Handbook.
[91] FSA CP 06/19, para. 6.63. Accordingly, the firm's Terms must state that nothing affects the Private Client's statutory rights.

8.4.7.1 Two-way consent

The following require some form of express consent from the client:

- Expertising a Retail Client up to Professional Client (COBS 3.5.3, 8.3.2.8). There must be a signature 'separate from any client agreement',[92] for example, in a separate additional signature clause or email confirmation.
- Opting up a Professional Client to Eligible Counterparty (8.3.3.3) (COBS 3.6.3). This requires 'express confirmation' which 'mean[s] some form of acknowledgement or active demonstration of consent by the client . . . [which] cannot be obtained by . . . silence or lack of objection'[93] or by 'a course of dealing after being sent a "one-way" notification'.[94] In other words, there must be a signature, an email confirmation or an oral statement supported by the evidence of a file note.
- Execution Policy (COBS 11.2.25, 11.2.26, 11.4.1) (13.2.3.1). The Execution Policy itself only requires 'prior consent of . . . clients', for which an agreement by course of conduct (within 8.4.7.2) would be sufficient. However, consent to executing transactions outside a regulated market or MTF,[95] which will usually also be contained in the Policy, requires 'prior express consent' which should be interpreted as equivalent to 'express confirmation' in the last point.[96] In relation to these consents, 'prior express consent . . . entails an actual demonstration of consent by the client which may be provided by signature . . . or an . . . electronic signature . . . by a click on a web page or orally' although, in contrast, 'prior consent may . . . be tacit and result from the behaviour of the client such as the sending of an order to the firm after having received . . . the firm's execution policy'.[97] Thus, FSA will not in practice accept that it is enough merely to send to the client an Execution Policy which states that each time the client places an order he is deemed to consent to orders being executed OTC.
- Professional Client consent to hold client assets with an unregulated firm in a non-EEA State (7.1.3.2) (CASS 6.3.4(2)).
- Professional Client consent to stocklending ('express prior consent') and signature by a Retail Client (7.1.3.3) (CASS 6.4.1).

---

[92] Implementing MiFID's Client Categorisation Requirements, FSA, August 2006, p. 37.
[93] Ibid, p. 38.   [94] FSA CP 06/19, para. 7.56.
[95] Such consent is required only 'where the relevant instruments are . . . admitted to trading on a regulated market or MTF' (CESR/07-320, May 2007, Q. 21.2). The rule does not apply where the instrument is only capable of being traded OTC, for example derivatives documented pursuant to an ISDA Master Agreement, or customer 'orders' are not 'executed' (13.2.2.1). Moreover, limit order exposure under COBS 11.4.1 (13.1.4.4) is not necessary if 'a client expressly instructs otherwise' and this also requires two-way consent.
[96] FSA CP 06/19, Annex 1, para. 9.16; CESR/07-050b, February 2007, para. 60.
[97] CESR/07-320, Q. 21.1, 21.3.

8.4.7.2 One-way consent

The following are subject only to notifications:

- Classification as a Retail or Professional Client or Eligible Counterparty (8.3) (COBS 3.3.1(1)).
- '[I]nform[ation] . . . about . . . (a) any right . . . to request a different categorisation; and (b) any limitations to the level of client protection that such a different categorisation would entail' (8.3.1, 8.3.2.6) (COBS 3.3.1(2)).
- The firm on its own initiative opts the client up to a category with a higher level of investor protection (8.3) (COBS 3.7.6(1)).
- Conflicts Policy (6.3.1.3) (COBS 6.1.4(8)).
- Inducements (6.3.2) (COBS 2.3.1(2).
- Client Asset and Client Money information (7.1.3.4, 7.2.3.4) (COBS 7.1.7).
- Other information disclosures (10.5.1, 10.5.2) (COBS 8.1).

In contrast, an agreement by course of conduct is required in relation to the agreement of the 'rights and obligations of the firm and the client' (8.4.1) (COBS 8.1.2, 8.1.4), this being an effective form of agreement under English Law, although a Continental branch of a UK firm or bank would need to ensure that it was also effective under applicable local law.

9
Principles of conduct

9.1 The FSA's 11 Principles

9.1.1 Policy

As explained in 2.5.8, 'principle-based regulation', while a cornerstone of the FSA's regulatory regime, is the wrong approach. Given that FSA's Principles were 'based on existing principles . . . issued by SIB . . . because of concern . . . that the existing rule books were too long and complicated and made it difficult to look at the underlying moral content of whether what was being done was right or wrong',[1] their precise meaning is impossible to pin down short of an enforcement action or their deriving content in the context of the more detailed rules from which, in their original form, they were summaries and never intended, as they are now, to be free-standing enforceable rules (DEPP 6.2.14). This Book therefore, tries to explain the Principles in that context where it exists:

1 Integrity

A firm must conduct its business with integrity.

Adopting the same words in the context of the rule responsibilities of Approved Persons, FSA considers that this Principle extends beyond misleading, fraudulent and dishonest behaviour to all forms of, as it were, 'really bad behaviour' (5.4.2).

2 Skill, care and diligence

A firm must conduct its business with due skill, care and diligence.

At first sight this seems to be a codification of the common law of negligence, but it is clear from the identical rule adopted for Approved Persons that in FSA's view it extends to any situation where a person 'gets it wrong' (5.4.2).

3 Management and control

A firm must take reasonable care to organise and control its affairs responsibly and effectively, with adequate risk management systems.

---
[1] Joint Committee Report, Vol. II, para. 224, FSA.

See 5.2.

4 Financial prudence

A firm must maintain adequate financial resources.

FSA has many miles of rules requiring detailed financial calculations by firms and what this Principle, as a free standing rule, requires beyond that detail is quite unclear.

5 Market conduct

A firm must observe proper standards of market conduct

See 12.6.

6 Customers' interests

A firm must pay due regard to the interests of its customers and treat them fairly.

See 9.2.

7 Communications with clients

A firm must pay due regard to the information needs of its clients, and communicate information to them in a way which is clear, fair and not misleading.

See 10.5.1.2.

8 Conflicts of interest

A firm must manage conflicts of interests fairly, both between itself and its customers and between a customer and another client.

See 6.3.1.

9 Customers: relationship of trust

A firm must take reasonable care to ensure the suitability of its advice and discretionary decisions for any customer who is entitled to rely upon its judgement.

See 11.2.1.

10 Customers' assets

A firm must arrange adequate protection for clients' assets when it is responsible for them.

See 7.1 and 7.2.

11 Relations with regulators

A firm must deal with its regulators in an open and cooperative way, and must disclose to the FSA appropriately anything relating to the firm of which the FSA would reasonably expect notice.

Individual Approved Persons are subject to an identical Principle (5.4.2). '[R]egulators . . . means, in addition to the FSA, other regulators with recognised jurisdiction in relation to regulated activities [4.2.I(1)], whether in the UK or abroad' (PRIN 3.4.5). This Principle requires the firm to make notifications to FSA beyond the detailed routine and ad hoc notifications set out in SUP 15, for example of 'any significant failure in the firm's systems or controls [or] any action which a firm proposes to take which would result in a material change in its capital adequacy or solvency' (SUP 15.3.8(2), (3)), 'any significant operational exposures that a firm has identified . . . and . . . any significant change to a firm's organisation, infrastructure or business operating environment' (SYSC 13.4.2). The frankness and completeness of the disclosure required by FSA under Principle 11 is connected with an additional rule under which 'A firm must notify the FSA of . . . a significant breach of a rule . . . or . . . Principle . . . by . . . the firm or any of its directors, officers, employees [or] approved persons . . . immediately it becomes aware . . . or has information which reasonably suggests, that any . . . [such] matter . . . has occurred, may have occurred or may occur in the foreseeable future' 'consider[ing] both the probability of the event happening and the severity of the outcome should it happen' (SUP 15.3.3, 15.3.11, 15.3.13). For this purpose, 'significance should be determined having regard to potential financial losses to customers or to the firm, frequency of the breach, implications for the firm's systems and controls and if there were delays in identifying or rectifying the breach' (SUP 15.3.12). Prompt notification has some benefit in an enforcement action (2.5.5) and the decision in practice on how quickly after discovery to notify will be linked to the firm's ability to articulate to FSA the causes of the breach and the steps it intends to take to remedy it, both of which FSA likes to see in the notification (SUP 15.3.14) and the firm will want to state in order to demonstrate the effectiveness of its systems and controls.

With the obligation to self-report, CESR was always clear that '[a] . . . firm must ensure that the competent authority is informed, without undue delay, of serious breaches of the conduct of business rules'[2] and although a self-reporting obligation 'is beyond the scope of the . . . implementing measures contemplated in the Directive . . . the imposition of such a requirement . . . is not excluded by . . . the Directive'.[3] Beyond mere self-reporting, though, 'we would like to encourage firms to report to us matters of suspicion in relation to peers [market abuse] . . . [T]here is [not] a formal reporting obligation . . . [W]e want . . . you to be good corporate citizens.'[4] There are few limits to principle-based regulation (2.5.8).

---

[2] 'A European Regime of investor protection: the harmonisation of COB Rules', CESR, April 02, para. 13. [3] CESR/04–261b, June 2004, p. 12.
[4] Market Abuse Policy and Enforcement in the UK, Sally Dewar, FSA Director, BBA Seminar, 22 May 2007.

In FSA's view '[t]he 11 Principles . . . are largely consistent with the high level requirements of MiFID . . . [and] we do not need to amend the text of the Principles in order to implement MiFID . . . This . . . will enable us to maintain the Principles as a consistent set of high-level standards.'[5]

9.1.2 Application

9.1.2.1 Clients

Pre-MiFID: Applying to the firm's infrastructure, Principles 3, 4 and 11 applied irrespective of the type of client dealt with. Principles 6, 8 and 9 only referred to 'customers' and, hence, applied only to Private Customers and Intermediate Customers. The rest applied to them and to Market Counterparties (who were within the definition of 'client'), although as regards the latter '[the] operation [of these Principles] in the interprofessional markets will be conditioned by the conventions of those markets and the presumed ability of participants . . . to protect their own interests'[6] and 'the only requirement of Principle 7 . . . is that a firm must communicate information to market counterparties in a way that is not misleading' (PRIN 3.4.1). Similarly, as regards Principles 6–10 the 'requirements depend, in part, on the characteristics of the client or customer concerned. This is because what is "due regard" (in Principles 6 and 7), "fairly" (in Principles 6 and 8), "clear, fair and not misleading" (in Principle 7), "reasonable care" (in Principle 9) or "adequate" (in Principle 10) will . . . depend on those characteristics' (PRIN 1.2.1).

MiFID: The Principles have exactly the same application, with the replacement of Market Counterparties, Intermediate Customers and Private Customers with Eligible Counterparties, Professional Clients and Retail Clients, respectively (PRIN 1–3). As regards an Eligible Counterparty, Principles 1, 2, 6 and 9 cease to 'apply in relation to a firm's conduct of business obligations', in line with MiFID's disapplication of the analogous conduct rules to Eligible Counterparties (COBS 1, Ann. 1, Part 1, para 1.1), but continue to apply 'in relation to other matters, such as client asset protections, systems and controls, prudential requirements and market integrity' (PRIN 4.1.4(2)), giving firms a compliance challenge in the training of staff.[7] 'Although Principle 8 does not apply to

---

[5] FSA CP 06/14, para. 8.2.   [6] FSA CP 13, September 1998, para. 19.

[7] Further complexity is to be added in that FSA 'propose, pending a more detailed review . . . in the fourth quarter of 2007, to retain [on and after 1 November 2007] the . . . [Pre-MiFID] application of the [P]rinciples to non-designated investment business' (FSA CP 07/16, para. 2.7), i.e. to Regulated Activities which are not Designated Investment Business (4.2.I(1)) being, in the Capital Markets context, deposit-taking (3.2.1.5). The significance is that, in this respect, the firm would not use the MiFID definition of Eligible Counterparty, but go back to the Pre-MiFID definition of Market Counterparty (8.3.3) (FSA CP 07/16, Ann. C).

eligible counterparty business [8.3.3], a firm will owe [MiFID] obligations in respect of conflicts of interest [6.3.2] . . . wider than those contained in Principle 8 . . . [which] apply to eligible counterparty business' (PRIN 4.1.5).

9.1.2.2 Business

Pre-MiFID: All of '[t]he Principles apply with regard to regulated activities generally [4.2.I(1)], but . . . with respect to accepting deposits [3.2.1.5] . . . the FSA will proceed only in a prudential context' (PRIN 1.1.3, 3.2.1), as explained in 9.1.2.3.

MiFID: The Principles continue to have exactly the same application.

9.1.2.3 Territorial scope

Pre-MiFID: For a UK firm or a UK branch of a non-EEA firm, Principles 6–10 applied only to 'activities carried on from an establishment maintained . . . in the UK' (PRIN 3.3.1), whereas Principles 3, 4 and 11 applied to the firm's Worldwide activities, including unregulated activities and activities of group members (PRIN 3.2.3), but '[t]his does not mean that, for example, inadequacy of a group member's risk management systems or resources will automatically lead to a firm contravening [the] Principle . . . Rather, the prudential impact of a group member's activities (and, for example, risk management systems operating on a group basis) will be relevant in determining the adequacy of the firm's risk management systems or resources' (PRIN 1.1.5). And Principles 1–3 applied to the firm's Worldwide activities, like Principle 5 'tak[ing] into account the standards expected in the market in which the firm is operating' (PRIN 1.1.6), but only in a 'prudential context', meaning if the 'activities . . . might reasonably be regarded or likely to have a negative effect on . . . confidence in the financial system . . . or . . . the ability of the firm to meet either . . . the "fit and proper" test [3.3] . . . or . . . the . . . requirements . . . relating to . . . financial resources'; otherwise, they applied only to 'activities carried on from an establishment maintained . . . in the United Kingdom' (PRIN 3.3.1).

A UK branch of an EEA firm had to comply with Principles 1, 2, 5 and 11 in a Worldwide context and Principles 6, 7 and 9 in its UK branch and, if a bank, Principle 4 in respect of its UK branch liquidity (PRIN 3.1.1, 3.3.1).

MiFID: The Principles continue to have exactly the same application (PRIN 4.1.2, 4.1.3). Thus, an EEA firm/bank 'is not subject to the Principles to the extent that it would be contrary to MiFID'.[8] See, generally, 4.2(r).

---

[8] FSA CP 07/16, Ann. AB, draft PERG Q.70.

9.2 Treating the customer fairly

In the New Settlement (2.4.3) SIB proposed, but subsequently dropped, a Core Rule regarding 'Legitimate expectations. A firm must not unfairly disappoint any customer who has a legitimate expectation that it will act . . . in a certain way; and it must ensure, accordingly, that any change in its business practices that could affect private investors is brought about only with adequate notice and adequate transitional provisions.'[9] Under FSMA, FSA has introduced a similarly intentioned and opaque Principle requiring the firm to 'pay due regard to the interests of its customers and treat them fairly', although initially this appeared to be regarded by FSA only as an agenda for action which would result in specific, and clearly understood, requirements. Thus, for example, the identified consumer need of 'making products and information easier . . . to understand' was to result in the use of the financial promotion rules (10.5) and FSA's Unfair Contract Terms powers (8.4.5) 'to promote the use of plain language' and a consideration of 'whether . . . there are products which, because of their inherent complexity or opacity, are unsuitable for sale to mass market retail customers'. Similarly, the need to 'keep . . . customers appropriately informed after the point of sale' was to result in 'review[ing] what mandatory information should be provided to retail customers after the point of sale . . . with a view to further consultation on any rules and guidance'.[10] Very quickly, however, it became polemicised because '[f]inancial services . . . inherently involve an imbalance of power and knowledge between the firm and the retail customer. This means that retail customers are not well placed to counteract any unfairness they face and it is important that firms take account of this positively in their dealings with customers'[11] and thus a general requirement to 'do the right thing' was imposed on firms:

> 'Fairness' is not a definitive concept. Instead it represents a series of values which help . . . [people] how to behave and treat others.
>
> . . . [I]t is difficult to define 'fairness' concretely . . . We have concluded . . . that because fairness is such a flexible and relative concept . . . generic guidance would not be helpful.[12]
>
> Treating customers fairly is . . . as much about attitudes and behaviour as it is about requirements.[13]
>
> As part of the move towards a more principles-based approach . . . we do not envisage introducing new rules as part of the TCF initiative;

---

[9] Principles and Core Rules, SIB Draft, 10 May 1989, Core Rule 17.
[10] Treating Customers Fairly after the Point of Sale, FSA DP, June 01, Chapter 5. Clearly, the consumer's expectation remains along these lines: see FSA Consumer Research 38, June 2005.   [11] Ibid, Ann. A, para. 4.5.   [12] Ibid, para. 3.3; Ann. A, paras. 8, 11, 15.
[13] Ibid, para. 3.10.

instead we want firms . . . to focus on the principles and the outcomes for consumers that we are looking to achieve . . .

Outcome 1: Consumers can be confident that they are dealing with firms where the fair treatment of customers is essential to the corporate culture . . .

Outcome 2: Products and services . . . in the retail market are designed to meet the needs of identified customer groups and are targeted accordingly . . .

Outcome 3: Consumers are provided with clear information and are kept appropriately informed before, during and after the point of sale . . .

Outcome 4: Where consumers receive advice, the advice is suitable and takes account of their circumstances . . .

Outcome 5: Consumers are provided with products that perform as firms have led them to expect, and the associated service is both of an acceptable standard and as they have been led to expect . . .

Outcome 6: Consumers do not face unreasonable post-sale barriers . . . to change product, switch provider, submit a claim or make a complaint.[14]

Outcomes 3 and 4 should be covered by the detailed rules referred to in 10.5 and 11.1, respectively, and the complaints part of 6 by the requirements to have 'effective and transparent procedures for the reasonable and prompt handling of complaints'.[15] For the rest, though, notwithstanding FSA's mandated full disclosure of risks (10.5.1.3), given its interpretation of the consumer protection Objective (2.5.1) so that 'it is only reasonable to expect consumers to exercise responsibility for their decisions if we address some of the inherent difficulties in the market',[16] consumers cannot be trusted to look after themselves. Or, put another way, the FSA's reversal of caveat emptor converts the traditional regulatory duty on the firm not to mis-sell into ensuring that customers do not mis-buy. This 'will include ensuring that the firm . . .

- maintains a balance between increasing sales and not exposing customers to inappropriate risks, particularly in the design and marketing of new products; [and]
- measures, monitors, controls and reviews the risks arising from products with both existing and potential new customers.

---

[14] Treating Customers Fairly – Towards Fair Outcomes for Consumers, FSA, July 2006, para. 1.9, Chapter 2.

[15] DISP 1.2.1. The detailed Pre-MiFID complaints handling rules have been, thus, simplified although in practice, given TCF (9.2), it is difficult to see how a firm could do anything less onerous.   [16] TCF, FSA, July 2006, para. 2.15.

Thus, FSA requires 'sales of the right products, to the right consumers at the right time',[17] judged by FSA ultimately with hindsight in an enforcement situation.

Since FSA imposes a requirement for such judgement to be exercised by the firm, it is not surprising that 'senior management has a key role to play in providing leadership . . . for delivering TCF . . . TCF is as much about staff behaviour and the culture and approach of the firm, as about systems and controls';[18] indeed, 'TCF . . . [i]s a key element to be embedded in . . . business cultures, and . . . to be taken forward as a senior management responsibility'.[19] Hence, in relation to Outcome 1:

> We have identified the key cultural drivers to be: leadership; strategy; decision making; controls; recruitment, training and competence; and reward . . .
>
> For each driver we have identified the associated indicators and contra-indicators of good behaviour. The framework will enable supervisors to assess the risk a firm's culture presents to treating customers fairly . . . We intend to integrate the culture framework into our ARROW risk assessment [5.6].[20]

The 'drivers', though, are extremely challenging to implement with anything approaching confidence. Take, for example, 'leadership' where, as with the other 'drivers', the real requirements are unknowable short of an enforcement action. The main indicator is that '[f]air treatment of customers is central to the behaviour and values of all managers . . . [and] they . . . apply appropriate controls and monitoring to ensure that the fair treatment of customers is determined by their staff' and, as a result, FSA wants to see that:

> Managers have established . . . values which reflect the fair treatment of customers. Their behaviours [must] support these values . . .
>
> Managers lead by example, by . . . inspiring staff to treat customers fairly.
>
> When management set plans . . . they are consistent with the firm's . . . values. They [must] give the fair treatment of customers appropriate prominence . . . Management [must] undertake monitoring to ensure that actions on the fair treatment of customers . . . are delivered.[21]

---

[17] A Strategic Approach to Treating Customers Fairly, Carol Sargeant, MD FSA, Retail Financial Services Forum, 15 October 2003.
[18] Treating Customers Fairly – Building on Progress, FSA, July 2005, para. 1.27.
[19] FSA Annual Report 2005/06, p. 27.
[20] Treating Customers Fairly – Culture, FSA, July 2007, pp. 6, 7.
[21] Ibid, pp. 21, 22. Part of monitoring is the development of management information (5.3.2.3), with the development of hard facts to analyse judgemental outcomes being required (Treating Customers Fairly – Guide to Management Information, FSA, July 2007).

In the absence of concrete rules or FSA's approval of the firm's procedures, an obligation to comply with the Principle is, in practice, reminiscent of a criticism that has been made of the contemporary formulation of the tortious negligence test as a 'situation . . . in which the court considers it fair, just and reasonable that the law should impose a duty of a given scope upon the one party for the benefit of the other':[22]

> No one would suggest that deciding a legal dispute is an easy task . . . [A] judge must establish . . . the true material facts. What is equally important is for the appropriate principles and rules of law to be identified. These principles and rules have to be applied to the facts . . . There is enough room for disagreement without having a question mark hanging over what the applicable rules and principles are and doubts about what they mean. Yet that is what has happened in ever-increasing areas of the law in recent years. It is a move away from principle and towards arbitrary judicial decision-making.
>
> One of the worst examples of this is the so-called 'fair, just and reasonable' test . . . The trouble is that 'fair, just and reasonable' is really a slogan rather than a test. It is simply too vague to use as a test, with the unfortunate results that are only too obvious.[23]

'Customers' include Intermediate Customers/Professional Clients as well as Private Customers/Retail Clients and so the Principle applies to them as well. Hence, it was used to discipline a firm which, having been offered a programme trade by an institutional customer, hedged its potential exposure in the market before it was awarded the trade and, thereby, moved the eventual strike price of the trade against the customer. 'The principle of fair treatment and effective management of the potential conflict [which Principle was used in another enforcement case: see 6.3.1.2] . . . require that a firm should not use . . . information [of the programme trade] for the purpose of its own trading to the detriment of the customer unless it has notified the customer that it intends to do so and that this may impact on the prices obtained . . . [A] firm is not prohibited from reasonable participation in the market prior to the award of a principal programme trade for which the firm has bid on a blind basis, if it can do so while maintaining fair treatment for its customer.'[24] The Principle also applies where 'product[s] . . . are sold . . . through . . . distribution channels'.[25] The provider:

(1) should identify the target market, namely which types of customer the product or service is likely to be suitable (or not suitable) for;

---

[22] *Caparo v. Dickman* [1990] 2 AC 605.
[23] *Principles of the Common Law*, Michael Arnheim, Duckworth, 2004, p. 275.
[24] Morgan Grenfell & Co Ltd., Final Notice, 18 March 2004, paras. 4.7, 4.8.
[25] FSA DP 06/4, September 2006, para. 1.3. For inducements, see 6.3.2(1), (3).

(2) should stress-test the product or service to identify how it might perform in a range of market environments and how the customer could be affected;
(3) should have in place systems and controls to manage adequately the risks posed by product or service design . . .
[4] When providing information to distributors . . .
- [•] should make clear if that information is not intended for customer use;
- [•] should ensure the information is sufficient, appropriate and comprehensible . . . including considering whether it will enable distributors to understand it enough to give suitable advice . . .

[5] When providing information to customers . . .
- [•] should pay regard to its target market, including its likely level of financial capability;
- [•] should take account of what information the customer needs to understand the product or service, its purpose and the risks . . .

[6] When selecting distribution channels . . .
- [•] should decide whether this is a product where customers would be wise to seek advice;
- [•] should review how what is occurring in practice corresponds to (or deviates from) what was originally planned . . . for distribution.[26]

And, for its part, the distributor:

(1) should consider, when passing provider materials to customers, whether it understands the information provided . . .
(2) should consider the nature of the products or services . . . and how they fit with the customer's needs and risk appetite . . .
(3) should consider any implied or express representation it made (during meetings, correspondence or promotional material, for example). Where a customer has reasonable expectations based on the prior statements of a distributor . . . the distributor should meet these expectations.[27]

FSA applies these obligations to the product provider where it is, in effect, using the distributor to sell its products, even if it categorises the distributor as its sole 'client' either because the distributor buys the product as principal (8.2.1) or acts as agent for the underlying customer rather than for the provider (8.2.2), and here the provider 'may ask itself whether the relative complexity of the [product] might lead it to consider that this product is one where customers would be wise [or should be told] to seek advice, or that it should use any other [distribution] channel where it can communicate relevant and complex information more effectively'.[28] If, alternatively, the

---

[26] Providers and Distributors, Regulatory Guide Instrument 2007, FSA 2007/41, paras. 1.17–1.20. [27] Ibid, paras. 1.23, 1.25.
[28] FSA DP 06/4, September 2006, Ann. 2, para. 5.16.

provider merely supplies a component of the product, say a derivative, which is packaged and sold by another firm, and 'might not know which application [the other firm] . . . intends to make of the derivative' then it is not 'responsible for treating customers fairly with respect to product design'.[29] Any greater involvement by the provider would appear to result in FSA applying the Principle.

Some Pre-MiFID conduct requirements have not been carried over into the post-MiFID FSA rules, for example, in derivatives dealing provisions as to margin and closing out a Private Customer's positions and realising his assets (FSA PM COB 7.8, 7.10). It may be, however, that FSA's expectations of 'treating the customer fairly' extend to the maintenance by the firm of such client protections.

9.3 The MiFID Principle

In effect, FSA appears to regard its existing 11 Principles as merely a lower level particularisation of the overriding MiFID conduct requirement that:

> A firm must act honestly, fairly and professionally in accordance with the best interests of its client. (COBS 2.1.1)

This applies to dealing with Retail Clients in all Designated Investment Business (4.2.I(1)), and with Professional Clients and Eligible Counterparties in MiFID Business and equivalent third country business (4.2.I(2), 4.2.III) (COBS 2.1.1). 'The requirement . . . overlap[s] to a large extent with our existing Principles . . . [and] does not appear to add anything to firms' existing duties, but . . . it might . . . [in its] reference to a firm acting "in the best interest of its clients".'[30] FSA has not explained what, in its view, this requires although its clarity can only rival the Principle of 'treating the customer fairly' (9.2).

---

[29] Ibid, paras. 5.10, 5.11. See, further: Platforms – the role of wraps and fund supermarkets, FSA DP 07/2, June 2007; The responsibilities of providers, distributors and platform providers, FSA DP 07/2, September 2007. [30] FSA CP 06/19, paras. 6.8, 6.14.

10
Marketing investments

10.1 The different regulatory regimes

Although now all of the rules on the marketing of investments are contained in, or derived from, FSMA, they differ as a result of the historical development and inter-action of different regulatory regimes for securities, collective investment schemes, bank deposits and investments generally. Figure 8 is a route map to the application of the current rules and cross-refers to the explanations in the following sections of this Chapter.

10.2 Securities

Ever since the beginning of the 20th century it was acknowledged that, notwithstanding 'that legislation cannot protect people from the consequences of their own imprudence, recklessness or want of experience', since subscribers cannot themselves enquire into the company's affairs, the principle of caveat emptor has a limited application and 'therefore the prospectus on which the public are invited to subscribe [should] not only not contain any misrepresentation but . . . satisfy a high standard of good faith . . . [and] disclose everything which could reasonably influence the mind of an investor of average prudence'.[1] The question has always been: What types of offer should trigger the mandatory prospectus contents rules? For almost 100 years the answer was: 'any prospectus, circular, notice, advertisement or other invitation, offering to the public for subscription or purchase any shares or debentures of a company' (1900 CA 30; substantially re-enacted in 1908 CA 285, 1929 CA 380(1), 1948 CA 455(1), 1985 CA 741), which included both an offer and an invitation to treat, as long as it was an offer to the public, not a private placement:

> 'The public' . . . is . . . a general word. No particular numbers are prescribed. Anything from two to infinity may serve . . . The point is that the offer is such as to be open to anyone who brings his money and applies in due form, whether the prospectus was addressed to him . . . or not. A private communication is not thus open.[2]

[1] Davey Report, paras. 4, 6. See 2.2.2. [2] *Lynde* v. *Nash* [1929] AC 158 at 167–8.

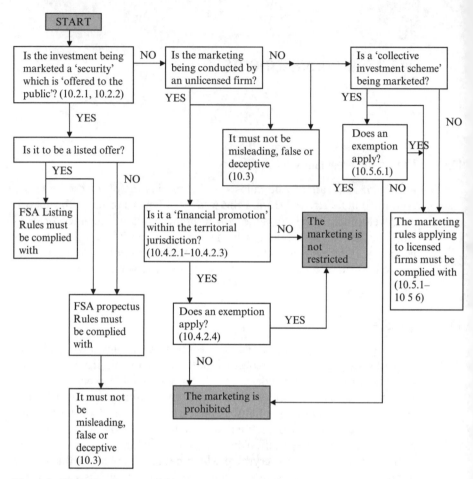

Figure 8 *Marketing investments*

However, there were placings where 'securities . . . are allotted . . . to a broker or issuing house . . . and then made available to members of the public, who make purchases through their stock brokers . . . [with] letters of allotment . . . renounced in favour of the public by the broker [or] issuing house . . . and the ultimate allotment is then made by the company to the purchasers'.[3] As a result, the rules distinguished true offers to the public using such a mechanism from genuine private placements:

> Any reference to offering shares or debentures to the public shall . . . includ[e] . . . offering them to any section of the public, whether

[3] Cohen Report, para. 22.

selected as members or debenture holders of a company . . . or as clients of the person issuing the prospectus or in any other manner . . . [This] shall not be taken as requiring any offer or invitation to be treated as made to the public if it can properly be regarded, in all the circumstances, as not being calculated to result, directly or indirectly, in the shares or debentures being available for subscription or purchase by persons other than those receiving the offer or invitation, or otherwise being a domestic concern of the persons making and receiving it. (1947 CA 68; re-enacted in 1948 CA 55, 1985 CA 59 and 60)

But it still had to be an offer for subscription for cash, not a share-for-share exchange[4] or an offer for sale (2.4.4(6), (7)) even though, with the latter '[i]t cannot . . . be right that, where the offerors are morally, although not in law, the agents of the company to place the shares with the public, the company . . . should be able to avoid their responsibilities'[5] and, hence, it was enacted that:

> Where a company allots . . . shares in or debentures of the company with a view to . . . those shares or debentures being offered for sale to the public, any document by which the offer for sale to the public is made shall . . . be deemed to be a prospectus issued by the company . . . as if the shares or debentures had been offered to the public for subscription. (1928 CA 32; substantially re-enacted in 1929 CA 38, 1948 CA 45, 1985 CA 58)

None of this, however, included a secondary offer by a shareholder where he had not received his allotment with a view to that offer (1948 CA 38; 1985 CA 56) because he would not have the information on the company necessary to satisfy the mandatory disclosure obligations. It did include, however, offers by non-UK companies unless confined to professionals, i.e. 'any person whose ordinary business or part of whose ordinary business it is to buy or sell shares or debentures, whether as principal or agent' (1928 CA 93; substantially re-enacted in 1929 CA 354, 1948 CA 417, 423(2), 1985 CA 72, 79(2)), this provision being the foundation of the London Euro-Securities Markets (2.4.1, 2.4.2).

The mandatory contents of a 'prospectus' 'represent[ed] a gradual accretion of provisions enacted over . . . 80-odd year[s] and are illogically arranged and extremely confusing',[6] all of the provisions being overlain by the European Single Market Directives on primary offers which, in their latest form, the 2003 Prospectus Directive, have at least introduced consistency and uniformity (2.2.2, 2.6(6), (7), 10.5.1.1):

> It is unlawful for transferable securities . . . to be offered to the public in the United Kingdom unless an approved prospectus has

---

[4] *Governments Stock Securities Co Ltd* v. *Christopher* [1955] WLR 238.
[5] Greene Report, para. 40.   [6] 1984 Gower, para. 9.04.

been made available to the public before the offer is made. (FSMA 85(1))

There are, thus, two issues.

10.2.1 Transferable securities

These are the following:

10.2.1.1 Shares

This is defined in the 1993 ISD (3.2.1.1), and includes a closed-ended collective investment scheme, but not: shares issued in substitution without any increase in share capital; a bonus issue; or shares issued in consideration of a takeover or merger, these being subject to the takeover rules (2.6(9)).

10.2.1.2 Debt securities

Again, these are as defined by the 1993 ISD (3.2.1.2), other than: 'money market instruments ... which have a maturity of less than 12 months'; Government debt; or debt securities 'issued in a continuous or repeated manner by a credit institution [and] ... the total consideration of the offer is less than 50 million Euros' and they 'are not subordinated, convertible or exchangeable' and do not give the right to subscribe for or acquire other types of securities and are not linked to a derivative instrument'.

10.2.1.3 Warrants

See 3.2.1.3.

10.2.1.4 Depositary receipts

See 3.2.1.4.

10.2.1.5 Options over shares or debt securities

For options generally, see 3.2.1.6.

In any of 10.2.1.1–10.2.1.5, there is an exemption if the total consideration for the offer is less than €2.5 million (FSMA 85(5), 102A(3), Sched. 11A; FSA Prospectus Rules 1.2.2).

10.2.2 Offer to the public

The concept under the Prospectus Directive is to the same effect as the previous rules explained above, except that it also includes a secondary offer by a shareholder since an 'offer to the public' is now defined as:

> a communication to any person which presents sufficient information on –

> (a) the . . . securities to be offered, and
> (b) the terms on which they are offered,
>
> to enable an investor to decide to buy or subscribe for the securities . . .
>
> The communication may be made . . . in any form . . . [and] by any means.

This 'includes a placing of securities through a financial intermediary' (FSMA 102B), with the intention that the intermediary sells on, and even a pure placing, subject to the exemptions referred to below. 'The definition is . . . capable of a wide variety of interpretations and . . . [one] concern [is] that the . . . definition . . . could capture screen trading'[7] and, hence, there is a specific exemption for 'a communication in connection with trading on . . . a regulated market [14.1] . . . [or] a multilateral trading facility [14.2]' (FSMA 102B(5)). Unfortunately, '[w]hile we will be happy to discuss particular circumstances . . . [FSA] will not be providing formal binding guidance on whether a particular set of circumstances amounts to a public offer'.[8] There are, however, a series of exemptions:

- An 'offer . . . made to or directed at qualified investors only', these being: institutions within the client categories in 8.3.2.1, 8.3.2.6 and 8.3.2.7; corporations which 'meet . . . two of . . .: an average number of employees during the financial year of 250, a total balance sheet . . . exceeding EUR 43,000,000 and an annual net turnover . . . exceeding EUR 50,000,000'; 'pension funds and their management companies'; and 'entities . . . whose corporate purpose is solely to invest in securities' such as SPVs within 8.3.2.3. A qualified investor firm can act as agent for its non-qualified investor client in receiving the offer. A further category, though, is 'an investor [which can be a company not meeting the above size requirements] registered on a register maintained by the [FSA who is] . . . resident in the United Kingdom . . . and meets . . . two of' conditions (a), (b) and (c) (referring to securities rather than any financial instruments) for becoming an expert investor set out in 8.3.2.8, the investor self-certifying to FSA that it meets the conditions and the issuer applying to access the register (FSA Prospectus Rules 5.4).
- An 'offer . . . made to or directed at fewer than 100 persons, other than qualified investors, per EEA State . . . [and] an offer . . . to trustees . . ., members of a partnership . . . or . . . two or more persons jointly, is to be treated as the making of an offer to a single person'. The numbers relate to offers or invitations to treat, not to acceptances (which may be less), although each set of offers is

---

[7] UK Implementation of the Prospectus Directive, FSA & HMT, October 2004, para. 4.10.
[8] LIST!, Issue 10, FSA, June 2005.

looked at separately, there being no 'require[ment for] the formal aggregation of the number of offerees during a 12 month period'.[9]

- 'The minimum consideration that may be paid by any one person . . . is at least 50,000 euros (or an equivalent amount)' aggregating 'any other offer . . . made . . . at any time within the . . . [last] 12 months' (FSMA 86, 87R).

10.3 Misleading etc marketing

From the 1930s the general criminal law was regarded as an insufficient deterrent in relation to fraudulent or misleading investment promotions[10] and, hence, a provision enacted in the 1930s[11] which continues in very similar form today and is unaffected by MiFID:

> a person who –
>
> (a) makes a promise, statement or forecast which he knows to be misleading, false or deceptive in a material particular; [or]
> (b) dishonestly conceals any material facts whether in connection with a statement, promise or forecast made by him or otherwise; or
> (c) recklessly makes (dishonestly or otherwise) a statement, promise or forecast which is misleading, false or deceptive in a material particular
>
> . . . is guilty of an offence if . . . [done] for the purpose of inducing, or is reckless as to whether it may induce, another person . . .
>
> [i] to enter or offer to enter into . . . a[n] agreement [for Regulated Activities within 4.2.I(1)]; or
> [ii] to exercise, or refrain from exercising, any rights conferred by a[n] . . . investment [within 3.2.1]. (FSMA 397(1), (2))

Heading (a) covers the deliberate release by a listed company of false information on the business.[12] Under heading (b), there can only be a dishonest concealment if 'there is a pre-existing duty under the general law to speak . . . such as [in] a contract of insurance where there is a duty of utmost good faith'[13] or, perhaps, where the 'treat the customer fairly' Principle applies (9.2). A statement is 'misleading' if there is 'a reasonable probability of confusion . . . having regard to the circumstances',[14] and can

---

[9] Explanatory Memorandum to the Prospectus Regulations 2005, HMT, May 2005, para. 7.4. [10] Greene Report, para. 92; Bodkin Report, paras. 24–8.
[11] A similar provision was enacted for deposit taking in 1987 Banking Act 35, and this is also covered by the current FSMA provision.
[12] FSA PN/106/2005, 7 October 2005; FSA PN/120/2005, 11 November 2005.
[13] *Aldrich* v. *Norwich Union* [2000] Lloyd's Rep. IR 1.
[14] *Re Bayer Product Limited's Application* [1947] 2 AER 188 at 190.

be 'false' even though literally true given what it omits, and is 'deceptive' if it induces a person to believe a thing to be true which is actually false, or vice versa, contrary to what the person deceiving knows or believes to be the case.[15] None of this applies if full disclosure is made in a way likely to come to the attention of the other party, whether or not there is a legal obligation to disclose. Under a predecessor section, some judges considered that in heading (c) 'the word "reckless" means not caring whether the statement, promise or forecast be true or false, and ... if an accused person honestly believed in the truth of what he had said or written he cannot be ... reckless'.[16] As a result, the words 'dishonestly or otherwise' were inserted into the provisions so that 'reckless ... mean[s] ... "careless", "heedless", "inattentive to duty" ... and ... cover[s] ... also the case where there is a high degree of negligence without dishonesty',[17] i.e. 'that it was a rash statement to make or a rash promise to give; and ... that the person ... had no real basis on which he could support the statement or the promise'.[18]

There must be, in [i], an 'agreement', although an agreement constituting arrangements (3.2.2.2) is sufficient, and for both [i] and [ii] there must be a 'purpose', which is almost an intention, rather than merely that the promise, statement etc has the effect referred to. There are defences for activities complying with FSA's Chinese Wall rules (6.3.1.3) and stabilisation and buy-back rules (12.3.7) (FSMA (397(4)), but if none apply it is a criminal offence, although there is no civil right of action by an investor who suffers loss as a result.[19] However, the offence is committed only if either:

(a) the statement, promise or forecast is made in or from, or the facts are concealed in or from, the United Kingdom or arrangements are made in or from the United Kingdom for the statement, promise or forecast to be made or the facts to be concealed; [or]
(b) the person on whom the inducement is intended to or may have effect is in the United Kingdom; or
(c) the agreement is or would be entered into or the rights are or would be exercised in the United Kingdom. (FSMA 397(6))

This gives statutory effect to a case under earlier legislation that held that with such 'result crimes ... the offence is committed in England ... if any part of the proscribed result takes place in England', it being enough to give the Courts jurisdiction that where a non-UK fund was sold in Germany to German investors, the application form, although completed in Germany, was received and processed in the UK.[20]

None of this is affected by MiFID.

---

[15] *Welham* v. *DPP* [1961] AC 103 at 126.   [16] *R.* v. *MacKinnon* [1958] 3 AER 657.
[17] *R.* v. *Bates* [1952] 2 AER 843 at 845.   [18] *R.* v. *Grunwald* [1960] 1 WLR 379 at 383.
[19] *Aldrich* v. *Norwich Union*.
[20] *R.* v. *Marcus* [1974] 3 AER 705; *Secretary of State for Trade* v. *Marcus* [1976] AC 35. For 'result crimes' see further 12.2.2.

10.4 Marketing by unlicensed persons

10.4.1 Marketing up to the end of the 20th century

From the 1940s there was a prohibition on the distribution of circulars inviting the entry into of agreements constituting dealing in securities and other business and 'containing . . . information calculated to lead directly or indirectly to the doing of any of those acts', irrespective of their accuracy, and subject to exemptions, for example in relation to registered prospectuses and authorised unit trusts and distribution only to professional investors (1939 PFI 13(1), 1958 PFI 14(1)). In the 1986 FSAct the marketing regime related to all forms of regulated activity (3.2.2) and sensibly divided into the only two, logical, types of marketing.

10.4.1.1 Written marketing

Territorial scope Subject to exemptions, 'no person other than an authorised person shall issue or cause to be issued an investment advertisement in the United Kingdom unless its contents have been approved by an authorised person' (1986 FSAct 57(1)). An advertisement was 'issued' not upon printing or production but when either offered or sent to recipients or, if sent in sealed form, when received. Thus, 'issued in the UK . . . has been widely interpreted by the market . . . [as] apply[ing] only to promotions received in the United Kingdom. The logic . . . is that an advertisement is not issued until it is communicated or received. The view is that . . . the section applies, first, to advertisements that originate in the United Kingdom and are sent within it and, secondly, to advertisements that originate outside the United Kingdom and are sent into it . . . [It] would not cover . . . promotions . . . that originate in the United Kingdom but are sent outside it.'[21]

The advertisement had to be issued/caused to be issued 'in the United Kingdom' although, for this purpose, 'an advertisement . . . issued outside the United Kingdom shall be treated as issued in the United Kingdom if it is directed to persons in the Untied Kingdom or is made available to them otherwise than in a newspaper, journal, magazine or other periodical publication published and circulating principally outside the United Kingdom' (1986 FSAct 207(3)). This followed the general criminal law approach for 'result-crimes' (12.2.2), although it posed significant challenges when the Internet was invented, because SIB's initial view that 'where an advertisement held anywhere on the Internet is made available to or can be obtained by someone in the United Kingdom (e.g. it can be pulled up on a computer screen in the UK) that advertisement may be viewed as having been issued in the United Kingdom'[22] resulted in the spectre of all financial providers

---

[21] Parl. Deb., House of Commons, Standing Committee A, FSMB, 30th Sitting, 2 December 1999, Minister, col. 1084.
[22] The Internet: Advertising into the UK, SIB General Letter, June 1996.

around the World having committed criminal offences. Accordingly, it formulated a more restricted enforcement approach under which 'FSA will consider the steps which a person has taken to avoid "issuing"... an investment advertisement in the UK ... including ... the extent to which the underlying investment or ... service ... was available to UK investors ... including ... through other media; ... the extent to which positive steps had been taken to ensure that UK investors did not obtain the investment service ... [and] the extent to which positive steps had been taken to limit access to the site ... include[ing] requiring pre-registration (and the issuing of passwords) ... As regards "directed at persons in the UK" ... FSA would take account of ... whether the site contains disclosures and wordings ... that the investment services were not available in those jurisdictions where the firm was not ... permitted ... to promote or sell the product[23] ... whether the ... site was written in a manner which made it clear that it was not aimed at UK investors ... [and] whether ... the site [has been advertised] in the UK.'[24] Similar issues arose in trying to rely on the exemptions for distribution solely to professionals [10.4.2.4] in that 'the ability to freely access material held on the Internet is problematic ... [since the] exemption depends on the advertisement being issued to a restricted ... class of persons ... [so that the] firm [must] ... restrict access to its site'.[25] And, for the same reason, '[a]ny Internet advertisement for an unregulated [collective investment] scheme should only be accessible by the persons to whom promotion is permitted [within 10.5.6.1]'.[26]

Where one firm (A) distributed advertisements, say brochures, to another firm (B) and B sent them to persons with whom it could rely on an exemption which A could not rely on, A had 'issued' the advertisements to the end recipients if either B was its agent for distribution or was remunerated for doing so or the advertisements had otherwise been 'caused' to be issued by A.

Scope of investment advertisements An 'investment advertisement' had two features. First, it had to be in the nature of an 'advertisement' and this 'includes every form of advertising, whether in a publication, by the display of notices, signs, labels or showcards, by means of circulars,[27] catalogues, price lists or other documents, by an exhibition of pictures or photographic or cinematographic films, by any sound broadcasting or television, by the

---

[23] 'A visitor to a firm's site should see the required risk warnings ... preferably on entering the site ... [It] is impractical to require firms to [insert] risk warnings ... on every page' (SFA BN 416, 25 August 1997).   [24] SIB GR 2/98, May 1998, paras. 15–17.
[25] SFA BN 416, 25 April 1997, p. 2.   [26] The Internet, IMRO, May 1997, p. 1.
[27] The wide definition of 'advertisement' was adopted because the 1958 PFI regulated only the distribution, or causing to be distributed, of 'circulars' which was not considered to include every type of advertisement, for example in newspapers, since they are 'published', not 'distributed' (Jenkins Report, para. 255; 1977 Cmnd. 6893, para. 19; 1982 Gower, p. 19, FN 26; 1984 Gower, para. 10.06).

distribution of recordings, or in any other manner' (1986 FSAct 207(2)). Thus, an advertisement was a repeated 'document which has the nature of a circular letter, including a letter which may be personalised to some extent if it is one of the series of such letters sent out with a common purpose . . . On the other hand, a genuinely individual letter dealing with matters personal to the writer and the receiver will not be an advertisement';[28] and 'pre-recorded messages [played over the telephone] are likely to be advertisements'.[29] More conventionally, and relating to advertisements in the Primary and Secondary Markets, an 'advertisement' included a newspaper advert of a firm's services generally or of a specific product, a research report, an indicative terms sheet for a product, a press release for a specific deal and, in a corporate finance context, pre-IPO adverts, prospectuses, sub-underwriting letters, circulars to shareholders and take-over documents (2.4.4 (6), (7), (9)).[30] It did not, however, include a defence document in a take-over because it would not lead to an 'investment agreement'. This the second requirement, i.e. the document had to be 'an . . . advertisement inviting persons to enter or offer to enter into an investment agreement . . . or containing information calculated to lead directly or indirectly to persons doing so'. An 'investment agreement' was 'any agreement the making or performance of which by either party constitutes an investment activity . . . within [3.2.2.1–3.2.2.6]' (1986 FSAct 57(2), 44(9)). 'Calculated to lead' 'may be read as likely to lead'[31] and, thus, an advertisement of a software system which, when operated by the investor, generated buy and sell recommendations 'w[as] clearly designed to encourage customers to believe that investing in the securities concerned was likely to be a profitable exercise, and to that extent was "calculated to lead" at least "indirectly" to them buying and selling such investments'.[32] Similarly, an advertisement containing merely attractively compiled information with an offer or invitation to treat, and even an invitation to a meeting at which an investment opportunity was to be discussed. And since 'investment advertisement' included an advertisement inviting entry into of an investment agreement, it followed that an agreement itself, if in the nature of an 'advertisement', would be caught.

Exemptions There were many exemptions, along the lines of those currently in place under FSMA for non-real time promotions (10.4.2.4).

Licensed firms The prohibition did not apply if either the issuer was licensed or the advertisement was 'approved' by a licensed firm because '[t]he objective is to ensure that all investment advertisements are subject

---

[28] SIB GR 4/94, July 1994, para. 6.   [29] SIB GR 3/91, June 1991, para. 12.
[30] *Re Chez Nico (Restaurants) Ltd.* [1991] BCC 736 at 752.
[31] SIB GR 4/94, July 1994, para. 11.
[32] In *Re Market Wizard Systems (UK) Ltd.* [1998] 2 BCLC 282, para. 52. See, further, 3.2.2.3.

to rules concerning form and content [10.5] and that a . . . [licensed] person . . . is responsible for ensuring that those rules are met'.[33]

Contravention Contravention was a criminal offence and, in addition, the person issuing the advertisement or causing it to be issued 'shall not be entitled to enforce any agreement to which the advertisement related' unless either 'the person against whom enforcement is sought . . . was not influenced . . . to any material extent, by the advertisement in making his decision to enter into the agreement . . . or . . . the advertisement was not misleading as to the nature of the investment [or] the terms of the agreement . . . and fairly stated any risks involved' (1986 FSAct 57(3)–(10)).

10.4.1.2 Oral marketing

Scope of unsolicited calls Again subject to exemptions, and although Professor Gower had said 'I wish that cold calling could be banned',[34] 'no person shall in the course of or in consequence of an unsolicited call . . . made on a person in the United Kingdom . . . or . . . made from the United Kingdom on a person elsewhere, by way of business enter into an investment agreement [within 10.4.1.1] with the person on whom the call is made or procure or endeavour to procure that person to enter into such an agreement' (1986 FSAct 56(1)). The policy was:

> a combination of two factors . . . first, that unsolicited calls afford an opportunity for bringing personal pressure to bear on individuals who have given little or no forethought to the purchase now urged upon them . . . and, secondly, that many investment transactions are complex relative to the financial sophistication of the individuals concerned and involve financial commitments that are large or long-term . . . all of which aggravate the dangers of an ill-considered transaction.[35]

An 'unsolicited call' was 'a personal visit or oral communication made without express invitation' (1986 FSAct 56(8)), 'express' being more than 'an implicit invitation to call, such as the supply of one's telephone number in a tear-off request to an advertiser for further information',[36] but less than an invitation made on the customer's own, unsolicited, initiative. Thus, firms relied on a provision in the Terms of Business that 'The Customer expressly requests the Firm to call with investment opportunities'. The definition was so wide that although the Government never intended it to catch a firm which was invited by the investor to talk about one investment and then switched the conversation to another,[37] the

---

[33] Parl. Deb., House of Lords, 20 October 1986, Minister, col. 37.
[34] 1984 Gower, para. 8.47.
[35] Regulation of the Marketing of Investment Products and Services, SIB, March 1990, para. 4.8.   [36] Ibid, para. 4.6.
[37] Parl. Deb., House of Lords, 23 July 1986, Minister, col. 350.

regulators considered that it 'covers not only cold calls in the colloquial sense but also the follow-up of referrals and calls made in response to an implicit invitation'.[38]

Territorial scope As a contrast to the investment advertisement prohibition which applied to advertisements issued in or into, but not from, the UK (10.4.1.1), this prohibition applied to calls made in or from, but not into, the UK and, further, there was no specific exemption for licensed firms.

Exemptions Since the prohibition was on both entering into the agreement and procuring or endeavouring to procure, it followed that both the agent making the call and its principal each needed an exemption on which they could rely. The policy, though, was to 'allow only three exceptions from the . . . ban on cold-calling:

(a) Calls on professional investors . . .
(b) Calls where the contract can be cancelled [10.5.6.4] . . .
(c) Calls made on a person with whom the caller has a written agreement that contemplates unsolicited calls.[39]

The scope of the exemptions was similar to that later permitted under FSMA (10.4.2.4).

Contravention Contravention was not a criminal offence but 'any investment agreement . . . entered into . . . shall not be enforceable' unless 'the person on whom the call was made was not influenced . . . to any material extent, by anything said or done in . . . the call' or 'following discussions between the parties . . . his entering into the agreement can fairly be regarded as a consequence of those discussions rather than the call . . . and [he] was aware of the nature of the agreement and any risks involved in entering into it' (1986 FSAct 56(2)–(6)).

10.4.2 The FSMA regime

Pre MiFID: Notwithstanding the practical workability of the 1986 FSAct regime, even in relation to the Internet, the Treasury and FSA could not resist a fundamental rewrite because '[e]xisting legislation distinguishes between the regulation of advertisements . . . and unsolicited calls . . . [FSMA] brings together the different regimes in a single cohesive framework which takes full account of . . . changing . . . technology . . . [and] defines financial promotion in terms which . . . covers . . . both issuing of advertisements and making unsolicited calls . . . The advent of email and

---

[38] FIMBRA Briefing No. 5, September 1991.
[39] Regulation of Investment Business – The New Framework, SIB and MIBOC, December 1985, para. 3.3.6.

the Internet has . . . lessened the differences between telephone calls and other media.'[40] But there were in fact 'considerable practical difficulties in combining the . . . separate oral and written regimes',[41] particularly in relation to the necessary exemptions which, although clothed in the most depressing complexity, essentially had to maintain the distinction if only because that is it the way the World is structured.

MiFID has not resulted in any changes to this regime as it applies to unlicensed firms. Indeed, although 'the government plans to . . . review the FPO [(10.4.2.4) with the] . . . aim . . . [of] reduc[ing] . . . the complexity and cost of marketing communications . . . [w]e expect the government to start work on this review . . . after MiFID has been implemented'.[42]

10.4.2.1 The scope of 'financial promotions'

The prohibition is that 'A person ('A') must not, in the course of business, communicate an invitation or inducement to engage in investment activity . . . unless –

(a) A is an authorised person; or
(b) the content of the communication is approved . . . by an authorised person.

To communicate 'includes causing a communication to be made' (FSMA 21(1), (2), (13)) which has the same meaning as in the 1986 FSAct (10.4.1.1), and 'engaging in investment activity' means 'entering or offering to enter into an agreement the making or performance of which by either party constitutes a[n] . . . activity [within 3.2.2.1–3.2.2.6]' (FSMA 21(8)–(11)), again the same as under the 1986 FSAct. Similarly, there has to be either an invitation (10.4.1.1) or, rather than 'information calculated to lead' to investment, its new formulation of an 'inducement'. This requires '[t]he material . . . to be clearly promotional, rather than simply informative'.[43] For the Government:

> There are different dictionary meanings of 'inducement' and one . . . is to 'bring something about or cause it to happen'. But there is a difference between the meaning that that word could be given on its own and the meaning that it . . . ha[s] in th[is] . . . context . . . [T]he Government do not believe that 'inducement' . . . will catch communications where the effect has been to prompt an investment decision regardless of the motivation of the communicator . . . '[I]nducement' in its . . . [FSMA] usage . . . incorporates an element of design or purpose on the part of the person making the communication . . . [T]here must be an element

---

[40] FSMB: A Consultation Document, HMT, July 1998, Part I, paras. 6.1, 6.2.
[41] FSMB: Progress Report, HMT, March 1999, paras. 10.1, 10.2.
[42] FSA CP 06/20, para. 2.3.2.
[43] Parl. Deb., House of Commons, Standing Committee A, FSMB, 9th Sitting, 20 July 1999, Minister, col. 326.

of persuasion contained in the communication . . . Our intention, in relying on 'invitation or inducement', has . . . been to capture the flavour of 'old' advertising and cold-calling . . . It follows that the [prohibition] . . . will not catch . . . public announcements [or] exchanges of draft share purchase agreements in corporate finance transactions.[44]

FSA agrees that 'it is . . . an objective test to decide whether a communication is . . . an inducement . . . [I]t must both have the purpose or intent of leading a person to engage in investment activity and be promotional in nature . . . [i.e.] the communicator intended the communication to persuade or invite the recipient to engage in investment activity . . . [and] the communication . . . seek[s] to persuade or incite the recipient to engage in investment activity . . . An inducement . . . [i]s a link in the chain . . . intended to lead ultimately to an agreement to engage in investment activity . . . Only those [links] that are a significant step in persuading or inciting . . . a recipient to engage in investment activity will be inducements' (PERG 8.4.4, 8.4.7). There is, thus, a distinction between: sources of information such as directory listings, mere links to another website, lists of historic prices and image adverts with no identified products or services which 'may involve an inducement (to contact the advertiser) but will be too far removed from any possible investment activity'; financial promotions such as live or indicative prices on a screen-based trading system, a prospectus and a direct offer advert with a form to complete; and possible financial promotions, depending on context and content, such as 'tombstone' advertisements (announcement of the firm's past achievements), invitations to attend meetings or receive calls or visits, and customer agreements with an explanation of their terms, effects and/or consequences (PERG 8.4.9–8.4.11, 8.4.13, 8.4.19, 8.4.20, 8.4.25, 8.4.26). And, of course, a financial promotion can be in any of the previous forms, written or oral.

Only communications 'in the course of business' are caught, not 'personal communications, such as informal conversations or communications',[45] and this 'requires a commercial intent on the part of the communicator. This does not . . . have to be . . . carrying on regulated activities [3.2.7] . . . [nor] in the course of carrying on activities as a business in their own right.' (PERG 8.5.2)

10.4.2.2 A chain of 'communicators'; and 'approval'

As with the previous regime, firm A might be liable for the communication of a written promotion to the end recipient through firm B. However, now the regulatory view is that 'because . . . communicate includes causing to communicate', if there is one exemption that the communicator can rely on, then this will 'frank' the causing to communicate such that the causer

---

[44] Parl. Deb., House of Lords, 18 May 2000, Minister, col. 387.
[45] Financial Promotion – Third Consultation Document, HMT, October 2000, para. 2.19.

can also, in effect, rely on it (PERG 8.6.7). If, alternatively, A is a licensed firm, originally it appeared that 'provided that the financial promotion which [B] . . . communicate[s] is still in the form originally approved or communicated by [A] . . . then . . . [B] will not be caught by the financial promotion restriction'.[46] However, in FSA's view, B 'communicates' and 'approval [by A] . . . must be specifically for the purpose of enabling the financial promotion to be communicated by unauthorised persons . . . [I]t will not be enough that an authorised person has ensured that the financial promotion complies with . . . [FSA rules] purely so that he can communicate it himself . . . An unauthorised person may pass on a financial promotion made . . . by an authorised person . . . [only if the] authorised person . . . also . . . approved its content . . . for th[at] . . . purpose' (PERG 8.9.1, 8.9.3. See also FSA PM COB 3.12.1(3)), which may seem a rather technical view. However, 'approval', as under the 1986 FSAct, can be given in relation to all products and services except a collective investment scheme 'if [the authorised firm] would be prohibited . . . from effecting the communication himself' (FSMA 240. See also, COBS 4.10.3(4)), i.e. if it could not rely on any of the exemptions in 10.5.6.1 were it to itself make the particular communication. Such restriction, which existed under the 1986 FSAct, has always been regarded as 'effectively an adjunct to [the restriction on authorised firms in 10.5.6]'.[47] Nor can a 'real time promotion' (10.4.2.4) be approved (FSA PM COB 3.2.4(2), 3.12.2; COBS 4.10.4).

10.4.2.3 Territorial scope

Like the 1986 FSAct, the financial promotion 'prohibition appl[ies] . . . to all communications originating inside the United Kingdom',[48] made in or from the UK. It also applies to all communications made into the UK. However, it does not apply to 'non-real time communications' if either the 'communication . . . is [only] made . . . to a person who receives the communication outside the United Kingdom' or it 'is directed . . . only at persons outside the United Kingdom', the previous enforcement criteria being codified so that there are five criteria for whether such a communication is 'directed at' the UK:

(a) the communication . . . indicat[es] . . . that it is directed only at persons outside the United Kingdom;
(b) the communication . . . indicat[es] . . . that it must not be acted upon by persons in the United Kingdom;
(c) the communication is not referred to in, or directly accessible from, any other communication made to a person . . . in the United Kingdom . . .

---

[46] Ibid, para. 2.17.   [47] SIB CP 83, August 1994, para. 10.
[48] Parl. Deb., House of Commons, Standing Committee A, FSMB, 10th Sitting, 22 July 1999, Minister, col. 351.

(d) there are in place proper systems and procedures to prevent recipients in the United Kingdom . . . engaging in the investment activity to which the communication relates . . .
(e) the communication is included in . . . a website . . . or periodical publication . . . [or] broadcast . . . principally for reception outside the United Kingdom. (2005 FPO 12(1)–(4))

The procedure in condition (d) 'may be conducted manually using a questionnaire or electronically through password-protected access . . . or . . . software to recognise and reject United Kingdom addresses' (AUTH, 2003, Ann., 1.12.22) and, with condition (e), 'it will be one indication that a financial promotion in a website is directed into the UK if the website is registered with a UK search engine' (PERG 8.12.8). Thus, a 'disclaimer [alone] . . . stating that material on the site was not . . . meant to be viewed by persons in the UK' is insufficient because 'the UK viewer is not prevented, but only discouraged, from viewing'.[49] If conditions (a)–(d) are met by a communication originating in the UK, or conditions (c) and (d) by a communication originating outside the UK, it is conclusive that such a communication is not directed at the UK; otherwise, conditions '(a) to (e) are . . . to be taken into account in determining whether or not a communication is to be regarded as directed at . . . the United Kingdom' (2005 FPO 12).[50]

10.4.2.4 Exemptions

Because of the extreme width of the term 'financial promotion' it has become necessary to provide over 60 detailed, complex and sometime random exemptions, some applying to oral communications only, some to written communications only, and some to both, but all resting upon the complex distinction between 'real time communications' (which can be 'solicited' or 'unsolicited') and 'non-real time communications', aka oral and written communications, respectively. FSA guidance states that 'Any one particular communication will either be real time or non-real time but not both' (PERG 8.6.10(1)).

'Real time' This is 'any communication made in the course of a personal visit, telephone communication or other interactive dialogue' (2005 FPO 7(1)). A telephone conversation includes a scripted call (PERG 8.10.4): 'the financial promotion is the words spoken during the conversation and not the script'[51] and, because it must be 'interactive', a speech is not real time

---

[49] Treatment of material on Overseas Internet Worldwide Web Sites, FSA, 28 May 1998, para. 12.
[50] These provisions give effect to 2000 FSMA 21(3): 'in the case of communications originating outside the United Kingdom . . . only if the communication is capable of having an effect in the United Kingdom' and, if the test is satisfied, 'it is irrelevant whether the communication [actually] has an effect' (PERG 8.8.1).
[51] CP 104 – Responses on Financial Promotion, FSA, 20 December 2001, p. 18.

Marketing investments

and nor is its recording, even if relayed live although, and this strains credulity, if the promoter 'answer[s] questions from the audience . . . in a way that . . . does not call for any intervention . . . [it] will be a non-real time communication. On the other hand, the question may call for . . . a conversation with the questioner, in which case the communication will be . . . real time' (PERG 8.10.6) and solicited, although goodness knows what its status is when heard by the other members of the audience. Each communication must, of course, come within an applicable exemption unless made by an authorised firm.

'**Solicited**' It is solicited where 'the . . . call, visit or dialogue . . . was initiated by the recipient of the communication . . . or . . . takes place in response to an express request from the recipient' (2005 FPO 8(1)) and 'a person is not to be treated to expressly requesting a call, visit or dialogue (i) because he omits to indicate that he does not wish to receive [it or] . . . (ii) because he agrees to standard terms that state that such a visit, call or dialogue will take place; unless he has signified clearly that, in addition to agreeing to the terms, he is willing for them to take place' (2005 FPO 8(3)(a)), thus requiring a revision to the 1986 FSAct practice (10.4.1.2) since, in FSA's view, a customer's signature to a standard terms of business letter is not sufficient, but the customer would have to sign the letter twice, the second time at a specific paragraph consenting to receive calls or visits. As regards (i), 'the mere failure . . . to tick a box which says "tick here if you do not wish to receive further promotions" will not be sufficient to indicate that that person has consented to further calls being made'.[52] Switching the conversation is now clearly caught since 'a communication is solicited only if it is clear from all the circumstances when the call, visit or dialogue is . . . requested that during the course of the call, visit or dialogue conversations will be made concerning the kind of . . . activities or investments to which the communications in fact made relate' (2005 FPO 8(2)(b)).

'**Unsolicited**' An unsolicited communication is one which has not been solicited by the recipient.

'**Non-real time**' This category 'include communications made by letter or e-mail or contained in a publication' and, otherwise, 'the [following] factors . . . are to be treated as indications that a communication is . . . non-real time . . .

   (a) the communication is made to or directed at more than one recipient in identical terms . . .
   (b) the communication is made or directed by way of a system which . . . creates a record of the communication which is available to

---

[52] Financial Promotion – Second Consultation Document, HMT, October 1999, para. 2.31.

the recipient to refer to at a later time ... [and/or] does not enable or require the recipient to respond immediately to it. (2005 FPO 7(3)–(5))

Exemptions The conditions of each exemption need to be very carefully considered before relying on it, and their application in the Capital Markets context is best understood through Figure 9, always remembering that exemptions can be combined in respect of a single promotion (2005 FPO 11).

10.4.2.5 Contravention

Contravention is a criminal offence in relation to any type of promotion, in contrast to the 1986 FSAct regime, unless '(a) ... he believes on reasonable grounds that the content of the communication was prepared, or approved ... by an authorised person ... or (b) ... he took all reasonable precautions and exercised all due diligence to avoid committing the offence' (FSMA 25). The Government did not consider that paragraph (a) provides a defence where an unauthorised firm 'caused' an authorised firm to issue a written promotion and the latter did not state on it that, as well as issuing it, it had also approved it for issue (10.4.2.2). Hence, there is a specific exemption for 'a communication caused to be made ... by an unauthorised person which is made ... by an authorised person ... [if] the authorised person prepared the content of the communication' (2005 FPO 17A). In addition to an offence, any resultant agreement cannot be enforced unless, with much more discretionary criteria than under the 1986 FSAct, 'the court ... is satisfied that it is just an equitable in the circumstances ... hav[ing] regard to ...

[1] If the applicant made the unlawful communication ... whether he reasonably believed that he was not making such a communication.
[2] If the applicant did not make the unlawful communication ... whether he knew that the agreement was entered into in consequence of such a communication. (FSMA 30(2), (4)–(7))

10.5 Marketing by licensed persons

10.5.1 Full disclosure

10.5.1.1 Common law

Traditionally at common law the Victorian capitalist principle of caveat emptor ('let the buyer beware') has meant that there is no duty in marketing literature, or otherwise, to disclose anything in particular about the product or service, it is simply that, as the general law developed, what is stated must not be deceitful or fraudulent (and 'fraud is proved when ... a false representation has been made (1) knowingly, or (2) without belief in its truth, or (3)

Marketing investments

EXEMPTION				APPLIES TO COMMUNICATION WHICH IS:		
				REAL TIME AND:		NON-REAL TIME
				UNSOLICITED	SOLICITED	
EXEMPTION BY TYPE OF RECIPIENT						
1	Professional investor (2005 FPO 19, 49). Generally, these follow the Pre-MiFID categories of Intermediate Customer (8.3.2)			✓	✓	✓
2	Personalised communication (2005 FPO 28, 28A)			✓	✓	✓
3	Individuals (2005 FPO 48, 50, 50 A)	(a)	Certified high net worth	✗	✓	✓
		(b)	Sophisticated	✓	✓	✓
		(c)	Self-certified sophisticated	✓	✓	✓
EXEMPTION BY TYPE OF COMMUNICATOR						
4	Introducer (2005 FPO 15)			✓	✓	✓
5	Overseas firm (2005 FPO 30-33)	(a)	Made from outside UK	✗	✓	✗
		(b)	Customer previously non-UK resident	✓	✗	✓
		(c)	Knowledgeable investor	✓	✗	✗
6	Passported firm (2005 FPO 20B, 36)	(a)	E-Commerce (10.5.4)	✓	✓	✓
		(b)	Other	✗	✓	✓
7	Corporations (2005 FPO 42, 43, 45, 52, 59)	(a)	To securities holders	✗	✓	✓
		(b)	Annual report and accounts	✗	✗	✓
		(c)	Private placement	✗	✓	✓
		(d)	To group companies	✓	✓	✓
8	CIS, to unitholder (2005 FPO 40, 44)			✗	✓	✓
9	Trustee, to fellow trustee, settler or beneficiary (2005 FPO 53, 54)			✓	✓	✓
10	Follow-up communication (2005 FPO 14)			✗	✓	✓
11	Customer to firm (2005 FPO 13)			✓	✓	✓
SPECIFIC CAPITAL MARKETS EXEMPTIONS						
12	Takeovers (2005 FPO 62-66)			✓	✓	✓
13	Securities offers (2005 FPO 29, 67-71), generally a registered prospectus			✗	Depends	✓
14	New Issues (2005 FPO 29, 67-71)	(a)	Listed securities		✗	✗	✓
		(b)	Unlisted securities		✗	✗	✓
		(c)	Collective investment scheme	(i) Authorised unit trust/OEIC	Promotions must be by an authorised person		
				(ii) Recognised scheme			
				(iii) UCITS (2005 FPO 36)	✗	✓	✓
EXEMPTIONS BY TYPE OF PROMOTION						
15	Generic (2005 FPO 17)			✓	✓	✓
16	One-off (2005 FPO 28)			✗	✓	✓

Figure 9 *Financial promotion exemptions*

recklessly, careless whether it is true or false')[53] or in breach of contract,[54] or in breach of a fiduciary relationship,[55] or in negligent breach of a duty of care[56] such that that which is stated is not true, complete and accurate. It was because of these limitations on the requirement to state anything in particular that prospectus law, first, imposed its own standard of liability and, second, detailed lists of disclosures that needed to be made in the prospectus (2.2.2, 10.2) and, third, on top of that, in its current formulation, requires that 'the prospectus contains . . . the information necessary to enable investors to make an informed assessment of . . . the assets and liabilities, financial position, profits and losses and prospects of the issuer . . . and . . . the rights attaching to the . . . securities'. Similarly, in listed offers, listing particulars must 'contain all such information as investors and their professional advisers would reasonably require, and reasonably expect to find there, for the purpose of making an informed assessment of' such matters (FSMA 80 (1), 87A (1), (2)). The same three results have been reached in relation to authorised unit trusts and OEICs which can be marketed to the general public (2.6 (10), 10.5.6.1) (COLL 4.2.2, 4.2.4, 4.2.5) where the prospectus 'must . . . not contain any provision which is unfairly prejudicial to the interests of unit holders' and, after a long list of mandatory contents, must 'contain . . . [a]ny other material information . . . including but not confined to . . .

(a) information which investors and their professional advisers would reasonably require, and reasonably expect to find in the prospectus, for the purpose of making an informed judgement about the merits of investing in the . . . fund and the extent and characteristics of the risks accepted by so participating; [and]
(b) . . . any risks which investment in the . . . fund may reasonably be regarded as presenting for reasonably prudent investors of moderate means. (COLL 4.2.2(2)(a) 4.2.5(27))

10.5.1.2 The Principles

Pre-MiFID: For similar reasons, other written offers to buy or sell securities required detailed disclosures by licensed dealers under the 1939 PFI and 1958 PFI (1939 LDRs 2, 5; 1960 LDRs 1, 2, 17), leading eventually to a requirement to 'disclose sufficient information about the investment to provide a person such as the persons to whom the offer is addressed with an adequate and reasonable basis for deciding whether or not, and on what terms, to accept the offer', although 'a licensed dealer shall not be taken to have committed a breach of this rule if he can establish that he took all reasonable care to ensure that the offer document satisfied its requirements' (1983 LDRs 9(1)). For the 1986 FSAct regulators, the same sentiment was best expressed

---

[53] *Derry* v. *Peek* (1889) 14 App. Cas. 237. [54] *De La Bere* v. *Pearson* [1908] 1 KB 280.
[55] *Nocton* v. *Lord Ashburton* [1914] AC 932.
[56] *Hedley Byrne & Co Ltd.* v. *Heller & Partners Ltd.* [1964] AC 465.

in one of their rules that 'All advertisements should be legal, honest, decent and truthful, clear and precise and in no way false and tendentious'.[57] The effect of the Licensed Dealers Rule is achieved in FSA's current Principle that: 'A firm must pay due regard to the information needs of its clients and communicate information to them in a way which is clear, fair and not misleading' (9.1). '[C]lear . . . emphasise[s] . . . clear and understandable' and only the second part on communications applies in relation to a Market Counterparty (9.1.2.1). Moreover, '[w]hat is judged misleading will . . . be conditioned by the particular knowledge and experience of the counterparty. So it will take a lot to mislead a market counterparty.'[58] 'If a firm volunteers information to a market counterparty . . . the firm would not advise [it] . . . about the reliability, relevance or importance of that information. Silence . . . does not result in a breach of [the] Principle . . . unless . . . it results in a communication . . . being misleading . . . It is for a firm to decide whether it wishes to provide information to a market counterparty' (FSA PM MAR 3.4.6, 3.4.7(1)). In addition, 'A firm must conduct its business with due skill, care and diligence' (PRIN 2.1.1, Principle 2), which is interpreted by FSA as requirements 'to inform . . . a customer . . . of material information . . . [the person dealing with the customer] was aware, or ought to have been aware, of' and 'to explain the risks of investment to a customer' (APER 4.2.3, 4.2.4(1)), this being FSA's interpretation of the equivalent Principle applying to Approved Persons) (5.4.2). Harking back to its Objectives (2.5.1):

> We want consumers to take responsibility for their own financial decisions. To do this they need material on products which is clear, fair and not misleading.[59]

Thus, '[o]ur financial promotions work forms part of our overarching theme of Treating Customers Fairly [9.2]'.[60]

MiFID: These Principles continue (9.1).

10.5.1.3 The rules

Pre-MiFID: One rule stated that 'When a firm communicates information to a customer, the firm must take reasonable steps to communicate in a way which is clear, fair and not misleading . . . hav[ing] regard to the customer's knowledge of the . . . investment business to which the information relates' (FSA PM COB 2.1.3, 2.1.4) and, to emphasise the point, with promotions within 10.5.2.1, 'A firm must be able to show that it has taken reasonable steps to ensure that a non-real time financial promotion is clear, fair and not misleading', which meant that, for example, 'a comparison or contrast

---

[57] FIMBRA Draft Rules, June 1987, App. 4.
[58] The Principles for Businesses, FSA PS, October 1999, paras. 35–36.
[59] Annual Report 2002/03, FSA, p. 35.
[60] Financial Promotions: Taking Stock and Moving Forward, FSA, February 2005, p. 5.

must ... compare investments or services meeting the same need or ... purpose' and be 'objective ...; not create confusion ...; not discredit or denigrate ...; not take unfair advantage of the reputation of a ... competitor; not present investments or services as imitations ...; and indicate ... clear[ly] ... the date on which the offer ends or ... i[f] subject to ... availability' (FSA PM COB 3.8.4). Moreover, the firm had to ensure that:

(a) its promotional purpose is not ... disguised or misrepresented;
(b) any statement of fact, promise or prediction is clear, fair and not misleading and discloses any relevant assumptions;
(c) any statement of opinion is honestly held ...
(d) the facts on which any comparison or contrast is made are verified ... and ... [it] is presented in a fair and balanced way ...
(e) it does not contain any false indications ...
(h) it does not omit any matters the omission of which causes the financial promotion not to be clear, fair and not misleading; and
(i) the accuracy of all material statements of fact ... can be substantiated. (FSA PM COB 3.8.5)

Given the problems with equity return of capital products in the early 1990s,[61] 'the description of an investment as 'guaranteed' should only be used where there is a legally enforceable agreement with a third party' and all of this was to be judged having regard to the audience targeted (FSA PM COB 3.8.7(1), (2)). In other words, 'the question whether ... [it] is misleading may be determined by reference to ... [what has] been omitted ... as well as by reference to [its] content and form ..., the context in which it is issued, the general impression which it creates and the likelihood of any person being misled',[62] for example in 'promot[ing] ... "high income" investments ... emphasis should not be placed on the "income" offered, without equal prominence being placed on the risks and nature of the product'.[63] Overall:

> A financial promotion should clearly indicate what the product or service is ... in a way that is relevant and meaningful to the ... intended customer. It is not necessary, however, and in some cases not helpful, to describe the product in technical terms as many customers will not understand such a description ... Statements should not mislead the customer into believing something that is ... highly unlikely ... For example ... it would usually be misleading to suggest that it is possible to take no risk and still receive a high return.[64]

FSA was not slow to take enforcement action for breach of these requirements and held firms to a higher standard the more risky and illiquid the

---

[61] Sales check on equity schemes, Independent, 8 February 1993.
[62] Rules of LAUTRO, August 1987, rule 6.3(3).   [63] SFA Briefing, 7 December 1993, p. 8.
[64] Financial Promotions: taking stock and moving forward, FSA, February 2005, pp. 12, 15–16.

investment advertised.⁶⁵ And to ensure its truth and say it a third time, a 'specific non-real time . . . promotion', being one 'which identifies or promotes a particular investment or service', 'must . . . include a fair and adequate description of: (a) the nature of the investment or service; (b) the investment . . . [and] (c) the risks involved', FSA providing detailed guidance in relation to certain products (FSA PM COB 3.8.8, 3.8.9; COB 3, Ann. 4).

On top of all this, where the firm intended to 'make a personal recommendation . . . or act as a discretionary . . . manager . . . or arrange . . . or execute a deal in a warrant or derivative . . . or engage in stocklending' it had to 'take reasonable steps to ensure that the private customer understands the nature of the risks involved' which, although FSA only said 'include[s]' the giving, and in some cases signature by the customer, of mandated risk warnings (FSA PM COB 5.4.3–5.4.13; COB 5, Ann. 1, 2), in practice was often treated by the market as exhaustive. With discretionary portfolio management the risks in the portfolio can change over time and if they do 'customers shall . . . be notified promptly'.⁶⁶ Moreover, in the context of promotions:

> Where firms are exposing the general public, as opposed to a limited class of investor, to a particular promotion they should not assume that the inherent risks of a product or service will be understood by all. We require that financial promotions present a balanced indication of the product, but they do not necessarily need to be all-encompassing . . . we do not expect every possible risk to be described in a short advert.⁶⁷

> We have considered whether we should mandate specific language for risk warnings . . . [T]his would not be particularly effective, as risk warnings tend to be clichés unless the wording is tailored appropriately . . . [I]t would be more customer friendly to allow firms to tailor the wording to the types of investment being advertised and the tone of their advertisements.⁶⁸

There were, however, further risk warning requirements where business for a Private Client was to be conducted from outside the UK (FSA PM COB 5.5.7). In giving any such risk warnings, the regulators have always taken the view that where they 'were either subsumed by other information, or . . . included in print so small that they could easily be overlooked . . . or dismissed as unimportant . . . [they] fall short of . . . the "fairness" test'.⁶⁹

---

⁶⁵ See Final Notices for: Highbury Financial Services Ltd., 3 March 2005 (penny shares); City Index Ltd., 22 March 2005 (spread betting); Courtover Investment Management Ltd., 29 April 2005 (unlisted shares); Helmscott Investment Analysis Ltd., 13 January 2005. See also the following FSA Press Notices: 37/2003, 136/2003, 14/2004, 111/2004.
⁶⁶ FSA PN 52/2004, 10 June 2004.
⁶⁷ Financial Promotions: taking stock and moving forward, FSA, February 2005, pp. 12, 13.
⁶⁸ The FSA's regulatory approach to financial promotions, FSA, April 2002, para. 4.10.
⁶⁹ The IMRO Reporter, Issue 4, October 1992, p. 10.

And, notwithstanding risk warnings, a 'suitability' test, in relation to the particular client, may have been necessary (11.2.2).

MiFID: Overall, 'A firm must ensure that a communication of a financial promotion is fair, clear and not misleading' and, while there is a change from the Pre-MiFID taking of 'reasonable steps', all of the Pre-MiFID Rules, guidance and enforcement actions are relevant to its meaning (COBS 4.2.1(1), 4.2.4, 4.2.5) if only because FSA has stated in relation to the change of standard that 'we take a risk-based and proportionate approach and use discretion in our dealings with firms'.[70] In particular, there is an explicit recognition that 'a communication addressed to a professional client may not need to include the same information, or be presented in the same way, as a communication addressed to a retail client' (COBS 4.2.2). And the general nature of the risk warning requirement is also more explicit since 'A firm must provide appropriate information in a comprehensible form to a client about . . . investments and proposed investment strategies; including appropriate guidance on and warnings of the risks associated with . . . those . . . investments or . . . strategies . . . so that the client is reasonably able to understand the nature and risks of the services and . . . investments . . . and, consequently, to take investment decisions on an informed basis', the rule applying to MiFID Business (4.2.I(2), 4.2.III) and, otherwise, 'business carried on for a retail client in relation to a derivative, a warrant or stocklending' (COBS 2.2.1). FSA no longer mandates the form of derivatives risk warnings and the previous, standard form, approach is inadequate in the context of such a wide-ranging and purposive disclosure requirement. In addition, although only a sub-set of the preceding rule and, to that extent, a repetition of it, where the firm carries on MiFID Business or equivalent third country business (4.2.I(2), 4.2.III) with a Retail or Professional Client or, otherwise, 'mak[es] a personal recommendation [11.2] . . . [or] act[s] as a discretionary investment manager . . . [or] arrang[es] [3.2.2.2] [or executes] a deal in a warrant [3.2.1.3] or derivative [3.2.1.6–3.2.1.8] or engage[es] in stocklending activity [7.1.3.3]' with a Retail Client, it 'must provide [the] client with a general description of the nature and risks . . . [which]:

(1) explain[s] the nature of the . . . investment, as well as the risks . . . in sufficient detail to enable the client to take investment decisions on an informed basis; and
(2) include, where relevant . . . an explanation of leverage . . . volatility . . . and any limitations on the available market . . . contingent liabilities . . . and . . . any margin requirements. (COBS 14.3.2. See also 14.3.3–14.3.11)

---

[70] FSA PS 07/6, para. 26.10. Accordingly, even though the promotion is otherwise exempt it would still require to be 'fair, clear and not misleading' (FSA CP 07/16, Ann. M, draft COBS 4.2.2(2)).

Like the Pre-MiFID rule, these rules require the firm to consider all products and services and, in respect of all of them, give to the client a risk warning nuanced by reference to the type of client, being Professional and/or Retail. Although for the purpose of the appropriateness obligation the firm can 'assume that a professional client has the necessary experience and knowledge' (COBS 10.2.1(2)(b)) and, indeed, this is part of the MiFID definition of Professional Client (11.4.2.1), no such assumption can be made for the purposes of the risk warning requirement. It is simply that a Professional, depending on its actual knowledge and experience in relation to the particular product or service, may need a different type of risk warning than a Retail Client. And, notwithstanding risk warnings, a 'suitability' or 'appropriateness' assessment, in relation to the particular client, may be necessary (11.2.2, 11.4).

10.5.2 Specific disclosures

From the beginning under the 1986 FSAct, and continuing today, the policy was that '[a]dvertisements will have to be fair, accurate and complete. The severity of the application of these principles will vary according to the form of advertisement . . . the simplest requirement being for advertisements which carry little or no message, and the most severe to advertisements which seek money "off the page" (i.e. clip-out coupons). Advertisements will have to be appropriate to the degree of sophistication of those to whom they are directed.'[71]

10.5.2.1 Application

Pre-MiFID: These disclosures applied in respect of all 'financial promotions' communicated or approved by all firms, including passported firms acting cross-border into the UK (FSA PM COB 3.1.1, 3.1.2; 2005 FPO 36) except:

- deposit promotions, when only the following applied:
  - 10.5.1.3;
  - if a 'structured deposit', i.e. 'a deposit . . . under which any interest or premium will be paid, or is at risk, according to a formula which involves the performance of (a) an index (other than money market indicia); (b) a stock . . . or (c) a commodity': 10.5.2.2, 10.5.2.3, 10.5.2.4 (FSA PM COB 3.2.3);
- any exempt promotion within 10.4.2.4 (FSA PM COB 3.2.4, 3.2.5(2));
- any promotion only to Market Counterparties or Intermediate Customers (FSA PM COB 3.2.4, 3.2.5(1), 3.2.8(3), 3.5.6, 3.5.7);
- an 'image advertisement' (FSA PM COB 3.2.4, 3.2.5(5), 3.2.7(3)(b), (c));

---

[71] Regulation of Investment Business – The New Framework, SIB and MIBOC, December 1985, para. 3.33.3.

- a 'one-off' real time promotion (FSA PM COB 3.2.5(4), 3.2.7(3)(a));
- handing on another firm's non-real time promotion if the firm 'takes reasonable care to [1] establish that [the] other firm . . . has already confirmed . . . compliance . . . with [FSA's rules and 2] communicates the . . . promotion only to recipients of the type for whom it was intended' (FSA PM COB 3.6.5).

The territorial scope was as in 10.4.2.3 (FSA PM COB 3.1.2(3), 3.3).

MiFID: These rules, and the general 'fair, clear and not misleading requirement' referred to in 10.5.1.3, apply to a 'communication' (which is not defined and therefore should be widely interpreted in accordance with its normal meaning) and, if different, a 'financial promotion' (which has the meaning in 10.4.2.1) issued, made or approved in relation to any Regulated Activity (4.2.I(1)) (COBS 4.1.1, 4.1.4, 4.1.6). The territorial scope, where it relates to MiFID Business, is as in 4.2(e)(i) and, otherwise, 4.2(e)(ii) although, in either case (within that territorial application), the rules only apply:

- with a written communication: if made solely within the UK; and
- with a cold call: if made in or from the UK.

In either case the rules apply to dealing with Retail or Professional Clients (COBS 1, Ann. 1, Part 1, para. 1.1; COBS 4.1.8–4.1.10) (8.2.1) and while there are some exceptions for prospectuses (COBS 4.5.1(3)(b), 4.7.1(3)(a)), there are, in a Capital Markets context, some, but not general, exclusions for exempt promotions within Figure 9 (COBS 4.1.1(2), 4.2.1(2), 4.5.1(3)(a), 4.6.1(3)(a), 4.7.1(4)(a), 4.8.1(1), 4.9.1(3)(a)). FSA acknowledges this change and states that '[w]here [an FPO] . . . exemption would otherwise apply, firms . . . will need to consider the proportionality of the . . . rules when designing compliance procedures for these promotions. For example, where a promotion . . . [Pre-MiFID] falls within exemptions due to the client being . . . sophisticated . . . we would not expect firms to change practices . . . Promotions . . . should be proportionate to the type of consumer and the nature of the product.'[72]

The rules referred to in 10.5.2.2–10.5.2.4 and 10.5.3 'are only applicable to financial promotions addressed to, or likely to be received by, retail clients'.[73] The rules apply 'to a firm . . . communicating with a client' (COBS 4.1.1(1)), which means any recipient (COBS 3.2.1(3)), so that 'firms need to ensure for themselves that all . . . promotions . . . satisfy the . . . rules . . . They cannot rely on another firm to have carried out the . . . exercise but must design a proportionate confirmation of compliance system of their own.'[74]

---

[72] FSA PS 07/6, para. 26.8.
[73] FSA CP 07/16, para. 7.4; Ann. M, COBS 4.2.2(2), 4.6.1(3)(d), 4.8.1(3), 4.9.1(3)(d).
[74] FSA PS 07/6, para. 26.8. See also COBS 4.10.

Marketing investments

10.5.2.2 Disclosures

Pre-MiFID: A number of specific disclosures had to be made:

- Non-real time promotions: 'the name of the firm . . . and either an address of the firm or a contact point from which an address is available' (FSA PM COB 3.8.2, 3.8.3); in relation to comparisons and contrasts with other investments and services (FSA PM COB 3.8.5(2)); and in relation to investments and services of non-UK firms (FSA PM COB 3.12.6).
- Real time promotions: no information beyond that required by 10.5.1.3 needed to be given, but there were rules about how to conduct the meeting/conversation (FSA PM COB 3.8.22–3.8.25) which were extremely similar to the rules under the 1986 FSAct.[75]
- Any promotion: details on the firm (FSA PM COB 5.5.3–5.5.5).

MiFID: The rules are quite similar (COBS 4.8, 6.1.4(1)).

10.5.2.3 Specific promotions

Pre-MiFID: 'Specific' non-real time promotions, which 'identif[y] or promote . . . a particular investment or service', had to disclose conflicts in terms of positions and material interests (6.3.1.2) and produce past performance information in particular ways (FSA PM COB 3.8.10–3.8.16).[76]

MiFID: There is no distinction between specific and general promotions, just requirements generally in relation to disclosure of compensation and past performance information and disclosures where the provider is outside the UK and (with Retail Clients) fair presentation and understanding, comparative information[77] and references to tax (COBS 4.4–4.6, 4.9).

10.5.2.4 Direct offer promotions

Pre-MiFID: A 'direct offer' promotion was non-real time and:

(a) contains an offer by the firm . . . to enter into a[n] . . . agreement with anyone who responds . . . or . . . an invitation to anyone who responds . . . to make an offer . . . to enter into a[n] . . . agreement; [and]
(b) specifies the manner of response or includes a form in which any response is to be made. (FSA PM GLOSSARY, def. of 'direct offer financial promotion').

---

[75] See, for example, SIB Conduct Rules, 7 October 1987, 2.15.
[76] For the policy here, see FSA CP 132, April 2002, Chapters 2 and 4; FSA Consumer Research 21, May 2003; FSA CP 183, May 2003; Standardising Past Performance, FSA PS, December 2003.
[77] For control of misleading comparative advertising, see SI 1988/915, SI 2000/914, SI 2003/3183; Directives 1984/450/EEC, 1997/55/EC.

Ever since such rules were introduced under the 1986 FSAct, '[t]he main point of the[m] . . . is to identify . . . products which can be sold impersonally, purely on the basis of disclosure . . . [without] know your customer and suitability rules apply[ing] . . . The[se] provisions . . . create a distinction which is in some respects analogous to that between prescription-only medicine and those which can be bought over-the-counter.'[78] Over the years the list of restrictions diminished so that under FSA's Pre-MiFID Rules the only restrictions were on derivatives and warrants unless 'the firm . . . has adequate evidence to suggest that the investment may be suitable for the person to whom the promotion is communicated' (FSA PM COB 3.9.5), which necessitated a suitability enquiry (11.2.2). In all cases various disclosures had to be made about the offer, execution-only services, investments which fluctuate in value, taxation and 'structured capital at risk products' or SCARPS, i.e. 'a product, other than a derivative, which provides an agreed level of income or growth . . . and . . . (a) the customer is exposed to a range of outcomes in respect of the return of initial capital invested; (b) th[at] return . . . is linked to the performance of a . . . factor . . . and (c) if the performance is [not] within specified limits . . . the customer could lose . . . the initial capital invested' (FSA PM COB 3.9.6, 3.9.12, 3.9.14, 3.9.15, 3.9.19, 3.9.20, 3.9.31, 3.9.32). This, however, does not include single index tracking funds which involve no pre-set formulae or set performance limits[79] nor 'deposits or other 100% capital secured products . . . [and] OEICS or other open-ended funds'.[80] SCARPS linked to a stock market index or basket were popular in the late 1990s, with investors losing money in the market crash in the early 2000s and, hence, whereas 'in December 1999 . . . FSA commissioned research found that . . . literature for these products w[as] not felt to be misleading',[81] by the end of 2002 '[t]he Financial Services Authority is warning consumers to be careful when investing in income bonds that promise income but carry a high risk that investors may not receive back all, or any, of their original investment' because 'the average age of investors in [such] precipice bonds is over 60'.[82] Two months later '[t]he FSA considers it is very important that . . . prospective investors are given a clear explanation of the risks of investing'[83] because these products 'present a significant risk to an investor's capital and it is essential that consumers understand and accept these risks before they buy . . . [a] concern . . . heightened by the fact that relatively few SCARPS are sold as a result of consumers receiving advice . . . If consumers are not getting personally tailored financial advice, then an adequate explanation of risk is particularly important as they will be relying solely on the

---

[78] Regulation of the Marketing of Investment Products and Services, SIB, March 1990, para. 5.4.   [79] FSA CP 188, July 2003, para. 4.3.
[80] FSA Feedback on CP 188, January 2004, para. 3.2.
[81] Annual Report 1999/2000, FSA, pp. 15–16.   [82] FSA PN/122/2002, 15 December 2002.
[83] FSA GN 7, February 2003, para. 3.1.

literature they receive.'[84] Accordingly, enforcement action was taken not only against a financial intermediary who used 'misleading descriptions . . . of the true risk of the precipice bonds'[85] but also Lloyds TSB Bank plc where it sold such a product through its branch network when 'there was not sufficient specific training of . . . financial consultants in terms of the suitability of the . . . [product] for investors' so that the 'sales . . . process did not identify potential unsuitable sales'.[86]

MiFID: Although the restriction for derivatives and warrants has been done away with, it has been replaced with an analogous 'appropriateness' obligation which applies to all MiFID instruments (3.2.1) and other regulated derivatives (3.2.1.6–3.2.1.8, 11.4). Beyond this, the rules for direct offer promotions are very similar to the Pre-MiFID Rules (COBS 4.7).

10.5.3 Real-time promotions

Pre-MiFID: Continuing a policy that had started as early as the 1939 LDRs, FSA provided that a licensed firm could make an unsolicited real-time promotion only in accordance with the exemptions in 10.4.2.4 (FSA PM COB 3.8.21) or if it related to 'readily realisable securities', non-geared packaged products or a generally marketable packaged product which was not a 'higher volatility fund' or if 'the recipient has an established existing customer relationship . . . such that the recipient envisages receiving unsolicited real time financial promotions' (FSA PM COB 3.10.3).

MiFID: The rules are to similar effect (COBS 4.8).

10.5.4 Electronic Commerce

Pre-MiFID: The Electronic Commerce Directive was conceived in the late 1990s 'to encourage the vigorous growth of electronic commerce in Europe . . . [a] fast moving sector . . . [which] will have a considerable impact on Europe's competitiveness in global markets'[87] and overcome 'the . . . uncertainty in a number of areas about how existing legislation can be applied to the on-line provision of services . . . [given] divergent national legislation'.[88] The requirements imposed under the Directive are in addition to those referred to in 10.5.1–10.5.3 above and imposed in relation to 'information society services', being 'a service [such as a Regulated Activity within 4.2.I(1)] that: (a) is normally provided for remuneration; (b) is provided as a distance; (c) is . . . provided by means of electronic equipment for

---

[84] FSA CP 188, July 2003, paras. 3.5, 3.6.   [85] FSA/PN/076/2004, 1 September 2004.
[86] FSA/PN/098/2003, 25 September 2003.
[87] A European Initiative in Electronic Commerce, European Commission, COM (97) 157, 16 April 1997, p. 4.
[88] Proposal for a Directive, European Commission, COM (1998) 586, 18 November 1998 p. 3.

the processing . . . and storage of data; and (d) is so provided at the individual request of a recipient of the service' (GLOSS., def. of 'information society service'). There were three sets of requirements.

10.5.4.1 Provision of an 'information society service' by a UK, EEA or non-EEA firm from a UK establishment to a client in the UK or a non-EEA State

The following requirements were imposed:

- Information disclosure:
    - provider's name, address of UK establishment, e-mail address, regulatory status, FSA register number, VAT identification number;
    - if price or charges were referred to, 'do so clearly and unambiguously and . . . indicate whether . . . inclusive of tax';
    - any relevant code of conduct to which the provider subscribed and how to access it electronically (unless the contract was concluded by exchange of e-mails);
    - make the terms and conditions of the contract 'available in a way that allows a . . . recipient to store and reproduce them';
    - '[b]efore the recipient places the order:
        (a) the technical steps the recipient should follow . . . to conclude the contract;
        (b) . . . whether the provider will keep a record of the contract and whether it will be accessible to the . . . recipient;
        (c) the technical means of identifying and correcting input errors before the . . . recipient submits the order;
        (d) the . . . language in which the contract may be concluded.'

    If the recipient is not an individual acting in a private capacity, it could agree that the last three requirements above, and the requirements under 'Orders' below, did not apply.

- Commercial communications:
    - 'must be clearly identifiable as such';
    - the provider 'must be clearly identifiable';
    - 'promotional offers . . . must be clearly identifiable as such and any qualifying conditions . . . set out clearly and unambiguously';
    - if unsolicited, must be 'clearly and unambiguously identifiable' as such.
- Orders:
    - receipt must be 'acknowledged without delay' (unless the contract is concluded by email exchange);
    - the 'provider must . . . make . . . available to a . . . recipient, appropriate, effective and accessible technical means . . . to identify and correct technical errors before placing an order' (FSA PM ECO 3.1, 3.2, Ann. 1).–

Marketing investments

10.5.4.2 Provision of an 'information society service' by a UK, EEA or non-EEA firm from a UK establishment to a client in an EEA State

The following rules were disapplied:
- Packaged product disclosure rules (10.5.6.3).
- The rules referred to in 10.5.2.4.

Subject to that, all of the rules in 10.5.1.3 and 10.5.2 applied, ignoring the territorial scope referred to in 10.5.2.1 'as if the person to whom the communication is made or directed was in the United Kingdom' (FSA PM ECO 2.1 and 2.2).

Otherwise, the requirements were as in 10.5.4.1.

10.5.4.3 Provision of an 'information society service' by an EEA firm from an EEA establishment (other than the UK) to a client in the UK

Although not relevant to an otherwise licensed or passported firm, it is worth noting that the mere provision of an 'information society service' is exempt from licensing (RAO 72A), except insofar as the substantive activity carried on thereby would itself require licensing. This is part of the freedoms established by the Directive which uses the methodology of 'country of origin' and, as a result, apart from the provisions referred to below, the only other substantive FSA rule that applied was the Code of Market Conduct (12.5) (FSA PM ECO 1.1).

As regards these substantive requirements, on the basis that the State of establishment had implemented the Directive and the firm was complying with those requirements, then none of the financial promotion rules applied, and only the following did:

- For a specific non-real time financial promotion:
    (1) a description of:
        (a) the main features of the product or service;
        (b) the total price . . .
        (c) any risks associated with the specific features of the contract; and
    (2) the name and address and contact point of the person with whom the consumer would enter into a contract. (FSA PM ECO 1.2.1–1.2.10)
    [3] A statement . . . that past performance should not be seen as an indication of future performance. (FSA PM ECO 1.2.11).
- For a direct offer financial promotion of unregulated collective investment schemes, derivatives or warrants: mandated risk warnings (FSA PM ECO 1.2.13, 1.2.14).

MiFID: Although not affected by MiFID itself, the FSA has recast the provisions implementing the Directive so that they apply only to 'a person carrying on an electronic commerce activity from an establishment in the

United Kingdom' (COBS 1, Ann. 1, Part 3, paras. 7.1–7.5; COBS 5.2.1), i.e. to situations 10.5.4.1 and 10.5.4.2 in the Pre-MiFID Rules and all of the requirements in 10.5.4.1 are applied to both situations (COBS 5.2.2–5.2.9).

10.5.5 Distance marketing

Pre-MiFID: The Distance Marketing Directive related to 'any contract concerning financial services concluded between a supplier and a consumer under an organised distance sales or service-provision scheme run by the supplier who, for the purpose of that contract, makes exclusive use of . . . distance communications up to and including the time at which the contract is concluded'.[89]

10.5.5.1 Passported firms

As a result of the Directive, an EEA firm operating from an establishment in the EEA (other than the UK) which had implemented the Directive was exempt from all the rules in 10.5.1.2, 10.5.1.3 and 10.5.2 in making a 'distance contract' except:

- FSA PM COB 3.8.4 referred to in 10.5.1.3; and
- the rules referred to in 10.5.3; and
- FSA PM COB 3.9.4 referred to in 10.5.2.4; and
- the rules relating to promotion of unregulated collective investment schemes referred to in 10.5.6.1 (FSA PM COB 3.3.4A).

A 'distance contract' was 'a . . . contract concerning financial services, the making or performance of which constitutes a regulated activity [4.2.I(1)], concluded under an organised distance sales or service provision scheme run by the contractual provider of the service who, for the purpose of that contract, makes exclusive use . . . of . . . means of distance communication up to and including the time at which the contract is concluded', and 'means of distance communication' were 'any means used for the distance marketing of a service . . . which does not involve the simultaneous physical presence of [the] parties'. However, 'the firm must have put in place facilities designed to enable a retail customer to deal with it exclusively at a distance . . . If a firm normally operates face-to-face . . . the DMD will not apply. A one-off transaction affected exclusively by distance means . . . will not be a distance contract' (FSA PM COB 1.10.4(2)(a)). 'FSA expects [the DMD] to apply in only a small minority of cases, for example where the intermediary agrees to provide continuing advisory, broking or portfolio management services for a retail customer. The DMD is only relevant if: (1) there is a contract . . . in respect of the intermediary's mediation services . . . (2) the contract is a distance contract; and (3) the contract is concluded other than merely as a stage in the provision of another service by the intermediary' (FSA PM COB 1.10.6).

---

[89] Directive 2002/65/EC of 23 September 2002, Art. 2(a).

Marketing investments

10.5.5.2 UK and non-EEA firms

The rules in 10.5.1–10.5.3 applied in full. In addition, the 'firm must ensure that a retail customer is provided with all the contractual terms and conditions on which its services will be provided . . . in good time before the . . . customer is bound . . . by a distance contract . . . unless . . . the firm has an initial service agreement with the retail customer [i.e. Terms of Business: see 8.4] and the contract is in relation to a successive operation . . . under that agreement [e.g. portfolio management or buying/selling investments]' (FSA COB 3.9.7A).

10.5.5.3 Cancellation of contracts

There were rights to cancel 'distance contracts' for collective investment schemes within 14 days and in respect of other 'designated investment business' (4.2.I(1)) unless:

- 'the price depends on fluctuations in the financial marketplace outside the firm's control which may occur during the cancellation period;' or
- 'the performance of the distance contract has been fully completed . . . before the customer exercises his right to cancel;' or
- the 'firm has an initial service agreement with the customer and the contract is in relation to a successive operation . . . of the same nature under that agreement' (FSA PM COB 6.7.1(6), 6.7.5. For cancellation of packaged products, generally, see 10.5.6.4.)

These exemptions, in practice, meant that there was no cancellation right.

MiFID: The rules have been completely recast, so that FSA 'have not carried forward the bulk of earlier DMD guidance'[90] which does, however, remain relevant, and the rules apply to a UK, EEA or non-EEA firm acting in or from the UK (COBS 1, Ann. 1, Part 3, paras. 6.1–6.5). The term 'distance contract' has been redefined, so as to exclude it from virtually all Capital Markets activities, as 'any contract concerning financial services concluded between a firm and a consumer under an organised distance sales or service provision scheme . . . which . . . makes exclusive use . . . of . . . means of distance communication (that is, any means which, without the simultaneous presence of the firm and the consumer, may be used for the distance marketing of the service . . .). A contract is not a distance contract if: (a) making or performing it does not constitute . . . a regulated activity; (b) it is entered into on a strictly occasional basis outside a commercial structure dedicated to the conclusion of distance contracts; or (c) . . . consumer, and an intermediary acting for a product provider, are simultaneously physically present' (GLOSS., def. of 'distance contract'). And, even if within this, there are exemptions 'if a distance contract is

[90] FSA PS 07/6, para. 8.7.

concluded merely as a stage in the provision of another service' or if 'followed by successive operations' (COBS 5.1.7–5.1.11). If, however, it is within the rules then there are requirements as to disclosures and the terms and conditions used (COBS 5.1.1–5.1.6, 5.1.14–5.1.17) and cancellation rights apply (COBS 15.2.1).

10.5.6 Collective investment schemes

10.5.6.1 Prohibited marketing

The 1936 Anderson Committee found it 'difficult to believe that the sale of units [in schemes over the last five years] would have obtained such large dimensions had it not been . . . for the methods of advertising and salesmanship . . . employed . . . [which] have given to large numbers of small investors an exaggerated idea . . . of the attractiveness and . . . safety of an investment in Unit Trusts . . . [B]oth the capital value . . . and the rates of dividend paid . . . are subject to serious fluctuations. . . . Invitations . . . to the public to subscribe [shares] . . . are subject to elaborate regulations under the Companies Acts [2.2.2, 2.6.(6), (7), 10.2, 10.5.1.1] . . . [but] advertisement . . . of Unit Trust[s] . . . enjoy . . . a freedom that is not open to other investment channels.'[91] This, together with the 1937 Bodkin Report on Share Pushing (2.3) resulted in the 1939 PFI which provided that only a category of 'authorised' unit trusts could be sold to the public, authorisation being granted by the Board of Trade if the fund invested in a diversified portfolio of equities and bonds and was thus considered a safe investment. Otherwise, unauthorised schemes could only be sold to professional investors, an approach which was continued in the 1958 PFI and modified in the 1986 FSAct to allow unauthorised trusts to also be promoted to clients of licensed firms who 'will be required under the 'know your customer' principle [11.2.2] . . . to take reasonable care to establish that a client understands and can afford to take the higher risks involved in [such] a scheme',[92] notwithstanding that Professor Gower considered this:

> in danger of providing a bucket shops' charter . . . Not all investment businesses will be 'conscientious' in distinguishing between their 'knowledgeable' and ignorant clients and even the knowledgeable may be greedy, gullible or both . . . [K]nowledge is not to be equated with wisdom or caution.[93]

This 1986 FSAct approach continues under FSMA with restrictions on the marketing of collective investment schemes by both unlicensed firms (10.4) and by licensed firms. 'Unlike other . . . investments, units or shares in collective investment schemes are subject to product regulation. Collective

---

[91] Anderson Report, paras. 30, 31.   [92] 1985 White Paper, paras. 9.15–9.17.
[93] 1985 Gower, para. 5.12.

Marketing investments

investment schemes marketed to the general public need to operate within a regulatory environment that covers their operations and constitution, for example in relation to how they spread risks. That is why even authorised persons are generally permitted only to promote authorised or recognised schemes.'[94]

As regards marketing by licensed firms, the prohibition is that:

> An authorised person must not communicate an invitation or inducement to participate in a collective investment scheme.

'Communicate includes causing a communication to be made' (FSMA 238(1), (9)), all of these terms having the same meaning as in 10.4.2, except that this prohibition does not 'include a "business test" . . . because th[is] . . . restriction applies only to authorised firms which will, in any event, be acting in the course of business'.[95] There is a statutory right of action for contravention of the prohibition (FSMA 241).

The territorial application of the prohibition is as in 10.4.2.3 (FSMA 238(3); CIS FPO 8).

There are three sets of exemptions. The first set is contained in FSMA itself and relates to authorised unit trusts and OEICs, UCITs and recognised overseas schemes (FSMA 238(4); CIS FPO 30).[96] As regards the other exemptions, the regulatory policy has always been that 'unregulated schemes are not subject to . . . regulatory disciplines. There is no obligation to make available [a prospectus] . . . There are no controls over investment and borrowing powers: a scheme may . . . invest in . . . anything . . . And there are no controls over the pricing of units . . . to ensure that unit holders can redeem their units at a price related to net asset value.'[97] This approach continues such that hedge funds, for example, can be marketed only within the following exemptions, although a class of publicly marketable funds of hedge funds is likely.[98] The second set of exemptions is made by the Treasury, uses the 'real time'/'non-real time' terminology, and contains Exemptions 1, 3(a)–(c), 4, 5(a), (b), 6(b), 7(d), 8, for unregulated schemes, 9, 10, 15 and 16 from Figure 9 in 10.4.2.4, although the applicable conditions sometimes vary (CIS FPO). The third set of exemptions appeared in the FSA Pre-MiFID conduct rules and permitted promotion:

---

[94] Financial Promotion – Third Consultation Document, HMT, October 2000, para. 4.4.
[95] Financial Promotion – Second Consultation Document, HMT, October 1999, para. 5.4.
[96] For the conditions to be satisfied in obtaining authorisation/recognition, and the prospectus to be published by UK schemes, see COLL and 10.5.1.1. A 'qualified investor scheme' can only be promoted within the second and third set of exemptions (COLL 8.1.3; FSA PM COB 3.11.6; FSA CP 07/9, Ann. C, COBS 5.9).
[97] SIB CP 32, January 1990, para. 3.
[98] See FSA DP 16, August 2002; FSA Feedback Statement, March 2003; FSA DP 05/3, June 2005; FSA FS 06/3, March 2006; FSA DP 05/4, June 2005; FSA FS 06/2, March 2006; FSA CP 07/6, March 2007.

- to existing or former unit holders (within the previous 30 months) of that scheme or 'any other ... scheme whose underlying property and risk profile are both substantially similar ... The property of a ... scheme is "substantially similar" to ... another ... scheme if in both ... the objective is to invest in ... (a) on-exchange derivatives or warrants; [or] (b) on-exchange ... securities; [or] (c) the property market ... [or] (f) unlisted investments ... The risk profile ... will be substantially similar ... only if there is such similarity in relation to both liquidity and volatility';
- of any scheme to 'a person ... for whom the firm has taken reasonable steps to ensure that investment in the ... scheme is suitable ... and ... who is an "established" or "newly accepted" customer of the firm or of ... the ... group', an 'established' customer being 'an actual customer' and 'a 'newly accepted' customer [being where] ... a written agreement ... exists between the customer and the firm ... [which] has been obtained without any contravention of [this prohibition]' (FSA PM COB 3.2.4(1), 3.3.3(1), 3.11, Ann. 5). The original SIB exemption on which this was based required the firm to have 'dealt with or for or arranged a deal for the [existing] customer at least once in the last 12 months',[99] but this did not appear in the FSA Pre-MiFID version, although generally '[t]he function of the ... exemption is to allow promotion ... to clients with whom a firm has a settled, ongoing relationship. The exemption was not designed to ... permit ... promotion to such members of the general public as can be prevailed upon to sign a customer agreement as a prelude to the promotion of specific schemes.'[100]

MiFID: The FSMA and Treasury exemptions continue and, in addition, FSA has taken the view that its exemptions are not affected by MiFID and, accordingly, the 'intention [is] to retain the substance of the ... provisions relating to the promotion of Unregulated ... CISs'.[101] Accordingly, FSA's exemptions are repeated, together with two new ones:

- of any scheme in which only Professional Clients or Eligible Counterparties can invest; and
- of any scheme to an investor assessed by the firm as expert to understand the risks involved in the scheme (8.3.2.8).[102]

10.5.6.2   Polarisation

Pre-MiFID: Collective investment schemes and life insurance sold as a savings medium are economically very similar products and their sales techniques often identical and severely criticised by Professor Gower in the

[99] SIB CP 32, January 1990, Ann., Note 8.   [100] Ibid, para. 11.
[101] FSA CP 07/9, para. 17.2.   [102] Ibid, Ann. C, draft COBS 5.9.

early 1980s. There were so-called tied intermediaries, a direct sales force of self-employed salesman remunerated solely by commission on sales and 'recruited . . . from those without relevant prior experience or educational qualification . . . [and] concentrate . . . on "cold calling" door-to-door or by telephone to prospects' houses or places of work . . . [Products sold] may not be what are best suited to the needs of his clientele . . . Tied salesman are generally not totally forbidden from selling products of another company . . . This blurs the distinction between sales forces and so-called "independent intermediaries"', although they were little better. '[M]ost members of the public probably assume that . . . an [independent intermediary] will be free from any inducement to recommend a [product] . . . other than that which he thinks best suited to the client's need . . . In fact the broker is likely to be subject to the same inducements in favour of particular . . . companies as a direct salesman . . . [since] some . . . [products and] companies pay larger commissions than others.'[103] The conclusion was that these products were 'sold through intermediaries [tied or independent] many of whom lack the qualifications to give adequate advice and all of whom are remunerated on a basis which faces them with conflicts between their interests and their duty'.[104] The competence issue resulted, under the 1986 FSAct, in a training regime (5.2.4) and, as regards authorised collective investment schemes (and insurance products), 'intermediaries would have to choose whether they wish to be categorised as independent intermediaries or as company representatives' and once tied the 'representative [must] act . . . for only one . . . unit trust manager',[105] rather than be multi-tied to a number because 'the risk of confusion on the part of the investor . . . is too great, and . . . disclosure cannot provide an adequate safeguard'.[106] To avoid any confusion an intermediary was 'require[d] to disclose his status to a prospective) investor'[107] in a Buyer's Guide (later renamed a Client's Guide) which was 'a statement which sets out in concise, objective, readily understandable manner, the essential characteristics of both a company representative and an independent intermediary and which identifies the category in which the adviser falls'.[108] As one SRO mandated the form of disclosure:

> Advisers . . . are of two types: *EITHER* Representatives of a particular company *OR* Independent . . . [T]he representative of a particular company . . . will act on its behalf, in the sense that he will recommend a product that is picked out from the range of those offered by that particular company . . .

---

[103] 1984 Gower, paras. 8.11, 8.12, 8.14, 8.17.   [104] Ibid, para. 8.19.
[105] Life Assurance and Unit Trusts, MIBOC and SIB, December 1985, paras. 24, 36.
[106] Life Assurance and Unit Trusts and the Investor, SIB and MIBOC, April 1986, para. 35.
[107] Life Assurance and Unit Trusts, MIBOC and SIB, December 1985, para. 76.
[108] SIB CP 23, May 1989, para. 31.

An Independent Adviser acts on his client's behalf in recommending the product picked from the range of all the companies that make up the marketplace.[109]

In practice this achieved little because although '[c]larity is supposed to emerge from . . . the Client's Guide . . . information overload . . . obscures the essential message'[110] or, as one commentator put it, 'the most nonsensical piece of paperwork that any fool could have ever dreamed up'.[111] A company representative had to 'recommend what he genuinely believes is the best product offered by his company or group for the investor'[112] such that 'best advice requires to be applied across the entire product range of a marketing group'.[113] However, '[t]he company representative is the agent of the [product company] he represents . . . [and is a] retailer . . . [The client has] the right to expect the agent to comply with good retailer standards . . . If he wants advice going wider than that, he should approach an independent intermediary'[114] who had 'to seek out and recommend what they genuinely believed to be the best product available from any company in the market'.[115] His independence was, initially, preserved by a Maximum Commission Agreement and two rules. First, a ban on 'induc[ing an independent intermediary] to introduce business . . . by . . . the making of gifts . . . or . . . by providing . . . any . . . benefit or reward other than . . . the payment of commission . . . no part of which is calculated by reference to the size or volume of other transactions entered into . . . by the [product company] as a consequence of introductions by [the intermediary]',[116] so-called volume overriders (although this was later deleted in favour simply of reliance on the general inducement rule in 6.3.2).[117] Second, there was a rule prohibiting the sale of a product of a connected company if there was an unconnected product 'which would be likely to secure [the client's] investment objectives as advantageously',[118] so that the connected product had to be better than anything else available.

SIB maintained these rules throughout the 1986 FSAct regime since 'it believes that there are demonstrable benefits to investors . . . from maintaining sharp distinctions between how business is conducted at the two poles'[119] and the independent intermediaries 'regard independence as their unique selling proposition',[120] although it allowed differential pricing

---

[109] LAUTRO (Disclosure of Status etc) Rules 1989, 26 September 1989, Sched. 1.
[110] Curbing the Sale of Unsuitable Products: A Report to the SIB, Tim Miller, May 1993, para. 4.   [111] Consultation with Members, FIMBRA Newsletter, December 1990, p. 3.
[112] Regulation of Investment Business – The New Framework, SIB and MIBOC, December 1985, para. 3.33.16.   [113] Selling Practices Rules, LAUTRO, 3 July 1987, para. 3.
[114] Retail Regulation Review, The Clucas Report, March 1992, paras. 5.37–5.39.
[115] Regulation of Investment Business – The New Framework, SIB and MIBOC, December 1985, para. 3.33.16.   [116] SIB Conduct Rules, 7 October 1987, 2.04(2).
[117] SIB CP 60, March 1992, paras. 51–52.   [118] SIB Conduct Rules, 7 October 1987, 5.03(1).
[119] Retail Regulation Review, Discussion Paper 2, SIB, September 1991, para. 22.
[120] Watchdog must be ready to bite, FT, 9 August 1991.

between different tied outlets or different tied and independent outlets when the OFT regarded its prohibition as anti-competitive.[121] FSA initially maintained SIB's rules under FSMA although against the background of media comment that 'the current regime is against the public interest',[122] the OFT's view that 'the rules restrict or distort competition to a significant extent'[123] and the chronic need for consumers to make appropriate financial provision, FSA 'concluded that the best option for change is a package providing for full abolition [of the rule] together with some related and necessary changes'.[124] Even from a narrow regulatory perspective:

> The evidence ... is that consumers do not shop around yet the company representatives can only offer one brand of product. In a climate in which many packaged products are sold not bought, the whole tenor of the market is one of the representatives looking for customers rather than customers looking for representatives ... [I]f a representative could select from a more comprehensive set of products, there will be a number of occasions when the recommendation matches the customer's need more accurately than if the choice was made from fewer products.[125]

FSA's conclusion was that 'polarisation delivers insufficient benefits to justify it'[126] and so the following regime was implemented:

Product range The firm had to decide upon both 'the scope of the advice ... given ... [i.e.:]

i) the whole market (or a sector of the whole market); [or]
ii) from a limited number of product providers; or
iii) from a single product provider,

[and its r]ange of products ... [W]hen a firm advises on products from a single ... or ... limited range of product providers, its range ... will comprise some or all of the products offered by the providers selected ... If a firm offers advice from the whole market, its [range] ... will be all ... firms who manufacture products ... [A] firm [can] ... offer whole of market and more restricted advice ... Once an adviser has disclosed what scope a customer will be offered ... then he ... will ... be required to complete the advice process by selecting the best product from within that range.[127]

---

[121] The marketing and sale of investment-linked insurance products, OFT, March 1993; HMT PR 89/93, 22 July 1993; SIB CP 77, January 1994.
[122] Time to tear up the Retail Financial Services Rulebook, Sunday Times, 9 November 1998.
[123] The Rules on Polarisation of Investment Advice, OFT, August 1999, para. 9.2.
[124] FSA CP 121, January 2002, para. 4.75.   [125] FSA CP 80, January 2001, paras. 4.2, 4.4.
[126] FSA CP 121, January 2002, para. 4.5.
[127] FSA CP 166, January 2003, para. 3.4, 3.8, 3.9, 7.1, 7.5. This was implemented in FSA PM COB 4.3.9(3), 4.3.14, 4.3.15, 5.1.6A–5.1.6G, 5.1.7–5.1.11, 5.2.12–5.2.18, 5.3.5, 5.3.5A, 5.3.8A, 5.3.8B, 5.3.14, 5.3.16, 5.3.18A–5.3.18C, 5.3.30.

A product provider could 'adopt' the products of other providers without limit (FSA PM COB 5.1.12–5.1.23, 5.2.12–5.2.18, 5.3.5, 5.3.5A, 5.3.14, 5.3.16, 5.3.18A–5.3.18C, 5.3.30).

Independence There was 'a restriction on a firm from holding itself out as "independent" . . . unless it both offers whole-of-market advice and . . . the choice of paying a fee for advice' rather than the intermediary receiving commission.[128] And although the general inducements rule (6.3.2) continued to apply, because 'indirect benefits bias . . . advisers' advice',[129] additional guidance was provided on it (FSA PM COB 2.2.6, 2.2.7).

Disclosure There was an initial disclosure document mandated by FSA providing 'key information to consumers to help them decide whether the services offered by a firm are right for them'[130] and '[a] Guide to the cost of our services' or 'menu' document disclosing 'the cost of advice . . . [and] aimed at getting consumers to appreciate that it is they who ultimately pay for the advice, regardless of the payment method'.[131] 'When a customer goes to see a firm . . . the adviser will first need to make clear which scope of advice he . . . will advise the customer about . . . [T]his will be achieved through the . . . initial disclosure document . . . [which] will need to be appropriate to the particular range being offered to that customer. So . . . if a firm has a number of different ranges, it will need to have a corresponding number of different . . . documents.'[132]

Advice There was 'a single standard of suitability for all firms . . . link[ed] . . . to the range of products on which a firm is advising':[133]

> A firm must take reasonable steps to ensure that if . . . it makes any recommendation to a private customer . . . the advice or transaction . . . is suitable for the client [11.2.2]. If the recommendation relates to a packaged product . . . it must . . . be the most suitable from the range of packaged products on which advice . . . is given to the client . . .

> A firm which holds itself out as giving personal recommendations . . . from the whole market . . . must not give any such recommendation unless it . . . has carried out a reasonable analysis of a sufficiently large number of packaged products which are generally available. (FSA PM COB 5.3.5, 5.3.10A)

---

[128] FSA CP 166, January 2003, para. 5.4. This was implemented in FSA PM COB 5.1.11A, 5.1.11B.   [129] Ibid, para. 9.2.   [130] Ibid, para. 8.14.

[131] FSA CP 04/3, February 2004, para. 2.5. The requirements for these documents were implemented in FSA PM COB 4.3 and Ann. 4–9, and 5.7.5–5.7.16.

[132] Ibid, paras. 3.9, 7.4.

[133] Ibid, para. 5.16. This was implemented in FSA PM COB 5.1.12–5.1.23, 5.2.12–5.2.18, 5.3.5, 5.3.5A, 5.3.10A, 5.3.10B, 5.3.14, 5.3.16, 5.3.18A–5.3.18C, 5.3.30.

MiFID: This regime is maintained, notwithstanding MiFID (subject to 'a retail distribution review') with some simplifications.[134] Accordingly, a notification has been made by FSA to the European Commission under Article 4 of the Level 2 Directive (2.6).[135]

10.5.6.3 Product disclosure

Regulators have always insisted upon product disclosure in relation to packaged products sold to the public because the ultimate benefit the investor obtains is unknown and unknowable at the outset and all depends upon investment performance. There are three forms of disclosure:

- Prospectus: A prospectus, with mandatory contents, must be produced for an authorised unit trust/OEIC and a UCITS (COLL 4). This continues unchanged under MiFID.
- Key features, Simplified Prospectus, Projections: Since the mid-1980s there have been, literally, dozens of attempts by regulators to introduce meaningful and understandable disclosure requirements for packaged products, the FSA's Pre-MiFID attempt (FSA PM COB 6) being carried over under MiFID (COBS 13, 14) with an appropriate notification made under Article 4 of the Level 2 Directive.[136]
- Financial Promotions: This does not impose a requirement to produce a document, but any promotion referring to packaged products must comply with the general financial promotion requirements and, in addition, certain special requirements, which are, in most respects, carried over under MiFID (FSA PM COB 3.8.13, 3.8.13A, 3.8.14 (past performance), 3.8.19, 3.8.20 (specific promotions), 3.9.23, 3.9.25 (direct offer promotions), 3.14.5 (interest); COBS 4.5) (10.5.1–10.5.5).

10.5.6.4 Cancellation

The sale of packaged products has been for decades subject to cancellation ('cooling off') rules which continue under MiFID with some amendment (FSA PM COB 6.7; FSA 15),[137] having been originally introduced because '[t]he most effective protection against ... cold calling ... is ... the willpower to hang up or close the door. But considerable protection can be provided through a 'cooling off' period.'[138]

---

[134] FSA CP 06/19, paras. 11.5–11.40; FSA PS 07/14, Chapter 3; COBS 6.2–6.4.
[135] Notification of Certain Requirements relating to the Market for Packaged Products, FSA, September 2007.   [136] Ibid; FSA CP 06/19, pp. 119–132 FSA PS 07/14, Chapter 6.
[137] FSA CP 06/19, pp. 133–137. For cancellation in relation to distance marketing, see 10.5.5.3.   [138] 1985 White Paper, para. 12.7.

11
Advising clients

11.1 General law

The supply of services, such as giving advice, whether on an ad hoc or discretionary or non-discretionary basis, is subject to a duty of reasonable care as a matter or contract, tort and statute:

> it was . . . within the scope of the defendant bank's business to advise on all financial matters and . . . there is a duty to the plaintiff to advise him with reasonable care and skill.[1]

> the liability of stockbrokers . . . did not differ from commodity brokers: . . . in contract . . . stockbrokers are liable for failing to use that skill and diligence which a reasonably competent and careful stockbroker would exercise . . . [T]he principle in *Hedley Byrne & Co Limited* v. *Heller* . . . would apply were there no contract and were a stockbroker negligently to give advice . . . [A] broker cannot always be right in the advice that he gives in relation to so wayward and rapidly changing a market as the commodity futures market. An error of judgement . . . is not necessarily negligent . . . even if he advised . . . [on] the transaction which produced the loss.[2]

> In a contract for the supply of a service where the supplier is acting in the course of a business, there is an implied term that the supplier will carry out the service with reasonable care and skill. (1982 Sale of Goods and Supply of Services Act 13)

The latter 'duty . . . may . . . be negatived or varied by express agreement, or by the course of dealing between the parties' (SOGASA 16 (1)). Like negligence at common law, this duty to take care extends into all of the firm's services and, as with the regulatory definition of 'client', it probably does not distinguish between MiFID services and activities (8.2.1). The duty can be disapplied by Statutory Instrument although the only relevant disapplication is in relation to directors' duties because that standard of care is closely defined by case law and under the 2006 Companies Act (5.3.2.5).[3]

---

[1] *Woods* v. *Martins Bank Limited* [1958] 3 AER 166 at 172.
[2] *Stafford* v. *Conti Commodity Services Limited* [1981] 1 AER 691 at 695–696.
[3] 1982 SOGASA 12(4); SI 1982/1771.

Moreover, where a fiduciary relationship exists (6.2.1), the consequent fiduciary duty may be to give advice, and this imports very similar standards (6.2.2.3).

11.2 The Regulated Activity

'Investment advice' is a regulated activity with a defined meaning (3.2.2.3), the standard for the giving of which has itself been defined by the regulators since the early 1980s in a manner intended to build upon the general law[4] and enable the regulator to take enforcement action for breach. It is based upon the policy that '[n]o investment business should recommend a client to engage in a particular transaction unless it has an adequate and reasonable basis for its recommendation, bearing in mind the nature of the investment and the circumstances of the client . . . This "know your customer" principle would require an investment business to satisfy itself that a particular recommendation . . . is suitable, bearing in mind the nature, circumstances and experience of the client and the client's expressed investment objectives. In many cases this would be no more than performance of an agent's duty of skill, care and diligence . . . where . . . clients rely on [the firm's] skill and judgement.'[5] 'Th[e] firm should vindicate his trust by tailoring its advice to his needs, even if it is . . . "dealing as principal" with him.'[6] FSA has two rules reflecting this policy.

11.2.1 The Principle

Pre-MiFID: Under the heading 'Customers' relationships of trust', the Principle provides: 'A firm must take reasonable care to ensure the suitability of its advice and discretionary decisions for any customer who is entitled to rely upon its judgement' (PRIN 2.1.1 Principle 9). FSA's original draft provided that 'A firm must keep faith with any customer who is entitled to rely upon its judgement', 'designed to reflect the fiduciary or "trust-based" nature of many relationships . . . with the customer trusting the firm to give advice (or provide a portfolio management service) reflecting

---

[4] The first attempt was in 1983 LDRs 10: any 'recommendation to [a] person who might reasonably be expected to rely thereon . . . [must have] an adequate and reasonable basis . . . [i.e.] the . . . [firm] has given the matter such consideration and conducted such investigation of the investment as is reasonable in the circumstances, having regard to the suitability for the person . . . to whom the recommendation is addressed'. Although not an 'enactment', this was probably intended to build on 1982 SOGASA 16(4): 'This Part . . . has effect subject to any other enactment which defines . . . the rights, duties or liabilities arising in connection with the service.' For SIB's rules, see 2.4.3.

[5] 1985 White Paper, paras. 7.13–7.14.

[6] Regulation of the Marketing of Investment Products and Services, SIB, March 1990, para. 3.3.

his . . . personal situation and needs',[7] although this was changed because commentators 'found the phrase "keep faith" . . . unclear . . . We have therefore redrafted it . . . focusing on the "suitability" concept. While this may appear to narrow the Principle's overall effect, it still retains the main intention of the original draft' and 'extends beyond fiduciary relationships [6.2.1] to include other activities where the customer is entitled to rely upon the judgement of the firm.'[8] The Principle did 'not require a firm to assess . . . suitability of a particular transaction for . . . a market counterparty' (FSA PM MAR 3.4.3), but applied to both Private and Intermediate Customers, if only because the originally proposed application of the rule in 11.2.2 to Intermediates was withdrawn notwithstanding that FSA originally 'took the view that, where a customer has given discretion to a firm . . . the customer, whether private or intermediate, has a valid expectation that the firm will act in a way which is suitable for each customer's circumstances. This expectation similarly reflects his legal position [as an agent]. Many . . . argued that this approach did not take sufficient account of the ability of intermediate customers to look after their own interests, or a need to draw a distinction between regulatory obligations and those duties which exist under general law. In the light of these comments, we have concluded that there is no regulatory justification for extending the . . . suitability rule to intermediate customers.'[9] The Principle required a 'know your customer' enquiry, as in 11.2.2.1, upon which to base the suitable advice (FSA PM COB 5.2.4), particularly since the previous SIB Principle required that 'A firm should seek from customers it advises or for whom it exercises discretion any information about their circumstances and investment objectives which might reasonably be expected to be relevant'.[10] It also required the giving of suitable advice as in 11.2.2.2 (FSA PM COB 5.3.4). Both obligations had to be performed according to the standard of Principle 2 requiring the firm to 'conduct its business with due skill, care and diligence (9.1).

MiFID: This continues unchanged, although the rule in 11.2.2 now also applies to Professional as well as Retail Clients, since the MiFID suitability rule is a particularisation of its principle requiring a firm to 'act honestly, fairly and professionally in accordance with the best interests of the . . . client' (9.3). Thus, for example, 'where a firm lends money to enable a client to carry out a transaction',[11] this principle gives rise to a suitability enquiry because margin lending 'may change the risk profile and complexity of the relevant transaction . . . and . . . may or may not be suitable for the client'.[12]

---

[7] FSA CP 13, September 1998, para. 36.
[8] The FSA Principles for Businesses, FSA PS, 1999, para. 41.
[9] Conduct of Business Sourcebook, FSA PS, February 2001, paras. 5.43–5.44.
[10] Statements of Principle, SIB, 1990, Principle 4.   [11] CESR/05-291(b), April 2005, p. 22.
[12] CESR/05-164, March 2005, pp. 5–6.

11.2.2 The Rule

Pre-MiFID: Where the firm 'gives a personal recommendation . . . or . . . acts as an investment manager for a private customer' 'it must take reasonable steps to ensure that it is in possession of sufficient personal and financial information about that customer relevant to the services that the firm has agreed to provide' and 'take reasonable steps to ensure that . . . the advice . . . or transaction is suitable for the client . . . hav[ing] regard to . . . the facts disclosed by the client . . . and . . . other relevant facts about the client of which the firm is, or reasonably should be, aware' (FSA PM COB 5.2.1, 5.2.5, 5.3.1, 5.3.5). Moreover, 'A firm which acts as an investment manager for a private customer must take reasonable steps to ensure that the . . . portfolio . . . remains suitable' (FSA PM COB 5.3.5(4)), which means 'keep[ing] the customer's portfolio under review to ensure that the portfolio as a whole and the investments contained within it remain suitable'.[13] Such an express requirement was necessary because at general law, subject to the express terms of the management agreement, '[i]f a bank official gives . . . advice . . . the Court may be prepared to say that while offering advice in circumstances in which the adviser knew that it would be relied upon he undertook to exercise reasonable care . . . That does not mean that if reasonable care is exercised when the advice is given the bank . . . has assumed a further continuing obligation to keep the advice . . . under review and, if necessary, to correct it in the light of supervening events.'[14]

MiFID: The duty now applies, as explained in 4.2(n)(i), in favour of both Retail and Professional Clients (8.2.1) in relation to both a 'personal recommendation' and investment management and is to the same effect as the Pre-MiFID Rules since 'A firm must take reasonable steps to ensure that a personal recommendation, or decision to trade, is suitable for its client . . . [having] obtain[ed] the necessary information regarding the client's: (a) knowledge and experience in the investment field relevant to the . . . investment or service; (b) financial situation; and (c) investment objectives' (COBS 9.1.1, 9.1.3, 9.2.1). Hence, FSA's statement 'that . . . in substance there need be no material difference between the MiFID and [pre-MiFID] . . . suitability standard as far as retail clients are concerned'[15] and 'If a firm does not obtain the necessary information . . . it must not make a personal recommendation . . . or take a decision to trade' (COBS 9.2.5) so that 'the . . . firm has to assess whether the information received is sufficient'.[16] Although the Principle in 11.2.1 always applied to Intermediate Customers, in practice the view was taken, sometimes incorrectly,

---

[13] SFA Briefing 5, May 1993, Section 2.
[14] *Fennoscandia Limited* v. *Clarke* [1999] 1 AER 365 at 368.
[15] FSA CP 06/19, para. 14.25.   [16] CESR/05-350, 16 May 2005, p. 11.

that since it was limited to 'a . . . customer who is entitled to rely upon [the firm's] judgement', Intermediate Customers did not place such reliance. Now, however, the rule applies without any qualification to Professional Clients in the Secondary Markets and even in the Primary Markets (if given to the client in its 'capacity as investor', rather than issuer or bidder in a takeover, and amounting to a 'personal recommendation'). The introduction of such an obligation into the Dealing Room poses compliance challenges given how traders' and salesmens' language can easily shade from the imparting of information and 'market colour' into a 'personal recommendation' (3.2.2.3). That said, and particularly with Professional Clients, there is in practice 'a range of advice [sought], from comprehensive and sophisticated to "limited advice" (i.e. where a client requests advice on a limited range of products or strategies)'[17] although, even with such limited advice, 'suitability' will still have to be achieved in that context unless the firm decides, and trains staff accordingly, never to give 'personal recommendations'. The issue needs to be considered throughout the firm's activities with Professional Clients, for example 'marketing roadshow Q&A sessions [in corporate finance], brainstorming with clients, market speculation, market "colour/context" conversations [in the Dealing Room], risk management hedging [in structured products], or discussions on trading strategies [in the Dealing Room]'.[18] 'It is possible . . . for a firm to provide information or opinions . . . without going as far as to "recommend" them or to provide a "personal" recommendation . . . [and] the position of the firm will be reinforced if it makes it clear to the client that in providing the information it is not providing a recommendation', for example, in the Terms of Business (8.4). 'But if it is clear from the circumstances that the firm is making a personal recommendation, a "disclaimer" . . . will have no effect'[19] and the firm must assess suitability in the context of the service it is providing. The obligations of an investment manager are to similar effect as to the Pre-MiFID Rules (COBS 9.3.1(2), 9.3.2), so that the 'firm . . . must take reasonable steps to ensure that the portfolio . . . remains suitable'.[20] In any event, and this is obvious from a regulatory policy perspective, the firm need not assess suitability where another EEA firm has already done so (COBS 2.4.4(2)(b), 2.4.5(1)).

Under both the Pre-MiFID and MiFID Rules there are, thus, two aspects.

11.2.2.1 Know-your customer

Pre-MiFID: Suitable advice had to be based on 'facts about the client of which the firm is, or reasonably should be, aware', thus necessitating a

---

[17] FSA CP 06/19, para. 4.24.   [18] Ibid, para. 14.26.   [19] FSA PS 07/2, para. 5.4.
[20] CESR/04-562, October 2004, p. 44.

rigorous due diligence which 'may vary significantly depending on the type of customer concerned' and 'should, at a minimum, provide an analysis of . . . personal and financial circumstances leading to a clear identification of . . . needs and priorities so that, combined with attitude to risk, a suitable investment can be recommended', although '[i]n assessing whether a . . . customer can afford an investment, due regard should be given to . . . current level of income and expenditure and any likely future changes' (FSA PM COB 5.2.8, 5.2.11), and in all cases the firm 'should keep its information about the customer under regular review' and keep records (FSA PM COB 5.2.6, 5.2.9). The policy was clear:

> Advisors must find out as much as possible about their clients' finances . . . They need to know about your earnings, what rate of tax you pay, if you have a mortgage, life assurance or a pension and whether you have a family. They will also ask whether you are looking for short term gain or an income . . . or whether you are saving for your old age.[21]

In practice, '[a] firm can . . . send . . . the customer . . . a questionnaire for completion',[22] although '[t]here is no requirement . . . to obtain the . . . customer's consent in writing to a customer information record' but '[f]irms may send the customer a copy of' it (FSA PM COB 5.2.13(1)(c), (d)). There were three issues. First, whether a pro-forma approach to the client's investment objectives, including a choice of acceptable risk as 'High', 'High/Medium', 'Medium', 'Medium/Low' or 'Low', was accurate or, indeed, intelligible to the client. It always needed a very clear explanation both in writing and, following appropriate training of the salesmen, orally, if only because 'what might constitute a high/medium/low risk . . . will differ according to the type of customer concerned, the markets in which the firm operates, and its approach to investment strategies. In agreeing with its customer a set of investment objectives, a firm should come to an understanding of how those objectives should be met.'[23] This, of course, links into, but cannot be replaced by, the giving of appropriate risk warnings (10.5.1.3). Second, how to comply with the regulator's expectation that '[a] firm must ensure that the information which it has about a customer is correct'[24] and, where it is not, how to persuade the regulator that 'reasonable steps' were taken in the construction of the fact-find document, instructions to the client and training of the salesman given that, for example, 'investors have a vital role . . . in indicating their objectives as accurately as possible . . . The advisor . . . ha[s] a clear responsibility for trying to find out the objectives and for assisting the investor in formulating them . . . but at the end of the

---

[21] Buying Investments from an Independent Adviser, FIMBRA, April 1992.
[22] Conduct of Business Rules, July 1987, TSA, Rule 38(8).
[23] Customer Understanding and Suitability, SFA Update 20, July 1999, pp. 6–7.
[24] SFA Briefing 5, May 1993, Section 2.

day the investor is the only person who knows what is really required . . . One of the disadvantages of the customary "Fact Find" procedures, or the standard questionnaire . . . is that they can become a routine bit of form filling.'[25] And, third, in this process although '[a] firm will be taken to be in compliance with any rule . . . that requires a firm to obtain information to the extent that the firm can show that it was reasonable to rely on information provided to it in writing' by the client or his agent (FSA PM COB 2.3.3), since the SRO Rule under the 1986 FSAct that '[a] firm is entitled to rely without further enquiry on any information which it receives'[26] was not adopted by FSA, the firm had to be cautious in demonstrating 'reasonableness', at least considering the answers given to a questionnaire and following up on unconvincing, ambiguous or contradictory answers.

MiFID: The extent and due diligence nature of the fact-find continues since the firm 'must obtain from the client such information as is necessary for the firm to understand the essential facts about him' (COBS 9.2.2(1)), and 'we do not propose to prescribe how the necessary information . . . is obtained and documented'.[27] There are three areas of enquiry. First, the client's investment objectives. 'Th[is] information . . . must include, where relevant, information on the length of time for which he wishes to hold the investment, his preference regarding risk taking, his risk profile, and the purposes of the investment' (COBS 9.2.1(2), 9.2.2(2)). All the Pre-MiFID issues on choice of appropriate risk thus continue to apply, although not all of these factors will be 'relevant' to Professional Clients in all circumstances, for example in the Dealing Room, notwithstanding FSA's statement that '[n]ecessary information for a professional client . . . will include the client's investment objectives'.[28] Second, information on the client's financial situation 'must include, where relevant, information on the source and extent of his regular income, his assets, including liquid assets, investments and real property, and his regular financial commitments' (COBS 9.2.1(2)(b), 9.2.2(3)), which represents no change from the Pre-MiFID rule. Of course, it presents challenges for how to assess such factors in relation to Professional Clients, since the rule was clearly drafted with the Retail Client in mind, and such factors may well not be 'relevant' in a Dealing Room environment once it is assessed that the Professional Client is good for the credit risk, although these and the other factors obviously are 'relevant' in relation to structured products. That said, with a Professional Client within 8.3.2.1–8.3.2.7 'the firm is entitled to assume that the client is able financially to bear any related investment risks' (COBS 9.2.8(2)).

The third enquiry relates to the client's knowledge and experience relevant to the investment or service. As with the Pre-MiFID rule, MiFID

---

[25] IMRO Bulletin 16, 31 May 1991.
[26] Conduct of Business Rules, TSA, July 1987, Rule 38(9).
[27] FSA CP 06/19, para. 14.13.
[28] Ibid, para. 14.17.

requires risk disclosures (10.5.1.3) but this requirement goes further in that the 'firm must obtain from the client such information as is necessary for the firm to . . . have a reasonable basis for believing . . . that the . . . transaction . . . is such that [the client] has the necessary experience and knowledge in order to understand the risks involved in the transaction or in the management of his portfolio' (COBS 9.2.1(2)(a), 9.2.2(1)) which has nothing to do with suitability as traditionally understood. Rather, '[i]n the case of investment advice, the client must evaluate the advice . . . and decide whether to enter into a transaction . . . In the case of a portfolio management service . . . the knowledge and experience of the client . . . is relevant in respect of the determination whether the client is able to understand the implications of the service he is to be provided with and to evaluate that service once it has been provided.'[29] In making this assessment 'The information [to be obtained] . . . includes . . . information on:

(1) the type of service, transaction and . . . investment with which the client is familiar; [and]
(2) the nature, volume, frequency of the client's transactions . . . and the period over which they have been carried out; [and]
(3) the level of education, profession or relevant former profession of the client.

With 'a professional client . . . [the firm] is entitled to assume . . . the client has the necessary level of experience and knowledge' (COBS 9.2.3, 9.2.8(1)). Since the firm is also able to assume that the Professional Client can bear the financial risk, that leaves only due diligence on its investment objectives. As those are, obviously, best known to the client itself, it is odd that the rules do not permit them to be assumed as well. And, as regards Retail Clients, there is the difficulty that where the Client has no knowledge or experience of the particular investment, for example a derivative, then the firm would appear unable to provide a recommendation, which cannot be the intention of the rules.

Records must be kept (COBS 9.5). It is implied that the information must be regularly reviewed, and the Pre-MiFID issues about the correctness of the information held continue since 'A firm is entitled to rely on the information provided by its clients unless it is aware that the information is manifestly out of date, inaccurate or incomplete' (COBS 9.2.6). Where the client acts through an agent, if the agent is a UK or EEA firm or a non-EEA licensed firm, it 'may rely upon any information about [a client] transmitted to it by' the agent. With any other agent, if unconnected with the firm then reliance must be 'reasonable' which '[i]t will generally be . . . unless it is aware or ought reasonably to be aware of any fact that would give reasonable grounds to question the accuracy of that information'

---

[29] CESR/05-291(b), April 2005, p. 27.

(COBS 2.4.4, 2.4.6–2.4.8). The drafting here is unnecessarily convoluted and in practice it must be reasonable to rely upon a duly constituted agent which means that, as has always been prudent, the firm should generally seek evidence of the agent's appointment or, where it is for example a fund manager, at least take an appropriate warranty of authority in the Terms of Business (8.4).

Anti-Money Laundering: This type of 'know-your customer' inquiry is quite different from the inquiry, under the same name, pursuant to anti-money laundering laws and regulations. This inquiry, also performed at client take-on, is to establish the identity of the client and source of funds to prevent the firm being used to launder the proceeds of crime. Caught up with terrorist funding concerns, the objectivity of both the rules made and rule-makers may sometimes be questioned. Criminal property is 'a person's benefit from criminal conduct', itself defined as 'conduct which –

(a) constitutes an offence in any part of the United Kingdom, or
(b) would constitute [such] an offence . . . if it occurred there. (2002 Proceeds of Crime Act 340)

Thus, under (b), it need not be an offence in the place where it was committed; and (a) covers any offence. There are, then, three separate offences: concealing, disguising, converting, transferring or removing criminal property; being party to an agreement known or suspected to facilitate the acquisition, retention or control of criminal property; and 'if [a person] . . .

(a) knows or suspects, or . . . has reasonable grounds for knowing or suspecting, that another person is engaged in money laundering [; and]
(b) . . . the information on which his knowledge or suspicion is based . . . came to him in the course of . . . business . . . [and]
(c) . . . he does not make the required disclosure [to the firm's MLRO or to SOCA, The Serious Organised Crime Agency] as soon as practicable after the information comes to him. (2002 POCA 327, 328, 330, 331, 333)

As regards (a), 'knowledge means actually knowing something to be true . . . Suspicion is more subjective . . . [and] has been defined by the courts as . . . extending beyond speculation . . . and . . . [a]lthough . . . [it] requires a lesser factual basis than . . . a belief, it must nonetheless be built upon some foundation . . . [R]easonable grounds . . . introduces an objective test of suspicion . . . met when there are . . . facts . . . known . . . from which a reasonable person . . . would have inferred knowledge, or formed the suspicion.'[30]

The firm must have 'systems and controls that . . . enable it to identify, assess, monitor and manage . . . the risk that . . . [it] may be used to further

---

[30] JMLSG Guidance Notes, January 2006, Part I, paras. 7–8, 7.9, 7.13.

money laundering' (SYSC 6.3.1. See also: SYSC 6.3.2–6.3.10). These systems should be constructed in compliance with:

- The Money Laundering Regulations 2003, SI 2003/3075, replaced from 15 December 2007 by The Money Laundering Regulations 2007, SI 2007/2157 (which implement the Third Money Laundering Directive); and
- the detailed procedures and views expressed in the JMLSG Guidance Notes. To Reflect the Third Money Laundering Directive,[31] a June 2007 Consultation Draft consolidates a 'risk-based approach' which FSA itself endorses[32]. Of course, a risk-based approach to the implementations of systems and controls is one thing when the firm is talking to FSA supervisors; it is quite different when the risks have actually materialised (2.5.8, 5.6); and
- FSA's expressed views over time;[33] and
- FSA's enforcement cases.[34]

These systems must comprise, in summary:

- identification procedures; and
- record-keeping procedures; and
- monitoring procedures;[35]
- internal and external (Suspicious Activity Reports or SARs) reporting procedures; and
- employee training.

None of this is affected by MiFID.

11.2.2.2 Suitability

Pre-MiFID: 'The nature of the steps firms need to take will vary greatly, depending on the needs and priorities of the . . . customer, the type of investment of service . . . and the nature of the relationship between the firm and the . . . customer' (FSA PM COB 5.3.4). However, '[i]f a . . . customer declines to provide relevant . . . information [under 11.2.2.1], a firm should not . . . provide the service . . . without promptly advising the customer that the lack of such information may affect adversely the quality of

---

[31] Directive 2005/60/EC.
[32] Keynote address on anti-money laundering and financial crime, Philip Robinson, Director FSA, City and Financial Annual Financial Crime Conference, 5 July 2007. For supranational standards, see Guidance on Risk-Based Approach, Financial Action Task Force (FATF), July 2007.
[33] See for example: FSA CP 30, October 1999; FSA CP 46, April 2000; FSA PN/101/2001, 30 July 2001 (NCIS); Money Laundering, FSA, 2002 (retail banking; on-line broking; spread betting); FSA DP 22, August 2003; FSA CP 05/10, July 2005; Review of private banks' anti-money laundering systems and controls, FSA, July 2007.
[34] See, for example: FSA/PN/123, 2002; PN/08/2003; PN/132/2003; PN/001/2004; PN/035/2004; PN/077/2004; PN/117/2005.
[35] Automated Anti-Money Laundering Transaction Monitoring Systems, FSA, July 2007.

the services which it can provide. The firm should consider sending written confirmation of that advice' (FSA PM COB 5.2.7). Similarly, if the client rejected the firm's advice and instructed it to deal in circumstances where the firm had advised that the client should not, the rule under the 1986 FSAct, which FSA did not adopt, was that 'the firm should explain that it will only accept the order on an execution-only basis . . . [and] should make a record of the conversation'.[36]

Like packaged product salesmen advising within their product range (10.5.6.2), 'it cannot be suitable to recommend one type of investment when another . . . would plainly be more appropriate for the customer . . . This presupposes on the part of firms a certain degree of general knowledge of alternative vehicles.'[37] But the regulator's standard is little different from the general law (11.1) since 'suitability of a . . . recommendation cannot be judged with the wisdom of hindsight (i.e. according to how the investment has turned out) but only by reference to what was known (or ought reasonably to have been known) to the advisor at the time of making the recommendation'[38] and 'there is not necessarily any one recommendation which would constitute "best advice" at any given time. Judgements . . . will inevitably vary, and there is an element of subjective judgement in most recommendations.'[39] The Court itself will judge suitability in the light of the general law reasonableness test[40] so that, applying the general law test for a professional:

> In the ordinary case which does not involve any special skill, negligence . . . means . . . [s]ome failure to do some act which a reasonable man in the circumstances would do, or doing some act which a reasonable man in the circumstances would not do . . . How do you test if this act or failure is negligent? In the ordinary case . . . you judge that by the action of the man in the street . . . But where you get a situation which involves the use of some special skill or competence, then the test whether there has been negligence . . . is not the test of a man on the top of the Clapham omnibus, because he has not got the special skill. The test is the standard of the ordinary skilled man exercising and professing to have that special skill. A man need not possess the highest expert skill at the risk of being found negligent. It is . . . sufficient if he exercises the ordinary skill of an ordinary competent man exercising that particular art.[41]

As a result, FSA would not provide detailed guidance and go beyond the general formulation in the rules. Indeed, it viewed it as almost an aspect of 'treating the customer fairly' (9.2). 'Consumers rightly expect those who

---

[36] SFA BN 139, 16 July 1993.
[37] Regulation of the Marketing of Investment Products and Services, SIB, March 1990, para. 3.7.   [38] Ibid.   [39] Guidance on Best Advice, FIMBRA, July 1988, para. 1.
[40] *Morgan Stanley* v. *Alfio Puglisi* [1998] CLC 481.
[41] *Bolam* v. *Friern Hospital* [1957] 1 WLR 582.

advise and sell financial services products . . . to give them appropriate advice and sell them a suitable product. In short, they expect financial firms to give them a fair deal. Our rules . . . make it clear . . . that this is what we expect . . . There are those who feel strongly that the regulator should define or catalogue "mis-selling" in such a way as to give certainty about what is expected of firms . . . However, it would not be practicable or ultimately desirable for the FSA to provide an exhaustive set of specifications by way of safe harbour.'[42] It all comes down to a matter of proof and, in practice, the firm should keep a record of advice given and (a counsel of perfection) the reasons for that particular advice, although other than in respect of packaged products there was no specific regulatory requirement for a 'suitability letter' (FSA COB 5.3.10A, 5.3.10B, 5.3.14–5.3.18B).[43] This is because 'one aspect above all [is] the most difficult – deciding what really happened . . . when a decent honest investor met a decent honest adviser and they both did their best to get the thing right, only to find a little while later that they had wholly inconsistent versions of what was said and done . . . Only God knows what actually happened'[44] unless some form of record, written or taped, has been kept.

MiFID: Now, although the rule is categoric that 'If a firm does not obtain the necessary information to assess suitability, it must not make a personal recommendation . . . or take a decision to trade' (COBS 9.2.5), FSA 'do not see [this] . . . as fundamentally different in its desired outcome from . . . [the Pre–MiFID] Rule',[45] and if the client rejects the firm's advice, the position remains as before. The MiFID Rules do not affect the standard by which suitability will be judged since 'A firm must . . . have a reasonable basis for believing . . . that the . . . transaction . . . recommended . . . meets his investment objectives . . . [and] is such that he is able financially to bear any related investment risks' and 'A transaction may be unsuitable . . . because of the risks . . . involved, the type of transaction, the characteristics of the order or the frequency of the trading' (COBS 9.2.2(1), 9.3.1(1)). 'Reasonableness' is to be judged in the context of the particular service being provided to the client, and will therefore differ as between a Private Bank advisory service to a Retail Client, who wants advice in the context of his entire financial affairs, at one end of the spectrum, and 'advice' given in a Dealing Room to a Professional Client who is interested merely in the salesman/trader's views on the contemporaneous market, irrespective of its financial situation or investment objectives which the client itself assesses, at the other end. In other words, 'how a client's knowledge and experience

---

[42] FSA PN/052/2003, 17 April 2003.
[43] For an assessment of the benefits, see Assessment of the FSA suitability letter, Oxera, April 2007.
[44] Annual Report 1995/1996, The Investment Ombudsman, April 1996, p. 11.
[45] FSA PS 07/2, para. 5.7.

might need to be taken into account . . . will vary . . . according to the nature of the client, the nature . . . of the service . . . the products . . . and so on . . . [I]n practice, the necessary information that must be obtained . . . may be calibrated according[ly although] . . . there is an irreducible minimum level of information without which it is not possible to provide a personal recommendation. MiFID . . . accommodates a range of advice, from comprehensive and sophisticated to "limited" . . . [I]t is possible . . . to focus the scope of . . . advice to suit the information the client wishes to disclose. For example, advice could be given in relation to just part of a client's portfolio.'[46]

The rules still require a 'suitability letter' to be sent to clients only in respect of packaged products[47] and while FSA was originally going to require a record to be kept of 'each . . . suitability assessment',[48] it never made such an express rule, relying instead on the general MiFID record-keeping requirement (5.5) (COBS 9.5.1) which firms can interpret 'in a proportionate and beneficial manner where personal recommendations are made to professional clients'.[49]

11.3 Execution-only services

Pre-MiFID: The suitability obligation applied only where the firm's service was the giving of advice. Thus, where the firm conducted an 'execution-only transaction' for the client, being 'a transaction executed . . . upon the specific instructions of the client where the firm does not give advice', it 'is not . . . required to obtain any personal or financial information about the customer' (FSA PM COB 5.2.2). The policy was that:

> Where an investor can be assumed to be self-reliant and not dependant on the firm's judgement it is inappropriate for the know-your-customer and suitability obligations to apply.[50]

MiFID: This continues to be the position, such that the 'appropriateness' obligation in 11.4 does not apply, only if the three conditions in 11.3.1–11.3.3 are satisfied.

11.3.1 The service relates to 'non-complex' investments

These are defined as '(a) shares admitted to trading on a regulated market or an equivalent third country market . . . in the list . . . published by the

---

[46] FSA PS 07/6, para. 12.12. For FSA's concerns about quality of advice, see A Review of Retail Distribution, FSA DP 07/1, June 2007; Platforms: the role of wraps and fund supermarkets, FSA DP 07/2, June 2007.
[47] COBS 9.4; FSA CP 06/19, Chapter 14; FSA PS 07/14, Chapter 4.
[48] FSA CP 06/19, Ann. 6, rule 10.5.1(2). [49] FSA PS 07/6, para. 12.12.
[50] Regulation of the Marketing of Investment Products and Services, SIB, March 1990, para. 3.4.

European Commission . . . or (b) money market instruments, bonds or other forms of securitised debt (excluding those . . . that embed a derivative); or (c) . . . UCITs . . . or (d) other non-complex financial instruments' (COBS 10.4.1). It is a 'non-complex' instrument only if '[i] [it] is not a derivative or warrant . . . [ii] there are frequent opportunities to dispose of, or redeem or otherwise realise the investment at prices that are publicly available to the market . . . [iii] [it] does not involve any actual or potential liability for the client that exceeds the cost of acquiring the instrument . . . and . . . [iv] adequately comprehensive information on its characteristics is publicly available and is likely to be readily understood so as to enable the average retail client to make an informed judgement as to whether to enter into a transaction in that instrument' (COBS 10.5.5). A listed share (3.2.1.1) or UCITs is clearly 'non-complex', but so is any other collective investment scheme (3.2.1.9), even a hedge fund and even if it invests solely in derivatives, because the scheme is not itself a derivative and most funds can satisfy [ii] – [iv]. Requirement [ii] depends on the nature of the fund and investors involved: a six month redemption period may be 'frequent' for Professional Clients, but not for Retail Clients. And requirement [iii] covers anything beyond the cost of the unit, however expressed. Any other instrument which is, or is an embedded form of, investment within 3.2.1.2, 3.2.1.3 or 3.2.1.6 – 3.2.1.8 is 'complex' since, from a policy perspective, 'their value is derived from another financial instrument or asset, adding a level of complexity to the understanding of the characteristics and valuation of those instruments'[51] and rendering an 'appropriateness' enquiry necessary (11.4). Thus, in FSA's view, a convertible bond is 'complex'. It is only with 'the structure of "non-complex" instruments . . . [that are] so simple that clients can be expected to easily understand the characteristics and risks associated with them . . . [that the] "appropriateness" test should not therefore be necessary'.[52]

11.3.2 The 'service is provided at the initiative of the client'

It will not be at the client's initiative if 'in response to a personalised communication from . . . the firm' but will be if 'the client demands it on the basis of a . . . promotion . . . that . . . is general and addressed to the public or a larger group . . . of clients' (COBS 10.4.1, 10.5.1–10.5.3). 'The fact that a directed communication contains the name and address of the recipient will not . . . be sufficient to make it personalised . . . Equally, the fact that is does not include a name and address may not prevent it from being regarded as personalised; a generic "flyer" which might otherwise be non-personal could become personalised if accompanied by a covering letter which clearly referred to the personal circumstances of the recipient.'[53]

[51] European Commission MEMO/06/57, 6 February 2006, Q. 1.4.7. [52] Ibid, Q. 1.4.6.
[53] FSA CP 06/19, para. 15.26.

Moreover, 'if a series of communications led up to a transaction . . . it is the response to the first . . . that will determine whether an appropriateness test is required. For example, if the original communication was a newspaper advertisement, we would not see a[n appropriateness] test as being triggered by any personalised communication that follows the client's response to the advert.'[54] This is all very well in theory, but, of course, in practice 'if clients provide instructions via telephone or email it will not always be clear whether they are responding to a financial promotion',[55] thus requiring the firm to set up a filtering or, at least, questioning procedure following the issue of such personalised promotions.

11.3.3 Risk Warning

'[T]he client has been clearly informed . . . that . . . the firm is not required to assess the suitability of the instrument or service . . . and therefore he does not benefit from the protection of the rules on assessing suitability' (COBS 10.4.1(1)). This is different from the risk warning required under 10.5.1.3.

11.4 Appropriateness

This is a new obligation under MiFID which did not exist before.

11.4.1 Application

Unless it is permitted MiFID execution-only business within 11.3, the appropriateness rule applies in two situations. First, it 'applies to a firm which provides . . . MiFID business or equivalent third country business [[4.2.I(2), 4.2.III] within 4.2(n)(ii)] other than making a personal recommendation and managing investments' (COBS 10.1.1), in other words, whenever the firm deals as principal, executes deals as agent or receives and transmits orders, whether in Primary or Secondary Market MiFID Business activities, with Professional or Retail Clients (8.2.1). Thus, in the Primary Markets the obligation can arise in relation to the MiFID activities of underwriting and placing. For other Regulated Activities (4.2.I(1)), i.e. 'firms carrying out a mix of MiFID and non-MiFID business . . . [who see] benefits in a consistent approach across all their business . . . [they] can . . . apply the test . . . if they so wish' or to allow another firm to rely on them (COBS 10.1.3).[56]

It also applies to dealing in any derivatives and warrants with a Retail Client as a result of a direct offer financial promotion (COBS 10.1.2), which replaces an analogous pre-MiFID rule (10.5.2.4).[57]

---

[54] Ibid, para. 15.27.   [55] Ibid, para. 15.9.   [56] FSA PS 07/6, para. 13.10.
[57] FSA CP 06/19, para. 15.8.

11.4.2 The Obligation

11.4.2.1 Assessing appropriateness

The 'firm must ask the client to provide information regarding his [relevant] knowledge and experience . . . so as to enable the firm to assess whether the service or product . . . is appropriate for the client . . . includ[ing] . . . information on:

(1) the types of service, transaction and . . . investment with which the client is familiar; [and]
(2) the nature, volume, frequency of the client's transactions . . . and the period over which they have been carried out; [and]
(3) the level of education, profession or relevant former profession of the client. (COBS 10.2.1(1), 10.2.2)

One reading is that the obligation is to obtain this 'information . . . so as to enable the firm to assess . . . appropriate[ness]', the information in (1), (2) and (3) being only part of the assessment and, thus, other information also being necessary, and the appropriateness assessment itself being something beyond merely assessing knowledge and experience. On this view, '[w]hen assessing appropriateness a firm . . . must determine whether the client has the necessary experience and knowledge in order to understand the risks involved' and the fact that it 'may assume that a professional client has the necessary experience and knowledge' (COBS 10.2.1(2)) does not constitute a total exemption from the rule. However, because 'a professional client . . . is a client who possesses the experience, knowledge and expertise to make his own investment decisions',[58] 'CESR . . . believes that a . . . firm should be deemed to have satisfied its obligations . . . in relation to a professional client by determining the professional status of that client'.[59] FSA agrees. 'Provided that a firm has categorised a professional client in accordance with the relevant requirements, we do not envisage the firm generally needing to obtain additional information from the client . . . for the purposes of the appropriateness test.'[60] Thus, 'the two tests are different in the degree of information gathering and the rigour of the assessment which is necessary. The "appropriateness" test is less wide-ranging than the suitability test. Firms are only required to assess whether the client has the knowledge and experience necessary to understand the risks in relation to the . . . product or service . . . For the purpose of the suitability test, the firm also has to collect

---

[58] CESR/05-291b, April 2005, p. 25. Indeed the MiFID definition of 'Professional Client', in the lead-in to the various categories in 8.3.2, is 'a client who possesses the experience, knowledge and expertise to make its own investment decisions and properly assess the risks that it incurs' (MiFID, Ann. II). [59] CESR/05-290b, April 2005, p. 30.
[60] FSA CP 06/19, para. 15.11.

additional information about the client's financial situation and investment objectives.'[61] Nonetheless, the 'complexity' of these investments, the general MiFID principle (9.3), and the FSA Principle requiring firms to 'treat the customer fairly' (9.2) must, prudently interpreted, mean that the firm ought to approach its appropriateness obligation as requiring an overall determination of whether the particular type of investment is 'appropriate' for the Retail Client and, with Professional Clients, at least that the firm does not possess information indicating that the transaction is 'inappropriate'.

This can be determined, rather than on a transaction-by-transaction basis, at the start of the client relationship (COBS 10.4.2), either in relation to the particular instrument (for example, LME copper contracts are 'appropriate' for a tin can manufacturer) or client strategy (for example, if the client ticks 'speculator', rather than 'hedger' on the fact-find and warrants his total net worth and the amount of money he can afford to lose, then dealing in derivatives up to that amount is 'appropriate' for him). In any event, the Retail Client must possess sufficient knowledge and experience, which produces the slightly curious result that, if he does, he could probably be expertised up to Professional Client (8.3.2.8), such that the appropriateness obligation would not apply on the regulators' interpretation, and if he does not possess such knowledge and experience then the investment can only be sold to him on an advisory or discretionary basis, notwithstanding the necessary risk warnings (10.5.1.3). Truly, this rule protects investors from themselves. It is, thus, another example of the trend towards regulation not simply of mis-selling, but also of mis-buying (9.2).

11.4.2.2 Assessing knowledge and experience

The firm may, if reasonable, decide 'that the client's knowledge alone is sufficient' or conversely 'infer knowledge from experience' (COBS 10.2.6), if sufficiently extensive, and even, although it should be cautious, 'seek . . . to increase the client's level of understanding . . . by providing information to him' (COBS 10.2.7), but avoid a recommendation requiring suitability (11.2), which could be coupled with an on-line examination. The requirement to 'determine whether the client has the necessary experience and knowledge in order to understand the risks' (11.4.2.1), means that the particular client (type) actually does understand them, although FSA's view is less than clear: 'it is difficult to determine "understanding" but this is not what MiFID requires. However, a purposive reading of the obligation to determine "knowledge" suggests that a firm ought to have a reasonable basis for determining that the client is able to understand the risk.'[62]

---

[61] European Commission MEMO/06/57, 6 February 2006, Q. 1.4.7.
[62] FSA PS 07/2, para. 6.7. See, on FSA's website, the 'appropriateness test' – Case Studies.

Advising clients

11.4.2.3 Information relied upon

The firm can 'rely on the information provided by a client', i.e. in some form of fact-find at client take-on, 'unless it is aware that the information is manifestly out of date, inaccurate or incomplete' (COBS 10.2.4) and on other 'information it already has in its possession' (COBS 10.2.5) or on a suitability or appropriateness assessment carried out by another EEA firm (COBS 2.4.5, 10.1.3).

11.4.2.4 Where the product or service is appropriate

Here, 'there is no duty to communicate this to the client' (COBS 10.2.8).

11.4.2.5 Where the product or service is not appropriate

In this situation 'the firm must warn the client' even 'in a standardised format' (COBS 10.3.1) and, in FSA's initial view, if 'the client asks the firm to proceed with the transaction, the firm should consider whether it would be in the client's best interests to proceed'[63] which is clearly the correct view given the MiFID general principle (9.3). However, in response to industry comment 'that this could be read as "raising the bar" on what . . . MiFID' requires,[64] FSA has confused the position in its final rule under which 'If a firm provides a warning and the client asks the firm to proceed . . . it is for the firm to consider whether to do so, having regard to the circumstances' (COBS 10.3.3), although FSA indicate the continuing relevance of their initial view.[65] If the transaction/service is not 'appropriate' and the firm warned the client but proceeded nonetheless, it is difficult to see how (in a case where substantial loss was in fact caused to the client) FSA will say that, in hindsight, the firm 'treated the customer fairly' (9.2). If appropriateness is performed at client take on (11.4.2.1), then clearly there can be no question of proceeding if this service/transaction type is determined to be inappropriate.

11.4.2.6 Record keeping

The firm must keep a written record of the information obtained to perform the assessment (11.4.2.1) and initially FSA was going to require a record of 'each appropriateness assessment',[66] the burden of which would have encouraged assessing appropriateness at the start of the client relationship, rather than on a transaction-by-transaction basis. In its final formulation, the 'firm is required to keep orderly records' (COBS 10.7.1), which is unclear with regard to Retail Clients, although with 'record-keeping in respect of professional clients . . . if a firm has . . . properly documented . . . records for the categorisation of clients as professional, it should not routinely be necessary to record additional information or assessment for the purposes of the appropriateness test'.[67] This may not be

---

[63] Ibid, Ann. 3, COBS 11.3.3. [64] Ibid, para. 6.8. [65] FSA PS 07/6, para. 13.9.
[66] FSA CP 06/19, Ann. 6, COBS 11.7. [67] FSA PS 07/2, para. 6.9; FSA PS 07/6 para. 13.9.

correct in the application of the test to the particular client as explained in 11.4.2.1 and, in any event, to minimise litigation risk with such a new regulatory requirement, prudently records of the whole process should be kept.

11.5 Margin Lending

11.5.1 Consumer Credit

The only restriction on lending money, subject as explained in 11.5.2, is in consumer credit legislation which regulates 'an agreement between an individual ... and any other person ... by which the creditor provides the debtor with credit of any amount', 'credit' being 'a cash loan, and any other form of financial accommodation', 'not exceeding £25,000' (1974 CCA 8(1), (2), 9(1)). The £25,000 limit will be removed from April 2008 (2006 CCA 2(1)(b)) and, in respect of margin lending, reliance will have to be placed upon an exemption in favour of a high net worth individual who is certified by an independent accountant as having either an income of not less than £150,000 per annum or net assets of at least £500,000.[68]

11.5.2 Securities Regulation

Pre-MiFID: Lending to customers on their securities purchases, and taking security over the investments, has always been regarded by regulators as so severely increasing the customer's risk that, for example, the 1939 LDRs prohibited a licensed dealer entering into any transaction 'on terms involving payment by instalments', subject to a narrow exemption for lending on prescribed terms (1939 LDRs 13). Similarly, under the 1986 FSAct, TSA provided that 'A firm may not borrow money for a private customer unless the customer has specifically authorised it',[69] although for SFA 'in addition to obtaining the customer's consent, firms should assess whether the loan or credit is suitable for the customer'.[70] Thus, not itself a Regulated Activity (3.2.2.2), FSA, continuing this policy, required that:

> A firm ... must not lend money or grant credit to a private customer (or arrange for any other person to do so) ... unless:
>
> (1) the firm has made ... an assessment of the customer's financial standing ... [and]
> (2) the firm is taking reasonable steps to ensure that the arrangements ... are suitable ... and
> (3) the ... customer has given his prior written consent. (FSA PM COB 7.9.3)

---

[68] The Consumer Credit (Exempt Agreements) Order 2007, SI 2007 1168. There is an analogous exemption in relation to financial promotions in 2005 FPO 48: see Figure 9 in 10.4.2.4. [69] TSA Rule Amendments, Notice 3, 24 March 1988.
[70] SFA BN 84, 12 June 1982, rule 5–27.

MiFID: Although the Pre-MiFID Rule has not been carried over, 'granting credits or loans to an investor to allow him to carry out a transaction' is MiFID Business (4.2.I(2), Ancillary Service (2)) and subject to not only the Principle of 'treating the customer fairly' (9.2) (which probably would be taken to import elements (1) and (2) of the Pre-MiFID Rule), but also to the conduct rules (COBS 1, Ann. 1, Pt. 1, para. 5) and, hence, has become part of the suitability and appropriateness assessments (11.2, 11.4).

12
Improper behaviour in dealing and executing orders

12.1 Introduction

Executing transactions in the 'proper' manner in relation to both Exchange and MTF rules (14.1, 14.2) and the regulator's rules in respect of such matters as order execution and best execution (13.1, 13.2) is one thing, but there is a further issue, in terms of market integrity in its widest sense: Ought the transaction to be carried out at all? In other words, the transaction must not constitute, or be part of, insider dealing, market manipulation or market abuse. None of this is affected by MiFID.

12.2 Insider dealing

Any form of express outlawing of insider dealing took a long time to find its way onto the Statute book. The 1962 Jenkins Committee recognised the mischief that 'a director who has . . . acquired . . . a particular piece of information materially affecting the value of the securities of his company . . . will incur no liability . . . if he buys or sells such securities'[1] and a 1977 Department of Trade Report agreed: '[p]ublic confidence in directors and others closely associated with companies requires that such people should not use inside information to further their own interests . . . That insider dealing is wrong is widely accepted and . . . [should be made] a criminal offence . . . [With] market transactions . . . it will not . . . be practicable to identify a victim who has suffered as a result of insider dealing. This rules out any adequate civil law remedy that would compensate the victim and is a further reason why criminal sanctions are called for.'[2] The original offence in 1980 CA (re-enacted in 1985 CA) thus required the insider to have a close connection to the company, and the 1989 Insider Dealing Directive[3] broadened it into a Single Market measure to protect the market generally or, as the DTI restated the objective:

> The Government is committed to the operation of the open market. Open markets mean not only free markets but informed and fair markets in whose workings the . . . investor can have confidence. By misusing inside information the insider is in breach of his moral and . . . legal

---

[1] Jenkins Report, para. 89.   [2] Cmnd 7037, Department of Trade, 1977, paras. 22–24.
[3] 1989/542/EEC.

obligations to the source of the information. Market professionals may take steps to avoid being damaged by insiders by setting less attractive terms on which they are prepared to do business. If investors believe that others are making improper use of inside information then they may be less prepared to invest themselves, thus damaging the market.[4]

This resulted in the CJA which made two fundamental changes. First it provided that the information could relate not only to the company, but also to its securities and allied derivatives, and, second, it broadened the necessary 'connection' of the insider to include any person who held the information by virtue of his employment. The combined effect of these changes was to convert the criminal offence from a control over corporate issuers into a control over securities markets which, at least for some, lost its moral basis and cast doubt on the criminalisation process, as is explained in Figure 10.

Each of the boxes in Figure 10 is explained in the following paragraphs.

12.2.1 An individual

Since 'companies can only act through individuals . . . the Government has concluded that it is more appropriate for the criminal law on insider dealing to focus on the individual who misuses the inside information'.[5] 'The provisions required to bring companies within the scope of the offence would be very complex and we do not think that by focussing solely on individuals we should be likely to miss any culpable persons.'[6]

12.2.2 Territorial jurisdiction

In general, '[t]here is a presumption that, in the absence of the contrary intention express or implied, United Kingdom legislation does not apply to foreign persons or corporations outside the UK whose acts are performed outside the UK'[7] because '[i]t would be an unjustifiable interference with the sovereignty of other nations . . . if we were to punish persons for conduct which did not take place in the United Kingdom and had no harmful consequences there'.[8] 'This . . . is subject to some modification in . . . "result-crimes" – that is, crimes that require for their completion not only conduct of a specified nature but also that a particular result shall follow from that conduct. In such crimes our courts have jurisdiction if some part of the prohibited result takes place in this country.'[9] The CJA

---

[4] The Law on Insider Dealing – A Consultative Document, DTI, December 1989, para. 1.1.
[5] Ibid, para. 2.29.
[6] Cmnd 7037, The Department of Trade, 1977, para. 29. The firm itself may breach Principles 3 (5.2) or 5 (12.6).
[7] *Arab Bank plc* v. *Mercantile Holdings Limited* [1994] Ch. 71 at 82. See also *Bennion*, section 106.   [8] *Treacy* [1971] AC 537 at 561.
[9] LC Report No. 180, 27 April 1989, paras. 2.1–2.2.

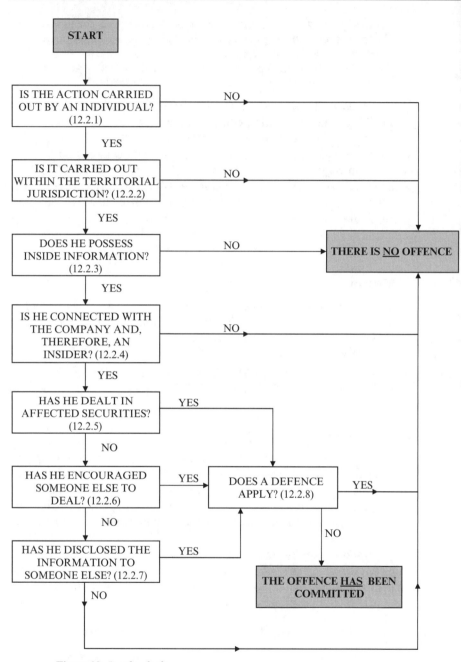

Figure 10 *Insider dealing*

adopts these principles so that the dealing offence (12.2.5) is committed if, with a UK market, the defendant dealt from anywhere in the World and, with an EEA market, was either in the UK or dealt through a firm in the UK; and the other offences (12.2.6, 12.2.7) are committed if the defendant was in the UK or the person counselled or in receipt of the information was in the UK (CJA 62).

12.2.3 Inside information

This 'means information which –

(a) relates to particular securities or to a particular issuer . . . or . . . issuers of securities and not to securities generally or to issuers of securities generally;
(b) is specific or precise;
(c) has not been made public; and
(d) if it were made public would be likely to have a significant effect on the price of any securities. (CJA 56(1))

Paragraph (a) allows the information to relate to the listed securities themselves or to a warrant, depositary receipt or derivative over them (3.2.1.3, 3.2.1.4, 3.2.1.6–3.2.1.8) or to any of their issuers but excludes, for example in relation to an oil exploration company, information on the oil industry, global energy trends or oil producers generally. However, 'information shall be treated as relating to an issuer . . . not only where it is about the company but also where it may affect the company's business prospects' (CJA 60(4)). With paragraph (b), 'specific' is broader than 'precise' so that 'specific information might typically be that a bid was going to be made. Precise information would be the price at which the bid was going to be made',[10] and 'business is down on last year' is 'specific' but, without figures, is not 'precise'. However, depending upon how the statement is made and its formulation, 'specific or precise' 'is intended to . . . ensur[e] . . . that mere rumour and untargeted information is not [caught]'.[11]

In relation to paragraph (c), 'Information is made public if . . . (a) it is published in accordance with the rules of a regulated market . . . [or] (b) it is contained in records . . . open to . . . the public . . . [or] (c) it can be readily acquired . . . or (d) it is derived from information which has been made public' (CJA 58(2)). Moreover, 'Information may be treated as made public even though . . . (a) it can be acquired only by persons exercising diligence or expertise; (b) it is communicated to a section of the public and not to the public at large; (c) it can be acquired only by observation; (d) it is communicated only on payment of a fee; or (e) it is published only outside the United Kingdom' (CJA 58(3)). Thus, the work product of a research analyst is excluded in the absence of a 'tip off' from the company. And, in

---

[10] Parl. Deb., House of Commons, Standing Committee B, 10 June 1993, Minister, col. 176.
[11] Parl. Deb., House of Lords, 3 December 1992, Minister, col. 1501.

determining whether, under paragraph (d), the information if made public 'would be likely to have a significant effect on . . . price', '[i]t is not possible to define any theoretical percentage movement in a share price which will make a piece of information price sensitive . . . since it is . . . necessary to take into account a number of factors . . . which cannot be captured in a mechanical formula. These include the price and volatility of the share and prevailing market conditions.'[12]

Thus, for example, 'inside information' can include: a company's imminent profits warning;[13] information disclosed in the company's briefings to analysts[14] since, although '[t]he Government attaches considerable importance to good communications between companies and the City, and believes that the practice of explaining the details of company operations to analysts and fund managers has an important part to play in this . . . it is equally important to ensure that price sensitive information is not selectively disclosed';[15] and information on actual or imminent client, counterparty or proprietary transactions and/or the intention to hedge them. Listed companies, of course, are under their own obligations to 'inform the public as soon as possible of inside information which directly concerns the . . . issuer'[16] and, thus, must 'establish effective arrangements to deny access to inside information to persons other than those who require it for the exercise of their functions within the issuer' (DTR 2.6.1) which includes not selectively briefing analysts. As a result, on their side, '[a]nalysts should refrain from putting an issuer in a position where it would be in breach of the . . . rules. For instance, analysts should not demand that an issuer corrects its reports or persist in asking questions in briefings where this would involve the issuer disclosing inside information.'[17] Moreover, in order that FSA can more readily identify the source of leaks, 'issuers . . . [and] persons acting on their behalf [such as investment banks, must] . . . draw up a list of those persons working for them . . . who have access to inside information . . . contain[ing] . . . the identity of such persons having access . . . [and] the reason why such person is on the insider list . . . and . . . the date on which the insider list was created and updated' (DTR 2.8.1, 2.8.3). FSA interprets this in a minimalist manner:

> staff need only be included in the insider list if . . . they have access to inside information . . . and . . . they are acting on behalf of the issuer. So it is . . . deal teams and client-facing staff who generally should be

---

[12] Guidance on the Dissemination of Price Sensitive Information, LSE, February 1990, paras. 8–9.   [13] *Mackie* v. *Her Majesty's Advocate* 1995 SLT 110.

[14] Guidance on the Dissemination of Price Sensitive Information, LSE, February 1994, February 1995 and July 1996 Editions.

[15] 1989 DTI CD, para. 2.5. For the issuer's disclosure obligations, see DTR 4; LIST!, Issue 14, FSA, December 2006; Davies Review of Issuer Liability: Final Report, June 2007.

[16] Directive 2003/6, Art. 6. See also DTR; CESR/06–562b, July 2007, paras. 2.1–2.12.

[17] LIST!, Issue 9, FSA, June 2005, para. 4.2.

included . . . [S]omeone . . . in a 'control room' . . . would not be acting on behalf of an issuer . . . despite . . . having access to inside information. Similarly, . . . senior management . . . unless . . . working on an assignment for an issuer . . . Administrative staff . . . would not meet the . . . test . . . [unless] clearly . . . attributed to the account of a particular client.[18]

What information about . . . their reason for being on the list needs to be provided? . . . [Only] a statement that the person is on the list because he has access to the inside information in question.[19]

Such an approach is necessary because 'it is questionable if a list can provide guidance as to whether a particular person has in fact received particular information. Lists seldom appear to provide valuable information about the "true" insider traders.'[20]

12.2.4 Connection

A person is an insider 'only if . . . it is, and he knows that it is, inside information, and . . . he has it, and knows that he has it, from an inside source . . . [i.e.] –

(a) he has it through . . . being a director, employee or shareholder of an issuer . . . or . . . having access to the information by virtue of his employment, office or profession; or
(b) the direct or indirect source of his information is a person within paragraph (a). (CJA 57)

Although paragraph (a), in effect, 'adopt[s] a wide . . . approach . . . that an insider is anyone who has inside information' which could result in 'a . . . range of individuals who would be in some doubt as to whether they were committing a criminal offence',[21] this is tempered by the requirement for positive knowledge as to the status of the information. Similarly, the lack of any necessary connection between the employee and the issuer. This formulation was deliberate to avoid one of the 1980 CA tests of 'insider' which was 'any individual who has information which he knowingly obtains directly or indirectly from another individual who is connected with a particular company', although the Court held this to include passive receipt because 'as far as gaining an unfair advantage of . . . the other party to a

---

[18] Ibid, paras. 12.2–12.4.
[19] Market Watch, Issue 12, FSA, June 2005, Q. 13. That said, FSA has recently criticised City practices as lax and leading to leaks so that '[f]irms should generally be applying more rigour in deciding who need[s] to know about a deal . . . Leakage of information could suggest a wider systems and controls weakness [5.2]' (Market Watch, Issue 21, July 2007, pp. 3, 4). For industry guidance, see Guidelines on the requirement to maintain insider lists, GC100 Listing Rules Working Group, May 2007.
[20] Market abuse: a first evaluation, European Securities Markets Expert Group (ESME), 6 July 2007, p. 1.   [21] Cmnd 7037, 1977, DTI, para. 27.

transaction is concerned, it makes no difference to the person cheated whether the information upon which the "tipee" is basing the cheating was sought out by him or came his way by unsolicited gift'.[22] 'The object of the legislation must be partially defeated if the narrow meaning of "obtained" is adopted'[23] and, as a result of paragraph (b), it is irrelevant whether or not the information reached the individual from the issuer since the policy is that 'secondary insiders should . . . know that they are in possession of inside information, and know that the original source . . . was a primary insider . . . [but] the secondary insider need [not] know exactly which primary insider was the source'.[24]

12.2.5 Dealing

The instrument dealt in must be: a share in a closed-ended (3.2.1.1) or open-ended (3.2.1.9) company or debt security (3.2.1.2), in either case listed or traded on an EEA Exchange; or a warrant (3.2.1.3) or depositary receipt (3.2.1.4) itself so listed or traded or over any such share or debt security; or an option (3.2.1.6) which is itself listed or traded or over any such share, debt security, warrant or depositary receipt or future or CFD referred to below; or a future (3.2.1.7) which is itself listed or traded or over any of the above instruments or CFD referred to below; or a contract for differences (3.2.1.8) which is itself listed or traded or over fluctuations in prices of any such other instrument (CJA 54, 60(2) and Sched. 2; Insider Dealing (Securities and Regulated Markets) Order 1994, SI 1994 187).

Prohibited dealing is buying or selling such instruments either 'on a regulated market' (set out in SI 187) or as or through a 'professional intermediary' (a firm, whether in the UK or abroad, acting as principal, agent or arranger) (CJA 52(1), (3), 59). Buying and selling includes doing so as principal, agent or arranger (3.2.2.1, 3.2.2.2) or through an agent or nominee (CJA 55).

12.2.6 Encouraging

Whereas 1980 CA prohibited 'counsel[ling] or procur[ing] any other person to deal',[25] the CJA has the wider prohibition of 'encourag[ing] another person to deal . . . knowing or having reasonable cause to believe that the dealing would take place' (CJA 52(2)(a)) and although it is unclear when disclosure within 12.2.7 becomes 'encouraging', it probably requires an additional purposive act which may, in practice, be no more than the tone of voice in which the disclosure occurs. This catches honest and complete discussions with prospective underwriters, sub-underwriters, placees and investors, such as during a roadshow, subject to the defences of equality of

---

[22] *Re A-G Reference (No. 1 of 1988)* [1989] 2 WLR 195 at 204. See 1980 CA 68(3).
[23] Ibid.   [24] 1989 DTI CD, para. 2.28.   [25] 1980 CA 68.

information (12.2.8.3) and market information (12.2.8.6) or placing the recipient under a clear confidentiality and 'no use' undertaking, perhaps in writing.[26] It also catches a star analyst's research report, subject to its publication achieving the making public of the recommendation within 12.2.3. Generally, though, under this heading there is no requirement for the person encouraging to be himself prohibited from dealing or even that he actually passes on inside information, as opposed to saying, for example, 'company X is doing some really interesting things that make its shares worth buying'.

12.2.7 Disclosure

Similarly, even though he might not himself be prohibited from dealing, it is an offence to 'disclose ... the information', even without reasonable cause to believe that the recipient might deal, 'otherwise than in the proper performance of the functions of his employment, office or profession' (CJA 52(2)(b)), for example, in seeking underwriters or sub-underwriters or placees although, as with encouraging, it is good practice to put the recipient under a 'no use' obligation.

12.2.8 Defences

The defendant has to himself prove whether he can fit himself within one of the many defences.[27]

12.2.8.1 Not with a view to profit

It is a defence to the offences in 12.2.5, 12.2.6 and 12.2.7 'that he did not at the time expect the dealing to result in a profit attributable to the fact that the information ... was price sensitive' (CJA 53(1)(a), (2)(a), (3)(b)). The application of the 1980 CA defence of 'doing any particular thing otherwise than with a view to ... profit'[28] was unclear where the defendant's primary purpose, as opposed to aim, was not to so make a profit. In contrast, the formulation in the CJA exempts an expectation resulting from a number of different things, only one of which is the holding of inside information and an expectation irrespective of the motive or intention in acting, thus limiting insider dealing to its policy aim of taking advantage of inside information for gain. The defence can, on this basis, operate whether, for example, the purchase is for investment purposes or speculative.

---

[26] For the type of practice occurring in the market here, see the Final Notice attached to FSA PN/677/2006. For precedent wording, see Consultation Paper: Confidentiality Agreements in Corporate Finance Transactions, Financial Law Panel, September 2000 which does not refer to the use of such agreements to prevent breach of the CJA, as opposed to the breach of confidentiality obligations.

[27] *R. v. Cross* [1990] BCC 237 at 244.   [28] 1980 CA 68 (8)(a).

12.2.8.2 Information irrelevant

The offences in 12.2.5 and 12.2.6 are not committed if 'he would have done what he did even if he had not had the information' (CJA 53(1)(c), (2)(c)). This was intended as a 'defence . . . [for] actions done in good faith by individuals who have a conflict of obligations'[29] and, thus, covers acting under a legal duty, for example where a broker–dealer is contractually bound to accept orders or a discretionary portfolio manager is contractually bound to invest the portfolio, in each case notwithstanding the holding of inside information. It also exempts dealing as a result of a predetermined, articulated and documented trading strategy, whether or not automated, where the inside information is received extraneous to and in the course of the strategy.

12.2.8.3 Widely disclosed information

Although less than having made the information public within 12.2.3, it is a defence to the offences in 12.2.5 and 12.2.6 'that at the time he believed on reasonable grounds that the information had been disclosed widely enough to ensure that none of those taking part in the dealing would be prejudiced by not having the information' (CJA 53(1)(b), (2)(c)). This 'defence would be applicable to properly conducted corporate finance transactions such as underwriting offers of listed securities'[30] where both parties had the information even though one of them had disclosed it to the other, under a confidentiality agreement, for the purpose of the dealing. Thus the defence was relied on in the SBC – Trafalgar House Takeover in relation to the CFD entered into between SBC and Trafalgar House, and although pre-cleared by the Panel under the Takeover Code[31] was regarded by SIB as 'risk[ing] . . . involving conduct which is in breach of . . . Principles'[32] and, hence, was one of the drivers in the formulation of the Market Abuse regime (12.5.3.1).

12.2.8.4 Unexpected dealing

It is a defence to the offence in 12.2.7 'that he did not at the time expect any person, because of the disclosure, to deal' (CJA 53(3)(a)).

12.2.8.5 Market makers

Market makers have a defence to the offences in 12.2.5 and 12.2.6 for anything done 'in good faith in the course of . . . business as a market maker' (CJA, Sched. 1, para. 1), in other words the information must be 'of a

---

[29] 1989 DTI CD, para. 2.31.
[30] Parl. Deb., House of Lords, 26 July 1993, Minister, col. 1070.
[31] Takeover Panel Notice 1995/1. Now there are Code Rules prohibiting this. See, for example, Derivatives and Options Regime: 2007 Review, Takeover Panel 2007/15, 29 June 2007. [32] SIB PN/012/95, 13 February 1995.

description which it would be reasonable to expect him to obtain in the ordinary course of that business'.[33] Most exchanges now are order rather than quote driven and this defence is of little application since it defines a market maker as 'a person who . . . holds himself out . . . as willing to acquire or dispose of [investments]' (CJA, Sched. 1, para. 1(2)), although it was used in the SBC – Trafalgar House Takeover in relation to the hedging of the CFD once entered into by SBC (12.5.3).

12.2.8.6 Market dealing

'Market information' is information that relates solely to instruments bought or sold or to be bought or sold, in terms of that fact, and the number, price and identity of the parties. There are two defences in relation to the offences in 12.2.5 and 12.2.6 as regards the use of that information. First, if 'it was reasonable . . . to have acted as he did despite having that information' (CJA, Sched. 1, paras. 2, 4). 'Reasonableness' is always a difficult concept to apply but given the Government's view that 'bought deals, stake building and the like, are well-established and respectable City practices, and accordingly it is difficult to conceive that they would not be considered to be reasonable activities',[34] best market practice would permit: obtaining a confidentiality undertaking before disclosing the information in relation to, for example, an underwriting, sub-underwriting or placing or a roadshow for a new issue; a broker–dealer accepting and executing orders notwithstanding his knowledge of the potential effect of other clients' orders or house positions; and bona fide hedging or unwinding of transactions, notwithstanding their likely effect on the market (subject to market abuse: 12.5.3.1).

And, second, there is a defence if 'he acted . . . in connection with an acquisition or disposal which was under consideration or . . . negotiation, or in . . . course . . . and with a view to facilitating the accomplishment of the acquisition or disposal' and the information related solely to that operation (CJA, Sched. 1, paras 3, 4). This covers a bidder making the takeover offer or soliciting irrevocable undertakings or making market purchases, but not, as in the SBC – Trafalgar House Takeover (12.5.3), entering into contracts for differences giving him an economic exposure to the share price of the target since although connected with the bid it does not facilitate it. It would also exempt carrying out or implementing a placing or a block trade or a bookbuild in relation to a large holding.

12.2.8.7 Stabilisation

Stabilisation (12.3.7) in compliance with FSA's rules is a defence to the offences to 12.2.5 and 12.2.6 (CJA, Sched. 1, para. 5).

---

[33] 1980 CA 68(8)(c), (9).
[34] Parl. Deb., House of Lords, 3 December 1992, Minister, col. 1502.

12.2.8.8 Chinese Wall

There is no express defence in the CJA for information the other side of a Chinese Wall (6.3.1.3) because, given its existence, information cannot flow over the Wall so that the individuals dealing are not doing so in possession of inside information, and the firm itself cannot be liable (as explained in 12.2.1).

12.3 Market manipulation

In the absence of fraud, which was extremely difficult to prove, originally the only prohibition on market manipulation was in the rules of the London Stock Exchange which prohibited its members 'knowingly or without due care deal[ing] in such a manner that shall promote or assist in the promotion of a false market', being 'a market in which a movement of the price of a share is brought about . . . by contrived factors, such as the operations of buyers and sellers acting in collaboration with each other, calculated to create a movement of price which is not justified by assets, earnings or prospects'.[35] Then, in the 1986 FSAct the Government decided that '[i]t will be a criminal offence for any person knowingly or recklessly to engage in any act, device, scheme, practice or course of conduct . . . which is likely to defraud, deceive or mislead'[36] which resulted in a provision later carried over into FSMA:

> Any person who does any act or engages in any course of conduct which creates a false or misleading impression as to the market in or the price or value of . . . investments [3.2.1] is guilty of an offence if he does so for the purpose of creating that impression and of thereby inducing another person to acquire, dispose of, subscribe for or underwrite that investment or to refrain from doing so or to exercise, or refrain from exercising, any rights conferred by those investments. (FSMA 397(3))

This is analysed in Figure 11. Each of the boxes in Figure 11 is explained in the following paragraphs.

12.3.1 Act or course of conduct

This requires either a positive 'act' or a failure to do something where there is a legal duty to do so, for example, a listed company's failure to disclose to the market a material event within 12.2.3, although it is possible to conceive of an ongoing failure to disclose in the absence of the legal duty to do so amounting to a 'course of conduct'. In any event, the 'act or course of conduct' must 'create' the impression referred to in 12.3.2, i.e. be the direct or indirect reason why the impression exists.

---

[35] Rules and Regulations of The Stock Exchange, 11 February 1975, Rule 73b. See, now, LSE Post MiFID Rules 3300, 3301.   [36] 1985 White Paper, para. 7.5.

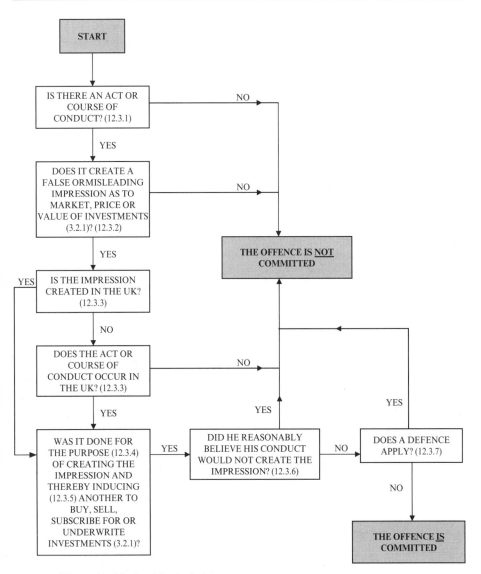

Figure 11 *Market Manipulation*

12.3.2 False or misleading impression

The impression created must be 'false of misleading'. It follows that real market activity, with the purchaser or seller entering into real, on-risk transactions, cannot amount to market manipulation, no matter how extreme those transactions in terms of volume and their effect on market price, even involving the pre-hedging of underlying shares on a proposed issue of convertible bonds which has not yet been announced to the market. This is contrary to the view of one MP when the 1986 FSAct was going through Parliament:

> the wording ... worries some dealers and brokers who, in discharging ... an order on behalf of a client, may have to go into the market and acquire parcels of shares at different prices ... sell[ing] some shares in order to make a market in which they will later be buyers, or vice versa ... The various ... ways in which professionals ... give ... a misleading view of what they are up to and what they believe the market price ... to be, are and ought to be legitimate means of trading.[37]

Moreover, the impression must actually exist in the minds of the persons induced, and there is no test of what the hypothetical reasonable person would believe, the impression created on private and professional investors differing. Such false or misleading impressions are typically created by, for example: 'talking up' (where a corporate finance firm conducting a blind written auction sale tells the only sealed bidder that it is going to have to bid higher to secure the purchase); 'wash sales' (a simultaneous sale and purchase between two colluding parties without any change in beneficial ownership, in order to create the illusion of liquidity) as contrasted with 'bed and breakfast' transactions (where, to crystallise tax or accounting treatment, a holder of securities sells them and minutes or hours later buys them back on the market having been exposed to the risk of price changes in the interim); and 'hold harmless' transactions (where, for example, in a takeover a bidder procures a third party to buy the target or bidder shares or sell a competing bidder's shares with the intention of affecting the price, in each case with an undisclosed indemnity to cover losses). At one point, it was even considered to apply to announcements of the success of bond issues:

> 'The deal had a slow reception but will go retail after a few days' – [means] 'We still own the bond, but hope we can flog a few to innocent investors. This will take a while'.

> 'We thought the pricing was fair' – [means] 'It was tight as hell, but co-managers had to come in for relationship reasons'.

> 'It was a blow-out, sold out within two hours' – [means] 'All the paper has been sold PA [i.e. to the manager itself] to boost the salaries of the new issue traders'.[38]

12.3.3 In the UK

Again, using the general territorial presumptions of criminal offences (12.2.2), either the conduct has to occur in the UK or the impression be created here (FSMA 397(7)).

---

[37] Parl. Deb., House of Commons, Standing Committee E, 4 March 1986, Anthony Nelson, col. 432.   [38] Lies, damned lies and Euro bonds, FT, 10 August 1989.

12.3.4 Purpose

A 'purpose' is less than knowledge of the actual effect[39] and requires 'that the person did the act or engaged in the course of conduct deliberately to create the impression . . . and . . . intended . . . to induce another . . . [but not] that the accused intended the impression to be false or misleading. On the other hand, the accused should not be regarded as having committed an offence if the false or misleading nature of the impression he has created was inadvertent.'[40] As a result, there cannot be a 'purpose' to mislead if full disclosure of the relevant facts is made to the market although, in that event, a false or misleading impression within 12.3.2 would not have been created in the first place. Otherwise, 'purpose' would be judged in relation to either the defendant's subjective intention or whether, objectively, his actions amounted to such a 'purpose' (1967 Criminal Justice Act 8).[41]

12.3.5 Inducing

No one need actually be induced to act but, rather, there must a purpose of inducing others to so act.

12.3.6 Reasonable belief

This defence applies if the defendant 'reasonably believed that his act or conduct would not create an impression that was false or misleading' (FSMA 397(5)(a)), i.e. only if the defendant addressed his mind to whether or not there was a market manipulation. Otherwise he cannot 'prove that he reasonably believed', reasonableness in practice being based upon the known level of knowledge or disclosure already existing in the market.

12.3.7 Defences

There are two further defences. First, 'that he acted or engaged in the conduct in conformity with control of information rules' (6.2.3.2, 6.3.1.3) (FSMA 397(5)(c); SYSC 10.2.3(1)) and, second, 'that he acted or engaged in the conduct in conformity with the relevant provisions of Commission Regulation No. 2273/2003 . . . for . . . stabilisation' (FSMA 397(5)(d))[42] which 'permit firms to support the price of new issues . . . The policy rationale . . . is . . . to underpin and support the new issue market. Stabilisation activity is potentially manipulative in that it may support

---

[39] Parl. Deb., House of Lords, 27 October 1986, Lord Edmund-Davies, col. 530.
[40] Ibid, Minister, col. 534.   [41] *Smith & Hogan*, pp. 84–89.
[42] There is a further exemption in the Regulation for buy-back programmes (MAR 1, Ann. 1).

the price of a security above that which would otherwise prevail if the market were left to find its own level. The rationale . . . stems from . . . the benefit to the issue of support to the price which facilitates the raising of capital by issuers . . . and . . . the benefit to the market as a whole of support to the price of new issues during the step change increase in supply . . . [N]ew securities . . . may result in temporary over-supply . . . leading to an artificially low market price during and immediately after issue . . . Price stabilising . . . involves . . . supporting the price . . . for a limited period.'[43] Market practice, and hence permitted stabilisation, differs between equity and debt issues, although in both cases there must be a 'significant distribution' for the rules to apply, i.e. 'an initial or secondary offer . . . publicly announced and distinct from ordinary trading both in terms of the amount in value of the securities offered and the selling methods employed' so that, for example, 'block trades are not considered as a significant distribution . . . [but as] strictly private transactions' (GLOSS, def. of 'significant distribution'; MAR 2.2.6). The effect of both sets of rules, though, is that 'the manager . . . may go into the market to buy . . . securities which he is himself offering, in order to . . . maintain the market price . . . only if the stabilising period is still running, . . . he has taken the necessary preliminary steps . . . (relating to warnings of the possibility of stabilisation action, knowledge of other changes in prices, and records of action taken) and only so long as the limits . . . as to the maximum price at which stabilising action may be taken are not exceeded'.[44] Thus, in respect of all stabilised securities there are detailed disclosure requirements (MAR 2.3.5–2.3.9, 2.3.11(f)). The rules apply in relation to shares, bonds, government securities, warrants and depositary receipts (3.2.1.1–3.2.1.4) 'that have been admitted to trading on a regulated market' (14.1), and also in modified form to all investments traded anywhere (MAR 2.2.1(2), 2.4), wherever in the World the stabilisation is conducted, although stabilisation carried out in accordance with US, Japanese or Hong Kong rules is also provided with a defence (MAR 2.1.3, 2.5).[45]

12.3.7.1 Equity

Here 'it is normal to over-allot . . . leav[ing] the lead manager with a net short position . . . having pre-sold more than 100% of the issue. Thereafter, when the issue begins to trade . . . the lead manager can buy in . . . securities . . . to close his short position . . . run[ning] . . . the risk that, if sufficient stock is not sold by the original investors to enable him to close

---

[43] FSA CP 40, January 2000, paras. 1.3, 1.4, 2.4.
[44] COB Rules: a new approach, SIB, November 1988, Rule 14–02, Principle of Conduct 81.
[45] This defence applies in relation to market manipulation under FSMA 397(5)(b), but not market abuse within 12.5 (MAR 2.5.1(1)).

the short position, the price will move against him . . . It is therefore usual for . . . the issuer to agree in advance that the lead manager should have an option to acquire further securities from the issuer at the offer price . . . a Green Shoe option . . . [Also] the . . . stabilising manager actively goes into the market to support the price of the stock.'[46] The rules define the 'greenshoe option' as 'an option granted by the offeror . . . for the purpose of covering overallotments, under the terms of which [the manager] . . . may purchase up to a certain amount of . . . securities at the offer price for a certain period' (GLOSS, def. of 'greenshoe option') and provide that 'securities may be overallotted only during the subscription period and at the offer price', 'the greenshoe option may be exercised . . . only when . . . securities have been overallotted . . . [and its] exercise period must be the same as the stabilisation period' and 'the greenshoe option may not amount to more than 15% of the original offer' and 'a position resulting from . . . overallotment . . . which is not covered by the greenshoe option may not exceed 5% of the original offer' (MAR 2.3.11). As a result, this 'limit[s] the ability to have a naked short position (i.e. a short not covered by a greenshoe) to 5%. Sales that establish a short position other than through an overallotment of securities cannot themselves be for the purpose of price support [within the defence and] . . . run the risk of depressing the price.'[47] The practice of 'refreshing the greenshoe is . . . selling securities that ha[ve] . . . been acquired as a result of stabilising activities to flatten a firm's position in anticipation of having to conduct further stabilising purchases . . . This might involve establishing a short position for a second time which would be filled through [further] stabilising purchases . . . While . . . the [defence] . . . does not [cover] . . . refreshing the greenshoe, there are circumstances where removing a short position would . . . fall within [it].'[48] Again there may be 'the need to sell securities which had been acquired as a result of stabilising purchases with a view to re-establishing a short position in case further stabilising purchases were needed . . . [or] in a choppy market . . . the . . . manager might have overallotted . . . 15% and the price . . . then rises above the issue price, triggering the exercise of the greenshoe option. If the price subsequently fell, stabilising purchases may be required which would be easier if a short position could be [re-]established . . . [N]one of the[se] scenarios . . . are clearly . . . covered by the . . . [defence] but this does not mean that the behaviour is itself abusive . . . [and] should be conducted in a way which minimises market impact.'[49] The stabilisation period for an IPO is the 30 days from commencement of trading and, for a secondary offer, 30 days from public announcement of

---

[46] FSA CP 40, January 2000, Ann. D, para. D3.
[47] Market Watch, Issue 12, FSA, June 2005, pp. 4–5.
[48] FSA PS 05/3, March 2005, para. 2.8.
[49] Market Watch, Issue 12, FSA, June 2005, p. 3.

the price (MAR 2.3.4(2), (3)). In respect of the shares offered and any 'associated interests', being derivatives over them (GLOSS, def. of 'associated instruments'), 'any purchase or offer to purchase . . . exclusively for supporting the market price of those . . . securities . . . due to a selling pressure in such securities', which may be on-exchange or off-exchange, must 'be executed above the offering price' (GLOSS, def. of 'stabilisation'; MAR 2.1.6, 2.3.10(1)) so that activities 'not directly related to the purpose of stabilisation activities' are not within the defence (MAR 2.2.7).

12.3.7.2 Bonds

'In the bond market, stabilisation . . . is no longer practiced . . . [T]he syndicate . . . offer bonds . . . using the "fixed price re-offer" approach . . . at a given price. When the issue is declared "free to trade" . . . the bonds may then be supported by buying at prices . . . at or below the previously given price . . . [T]he focus of pricing is usually on the spread over a benchmark bond at which the new bond is expected to trade. The lead manager will . . . price the issue at a price comparable with similar credits in the market. Any support . . . is likely to focus on maintaining or reducing the spread between the bond and the benchmark', whereas in equity the focus 'is . . . on the outright price of the stock.'[50] With convertible bonds (3.2.1.2), the stabilising period starts on the day of public disclosure of the final offer terms and ends on the earlier of 30 days after the issuer receives the proceeds and 60 days after allotment, whereas with other bonds it ends on the same day but '[s]tart[s] on the date of . . . public disclosure of the terms of the offer . . . (i.e. including the spread to the benchmark . . . once it has been fixed)' (MAR 2.3.4(4), (5)). With straight bonds there is no limit on the price at which 'any purchase or offer to purchase . . . securities, or any transactions in associated instruments' (being derivatives over the securities or bonds issued by the same issuer), which can be on-exchange or off-exchange, can occur as long as the activities are 'directly related to the purpose of stabilisation activities'. However, with convertible bonds such transactions in those bonds, derivatives over them or underlying securities 'shall not in any circumstances be executed above the market price of those instruments at the time of the public disclosure of the final terms of the new offer' (GLOSS, defs. of 'stabilisation' and 'associated instruments'; MAR 2.1.6, 2.2.7, 2.3.10(2)). Different provisions were necessary for convertibles because although '[n]o problem arises in the case of a stabilising . . . transaction which relates to the two [instruments] combined . . . [a] problem does arise in identifying appropriate limits to . . . transactions which relate to one element only of the combined unit'.[51]

---

[50] FSA CP 40, January 2000, Ann. D, paras. D4–D6.
[51] Further sundry proposed amendments to the Rulebook, SIB, June 1988, para. 20.

12.4 A principle of conduct and the need for an administrative remedy

There has always been a market expectation that 'A dealer should . . . act in conformity with the principles of good conduct already applying in the securities market . . . [and] avoid any practice which might lead to a false market'[52] and this was reflected in Exchange rules such as the LSE's quoted in 12.3 and the 1983 LDRs: '[t]o the extent that there exist generally accepted standards as to what constitutes good market practice . . . a licensed dealer shall comply with such standards'. Hence, for the Government under the 1986 FSAct there would be 'a principle of fair dealing . . . [which] would be the basis of specific rules'[53] and SIB stated at the front of its original Rulebook that '[t]he objectives of these rules are to ensure that a [firm] . . . complies with best market practice'.[54] In the New Settlement this became a Principle (2.4.3) that 'A firm should comply with high standards of market conduct and with any code or standard which has been . . . endorsed for the purpose of this principle'.[55] SIB endorsed both the Takeover Code (2.4.4(9)) and the Bank of England's Grey Book (13.1.5),[56] because 'there is now greater emphasis given . . . to the significance of markets . . . [and the] principle . . . provide[s] . . . a clear focus . . . for rules on reporting of off-exchange transactions, and on insider dealing and market manipulation'.[57] From the beginning, though, the Principle was of uncertain application and used by the regulator against any behaviour which it considered undesirable. Hence, SIB's difficulties in explaining the meaning of a 'proper trade' in the context of on-exchange derivatives:

> one way in which a firm may fail to observe high standards of market conduct is by effecting . . . improper trades . . . A trade must be entered into for proper trading purposes . . . [H]edging, investment, speculation, price-fixation, arbitrage, delivery, market making or . . . executing customer orders which appear to be for one of these purposes, can all be proper trading purposes . . . [A] proper trade must involve . . . entering into a [transaction] . . . (either for proprietary account or in execution of a . . . [customer] order) which . . . open[s] a new position and thereby creat[es] an exposure to market risk . . . or . . . clos[es] out a position and thereby remov[es] (further) market risk. A trade is improper if it is entered into in conjunction with a separate arrangement with another person . . . which has the effect of reducing or removing . . . market risk . . . [for example] agreements to indemnify a counterparty against loss or . . .

[52] Code of Conduct, Council for The Securities Industry, May 1980, paras. 1–2.
[53] 1985 White Paper, para. 7.5(i).
[54] The Financial Services (Conduct of Business) Rules 1987, 7 October 1987, Introduction, p. 3.11.   [55] Statements of Principle, SIB, 1990, Principle 3.
[56] The Financial Services (Statements of Principle) (Endorsement of Codes and Standards) Instrument 1995.   [57] SIB CP 33, June 1990, para. 16.

(i) pre-arranged trades . . . which are not exposed to any . . . pricing mechanism . . .
(iii) accommodation trades (usually non-competitive trades entered into with a view to assisting another party to conceal an abuse);
(iv) wash trades (whereby a false impression of trading activity is deliberately created).[58]

SIB's ideas for the equity markets were hardly any clearer. It concluded that '[short] selling stock . . . in anticipation of buying it later at a lower price' was not improper'[59] even though it 'may add significantly to downwards pressure in a market that is already falling' because it is 'a legitimate investment activity . . . enabling investors to establish an exposure that reflects their opinion of a security's value . . . and . . . assist[s] market efficiency by . . . enabling the market price to reflect a full range of investor perceptions; facilitat[es] arbitrage, e.g. between the futures and cash markets; [and] add[s] to market liquidity'.[60] Beyond this it concluded that '[i]n order to secure a market which is not misled, manipulated or abused, SIB will work with other regulators to define what is, and what is not, acceptable conduct'.[61]

Thus, in the early 1990s there was a lack of enforcement action and, in the context of market fragmentation away from the LSE, SIB saw 'a need for regulation to be able to provide a more credible alternative . . . to the criminal process'.[62] '[M]arket abuse has to be more clearly defined . . . it's got to be made easier to detect . . . [a]nd . . . once detected, there has to be efficient means for dealing with guilty parties',[63] in other words administrative fines.[64] And whereas for the Conservative Government 'some form of civil penalty . . . impose[d] . . . in the public interest . . . is the classical reason for creating a criminal offence' so that '[t]he Government accordingly believe that the criminal law remains appropriate',[65] to the Labour Opposition '[a]t the moment there is little chance of City crime being detected, even less chance of prosecution, and those convicted have a good chance of walking free from court'.[66] When elected, the new Labour Minister 'said there had been only 17 prosecutions for insider dealing since 1990, 12 of which had been successful. "I do not think anyone can seriously maintain that 17 is the

---

[58] SIB GR 2/93, April 1993, paras. 6, 11–14.
[59] Regulation of the UK Equity Markets, SIB DP, February 1994, paras. 4.34–4.40.
[60] SIB CP 100, November 1996, paras. 61, 70.
[61] Regulation of the UK Equity Markets, SIB DP, February 1994, App. 2, para. 13.
[62] Ibid, para. 8.12.
[63] Regulation in a Changing Market Environment, Andrew Large, Chairman SIB, at Equity Markets Regulation Conference, 26 May 1994.
[64] SIB PN/012/94, 7 March 1994.   [65] Company Investigations, DTI, August 1990, p. 18.
[66] Alistair Darling, Labour City Spokesman, quoted in Labour calls for shake-up of City Regulator, FT, 20 September 1994.

number of times that insider dealing has occurred in the last eight years", he said.'[67] This was compounded by the frustration of SIB and the SROs in not being able to take enforcement action against licensed firms like SBC over the Trafalgar House takeover of Northern Electric (12.5.3.1), the uncertainty of the market in the pre-hedging of programme trades as the result of the SBC/KEPIT case (12.5.5.1), the international and unregulated aspects of the Sumitomo copper squeeze on the LME (12.5.5.1), the fact that genuine, albeit aggressive, trading affecting prices was not criminal market manipulation (12.3.2) and uncertainty over the propriety of short selling and stock borrowing (12.5.5.1). As a result of all this, the following features were built into the market abuse regime.

12.4.1 An administrative offence

The criminal law, with imprisonment of individuals as a sanction (CJA; FSMA 397) did not really focus the minds of corporations, while 'the power to levy fines . . . [with] a code of market conduct, produced by the FSA, setting out behaviour which would be acceptable in the markets'[68] would do so, particularly since '[t]here will be no limit on fines, so serious abuse will get a serious fine'.[69]

12.4.2 The burden of proof

Criminal offences require proof 'beyond reasonable doubt' and 'the quantum of proof required is a high one, for the tribunal must be satisfied beyond reasonable doubt that the accused is guilty',[70] 'not proved beyond all doubt',[71] so that in its classical formulation 'it is sufficient for [the defendant] to raise a doubt as to his guilt'.[72] In contrast, the lower civil law standard is the 'balance of probabilities' and that is the standard to be applied in market abuse cases,[73] although as the Courts apply it:

> The balance of probability standard means that a court is satisfied an event occurred if the court considers that, on the evidence, the occurrence of the event was more likely than not. When assessing the probabilities the court will have in mind as a factor, to whatever extent is appropriate in the particular case, that the more serious the allegation

---

[67] FSA to get more power to tackle insider dealing, FT, 7 May 1998.
[68] HMT News Release 69/98, 6 May 1998.
[69] FSA to get more power to tackle insider dealing, FT, 7 May 1998. For FSA's enforcement discretion generally with market abuse, see DEPP 6.2.1, 6.2.2, 6.3.2, 6.4, 6.5; EG 2.5, 7.1–7.5.
[70] *Criminal Law – The General Part*, Glanville Williams, 2nd edn., Stevens, 1961, p. 871.
[71] *The Proof of Guilt*, Glanville Williams, Stevens, 1955, p. 134.
[72] *Woolmington* [1935] AC at 481.
[73] *Davidson* v. *FSA*, Financial Services Tribunal, 2006, Decision 031; *Legal and General* v. *FSA*, 2005, Decision 015; *Arif Mohammed* v. *FSA*, 2005, Decision 012.

the less likely it is that event occurred and, hence, the stronger should be the evidence before the court concludes that the allegation is established on the balance of probability.[74]

Market abuse 'is a very grave charge . . . [C]ompelling evidence must be adduced if it is to be established. Put another way, if one applies the "sliding scale" . . . the slide must be very close to the upper end of the scale. In a practical sense . . . it is difficult to draw a meaningful distinction between [this] standard . . . and the criminal standard.'[75]

12.4.3 Intention

Notwithstanding the precise definition of the criminal offence, '[t]he principle of mens rea . . . stat[es] that defendants should only be held criminally liable for events or consequences which they intended or knowingly risked',[76] and 'regulators hate the concept of intent because it is virtually impossible to prove'.[77] Accordingly, '[t]he aim of the . . . regime is . . . to protect people's confidence in the trueness and fairness of financial markets . . . focu[sing] on the effect of . . . behaviour not the intention behind that behaviour. This is because the unintended effects of behaviour can undermine the proper operation of a market.'[78] Similarly, '[i]t is not . . . necessary to show that . . . conduct was dishonest, nor that he gained by it; dishonesty and gain (or intended gain) may be common features of market abuse, and may constitute evidence of it, but they are not . . . essential ingredients'.[79] Thus, market abuse 'does not require the person engaged in the behaviour . . . to have intended to commit market abuse' (MAR 1.2.3), although in practice '[w]hen it decides to take action for behaviour appearing to the FSA to amount to market abuse . . . the FSA may take into account . . . whether the behaviour was deliberate or reckless' and 'the factors which may be relevant when it sets the amount of a penalty' include, similarly towards the top of the list, '[t]he extent to which the behaviour was deliberate or reckless' (ENF 14.4.2(1)(b), 14.7.4(2)).[80] In practice, how else is it possible to distinguish 'good', albeit accidental, from 'bad' behaviour deserving of censure? It is for this reason that, as explained in 12.5, the drafting of the substantive market abuse offence includes at various points intention-like requirements.

---

[74] *Re. H* [1996] 1 AER 1 at 16–17.
[75] *James Parker* v. *FSA*, Financial Services Tribunal, 2006, para. 23.
[76] *Principles of Criminal Law*, Andrew Ashworth, Oxford, 3rd edn., 1999, pp. 87–88.
[77] Joint Committee Report, Vol. II, Minutes of Evidence, 25 March 1999, para. 247, Executive Director LME.
[78] FSMB – Progress Report, HMT, March 1999, para. 13.5.
[79] *James Parker* v. *FSA*, Financial Services Tribunal, 2006, para. 126.
[80] This will continue under FSA's restructuring of the Enforcement Manual. See DEPP 6.2.1(1)(a).

That said, as an effects-based offence it will often be appropriate to infer from the facts the satisfaction of various elements of the offence, for example that, in misuse of information (12.5.3), the defendant dealt 'on the basis' of inside information.[81]

12.4.4 Affected persons and certainty

The Principle of 'high standard of market conduct' applied only to licensed firms yet something of that nature, or vagueness, would enhance enforcement against unlicensed persons. On the one side, the criminal law was both too widely drawn (in the market manipulation offence), and too narrow and precise (in the insider dealing offence), in both cases rendering successful prosecution extremely difficult given 'the principle of strict construction . . . [under which] any doubt in the meaning of a statutory provision should . . . be resolved in favour of the defendant'.[82] Moreover, while the market manipulation offence could be committed by an individual or, under usual principles of vicarious responsibility in criminal law, his employer, the insider dealing offence could be committed only by an individual (12.2.1). The 2001 Market Abuse regime, applying to corporations as well as individuals, would thus be drafted in a much more 'principle-based' manner (cf 2.5.8), which has been compounded by the revisions made in 2005 as a result of the Market Abuse Directive.

12.4.5 Multiple jeopardy

Just in case, the Government and FSA between them ended up with a number of overlapping regimes: the criminal laws of insider dealing and market manipulation,[83] and the civil law administrative Market Abuse regime, applying to licensed and unlicensed persons; the Principle of market conduct applying to licensed persons; and the Exchange rules applying to Exchange members.

12.5 The market abuse regime

In both its original FSMA formulation, and its revision upon adoption of the Market Abuse Directive, the regime is best understood through Figure 12. The regulators maintain, at least in relation to the original 2001 Market Abuse Code, that '[t]he Code . . . provides a clear statement of the standards we expect to see in UK markets'[84] if for no other reason than that '[m]arket participants have a common core understanding of the kinds of behaviour which constitute abuse of the markets as a result of well

---

[81] For an example, see *James Parker* v. *FSA*, Financial Services Tribunal, 2006, para. 138.
[82] *Principles of Criminal Law*, Andrew Ashworth, p. 80.
[83] FSA has criminal enforcement powers: EG 12.   [84] FS PN/047/2001, 30 April 2001.

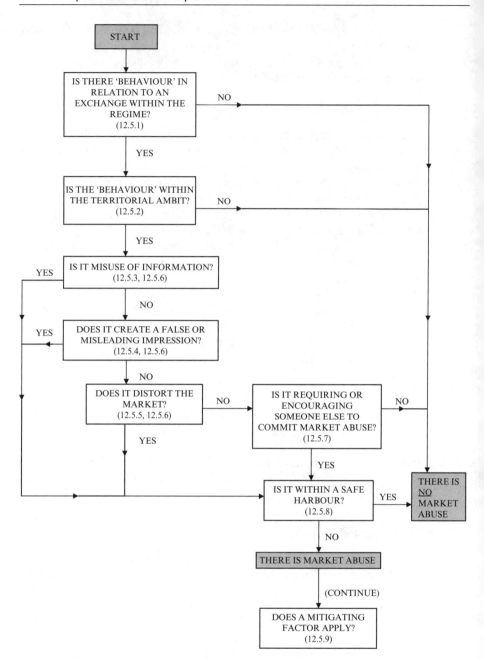

Figure 12 *Market abuse*

understood market conventions and expectations and particular regulatory cases'.[85] The reader must decide whether this has been achieved given that, from the market perspective, 'it is very important for firms and individuals that the behaviour expected of them should be clearly described . . . [and] that the types of behaviour which are to be subject to fines . . . should be foreseeable in advance. Indeed, since the primary purpose of the . . . offence is to deter behaviour which is damaging to UK markets, it would be perverse if there was uncertainty about the conduct which will be subject to FSA disciplinary action.'[86]

12.5.1 'Behaviour' in relation to an exchange

Unlike insider dealing (12.2.1), market abuse applies 'to conduct by any person (whether an individual or a corporate entity)' and, like the criminal offences, 'to both regulated and unregulated persons'.[87] '[B]ehaviour includes action or inaction' 'whether by one person alone or by two or more persons jointly or in concert' (FSMA 118(1), 130A(3)), and whether or not there is a legal obligation to act,[88] provided that it falls within one of the three headings of market abuse in 12.5.3, 12.5.4 or 12.5.5. It must occur in relation to any investment (within 3.2.1.1–3.2.1.4, 3.2.1.6–3.2.1.9) traded, or in respect of which a request for admission to trading has been made, on a UK recognised investment exchange[89] or OFEX or, in relation to the headings of market abuse in 12.5.3.1, 12.5.3.2, 12.5.4.1, 12.5.4.2, 12.5.5.1 and 12.5.5.2, a regulated EEA market (FSMA 118(1); FSMA 2000 (Prescribed Markets and Qualifying Investments) Order 2001, SI 2001/996) or, in relation to 12.5.3.3, 12.5.4.3 and 12.5.5.3, any such UK recognised investment exchange 'accessible electronically in the United Kingdom' even though not established here (FSMA 118A(2)). '[T]he intention . . . is to capture "when issued" or grey market trading . . . before admission takes place . . . [because s]uch trading could have an impact on the price at which the . . . investment starts to trade',[90] although if the behaviour occurs before a request for trading has been made, market abuse is committed only 'if [the behaviour] . . . continues to have an effect once an application has been made' (MAR 1.2.5).

Inaction is caught only 'if the person concerned has failed to discharge a legal or regulatory obligation [to act] . . . or . . . if the person concerned has created a reasonable expectation of his acting in a particular manner, as a result of his representations . . . in circumstances which give rise to a duty

---

[85] FSMB: Government Response to the Reports of the Joint Committee, HMT, 17 June 1999, Pt. 2, para. 3.   [86] Joint Committee Report, Vol. II, App. 65, para. 1.
[87] FSA CP 10, June 1998, Pt. 1, para. 3.
[88] FSA MAR Release 001, 1 December 2001, 1.3.2.
[89] These are: EDX London Ltd., ICE Futures, LIFFE, LSE, AIM, PLUS Markets, LME, virt-x.
[90] UK Implementation of The Market Abuse Directive, HMT & FSA CD, June 2004, para. 4.19.

or obligation to inform those to whom he made the representations that they have ceased to be correct, and he has not done so' (MAR 1.2.6), thus extending the position under the criminal law of market manipulation (12.3.1). However, whether action or inaction, it need only be 'in relation to' an investment which is within the scope of the regime (FSMA 118(1)(a)), thus catching:

(1) a physical commodity which is the subject-matter of an exchange-traded . . . futures contract . . .
(2) the constituent shares of . . . an exchange-traded option . . .
(3) a bond which is convertible or exchangeable into shares which are [listed] . . .
(4) a bond deliverable . . . [under] an exchange-traded bond futures contract;
(5) an OTC . . . swap . . . priced in accordance with a [listed] . . . investment;
(6) spread bet on . . . [listed] investments; and
(7) equity warrants on . . . [listed] investments.

That said, a mere 'correlation between the product (or its price or value) and the . . . [listed] investment' may not be enough. 'For example, silver will not be [caught] . . . in relation to shares in silver producing companies.'[91]

In any event, and this was a key reason for the creation of the market abuse regime (12.4.3), the offence 'does not require the person engaging in the behaviour . . . to have intended to commit market abuse' (MAR 1.2.3).

12.5.2 Territorial ambit

In relation to an EEA regulated market the behaviour in 12.5.1 must occur 'in the UK' but, in relation to UK Exchanges, it can occur anywhere in the World (FSMA 118A(1)), which is consistent with the approach taken in the criminal laws of insider dealing and market manipulation (12.2.2, 12.3.3). Nontheless, the overall scope of the regime may be viewed as draconian since it 'applies extraterritorially . . . [and is] a scheme for punishing people who may be abroad, who may not be taking any active part in any market in this country, who have not done anything illegal [in their own country], whose conduct is innocent, who are under no duty to act when they are accused of failing to act, and nevertheless punishing them for such conduct'.[92]

12.5.3 Misuse of information

The underlying policy is different from that used now to justify criminal insider dealing legislation (12.2): 'market users rely on the timely dissemination of . . . information . . . they . . . reasonably expect to

---

[91] FSA CP 59, July 2000, Ann. A, paras. 1.12.8–1.12.10.
[92] Joint Committee Report, Vol. II, Minutes of Evidence, 15 April 1999, para. 433.

receive. Those who possess . . . information ahead of general dissemination should, therefore, refrain from basing their behaviour on that information . . . Otherwise, the confidence of market users . . . will be undermined.'[93] Before the Market Abuse Directive this heading of market abuse was included in the original regime because of the 1994 bid by Trafalgar House for Northern Electric where SBC Corporate Finance Department entered into a cash-settled CFD (3.2.1.8) under which if, prior to the bid being made, the market price of Northern Electric shares increased, SBC would pay the difference to Trafalgar House. There was no insider dealing by the Trafalgar House directors who signed the CFD on behalf of the company because although they had inside information on the impending bid and were encouraging the company itself to deal in the CFD, there was full equality of information with SBC (12.2.8.3). The Corporate Finance Department entered the CFD into SBC's central risk database without expressly referring to Northern Electric and SBC's market makers, the other side of a Chinese Wall, hedged the disaggregated risk on the entire SBC trading book without any knowledge of Northern Electric and, hence, Corporate Finance personnel had not disclosed the inside information (12.2.7) and, in any event, the market makers could rely on the defence of bona fide market making (12.2.8.5). As a result, with no breach of the criminal law, Trafalgar House could afford to wait and see whether to make the bid and there was no breach of the Principle relating to 'high standards of market conduct' (12.4) because there was no precedent in the market and all parties involved had obtained legal opinions as to compliance with the criminal law.[94] Nonetheless, SIB so disliked this transaction that for the future it provided in guidance that '[e]ntering into transactions of th[is] . . . kind . . . risks . . . conduct which is in breach of the . . . Principles,'[95] because 'it is not acceptable for a firm to use derivatives to . . . enable a customer to buy or sell an indirect stake where the firm knows . . . that as a result of inside information the customer could not properly do so on the open market'.[96] The end result, under the then formulation of the Principle, was that '[t]ranslated into plain English . . . [such a transaction] is illegal – "is" being the operative word . . . for that is not what the law actually says, it is what SIB believes it should say'.[97] Thus, the need for this heading of market abuse, which was also drafted to include the improper use of confidential information which, although a breach of 'high standards of market conduct' by an

---

[93] FSA MAR release 001, 1 December 2001, 1.4.3.
[94] House of Commons, Treasury and Civil Service Committee, Minutes of Evidence, 10 May 1995, paras. 4615 and 4634.   [95] SIB PN/012/95, 13 February 1995, para. 6.
[96] Equity-related Derivatives: Use of Inside Information, SIB, December 1996, para. 7. Now, in addition, the Takeover Code contains rules regulating the use of derivatives in takeovers.
[97] Gobbledygook, chinese walls and the SIB, The Independent, 14 June 1996.

investment bank when using confidential information obtained by its client bidder on a target, was not clearly an offence by the client in the absence of express knowledge.[98]

There are, actually, three headings of market abuse constituting misuse of information.

12.5.3.1 Dealing

It is market abuse for 'an insider . . . [to] deal . . . , or attempt . . . to deal, in' an investment within 12.5.1 'or [in] a related investment', being 'an investment whose price or value depends on the price or value of th[at] . . . investment', i.e. a derivative within 3.2.1.6–3.2.1.8, 'on the basis of inside information' (FSMA 118(2), 130A(3)). This requires that 'the inside information is the reason for, or a material influence on, the decision to deal', rather than that:

- 'the decision . . . was made before the person possessed the . . . information' (MAR 1.3.3) (cf. 12.2.8.2). This requires that 'the person had taken a firm decision to deal . . . and . . . the term[s] of . . . the transaction . . . did not alter after the receipt of the information';[99] or
- 'the . . . dealing [is] to satisfy a legal or regulatory obligation which comes into being before . . . possess[ion of] the . . . information' (MAR 1.3.4) (cf. 12.2.8.2). This 'include[es a] . . . contractual . . . obligation';[100] or
- 'none of the individuals in possession of the . . . information . . . had any involvement in the decision . . . or . . . influence[d] . . . the decision . . . or . . . had any contact with those who were involved in the decision . . . whereby the information could have been transmitted . . . [i.e.] the . . . information is held behind an effective Chinese Wall [within 6.3.1.3]' (MAR 1.3.5). (cf. 12.2.8.8)

Unless within one of these exceptions, the dealing must be based on inside information, defined as 'the reason for, or a material influence on, the decision to deal', in effect 'one of the reasons for the behaviour, but [it] need not be the only reason'.[101] In practice, a person could only base his actions on information if he intended to do so, notwithstanding the supposed absence of a requirement for intention (12.5.1). And 'dealing . . . means acquiring or disposing of the investment whether as principal or agent or directly or indirectly' (FSMA 130A(3)), for example using a derivative or financial spread bet. Thus, misusing information includes: a listed company secretary selling his shares in the company when he 'became aware that . . . revenues were likely to be significantly below

---

[98] SFA BN 522, 16 September 1999.
[99] FSA MAR release 001, 1 December 2001, 1.4.22. [100] Ibid, 1.4.20.
[101] FSA CP 59, July 2000, Ann. A, para. 1.5.5(1).

expectations . . . and [b]efore this news was released to the market';[102] staff in a listed company buying shares while in possession of unannounced financial information;[103] an analyst trading on the basis of unannounced inside information 'on a bid for the company illegitimately passed to him by . . . [the] finance director';[104] an external auditor trading on inside information obtained during the audit;[105] and a hedge fund, having received from an investment bank clearly confidential information on a potential issue of convertible preference shares, trading in the underlying shares based on that inside information.[106]

An 'insider' is a director or 'member of . . . management . . . of an issuer', a shareholder, 'a . . . person who has inside information . . . as a result of having access to the information through the exercise of his employment, profession or duties' and anyone who obtains the information criminally or who 'knows, or could reasonably be expected to know, [that it] is inside information' (FSMA 118B), i.e. 'if a normal and reasonable person in . . . [his] position . . . would know or should have known that the person from whom he received it is an insider . . . and . . . that it is inside information' (MAR 1.2.8). This is wider than the knowledge required for the purpose of the criminal offence (12.2.4) and establishes, by implication, that 'insiders' under the other categories do not need to know that the information they possess is 'inside information'.

'Inside information' in relation to financial instruments is defined in a very similar manner to the definition used for the purpose of the criminal offence (12.2.3) as 'information of a precise nature which –

(a) is not generally available;
(b) relates, directly or indirectly, to one or more issuers . . . or . . . investments, and
(c) would, if generally available, be likely to have a significant effect on the price of the . . . investments or . . . an investment whose price or value [i.e. a derivative] depends on the price or value of the . . . investment. (FSMA 118C(2), 130A(3))

'Information is precise if it . . . indicates circumstances that exist or may reasonably be expected to come into existence or an event that has occurred or may reasonably be expected to occur, and . . . is specific enough to enable a conclusion to be drawn as to the possible effect of those circumstances . . . on the price of . . . investments' (FSMA 118C(5)). Depending upon its nature, this could include a rumour such as that a particular company has been targeted for a takeover if 'there is firm and objective evidence', but not

---

[102] FSA PN/013/04, 10 February 2004.
[103] FSA PN/069/04; FSA PN/063/04; FSA PN/141/05; James Boyd Parker, Final Notice, 6 October 2006.   [104] FSA PN/107/04, 16 December 2004.
[105] FSA PN/034/05, 6 April 2005.
[106] FSA PN/077/06; *Jabre* v. *FSA,* Financial Services Tribunal, 10 July 2006. Similarly if the proposed issue was cancelled and not disclosed to the market.

'vague market rumours, or the fact that two company directors had been observed having lunch together'.[107]

As regard paragraph (a), relevant 'factors are . . .

(1) whether the information has been disclosed to a . . . market . . .
(2) whether the information is contained in records which are open to . . . the public;
(3) whether the information is otherwise generally available, including through the Internet, or some other publication (including . . . on payment of a fee), or is derived from information which has been made public;
(4) whether the information can be obtained by observation . . . For example, if a passenger on a train passing a burning factory calls his broker and tells him to sell shares in the factory's owner, the passenger will be acting on information which is generally available.

Information can be generally available even though it 'became public through an incorrect disclosure by the issuer or . . . a third party'.[108] Also relevant is 'the extent to which the information can be obtained by analysing or developing other information which is generally available', i.e. 'Information which can be obtained by research or analysis . . . is to be regarded . . . as being generally available' (MAR 1.2.12, 1.2.14; FSMA 118C(8)) because, as with criminal insider dealing (12.2.3), it should not be improper for a research analyst to draw informed conclusions from information which is not itself price sensitive. It follows that 'a firm which trades ahead of the publication of its own research report will not have engaged in market abuse',[109] subject always to the star analyst whose view can move a market, and to the requirements of 'front running' (6.3.4.2) and 'treating the customer fairly' (9.2).

And for this purpose, 'it is not relevant that the information is only generally available outside the UK . . . [or] that the observation or analysis is only achievable by a person with above average financial resources, expertise or competence' (MAR 1.2.13). Thus, whether information is 'generally available' for the purpose of market abuse is, in practice, the same as the test for whether information has been 'made public' for the purpose of the criminal offence (12.2.3). However, paragraph (b) allows the information to relate to issuers or securities generally, whereas the criminal offence covers only particular issuers or securities (12.2.3).

Paragraph (c) is satisfied 'only if it is information of a kind which a reasonable investor would be likely to use as part of the basis of his investment decision' (FSMA 118C(6)) and, as with the criminal law (12.2.3), a theoretical percentage movement in price cannot be defined. 'It is a question of determining the degree of probability with which at that point in time such an effect could reasonably have been expected. The . . . test is "likely" so . . .

---

[107] CESR/06-562b, July 2007, para. 1.5; FSA CP 59, July 2000, para. 6.21.
[108] CESR/06-562b, July 2007, para. 1.9.   [109] FSA CP 59, July 2000, para. 6.38.

the mere possibility that a piece of information will have a significant price effect is not enough . . . but . . . it is not necessary that there should be a degree of probability close to certainty.'[110] The requirement of likely significant price effect means that, in practice, '[s]omething would only constitute inside information if it was sufficiently material'.[111]

In contrast, 'inside information' in relation to commodity derivatives means 'information of a precise nature which –

(a) is not generally available,
(b) relates directly or indirectly to . . . such derivatives, and
(c) users of markets on which the derivatives are traded would expect to receive in accordance with any accepted market practices on those markets. (FSMA 118C(3))

An example of breaching paragraph (c) would be where '[b]efore the official publication of LME stock levels, a metals trader learns . . . that there has been a significant decrease in the level of LME aluminium stocks . . . [and the] trader buys a substantial number of futures in that metal on the LME' (MAR 1.3.21). However, there are 'differences in the definition of inside information for commodity derivatives and for other financial instruments . . . [Thus a] person [is caught if he] deals . . . in the equities of XYZ plc, a commodity producer, based on inside information concerning that company . . . [But a] person [who] deals in a commodity futures contract . . . based on the same information [is only caught] provided . . . the information is required to be disclosed under the rules of the relevant . . . market' (MAR 1.3.23). It follows that there can be 'inside information' for the purposes of the securities market even though there is no legal obligation to disclose and no user of the market would, in practice, expect to receive disclosure, the test being solely the effect on the price if disclosure is not made. Thus, for example, listed companies cannot always rely solely on the rules in DTR (12.2.3) to avoid a disclosure obligation.

Moreover, 'inside information' can also be 'related to . . . [a] client's pending orders . . . [if] –

(a) . . . of a precise nature,
(b) . . . not generally available,
(c) [it] relates, directly or indirectly, to one or more issuers . . . or . . . investments, and
(d) would, if generally available, be likely to have a significant effect on the price of those . . . investments.

Here, though, '[i]nformation would be likely to have a significant effect on price . . . only if it is information of a kind which a reasonable investor would be likely to use as part of the basis of his investment decision' (FSMA 118C(4), (6)) which depends on '[t]he order's . . . size . . . the liquidity of the

[110] CESR/06-562b, July 2007, para. 1.12.   [111] Ibid, para. 1.15.

market . . . the price limit for the order and . . . whether the order is likely to influence the behaviour of the market participants'.[112] A 'pending order' exists if 'a transaction is not immediately executed . . . and . . . the [firm] . . . has taken on a[n] . . . obligation relating to the manner or timing of . . . execution' (MAR 1.2.16). 'Thus . . . merely . . . contacting various brokers to establish at what price they are prepared to buy or sell . . . would not in itself constitute a client's pending order as no order has been placed.'[113] Similarly, '[t]he test for the precise nature of information . . . is more likely to be satisfied . . . the more defined are the order's size, price limit and execution period'.[114] To this extent, the regime is a control not only on market abuse, but also on customer abuse.

These three types of 'inside information' have the result, collectively, that market abuse 'misuse of information' covers all 'inside information' under the criminal law in relation to securities (12.2.3) and expands into similar coverage in relation to all other traded 'investments' (3.2.1.1–3.2.1.4, 3.2.1.6–3.2.1.9).

This heading of 'misuse of information' was designed to catch the SBC – Trafalgar House situation explained above (MAR 1.3.2(3)) and also, confusing market regulation with customer regulation, dealing ahead of a customer transaction (MAR 1.3.2(2), 1.3.22) unless it is '[t]he dutiful carrying out of . . . an order' which depends on 'whether the [firm] . . . has agreed with its client it will act in a particular way . . . whether the [firm]'s . . . behaviour was with a view to facilitating . . . the effective carrying out of the order . . . the extent to which the [firm]'s . . . behaviour was reasonable by the proper standards of conduct of the market . . . and . . . proportional to risk undertaken . . . [and] whether . . . the trading either has no impact on the price or there has been adequate disclosure to that client that trading will take place' (MAR 1.3.2(2), 1.3.12, 1.3.15). This is necessary given that customer information is one type of 'inside information'. Thus, 'legitimate trading and hedging activity involving the use of trading information is . . . acceptable'.[115] It also catches: an investment bank acting for a bidder in a takeover which buys target investments for itself; a person who learns of the bid before it is launched and buys target investments; and dealing in a company's shares knowing about significant but unannounced business developments (MAR 1.3.2(4), 1.3.20). But there are effectively a number of defences which are somewhat different from the criminal law (12.2.8) given the different scope of the offence:

Widely disclosed information Unlike the criminal law (12.2.8.3) there is no defence for information held by both parties to a transaction, which saved SBC in the Trafalgar House case, unless it is 'generally available' so as not to be 'inside information' in the first place.

---

[112] CESR/06-562b, July 2007, para. 3.13.   [113] Ibid, para. 3.8.   [114] Ibid, para. 3.16.
[115] FSA PS 05/3, March 2005, para. 2.5.

Market makers; market dealing The criminal defences (12.2.8.5, 12.2.8.6) have been substantially altered so that there is no defence for the use solely of 'market information', although there is an identical definition of 'trading information' used in a statement that '[t]he following . . . [is] market abuse . . . dealing on the basis of inside information which is not trading information' (MAR 1.3.2(1)) which itself implies, albeit weakly, that 'trading information' is not inside information. However, there are certain defences where 'A person . . . [having] form[ed] an intention to buy or sell a[n] . . . investment . . . carries out his own intention' (MAR 1.3.6), for example making a takeover bid or carrying out any other Primary or Secondary Market transaction of one's own, and where it interacts with clients trading, a broker–dealer 'deal[s] . . . on their own account' (or a person underwrites a new issue) provided that the inside information is limited to 'trading information' and either 'the . . . trading . . . is carried out . . . to hedge a risk . . . or . . . the . . . inside information [is] . . . a client's [executed] transaction . . . information about [which] is not, or is not yet, required to be published . . . or . . . if the . . . trading . . . is connected with a transaction entered into or to be entered into with a client . . . the trading either has no impact on the price or there has been adequate disclosure to that client that trading will take place . . . or . . . the . . . behaviour was reasonable by the proper standards of behaviour of the market . . . and . . . executed in a way which takes into account the need for the market as a whole to operate fairly and efficiently' (MAR 1.3.6–1.3.10). This, in practice, permits a firm trading with a client as principal and, based on the information of that trade, hedging its risk in the market or, to fulfil a client order, trading in the market.

In this context, the question arises of the correct procedure to be adopted in a block trade amounting to inside information where 'there are several . . . transaction structures . . . [S]ome vendors . . . approach a bank's trading desk . . . [for] the block . . . [to] be disposed of as part of normal trading activity . . . [O]thers . . . approach the bank's equity capital markets department . . . to agree . . . a bought deal . . . (where the bank buys the shares as principal . . . and on-sells them) or an accelerated bookbuild (where the bank builds a book of demand . . .).' With bought deals and accelerated bookbuilds the bank will approach clients to gauge interest and make them insiders on confidentiality agreements which FSA 'consider . . . is reasonable practice and is conducted to facilitate a transaction' [cf. 12.5.7]. Thereafter 'there . . . [are] a diverse range of practices . . . include[ing] . . . [a]lways issuing a press release in advance . . . [and n]ever making an announcement . . . [W]here firms disclose inside information solely to offer the stock . . . this could . . . be considered as disclosure in the proper course of the exercise of employment, profession or duties [if] . . .

- The information disclosed consists only of trading information.
- The information is disclosed only to the extent necessary . . . to offer the investment . . .
- It is reasonable . . . to enable the proper functions of their employment, profession or duties.[116]

FSA is proposing to make this view part of its Code of Market Conduct with the caveat that it 'is intended only to apply to an actual offer of the investment. It is not intended to apply to a disclosure of trading information to gauge potential interest . . . or to help establish the likely price'[117] which would have to be subject to confidentiality agreements as explained above and in 12.5.3.2.

Stabilisation This defence is carried over from the criminal law (12.2.8.7, 12.3.7) and there is a defence for buy-back programmes (MAR 1.10.1).

Chinese Wall This defence is provided since, unlike the criminal law (12.2.8.8), corporations themselves can commit market abuse (MAR 1.10.2(1)).

Not with a view to profit; information irrelevant These defences have not been carried over from the criminal law (12.2.8.1, 12.2.8.2) since, if asserted with proof, they are extremely difficult for the prosecution to rebut and are not really consistent with a regime which is not based upon intent.

Takeovers There are, however, detailed defences in relation to takeover activity (MAR 1.3.17–1.3.19).

12.5.3.2 Disclosure

As with the criminal law (12.2.7), and to similar effect, market abuse is also committed if 'an insider discloses inside information [both terms being explained in 12.5.3.1] to another person otherwise than in the proper course of the exercise of his employment, profession or duties' (FSMA 118(3)). Disclosure is 'proper' only if 'to a Government department . . . or . . . regulatory body' or if 'permitted by the rules of a . . . market . . . the FSA or the Takeover Code' or 'accompanied by the imposition of confidentiality requirements . . . and . . . reasonable and . . . for the purposes of facilitating any commercial, financial or investment transaction' (MAR 1.4.3, 1.4.5) such as disclosure to potential placees or underwriters.[118] In this context the firm must '[n]ot pass . . . information to individuals unless they are first clearly made aware of their responsibilities for handling sensitive information' so that 'reliance . . . [cannot be] placed on confidentiality

---

[116] Market Watch, Issue 20, May 2007, pp. 2–3. This view is repeated in Quaterly Consultation (No. 13), FSA, July 2007, pp. 19–22. See also: CESR/06-562, November 2006. [117] Market Watch, Issue 21, July 2007, pp. 7, 10.
[118] As by the investment bank in FSA PN/077/06, 1 August 2006.

letters without any assurance that a firm to whom information was passed had the necessary controls to keep the information confidential'.[119] All other disclosure is prohibited, for example, 'selective briefing of analysts' (MAR 1.4.2) and an investor in a company, having improperly obtained inside information on his business, posting that information on an Internet bulletin board 'prompted by a desire to "ramp up" the price of . . . [the] shares'.[120]

12.5.3.3 The 'regular user'

Moreover, it is also market abuse 'where the behaviour [not falling within 12.5.3.1 or 12.5.3.2] . . .

(a) is based on information which is not generally available to those using the market but which, if available to a regular user of the market, would be, or would be likely to be, regarded by him as relevant when deciding the terms on which transactions . . . should be effected, and

(b) is likely to be regarded by a regular user of the market as a failure on the part of the person concerned to observe the standard of behaviour reasonably expected of a person in his position in relation to the market. (FSMA 118(4))

The concept of the 'regular user' is explained in 12.5.6. The 'behaviour' can be dealing or disclosing and the information is either not 'inside information' within 12.5.3.1 and 12.5.3.2 (MAR 1.5.2, 1.5.3, 1.5.8) and/or not dealing within 12.5.3.1 (MAR 1.5.10), for example, 'icing' stock or a fixed-odds, rather than spread, bet or a physical commodity trade. This heading catches behaviour in relation to the underlying asset of the investment, for example, a share underlying a warrant or a bond underlying a derivative, or a linked asset 'whose price or value is expressed by reference to the price or value of the . . . investments', for example a commodity priced by reference to a listed commodity derivative such as on the LME, or an 'investment (whether or not [itself within 12.5.3.1] . . .) whose subject matter is the . . . investment', such as an off-exchange derivative over the exchange traded investment (FSMA 118A(3)). The same defences as in 12.5.3.1 apply (MAR 1.5.9). Whether information is 'generally available' and the behaviour 'based on' the information is determined as in 12.5.3.1 and to be 'relevant' it must be 'reliable . . . and [from a] . . . reliabl[e] . . . source . . . new . . . information; [and] . . . in the case of . . . possible future developments . . . provides . . . with reasonable certainty, grounds to conclude that the possible future development will . . . occur' (MAR 1.5.4–1.5.6). There is a large overlap with the offence in 12.5.3.1 since '[e]xamples of relevant information' include, in relation to company securities, 'information concerning the business affairs or prospects of the company . . . [and] in relation to a derivative

---

[119] Quarterly Consultation (No. 13), FSA July 2007, App. 5, draft MAR 1.4.5A.
[120] David Isaacs, Final Notice, 28 February 2005, para. 45.

relating to a commodity . . ., information . . . affecting the deliverable supply of the commodity . . . and . . . [generally] information as to official statistics, and fiscal and monetary policy announcements'.[121]

FSA interprets the standards in (b) as including 'whether a regular user would reasonably expect the relevant information to be disclosed to users of the . . . market' which he will do if there is either a legal or regulatory requirement to do so or 'the . . . information is routinely the subject of a public announcement' (MAR 1.5.7). The inclusion of commodity markets in the regime (12.5.1) such as LME and LIFFE, means that with, for example, an LSE listed commodity producer, there can be relevant information on its production supplies which is discloseable in relation to its listing, but not significant in relation to the commodity market such that it can still hedge its commodity position before making public disclosure.[122] Information which is 'routinely the subject of a public announcement' includes 'official announcement[s] by governments, central monetary or fiscal authorities . . . [and] changes in published credit ratings of companies . . . [and] changes to the constituents of a securities index'[123] and 'economic and survey data series such as consumer confidence indexes, published by private sector bodies'.[124]

This category of market abuse was carried over, like the categories in 12.5.4.3 and 12.5.5.3, from the pre-Market Abuse Directive regime because '[t]he Government wishes to maintain the current scope of prohibited behaviours',[125] even though no-one could accurately articulate what was caught in addition to the Directive headings. For this reason it ceases on 30 June 2008 (FSMA 118(9)) and '[b]efore May 2008 we will conduct a review of the impact of the provisions . . . to establish whether the expected benefit . . . has exceeded the cost'.[126]

12.5.4 False or misleading impression

At a policy level, 'markets provide a mechanism by which the price or value of investments may be determined according to the market forces of supply and demand . . . [M]arket users . . . expect the price . . . to reflect the proper operation of market forces . . . Improper conduct which gives market users a false or misleading impression results in market users no longer being able to rely on the price formed in markets . . . as a basis for their investment decisions. This will undermine confidence in the integrity of the . . . market and overall market activity may decrease and transaction costs may rise . . . to the detriment of market users, including investors.'[127] There are three

---

[121] FSA CP 59, July 2000, Ann. A, para. 1.5.12. [122] Ibid, paras. 6.28–6.33.
[123] Ibid, Ann. A, para. 1.5.17. [124] Market Watch No. 1, FSA, September 2001, p. 2.
[125] UK Implementation of the Market Abuse Directive, HMT & FSA CD, June 2004, para. 3.7. [126] Feedback Statement, HMT, February 2005, para. 9.
[127] FSA MAR release 001, 1 December 2001, 1.5.3.

overlapping headings of such market abuse which, together, are broader than the 'act or course of conduct' required under the criminal law of market manipulation (12.3).

12.5.4.1 Trading

It is market abuse to trade so as to 'give . . . a false or misleading impression as to the supply of, or demand for, or as to the price of . . . investments' (FSMA 118(5)(a)). Like the criminal offence of market manipulation (12.3.2), which is relevant to the construction of this requirement, there must be a 'false or misleading impression' so that real trading activity is not caught (and, hence, the distortion offence in 12.5.5). This catches artificial transactions generally, with no requirement for a materially false or misleading impression, including:

- 'wash trades . . . A sale or purchase of a[n] . . . investment where there is no change of beneficial interest or market risk, or where the transfer . . . is . . . between parties acting in . . . collusion' (MAR 1.6.2(2). See also, MAR 1.6.15). This does not include stocklending/repo's (MAR 1.6.3) because here there is 'a genuine change in . . . beneficial interest or the taking of risk, if only for a short period of time';[128]
- 'painting the tape . . . entering into a series of transactions that are shown on a public display for the purpose of giving the impression of activity or price movement' (MAR 1.6.2(3));
- 'entering orders into an electronic trading system, at prices which are higher than the previous bid . . . and withdrawing them before they are executed, in order to give a misleading impression that there is demand for . . . the . . . investment at that price' (MAR 1.6.2(4));
- 'transactions . . . designed to conceal . . . ownership, so that disclosure requirements are circumvented by the holding of . . . investments in the name of a colluding party, such that disclosures are misleading in respect of the true underlying holding'.[129]

Beyond this, it is a judgment depending upon 'the extent to which orders . . . or transactions . . . represent a significant proportion of a daily volume . . . [and/or] lead to a significant change in . . . price . . . [and/or] lead to no change in beneficial ownership . . . [and/or] include position reversals in a short period . . . [and/or] are concentrated within a short time span . . . and lead to a price change which is subsequently reversed . . . [and/or] are undertaken . . . around a specific time when reference prices, settlement prices and valuations are calculated and lead to price changes' (MAR 1.6.9). This will depend on 'the experience and knowledge of the users of the market in question; . . . the structure of the market,

---

[128] FSA CP 10, June 1998, Pt. 1, para. 39.
[129] FSA MAR release 001, 1 December 2001, 1.5.14(2).

including its reporting . . . and transparency requirements; . . . accepted market practices; . . . the identity and position of the person responsible . . . and . . . the . . . visibility . . . of the person's activity'.[130] And, of course, the judgment is always influenced by whether 'the person has an actuating purpose . . . to induce others to trade' and whether 'the transaction was executed in a particular way with the purpose of creating a false or misleading impression' (MAR 1.6.5(1), (3)). It follows that a false or misleading impression will not, without more, be created simply because of 'transactions which effect the taking of a position, or the unwinding of a position taken, so as to take legitimate advantage of . . . differences in . . . prices . . . or transactions which . . . lend . . . or borrow . . . investments . . . so as to meet an underlying . . . demand' or '[m]aking a report or disclosure . . . in accordance with . . . applicable legal or regulatory requirement[s]'.[131]

The criminal law defences of stabilisation and Chinese Walls (12.3.7) apply (12.5.8.1, 12.5.8.2) and, in addition, there is a defence for a trade carried out 'for legitimate reasons and in conformity with accepted market practices', although the only accepted practice is the LME market aberrations regime (FSMA 118(5); MAR 1.6.14).

12.5.4.2 Disseminating information

A further heading of market abuse is 'the dissemination of information . . . which gives . . . a false or misleading impression as to a[n] investment by a person who knew or could reasonably have been expected to have known that the information was false or misleading' (FSMA 118(7)). It is a defence if the relevant information was the other side of a Chinese Wall (MAR 1.8.5) but, otherwise, examples of this type of abuse are:

- 'a person responsible for the content of information submitted to a regulatory information service submits information which is false or misleading . . . and that person is reckless' (MAR 1.8.6(2)). The policy here is that 'Users of such information should be able to rely on the accuracy and integrity of information carried through these channels. It is, therefore, appropriate that those who disseminate information through them, for example, the company itself . . . take reasonable care.'[132] Examples are: the holder of derivatives over a company's shares notifying it, wrongly, of a physical shareholding;[133] a corporate finance firm falsely announcing to the market that the full issue has been placed;[134] and a listed oil company making 'false or misleading announcements in relation to its . . . reserves . . . between 1998 and 2003';[135]

---

[130] Ibid, 1.5.5.   [131] Ibid, 1.5.24, 1.5.25.   [132] Ibid, 1.5.20.
[133] Indigo Capital and Robert Bonnier, Final Notice, 21 December 2004.
[134] Hoodless Brennan, Final Notice, 17 December 2003.
[135] FSA PN/074/04, 24 August 2004.

- 'a person posts information on an Internet bulletin board . . . which contains false or misleading statements about the takeover of a company . . . and the person knows that the information is false or misleading' (MAR 1.8.6(1));
- the 'dissemination of . . . false or misleading . . . rumours';[136]
- failing to disclose, or incorrectly disclosing shareholdings.[137]

The requirement for knowledge of the falsity imports intention, to be judged by the test of 'a normal and reasonable person', which includes being 'reckless as to whether the information is false or misleading' (MAR 1.8.4, 1.8.6(2)).

12.5.4.3 The 'regular user'

Any 'behaviour (not falling within [12.5.4.1 or 12.5.4.2] . . .) [which] is likely to give a regular user of the market a false or misleading impression as to the supply of, demand for or price or value of . . . investments . . . and [which] . . . is likely to be regarded by a regular user of the market as a failure on the part of the person concerned to observe the standard of behaviour reasonably expected of a person in his position in relation to the market' is market abuse (FSMA 118(8)(a)). The concept of the 'regular user' is explained in 12.5.6. This heading of market abuse appears to bring in the pre-Market Abuse Directive test which required 'behaviour . . . likely to give rise to, or to give an impression of, a price or value or volume of trading which is materially false or misleading . . . and . . . in order to be likely, there must be a real and not fanciful likelihood that the behaviour will have such an effect, although the effect need not be more likely than not'.[138] Although the clarity of the double negative is impressive, FSA explained it as follows:

> Court . . . definitions of 'likely' . . . range from a 'bare possibility', 'possible but not probable' to 'probable' (that is, more likely than not). The FSA has . . . concluded that the appropriate definition . . . is . . . that there must be a 'real and not fanciful likelihood'. This is more than a 'bare possibility' but less than 'more likely than not'.[139]

It all depends on 'the experience and knowledge of the users of the market . . .; the structure of the market, including its reporting, notification and transparency requirements; the legal and regulatory requirements of the market; the . . . position of the person responsible; and . . . the visibility or disclosure of the person's activity' and whether 'the transaction is executed

---

[136] European Council Common Position – Draft Statement of the Council's reasons, 1 July 2002, para. III(b).
[137] For the disclosure requirements, see DTR 5; LIST!, Issue 14, FSA, December 2006.
[138] FSA MAR release 001, 1 December 2001, 1.5.4. This seems to follow from the UK's example on p. 78 of CESR/07-429, July 2007.
[139] Feedback on CP 59 and CP 76, FSA PS, April 2001, para. 4.10.

in a way which takes into account the need for the market as a whole to operate fairly and efficiently'. Two obvious examples are 'the movement of physical commodity stocks . . . creat[ing] . . . a misleading impression . . . and . . . the movement of an empty cargo ship creat[ing] . . . a false . . . impression as to . . . supply' (MAR 1.9.2, 1.9.4, 1.9.5(2)). It is difficult to understand what this heading covers in addition to 12.5.4.1 and 12.5.4.2 other than such conduct which is not a transaction or the positive dissemination of information.

The only defences are under the LME market aberrations regime and information the other side of a Chinese Wall (MAR 1.9.3, 1.9.5(6)).

This heading of market abuse ceases to have effect on 30 June 2008 (FSMA 118(9)), as explained in 12.5.3.3.

12.5.5 Distortion

'[B]ehaviour that interferes with the proper operation of market forces . . . undermines confidence in the . . . markets and damages efficiency to the detriment of market users, including investors.'[140] This heading of market abuse was considered necessary because, as explained in 12.5.5.1, the criminal law of market manipulation (12.3.2) catches only 'conduct which creates a false or misleading impression', not actual on-risk trading activity, no matter how aggressive or manipulative. Again, though, there are three somewhat overlapping headings.

12.5.5.1 Trading

It is market abuse to trade so as to 'secure the price of . . . investments at an abnormal or artificial level' (FSMA 118(5)(b)). The regulatory difficulty is to distinguish, on some sort of objective (or, at least, social consensus) basis, 'normal' from 'abnormal' price changes. Hence, FSA acknowledges that:

> It is unlikely that the behaviour of market users when trading at times and in sizes most beneficial to them (whether for the purpose of long-term investment objectives, risk management or short-term speculation) and seeking the maximum profit from their dealings will of itself amount to distortion. Such behaviour, generally speaking, improves the liquidity and efficiency of markets. It is unlikely that prices in the market which are trading outside their normal range will necessarily be indicative that someone has engaged in behaviour with the purpose of positioning prices at a distorted level. High or low prices relative to a trading range can be the result of the proper interplay of supply and demand. (MAR 1.6.7, 1.6.8)

The judgment, however, is extremely difficult and, notwithstanding that intention is supposed to be irrelevant to the regime, as explained in 12.5.1,

---

[140] FSA MAR release 001, 1 December 2001, 1.6.3.

'[i]n the opinion of the FSA the following factors are to be taken into account . . .: if a person has an actuating purpose . . . to . . . position or move the price . . .; if the person has another, illegitimate, reason', such intention being determined, at least in part, by whether 'the transaction is pursuant to a prior . . . obligation . . .; [and whether the transaction] is executed in a way which takes into account the need for the market as a whole to operate fairly and efficiently . . . [or] opens a new position, so creating an exposure to market risk, rather than closes out a position' (MAR 1.6.5, 1.6.6). There are two classic methods of distorting the market.

Price positioning This category of market abuse was included in the original pre-Market Abuse Directive regime as a result of some unsatisfactory cases in the 1990s. In one case KEPIT, an investment trust was liquidating its portfolio and, without disclosing its contents, asked for bids from a number of investment banks, the SBC bid being accepted at 12.03pm at a market price to be fixed at 12.15pm. However, 'SBC was . . . able to guess at the constituent stocks of the . . . portfolio . . . [and] between . . . [12.03] and [12.15], the manner in which SBC sold a very large volume of stocks substantially contributed to a significant downward impact on the prices of some of those stocks' with SBC, as a result of a negotiated settlement, being disciplined by SFA for breach of the Principles on due skill, care and diligence and conflict of interest (6.3.1.2).[141] Since 'SFA makes no criticism of reasonable participation in the market for risk management purposes in the conduct of programme trades'[142] and the action was not concluded for breach of 'high standards of market conduct' (12.6), this left great uncertainty in the market which was not dispelled by FSA guidelines that '[p]rogramme trading . . . [is in] two categories . . .

- 'Risk trades'. . . A firm will tender to acquire the portfolio . . . as principal, quoting a premium [on a sale to the client] or discount [on a purchase] to a price prevailing in the market at a designated strike time.
- 'Agency trades' . . . The broker will tender . . . on the basis that it will purchase or sell it . . . at the best price available in the market . . . [for a]n agreed commission . . .
  [T]he . . . Principles . . . restrict the firm from . . . taking a position for its own book . . . ahead of the strike time unless it can provide fair treatment for its customer . . . [including] the explicit consent of suitably informed customers.[143]

Similarly, when two traders in JP Morgan deliberately placed trades at the close of the LSE market in order to depress the FTSE 100 Index so that the bank would not have to pay out under a barrier option with an institutional customer at a particular level of the Index, while this was a breach of the LSE rule that 'A member firm . . . shall not do any act or engage in any

[141] SFA BN 438, 28 August 1997.   [142] Ibid.   [143] SFA BN 500, 13 November 1998.

course of conduct the sole intention of which is to move the Index value', it was not criminal market manipulation because they were genuine trades (12.3.2) and action for breach of 'high standards of market conduct' was taken only against the traders.[144] Again, SIB wanted the ability to go against both the firm and the individuals under a clearer administrative offence.

SIB was also concerned that 'there would be scope . . . for stock to be borrowed simply to deprive others of its use . . . thereby creating possible settlement problems and increasing the cost of borrowing'[145] and, in addition, 'If a person were intent on manipulating the price of an equity, or [a derivative] . . . priced by reference to it, stock borrowing could . . . assist such a scheme. The manipulator would be able either directly in the equity, or indirectly through a derivative, to profit from any price movements arising from the restrictions in supply' and, hence, for SIB, borrowing was proper only where the borrower 'use[s] it to meet a [short sale] delivery obligation, or to replace an existing borrowing or to on lend'.[146] However, since no 'false or misleading impression' was created, it was not criminal market manipulation (12.3.2) and, therefore, required to be 'market abuse'.

Price positioning catches, in FSA's view:

- 'buying or selling . . . investments at the close of the market with the effect of misleading investors who act on the basis of closing prices' (MAR 1.6.2(1)), for example, 'a trader buys a large volume of commodity futures . . . just before the close of trading . . . [with the] purpose . . . to position the price of the commodity futures at a[n] . . . abnormal or artificial level so as to make a profit from . . . [a connected] position' or 'a trader holds a short position that will show a profit if a particular . . . investment . . . falls out of . . . [an] index . . . [which] depends on the closing price of the . . . investment. He places a large sell order . . . just before the close of trading . . . [with the] purpose . . . to position the price . . . at a[n] . . . abnormal or artificial level so that the . . . investment will drop out of the Index' (MAR 1.6.15(2), (3));
- 'transactions or orders . . . that secure a dominant position over the supply of . . . a[n] . . . investment and which have the effect of fixing . . . purchase or sale prices or creating other unfair trading conditions';

---

[144] SFA Disciplinary Appeal Tribunal, Fleurose Case, Judgment, 7 May 1999; Judgment, 29 June 1999; *Fleurose* [2001] EWHC 1085. See also: SFA PN, 26 September 2000 where 'Nomura's strategy . . . was . . . designed to drive down the [Index] by the aggressive selling of shares shortly before the close [of the Exchange and] . . . did not observe high standards of market conduct'.
[145] Stock Borrowing and Shortselling, SIB CP 100, November 1996, para. 20.
[146] Stock Borrowing and Repo in UK Equities: Market Conduct, SIB, October 1997, Ann. A, paras. 14, 15.

- 'entering orders into an electronic trading system, at prices which are higher than the previous bid . . . in order to move the price';
- 'parties, who have been allocated . . . investments in a primary offering, colluding to purchase further . . . investments when trading begins, in order to force the price . . . to an artificial level and generate interest from other investors, and then sell'; and
- 'trading on one market . . . with a view to improperly influencing the prices of the same or a related . . . investment that is traded on another . . . market' (MAR 1.6.4(1), (3), (5), (7)).

The difficulty, again, is distinguishing 'normal' from 'abnormal' trading activity particularly since '[t]here is a spectrum of views as to what distortion means. Some . . . say that "distortion" only occurs when price movements are outside the range . . . routinely observed . . . Others . . . that any price which does not represent a perfectly competitive market is a distorted price.'[147] Thus, depending on the circumstances, 'distortion' could arise with any proprietary dealing, arbitrage or hedging. Hence, although regard can be had to 'the extent to which the person had a direct or indirect interest in the price . . . of the . . . investment . . . [and] the extent to which price . . . movements . . . are outside their normal . . . range . . . and . . . whether [the] person has successively and consistently increased or decreased . . . the price he has paid' (MAR 1.6.10), it always comes down to a question of intention. Or, rather, as expressed in the pre-Market Abuse Directive rules, the offender must 'enter . . . into a transaction . . . with the purpose of positioning the price . . . at a distorted level (the purpose need not be the sole purpose for entering into the transaction, but must be an actuating purpose)', i.e. 'a purpose which motivates or incites [the] person to act',[148] which was probably best understood as intention. Thus, the rule 'does not restrict market users trading significant volume where there is a legitimate purpose for the transaction . . . and where the transaction is executed in a proper way . . . which takes into account the need for the market as a whole to operate fairly and efficiently . . . Such behaviour is unlikely to distort the market . . . even if it causes the market to move. But trading significant volumes with the purpose of controlling the price . . . and positioning it at a distorted level will amount to market abuse.'[149] Accordingly, FSA's enforcement cases show that price positioning can occur where: a majority shareholder, placing its issued shares through an intermediary, enters into a spread bet over the company's shares with a firm which it knows will hedge its risk in the market and, thus, affect the price;[150] a firm carries out a non-UK affiliate's instruction to buy 500,000 shares in a particular listed

---

[147] FSA CP 59, July 2000, para. 6.72.   [148] FSA MAR release 001, 1 December 2001, 1.6.9.
[149] Ibid, 1.6.10.
[150] Paul Davidson, Nigel Hare, Ashley Tatham, Warning Notice, 28 August 2003. See also *Paul Davidson and Ashley Tatham* v. *FSA,* Financial Services Tribunal, 2006.

company in order to achieve a closing price higher than the market price at the time the order was placed;[151] and a broker enters into contracts to buy a company's shares amounting to 252% of its issued capital.[152] However, short selling on its own is not market abuse but, rather, 'a legitimate investment strategy that can contribute to market efficiency' even though it can be 'used . . . to drive down prices' because 'a significant part of short selling . . . is driven by a variety of trading strategies that have nothing to do with . . . such "bear raid[s]"'.[153] Nor was there market abuse, or a breach of the Principle (12.6), where a dealer on an electronic trading platform developed a 'strategy . . . [to] create a "basis position" whereby it became long in [i.e. purchased] . . . bonds, and short [i.e. sold] . . . futures, then on a given day close[d] out the . . . futures position . . . leaving a . . . [bond] position; and then [sold] . . . quickly the . . . [bond] position on [the electronic platform] . . . On . . . 2 August 2004 between 09:12 and 10:29 the desk bought 62,214 futures contracts on Eurex . . . [and] between 10.28 and 10.29 . . . sold €11.3 billion of bonds in 18 seconds, which was equivalent to an average day's trading volume on the platform, and also sold . . . [another] €1.5 billion [bonds] on other . . . markets . . . This left [the dealer] . . . with an unexpected short position which was closed out at 11.25 through the purchase of €3.8 billion of bonds on [the platform], thus buying . . . back at a lower price some of the bonds it had earlier sold, further adding to their profit. The effect was a temporary disruption to the volume of bonds . . . traded on the platform [and] sharp falls in bond prices.'[154]

An abusive squeeze This was originally included as a result of the activities of Hamanaka, the lead metals trader at Sumitomo, based in Tokyo, who falsified his positions over a ten year period in an attempt to corner the global copper market, including on the LME, causing Sumitomo just over $2.5 billion in losses in respect of a massive long (purchase) position of LME futures copper contracts under which Sumitomo had the right to insist on delivery of copper in an amount greatly in excess of total LME warehouse stocks. As a result, the price of LME copper contracts was much higher than it would otherwise have been without this squeeze, which was important because 95% of the World's non-ferrous metal trading occurred on the LME.[155] The difficulty was that no one regulator had jurisdiction over all of Hamanaka's activities: he was, from a UK perspective, unregulated; his OTC trades in the UK were regulated only insofar as he used SFA-regulated firms; SIB regulated only the LME; and the LME regulated only its market

---

[151] FSA PN/53/03, 23 April 2003.
[152] Evolution Beeson, Final Notice, 12 November 2004.
[153] Short Selling, FSA DP, October 2002, paras. 4.1, 4.14.
[154] PN/072/2005, 28 June 2005.   [155] A Review of the Metals Market, SIB, August 1996.

members and not their clients. Hamanaka used a large number of intermediaries to disguise his overall positions and 'build up a sizeable unregistered position by splitting it between a number of different LME Members in amounts insufficient to trigger mandatory notification. In addition, the true extent of the . . . customer's economic interest would be unknown . . . [since] he . . . also held . . . positions in the OTC derivatives market . . . [and] with other Exchanges. In addition . . . the LME does not . . . have access to information regarding . . . positions held . . . in the underlying physical cash market.'[156] Moreover, the criminal law on market manipulation was not breached because, as genuine trades subject to market risk, no 'false or misleading impression as to the market in or the price or value of . . . investments' was created (12.3.2); rather, 'the price reflects the interplay of buying and selling interests. But this . . . is an abuse, for several reasons:

- the price no longer reflects . . . the natural buying and selling interests, based on fundamentals, but instead reflects a short-term desire to influence the price and so to profit at the expense of others . . .
- it distorts the ordinary operation of the market, making it more difficult for users to get their business done; and
- it calls into question the market's fairness, suggesting that other market users are at the mercy of those whose size enables them to move the price.[157]

Thus, SIB wanted the ability to take direct action for a market squeeze, whether or not the perpetrator was based in the UK, against both the perpetrator and any intermediaries. As a result, the offence is defined as follows. '[A]n abusive squeeze . . . is . . . [where] a person [with] . . . a significant influence over the supply of . . . a[n] investment or the underlying product if a derivative . . . [and] a position (directly or indirectly) in an investment under which quantities of the . . . investment or product in question are deliverable . . . engages in behaviour with the purpose of positioning at a distorted level the price at which others have to deliver, take delivery or defer delivery to satisfy their obligations' (MAR 1.6.4(4)). Another example is where '[a] trader with a long position in bond futures buys or borrows a large amount of the cheapest to deliver bonds [under that futures contract] and . . . refuses to re-lend those bonds . . . His purpose is to position the price at which those with short positions have to deliver to satisfy their obligations at a materially higher level, making him a profit from his original position' (MAR 1.6.16). Of course, '[s]queezes occur relatively frequently when the proper interaction of supply and demand leads to market tightness, but this is not of itself abusive' and 'having a significant influence over the supply of . . . an investment . . . is not of itself abusive'. It

---

[156] A Review of the Metals Market: Analysis of Responses, SIB, December 1996, paras. 5.14–5.15.   [157] A Review of the Metals Market, SIB, August 1996, para. 3.17.

all depends on 'the extent to which a person is willing to relax his control [or to lend] . . . to help maintain an orderly market . . .; the extent to which the person's activity . . . risks causing settlement default by other[s] . . . on a multilateral basis and not just a bilateral basis' because he will not excuse his individual counterparty from his delivery obligations; 'the extent to which prices . . . [in the particular] market diverge from . . . prices [elsewhere] . . . .; and . . . the extent to which the spot . . . market compared to the forward market is unusually expensive or inexpensive' (MAR 1.6.11, 1.6.12). Again, it must come down to intention and, even then, one can sympathise with the comments in 1999 of the then senior non-executive LME Director on the FSA's initial draft Market Abuse Code:

> I have spent ten years looking at that subject [i.e. abusive squeezes] from the London Metal Exchange Boardroom and I do not find clarity in . . . [the Code] on the basis I would be comfortable to tell anybody they had breached a clear provision of law.[158]

Defences There is a defence for a trade carried out 'for legitimate reasons and in conformity with accepted market practices', but the only such practice is the LME market aberrations regime (FSMA 118(5); MAR 1.6.14).

12.5.5.2 Fictions

Market abuse is committed by trading 'which employ fictitious devices or any other form of deception or contrivance' (FSMA 118(6)), i.e. trading 'preceded or followed by dissemination of false or misleading information . . . [or] research or investment recommendations which are erroneous or biased or demonstrably influenced by material interests', for example:

- [•] pump and dump . . . taking a long [purchase] position . . . and then disseminating misleading positive information about the . . . investment with a view to increasing its price;
- [•] trash and cash . . . take a short [sold] position . . . and then disseminating misleading negative information about the . . . investment, with a view to driving down its price [and buying in the investment to settle the sale contract]. (MAR 1.7.2(3), (4), 1.7.3)
- [•] Opening a position and closing it immediately after its public disclosure.[159]

The phrase 'employ fictitious devices' implies an intention.

12.5.5.3 The 'regular user'

Any 'behaviour (not falling within [12.5.5.1 or 12.5.5.2] . . .) [which] would be . . . regarded by a regular user of the market as behaviour that would distort . . . the market . . . and . . . as a failure on the part of the person

---

[158] Joint Committee Report, Vol. II, Minutes of Evidence, 25 March 1999, para. 221.
[159] CESR/ 04-505, November 2004, para. 4.13(e).

concerned to observe the standard of behaviour usually expected of a person in his position in relation to the market' is market abuse (FSMA 118(8)(b)). The concept of the 'regular user' is explained in 12.5.6 although, given the lack of clarity as to what this heading of market abuse is intended to cover beyond 12.5.5.1 and 12.5.5.2 (the only articulated example appearing to be 'inaction which leads to the distortion of a market'),[160] FSA prescribes 'factors to be taken into account'. These are whether the transaction is 'pursuant to a prior . . . obligation . . . [or] executed in a way which takes into account the need for the market as a whole to operate fairly and efficiently' (which all depends on 'the characteristics of the market . . . [and] the position of the person in question . . . [and whether] the transaction complied with the rules of the . . . market'), the only defence being compliance with the LME market aberrations regime (MAR 1.9.3, 1.9.5). It is very similar to the pre-Market Abuse Directive test generally which required 'behaviour, interfer[ing] . . . with the proper operation of market forces with the purpose of positioning prices at a distorted level. This need not be the sole purpose of . . . the transaction . . . but must be an actuating purpose', i.e. 'a purpose which motivates or incites a person to act', probably best regarded as intention, 'and . . . in order to be likely, there must be a real and not fanciful likelihood that the behaviour will have such an effect, although the effect need not be more likely than not',[161] this phrase defying interpretation.

This heading of market abuse ceases to have effect on 30 June 2008 (FSMA 118(9)) as explained in 12.5.3.3.

12.5.6 The reasonable and regular user

Under the Market Abuse Directive regime, the 'regular user' is relevant to only three subsidiary headings of market abuse which are not derived from the Directive (12.5.3.3, 12.5.4.3, 12.5.5.3). Given this subsidiary role of the 'regular user', all the FSA now say is that he is 'a hypothetical reasonable person who regularly deals on the [relevant] market . . . The presence of the regular user imports an objective element . . . while retaining some subjective features of the market for the investments in question' (MAR 1.2.21. See also: FSMA 130A(3)). Originally, though, in the 2001 regime, in relation to all headings of market abuse, '[b]ehaviour will amount to market abuse only where it would be likely to be regarded by a regular user as a failure on the part of the person . . . concerned to observe the standard of behaviour reasonably expected of a person in his . . . position in relation to the market', in other words 'whether a hypothetical reasonable person . . . would regard the behaviour as acceptable in the light of all the relevant circumstances'.[162] This required FSA to bring some realism to a supposedly

[160] UK Implementation of the M.A.D., HMT & FSA CD, June 2004, para. 3.23. See, also, CESR/07-429, July 2007, p. 78.   [161] FSA MAR release 001, 1 December 2001, 1.6.4.
[162] FSA MAR release 001, December 2001, 1.2.1, 1.2.2.

non-intention based regime (12.4.3, 12.5.1) and a regime which made little attempt to validate normal market practices, such that the regular user 'has to be . . . the cousin of the courts' reasonable man. He represents the distillation of the standards expected by those who regularly use the market.'[163] Accordingly, in applying the regular user test regard had to be had to:

- 'the characteristics of the market in question . . . and the users of the market . . . For example, the disclosure standards . . . expected in equities markets differ from those expected in commodities markets. Consequently, different standards . . . apply to the use of non-public information in different markets.'[164] This particular distinction is now reflected in the definition of 'inside information' (12.5.3.1); and
- 'the position of the person in question and the standards reasonably to be expected of that person . . . in the light of that person's experience, level of skill and standard of knowledge';[165] and
- 'the rules and regulations of the market' and 'the extent to which the behaviour is in compliance with' those rules, particularly where 'the person is based overseas . . . [and] is in compliance with the standards prevailing in that overseas jurisdiction';[166] and
- (almost a policy that) '[a] mistake is unlikely to fall below the objective standards expected where the person . . . has taken reasonable care to prevent . . . such mistakes'.[167]

These statements no longer appear in the Market Abuse Code but, in practice, it is hard to see how the regime can be operated unless the regulator has regard to them. Of course, the issue always was 'whether there are absolute or only relative standards . . . in terms of what people regard as normal',[168] although '[w]ere the market abuse regime to allow the FSA to take action solely in the light of its own view of what are the proper standards, what market participants thought was right or wrong . . . would be neither here nor there'.[169] Nonetheless, FSA set out its factors in the context of an overarching distinction between 'accepted' and 'acceptable' conduct, which followed the redrafting of the Principle from 'high' to 'proper' standards of market conduct (12.6), so that although 'FSA does not anticipate that divergence between standards that are generally accepted by users of the market and the standards accepted by the regular user will be frequent . . . the FSA may identify a practice which is accepted in the market, but which, in the FSA's opinion, is

---

[163] Parl. Deb., House of Commons, Standing Committee A, FSMB, 29th Sitting, 2 November 1999, Minister, col. 655.
[164] FSA MAR release 001, December 2001, 1.2.3(1), 1.2.7.   [165] Ibid, 1.2.3(4).
[166] Ibid, 1.2.3(2), 1.2.8.   [167] Ibid, 1.2.6.
[168] Parl. Deb., House of Lords, 21 February 2000, col. 32.
[169] Parl. Deb., House of Lords, 21 March 2000, Minister, cols. 228–229.

likely to fall short of the standards expected by the regular user'.[170] Such righteousness will continue, particularly in the absence of the regular user.

12.5.7 Requiring or encouraging

As well as directly engaging in market abuse, the regime prohibits action or inaction (12.5.1) which 'require[s] or encourage[s] another person . . . to engage in behaviour which . . . would amount to market abuse' (FSMA 123(1)(b)), for example: 'an analyst . . . telephones the finance director at [a] PLC and presses for details of the profit . . . from the latest unpublished management accounts' (MAR 1.4.7) or 'selective disclosures of information' unless 'accompanied by a statement . . . that the information is given in confidence and that the recipient should not base any behaviour in relation to the . . . investment . . . on the information until after the information is made generally available'.[171] But it does not catch 'pass[ing] . . . information which is . . . not generally available to:

- [•] employees . . . where the possession of the information . . . is necessary for the proper performance of th[eir] function; or
- [•] professional advisers . . . for the purpose of obtaining advice; or
- [•] any person with whom he is negotiating . . . any . . . transaction . . . for the purpose of facilitating the proposed transaction; or
- [•] any person from whom he is seeking . . . an irrevocable commitment . . . in relation to a . . . takeover . . . or . . .
- [•] any government department . . . or regulatory body or authority for the purpose of fulfilling a legal or regulatory obligation.[172]

'A particular issue is whether intermediaries have any responsibility to satisfy themselves that their customers' transactions will not give rise to market abuse'[173] and, in FSA's view, 'where an intermediary receives an order . . . with no indication that the transaction . . . is . . . abusive . . . the mere execution of the order will not of itself constitute the intermediary requiring or encouraging the customer to engage in . . . market abuse. However, [if] . . . the intermediary executes a transaction when it knows, or ought reasonably to know, that . . . the transaction . . . will . . . abuse the market . . . the intermediary's behaviour will amount to [the primary offence of] market abuse.'[174] Thus, client transactions through firms' electronic systems, whether an MTF (14.2) or direct market access to an Exchange (13.2.3.4), require some filters and controls. And, as a result of the Market Abuse Directive, a firm executing transactions must notify

---

[170] FSA MAR, release 001, December 2001, 1.2.11.   [171] Ibid, 1.8.5.   [172] Ibid, 1.8.6.
[173] FSA CP 59, July 2000, para. 6.85.
[174] FSA CP 76, November 2000, Ann. A, para. 1.8A2.

FSA if it 'has reasonable grounds to suspect that the transaction might constitute market abuse' (SUP 15.10.2) although 'we are not trying to trip firms up . . . [so] there is no requirement for firms to have electronic transaction surveillance systems . . . [or] to go back and retroactively review transactions', although 'we expect firms to inform us of suspicious transactions by their clients'.[175]

12.5.8 Safe harbours

12.5.8.1 Compliance with the stabilisation and buy back rules

See 12.3.7 (FSMA 118A(5)(b); MAR 1.10.1, 2.2.4).

12.5.8.2 Chinese Walls

Information held the other side of a Chinese Wall (6.2.3.2, 6.3.1.3) is not taken into account in determining whether, if it was not so held, it would be market abuse (FSMA 118A(5)(a); MAR 1.10.2(1)).

12.5.8.3 Listed company disclosure

Disclosure in accordance with DTR (12.2.3), including the ability to withhold information, does not constitute market abuse (FSMA 118A(5)(a); MAR 1.10.2(2)).

12.5.8.4 Takeover code

'Behaviour conforming with . . . the rules of the Takeover Code about the timing, dissemination or availability, content and standard of care applicable to a disclosure, announcement, communication or release of information, does not, of itself, amount to market abuse' (MAR 1.10.4; FSMA 120).

12.5.9 Mitigating factors

Notwithstanding the occurrence of market abuse, FSA 'may not impose a penalty . . . if . . . there are reasonable grounds for it to be satisfied that:

(a) he believed, on reasonable grounds, that his behaviour did not [amount to market abuse] . . . or
(b) he took all reasonable precautions and exercised all due diligence to avoid behaving in a way which [amounted to market abuse]. (FSMA 123(2))

In the original 2001 Market Abuse regime, this was introduced as a sop to the industry for the supposed lack of intent in the offence (12.4.3, 12.5.1) and in deciding whether to accept it as a defence in any particular case FSA,

---

[175] Market Watch 12, FSA, June 2005, p. 2. Crime in the financial markets, Philip Robinson, Director FSA, speech, 5 September 2007.

unsurprisingly given the drafting, in effect apply their understanding of the reasonable user test (12.5.6) (ENF 14.5.1; DEPP 6.3.2) which, almost by definition, does not excuse mere ignorance.

If a mitigating factor does not apply, FSA can impose a fine, but transactions are not unenforceable (FSMA 123(1), 131).

12.6 The Principle

In 2001, SIB's Principle requiring 'high standards of market conduct' (12.4), which required attaining the level of the firm's peer group in the relevant market, was replaced by FSA with the much more judgemental 'proper standards of market conduct' (9.1) so that 'FSA will take into account the standards expected in the market in which the firm is operating'.[176] 'Any behaviour which constitutes market abuse . . . will also constitute a breach of [the] Principle' (ENF 14.8.1) '[r]egardless of whether a security is technically within the scope of the market abuse regime',[177] although the 'Principle . . . is broader . . . than the market abuse regime . . . [and] directed generally at all behaviour which may fall short of proper standards of market conduct'.[178] Thus, in line with its general policy of principle-based enforcement (2.5.8), FSA found a breach of the Principle where: an investment bank, carrying out a firm underwritten placing of shares for an investor, bought shares in the market through a third party broker having 'a material effect on the market price of the . . . shares', raising it to the underwritten level so that the bank did not show a loss on the placing and 'investors and potential investors [in the placing] did not obtain a full understanding of the nature of the demand for . . . shares';[179] an analyst released the conclusions in his report to selected clients in advance of publication to clients generally;[180] and a salesman in a broker–dealer mistakenly thought he had inside information on a company and disclosed it to clients because '[i]t is an important part of maintaining confidence in the financial system that all approved persons . . . are alert to warning signals that they may be the recipient of inside information and . . . follow appropriate compliance procedures'.[181]

A particular aspect of this Principle Pre-MiFID was that 'A firm should not enter into a transaction which it knows . . . or . . . ought reasonably to have realised is improper, whether on its own account or through a third party . . . [and] a good indication that the purpose may be

---

[176] Principles for Businesses, FSA, 1 December 2001, 1.1.6.
[177] Market Watch 5, FSA, October 2002, p. 2.
[178] FSA CP 59, July 2000, Ann. A, para. 1.10.3(3).
[179] Deutsche Bank AG, Final Notice, 10 April 2006, para. 13.26.
[180] FSA PN/036/07, 20 March 2007.
[181] Sean Julian Pignatelli, Final Notice, 20 November 2006, para. 43.

improper is if the transaction is undertaken at a price other than . . . the prevailing market price' (FSA PM MAR 3.5). Accordingly, 'a firm must not enter into, as agent or principal, a non-market price transaction', being 'a transaction where . . . the dealing rate or price paid by the firm or its client differs from the prevailing market rate or price to a material extent . . . or . . . the firm or its client otherwise gives materially more or less in value than it receives in return', 'unless it has taken reasonable steps to ascertain that the transaction is not being entered into for an improper purpose' (FSA PM MAR 3.5.4; FSA PM COB 7.15.3). Structured transactions may have individual components which are not at market price but in the particular circumstances, overall, it may be justified, and 'improper purposes' include 'fraud; . . . disguising or concealment of the nature of a transaction or . . . profits, losses or cash flows; transactions which amount to market abuse; . . . and "window dressing" . . . to disguise the true financial position of the person concerned' (FSA PM MAR 3.5.8–3.5.12, 3.5.13). The 'reasonable steps require a procedure to identify, examine and review such transactions' (FSA PM MAR 3.5.7). Although these rules were deleted under MiFID (13.1.5), they should still be considered to reflect the effect of the Principle to observe 'proper standards of market conduct'.

12.7 The future

FSA's 2007/08 Business Plan is clear that:

> we are . . . committed to stepping up our efforts to prevent, detect and prosecute market abuse and other forms of financial crime.[182]

This needs to be understood in context. 'Our market cleanliness statistics . . . have indicated that the level of informed price movements ahead of takeover announcements . . . remains a cause for concern'[183] and 'it seems likely that inherent in these numbers is the unacceptable practice of trading on inside information'.[184] Thus, notwithstanding the radical shift in 2001 away from traditional (criminal) standards of intention and proof (12.4), it may be that the Market Abuse regime has not achieved its objectives. As the FSA also put it:

> successfully prosecuting market abuse is not straightforward. The perpetrators may be in a ring designed to disguise the identify of both the intermediaries and the beneficiaries and some may operate from abroad. Market abuse can be a very sophisticated activity where complex derivative transactions which are not easily visible to the

---

[182] Business Plan, 2007/8, FSA, p. 10.   [183] Market Watch, Issue 21, July 2007, p. 1.
[184] Reflections of a soon-to-be-former regulator, John Tiner, CEO FSA, at ABI Annual Conference, 2 July 2007, p. 5.

market or us may be used. And the standards of evidence to prosecute successfully market abuse are high and reliance on circumstantial evidence can seriously weaken a case . . . To help the FSA build a strong case we would like to be granted formal powers to offer immunity in exchange for hard evidence and I would urge the government to accede to this request.[185]

[185] Ibid. Moreover, about one-third of Enforcement Division staff are being 'upgraded' in 2007 as 'essential in a principles-based world' (2.5.8) (Enforcement shake-up at UK watchdog, FT, 15 August 2007).

13
Dealing and executing orders

13.1 Transactions

Much of banking, investment banking, broking and dealing is a process and to that extent regulatory compliance, which is derivative of commercial operations in that it regulates a commercial activity, is itself a process. The way the firm executes transactions, both for itself and clients, is a paradigm example of this; and so, as with all law and regulation, that of transaction execution is best understood by placing it in the context of the commercial activity.

13.1.1 Pre-transaction

The firm may have actively promoted the product or service to the client (10), but will have in any event gone through the client categorisation and take-on process (8.1–8.4) which may have resulted in the giving of advice or exercise of discretion on the client's behalf (11.1, 11.2) unless it was an execution-only client (11.3, 11.4). Alternatively, there may be no client involvement whatsoever, it being a proprietary transaction solely for the firm's own account.

13.1.2 The order to deal

Pre-MiFID: The firm, obviously, should only 'undertake transactions . . . having received authority to do so from the . . . customer',[1] the client's order having been communicated to the firm or a discretionary decision to deal taken by the firm, in either case resulting in the need for the firm to have created, and kept for three years, a detailed record of '(a) the customer name . . . (b) the date and time . . . (c) the . . . employee who received the . . . order or made the decision . . . (d) . . . the . . . investments . . . and . . . number . . . or total value . . . (e) whether . . . a purchase or sale . . . (f) any other instruction received' and (g) if the order was received over the Internet in response to a displayed price, 'the firm should record the price, even if only indicative' (FSA PM COB 7.12.1(1), 7.12.3–7.12.5, 7.12.9, 7.12.10, 7.12.11; FSA PM COB, Sched. 1).

---

[1] SFA BN 131, 26 April 1993.

Dealing and executing orders

MiFID: Again, the firm must only deal if authorised (COBS 11.3.1(1)) and, as regards record keeping, which is now a five year obligation, while Pre-MiFID item (c) is no longer required but could be continued with, in addition to (a), (b) and (d)–(g), the record must specify 'the nature of the order if other than buy or sell' and 'the type of the order' ('for example, a limit order or a market order'), a 'buy/sell indicator . . . Instrument identification . . . Price notation [i.e. currency or percentage price of a debt instrument] . . . Quantity . . . [and] Quantity notation [i.e. number or nominal value]' and, strangely for an order as opposed to execution, the 'Unit Price' (COBS 11.3.2(1), 11.5.1, 11.5.4).

13.1.3 The decision on how to deal

Pre-MiFID: A discretionary decision taken by the firm will have resulted from 'suitable advice' (11.2) as may an order received from a customer, or it may simply be execution-only (11.3). In any of these cases the firm had to decide, first, whether to itself execute the transaction, second, if so, whether as principal or as disclosed or undisclosed agent, third, if not, whether to 'instruct [i.e. arrange for: 3.2.2.2] . . . another person to execute' as its agent or, fourth, merely 'pass . . . a customer order to another person for execution' and, fifth, if it is to execute as agent, whether or not to aggregate it with another client or own account order (GLOSS, def. of 'execute'). These decisions were determined by the firm's abilities as reflected in the service which it contracted to the client to provide and recorded in its customer documentation (8.4). If it passed the order to another for execution, it had to record and keep for three years in relation to customer orders '(a) the name of the person instructed; (b) the terms of the instruction; and (c) the date and time' (FSA PM COB 7.12.1(3), 7.12.3, 7.12.4, 7.12.6(3), 7.12.11), while it could aggregate orders only if 'it is likely that the aggregation will not work to the disadvantage of each of the customers concerned . . . and . . . it has disclosed . . . to each customer concerned . . . in the terms of business, that the effect of aggregation may work on some occasions to its disadvantage' and it made, and kept for three years, 'a record of the intended basis of allocation' (FSA PM COB 7.7.4, 7.7.14(2), (3), 7.7.18; FSA PM COB, Sched. 1). From a policy perspective, the aggregation rule was viewed as an application of the conflicts rule (6.3.1) since it 'allows a firm to have regard to the advantages likely to enure to a customer in connection with future transactions . . . [although] a particular customer may be disadvantaged by being included in the amalgamation . . . This is justified where the customer can expect countervailing advantages in future allocations. A customer can have this expectation only if future allocations are made fairly from time to time so that advantages and disadvantages . . . are spread evenly amongst the firm's customers generally.'[2] 'The advantages

---

[2] SIB Conduct Rules, 7 October 1987, 5.04(4), Practice Note 3.

envisaged are either that there would be no transaction at all (e.g. . . . large placings) or that best execution would be achieved (e.g. if large transactions entailed lower commissions).'[3] It follows that in practice '[a] firm should only aggregate customers' orders where it believes on reasonable grounds that this is in the overall best interests of its customers'.[4]

MiFID: A discretionary decision must still have resulted from 'suitable advice' as may an order received from a client, but now there is a more limited class of execution-only transactions, with any order for an instrument with a derivative component having to be subject to the 'appropriateness' test (11.3, 11.4).[5] Subject to that, as before, the firm can either execute the transaction itself or pass to another for execution in which case it must record, and keep for five years, exactly the same information as before and can only aggregate if it satisfies the same conditions (COBS 11.3.7, 11.5.3).

13.1.4 Executing transactions

13.1.4.1 Application

Pre-MiFID: The rules referred to in 13.1.4.2–13.1.4.5 applied where the firm itself executed the transaction within 13.2.2.1.

MiFID: The application remains the same in terms of execution of orders (13.2.2),[6] except that it also includes order passing if reception and transmission of orders (3.2.2.2) (COBS 11.1.1, 11.3.13) and the rules apply only to dealing with or for Retail and Professional Clients (COBS 1, Ann. 1, Part 1, para. 1.1) (8.2.1). For the general application of the rules, see 4.2(o).

13.1.4.2 Priority of dealing

Pre-MiFID: The 'firm must execute customer orders and own account orders . . . fairly and in due turn' (FSA PM COB 7.4.3), since '[i]t is unfair to put the firm or another customer . . . into a transaction ahead of a customer who ought to have priority'.[7] For this purpose the firm could treat group employees, pension schemes and collective investment schemes as third party customers (FSA PM COB 7.7.10) and could nonetheless:

(1) execut[e]:
   (a) a prior own account order ahead of a subsequent . . . customer order . . . [and]
   (b) a . . . [subsequent] customer order when the person dealing for the customer neither knew a or ought reasonably to have known

---

[3] SIB Conduct Rules, draft September 1986, Explanatory Memorandum, para. 3.3.1
[4] SFA Rules Release 1, 6 December 1991, Rule 5–42, Guidance.
[5] Client consent may be necessary to deal off-exchange (8.4.7.1, 3rd bullet point).
[6] FSA CP 06/19, para. 16.31.
[7] COBS: A New Approach, SIB, November 1988, draft Rule 3.04.

of an earlier unexecuted . . . customer order [because he was the other side of a Chinese wall but, probably, not simply because he was on a different desk on the trading floor];
(2) postpon[e] . . . a . . . customer order when the firm has taken reasonable steps to ensure that execution of another customer order ahead of that customer order is likely to improve the terms on which the . . . [first] order is executed (. . . the firm . . . ensur[ing] . . . that the [second] customer . . . is also being treated fairly [9.2]). (FSA PM COB 7.4.3, 7.4.4)

Exception (2) required caution in practice. The rule, however, applied only where the firm 'executed' a 'customer order' within 13.2.2.1.

MiFID: Where the firm executes or procures another firm to execute (COBS 11.3.13), i.e. receives and transmits or passes on an order, the application of the equivalent MiFID Rules is probably the same, and also in relation to RFQ business (13.2.2.1). One rule, which applies where the 'firm . . . is authorised to execute orders on behalf of clients' (defined as 'acting to conclude agreements to buy or sell . . . instruments on behalf of clients' and therefore implying a similar distinction as with the Pre-MiFID definition of 'execute' 'client orders'), requires the firm to 'implement procedures . . . which provide for the prompt, fair and expeditious execution of client orders, relative to other client orders or the trading interests of the firm. These procedures . . . must allow for the execution of otherwise comparable client orders in accordance with the time of their reception by the firm' (COBS 11.3.1). Similarly, 'A firm must . . . carry out otherwise comparable client orders sequentially and promptly unless the characteristics of the order or prevailing market conditions make this impracticable, or the interests of the client require otherwise' (COBS 11.3.2(2)). 'Promptly' is interpreted as 'a flexible, not rigid, standard and means as soon as reasonably possible depending on the circumstances'.[8]

13.1.4.3 Best execution

See 13.2.

13.1.4.4 Timely execution

Pre-MiFID: A 'customer order', as explained in 13.1.4.1 and 13.1.4.2, if capable of immediate execution and not subject to a condition such as a price limit which had not been reached, had to be 'execute[d] . . . as soon as reasonably practicable unless . . . [the] firm has taken reasonable steps to ensure that postponing . . . execution . . . is in the best interests of the customer', for example 'a foreseeable improvement in . . . liquidity . . . is likely to enhance the terms on which the firm executes' or 'executing the order as a

---

[8] FSA CP 06/19, para. 16.61.

series of partial executions over a period . . . is likely to improve the terms' or 'the deal was part of an aggregated transaction' within 13.1.3 (GLOSS., def. of 'current customer order'; FSA PM COB 7.6). It has always been difficult to understand how aggregation, which only has to not operate to the customer's disadvantage (13.1.3), is really 'in the best interests of the customer'. Receipt of an order outside the relevant market's trading hours had to result in execution upon opening the next day (FSA PM COB 7.6.6(1)).

Once the transaction was executed, whether for a customer or own account, the firm had to record 'as soon as practicable', and retain for three years, '(a) the name . . . and account number of the client (if any) . . . (b) the name of the counterparty, if known . . . (c) the date and, if available, the time of the transaction . . . (d) the identity of the employee executing . . . (e) . . . the . . . investment . . . and . . . number . . . or total value . . . (f) the price and other significant terms (including exchange rate details if relevant) and (g) whether . . . a purchase or a sale' (FSA PM COB 7.12.1(2), (4), 7.12.3, 7.12.4, 7.12.6(2), 7.12.8, 7.12.11).

MiFID: Where the firm executes or procures another firm to execute (COBS 11.3.13), immediate execution continues to be required, as for the Pre-MiFID Rules and the record keeping, now for five years, is the same except, in addition, the MiFID Rules require 'Price notation [i.e. currency of price; percentage value of debt instrument] Quantity notation [i.e. units or nominal value] Venue identification [13.2.3]' and 'the nature of the transaction if other than buy or sell', for example, option exercise (COBS 11.3.2(1), 11.5.2, 11.5.4). In addition, there is a new rule which applies to 'limit orders', being 'an order to buy or sell . . . at a specified price level or better and for a specified size', although this does not include '"stop orders" and "contingent orders" . . . A "stop order" is . . . to buy or sell a share once the price . . . reaches a specified price, known as the stop price. When the specified price is reached, the stop order becomes a market order. The intention . . . is not to execute at the current prevailing market conditions, but rather, it is to limit a loss or protect a profit in volatile market conditions . . . A "contingent order" is an order whose execution depends upon the execution and/or the price of another security.'[9] Under this rule, 'in respect of shares admitted to trading on a regulated market [14.1] which are not immediately executed' the firm must 'mak[e] public immediately that . . . order in a manner which is easily accessible to other market participants', i.e. send it to a regulated market or MTF (COBS 11.4). In publishing, the firm must 'ensure barriers to the accessibility . . . of the information are not erected', although '[t]he system used . . . does not need to have execution functionality'.[10] The rule does not apply if 'a client expressly instructs otherwise', which can be generally in Terms of Business

---

[9] FSA CP 06/19, paras. 16.82–16.83.   [10] Ibid, paras. 16.79, 16.86.

(8.4.2) or the 'order ... is large in scale compared with normal market size' (COBS 11.4). In seeking client consent in Terms of Business, the firm should consider whether this 'treats the customer fairly' (9.2).[11] Moreover, 'A firm must ... inform a retail client about any material difficulty relevant to the proper carrying out of orders promptly' (COBS 11.3.2(3)), which represents good market practice.

13.1.4.5 Allocation

Pre-MiFID: A rule on timely allocation of aggregated orders was introduced under the 1983 LDRs in the context of investment management to stop the practice of effecting bulk purchases without a clear idea of which clients the firm was dealing on behalf of, on the basis that if the price increased, the licensed dealer would take the securities for its own account, sell them and keep the profit, but if they went down in value, the securities would be allocated to clients (1983 LDRs 14(3)). This rule was carried over by SIB under the 1986 FSAct so that '[t]he practice of dealing for a suspense account for later appropriation will thus be banned'.[12] Accordingly, 'allocation must be ... to the account of the customer on whose instructions the transaction was executed'.[13] Aggregated orders (13.1.3) may be executed all at once, partially over a period or, ultimately, in full or only in part, necessitating allocation, in whole or in part, to each of the clients aggregated. For this purpose, the firm could treat group employees, pension schemes and collective investment schemes as third party customers and needed a written allocation policy which reflected the rule that 'it must ... not give undue preference to the firm or to any [client] ... and ... where [it had aggregated a customer and own account order] ... if the aggregate total of all orders cannot be satisfied', 'give priority to satisfying customer orders' (FSA PM COB 7.7.9, 7.7.10). 'The point of th[is] rule ... [is] to prevent firms from taking advantage of their control over their customers' transactions to favour unfairly either themselves or a particular customer.'[14] Thus, in the firm's policy, '[o]ne interpretation of "fair" would be rateable'.[15] Aggregated orders, whether in the Secondary Market or 'new issues'[16] had to be 'promptly allocate[d]' which meant 'within five business days if ... only intermediate customers are concerned ... and ... each of them has agreed' and, otherwise, 'within one business day' (FSA PM COB 7.7.5, 7.7.6). For this purpose, 'All transactions in a series ... executed within the one business day, may be treated as ... executed at the time of the last transaction' and, if executed over more than one day, each day's

[11] FSA PS 07/2, para. 7.12.
[12] Regulation of Investment Business – The New Framework, SIB and MIBOC, December 1985, 3.33.13.   [13] SFA Rules Release 1, 6 December 1991, Rule 5.40.
[14] SIB Conduct Rules, Draft: May 1986, Explanatory Memorandum, para. 3.22.
[15] IMRO Rules, Final Proof: 18 November 1987, Rule 10.02, Commentary.
[16] IMRO Reporter 10, February 1995, p. 7.

transactions had to be allocated separately (FSA PM COB 7.7.6(4), (5)). Re-allocations were permitted only for errors or if 'the order is only partially executed resulting in an uneconomic allocation to some customers' (FSA PM COB 7.7.11) and both allocations and re-allocations had to be at either the executed price or a volume weighted average (VWAP) (FSA PM COB 7.7.12, 7.7.13). For example, if Transaction 1 is 100 shares at £1 each, and Transaction 2 is 400 shares at £2 each then:

$$\text{VWAP} = \frac{(100 \times £1) + (400 \times £2)}{500} = £1.80$$

Records had to be kept for three years of 'the identity of each client concerned, whether the transaction is . . . in whole or in part for a discretionary managed portfolio' and '(1) the date and time of allocation; (2) the . . . investment; (3) the identity of each customer . . . concerned; [and] (4) the amount allocated to each . . . and to the firm' and 'the basis of and reason for any re-allocation' (FSA PM COB 7.7.14–7.7.18, 7.12.7; FSA PM COB Sched. 1).

MiFID: Allocation, where the firm executes the transaction or instructs another firm to execute (COBS 11.3.13), continues to be required to be 'prompt' (COBS 11.3.2(1)), i.e. 'as soon as reasonably possible depending on the circumstances',[17] 'consider[ing] market practices (provided such practices do not interfere with the requirement promptly and correctly to deliver the financial instruments or funds to the account of the client)'.[18] With aggregated orders, while there is nothing to prevent connected persons being treated as 'customers',[19] partial executions continue to be required to be 'allocate[d] . . . in accordance with [the firm's] . . . order allocation policy' and, where own account orders are aggregated with client orders, the firm 'must allocate' . . . to the client in priority to the firm' unless 'the firm is able to demonstrate on reasonable grounds that without the combination it would not have been able to carry out the order on such advantageous terms, or at all, [in which case] it may allocate . . . for own account proportionally, in accordance with its order allocation policy' (COBS 11.3.8–11.3.10). The timing and pricing of allocation is not specified and, therefore, firms can continue to comply with the Pre-MiFID requirements if only because FSA views the express inclusion of them in the Rules as having been 'safe harbours . . . [which] will be super-equivalent . . . because there may be circumstances

---

[17] FSA CP 06/19, para. 16.61; FSA PS 07/6, para. 14.24.   [18] FSA PS 07/6, para. 14.28.

[19] FSA '[c]onsider an own account transaction . . . to be one that a firm executes for its "own" benefit. Therefore, if . . . the affiliate's interests (regarding aggregation and allocati[on] . . .) are separate from those of the firm, then that affiliate's order is likely to be a "client order"' (FSA PS 07/6, para. 14.35).

in which a firm could satisfy MiFID's requirement for prompt allocation even if it did not meet the time limits set in [the Pre-MiFID] . . . Rules'.[20] Re-allocation is prohibited if 'detrimental to the client' (COBS 11.3.11, 11.3.12), which should be interpreted as requiring compliance with the Pre-MiFID Rules.

13.1.4.6 Confirms

The client needs to know when, and on what terms, his transaction has been completed and, for this purpose, the firm will send to him a confirmation or contract note. There are three issues.

When must a confirm be provided? Pre-MiFID: A firm had to provide a confirm 'when it executes a sale or purchase of a[n] . . . investment with or for a customer', 'execute' having the meaning explained in 13.1.4.1. The last in a series of transactions could be taken as the time of execution as could allocation of an aggregated order and 'When a firm executes a transaction outside normal market hours, the transaction . . . [i]s executed on the following business day', and any right to cancel (10.5.5.3, 10.5.6.4) was ignored (FSA PM COB 8.1.1, 8.1.12, 8.1.13). There were exemptions for regular savings plans for regulated collective investment schemes and investment trusts and if periodic statements containing the same information were provided and the customer agreed (FSA PM COB 8.1.6–8.1.9).

MiFID: The obligation to provide a confirm applies whenever a firm 'has carried out an order in the course of its designated investment business [4.2.I(1), 4.2(p)] on behalf of a client' and relates to 'the execution of the order' (COBS 16.2.1(1)), even by someone else where the firm arranged the transaction or received and transmitted the order (3.2.2.1, 3.2.2.2). It is implicit that an 'order' relating to a series of transactions or aggregated can be treated as before (COBS 16.2.1(1), 16.2.3). The only exemptions are in relation to portfolio management services if a third party (i.e. an executing broker) provides the confirmation, regular savings plans for collective investment schemes, Eligible Counterparties and if, in respect of business which is not MiFID Business or equivalent third country business (4.2.I(2), 4.2.III), 'the firm has agreed with the client (in the case of a retail client, in writing with the client's informed consent) that confirmations need not be supplied' (COBS 16.2.1(2), (3), (5), 16.2.6(1); COBS 1, Ann. 1, Pt. 1, para. 1.1).

When and how must a confirm be despatched? Pre-MiFID: The confirm had to be despatched 'promptly' either to the client or its agent, other than the firm or an associate, thus preventing the use of a hold mail system, and

---

[20] FSA CP 06/19, paras. 16.65–16.66. That such practices can continue is acknowledged in FSA PS 07/6, paras. 14.29–14.33.

either in paper or electronic form or 'by posting a confirmation on its website' although '[i]f the private customer has not accessed his confirmation within five days . . . the firm should send the confirmation to him' (FSA PM COB 8.1.3, 8.1.4). The FSA's interpretation of 'prompt despatch' followed commercial reality, i.e.: with regulated collective investment schemes, 'the business day following the day the . . . price was determined'; with derivatives and stockloans, where a detailed schedule to an industry standard agreement like an ISDA would need to be drafted, 'as soon as practicable in accordance with proper standards of market practice'; and with securities, next business day after execution or, where the firm used an agent to execute, the business day following receipt of the agent's confirm because a firm could simply forward on that confirm instead of having to provide its own (FSA PM COB 8.1.5(1)(c), (2)).

MiFID: The Professional Client must receive the confirmation 'promptly', which is to be interpreted as with the Pre-MiFID Rule, and the Retail Client must be sent it 'as soon as possible and no later than the first business day following . . . execution', or receipt of the confirmation from an executing broker (COBS 16.2.1(1)), which will be challenging where a schedule to an industry standard agreement needs to be completed. The confirm can be sent to the client's agent (COBS 2.4.9, 16.2.5) and, in any case, provided in paper or electronic form or through a website provided that such site 'enables the recipient to store [such] information . . . in a way accessible for future reference' (COBS 16.2.1(1), reference to 'durable medium').

What are the necessary contents of the confirm? Pre-MiFID: The contents were mandated by FSA, with different information permitted only if 'the customer has agreed . . . (in the case of a private customer, agreed in writing . . .)' or 'anyone fails to supply information which the firm requires . . . provided that the fact of its omission is stated' or if necessary for 'a series of transactions or aggregate[d] orders . . . to ensure that the information is clear, fair and not misleading' (FSA PM COB 8.1.5(1), 8.1.10, 8.1.11).

MiFID: Professional Clients' confirmations must contain 'the essential information concerning . . . execution' which is to be construed in the context of the general obligation 'that a client receives adequate reports on the services provided' (COBS 16.1.1, 16.2.1(1)(a)), being at least the investment transacted, price and counterparty (i.e. whether the firm acted as principal ('sold to you') or agent ('bought for you')) and any materially unusual terms given market practice (cf. COBS 16.2.3A). In contrast, Retail Clients' confirmations must contain 'such of the trade confirmation information as is applicable'.[21] In both cases, there are no exceptions. The 'trade

---

[21] Ultimately, FSA withdrew its 31 January 2007 super-equivalent Notification under Article 4 in respect of some of these contents requirements: FSA PS 07/14, pp. 24–25.

confirmation information' is derived from the transaction reporting information (13.4.2) and it is clear from that information that 'as applicable' permits a firm to omit an item only if, in its own terms as written, that item does not apply to the particular transaction.[22] Referring to the COBS 16, Ann. 1 requirements, which are themselves numbered and noted below, those contents requirements differ from the Pre-MiFID contents as follows:

- Some of the MiFID contents were not previously required: COBS 16, Ann. 1, Items 5, 6, 9, 17. An example is 'venue identifier' and, as a result, '[w]here multiple venues were used to fulfil an order . . . [the] Firm . . . may . . . provid[e] separate contract notes . . . for each tranche or . . . includ[e] all venues and all trading times on one contract note'.[23]
- Conversely, a lot of the Pre-MiFID contents are no longer required (FSA PM COB 8.1.15(9)(b), 8.1.16(3),(5), (7), (8), 8.1.17, 8.1.18(3)).
- And there are a large number of common requirements, although the detailed wording is often slightly different: COBS 16.2.3A(1)(a), (b), (c), (2),(3); COBS 16, Ann. 1, Items 1–4, 7, 8, 10–16.[24]

As a result, and FSA is understood to be in agreement with this interpretation, referring to the COBS 16, Ann. 1 requirements:

1. (firm identification): this can be the firm's FSA reference number or name.
2. (client designation): this can be the client's name or account/reference number.
3. (trading day).
4. (trading time): this should be in hours and minutes, but need not be in seconds. With a series of transactions, no times need be shown, just a statement that they are available on request.
5. (type of order): examples are limit and market orders.
6. (venue): this should use an FSA Code or 'OTC'. Where the firm executes through another, it may not be able to determine the venue (for example, that other acting as systematic internaliser or on-exchange) until it receives that other's own confirm. With a series of transactions on different venues, none need be shown, just a statement that they are available on request (see above).
7. (instrument identification): an FSA identification code or instrument description can be used.
8. (buy/sell indicator).
9. (nature of order if not buy/sell): for example, a put or call option.
10. (quantity).

---

[22] Level 2 Directive, Art. 40(4); COBS 16, Ann. 1, heading reference to 'where relevant'; FSA PS 07/6 para. 19.9.   [23] FSA PS 07/6, para. 19.11.
[24] Contrast, FSA PM COB 8.1.15(1), (4), (5), (7), (8), (9)(a), (10), (11), 8.1.16(1), (2), (4), (6), (9), 8.1.18(1), (2), (4), 8.1.19.

11 (unit price): this excludes commission/accrued interest. With a bond (3.2.1.2) it can be expressed as a £ amount or %. If executed in tranches, the price of each tranche or the average can be given.
12 (total consideration).
13 (commission/expenses): Where the firm owes best execution (13.2), any firm/associate mark-up/down must be included because this is a 'commission or charge'.[25]
14 (FX rate): best execution is owed (13.2.1).
15 (client's settlement responsibilities): this requires the settlement due date. All other responsibilities can appear in the Terms of Business (8.4).
16 (firm/associate/another client was counterparty).

For derivative transactions and options exercise, see in addition COBS 16.2.3A.

13.1.4.7 Settlement

The transaction will be settled in accordance with the client's instructions, the customer documentation, the client's custody arrangements and, under FSA MiFID Rules, reflecting market practice under which 'firms are already meeting this standard'.[26] 'Where a firm is responsible for overseeing or arranging the settlement of an executed order, it must take all reasonable steps to ensure that any . . . instruments or . . . funds received in settlement . . . are promptly and correctly delivered to the account of the appropriate client' (COBS 11.3.4).

13.1.5 Own account dealing

Pre-MiFID: Under the PFI dealing solely with professional investors was exempt (8.1) and while a licence was required under the 1986 FSAct (3.2.2.1), if the dealings were solely in the wholesale money markets there was an exempt status of Listed Money Market Institution subject to Bank of England supervision and compliance with its Grey Book and London Code of Conduct rules (1986 FSAct, Sched. 5). These included rules on market conventions, customer categorisation, dealing conventions, conflicts of interest, non-market price transactions and taping. Under FSMA, FSA did away with this status[27] but considered that 'there is a need to ensure a level playing field amongst professionals who are equally expert' and, hence, 'a new Code'[28] with 'three main purposes: to increase certainty by amplifying the Principles

---

[25] FSA PS 07/14, para. 7.3.   [26] FSA CP 06/19, para. 16.69.
[27] However, a Non-Investment Products Code, based on the earlier Grey Book, was retained for non-investment products, namely: sterling and foreign currency wholesale deposits, gold and silver bullion deposits and spot and forward FX. The Code is being retained following the implementation of MiFID.
[28] Differential regulatory approaches, FSA DP, October 1998, para. 3.7; The Future Regulation of Inter-Professional Business, FSA, June 1999, para. 26.

[9.1] as they apply to inter-professional business; to set out rules for inter-professional business in cases where it is not appropriate to rely on the Principles alone; and to set out the FSA's understanding of certain market practices and conventions'.[29] It was not really a 'Code', but a curious, slightly random, mixture of rules, quasi-rules and regulatory expectations which applied to all firms in respect of dealing as principal or agent, arranging deals and 'giving transaction-specific advice' (3.2.2.1, 3.2.2.2, 3.2.2.3), except custody and corporate finance, in or from the UK, with or for a Market Counterparty (FSA PM MAR 3.1.3–3.1.4). Thus, '[t]he [conduct of business rules] appl[y] to the customer-facing relationship and the [IPC] applies to the market-facing elements of any transaction',[30] being:

(i) The Principles
These applied only in part (9.1).

(ii) Clarity of role
'A firm should take reasonable steps to ensure that it is clear to the market counterparty whether it is acting on its own account, as agent, or as arranger before it enters into a transaction' (FSA PM MAR 3.4.10).

(iii) Inducements
Although this more limited rule provided only that 'A firm should take reasonable steps to ensure that it . . . does not offer, give, solicit or accept an inducement if it is likely to conflict to a material extent with any duty which a recipient firm owes to another person' (FSA PM MAR 3.4.14), in practice it was interpreted in line with the wider-ranging conduct rule (6.3.2).

(iv) Non-market price transactions
See 12.6.

(v) Taping
Taping of the dealing room telephones was encouraged by a provision that 'A firm should implement appropriate systems and controls with a view to ensuring that the material terms of all transactions . . . are promptly and accurately recorded . . . [by] voice recordings . . . [or] written trading logs or blotters' (FSA PM MAR 3.6.3). Beyond this there was no regulatory requirement to record.

(vi) Market conventions
Some of these were rather detailed (FSA PM MAR 3.7; FSA PM MAR 3, Ann. 3).

MiFID: As a result of the rule regime for Eligible Counterparties (8.1) and since 'the case for retention of . . . [the IPC] is weak [in that] . . . some of the provisions will be unnecessary, given MiFID requirements . . . and . . .

---

[29] FSA CP 47, May 2000, para. 1.15.   [30] FSA CP 43, May 2000, para. 2.7.

others refer to market practices that have become standard and therefore, there is no longer any need for [them]',[31] FSA decided not to carry over the IPC regime as a whole to principal dealing generally, only certain rules[32] as follows:

(i) The Principles
These continue to apply (9.1).

(ii) Clarity of role/(iv) Market conventions
Although these requirements have not been carried over, in practice they should be considered to be part of meeting 'proper standards of market conduct' (12.6).

(iii) Inducements
The general rule applies (6.3.2).

(iv) Non-market price transactions
Again, although not expressly carried over, in practice this rule should be continued to be followed as a 'proper standard of market conduct' (12.6) since 'the IPC ... provisions ... are ... covered by high level FSA Principles ... Notably, this includes the provision on non-market-price transactions.'[33]

(v) Taping
It is proposed that all telephone conversations and electronic communications, where the firm deals as principal or agent or arranges a transaction in any investment within the market abuse regime (12.5), must be recorded and kept for three years[34] because '[t]he prevention, protection and deterrence of market abuse is a key priority for the FSA. Good quality recordings of voice conversations and of electronic communications assist firms and the FSA in the detection of inappropriate behaviour, and its investigation and punishment ... We propose firms be required to record telephone lines used for ... conversations that involve the receipt of client orders and the negotiating, agreeing and arranging of transactions across the equity, bond and financial commodity and derivatives markets ... [E]lectronic communications ... include fax, email, client and instant messaging ... Activities within the scope of our proposals include proprietary trading and other principal dealing and agency broking and the associated sales functions.'[35] The requirement is articulated as part of FSA's anti-market

---

[31] Implementing MiFID's Client Categorisation Requirements, FSA, August 2006, para. 6.11.
[32] Ibid, para. 6.10; FSA CP 06/19, paras. 7.1 02–7.1 08; FSA PS 07/6, paras. 7.9–7.12.
[33] FSA PS 07/6, para. 7.12.
[34] FSA CP 07/9, Ann. C, draft COBS 12.8. CP 07/9 does not specify a date for implementation of this requirement. It goes far beyond market practice (LSE Post-MiFID Rules 4170, 4171).   [35] Ibid, paras. 19.1, 19.4, 19.5.

abuse efforts presumably because, otherwise, it would be 'super-equivalent' for a passported UK branch of an EEA firm (4.2(a)). In any event, the tape might constitute the suitability record where personal recommendations are given in the Dealing Room (11.2.2.2).

13.2 Best execution

13.2.1 Policy

The LDRs were silent on any duty to obtain best execution, but market practice from the early 1980s was that 'A dealer who acts as agent for his client should endeavour to deal on the best basis for the client'[36] and, following that, SIB, under the 1986 FSAct, regarded the conduct rules in general, and best execution in particular, as 'restat[ing] certain basis duties of an agent . . . The best execution rule . . . require[s] a firm to execute clients' orders on the best available terms . . . attempt[ing] to reconcile the fiduciary duty owed by a firm . . . with the fact that the firm . . . may also [act as] . . . principal . . . The . . . effect is to require the firm to execute the transaction [as agent] with another counterparty unless the client would receive at least as good a deal from the firm itself.'[37] Under MiFID, a similar result was to be reached in a Single Market context:

> 'Best execution' rules are important . . . The operation of an integrated financial market requires that orders to buy and sell . . . interact effectively, freely and instantaneously with each on a cross-border basis. Requiring . . . firms . . . to route orders to the venues offering the best prices will ensure that liquidity responds quickly to price differentials.[38]

13.2.2 When the best execution obligation applies

13.2.2.1 Generally

Pre-MiFID: It followed from the policy basis of best execution that the rule would apply where the firm 'receiv[ed] a customer order to effect a transaction as agent, or . . . in circumstances giving rise to similar duties . . . (i.e. a riskless principal transaction)'[39] and, hence, the rule applied if three conditions were satisfied (FSA PM COB 7.5.1).

First, the firm had to 'execute' a transaction, i.e. enter into the contract of acquisition or disposal, either as principal (with the client) or as agent

---

[36] Code of Conduct for Dealers, Council for the Securities Industry, May 1980, para. 5.
[37] Regulation of Investment Business – The New Framework, SIB and MIBOC, December 1985, para. 3.33.8.
[38] Proposal for a Directive Modifying Directive 93/22/EEC, European Commission, 3 September 2002, Detailed Commentary, para. 4.2.
[39] SFA BN 488A, 22 September 1998.

(for the client), whether on-exchange or off-exchange, and (where acting as agent for the client) whether direct with the counterparty or through the agency of another firm by 'instructing [that firm] . . . to execute the transaction' (GLOSS, def. of 'execute'). The rule did not, therefore, apply where the firm either passed on the order to another firm to execute or merely arranged the transaction (contrast 3.2.2.1 and 3.2.2.2).

Second, the execution of the transaction had to relate to a 'customer order', defined, in relation to a 'customer' (8.2), as acting as agent or pursuant to discretion or 'any other order . . . in circumstances giving rise to duties similar to those arising on an order to execute a transaction as agent' (GLOSS, def. of 'customer order'). In practice, this was interpreted as excluding so-called Request for Quote (RFQ) fixed income securities markets where the firm always dealt as principal and the client merely asked for a price ('take-it-or-leave-it'). 'Whether a firm owes agency-type duties . . . will be determined by:

(1) the written terms of business . . .
(2) the course of dealings between the firm and the customer . . . and
(3) the customs and practices of the market . . .

> There is a distinction between a firm simply dealing as principal and . . . accepting a customer order. A clear example of a simple principal-to-principal deal is when a firm carries out a . . . transaction with a customer at the firm's quoted price. A clear example of a firm accepting an 'order' would be undertaking . . . to buy . . . in the market, before selling . . . to the customer . . . [B]oth cases . . . [are] on a principal-to-principal basis. However, in the second example the firm will have accepted an 'order'.[40]

Third, the best execution obligation applied in relation to securities and derivatives (3.2.1.1–3.2.1.4, 3.2.1.6–3.2.1.9), dealt in on-exchange or OTC, and to the spot FX conversion on a best execution transaction 'to ensure that the benefit which a customer receives from a transaction . . . is not lost by his being given a poor rate in respect of the foreign exchange element',[41] but not to 'the purchase of or sale of units in a regulated collective investment scheme from or to the operator of that scheme'. The only exemptions were where an Intermediate Customer, other than the trustee of an occupational pension scheme, contracted out or 'the firm relies on another [firm] . . . to provide best execution, but only if it has taken reasonable care to ensure that [it] will do so' (FSA PM COB 7.5.2–7.5.4), '[f]or instance, . . . an investment manager . . . may . . . instruct . . . another firm [which] . . . is . . . subject to a best execution obligation to the investment manager'[42] under contract or regulation.

---

[40] SFA BN 578, 16 March 2001, p. 2.
[41] TSA Rules, July 1987, Vol. 2, Chapter XII, para. 25; Cf. FSA PM COB 7.5.6(2).
[42] Best Execution, FSA DP, April 2001, para. 4.15.

MiFID: The obligation is to 'take all reasonable steps to obtain, when executing orders, the best possible result for . . . clients', the analogous term 'execution of orders on behalf of clients' meaning 'acting to conclude agreements to buy or sell . . . financial instruments [3.2.1.1–3.2.1.4, 3.2.1.6–3.2.1.9] on behalf of clients'. It is clear that this obligation 'applies in relation to all types of financial instruments' including derivatives and spread bets (COBS 11.1.1),[43] and FX which is not itself an 'investment' (3.2.1.7) but is 'connected to the provision of investment services' (4.2.I(2)) (COBS 11.1.1(1)).[44] It also 'should apply to a firm which owes contractual or agency obligations to the client' and '[d]ealing on own account with clients . . . should be considered as the execution of client orders, and therefore subject to . . . best execution' (COBS 11.2.1–11.2.3, 11.2.5; GLOSS, def. of 'execution of orders on behalf of clients'). On this basis, RFQ (request for quote) markets appear to be subject to a best execution obligation, unless the firm is dealing only with Eligible Counterparties (8.1, 8.3.3), since the Pre-MiFID Rule 'that . . . [Intermediate] clients . . . can agree to forgo best execution . . . [does] not . . . [remain] under . . . MiFID'.[45] This would cause enormous difficulties in the non-price transparent fixed income instruments markets where the client, in effect, receives a 'take-it-or-leave-it' price from the firm. FSA's first attempt to rationalise its way out of this unintended consequence was that in such markets there is no 'client' because the firm is only conducting an 'activity' and not providing a 'service', with the 'consequence . . . that when a person . . . deals with [the] . . . firm, whose business is to deal on a quote-driven basis and who has not agreed to act on behalf of that person . . . that person may not receive the benefit of any of the client facing protections'.[46] This failed (8.2.1). Its next argument had more credibility. 'Our approach to implementing the MiFID best execution requirements in the context of quote-driven markets indicates the scope of the requirement may be subject to . . . whether a firm . . . is executing an order . . . [This] question . . . will turn on what

---

[43] It is proposed that there should be an exemption for non-financial spread bets (FSA CP 07/9, Ann. B, COBS 12.1.6) but not others (FSA PS 07/15, paras. 7.10–7.13).

[44] This version of COBS 11.1.1(1) appears in FSA PS 07/6, applying the best execution rule 'to . . . MiFID business . . . [and] equivalent . . . third country business'. FSA CP 07/9, in contrast, redrafts the rule to apply 'to a firm' without specifying the applicable business, although this change is proposed 'to extend the . . . best execution . . . rule . . . to cover non-MiFID firms and business where the business involves the execution of orders . . . The orders covered relate only to MiFID financial instruments' (FSA CP 07/9, para. 13.2). Although FX which is an ancillary service is still included because of the wide scope of COBS 11.2.1; otherwise there would be no need to exclude non-financial spread bets, as explained in FN42; and treating the customer fairly (9.2) would appear not to permit the spot FX element to deny overall best execution), FSA in practice does not regard it as included (cf. COBS 11.2.5, first sentence). It follows that there is no best execution obligation in relation to margin lending (4.2.I(2), ancillary service (2); 11.5).

[45] FSA CP 06/19, paras 16.21–16.22.   [46] Ibid, para. 7.98.

responsibilities (if any) the firm has agreed to undertake to its customer . . . [and] whether . . . [it is] executing an order for a person who expects it to deliver best execution . . . [I]t will normally be possible for the issue to be determined by reference to the firm's terms of business and whether . . . the customer is looking to deal merely on the basis of the published quote, or is asking the firm to execute an order on its behalf . . . [Where] the dealing firm . . . provides . . . . published quotes or [a] request for quote service . . . clients . . . will not . . . give "orders" to the firm . . . [I]t does not make sense to require a dealing firm to deliver best execution if the customer is relying on its due diligence in deciding to buy or sell a financial product from or to a firm. This will apply in respect of all dealers including those which provide continuously published quotes or a "request for quote" service . . . This approach will be possible in both wholesale and retail markets.'[47] The European Commission, however, while agreeing with the conclusion, rejected FSA's reasoning since 'we do not believe it is useful to focus on the question of when an order arises . . . [because MiFID] clarifies that whenever a firm deals on own account with a client there should be considered to be an order'. For the Commission, 'the key concept to focus on . . . is the execution of orders on behalf of clients . . . [because] the definition of ['execution of orders on behalf of clients'], . . . refers specifically to a firm acting to conclude agreements to buy or sell financial instruments on behalf of clients, and the description of the relevant investment service in . . . MiFID [i]s the "execution of orders on behalf of clients". Both provisions support the idea that the requirement that the order is being executed on behalf of the client is integral to the concept of best execution . . . MiFID provides . . . [that] execution of orders on behalf of clients . . . will typically be present in . . . situations where "contractual or agency obligations are owed by the firm to the client" . . . [T]he scope of best execution requirements in relation to dealing on own account is limited to . . . where the firm is acting on behalf of the client.'[48] The distinction is between a client instruction to 'get for me', which is subject to best execution, and 'sell to me', which is not. Thus, 'transactions based on a client's request . . . to buy or sell . . . for him will always fall within . . . execution of an order on behalf of a client . . . includ[ing] . . .

- Executing a client order by dealing as agent for a client . . .
- Executing a client order against the firm's own proprietary position . . . where the firm is making a decision as to how the order is executed: e.g. where it is 'working the order' on the client's behalf . . .
- Executing a client order by dealing as a riskless principal on behalf of the client . . .

---

[47] Ibid, paras 16.24–16.26, 16.31.
[48] European Commission Working Document ESC-07-2007, 19 March 2007, paras 1, 4, 5.

Transactions based on a specific request by the client to buy or sell . . . from the . . . firm, or on the acceptance by the client of an offer made by the firm . . . will typically not fall within the concept of execution of an order on behalf of a client unless . . . the firm should properly be regarded as acting on behalf of the client . . . This includes . . . where the firm engages in proprietary trading by quoting on a 'request for quote' basis . . . [or] a market maker . . . displays its quotes and [the] client . . . 'hits' the quote displayed . . . [W]hether the execution of the client's order can be seen as truly done on behalf of the client . . . depends on whether the client legitimately relies on the firm to protect his or her interests in relation to pricing and other elements of the transaction . . . that may be affected by the choices made by the firm when executing the order . . . [This depends on]:

- whether the firm approaches . . . the client or the client instigates the transaction by making an approach to the firm . . . [W]here the firm approaches a retail client and suggests [to] him to enter into a specific transaction it is more probable that the client will be relying on the firm to protect his or her interests . . .
- . . . market practice . . . [In] the wholesale OTC derivatives and bond markets buyers . . . 'shop around' by approaching several dealers for a quote, and . . . there is no expectation . . . that the dealer chosen . . . will owe best execution . . .
- the terms of any agreement between the client and the . . . firm [8.4] will also be relevant, but not determinative . . . [if] otherwise than in accordance with economic reality . . .

These factors are likely to support the presumption that, in ordinary circumstances, a retail client legitimately relies on the firm to protect his or her interests . . . [but] in the wholesale markets clients do not.[49]

Thus where, for example, a Private Bank distributes to its Retail Clients a structured product (which is not highly customised within 13.2.3.2) put together by an Investment Bank, even though it may be offered to the client on a take-or-leave-it basis, given the relationship with, and expectation of, the Retail Client, best execution will be owed by the Private Bank. In practice, this might well be difficult in view of the absence of transparent information in the market on comparable products and, therefore, price. But even in the wholesale RFQ market, best execution might on occasion apply if the client requests it or the order is so large that, from a risk perspective, the firm cannot simply give a price and must 'work the order' to lay off its risk, which would give rise to a need to train front office staff in when they need to apply best execution.

FSA's conclusion is that '[w]hile the Commission's approach differs in some respects from the view we expressed . . . its outcomes are consistent

---

[49] Ibid, paras 6–9. FSA agree (PS 07/15, paras. 3.6, 3.9). See also: 13.4.2; TRUP, pp. 11, 14, 22, 24.

with our opinion. So we presently see no need to develop further a separate legal analysis and we intend to proceed on a basis that is in line with the Commission's approach.'[50]

13.2.2.2 Booking

An investment banking group with international operations will often have the situation where its operation in Country A, which may be an affiliated company (Affiliate A) or a branch (Branch A), has the relationship with Customer A in that country and advises, negotiates and enters into a transaction with Customer A, but does it for the account of the UK Operation which has the necessary regulatory capital. The transaction is said to be 'booked' to the UK Operation which becomes the counterparty to Customer A and is named as such on the confirm (13.1.4.6). The issue is which entity in which location is treated as having 'executed' the transaction so as to have the best execution obligation.

Pre-MiFID: Where the operation in Country A was Affiliate A and 'the actual contract is between the firm in the United Kingdom and [Customer A, FSA's best execution rule] . . . will apply to [the UK Operation] . . . because . . . [its] . . . entry into the contract amounts to dealing [within 3.2.2.1; and to "executing" within 13.2.2.1] and that dealing is done from an establishment maintained by the firm in the United Kingdom' (FSA PM MAR 3, Ann. 1, para. 9(1)). Accordingly, Affiliate A had to ensure, in practice, that it executed the transaction in accordance with the FSA's best execution rules. In contrast, if the Country A operation was Branch A then 'the booking is merely an internal accounting exercise, and the transaction has no other United Kingdom connection . . . [The best execution rule will not apply to the UK Operation] because, even though [it] . . . is party to the contract and is carrying out a dealing transaction, all the dealing activity takes place at the foreign branch. A mere bookkeeping entry in the United Kingdom, not involving the [customer] . . . in any way, does not mean that the dealing activity is carried on from the establishment maintained by the firm in the United Kingdom. It is carried on from the overseas branch' (FSA PM MAR 3, Ann. 1, para. 9(2)). This was FSA's clear conclusion even though 'executing' a transaction means (1) giving a price (2) agreeing the transaction with the client or counterparty and (3) going on risk for the transaction, and the UK Operation may in practice give a price to Branch A, certainly agrees the transaction through Branch A and goes on risk, such that the dealing activity in fact occurred in the UK (3.2.2.1).

MiFID: The UK Operation is 'executing orders' within 13.2.2.1 (even though 'dealing on own account' (4.2.I(2))) where Affiliate A books a

---

[50] FSA PS 07/6, para. 14.5.

transaction to it and the analysis in the last sentence applies where Branch A does so, the FSA Guidance not having been carried over under MiFID.

13.2.2.3 Capital markets transactions

Pre-MiFID: The best execution obligation applied where the firm executed a customer 'order' which was not the case in relation to new capital raisings by a corporate issuer although, in any event, the best execution rule was disapplied to 'corporate finance business' (15.3.1.2) (FSA PM COB 1.6.4). There was a specific rule about the systems and controls to be adopted in pricing new issues (6.3.5) and a general law duty of care to fix the price at the correct level (11.1).[51] Where an existing shareholder, though, sold a block of shares or the firm did a bought deal with the company or a bookbuild (2.4.4(6), (7)) and existing shares were being traded in the market, there would have been an 'order' although the rule was disapplied (FSA PM COB 1.6.4).

MiFID: There are three arguments as regards any duty which the firm owes to the corporate finance client. First, the best execution rule applies only to 'executing orders ... for ... clients' which is closely related to the MiFID Business category of 'Execution of orders on behalf of clients' (4.2.I(2)), defined as in 13.2.2.1. This is to be contrasted with two separate MiFID Business categories which cover corporate finance: 'underwriting ... and/or placing on a firm commitment basis' and 'placing ... without a firm commitment basis'. It is, therefore, highly arguable that the best execution obligation does not apply to capital market transactions. And, even if it does, second, with new capital raisings, again, there is no 'order', although with block trades, bought deals, bookbuilds and placings (whether the firm acts as agent or principal), acquiring a strategic stake/company or share buy-backs where the price is being built around the market price, the firm can be said to be 'executing orders' except on the resale of a block trade bought as principal (FSA CP 07/15, paras. 4.4, 4.5). Nonetheless, in practice, given the unique and particular circumstances of each market operation, the execution factors (13.2.3.1) can be applied so that the best execution obligation is discharged. And third, there is a disapplication of the best execution rule to corporate finance, but only insofar as such business is not within MiFID (COBS 18.3.3),[52] which is difficult to understand since non-MiFID corporate finance is limited to advisory services (15.3.2.1).

Of course, where the firm acts for a client purchasing securities in such a corporate finance transaction, the best execution obligation will apply unless the client is a 'corporate finance contact' (15.3.2.2).

---

[51] For a US analogy, see *EBCI* v. *Goldman Sachs & Co*, New York Court of Appeal, 7 June 2005.

[52] This rule is proposed in FSA CP 07/9, Ann. C as 19.3.3, but will be renumbered.

13.2.2.4 Stocklending and repo's

See 16.3.3.1.

13.2.2.5 Counterparty type

Pre-MiFID: Best execution did not apply if the transaction was with a Market Counterparty or, if with an Intermediate Customer, it contracted out (FSA PM COB 7.5.1, 7.5.3, 7.5.4(2)).

MiFID: There is no ability to contract out with a Professional Client, but the obligation does not apply in favour of Eligible Counterparties (8.2.1) or as between participants on a regulated market or MTF (COBS 1, Ann. 1, Part 1, paras 1.1, 3.1, 4.1).

13.2.3 Achieving best execution

13.2.3.1 Generally

Pre-MiFID: The firm was required to 'take reasonable care to ascertain the price which is the best available . . . in the relevant market at the time for transactions of the kind and size concerned . . . and . . . execute the . . . order at a price which is no less advantageous . . . unless . . . it would be in the customer's best interests not to do so', for example, the 'firm has a continuing relationship with the customer and reasonably expects that it will be able to secure compensating advantages for the customer in other transactions' (FSA PM COB 7.5.5, 7.5.8) although to rely on this a firm 'would need good grounds for foreseeing such compensating advantages'.[53] It was a duty of reasonable care which 'does not mean that the rule imposes an absolute obligation to secure the best market price',[54] rather 'a duty of care . . . similar to that which an agent owes a principal' so that '[a] firm does not contravene this rule . . . by reason of any action which it takes in good faith if . . . having regard to common market practices, market conditions, the . . . relevant customer document . . . and any other relevant consideration . . . it was reasonable for the firm to act in that way'.[55] The firm must 'take into account such factors as: price transparency; liquidity; volatility; the size and time of the transaction; any special circumstances relating to the transaction; and market conditions generally',[56] thus producing 'a price which is fair and reasonable to the customer'.[57] For the purpose of such 'reasonable care', a firm:

---

[53] IMRO Rules, 17 February 1987, Chapter IV, Rule 2.03.
[54] TSA Rules, July 1987, Guide to Conduct of Business Rules, para. 23.
[55] COBS, TSA, Draft 8 May 1987, Rule 18(9).
[56] Amendments to rules proposed to be brought into effect on 1 July, AFBD, June 1988, Rule 5.5.1, Practice Note.   [57] TSA BN 41, 11 November 1988, Sched. 1, para. 2.04.

(a) should disregard any [disclosed] charges and commissions...
(b) need not have access to competing exchanges [on which the investments are also traded] ... but if a firm can access ... different exchanges and trading platforms ... it should execute ... at the best price available...
(c) should pass on to the customer the price at which it executes...
(d) should not take a [principal] mark-up or mark-down from a price at which it executes as agent unless it executes as a principal and discloses it in the confirm.[58]

Moreover, the firm had to apply best execution to each investment in a programme trade and was treated as achieving best execution in shares traded on the LSE's SETS if it executed at the SETS price (FSA PM COB 7.5.6, 7.5.9). With investments traded on-exchange, while 'a firm can comply with th[e] rule by dealing at the best price displayed at the time'[59] because '[i]n markets where there is a single or central exchange, the comparison is the exchange price',[60] alternatively 'the firm [can] itself ... [be] the execution venue and counterparty to the customer ... [in which case the] firm ... must ... compl[y] ... with the best execution obligation. While any firm is able to internalise a transaction, it generally does so by reference to external prices ... So ... a firm's decision to internalise the transaction in no way diminishes its responsibility to review the execution alternatives available.'[61] As regards unlisted securities and OTC instruments, including derivatives, the regulators' formal position has always been that where it is 'not ... possible for a firm to survey the entire market [for example, because of the lack of transparency] ... a firm which surveys a representative sample of available sources will have made a sufficient effort',[62] but 'SFA would not consider that a firm has taken reasonable care to ascertain the best price available for a particular unlisted security where the firm approaches only one price source ... unless that source is the only one reasonably available in the market. In assessing reasonable care, firms should be aware of the danger of using a basis price as a reference point'.[63] '[I]n ... an over-the-counter ... market, the practice ... is to obtain three quotes from different market makers.'[64] Thus, 'some OTC derivative products ... may not be

---

[58] Hence, a net contract note (which shows the price dealt without splitting out the firm's mark-up/down from the best execution price) could not be issued to a customer to whom best execution was owed, only to an Intermediate Customer who waived best execution (FSA PM COB 8.1.15(11)(c)). Similarly, where best execution is owed a net contract note cannot be issued under MiFID (COBS 16, Ann. 1, Item 13).
[59] SIB Conduct Rules, Draft February 1986, Explanatory Memorandum, 3.19.
[60] Best execution, FSA DP, April 2001, para. 4.18.
[61] FSA CP 154, October 2002, paras 5.27, 5.28, 5.30.
[62] SIB Conduct Rules, 7 October 1987, Rule 5.04, Practice Note 1.
[63] SFA BN 485, 14 August 1998, pp. 2–3.
[64] Best Execution, FSA DP, April 2001, para. 4.18.

easy to assess in terms of best execution. It may not be possible to obtain a number of different price quotes. Firms may restrict the availability of [such] products . . . to . . . [Intermediate] customers . . . so that the best execution obligation can be waived.'[65]

MiFID: FSA has always considered the best execution rule criteria to be too narrow because '[c]ertain non-price aspects of order execution . . . can impact on price', '[e]xisting policy . . . does not require firms to have access to all available execution venues (or even a minimum number)' and '[an Intermediate] customer may waive . . . best execution . . . The original rationale . . . was that, in return, a customer may be able to negotiate finer rates or perhaps lower costs . . . [but they] rarely seek to forego their rights . . . on this basis. On the contrary, it is usually firms that tend to include the waiver in standard terms of business.'[66] Thus, FSA concluded that the rule 'should be restructured . . . [with] the emphasis . . . on achieving the "best result" . . . [which] involves more than price' and also that the rule should require 'provision of information to consumers on firms' execution arrangements; review [by firms] and, if necessary, changes to those arrangements; and monitoring the quality of execution achieved' and 'the ability for one firm to delegate its responsibility to deliver best execution to another should be removed'.[67] FSA's views are reflected in the two MiFID best execution rules.

Where the firm executes transactions Where the firm, typically a broker–dealer (although it could be a portfolio manager if, for example, it is executing directly onto an exchange through an electronic direct market access system supplied to it by a broker–dealer, or entering into an OTC derivatives transaction with a broker–dealer), 'executes orders' within 13.2.2.1, it 'must take all reasonable steps to obtain . . . the best possible result . . . taking into account . . . the execution factors:

(1) the characteristics of the client including the categorisation . . . as retail or professional; [and]
(2) the characteristics of the client order; [and]
(3) the characteristics of [the] financial instrument . . . [and]
(4) the characteristics of the execution venues to which the order can be directed . . . [being] a regulated market, an MTF, a systematic internaliser, or a market maker or other liquidity provider. (COBS 11.2.1, 11.2.6, 11.2.34)

For Retail Clients 'the best possible result' means 'total consideration, representing the price of the financial instrument and the costs related to execution', i.e. 'execution venue fees, clearing and settlement fees, and any

---

[65] Ibid, para 10.4.   [66] Best Execution, FSA DP, April 2001, paras 6.1, 8.2, 9.2.
[67] FSA CP 154, October 2002, paras 3.4.6, 4.3, 5.15.

other fees paid to third parties involved in the execution of the order',[68] and other factors 'may be given precedence over the immediate price and cost considerations only insofar as they are instrumental in delivering the best possible result in terms of the total consideration'. In contrast, for Professional Clients, although 'ordinarily . . . price will merit a high relative importance' (COBS 11.2.9) 'because in practice the firm is unlikely to be acting reasonably if it gives a low relative importance to the net cost',[69] '[s]peed, likelihood of execution and settlement, the size and nature of the order, market impact and any other implied transaction costs' and other 'considerations relevant to the execution of any order' can more easily override price (COBS 11.2.7, 11.2.8; GLOSS, def. of 'execution factors'). That said, 'in most circumstances price and cost will merit a high relative importance in obtaining the best possible result for professional clients, although there will be circumstances where other factors will be more important . . . [F]irms should weigh the factors in a manner that is appropriate to a particular type of client. For example . . . speed [may be] . . . paramount . . . [for] a hedge fund taking advantage of arbitrage opportunities . . . [C]ertainty of execution may be given a high weighting for highly structured derivative instruments.'[70] Thus, '[p]rice . . . is the first consideration . . . However, the best price . . . may not represent the best possible result . . . if it comes . . . with high costs, such as high . . . custody fees. Conversely . . . a venue that is especially good at managing trading in a fast moving market or trading in size may merit higher cost . . . The 'best price' . . . at a particular size . . . may be less than the size that the client wishes to trade . . . [and] if part of the order is executed at the indicated size, the price for subsequent executions may become less favourable (i.e. the market may "move") . . . Likelihood of execution. The best price [will] be illusory if the venue . . . is unlikely to complete the order. Likelihood of settlement. The best price may be . . . illusory if the venue . . . has a poor record for failed trades . . . [T]he relative importance of the factors . . . will depend on . . . Client characteristics . . . whether they are retail or professional and the nature of the execution services they require . . . For example . . . clients' trading objectives . . . ; Order characteristics . . . including size . . . instrument . . . settlement; and venue characteristics.'[71] In selecting a venue for a Retail Client order 'the firm's own commissions and costs for executing the order . . . must be taken into account' and the 'firm must not structure its commissions . . . to discriminate unfairly between execution venues', i.e. 'charge . . . a different commission or spread . . . that . . . does not reflect actual differences in the cost to the firm of executing on those venues', although the firm 'is not . . . require[d] . . . to compare the results

---

[68] CESR/07–320, May 2007, para. 11.1. This includes implicit costs, firm's charges (FSA PS 07/15, paras. 2.9, 3.12) or mark-up (p. 399, FN 57).   [69] CESR 07/320, para. 11.3.
[70] CESR/07-050b, paras. 29, 30.   [71] CESR CP 04-261b, pp. 72–73.

that would be achieved ... on the basis of its own execution policy and [charges] ... with results that might be achieved ... by any other firm on the basis of a different execution policy or [charges]' (COBS 11.2.10–11.2.13).

Pricing in relation to listed equities is relatively easy. Unlisted instruments with limited liquidity are more difficult and in relation to fixed income dealer markets FSA originally put forward 'a new option referencing dealer prices to robust benchmarks'[72] because of 'concerns about the validity of internal benchmarks in satisfying MIFID's best execution requirements ... [and] the extent to which a firm's internal models might take account of its own risk positions and ... distort the firm's perception of the best possible result'.[73] This was withdrawn because 'firms were strongly negative', which was an understatement, FSA now merely pointing out that 'firms ... [must] take all reasonable steps to obtain the best possible result ... whether or not the firm's quoted price was based on an internal pricing model'.[74] There has to be, in practice, some objectivity, i.e. benchmark, in how the firm derives the price.[75]

The firm must have a written 'order execution policy' which reflects 'arrangements [put in place] for complying with the obligation to take all reasonable steps to obtain the best possible result' and includes 'in respect of each class of financial instruments, information on the different execution venues ... and the factors affecting the choice', 'select[ing] the ... venues that enable [the firm] ... to obtain on a consistent basis the best possible result', and 'the relative importance of the execution factors, or at least ... the process by which [the firm] ... determines the relative importance of these factors' (COBS 11.2.14–11.2.16). Accordingly, the policy must 'set out the strategy of the firm, the key steps the firm is taking to comply with the overarching best execution requirement and how those steps enable the firm to obtain the best possible result'.[76] Although the firm does 'not ... [have] to include in its execution policy all available execution venues' (COBS 11.2.16(4)), this 'mean[s] that firms should include certain venues in their policy, not that the policy can omit other venues used by the firm. A firm may however in exceptional circumstances use venues not listed in its policy, for example ... to accommodate a client request to trade in an unusual instrument.'[77] Moreover, the policy must 'at least ... address the different classes of instruments for which it carries out orders ... (which would need to be further distinguished between exchange-traded ... and OTC products ...)' and 'address the distinction between retail and professional clients to the extent that the firm treats each category ... differently'.[78] In deciding which venues to include, the firm can ignore costs

---

[72] FSA DP 06/3, May 2006, para. 1.20.   [73] FSA CP 06/19, para. 16.47.
[74] Ibid, paras. 16.47, 16.49.   [75] CF. FSA PS 07/15, para. 2.11.
[76] CESR/07-320, May 2007, para. 4.1.   [77] Ibid, para. 4.3.   [78] Ibid, para. 7.3.

and commissions (COBS 11.2.17). There is, however, 'a distinction between the selection of venues to be included in the . . . policy and the choice between . . . venues contained in the policy for the execution of a particular transaction. When selecting venues to be included in its . . . policy, a firm should not take into account the fees and commissions that it will charge . . . [I]t should focus on the quality of execution available on the various venues. When choosing a venue for the execution of a particular client order (from . . . the venues . . . that are capable of executing such an order), the firm should take into account the effect of its own fees and commissions on the total consideration to the client.'[79] Thus, the policy needs to set up a procedural methodology for the firm to use in seeking to achieve the 'best result' such that the execution factors do not need to be applied separately in each transaction, so long as the system has addressed them generally, for example by identifying venue A to be used in transactions for financial instruments type X, and the firm will then have to ensure that front office staff are alert to any particular and unusual circumstances in relation to a particular transaction on that venue. In deciding this, there may be 'more than one trading venue that offers execution . . . on a consistent basis . . . [or] only one . . . venue . . . will deliver the best possible result on a consistent basis'.[80] The firm may 'select . . . only one execution venue if . . . it is able to obtain the best possible result on a consistent basis'[81] and, in any event, the requirement is for the firm to 'ensure that appropriate (execution) policies and/or arrangements are effectively implemented . . . not . . . to obtain the best possible result for each individual order'.[82]

All clients must be 'provide[d with] appropriate information on [the firm's] . . . order execution policy', i.e. a summary, in writing or on a website (8.4.7.1). For Retail Clients it must contain 'an account of the relative importance the firm assigns . . . to the execution factors, or the process by which the firm determines the relative importance of those factors; a list of the execution venues on which the firm places significant reliance . . . [and] a clear . . . warning that any specific instructions from a client [13.2.3.3] may prevent the firm . . . obtain[ing] the best possible result' (COBS 11.2.22, 11.2.23). In contrast, 'the "appropriate" level of information disclosure for Professional Clients is at the discretion of the . . . firm'.[83] The firm itself can be an execution venue, but if so it would not be sufficient merely to state that fact without going on to explain how in practice the firm will benchmark its price against other possible venues, i.e. how it will apply the 'execution factors' to ensure that its own execution is 'best' and,

---

[79] Ibid, paras. 12.1–12.3. Thus, where it deals as agent, the firm's fees and commissions are relevant to the determination of 'best result' (COBS 11.2.7, 11.2.10), as are any mark-up/down it applies where it deals as principal.
[80] CESR/07-050b, February 2007, para. 39.   [81] CESR/07-320, May 2007, para. 8.2.
[82] Ibid, para. 3.3.   [83] Ibid, p. 7.

therefore, that its own proprietary book is a proper choice of venue. The client must agree to the summary, which can be by course of dealing except in relation to 'prior express consent . . . to execute . . . orders outside a regulated market or an MTF' (8.4.7.1) (COBS 11.2.24–11.2.26). Thus 'MiFID aims to strike a balance between . . . disclos[ing] . . . a lengthy trading manual (which would be of limited utility to clients) and a description that is too high level to facilitate client understanding of a firm's execution process', in other words 'firms need to ensure that the execution policy disclosure is sufficient for consent to be valid'.[84]

The obligation generally is to take 'all reasonable steps' to obtain the best possible result and to 'apply . . . [the] execution policy to each client order . . . with a view to obtaining the best possible result . . . in accordance with that policy' (COBS 11.2.1, 11.2.16(3)). Hence, the firm must 'monitor the effectiveness of its . . . policy and assess the . . . venues . . . on a regular basis . . . to identify and, where appropriate, correct any deficiencies' at least annually (COBS 11.2.18, 11.2.27, 11.2.28). Moreover, it 'must be able to demonstrate to its clients, at their request, that it has executed their orders in accordance with its execution policy' (COBS 11.2.29). This has the result that 'information on execution quality will be essential'[85] and, hence, there is a need for appropriate record keeping or at least retrieval from public data systems. The best execution duty is one of reasonable care and this is the only practical way to comply with the fact 'that MiFID does not prescribe any particular method of monitoring . . . [but] indicat[es] that monitoring (and review) are two of the steps that firms should be taking to meet the overarching best execution requirement'.[86]

Portfolio managers and arrangers and transmitters of orders As part of the firm's obligation to 'act in accordance with the best interests of its clients' (9.3), when a portfolio manager or a firm acting as arranger places an order with, or transmits an order to, another firm for execution 'there is a continuum of responsibility'[87] and it must 'take all reasonable steps to obtain the best possible result for its clients', i.e. ensure that the other firm is obliged to provide best execution to it. With an EEA firm this means that the manager/arranger must not accept categorisation as an Eligible Counterparty (13.2.2.5) and with a non-EEA firm requires the imposition of contractual duties to MiFID best execution standards. The firm must also 'establish . . . a policy . . . identify[ing] . . . the entities with which the orders are placed', 'provide appropriate information to . . . clients on the policy' and monitor and review the effectiveness of the policy (COBS 11.2.32). The aim of this so-called 'second tier obligation' is to avoid 'a duplication of effort as to best execution between . . . [the manager/arranger] and any firm

---

[84] CESR/07–050b, paras. 50, 54. Also disclose '[w]here . . . best execution . . . do[es] not apply' (FSA PS 07/15, para. 3.6).   [85] CESR/07-050b, para. 89.
[86] CESR/07-321, p. 9.   [87] Ibid, p. 8.

to which [it] . . . transmits its orders for execution' (COBS 11.2.33). Hence, in a chain of execution there can be, for example, a portfolio manager/arranger subject to this requirement and a broker–dealer acting as agent, and treated as thereby executing the transaction through another broker–dealer which acts either as principal or as exchange member and is itself also treated as executing the transaction. As a result, the two broker–dealers can both owe best execution obligations except insofar as the intermediate broker–dealer is categorised as an Eligible Counterparty.[88] Nonetheless, the second tier obligation is a real one and not merely 'a "transmission" policy' so that 'a firm that transmits an order cannot delegate responsibility for selecting the "best" entities . . . [and must] determine that the entities it uses will enable it to comply with the overarching best execution requirement when placing an order with, or transmitting an order to, another entity for execution', although the manager/arranger's duty 'is relatively less onerous than' the executing firm's which 'is supported by the absence . . . of requirements for client consent [to the policy] and demonstration of compliance'.[89] Like the first tier obligation, the manager/arranger must put in place a policy which 'should set out the strategy of the firm, the key steps the firm is taking to comply with the overarching best execution requirement and how those steps enable the firm to obtain the best possible result', 'set out the entities the firm uses' and 'provide "appropriate information" on its policy to its clients'.[90] Of course, the manager/arranger may on occasion itself execute transactions, in which case it will need a policy complying with both the first tier and second tier obligations.

13.2.3.2 Highly structured transactions

Derivatives transactions structured to the particular circumstances and needs of an institutional client may consist of one or more components which make it very difficult, if not impossible, to apply a concept of best execution. The question is whether the obligation applies.

Pre-MiFID: The obligation applied, in particular because the length of time over which, and circumstances in which, the firm structured the transaction gave rise to fiduciary-type obligations (13.2.2.1), although in practice the criteria were not applied except perhaps to loosely argue that, given the absence of any transparent market benchmark price, the 'reasonable care' obligation was, loosely, discharged.

MiFID: This approach is now expressly sanctioned because 'given the differences in market structure or the structure of financial instruments, it may be difficult to identify and apply a uniform standard . . . for best execution that would be valid and effective for all classes of instrument. Best

---

[88] CESR/07-320, May 2007, paras. 9, 22.   [89] CESR/07-321, May 2007, pp. 3–4.
[90] CESR/07-320, May 2007, paras. 6.2, 6.4, 17.1.

execution obligations should therefore be applied in a manner that takes into account the different circumstances associated with the execution of orders related to particular types of financial instruments. For example, transactions involving a customised OTC financial instrument that involves a unique contractual relationship tailored to the circumstances of the client and the firm may not be comparable for best execution purposes with transactions involving shares traded on centralised execution venues' (COBS 11.2.5). It is, therefore, necessary to price in a way which 'treats the customer fairly' (9.2). This, though, applies only to highly structured transactions 'for which there is practically no liquidity. On the contrary, an OTC plain vanilla option on a single liquid share with a maturity of one month should not be considered as a customised instrument'[91] and nor should a derivative issued as one of the series, all such transactions being 'execution of a customer order' since the firm is on risk and the transaction is within categories (2) and (3) of MiFID Business in 4.2.I(2).

13.2.3.3 Specific instructions

Pre-MiFID: If the client gave specific instructions as to the price at which the transaction was to be executed, then the firm must have used 'reasonable care' within 13.2.3.1 if it executed at that price.

MiFID: It is expressly stated that the 'firm satisfies its obligations . . . to the extent that it executes an order . . . following specific instructions from the client' but, given the wider requirement to achieve 'best result' beyond price, only 'in respect of the . . . aspect of the order to which the client instructions relate'. Thus if, for example, the client specifies a price minimum on a sale, the firm retains its best execution duties as to venue and timing. Obviously, the 'firm should not induce a client to instruct it to execute an order in a particular way . . . when the firm ought reasonably to know that an instruction to that effect is likely to prevent it from obtaining the best possible result' (COBS 11.2.19–11.2.21). Even where the firm did not positively so encourage the client, whether a specific instruction is sensible must always be considered against the 'treat the customer fairly' standard (9.2) before it is accepted and executed.

13.2.3.4 Direct market access

With most Exchange dealing activity occurring remotely through electronic terminals, firms give direct access to their membership to their institutional clients who deal, in the firm's name, direct onto the Exchange. The client may even place the order through some form of algorithmic trading as to timing and quantity of execution. If the firm has a best execution obligation, it cannot in practice discharge it in these circumstances.

---

[91] European Commission Working Document ESC-07–2007, 19 March 2007, para. 12.

Pre-MiFID: In practice, since such clients were always Intermediate Customers, a waiver of best execution was obtained (13.2.2.1). In any event, given the nature of the service, it was hard to see how, as between the customer and the firm, the latter could have been said to 'execute' the transaction within 13.2.2.1.

MiFID: Since the 'client chooses to use a Direct Market Access system, such that he himself selects parameters of the trade . . . the dealer . . . will be treated as having satisfied its duty of best execution to the extent that the client has given specific instructions [within 13.2.3.3] by means of the DMA system'.[92] There may be a 'chain of execution', for example, a portfolio manager uses a broker–dealer's DMA system. Here, the broker–dealer has discharged its best execution responsibilities and the portfolio manager, using DMA, is itself executing the transaction within 13.2.3.1.

13.2.3.5   Single venue transactions

Some client orders are only capable of execution on a single venue, for example a particular LIFFE or LME derivative or a collective investment scheme (the choice between schemes being a suitability issue: 11.2) or even, unless the firm has access to another firm acting as systematic internaliser in that security, a security solely listed on the LSE or a contract for differences or spread bet which the firm offers only in relation to LSE listed securities.

Pre-MiFID: The price to be ascertained in relation to which 'reasonable care' was to be exercised (13.2.3.1) could only have been the price in relation to that single venue.

MiFID: Similarly, the execution factors in relation to which 'reasonable steps' are to be taken can lead only to that single venue.

13.3   Systematic internalisers

13.3.1   Introduction

A firm can deal as principal in one of three ways. First, it can, post-Big Bang (2.4.1), as a broker–dealer, deal with its client either as principal or as agent. Second, as the market maker on an Exchange it might, depending upon how the Exchange operates, deal as principal providing quotes, and thereby liquidity, to other market members, or as a 'specialist' taking up orders if unmatched in the market. And, third, on a more organised basis, it may maintain a significant 'book' of Exchange-traded investments and buy and sell from that book with clients rather than put their orders through the Exchange. As long as conflicts of interest are managed (6.2, 6.3.1), the

---

[92] European Commission Working Document ESC-07-2007, 19 March 2007, para. 11.

FSA, in line with earlier regulators, has never sought to regulate principal dealing, save for one rule which did not survive MiFID and required that where a firm sold to a Private Customer 'any security that is not traded on a . . . regulated market . . . and holds itself out as a market maker in that security' it must undertake to repurchase it for 'a reasonable price . . . [during] a period specified' (FSA PM COB 7.11).

13.3.2 The Investment Services Directive

In drafting the ISD, the Commission always wanted 'a rule aimed at enhancing price transparency by requiring brokers to route orders to organised markets in the absence of client instructions to the contrary',[93] and after long and acrimonious debate over whether it was correct to try to protect the central position of established Exchanges, the compromise was that:

> A Member State may require that transactions . . . must be carried out on a regulated market [14.1] [where]–
>
> – the investor . . . [is] habitually resident or established in that Member State, [and] . . .
> – the transaction . . . involve[s] an instrument dealt in on a regulated market in that Member State.
>
> Where a Member State applies [the last] paragraph . . . it shall give investors . . . the right . . . to . . . have the transactions . . . carried out away from a regulated market . . . subject to [specified conditions]. (1993 ISD 14(3), (4))

In addition, though, 'a Member State may not limit the right of [such] investors . . . to avail themselves of any investment service provided by a . . . firm . . . acting outwith that Member State' under the services passport (1993 ISD, Recital 34), i.e. dealing off-market and cross-border. The UK never imposed any such restriction, although 'LSE member firms are required to report to the LSE their bilateral trades which take place outside' the Exchange,[94] and lobbied for its removal in MiFID. The Commission considered that '[t]he main regulatory motive . . . [i]s to preserve overall market quality and efficient price formation. Widespread off-exchange order matching could reduce interactions between buy and sell interests, thereby rendering price-formation less efficient, increasing spreads and adverse price impacts . . . [since this] activity is not based on an open order book, through which potential trading interests are disclosed to other users.'[95] And for CESR members, although 'the ISD should not dictate market structures', '[t]here is no common view . . . concerning . . . a

---

[93] European Commission Discussion Document XV/839/88-EN, para. 7.
[94] FSA CP 06/14, para. 6.7.
[95] Revision of the ISD, European Commission, Second Consultation, Overview Paper, 25 March 2002, pp. 7, 10.

regulatory concentration requirement. Some members . . . believe that the concentration requirement is . . . important . . . to preserve market efficiency and investor protection. Some members believe that . . . concentration inhibits competition.'[96] The end result was the rules on systematic internalisation explained in 13.3.3 which, since they require the internaliser to make prices round about those of other venues, including the Exchange, (13.3.3.4) may not really represent a practical end to the concentration rule. It is justified by regulators for different reasons:

> MiFID transparency arrangements aim to ensure investors are fully informed as to the true level of potential or actual transactions in shares admitted to trading on an RM, no matter which trading venue is used for . . . execution . . . Furthermore, MiFID recognises that a consistent transparency regime across trading venues is essential to ensure that the price discovery mechanism in respect of shares is not undermined by the fragmentation of liquidity [in different trading venues] and that investors benefit from a high level of information no matter where they trade.[97]

At present the rules apply only to shares traded on regulated markets, 'not to . . . non-equity instruments, such as bonds and derivatives . . . This may be amended as a result of the Commission's review on whether the . . . requirements . . . should be extended to other . . . instruments.'[98]

13.3.3 MiFID

13.3.3.1 'Systematic internalisers'

The rules apply, as explained in 4.2(q), if the firm is a 'systematic internaliser' (MAR 6.1.1), i.e. a 'firm which, on an organised, frequent and systematic basis, deals on own account by executing client orders outside a regulated market [14.1] or an MTF [14.2]' (GLOSS, def. of 'systematic internaliser'). This is decided on a share-by-share basis such that the activity is 'organised, frequent and systematic' if '(a) . . . [it] has a material commercial role for the firm', i.e. 'is a significant source of revenue . . . or cost . . . tak[ing] into account the extent to which the activity is conducted or organised separately, the monetary value of the activity, and its comparative significance by reference both to the overall business of the firm and its overall activity in the market for the share concerned' '(b) the activity is carried out by personnel, or . . . an automated technical system, assigned to that purpose . . . [and] (c) the activity is available to clients on a regular or continuous basis' rather than 'on an ad hoc and irregular bilateral basis' (MAR 6.3.1, 6.3.2) 'carried out with wholesale counterparties and . . . part of a business relationship characterised by dealings above SMS [13.3.3.3] and outside systems used . . .

---

[96] Revision of the ISD, CESR, June 2002, paras. 13, 23.   [97] FSA CP 06/14, para. 16.1.
[98] Ibid, para. 16.5. As regards extension to fixed income markets, see CESR/07-284, May 2007; CESR 07-284b, CESR/07-538; EC Public Hearing, 11 September 2007.

for systematic internalisation'.[99] Although these are not part of the formal criteria, the original intention was that there should be 'both a threshold based on the rates of internalised order value of the firm . . . and a minimum value threshold' so that '[t]he following . . . [are] indicative that a firm is undertaking systematic internalisation . . . (a) the ratio of the value of [the firm's] client orders executed outside the RM or MTF to the total value of [the firm's] executed client orders . . . on a yearly basis is more than 15%; or (b) the ratio of the value of client orders [so] executed . . . to the total value of trading in shares on the most liquid market . . . on a yearly basis is more than 0.5%'.[100]

For this purpose, 'dealing on own account' 'is defined . . . as "trading against proprietary capital resulting in the conclusion of transactions" . . . [I]f a firm enters into matched back-to-back trades to execute a client order, this does not amount to dealing on own account. This contrasts with . . . where a firm enters into a position to execute an order on behalf of a client (at which time it has a[n] . . . "unmatched principal" position . . .) and subsequently hedges its exposure by taking a corresponding position in the market . . . [which is] dealing on own account.'[101] It follows that a firm offering RFQ facilities (13.2.2.1) may not be a systematic internaliser.[102]

FSA must be notified of the shares in which the firm is, or ceases to be, a systematic internaliser (MAR 6.4).

13.3.3.2 'Liquid share'

Notwithstanding that the share is listed, the obligations only apply if it is a 'liquid share' and FSA publishes a list of such UK listed shares on its website (MAR 6.5.1, 6.8.1(1), 6.8.2–6.8.5).[103] The reason is that 'MiFID recognises that SIs will only be able to carry the risks of maintaining a firm quote . . . if the share is sufficiently liquid to enable them to lay off their risk',[104] in other words, this requirement seeks 'the appropriate balance between . . . helping to integrate separate/fragmented liquidity pools, aid competitive price formation and lower search costs for participants . . . [and the] need to take into account the risks borne by systematic internalisers as a result of being required to continuously display quotes'.[105] FSA's determination is constrained by MiFID itself under which shares 'will [only] be considered to have a liquid market if they meet . . . quantitative criteria . . . that a share be traded daily and have a free float market capitalisation of at least €500 million . . . [and] an average daily number of transactions of at least 500 or an average daily turnover of at least €2 million . . . Under the[se] criteria . . . there would be about 500 European "liquid"

---

[99] FSA CP 06/14, para. 16.14.   [100] CESR/05-290b, April 2005, pp. 59–60.
[101] FSA CP 06/14, para. 6.11.   [102] FSA PS 07/2, para. 12.10.
[103] For liquid shares on all EU regulated markets, see CESR/07-450 and CESR/07-322, 3 July 2007.   [104] FSA CP 06/14, para. 16.17.   [105] CESR/04-562, October 2004, para. 64.

shares, of which UK shares would account for about a quarter.'[106] A free float means the shares are held by 'investors who are willing to sell them at any time without restriction',[107] thus excluding the holdings of pension funds, mutual funds and insurance companies. While this 'is not a perfect liquidity measure in that it is not focused on the more traditional liquidity dimensions (tightness, immediacy, depth, breadth, resilience, etc) . . . it . . . [is] a valuable proxy variable (and more valuable than straight market capitalisation) to identify the top liquid shares'.[108]

If it is a systematic internaliser, but 'there is no liquid market, the internaliser must disclose quotes to its clients on request' (MAR 6.5.2).

13.3.3.3 'Standard market size' (SMS)

Even if the firm would otherwise satisfy the definition of 'systematic internaliser', the rules will not apply if it only ever deals in that share in sizes larger than its SMS (MAR 6.1.1, 6.3.1(3)). FSA publishes on its website the SMS for each London listed share (MAR 6.8.1(3), 6.8.2) and this is calculated by reference to the average value of transactions (AVT) over the preceding 12 months. For example, if the AVT is under €10,000, then the SMS is €7,500; if between €10,000 and €20,000, it is €15,000; if between €70,000 and €90,000, it is €80,000 (MAR 6.8.6, 6.8.7).[109]

13.3.3.4 Publication of quotes

As regards price formation, the price quoted 'must reflect the prevailing market conditions for that share', i.e. be 'close in price to comparable quotes . . . in other trading venues' (MAR 6.7.1, 6.7.2(a)). 'For instance, if the share is . . . traded on the LSE order book . . . [FSA] would expect that the SI's quote would be as close to the best bid or offer on the LSE order book for the quantity of stock in question.'[110]

The firm must publish one or more firm bid or offer prices 'up to standard market size', which it 'may . . . update . . . at any time' but only 'under exceptional market conditions, withdraw a quote' (MAR 6.5.1–6.6.3). 'The quote can be in any size, from one share up to the SMS . . . While there is no obligation . . . to quote in size above SMS, firms may do so.'[111] Actual publication must be 'on a regular and continuous basis during normal trading hours . . . and . . . in a manner which is easily accessible to other market participants on a reasonable commercial basis . . . as close to real time as possible', which means 'as close to instantaneously as technically possible' (MAR 6.9.1–6.9.3). This is satisfied 'if it is made available . . . through . . . the facilities of a regulated market or an MTF . . . [or] the facilities of a third party . . . [or] proprietary arrangements' as long as the arrangements

---

[106] FSA CP 06/14, paras. 16.20–16.21.   [107] CESR/05-291b, April 2005, p. 45.
[108] Ibid, pp. 44–45.   [109] FSA CP 06/14, para. 16.23. See also CESR/07-322, July 2007.
[110] FSA CP 06/14, para. 16.19.   [111] Ibid, para. 16.18.

used 'facilitate the consolidation of the data with . . . data from other sources . . . [and] make[s] the information available to the public on a non-discriminatory commercial basis at a reasonable cost' (MAR 6.9.4).[112]

13.3.3.3.5 Accepting clients

The firm 'might decide to give access to . . . quotes only to retail clients, only to professional clients, or to both . . . [but can]not . . . discriminate within those categories of clients', particular investors being given access 'in an objective, non-discriminatory way . . . on the basis of [a] policy, including considerations such as . . . investor credit status; . . . counter-party risk; and final settlement of the transaction' (MAR 6.13).

13.3.3.3.6 Dealing price

With Retail Clients, the order must be executed as follows:

- If the order is in that size: at the price quoted.
- If the order is bigger than the highest quotation size, but smaller than SMS: 'that part of the order which exceeds the quotation size must . . . be executed at the quoted price'.
- If the order is between two quoted sizes: 'at one of the quoted prices' in compliance with the rules referred to in 13.1.3, 13.1.4.2, 13.1.4.4 and 13.2.3 and the limit order rule referred to in 13.1.4.4 (MAR 6.10.1, 6.12).

'This means that the SI cannot offer an improved price to retail clients. This rule aims to prevent the SI from discriminating between small investors, for example, by offering some of them undisclosed improvements to the prices it has publicly quoted.'[113]

As regards Professional Clients, the order must be executed as follows:

- If the order is in that size: at the price quoted or at a better price if (1) it is a portfolio trade (MAR 6.11) since '[i]t would be impracticable for SIs to conduct such transactions on the basis of the price they were quoting for any share in the basket . . . because portfolio transactions are normally priced as a percentage of the aggregate (and at the time unknown) mid-market value of the constituent stocks'[114] or (2) 'the order is . . . neither an order for . . . execution . . . at the prevailing market price, nor a limit order [within 13.1.4.4]' (MAR 6.11),[115] which 'allow[s] for the complex orders used by professional investors that are often executed on the basis of factors other than

---

[112] See, generally, CESR/07-043 and CESR 07-086, February 2007.
[113] FSA CP 06/14, para. 16.26.   [114] Ibid, para. 6.30.
[115] The rationale for this exception is that if '[a] systematic internaliser receives a limit order executable only at a more competitive price than its current quote, it should be required to modify its quote if it wishes to execute the limit order' (CESR/05-291b, April 2005, p. 50).

immediacy and the prevailing market price', for example 'an order for which the execution price is determined as an average of prices throughout the day (e.g. a volume weighted average price order) cannot be executed at the price quoted at the time the order is received'[116] or (3) the order is bigger than €7,500 and the better price 'falls within a published range close to market conditions' (MAR 6.11). 'This figure represents the size of order that MiFID has determined should be considered as that customarily undertaken by retail investors.'[117]

- If the order is bigger than the highest quotation size, but smaller than SMS: 'that part of the order which exceeds the quotation size must . . . be executed at the quoted price' or at a better price as permitted under the last point.
- If the order is between two quoted sizes: at one of the quoted prices as referred to above for Retail Clients or at a better price as permitted under the first point (MAR 6.11, 6.12).

For this purpose, a Professional Client can be treated as such 'irrespective of whether that client is acting for an underlying retail investor'. Thus, for example, '[i]ntroducing brokers . . . [can] aggregate orders, which may enable them to trade with SIs in sizes greater than €7,500 . . . [and] the ability to secure price improvement would be a factor which brokers could take into account in implementing their best execution . . . policies' (13.2.3.1).[118]

13.3.3.7 Deals undertaken

The firm can limit the number of transactions it undertakes both with an individual client (as long as it does it 'in a non-discriminatory way' based on matters such as credit rating and available inventory) and clients generally (again 'in a non-discriminatory way' set out in a published policy), if the firm 'cannot execute . . . [the number of] orders received without exposing itself to undue risk . . . [based on] the volume of . . . transactions, the capital . . . available to cover the risk . . . and the prevailing conditions in the market' (MAR 6.14).

13.4 Reporting

13.4.1 Trade reporting

As part of the market mechanism for the formation of prices, or the so-called post-trade transparency requirement, in relation to shares admitted to trading on a regulated market (14.1) there are two requirements. First,

---

[116] FSA CP 06/14, paras. 16.29, 16.31.   [117] Ibid, para. 16.28.
[118] Ibid, paras. 16.27–16.28.

the market itself must 'make public the price, volume and time of . . . transactions executed' while allowing 'deferred publication . . . in respect of transactions that are large in scale compared with the normal market size' (MiFID, Art. 45) 'between a . . . firm dealing on own account and a client of that firm . . . as they may be less easy to execute efficiently in a fully transparent environment. In particular, an intermediary that puts capital at risk to facilitate a large client trade may be disadvantaged if details of its position are published before it has had time to lay off . . . that risk. The new rules aim to ensure that the delay is no longer than is reasonably needed for a firm to work off its risk. This means that the minimum trade size qualifying for deferred publication, as well as the length of delay, will differ, depending on the liquidity of the stock . . . measured by the average daily volume of trading in that share.'[119] This is to accommodate block trades. The LSE, for example, has had rules on trade reporting and deferred publication for decades but these MiFID requirements necessitate some changes to those rules.[120]

Second, where a UK, EEA or non-EEA firm 'either on its own account or on behalf of clients, concludes transactions in shares admitted to trading on a regulated market outside a regulated market or MTF . . . in the United Kingdom', then it 'must make public the volume and price of those transactions and the time at which they were concluded' (MAR 7.1). In the absence of agreement between the parties, the obligation falls on the first firm in the following list involved in the transaction that is within the rule's application: seller as principal, seller as agent, buyer as agent, buyer as principal (MAR 7.2.5). Thus, unlike Pre-MiFID, an investment manager can find that it has to trade report, for example if a share listed on both the LSE and the New York Stock Exchange is sold to the manager by a US broker–dealer. The information must 'be made public as close to real-time as possible', i.e. within three minutes, subject to permitted deferred publication (MAR 7.2.1, 7.2.6–7.2.10; MAR 7, Ann. 1) and the FSA's Rules set out the detailed contents necessary and how they are to be made public, including through the services of a new status of Trade Data Monitor (MAR 7.2.2–7.2.5, 7.2.12, 7.2.12A, 7.2.14).[121]

---

[119] Ibid, paras. 14.40–14.41. For policy in relation to fixed income markets, see Non-Equity Market Transparency, European Securities Markets Expert Group (ESME), June 2007.

[120] MiFID Service and Technical Description, LSE, June 2007, section 3.3. See also LSE Notice N57/07, 1 August 2007.

[121] For the policy, see FSA CP 06/14, paras. 16.71–16.87; FSA PS 07/2, Chapter 13; FSA CP 07/16, Chapter 6 and Ann. 2. See also CESR/07-043 and CESR/07-086 of February 2007.

13.4.2 Transaction reporting

To support regulators' anti-market abuse efforts (12.5), and monitoring of compliance with transaction execution rules, MiFID requires reporting to FSA of transactions 'executed' as principal or agent (13.2.2.1), and not merely arranged (3.2.2.2),[122] in 'any financial instrument admitted to trading on a regulated market or a prescribed market [for market abuse purposes: 12.5.1] (whether or not the transaction was carried out on such a market) . . . or in any OTC derivative the value of which is derived from, or which is otherwise dependent upon, an equity or debt-related financial instrument which is admitted to trading on a regulated market or on a prescribed market' (SUP 17.1.4). This includes options, futures and CFDs, including spread bets, (3.2.1.6–3.2.1.8) not only over such instruments but also over indices some part of which relate to such instruments. That said, even though they are transactions in MiFID financial instruments, stock-borrows and repo's are not reportable. Only the opening of transactions is reportable, although 'transaction' should be widely construed to include, for example, '[t]he movement, relocation or transfer of financial instruments' (SUP 17.1.7). '[T]ransaction means a purchase and sale . . . and excludes . . . securities financing transactions; exercise of options or of covered warrants as well as primary market transactions' (SUP 17.1.1; GLOSS, def. of 'transaction'), but would include the purchase and sale of depository receipts (3.2.1.4) over such traded instruments. Moreover, CESR Members have agreed 'to collect . . . [only] the following: (a) Information relating to transactions conducted by . . . firms transacting directly with an execution venue (immediate market facing firms) . . . [and] (b) . . . transactions . . . where the . . . firm is undertaking the transaction for its own account (regardless of whether . . . executed on RM or MTF or outside them)', subject to review in 2009.[123] On this basis there would be a transaction reporting obligation where the firm used a non-EEA broker to execute a transaction locally in a dual (EEA and non-EEA) listed stock.[124]

The MiFID requirements differ from FSA's Pre-MiFID transaction reporting rules in two respects. First, 'as well as equity and debt instruments admitted to trading on a regulated market, reportable transactions . . . now include commodity derivatives, interest rate derivatives and foreign exchange derivatives contracts that are admitted to trading[125] . . . MiFID is also narrower . . . by requiring only transactions in financial instruments admitted to trading . . . to be reported . . . [rather than the Pre-MiFID] requirement to report transactions in non-EU securities that are not

---

[122] Market Watch 22, FSA, August 2007, p. 3.
[123] CESR/07–301, May 2007, pp. 5–6. See also: TRUP, p. 11; Market Watch 22, p. 6.
[124] Market Watch 22, p. 6.
[125] FSA is not implementing this, relying instead on an Exchange feed (TRUP, p. 9)

admitted to trading on an RM.' However, '[t]o avoid possible . . . blind spots in our monitoring of reportable transactions, we . . . propose . . . continued reporting of transactions in instruments admitted to trading on exchanges outside of the EEA the value of which is derived from, or otherwise dependent upon, an equity or debt related instrument admitted to trading on a UK regulated market or prescribed market'.[126] Second, 'MiFID . . . change[s] . . . requirements regarding Home State reporting . . . [Pre-MiFID] EEA passported branches . . . [were] required to report to their Home State. MiFID changes this so that EEA passported branches . . . [are] required to report to their Host State in respect of transactions executed . . . within the territory where the branch is established',[127] which could result in 'potential practical difficulties' for passported branches if 'all transactions executed . . . within the territory of the Member State where the branch is located, shall be reported to the Host . . . State . . . whereas other transactions shall be reported to the home Member State'. Accordingly, 'all transactions executed by branches could be reported to the host Member State . . . if the . . . firm elects to do so. In these cases transaction reports should follow the rules of the competent authority to which the report is made'.[128]

The obligation applies only to 'transactions executed in the United Kingdom' by a UK, EEA or non-EEA firm, including acting as manager of a CIS or pension scheme (SUP 17.1.1, 17.1.5), even if the transaction is booked to another location or entity (13.2.2.2). This includes a firm providing portfolio management services in the course of which it 'executes' transactions, but it 'may rely on a third party acting on the firm's behalf to make a transaction report to the FSA' (SUP 17.2.1) 'provided it has reasonable grounds to be satisfied that the other party (typically a sell-side broker) will make a transaction report to [FSA] or to another competent authority which, as to contents, will include all such information as would have been contained in a transaction report by the firm'.[129]

Reports must be made 'as quickly as possible and by not later than the close of the working day following the day upon which that transaction took place' and can be made through an approved 'reporting channel', FSA rules specifying the information to be filed (SUP 17.2–17.4).[130]

---

[126] FSA CP 06/14, paras. 17.11–17.12; FSA CP 07/16, para. 5.3. This is delayed until 2008 (Market Watch 22, p. 5).   [127] FSA CP 06/14, para. 17.29; TRUP, p. 12.
[128] CESR/07–301, May 2007, pp. 3–4. See also FSA CP 07/16, para. 5.5. This results from MiFID, Art. 32(7) (4.2(e)(i)).   [129] FSA PS 07/2, para. 14.8.
[130] See CESR/06–648b, December 2006; CESR/07–043, CESR 07–047, CESR/07–086 of February 2007; Market Watch 18, FSA December 2006; Market Watch 20, FSA, May 2007, p. 4; TRUP, Chapter 6; Industry Transaction Reporting-Assumptions, BBA, ICMA, 24 July 2007; Market Watch 22, FSA, August 2007, p. 3.

13.4.3 Reporting to clients

13.4.3.1 Confirms

See 13.1.4.6.

13.4.3.2 Periodic reporting

Pre-MiFID: Where a firm manages a client's investments then, commercially, it will need to give the client periodically statements of the assets managed and performance. Specific regulatory requirements on the periodacy and contents were imposed in the 1983 LDRs and carried over under both the 1986 FSAct and FSMA (FSA PM COB 8.2). Simplistically, the regulator can only build on the following formulation:

Initial value of portfolio at start of period	a
Plus assets added to portfolio during period	b
Less assets paid out/transferred during period	(c)
Plus income received	d
Less costs	(e)
Plus/Less valuation differences on assets at end of period	f/(f)
Value at end of period	g
	===

MiFID: Similarly, the requirements for a periodic statement are applied to 'a firm managing investments on behalf of the client', whether a Professional or Retail Client (8.2.1), although with the latter timing and contents are specified (COBS 16.3.1–16.3.3),[131] with special provisions for contingent liability derivatives transactions (COBS 16.3.6–16.3.9). One issue has always been so-called hold mail arrangements where 'long-standing clients . . . do not want to be "bothered by too many documents": in these cases the client executive acts as a filter to prevent "unwanted" information from reaching the client'[132] although, as with the Pre-MiFID Rules for Private Clients (even though Intermediate Customers were allowed to contract out: FSA PM COB 8.2.6(1)), this is permitted only with 'a client habitually resident outside the United Kingdom if the client . . . has so requested or the firm has taken reasonable steps to establish that he does not wish to receive it' (COBS 16.3.10(1)). Statements can, of course, be sent to a third party agent for the client (COBS 2.4.9).

A further statement, which can combined where portfolio management is carried on, must be sent by any 'firm that holds client . . . investments or client money' (7.1, 7.2) (COB 16.4).

---

[131] In respect of these requirements FSA withdrew its super-equivalent Notification under Article 4 of FSA, January 2007 (FSA PS 07/14, Chapter 7).
[132] SFA Briefing 5, May 1993, section 2.

14
Exchanges and MTFs

14.1 Regulated markets

MiFID allows regulated markets to themselves 'passport' by setting up branches in other Member States and allowing remote membership to firms from other Member States (MiFID Art. 33). As a result, there are detailed requirements as to authorisation of such markets, their controllers and systems and controls, trading of financial instruments, access rights and so-called 'pre-trade transparency', i.e. publication of bid and offer prices, and 'post-trade transparency' (13.4.1) (MiFID Arts. 33–47; Level 2 Regulation).[1]

Transactions between members of regulated markets are not themselves subject to most of the conduct rules (COBS 1, Ann. 1, Part 5, para. 4.1).

14.2 Multi-lateral Trading Facilities (Alternative Trading Systems)

14.2.1 The need for separate regulation

The operator of an ATS or MTF always required a license/authorisation under FSMA and its predecessor 1986 FSAct (3.2.2.7) and, accordingly, if operated by an Exchange, came within its exempt 'recognised investment exchange' (RIE) status (FSMA 285) or, if operated by a firm, under its general authorisation. However, because they were really quasi-exchanges, FSA perceived that such systems 'pose risks to our . . . objectives' (2.5.1), all of market confidence ('little public transparency of ATS activity leading to possible inefficiencies in the price formation process and so higher trading costs; variations in the extent to which operators comply with good practice in systems and controls, the monitoring of user activity, and arrangements for reporting of suspect transactions; and the possibility of traders trading in

---

[1] UK Implementation: The FSMA 2000 (Recognition Requirements for Investment Exchanges and Clearing Houses) (Amendment) Regulations 2006, SI 2006/3386; FSA CP 06/14, Chapter 14; The Markets (MiFID) Instrument 2007/13, FSA, Ann. E, amendments to REC; CESR/05-290b, April 2005. LSE rules: MiFID Service and Technical Description, LSE, June 2007; Notices N57/07, N63/07. See also Corporate governance of recognised bodies, FSA open letter, 8 June 2007; Investment Exchanges and Clearing Houses Act 2006; Notification Obligations under Act 2006, FSA CP, June 2007. UK regulated markets under MiFID will be the recognised investment exchanges (12.5.1, FN 89). Commodities markets: CESR/07-429, pp. 56–63.

transparent markets on the basis of information from trades only known to direct users of non-transparent ATSs, to the disadvantage of participants in the wider market'), consumer protection ('best execution where some activity is conducted on non-transparent ATSs') and financial crime ('lack of transparency of ATS trading, and the lack of a systematic approach to the monitoring and reporting of suspect transactions').[2] FESCO, the predecessor of CESR, saw exactly the same issues in the wider European context of the 'need to . . . maintain . . . an appropriate regulatory framework, that not only supports competition . . . but is also capable of addressing . . . new risks to investor protection, market integrity and financial stability' given '[i]ncreased competition in the provision of trading services, including the emergence of ATSs, [which] might lead to fragmentation of previously centralised markets into separate pools of liquidity',[3] '[t]he trend towards more automated, multilateral trading facilities . . . be[ing] . . . driven by market pressure to reduce transaction costs'.[4] With, for example, an 'MTF share market . . . unlike RM share markets, responsibility for . . . admission requirements [of shares to trading] . . . and enforcing continuing obligations on issuers, falls to the MTF. This means . . . that the MTF needs to monitor trading . . . for indications that price-sensitive information may be leaking into the market' and it can be difficult for 'a commercial organisation to watch over a share that trades on multiple venues (and which also may be traded via derivatives) . . . MiFID specifies no detailed transparency requirements for trading MTF shares . . . in contrast to . . . RM shares . . . [W]hile MTFs will be responsible only for trading on their own facilities, fragmentation of trading . . . could result in them having insufficient information on activity in the broader marketplace to assess . . . any disordliness in their own markets.'[5]

Under MiFID, the MTF has passporting rights (3.2.2.7).

14.2.2 Regulatory standards

As a result of these policy concerns, the rule requirements imposed on firms that operate ATSs/MTFs convert them into quasi-exchange regulators.

14.2.2.1 Systems and controls

Pre-MiFID: All of the infrastructure rules were imposed (5.2–5.5) (FSA PM MAR 5.5.3) because the 'firm . . . should be able to demonstrate . . . that the system is capable of delivering the proposed service, that there are satisfactory arrangements for the management of the technical operation

---

[2] FSA CP 153, October 2002, paras. 2.5–2.7.
[3] FESCO/00-064c, September 2000, paras. 3, 48. Cf. the debate on systematic internalisation: 13.3.1, 13.3.2.
[4] Trading transparency in the UK secondary bond markets, FSA DP, September 2005, para. 2.35.
[5] Trading of MTF shares: impact of proposed stamp duty changes, FSA DP 07/3, July 2007.

of [the] system and that there are satisfactory contingency arrangements in the event of system disruption' and, in particular, 'that there is clarity of obligations and responsibilities for the clearing . . . and settlement of transactions'.[6] Beyond this, the firm had to 'establish trading arrangements that result in fair and orderly trading', i.e. 'efficient pricing and the equitable treatment of users', and 'monitor user compliance with the contractual rules of the system'.[7]

MiFID: Although 'in practical terms there will be no substantive change for ATS operators covered by [the Pre-MiFID] provisions',[8] MiFID articulates these requirements in greater detail and, thus, while continuing to apply the infrastructure rules in 5.2–5.5 (MiFID Arts. 13, 14.1), the firm 'must have: (1) transparent and non-discriminatory rules and procedures for fair and orderly trading; (2) objective criteria for the efficient execution of orders . . . (4) transparent rules, based on objective criteria, governing access to its facility, which . . . provide that its members . . . are . . . [licensed] firms [or banks] . . . or other persons who . . . are fit and proper . . . [and] have a sufficient level of trading ability and competence . . . [and] have sufficient resources for the role they are to perform . . . and (5) . . . provide . . . sufficient publicly available information to enable its users to form an investment judgement' and 'clearly inform . . . users of their . . . responsibilities for the settlement of transactions . . . and . . . have in place the arrangements necessary to facilitate the efficient settlement of . . . transactions' (MAR 5.3.1, 5.4.1). 'MiFID allows . . . MTF operators to establish arrangements with central counterparties, clearing houses and settlement systems from other Member States.'[9] Thus, 'MTF operators . . . [are] required to establish transparent rules governing access to their facilities (equivalent to those required for RMs) and the financial instruments that can be traded on those facilities'.[10] The specific MTF rules apply as in Chapter 4.2(s).

14.2.2.2 Conduct rules

Pre-MiFID: The ATS operator had to comply with the Principles (9.1), while 'not[ing] . . . that some Principles are (partially) disapplied for clients that are market counterparties', and with all of the relevant conduct rules (6.3.1, 6.3.2, 6.3.3, 6.3.7, 8.3), including in particular terms of business (8.4), unless either its sole members were Market Counterparties or its sole business was operating an ATS, in which case substantially reduced rules applied (FSA PM MAR 5.5.3; FSA PM COB 1.2.1(2A), 4.2.17).

MiFID: Although operating an MTF is, as well as MiFID Business (4.2.I(2)), also Regulated Activity within 3.2.2.1 (if the MTF acts as agent) or 3.2.2.2 (if

---

[6] CESR/02-086b, July 2002, Standards 6, 7; FSA PM MAR 5.4.2.
[7] Ibid, Standards 1, 4; FSA PM MAR 5.4.2.   [8] FSA CP 06/14, para. 15.6.
[9] Ibid, para. 15.8.   [10] Ibid, para. 15.7.

it acts as arranger), FSA has disapplied most of the conduct rules as required by MiFID (MiFID Art. 14(3); COBS, App. 1, Part 1, paras. 2.1, 3.1). This leaves only Inducements (6.3.2), Soft Commission (6.3.3), Personal Account Dealing (6.3.7) and Client Categorisation (8.3), as well as the Principles (9.1) (on the usual cut down basis where a UK passported branch of an EEA firm/bank is concerned (9.1.2.3) (PRIN 4.1.4)) to be complied with. Thus, for example, the best execution rule is disapplied, but where participants in the system include Private Clients, would the 'treat the customer fairly' Principle (9.2) require Eligible Counterparty participants to apply best execution?

14.2.2.3 Market conduct

Pre-MiFID: All of the market conduct rules (12.1–12.6) applied to the way the system operated and the conduct it permitted (FSA PM MAR 5.5.3) because, more broadly, the 'firm . . . should . . . establish arrangements . . . to facilitate satisfactory monitoring of the markets in the instruments traded and the detection of market abuse' and if the ATS was 'trading in an investment traded on a regulated market . . . [it must] make publicly available . . . information about quotes and/or orders . . . [and] completed transactions' (FSA PM MAR 5.4.2).[11]

MiFID: The Market Conduct rules (12) continue to apply and, in addition, there are detailed rules requiring the operator to:

- 'regular[ly] monitor . . . the compliance by its users with its rules . . . and . . . monitor the transactions undertaken by its users . . . in order to identify breaches of those rules, disorderly trading conditions or conduct that may involve market abuse' (MAR 5.5.1). Thus, the MTF operator is required to be a regulator of its members who are no longer, solely, in a customer relationship under 14.2.2.2. This requires the operator to have both systems to prevent its MTF being used for market abuse in the first place (which given the width and unpredictability of the offence is challenging with an electronic system), and also to monitor transactions after the event, if only because the operator 'must . . . report to the FSA . . . disorderly trading conditions . . . and conduct that may involve market abuse' (MAR 5.6.1). In practice, FSA's sympathy for the operator in these situations may only go so far; and
- publicise prices on the system for quotes and orders (pre-trade transparency) and price, volume and time of transactions executed (post-trade transparency), whether or not the instruments are also traded on a regulated market (MAR 5.3.2–5.3.8, 5.7–5.9), although limited waivers are available.[12]

---

[11] CESR/02-086b, July 2002, Standards 3, 5.
[12] FSA CP 06/14, para. 15.11; FSA PS 07/2, para. 11.6.

14.3 Clearing services

Transactions conducted on a regulated market require, for efficient exchange of cash against title, a clearing house which takes responsibility for the processing, clearing and settlement of transactions. To reduce counterparty risk during the period after the transaction has been matched (i.e. confirmed as to parties and terms) and before it is settled, usually the clearing house receives a novation of the contract, thus becoming a principal seller to the buyer and a principal buyer from the seller, so that the firms exchange counterparty risk on each other for (minimal) credit risk on the clearing house. MiFID provides 'passporting' rights to the regulated markets (14.1) but effects only limited changes in respect of clearing houses so that:

> Member States shall require that investment firms from other Member States have the right of access to central counterparty, clearing and settlement systems in their territory for the purposes of finalising ... transactions ... Member States shall require that [such] access ... be subject to the same non-discriminatory, transparent and objective criteria as apply to local participants ... Member States shall not prevent regulated markets from entering into appropriate arrangements with a ... clearing house ... of another Member State. (MiFID Arts. 34, 46)

Yet, '[c]ross-border clearing and settlement requires access to systems in different countries and/or the interaction of different settlement systems', without which 'fragmentation in the EU clearing and settlement infrastructure complicates significantly the post-trade processing of cross-border securities transactions relative to domestic transactions', one significant barrier being '[n]ational restrictions on the location of clearing and settlement [which] typically require investors to use the national system'.[13] Accordingly, for many years a specific Directive was envisaged, although now a European Code of Conduct has been entered into between clearing systems which, as an industry solution, is intended 'to offer market participants the freedom to choose their preferred provider of [clearing] services ... and to make the concept of "cross-border" redundant for transactions between EU Member States'.[14] Only time will tell if an industry solution is really possible.

---

[13] Cross-Border Clearing and Settlement Arrangements in the EU, The Giovannini Group, November 2001, pp. (i), (ii), 46.

[14] European Code of Conduct for Clearing and Settlement, Federation of European Securities Exchanges, European Association of Central Counterparty Clearing Houses, European Central Securities Depositaries Association, 7 November 2006. See also The Second Giovannini Report, April 2003; Clearing and Settlement: The Way Forward, Charlie McCreevy, European Commissioner, 11 July 2006.

PART V
Application of rules to particular businesses

15
Corporate finance

15.1 Regulatory status

The commercial activities of new issues and M&A/takeovers (2.4.4(6), (7), (9)), together with general advice and counselling to corporations and public bodies, are reflected in the scope of MiFID Business covered by the Directive set out in 4.2.I(2):

- New issues
  Investment services and activities:
    (3) 'Dealing on own account'
    (6) 'Underwriting . . . and/or placing on a firm commitment basis'
    (7) 'Placing without a firm commitment basis'
  Ancillary services:
    (6) 'Services related to underwriting'
- M&A/takeovers
  Ancillary services:
    (3) 'Advice and services relating to mergers and the purchase of undertakings'
- General advice and counselling
  Ancillary services:
    (3) 'Advice to undertakings on capital structure' (MiFID Ann. 1, Section A, paras. (3), (6), (7); Section B, paras. (3), (6)).

A similar result was reached, Pre-MiFID, by the definition of Regulated Activities (4.2.I(1)), although this applies to corporate finance, the regulated activity of 'arranging deals' (3.2.2.2) and, in any event, a recommendation not to sell in a defence document is not 'investment advice' (3.2.2.3).

15.2 Infrastructure rules

As a result, a licence (authorisation) is required, bringing with it compliance with all of the infrastructure rules (5.2–5.5), including conflicts of interest (6.3.1) where there are particular requirements for corporate finance (6.3.5), and inducements (6.3.2).[1]

---

[1] For the policy, see FSA CP 06/19, para. 5.3.

15.3 Conduct rules

15.3.1 Pre-MiFID

It is misconceived to apply to corporate finance activities the full rigour of conduct rules since their starting point has always been Private Clients involved in Secondary Markets. On the one side, the corporate client of the investment bank is so large and sophisticated that the content of such rules as best execution and suitability is inappropriate; and, on the other side, the third party investors who buy investments in the course of the particular corporate finance operation have no relationship with the investment bank save that they rely on the publicly issued document (which has been prepared to the standard of prospectus law and/or the Takeover Code (2.2.2, 2.6(6), (7), (9), 10.2)). Accordingly, rules going back to the early days of the 1986 FSAct dealt with this problem in two ways:

15.3.1.1 A special definition of 'client'

The public was excluded from the 'clients' to whom the investment bank owed regulatory obligations by defining 'client' (8.2.1) as 'any person with or for whom a firm conducts . . . designated investment business [4.2.I(2)]', but 'does not include . . . a corporate finance contact' in respect of whom two conditions had to be satisfied. First, the contact had to arise in the course of 'corporate finance business', which was itself a complex definition. It sought to distinguish (1) Primary Market activities for corporates, Governments, issuers and strategic shareholders of 'offer, issue, underwriting, repurchase, exchange or redemption', 'the manner in which, or the terms on which . . . [an entity is] to be financed, structured, managed [or] controlled', a 'takeover . . . or . . . merger, de-merger, reorganisation or reconstruction', and whether as principal or agent, from (2) Secondary Market activities of buying and selling for investors (FSA PM GLOSSARY, defs. of 'client' and 'corporate finance business'). And, second, the 'corporate finance contact' was not in any type of special relationship with the firm, i.e. 'the firm does not behave in a way . . . which might reasonably be expected to lead that person to believe that he is being treated as a client . . . and . . . the firm clearly indicates . . . that it . . . is not acting for him . . . and will not be responsible to him for providing protections afforded to clients of the firm or be advising him on the relevant transaction' (FSA PM GLOSSARY, def. of 'corporate finance contact'). Thus, there was invariably an express statement to this effect in the prospectus or other publicly issued document. Overall, this would be achieved if '(a) the circumstances are such that [he] should realise (even taking into account any lack of sophistication on his part if he is a private customer) that . . . the firm is dealing . . . with [him] solely in his capacity as a member of the public ... and (b) there is no material difference in the way in which the firm communicates or deals with [him] and the way in which it communicates or deals with other members of the public ... and (c) the firm does not indicate that it considers that the recommendation or transaction ... [is] in [his] particular interests and ... [he] cannot reasonably expect the firm to have any responsibility ... to him to indicate whether or not it considers the recommendation or transaction to be in his own particular interest'.[2]

15.3.1.2 Applicable conduct rules

Where 'corporate finance business' was conducted with a corporate, Government, issuer or strategic shareholder, 'since the [conduct] rules have been written primarily for dealings in market securities, it is not surprising that they do not suit ... a relationship ... where ... advice is given by reference to the commercial and strategic requirements of a ... business rather than by reference to portfolio investment criteria'.[3] Accordingly, unless the corporate finance client was a Private Customer, in which case rules like suitability and understanding risk applied, the only rules that applied were: clear, fair and not misleading communications (10.5.1.3); inducements and soft commission (6.3.2, 6.3.3); exclusion of liability (8.4.5); personal account dealing (6.3.7); and research (6.3.4) (FSA PM COB 1.6), as well as the Principles (9.2) and market conduct (12.1–12.6).

15.3.2 MiFID

Although the same issue with the conduct rules remains and, of course, the nature of corporate finance market operations has not changed, MiFID does not expressly permit such modifications to its provisions and, accordingly, FSA 'will ... create a ... regime for firms outside the scope of MiFID who undertake corporate finance business that is not the same as that for firms inside the scope of MiFID'.[4] Thus:

15.3.2.1 Non-MiFID corporate finance

This is, effectively, the giving solely of advice within 4.2.I(2), ancillary service (3) which may amount to arranging deals (3.2.2.2), but goes no further and, in particular, does not amount to receiving and transmitting orders or acting as principal or agent in the issuance or selling of securities.[5] With such limited business, a very similar set of rules to those applied Pre-MiFID are proposed here.[6]

---

[2] TSA Notice 35, 5 October 1988, Sched. 2, para. 6.
[3] A Review of the Regulation of Corporate Finance Business of Advisory Firms, SCH Douglas-Mann, 19 March 1991, para. 5.13.1.   [4] FSA CP 07/9, para. 1.4.
[5] Cf. ibid, p. 15.   [6] Ibid, Ann. C, COBS 19.3.3, 19.3.4 (to be renumbered in 18).

15.3.2.2   MiFID corporate finance

'[T]here . . . [is] no scope to disapply . . . conduct of business rules which implement MiFID'.[7] Thus, the disapplication of most conduct rules from the relationship with the corporate finance client has been removed (COBS 18.3). As a result:

- The following obligations are owed: inducements (6.3.2); information on the firm, including its conflicts of interest policy and costs (COBS 6.1.4, 6.1.9); entry into of a customer agreement (8.4) (COBS 8.1.4(1)); personal account trading (6.3.7) (COBS 11.7.1); research (6.3.4) (COBS 12.1.2); risk warnings (10.5.1.3).
- Even if the advice given can be construed to be a 'personal recommendation' (3.2.2.3), the suitability rule (11.2.2) will, in practice, be complied with in the context of the way in which the corporate finance operations are conducted, and similarly any appropriateness obligation if such a recommendation is not given (11.4).
- The best execution obligation either does not apply or is satisfied in the course of the corporate finance operation itself (13.2.2.3).

As regards obligations owed to investors in the corporate finance transaction, the Pre-MiFID Rule continues with the exclusion of 'corporate finance contact' from the definition of 'client' (COBS 3.2.2), although the financial promotion rules (10.5) must be complied with (COBS 3.2.2).

---

[7] FSA PS 07/14, para. 8.7.

16
Broker-dealers

16.1 Regulatory status

The commercial activities of broker-dealers (2.4.4(8)) resolve themselves, in regulatory terms, into:

(a) buying and selling as principal or as agent (3.2.2.1); and
(b) arranging deals (3.2.2.2); and
(c) advising (3.2.2.3).

16.2 Infrastructure rules

All of the infrastructure rules apply (5.2–5.5, 6.3.1–6.3.4, 6.3.6, 6.3.7).

16.3 Conduct rules

As well as market conduct (12.1–12.6), there are three separate regimes.

16.3.1 Securities and derivatives broking and dealing

Here, all of the conduct rules in 7–11 and 13 apply.

16.3.2 Energy and oil markets

Where energy and oil market derivatives are MiFID Business (4.2.I(2)), 16.3.1 applies (subject to a very limited disapplication).[1] However, where they do not constitute MiFID Business but are still Regulated Activity (4.2.I(1)), FSA 'propose to maintain the policy approach reflected in ... [Pre-MiFID] COB',[2] such derivatives being where 'UK regulation does not contain exemptions as broad as those in MiFID for firms undertaking commodity and exotic derivatives business[3] and the definition of financial instruments in UK legislation covers a wider range of physically settled options on precious metals and a wider set of physically settled commodity futures than does MiFID'[4] as explained in 3.2.1.6 and 3.2.1.7.

---

[1] Contrast COBS 18.2 with FSA PM COB 1.6.6–1.6.12 (FSA PS 07/6, Chapter 21; FSA PS 07/14, Chapter 8).   [2] FSA CP 07/9, para. 2.3.   [3] See MiFID, Art. 2.1(k) and (l).
[4] FSA CP 07/9, para. 2.1.

Pre-MiFID: The regime related to on-exchange dealing with any type of client, OTC dealing 'with or for persons who are not individuals' and the establishment of collective investment schemes, originally in relation to derivatives over 'oil' (defined as 'mineral oil . . . and petroleum gases, whether in liquid or vapour form, including products and derivatives of oil') and later extended to 'energy' (which included 'coal, electricity, natural gas (or any by-product or form of any of them) . . . or a greenhouse gas emissions allowance . . . or a tradable renewable energy credit'). This was because 'it would not be appropriate to introduce the comprehensive regulatory regime needed elsewhere . . . [given] the absence of non-professional players . . . the high value of individual transactions; the need in many of the transactions to be able to make or take . . . physical delivery . . . [and] the strong "caveat emptor" ethos of the market'.[5] As a result, where the firm dealt as principal, the only conduct rules that applied related to exclusion of liability (8.4.5), unregulated collective investment schemes (10.5.6.1) and non-market price transactions (12.6); and, if it dealt as agent, in addition, it had to comply with the conduct rules on clear, fair and not misleading communications (10.5.1.3), financial promotions (10.5.2–10.5.5), conflicts (6.3.1), dealing ahead (6.3.4.2), research (6.3.4) and confirms (13.1.4.6) (FSA PM COB 1.6.6–1.6.12).

MiFID: A very similar application is to be continued for non-MiFID Business where, in addition, the Pre-MiFID best execution rule (13.2) is to be retained, including the ability of Professional Clients to contract out (COBS 18.2.3–18.2.9).[6] For MiFID Business the disapplication has been cut back because 'there . . . [is] no scope to . . . make concessions from . . . conduct of business rules which implement MiFID' (COBS 18.2)[7].

16.3.3 Stocklending

16.3.3.1 Dealing rules

Pre-MiFID: Although commercially a loan, in legal terms stocklending or repo is a transfer of securities and an agreement to re-transfer in the future equivalent securities, usually with a transfer (and subsequent re-transfer) of collateral (2.4.4(8), 3.2.2.1). Since all of the dealing rules would otherwise have applied, they were disapplied except for aggregation and allocation (13.1.3, 13.1.4.5). A stocklending programme, as investment management (3.2.2.4), unless total title transfer (7.1.2.6, 7.2.2.7) was subject to suitability and risk rules (FSA PM COB 1.6.2) and dividends to client money (7.2).

MiFID: There is no disapplication because 'there . . . [is] no scope to . . . make concession from . . . conduct of business rules which implement

---

[5] Consultative Document on the future regulation of the Oil Markets, SIB, February 1988, para. 11.   [6] FSA CP 07/9, Ann. C, draft COBS 19.2.3–19.2.9.
[7] FSA PS 07/14, para. 8.7.

MiFID'[8] and, therefore, the very limited disapplications (COBS 18.4) mean that the stockloan/repo must comply with the rules on dealing procedures (13.1), including confirms, notwithstanding periodic statements (COBS 16.4.5), although the best execution rule, even if technically applicable, will in practice be complied with when the factors (13.2.3.1) are applied to the nature of the transaction, particularly since it is the rate of return for the loan, rather than the market price of the securities per se, that is relevant; and, in any event, a client express instruction may be RFQ (13.2.2.1).[9]

16.3.3.2 Other rules

Pre-MiFID: The firm had to, in advance, notify a Private Customer that 'stocklending activity . . . may affect his tax position and . . . of the consequences of the stocklending activity' (FSA PM COB 5.4.10) which, in practice, meant:

Credit/Counterparty Risk

The possibility of default by a borrower . . .

Market/Collateral Risk

. . . not just the appropriateness of the type and volatility of collateral taken but also the appropriateness of the collateral arrangements in respect of any volatility in the investments . . .

Legal Risk

The . . . risk that . . . agreements may not establish the lender's right to realise the value of collateral upon the borrower's default . . .

Operational Risk

. . . [Lenders] may not receive income payments on the due date or may not receive notifications of corporate actions.[10]

In addition, the client's prior consent to stocklending was required and there were various other requirements when the firm lent securities from its safe custody (FSA PM CASS 2.5.4, 2.5.8–2.5.10, 2.5.12) as explained in 7.1.3.3.

MiFID: The requirements, generally, to give risk warnings (10.5.1.3) (COBS 18.4) means that there should be no change in the practice required by the Pre-MiFID Rules, and the MiFID Rules carry over certain aspects of the requirements where securities are lent from the firm's safe custody (CASS 6.4) as explained in 7.1.3.3.

---

[8] FSA PS 07/14, para. 8.7.
[9] FSA PS 07/15, paras. 4.11–4.13. Where the firm reinvests cash collateral, best execution applies.   [10] SFA BN 459, 6 February 1998, pp. 2–3.

17
Asset managers

17.1 Portfolio managers

17.1.1 Regulatory status

The activities of portfolio managers (2.4.4(11)) comprise, from a regulatory perspective:

- management (3.2.2.4); and
- advice (3.2.2.3); and
- buying and selling as agent and/or arranging deals (3.2.2.1, 3.2.2.2).

17.1.2 Infrastructure rules

All of the infrastructure rules apply (5.2–5.5, 6.3.1–6.3.4, 6.3.6, 6.3.7).

17.1.3 Conduct rules

All of the conduct rules apply (7–11, 13), the only special application being in relation to the so-called second tier best execution obligation (13.2.3.1).

17.2 Collective investment schemes

Although 'establishing, operating or winding-up a collective investment scheme . . . [and] acting as trustee of an authorised unit trust scheme . . . [and] acting as depositary or sole director of an open-ended investment company' is a Regulated Activity (3.2.2.5), MiFID exempts 'collective investment undertakings . . . whether coordinated at Community level [i.e. UCITS: 2.6(10)][1] or not and the depositories and managers of such undertakings' (RAO, Sched. 3, para. 1(h)). Hence, FSA 'propose to maintain the . . . [Pre-MiFID] concessionary treatment of CIS operators' whereby 'operators of regulated and unregulated CISs when undertaking scheme management activity . . . [could take advantage of] modifications in respect of best execution, suitability and order aggregation and allocation . . . [This regime] applie[d] COB provisions in a CIS environment where there are three parties . . . the operator, the scheme and the participants . . . rather

---

[1] For the extent of UCITS managers' activities, see SUP, App. 3.9.6.

than the usual two (firm/customer). Parts of COB that are applied include inducements, conflicts . . . best execution, aggregation and allocation, customer order and execution records and . . . [soft commission, and in addition] modifie[d] COB provisions regarding suitability (to require each transaction and the portfolio itself to be suitable for the scheme) and best execution (to allow funds for professionals only to be opted out) for unregulated schemes. As unregulated . . . schemes are outside . . . UCITS . . . they are also subject to specific requirements in respect of scheme documentation and reporting to clients'. Under the MiFID regime, FSA 'propose to apply the . . . [MiFID] equivalent of most of the [Pre-MiFID] . . . provisions . . . disapplying . . . [f]or example . . . Suitability . . . [which] is a statement of the obvious' and applying MiFID best execution, but retaining the ability of unregulated schemes to contract out .[2]

In addition, because they are also within the MiFID exemption, the Pre-MiFID limited conduct rules applying to collective investment scheme depositaries[3] and 'UCITS qualifiers', being 'authorised persons who . . . act as the trustee or depository of a UCITS fund established outside the UK and which is a recognised overseas . . . CIS . . . under section 264 of [FSMA:10.5.6.1]', will continue,[4] as will the disapplication of all conduct rules other than financial promotion to Investment Companies with Variable Capital (ICVCs).[5]

---

[2] FSA CP 07/9, paras. 8.1–8.4, 8.6, 8.7. See also: CP 07/9, Ann. C, draft COBS 19.5 (to be implemented as COBS 18.5); and, as regards best execution, FSA PS 07/6, paras 14.12–14.14.

[3] FSA PM COB 11; FSA CP 07/9, Ch. 6 and Ann. C, draft COBS 19.7 (to be implemented as COBS 18.7).

[4] FSA PM COB 1.9, 11; FSA CP 07/9, Chs. 6 and 11, Ann. C, draft COBS 19.7, 19.10 (to be implemented as COBS 18.7, 18.10); PERG 13.2, Q.6.

[5] FSA PM COB 1.9, 11; FSA CP 07/9, Chs. 6, 11, 12, Ann. C, draft COBS 19.7, 19.9, 19.10 (to be implemented as COBS 18.7, 18.9, 18.10).

18
Trustees

18.1 Trustees of collective investment schemes

See 17.2.

18.2 Custodians

18.2.1 Regulatory status

Custody of assets (2.4.4(11)) is subject to a separate category of licensable activity (3.2.2.6). The custodian will, inevitably, hold the assets, comprising physical custody or, more likely, rights against sub-custodians, depositories and clearing houses, subject to an express or implied trust.

18.2.2 Infrastructure rules

All of the infrastructure rules apply (5.2–5.5, 6.3.1–6.3.4, 6.3.6, 6.3.7).

18.2.3 Conduct rules

The custodian will need to comply with the detailed rules on holding client assets and client money (7.1, 7.2).

18.3 Other trustees

18.3.1 Regulatory status

Trustees, whether of private settlements or commercial trusts, such as trustees of securities issues and collateral arrangements (3.2.5.3), will be carrying on any combination of:

- buying and selling investments as principal (3.2.2.1); and/or
- management (3.2.2.4); and/or
- advice (3.2.2.3).

However, they may or may not be able to rely on the exemption for trustees from licensing (3.2.5.3).

18.3.2 Infrastructure rules

If licensed (authorised) the trustee must comply with all of the infrastructure rules (5.2–5.5, 6.3.1–6.3.4, 6.3.6, 6.3.7).

18.3.3 Pre-MiFD conduct rules

Trustees are highly regulated under general law and statute which covers most, if not all, of the areas that FSA seeks to regulate, 'for example: duties to safeguard trust assets . . . duties to invest trust property . . . duties to keep accurate records . . . duties on professional paid trustees to exhibit a high degree of care in the management of trust property . . . duties . . . of never self-dealing, and or being liable to account for profits . . . where there is a conflict between their fiduciary duties and their personal self-interest'.[1] Moreover, conduct rules drafted for an investor–broker relationship 'cannot be applied to trustees without amendment' in terms of who is to be regarded as the trustee's 'client' given 'that there may be a single beneficiary or many beneficiaries . . . [who] may be . . . well-known [or] . . . no more than identifiable . . . [or] wholly unknown, or . . . not yet existing'.[2] It is, therefore, possible to conclude 'that [the regulator] should disapply Rules either where they make no sense in the context of a trustee relationship or where they are not necessary for the purpose of investor protection. For example, it is not sensible to suggest that a trust deed should become a customer agreement . . . conflicts of interest should be regulated by trust law alone'[3] and Client Money Regulations, imposing a statutory trust (7.2.1), seem otiose. A large series of exemptions were provided under the 1986 FSAct, although these were progressively worn away until, immediately before MiFID was implemented, they were as follows.

18.3.3.1 The 'client'

As regards the trustee firm, the 'client', i.e. 'any person with or for whom a firm conducts . . . any regulated activity' (8.2.1), did 'not include . . . a trust beneficiary' (FSA PM GLOSSARY, def. of 'client'). Accordingly, any rule requiring 'information to, or . . . consent from, a customer' was to be interpreted as 'as many [co-]trustees as are required by the trust instrument' (FSA PM COB 11.2) and there was no need for a customer agreement (FSA PM COB 4, Ann. 1, para. (7)).

18.3.3.2 Bare trustees and trustees of securities issues

Because they did not engage, commercially, in investment management and were clearly regulated in their activities by trust law, these trustees were

---

[1] Report on Financial Services and Trust Law prepared for SIB and IMRO, Professor DJ Hayton, September 1990, para. 3.02.
[2] Trustees: IMRO Provisional Policy Statement, 16 February 1988.
[3] Special IMRO Bulletin: Rules for Trustees, 18 October 1988, p. 3.

subject to minimal conduct rules: inducements (6.3.2); soft commission (6.3.3); clear, fair and not misleading communication (10.5.1.3); exclusion of liability (8.4.5); financial promotions (10.5.1.3, 10.5.2–10.5.6); and conflicts (6.3.1). And, in each case, 'customer' in the relevant rule was construed as ' "trustee" or "trust", as appropriate' (FSA PM COB 11.5.1(1), 11.5.2).

18.3.3.3 Trustees with active portfolio management duties

'Active' trustees (i.e. other than bare trustees) who were subject to investment management duties as a matter of general trust law[4] were, in addition to the regulatory obligations under 18.3.3.2, also subject to rules on know-your-customer (11.2.2.1), suitability (11.2.2.2) and dealing, including best execution (13.1, 13.2) again with the 'customer' interpreted as 'trustee or trust, as appropriate' which, in the context of these rules, meant the trust (ignoring the metaphysical difficulty that the trust had no existence beyond the fiduciary relationship of the trustee itself to the assets held for the beneficiaries subject to the trust relationship) (FSA PM COB 4, Ann. 1, para. (7); FSA PM COB 11.5.1(2), 11.5.3). This was clearly appropriate, from a regulatory perspective once one ignored the trustee's general law duties as regards investment and the duty of care,[5] since this type of trustee was a 'managing trustee . . . [who] is his own discretionary portfolio manager'.[6] However, there are two other types of trustee. First, an 'arm's-length trustee' who 'delegates all decisions of a day-to-day nature to a professional investment manager, having laid down strategic guidelines . . . and . . . stipulated that he is to be consulted before action is taken in . . . specified situations, e.g. decisions affecting more than a specified percentage of the total value of investments' and, second, an 'advice-driven trustee' who 'himself . . . make[s] not just strategic decisions but also decisions of a day-to-day nature, though in making these latter decisions he always obtains advice [from a licensed firm] and acts within . . . such advice'.[7] Under the 1986 FSAct versions of trustee rules, such reliance by arm's-length and advice-driven trustees obviated their regulatory responsibility for suitability and execution, but FSA's policy was that '[a]lthough a firm may always delegate . . . that . . . does not affect the responsibility of the delegating firm',[8] particularly 'where the trustee firm undertakes substantial trustee business' (FSA PM COB 11.6.2). As a result, the disapplication was cut back into a rule that acknowledged that, in discharging its own responsibilities, the trustee would rely on analogous duties performed by the other licensed firm, and only permitted such reliance if 'the trustee firm could not reasonably be expected to discharge the responsibility itself

---

[4] *Trust & Trustees Cases & Materials*, EH Burn, 5th edn., Butterworths, 1996, Chapter 17; 2000 Trustee Act 3–7.   [5] 2000 Trustee Act 1–7.   [6] Hayton Report, para. 3.03(a).
[7] Hayton Report, para. 3.03(b), (c).   [8] FSA CP 45a, February 2000, para. 15.7.

[and] . . . the delegation is made in writing which . . . describes in adequate detail the regulated activities to be carried on by the [other firm which] . . . undertakes in writing to . . . comply with all rules relevant to the regulated activity in question . . . and is an appropriate person to perform the regulated activity' (FSA PM COB 11.6).

18.3.3.4 Client money and custody

These rules were partially disapplied (FSA PM CASS 2.1.16, 4.2.6).

18.3.4 MiFID conduct rules

Since the ISD/MiFID override (3.2.6) does not apply to trustees, FSA could have continued with the Pre-MiFID trustee regime. Instead though, it has taken the view that because, in regulatory terms, the trustee's Regulated Activities are no different from those of mainstream financial services providers all MiFID Business conduct and client asset rules must apply, unamended, to trustees: 'under MiFID there will be no scope to disapply . . . conduct of business rules which implement MiFID'.[9] As a result, the following rules apply in addition to the Principles (9.1, 9.3) (COBS 18.1): conflicts of interest (6.3.1); inducements (6.3.2), information on the firm, including its conflicts of interest policy and costs (COBS 6.1.4, 6.1.9); entry into of a customer agreement (8.4) (COBS 8.1.4(1)), which could be the trust deed or amendments or a notice supplemental to it; risk warnings (10.5.1.3); suitability (11.2.2); dealing (13.1.1–13.1.4) and best execution (13.2). To comply with its best execution and suitability obligations, the trustee would have to ensure that the broker–dealer/portfolio manager categorises it as a Professional Client (8.3.2.5) and not as an Eligible Counter Party (8.3.3) and so, in turn, owes the trustee the relevant duties (8.1). As regards the 'client', to whom the trustee owes the duties, the definition excludes 'a trust beneficiary' (GLOSS, def of 'client') which is not correct in all circumstances. Rather, 'where the firm . . . is . . . trustee . . . in most cases the beneficiary . . . will be its client. However, the position will not always be so clear . . . for example, if the trust is a purpose trust without clearly identified beneficiaries. In such cases it would be necessary for . . . firms . . . to consider the specific circumstances and interpret the Handbook provisions purposively',[10] which can be taken as license to interpret the 'client' in relation to each conduct rule in the Pre-MiFID manner.

In addition, the custody and client money rules apply (7.1.2.4, 7.2.2.6).

[9] FSA PS 07/14, para. 8.7.   [10] FSA CP 06/19, para. 7.49.

19
Retail intermediaries

19.1 Stockbrokers

19.1.1 Regulatory status

Although dealing mainly, if not exclusively, with Private/Retail Clients, the commercial activities of a Retail stockbroker are, in legal and regulatory terms, no different from those of a broker–dealer (16.1).

19.1.2 Infrastructure rules

All of the infrastructure rules apply (5.2–5.5, 6.3.1–6.3.4, 6.3.6, 6.3.7).

19.1.3 Conduct rules

As well as market conduct (12.1–12.6), and the Principles (9.1–9.3), all of the conduct rules apply (7–11, 13), the only special application being that if the broker only receives and transmits orders, rather than dealing as agent (dealing as principal being unlikely in practice), then the so-called second tier best execution obligation will apply (13.2.3.1).[1]

19.2 Packaged product intermediaries

19.2.1 Regulatory status

The commercial activities (2.4.4(10), 10.5.6.2) result, from a legal and regulatory perspective, in the following activities in relation to collective investment schemes (3.2.1.9) and savings insurance:

- arranging deals/receiving and transmitting orders (3.2.2.2); and
- advice (3.2.2.3).[2]

19.2.2 Infrastructure rules

All of the infrastructure rules apply (5.2–5.5, 6.3.1–6.3.4,[3] 6.3.6, 6.3.7).

---

[1] Understanding the basics of the new COBS sourcebook for retail markets, FSA, September 2007.

[2] Passporting (3.4) is available (Financial Advisers and Passporting, FSA Factsheet, August 2007; MiFID Permissions Guide – Update, FSA, September 2007, Chapters 3, 4).

[3] For disclosure of inducements in relation to personal recommendations of packaged products, see COBS 2.3.1(2)(b); FSA PS 07/14, paras. 2.3–2.7.

19.2.3 Conduct rules

All of the conduct rules apply (7–11, 13) although, in addition, there are a range of rules specifically tailored to packaged products:

- financial promotion (10.5.6.1, 10.5.6.3);
- polarisation (10.5.6.2);
- product disclosure (COBS 6, 13, 14.3.11, 14.3.12, 16.5, 19, 20);
- insurance mediation (COBS 7);
- suitability (COBS 9.3, 9.4, 9.6);
- cancellation (10.5.6.4) (COBS 15);
- after-sales disclosure of insurance products and claims handling (COBS 16.6, 17).[4]

[4] Ibid. A number of these provisions are 'super-equivalent'; Article 4 Notification of certain requirements relating to packaged products, FSA, September 2007.

Bibliography

Anderson Report: Report on Fixed Trusts, July 1936
Bennion: *Statutory Interpretation*, FAR Bennion, 4th edn., Butterworths, 2005
Bodkin Report: Report of the Departmental Committee, 1937, Cmnd. 5539
Bowstead: *Bowstead on Agency*, FR Reynolds, 17th edn., Sweet & Maxwell, 2001
Cohen Report: Report of the Committee on Company Law Amendment, June 1945
Davey Report: Report of the Departmental Committee under the Companies Acts 1862–1890, 1895
Goff and Jones: *The Law of Restitution*, R Goff and G Jones, 5th edn., Sweet & Maxwell, 1998
Greene Report: Report of the Company Law Amendment Committee, 1926
Hanbury: *Modern Equity*, GH Hanbury and J Martin, Sweet and Maxwell, 16th edn., 2001
Jenkins Report: Report of the Company Law Committee, June 1962
Joint Committee Reports: House of Lords and House of Commons Joint Committee on Financial Services and Markets, First Report, 27 April 1999, Vols. I and II; Second Report, 27 May 1999
Markesinis: *Tort Law*, RWM Dias, B Markesinis and S Deakin, 4th edn., Oxford, 1999
Meagher: *Equity, Doctrines and Remedies*, Meagher, Gummow & Lehane, Butterworths, 3rd edn., 1992
1982 Gower: Review of Investor Protection: Discussion Document, Professor LCB Gower, 1982
1984 Gower: Review of Investor Protection: Part I, Cmnd. 9125, LCB Gower, 1984
1985 Gower: Review of Investor Protection: Part II, LCB Gower, 1985
1985 White Paper: Financial Services in the UK: A new framework for investor protection, Cmnd. 9432, January 1985
Scott Report: Report of the Committee on Property Bonds and Equity-Linked Life Assurance, Cmnd. 5281, 1973
Smith & Hogan: *Criminal Law* JC Smith, 9th edn., Butterworths, 1999
Treitel and B Hogan *Law of Contract*, GH Treitel, 10th edn., Sweet & Maxwell, 1999

Index

abuse
  see market abuse
abusive squeeze, 368–370
action, right of
  see right of action
advertisement
  see financial promotion
advertising
  see financial promotion
advice
  appropriateness, 109, 318–324
  controlled functions, 132–135, 139–140
  definition, 81–82, 307
  execution-only, 147, 242, 292, 316, 318–320
  general law standard, 306–307
  independent financial advisers, 300–305
  regulated activity, 81–82, 306–307
  suitability, 307–318
advisory standards
  appropriateness, 318–324
  general law, 306–307
  Principle 9 (trust), 255, 307
  suitability, 307–318
agency dealing
  regulated activity, 79–80, 89–90
  single capacity / dual capacity, 150, 153, 158
agent
  appointed representative, 300–305
  client of firm as agent, 229–230, 263
  tied agent, 300–305
aggregation of orders, 152, 379–380, 383–385
allocation, 383–385
alternative trading system (ATS)
  see multi-lateral trading facilities
analyst
  insider dealing, 329, 330, 333, 354, 359, 373, 375
  market abuse, 329, 330, 333, 354, 359, 373, 375
  research, 151, 152, 155, 178–189
ancillary service, 101
annual report of FSA, 37–38
Anti-Money Laundering Directive, 58, 314–315
Anti-Terrorism, Crime and Security Act 2001, 167
APER
  1.1, 105
  3.1.4, 139
  3.1.8, 139
  3.3.1, 139
  4.1.5, 140
  4.1.6, 140
  4.1.11, 140
  4.2.3, 285
  4.2.4, 140, 285
  4.2.6, 140
  4.2.10, 140
  4.3, 140
  4.4, 140
  4.5.3, 136
  4.5.4, 136
  4.5.8, 137
  4.5.12, 136
  4.5.13, 136
  4.6.3, 136
  4.6.4, 136
  4.6.5, 137
  4.6.6, 136
  4.6.8, 137
  4.6.11, 136

441

Index

APER (*cont.*)
  4.6.13, 139
  4.6.14, 136
  4.7.3, 136
  4.7.4, 136
  4.7.6, 136
  4.7.7, 136
  application, 105
  Code of Conduct, 104
  Statements of Principle
    1, 140, 254
    2, 140, 254
    3, 140, 256
    4, 40–41, 140
    5, 135–139
    6, 135–139
    7, 135–139
APER Code of Conduct, 40–41, 135–140, 254, 256
appeal by firms, 39–43
appointed representative, 300–395
apportionment and oversight, 121–123, 136
appropriateness
  see advice
approved person
  code of conduct, 40–41, 135–140, 256
  controlled functions, 132–135, 139–140
  liability, 137–139, 140
  registration, 132–135, 139–140
  senior managers, 132–139
  Statements of Principle, 40–41, 135–140, 254, 256
  training, 136–137
arranging deals
  client assets, 200
  regulated activity, 80–81, 90
ARROW, 143, 261
asset managers
  see portfolio manager
assets
  see client money
  see also custody
associated instrument, 342
authorised persons
  see licensing

authorised unit trusts
  AUTS, 240, 284, 293, 299, 385, 432
  UCITS, 26–27, 59, 236, 240, 299, 385, 432

bank
  definition, 104
  see credit institution
Bank for International Settlements (BIS), 9
Banking Acts 1979, 1987, 24, 113, 270
Banking Coordination Directive
  see Banking Directives
Banking Directives, 58, 71, 91, 95, 232, 233
Barings, 114–116
Basel II, 119
BCD credit institution, 104
best execution
  application, 391–398
  booking, 396–397
  capital markets, 397–398
  direct market access (DMA), 406–407
  execution standard, 398–404
  policy (disclosure), 245, 247, 403–405
  request for quote (RFQ), 381, 391–396, 409, 431
  RTO standard, 229, 404–405
  single venue transaction, 407
  specific instructions, 406
  stocklending and repo's, 430–431
  structured transactions, 405–406
BIPRU firm, 104
body corporate
  see companies
bonds
  see debt securities
branch
  non-UK branch of EEA firm/bank, 99, 100, 102
  UK branch
    EEA firm/bank, of, 56–57, 99, 100, 103
    non-EEA firm/bank, of, 58, 99, 100, 103

Index

breach of statutory duty
  see right of action
broker–dealer, 25–26, 59
  conduct rules, 429–431
  conflicts, 146–193
  executing broker 230
  introducing broker, 230
  licensing, 79–82, 84–86, 89–91, 429
  systems and controls, 429
bundling, bundled brokerage
  see conflicts of interest, soft commission
burden of proof, 345–346
business planning, 120, 123
by way of business, 70, 83, 92

CAD full scope firm, 108
CAD investment firm, 104
call options
  see options
Capital Requirements Directive, 104, 118
Carrying on Regulated Activities by way of Business Order 2001, The, 70, 83, 92
CASS
  see client money
  1.2.2, 109, 199, 211
  1.2.3, 109, 199, 202, 216
  1.2.7, 109, 199, 200, 202, 210, 211, 212, 215
  1.2.8, 211, 212, 227
  1.2.9, 211
  1.2.10, 199
  1.2.11, 210
  1.2.12, 199, 210
  1.3.2, 211
  1.3.3, 211
  1.4.1–1.4.4, 211
  1.4.2–1.4.8, 200, 201, 212, 215
  2.1.1, 199, 200, 227
  2.1.2A, 109, 199
  2.1.5, 200
  2.1.6, 202
  2.1.9, 109, 199, 201
  2.1.10A, 199
  2.1.11, 203, 206
  2.1.13, 200
  2.1.14, 200
  2.1.15, 200
  2.1.15–2.1.20, 201
  2.1.21, 200
  2.1.22, 200
  2.1.23–2.1.26, 201
  2.2.4, 201
  2.2.18, 204
  2.2.20, 204
  2.2.21, 204
  2.3.2, 206
  2.3.3, 206
  2.3.12–2.3.21, 207
  2.4, 205
  2.5.2, 207
  2.5.3, 207
  2.5.4–2.5.14, 206
  2.5.9, 207
  2.6.2, 208
  2.6.6, 208
  2.6.10, 208
  3.1.1, 199, 277
  3.1.3, 201, 215
  3.1.4, 201, 215
  3.1.5, 202, 215
  3.1.7, 202, 215
  3.2.2, 202, 215
  4.1.1, 109, 211, 212, 227
  4.1.2, 109, 210, 215
  4.1.2C, 210
  4.1.3, 216
  4.1.7, 210
  4.1.8–4.14, 213
  4.1.15, 214
  4.1.18, 214
  4.1.19, 214
  4.1.20, 214
  4.1.21, 214
  4.1.23, 214
  4.1.27–4.1.29, 215
  4.2.3, 209
  4.2.4, 210
  4.3.3, 216
  4.3.5, 216
  4.3.9, 217
  4.3.10, 217
  4.3.12, 217
  4.3.19–4.3.25, 217

CASS (cont.)
  4.3.24, 217
  4.3.26–4.3.28, 218
  4.3.30, 217
  4.3.34, 218
  4.3.40, 218
  4.3.42, 218
  4.3.44, 218
  4.3.46, 218
  4.3.47, 218
  4.3.48, 218
  4.3.52, 217
  4.3.56, 218
  4.3.61, 217
  4.3.65, 220
  4.3.66, 220
  4.3.67, 220
  4.3.99, 217
  4.5, 211
  4.5.1, 211
  6.1.1, 199, 200, 227
  6.1.3, 201
  6.1.4, 202
  6.1.5, 202
  6.1.6, 202
  6.1.7, 208
  6.1.8, 202
  6.1.10, 201
  6.1.11, 201
  6.1.12, 200
  6.1.13, 200
  6.1.14, 200
  6.1.15, 202
  6.6.16, 202
  6.1.17, 199
  6.1.18, 199
  6.1.20, 199
  6.1.22, 198
  6.2.1, 199
  6.2.2, 199
  6.2.1–6.2.7, 204
  6.3.1, 204
  6.3.4, 205, 252
  6.4, 431
  6.4.1, 206, 252
  6.4.2, 206
  6.5.1, 204
  6.5.2, 204
  6.5.4–6.5.12, 208
  7.1.1, 210, 227
  7.1.1–7.1.6, 109
  7.1.2–7.1.7, 210
  7.1.6, 211
  7.1.8–7.1.11, 213
  7.1.12, 214
  7.1.13, 214
  7.1.16, 210
  7.2.1, 212
  7.2.2, 216
  7.2.3, 215
  7.2.6, 216
  7.2.7, 216
  7.2.8, 214
  7.2.9–7.2.11, 215
  7.2.12, 212
  7.2.14, 218
  7.2.15, 218
  7.3.1, 211
  7.4.1, 217
  7.4.1–7.4.6, 219
  7.4.7–7.4.10, 219
  7.4.11, 217, 219
  7.4.14–7.4.31, 217
  7.6.2, 221
  7.6.6, 221
  7.7, 211
  7.8.1, 219
  7.9, 211
  8.1, 200, 212
certificate of deposit
  see debt securities
charges (costs)
  amount, 162, 245
  disclosure, 140, 245, 247, 248
  inducements, 166–171
  soft commission, 108, 171–177
  volume overriders, 168, 171
Chinese Walls
  conflicts, 152, 153–156, 162–163, 187, 381
  insider dealing, 336, 339, 351, 352, 358, 362, 363, 374
  market abuse, 258, 336, 339, 351, 352, 362, 363, 374
churning
  see conflicts of interest

clearing houses, 80, 239
client
   agent for, 229–230, 263, 313–314, 323, 386, 417
   agreement
     see terms of business
   applicable rules, 226–228
   categorisation, 109, 230–241
   definition, 226–241, 437
   eligible counterparty
     firms, 240
     government bodies, 239–240
     large professionals, 240–241
     large undertakings, 240–241
   experts, 236–239
   intermediate customer
     clearing houses, 239
     collective investment schemes, 236
     corporates, 232–233
     exchanges, 239
     experts, 236–239
     firms, 234–236
     government bodies, 231–232
     insurance companies, 236
     packaged products, 236
     partnerships, 234
     SPVs, 233
     trustees, 234
     UCITS, 236
     unincorporated associations, 234
   market counterparty
     firms, 240
     government bodies, 239–240
     large intermediates, 240–241
     large undertakings, 240–241
   private customer, 231
   professional client
     clearing houses, 239
     collective investment schemes, 236
     corporates, 232–233
     exchanges, 239
     experts, 236–239
     firms, 234–236
     government bodies, 231–232
     insurance companies, 236
     packaged products, 236
     partnerships, 234
     SPVs, 233
     trustees, 234
     UCITS, 236
     unincorporated associations, 234
   retail client, 231
   reporting, 417
client assets
   see custody
client money
   accounts, 218–220
   application, 109, 210–212
     affiliates, 214
     banks, 212–213
     DvP, 214
     fiduciaries, 215
     firm's money, 214–215
     opt-out, 213
     passported branches, 216
     total title transfer, 215–216
   approved banks, 218–220
   CFTC, 221
   collective investment scheme, 210
   deposits, 69–71
   disclosures to client, 219–220
   fees, etc., withdrawal of, 214–215
   interest, 218
   nostro accounts, 212
   opt out, 213
   payments in and out, 217–218
   Principle 10 (assets), 198–199, 210, 285
   reconciliations, 220–221
   segregation, 216–217
   title, 208–211
   total title transfer, 215–216
   trust accounts, as, 208–211
COAF, 44
COBS
   1.1, 108
   1, Ann. 1, 106, 108, 248, 277, 290, 296, 297, 325, 380, 385, 398, 421
   2.1.1, 264
   2.1.2, 251
   2.1.3, 251
   2.2.1, 243, 248, 288
   2.2.2, 247, 248
   2.3.1, 108, 169, 170, 253, 437
   2.3.2, 171
   2.3.5, 169

COBS (*cont.*)
  2.3.6, 170
  2.3.8, 169, 171
  2.3.9–2.3.16, 171
  2.3.17, 141, 170
  2.4.3, 230
  2.4.4, 230, 310, 314
  2.4.5, 310, 323
  2.4.6–2.4.8, 314
  2.4.9, 386, 417
  3.1.1–3.1.5, 109
  3.2.1, 228
  3.2.2, 308
  3.2.3, 228, 230, 236
  3.3.1, 231, 235, 253
  3.3.2, 231, 428
  3.5.2, 232, 233, 234, 235, 236
  3.5.3, 238, 252
  3.5.4, 238
  3.5.8, 239
  3.5.9, 239
  3.6.1, 231, 239
  3.6.2, 234, 236, 240
  3.6.3, 240, 251
  3.6.4–3.6.6, 241
  3.6.7, 241
  3.7.1–3.7.3, 231, 235
  3.7.5, 235
  3.7.6, 253
  3.7.7, 235
  4.1.1, 227, 290
  4.1.4, 290
  4.1.5, 227
  4.1.6, 290
  4.1.8–4.1.10, 290
  4.2.1, 249, 288, 290
  4.2.2, 288
  4.2.4, 288
  4.2.5, 248, 288
  4.4, 291
  4.5, 291, 305
  4.5.1, 290
  4.6, 291
  4.6.1, 290
  4.7, 293
  4.7.1, 290
  4.8, 290, 293
  4.8.1, 290
  4.9, 291
  4.9.1, 290
  4.10, 290
  4.10.3, 279
  4.10.4, 279
  4.11, 141
  5.1.1–5.1.6, 298
  5.1.7–5.1.11, 298
  5.1.14–5.1.17, 298
  5.2.1, 296
  5.2.2–5.2.9, 296
  5.9, 299, 300
  6, 439
  6.1.4, 166, 247, 248, 253, 291, 437
  6.1.6, 248
  6.1.9, 437
  6.1.14, 248
  6.2–6.4, 305
  7.1.7, 220, 253, 439
  8.1, 253
  8.1.1, 109, 227, 243
  8.1.2, 247, 253
  8.1.3, 243, 249, 250
  8.1.4–8.1.6, 141, 227, 243, 247, 249, 253, 328, 437
  9.1, 108
  9.1.1, 109, 309
  9.1.3, 109, 309
  9.1.4, 109
  9.2.1, 227, 309, 312, 313
  9.2.2, 312, 313, 317
  9.2.3, 313
  9.2.5, 309, 317
  9.2.6, 313
  9.2.8, 312, 313
  9.3.1, 191, 310, 317
  9.3.2, 191, 310
  9.4, 318
  9.5, 141, 313
  9.5.1, 318
  10.1, 109
  10.1.1, 227, 320
  10.1.2, 320
  10.1.3, 323
  10.2.1, 289, 321
  10.2.2, 321
  10.2.4, 323

10.2.5, 323
10.2.6, 322
10.2.7, 322
10.2.8, 323
10.3.1, 323
10.3.3, 323
10.4.1, 319, 320
10.4.2, 322
10.5.1–10.5.3, 319
10.5.5, 319
10.7.1, 141, 323
11.1.1, 108, 109, 227, 380, 393
11.1.2, 109
11.1.3, 108
11.1.4, 108
11.1.5, 108
11.2.1–11.2.3, 393, 400, 404
11.2.5, 393, 406
11.2.6, 400
11.2.7, 401, 403
11.2.8, 401
11.2.9, 401
11.2.10–11.2.13, 402, 403
11.2.14–11.2.16, 402
11.2.16, 404
11.2.17, 403
11.2.18, 404
11.2.19–11.2.21, 406
11.2.22, 403
11.2.23, 403
11.2.24, 404
11.2.25, 252, 404
11.2.26, 252, 406
11.2.27, 404
11.2.28, 404
11.2.29, 404
11.2.32, 404
11.2.33, 405
11.2.34, 400
11.3.1, 379, 381
11.3.2, 379, 381, 382, 383, 384
11.3.4, 388
11.3.7, 380
11.3.8–11.3.10, 384
11.3.11, 385
11.3.12, 385
11.3.13, 380, 381, 382, 384
11.4, 382, 383
11.4.1, 252
11.5, 141
11.5.1, 379
11.5.2, 382
11.5.3, 380
11.5.4, 379, 382
11.6, 178
11.6.2, 108
11.7.1, 108, 193
11.7.2, 184
11.7.4, 193
11.7.5, 192
11.7.6, 192
12.1.2, 108, 328
12.1.3, 108
12.2.2, 184
12.2.3, 184
12.2.5, 184, 185, 186
12.2.7, 184
12.2.9, 184
12.2.10, 184
12.2.11, 186
12.2.12, 185
12.2.13, 186
12.3.2, 184, 186
12.3.4, 184, 186
12.4.3, 187
12.4.4, 187
12.4.5, 187
12.4.6, 187
12.4.7, 187
12.4.9, 188
12.4.10, 188
12.4.11, 188
12.4.12, 188
12.4.15–12.4.17, 189
13, 169, 305, 439
14, 305, 439
14.3.2, 288
14.3.3–14.3.11, 249, 288
15, 248, 298, 439
16.1.1, 227, 386
16.1.2, 227
16.2.1, 110, 385, 386
16.2.3, 385
16.2.3A, 386, 388
16.2.5, 386
16, Ann. 1, 399

Index

COBS (*cont.*)
  16.3, 417
  16.4, 417, 431
  16.5, 439
  16.6, 439
  17, 439
  18.1, 437
  18.2, 430
  18.3, 397, 427, 428
  18.4, 431
  18.5–18.10, 433
  19, 439
  20, 439
  TP1, 238
cold calling
  see financial promotion
COLL, 299
  4, 284, 305
Collateral Directive, 54
collective investment schemes
  as customer, 236
  best execution, 407
  definition, 76–79, 210
  limited liability partnerships, 65, 76–79
  limited partnerships, 65, 76–79
  marketing, 300–305, 318
  MiFID rules, 432–433
  open-ended companies, 299
  operating, etc. (regulated activity), 83–84
  partnerships, 65
  polarisation, 300–305
  regulated schemes, 240, 284, 293, 299, 385, 432
  'splits', 41–42
  UCITS, 26–27, 59, 236, 240, 299, 319, 432,
  unit trusts, 26–27, 284
  unregulated schemes, 240, 245, 279, 432
Collective Investment Schemes Order 2001, 79–79
commercial banks, 24, 58
commercial paper
  see debt securities
commission
  see charges

commission recapture
  see conflicts of interest, soft commission
Committee of Wise Men
  see Lamfalussy procedure
commodities
  see future
  see also options
common platform firm, 104
COMP, 94, 209, 245, 291
companies, 11, 78
Companies Act 2006
  3 (section), 65
  15 (section), 65
  16 (section), 65
  33 (section), 65
  174 (section), 139
  860 (section), 210
compensation scheme, 94, 209, 245, 291
complaints
  against FSA, 43–44
  by clients, 260
compliance risk function, 120, 123, 124, 134, 136
COND
  2.3, 94
  2.4, 94
  2.5, 94
confirms, 110, 385–388
conflicts of interest
  application, FSA SYSC, 105
  Chinese Wall, 152, 153–156, 162–163, 187, 271, 336, 339, 351, 352, 358, 362, 363, 374, 381
  churning, 108, 191, 317
  conflicts policy, 165, 166, 186
  corporate finance, 150, 151, 152, 169, 170–171, 189–191
  front running, 151, 354
  general law (fiduciary), 146–158
  inducements, 108, 141, 151, 162, 166–171, 277–278, 302, 304, 389, 390
  personal account dealing, 108, 191–193
  polarisation, 300–305

Principle 8 (conflicts), 159–166, 189,
    190–191, 244, 255, 262–263, 365
  regulatory rule, 158–166
  research, 151, 152, 155, 178–189
  soft commission, 108, 171–178
  volume overrides, 302
consumer credit
  see margin lending
Consumer Credit Acts, 324
consumer panel, 38–39
Consumer Protection Cooperation
    Regulation, 250
contract for differences, 75–76, 359,
    367, 393, 407
contract note
  see confirms
controlled functions, 123–125,
    132–135, 139–140
corporate finance
  conduct rules, 102, 310, 320, 383,
    397, 426–428
  conflicts, 150, 151, 152, 169,
    170–171, 189–191
  licensing, 79–82, 88–89, 90, 425
  market abuse, 334, 335, 357
  systems and controls, 425
corruptly, 167
cost–benefit analysis, 30, 36, 39
credit derivative
  see contract for differences
credit institution
  banks and banking, 24
  definition, 104
  deposits and deposit-taking business
    (regulated activity), 69–71
  EU Directives, 58, 102
  MiFID, application of, 98–110, 198,
  Principles, 110, 257–258
Criminal Justice Act
  52 (section), 332, 333
  53 (section), 333, 334
  55 (section), 332
  56 (section), 329, 345
  57 (section), 331
  58 (section), 329
  60 (section), 329, 332
  62 (section), 329
  Sched. 1, para. 1, 334, 335

Sched. 1, para. 2, 335
Sched. 1, para. 3, 335
Sched. 1, para. 4, 335
Sched. 1, para. 5, 335
current customer order, 382
custodians, 23, 27, 59, 84
custody
  application, 108, 198–202
  affiliates, 201
  depositary receipts, 201
  DvP, 200
  fiduciaries, 201
  introducers and arrangers, 200
  passported branches, 202
  temporary holdings, 202
  total title transfer, 195, 201–202
  collateral, 195, 201–202
  disclosures to clients, 206–208
  nominee, 203
  Principle 10 (assets), 198–199, 255
  reconciliations, 208
  regulated activity, 84
  reporting, 417
  segregation, 203–204
  stocklending, 205–206
  total title transfer, 195, 201–202
  tracing, 195–198
  trusts/title, 194–199, 203
  using custodians, 204–205
customer
  see client

damages
  civil law claim
    see right of action
  Compensation Scheme, 94, 209, 245,
    291
  Ombudsman, 45
  under statute (FSMA 150)
    see right of action
dealing
  agency cross, 153
  aggregation, 152, 379–380, 383–385
  allocation, 383–385
  best execution
    see best execution
  churning
    see conflicts of interest

449

Index

dealing (*cont.*)
  client reporting, 417
  confirms, 110, 385–388
  dealing as agent, 79–80, 89–90, 153, 379
  dealing as principal, 79–80, 89–90, 148, 150, 248, 379
  mark up/down, 157, 248
  own account, 388–391
  portfolio (programme) trade, 161, 262
  priority, 380–381
  riskless principal, 148, 150, 391, 394
  short selling, 160, 344, 345, 366, 368, 369
  systematic internalisers
    see systematic internalising
  timely execution, 381–383
  trade reporting, 413–414
  transaction reporting, 414–416
  working the order, 394, 395
dealing ahead
  see conflicts of interest, research
debenture
  see debt securities
debt securities
  investment, as, 67–69
  offer to the public, 10–11, 24–25, 58, 265–270
  prospectus, 56, 265–270
  public offers, offers not be treated as, 10–11, 24–25, 58, 265–270
  transferable security, as, 268
delegating, 116, 128–131
depolarisation, 300–305
deposit
  definition, 69–71
  deposit-taking, 69–71
  index linked, 75–76
depositary receipts, 69
DEPP
  3, 43
  4, 43
  5, 43
  6.2.1, 52, 53, 345, 346
  6.2.2, 345
  6.2.4–6.2.13, 135
  6.2.7, 139

  6.2.8, 139
  6.2.14, 46, 254
  6.3.2, 345, 375
  6.4, 345
  6.5, 345
  6.7, 43
derivatives
  contracts for differences, 75–76
  futures, 72–74
  options, 71–72
designated investment business, 101
direct market access, 373, 400, 406
directed commission
  see conflicts of interest, soft commission
Directions, legal effect of, 51
Directives, EU
  Anti-Money Laundering Directives, 58
  Banking Co-ordination Directive, 58
  Capital Requirements Directive, 104
  Distance Marketing Directive, 296–298
  E-Commerce Directive, 293–296
  Insider Dealing Directive, 58
  interpretation, 5–6, 54–55
  Investment Services Directive, 53, 59
  Lamfalussy Report, 9, 54–55
  Market Abuse Directive, 58, 347, 351
  passporting, 56–59
  procedure for making, 54–46
  Prospectus Directive and Regulations, 56
  single market, 53–59, 326, 391
  UCITS Directives, 26–27, 59
directors' liability, 137–139
dishonesty, 167
DISP, 260
distance contract, 297
distance marketing, 296–298
Distance Marketing Directive, 296–298
distortion
  see market abuse
DTR
  4, 330
  5, 363, 373
  12.2.3, 355, 374
durable medium, 249

Index

E-Commerce
  Directive, 293–296
  FSA Rules, 283, 293–296
EEA firm/bank, 56, 102, 104
EEA passport rights
  see passport
EG
  2.1, 39
  2.2, 39
  2.20, 47
  2.21, 46
  2.23, 52
  2.25, 52
  2.28–2.30, 53
  2.32, 132
  2.33, 40
  2.34, 40
  2.5, 345
  2.7, 143
  5, 43
  7.1–7.5, 345
  9, 135
  9.12, 139
  9.13, 139
  10, 247
  11, 247
  12, 347
electronic commerce, 293–296
Electronic Communications Act 2000, 249
eligible counterparty
  see client
equivalent third country business, 103
energy and oil markets, 429–430
enforcement, 15, 29, 39–43, 137–139, 256, 307, 347, 376–377
evidential provisions, legal effect of, 50
excluded activities, 88–90
exclusion/exemption clauses
  see terms of business, standard (unfair) terms
execution
  see dealing
execution factors, 401
execution of orders
  see dealing
execution of orders on behalf of clients, 393

execution-only services
  see advice, execution-only
exempt person, 92–93

fact find
  see advice
  see also suitability
fairly, duty to treat customers,
  see Principles, Principle 6
false or misleading impression
  see distortion
FESCO, 419
fiduciaries
  see conflicts of interest, general law
Financial Action Task Force (FATF), 315
financial instruments
  definition, 65–57
  see Regulated Activities Order
Financial Ombudsman Service, 45
financial promotion
  application, 109
  licensed persons
    collective investment schemes, 298–300
    direct offers, 291–293
    disclosure, 282–293
    distance marketing, 296–298
    electronic commerce, 293–296
    oral, 293
    Principle 7 (communications), 242, 246, 249, 255, 285
    specific promotions, 291
  misleading, etc., marketing, 270–271
  non-real time communication, 281–282
  real time communication, 280–281
  securities
    see Primary Markets, new issue
  unlicensed persons
    definition of 'financial promotion', 272–276, 277–279
    exemptions, 280–283
    territorial scope, 279–280
Financial Promotion Order, 279–283, 289
financial prudence (Principle 4), 255

451

Index

Financial Services Act 1986
  Gower Reports, 15–19
  New Settlement, 19–22, 27
  Principle 11 (relations with regulators), 40–41, 255–257
  reform of, 27–33
  Securities and Investments Board (SIB), 19, 20, 21
  SROs (Self Reporting Organisations), 17–19
Financial Services Action Plan (FSAP), 54
Financial Services and Markets Act 2000 (FSMA)
  2–6 (FSA Objectives), 33–36, 117, 226
  7–11 (consulting Panels), 38–39
  12–18 (inquiries), 44–46
  19 (carrying on regulated activities), 64, 71, 86
  21, 25 (promotion), 277, 280, 282
  22 (by way of business), 92
  23–29, 31, 37 (licensing), 93, 95
  34 (appointed representative), 92
  59 (approved persons), 132, 139
  80 (listing particulars), 284
  87A (prospectus approval), 284
  102 (exemptions), 269
  118(1) (market abuse), 349, 350
  118(2), 352
  118(3), 358
  118(4), 359
  118(5), 361, 362, 364, 370
  118(6), 370
  118(7), 362
  118(8), 363, 371
  118(9), 360, 364, 371
  118A(1), 350
  118A(2), 349
  118A(3), 359
  118A(5), 374
  118B, 353
  118C(2), 353
  118C(3), 355
  118C(4), 355
  118C(5), 353
  118C(6), 354
  118C(8), 354
  120 (code), 374
  123 (penalties), 373, 374, 375
  130A (interpretation), 349, 352, 353, 371
  131 (effect on transactions), 375
  138 (rules), 50, 226
  139 (client money), 209, 219
  148 (waivers), 49
  149 (evidential provisions), 50
  150, 151 (right of action)
    see right of action
  155 (consultation), 39
  157 (guidance), 50
  235–237 (collective investment scheme), 76–79
  238–241 (collective investment schemes), 279, 299
  264 (EEA schemes), 433
  285 (RIE), 418
  397(1), (2), (misleading, etc., marketing)
    see financial promotion, misleading, etc., marketing
  397(3) (market manipulation) 336–342, 345
    see *also* market manipulation, criminal offence
  418 (territoriality), 86–87
  Sched. 1 (FSA), 37, 38, 44
  Sched 3 (passporting), 96
Financial Services and Markets Tribunal, 39–43
Financial Services Authority (FSA)
  accountability to Treasury, 44–45
  annual report, 37–38
  complaints commissioner, 43–44
  consultation, 30, 36, 39, 52
  enforcement, 29, 39–43, 137–139, 307, 347, 376–377
  governance, 36–37
  guidance, 50–51
  immunity, 43–44
  judicial review against, 33
  Objectives, statutory, 33–36, 142–145, 226, 418–419
  principles of good governance, duty to follow, 35–37

Index

risk assessment, 142–145, 288, 315
rulebook, 45–53, 226
waiver power, rules, 48–49
Financial Services Compensation Scheme, 94, 209, 245, 291
FIT, 94, 133, 134
foreign exchange (FX), 26, 73, 74, 101, 102
freedom of establishment
  see passport
front running
  see conflicts of interest, research
FSA
  see Financial Services Authority
FSMA
  see Financial Services and Markets Act 2000
full credit, institution, 104
full scope BIPRU investment firm, 104
future, 72–74

gaming
  see wagering contracts
GEN
  2.2.1, 48
  2.2.4, 50
GLOSS definitions
  ancillary service, 101
  associated instrument, 342
  bank, 104
  BCD credit institution, 104
  BIPRU firm, 104
  CAD full scope firm, 104
  CAD investment firm, 104
  client, 226–230, 437
  common platform firm, 104
  credit institution, 104
  current customer order, 382
  designated investment business, 101
  distance contact, 297
  durable medium, 249
  EEA bank, 104
  equivalent third country business, 103
  execution factors, 401
  execution of orders on behalf of clients, 393
  financial instruments, 65–79
  full credit institution, 104
  full scope BIPRU investment firm, 104
  information society service, 294
  investment research, 183
  investment services and activities, 101
  outsourcing, 128
  prudential context, 104
  regulated activity, 101
  relevant person, 131, 161, 192
  research recommendation, 187
  stabilisation, 342
  systematic internaliser, 409
  tied agent, 93
  transaction, 415
  website conditions, 249
gold plating, 55–56, 118, 122, 129, 133, 171, 178, 184, 186, 391, 417
granting credit
  see margin lending
greenshoe option, 341
Grey Book, 343, 388
Guidance, legal effect of, 50–51, 180 FN 135, 186 FN 151

hedge funds, 26, 76–79, 233, 299, 319, 353, 401
hold mail, 385, 417
holder
  see options
Home/Host State, 56, 57, 86, 94–96, 102, 103

independent financial advisers, 300–305
inducements
  see conflicts of interest
industrial and commercial companies
  licensing, 79–80, 88–91
  role in the Capital Markets, 24
information barrier
  see Chinese Wall
information society service, 294
inside information
  see insider dealing

453

Index

insider dealing
  criminal offence
    ATS, 419
    burden of proof, 345–346
    dealing offence, 332
    defences, 333–336
    disclosure offence, 149, 333
    encouraging offence, 332–333
    history of offence, 326–327
    inside information, 329–332
    insider, 329–332
    insider list, 330
    regulated market, 332
    securities, 332
    territorial scope, 327–328
  market abuse
    ATS, 419, 421
    behaviour and investments, 349–350
    burden of proof, 345–346
    dealing, 352–358
    defences, 356–358
    disclosure, 358–359
    history of offence, 343–347
    inside information, 352–356
    price stabilisation, 335, 339–342
    regular user, 359–360, 363–364, 370–373
    territorial scope, 350
Insider Dealing Directive, 326–327
Insolvency Act 1986, 214 (section), 138
insurance companies, 23, 26–27, 91, 236
intention, 140, 339, 346–347
intermediate customer
  see client
International Organisation of Securities Commissions (IOSCO), 9
interpretation
  FSA Rules, of, 6–7, 49–53, 54–55
  statutory, rules of, 4–6
inter-professional business, 257, 388–389
introducers, 80–81, 200
introductions
  see arranging deals
investment advertisements, 272–293
investment advice

see advice
investment business
  see licensing, test
investment companies
  see collective investment scheme
investment firm, 56, 57, 59, 90–91, 95, 102
investment managers/management
  see portfolio manager
investment research
  definition, 183
  see research
investment services and activities, 101
Investment Services Directive (ISD), 53–59, 63, 408–409
investment trusts
  see companies
investments
  see Regulated Activities Order
investor, 22, 23, 79–80, 88–91
ISD/MiFID override, 90–91
issuer, 10–11, 79–80, 88–91

Joint Money Laundering Steering Group (JMLSG), 314–315
judicial review, 33

key features, 305
know-your-customer (KYC)
  see advice
  see also suitability

laddering, 189
Lamfalussy procedure, the, 9, 53–54
legal personality
  see companies
licensing
  offences, 92–93
  process, 94
  test
    by way of business, 92
    excluded activities, 86–90
    investment activities, 79–86
    investments, 65–79
    ISD/MiFID override, 90–91
LIFFE (London International Financial Futures Exchange), 360, 407

Index

limit orders, 382–3
limited liability partnership (LLP), 65, 76–79
limited partnership, 65, 76–79
Listed Money Market Institution (LMMI), 388
listing, 355
LME (London Metal Exchange), 355, 359, 360, 362, 364, 368, 369, 370, 371, 407
London Stock Exchange (LSE)
    Big Bang, 9–10, 16–17, 150, 153, 158
    recognised exchange, 360, 365, 399, 407, 408, 409, 414, 418

manager of collective investment scheme
    conduct rules, 300–305
    licensing, 83–84
    systems and controls, 342
MAR
    1.2.3, 346, 350
    1.2.5, 349
    1.2.8, 350, 353
    1.2.12, 354
    1.2.13, 354
    1.2.14, 354
    1.2.16, 356
    1.2.21, 371
    1.3.2, 356, 357
    1.3.3, 352
    1.3.4, 352
    1.3.5, 352
    1.3.6–1.3.10, 357
    1.3.12, 356
    1.3.15, 356
    1.3.17–1.3.19, 358
    1.3.20, 356
    1.3.21, 355
    1.3.22, 356
    1.3.23, 355
    1.4.2, 359
    1.4.3, 358
    1.4.5, 358
    1.4.5A, 359
    1.4.7, 373
    1.5.2, 359
    1.5.3, 359
    1.5.4–1.5.6, 359
    1.5.7, 360
    1.5.8, 359
    1.5.9, 359
    1.5.10, 359
    1.6.2, 361, 366
    1.6.3, 361
    1.6.4, 367, 369
    1.6.5, 362, 365
    1.6.7, 364
    1.6.8, 364
    1.6.9, 361
    1.6.10, 367
    1.6.11, 370
    1.6.12, 370
    1.6.14, 362, 370
    1.6.15, 361, 366
    1.6.16, 369
    1.7.2, 370
    1.7.3, 370
    1.8.4, 363
    1.8.5, 362
    1.8.6, 362, 363
    1.9.2, 364
    1.9.3, 364, 371
    1.9.4, 364
    1.9.5, 364, 371
    1.10.1, 358, 374
    1.10.2, 358, 374
    1.10.4, 374
    2.1.3, 340
    2.1.6, 342
    2.2.1, 340
    2.2.4, 374
    2.2.6, 340
    2.2.7, 342
    2.3.4, 342
    2.3.5–2.3.9, 340
    2.3.10, 342
    2.3.11, 340, 341
    2.4, 340
    2.5, 340
    2.5.1, 340
    5, 110, 420–421
    6, 110, 141
    7, 409–413
margin, 70, 73, 74, 114, 115, 197, 201, 207, 215, 217, 220, 221, 264, 288, 308

Index

margin lending, 24, 26, 80, 101, 102, 195, 324–325, 393
market abuse
 ATS, 419, 421
 behaviour, 349–350
 burden of proof, 345–346
 buy-back programmes, 358
 Chinese Walls, 351, 352, 358, 362, 363, 374
 conclusive provisions, interpretation of, 49–53, 54–55
 criminal offence
  insider dealing, 326–336
  market manipulation, 336–342
 disclosure, 358–359
 disclosure of interests in shares, and, 363 FN 137
 distortion
  abusive squeeze, 368–370
  fictions, 370
  price positioning, 365–368
 effects based, as, 346–347, 350
 exchanges, 349
 false or misleading impression, 360–364
 intention, 346–347, 350
 investments, 349–350
 misuse of information, 350–360
 penalties, 375
 prescribed markets, 349
 Principle 5 (market conduct), 255, 343, 347, 351, 365, 366, 368, 372, 375–376
 reasons for regime, 342–347
 regular user, 359–360, 363–364, 370–373
 reporting of suspicious transactions, 374
 requiring or encouraging, 373–374
 safe harbours (defences), 374–375
 stabilisation, 245, 271, 339–342, 374
 sunset clause, 359, 363–364, 370–371
 suspicious transactions, notification of, 374
 Take-over Code, and the, 343, 351, 356, 358, 374, 376
 territorial scope, 350
market confidence, 34–35
market counterparty
 see client
market maker, 89–90, 185, 186, 334–335, 351, 357, 395, 407
market manipulation
 criminal offence, 336–342, 366, 369
 market abuse, 360–371
marketing communication
 see financial promotion
mark-up/mark-down, 157, 248, 388, 401
MiFID override
 see ISD/MiFID override
misleading practices
 market abuse, 345–376
 market manipulation, 336–342
misleading statements, 270–271
misselling, 41, 270–271, 315–318
misuse of information, 350–360
money laundering, 58, 123, 314–315
Money Laundering Directives, 58, 314–315
money market instruments
 see debt securities
multi-lateral trading facilities (MTFs), 84–86, 110, 269, 373, 382, 397, 400, 409, 411, 415, 418–421

National Criminal Intelligence Service (NCIS)
 see Serious Organised Crime Agency
negligence
 Principle 2 (skill, care and diligence), 204, 254
 standard, 93, 130, 137–139, 158, 168, 206, 262, 284, 306, 307, 316
 tortious action, 246–247, 262
net contract note/confirm, 399
non-EEA firm/bank, 57, 58, 96–97
Non-investment Products (NIPs) Code, 388
non-market-price transaction, 375–376, 388, 389, 390
non-real-time communication, 281–282

offer to the public, meaning of, 10–11, 24–25, 58, 265–270

Ombudsman Scheme, 45, 245
open-ended investment companies (OEICs)
  see collective investment schemes
operational risk, 118–131
options, 71–72
override
  see ISD/MiFID override
overseas company/firm
  EEA firm/bank, 56
  non-EEA firm/bank, 57–58, 96–97
  overseas persons exclusion, 86–88
overseas persons exclusion, 86–88
outsourcing
  definition, 128
  see systems and controls
own account dealing, 79–80, 89–90
  see also conflicts

packaged products, 23, 26–27, 57–59, 76–79, 236, 300–305
painting the tape, 361
Part IV permission, 85, 86, 94
partnership, 77–78
passport, the EU
  branching/services, 56, 57, 86, 94–96, 102, 103, 202, 216
  non-EU firms, 58, 96–97, 103
  products, 56, 57
personal account dealing, 108, 191–193
personal recommendation
  see advice
place of business, 87
placing, 10–11, 24–25, 58
polarisation
  see collective investment schemes, polarisation
portfolio manager, 14, 27, 59
  as clients, 229–230, 234–236, 240
  conduct rules, 287, 288, 307–318, 385, 400, 404, 417, 432
  conflicts, 150, 151
  regulated activity, 82–83, 89, 432
  systems and controls, 432
portfolio (programme) trade, 161, 262, 345, 365, 399, 412
Practitioner Panel, 38–39
precipice bonds, 292–293

Prevention of Corruption Act 1906, The, 166–167
Prevention of Fraud (Investments) Acts 1939, 1958, The, 12–17, 86, 92, 140, 225, 272, 284, 293, 298, 307, 324, 343, 383, 388, 390, 417
price positioning, 365–368
price stabilising rules
  see stabilisation rules
Primary Markets
  approval of prospectus in another EEA State, 56–59
  best execution, 391–407
  corporate finance, 425–428
  disclosure, 10–11, 265–270
  exempt offers, 270
  listing, 355
  mutual recognition, 56–59
  new issue, 10–11, 24–25, 58, 265–270
  offer for sale, 10–11, 24–25, 58, 265–270
  transferable securities, 268
  see also financial promotion; market abuse
principal dealing
  regulated activity, 79–80, 89–90
  single capacity / dual capacity, 150, 153, 158
principle-based regulation, 45–49, 55, 256, 259–260, 347
Principles, 246, 254–264
  MiFID 'best interests' rule, 202, 264, 308, 322, 323, 404
  Principle 1 (integrity), 168, 254
  Principle 2 (skill, care, diligence), 204, 254, 285, 308, 365
  Principle 3 (management and control), 118, 254, 256
  Principle 4 (financial prudence), 255
  Principle 5 (market conduct), 255, 343, 347, 351, 365, 366, 368, 372, 375–376, 390
  Principle 6 (customers' interests), 168, 191, 216, 238, 241, 243, 248, 250, 251, 255, 270, 285, 316–317, 322, 323, 325, 354, 381, 383, 393, 406, 421

Principles (*cont.*)
   Principle 7 (communications), 242, 246, 249, 255, 285
   Principle 8 (conflicts)
     see conflicts of interest
   Principle 9 (trust), 255, 307
   Principle 10 (assets), 198–199, 210, 255
   Principle 11 (relations with regulators), 40–41, 255–257
   scope of, 110, 257–258
priority of dealing
private customer
   see client
Proceeds of Crime Act, 314–315
professional client
   see client
programme trade
   see portfolio (programme) trade
promissory note
   see debt securities
promotion
   see financial promotion
prospectus
   Directive, 56, 265–270
   see Primary Markets
prudential context, 104
pump and dump, 370
purpose
   see intention
put option
   see options

RAO
   see Regulated Activities Order
Reader's Guide, 50–51
readily realisable investments, 246, 293
real-time communication, 280–281
reception and transmission of orders
   best executions, 404–405
   see arranging deals
recognised clearing house (RCH), 239
recognised investment exchange (RIE), 239
record keeping, 140–141, 313, 318, 323, 378, 379, 380, 382, 384
regular user, 359, 363–369, 370–373

regulated activities
   advice, 81–82
   appointed representatives, 92–93
   authorised persons, 92–93
   by way of business, 70, 83, 92
   custody, 84
   dealing as agent, 79–80
   dealing as principal, 79–80
   deposit taking, 68, 75
   effect of unlicensed activities, 92–93
   exclusions, 68, 75, 83–90
   general prohibition, 92–93
   investment activities, 68, 75, 79–86
   investments, 65–83
   licensed persons, 92–93
   managing investments, 82–83
   MTF, 84–86
   occupational pension scheme, managing investments for, 82–83
   operating collective investment schemes, 83–84
   override, the ISD/MiFID, 90–91
   overseas persons exclusion, 86–88
   passported firm/bank, 94–96
Regulated Activities Order 2001
   art. 4 (override), 90–91
   arts. 5–9 (deposits), 68, 75
   art. 10 (insurance), 76
   arts. 14–20 (dealing as principal), 79–80
   art. 21 (dealing as agent), 79–80
   arts. 25–36 (arranging deals), 80–81
   art. 25D (MTF), 84–86
   art. 37 (managing investments), 82–83
   arts. 40–44 (custody), 84
   art. 51 (operating collective investment schemes), 83–84
   art. 53 (advice), 81–82, 307
   art. 66 (trustees), 83, 89
   art. 69 (group exclusion), 88
   art. 70 (sale of company), 88–90
   art. 72 (overseas persons), 86–88
   art. 72A (information society services), 295
   art. 76 (shares), 65–67, 268
   art. 77 (debt securities), 67–69, 268

Index

art. 78 (government, etc., securities), 68
art. 79 (warrants), 69, 268
art. 80 (depositary receipts), 69, 268
art. 81 (units in CIS), 76–79
art. 83 (options), 71–71, 268
art. 84 (futures), 72–74
art. 85 (contract for differences), 75–76
art. 89 (rights and interests), 83
Sched. 3, para. 1(h), 432
regulated activity, 101
see also Regulated Activities Order
regulated market
   generally, 269, 318, 382, 397, 400, 408, 409, 413, 415, 418, 422
   market abuse, 329, 349
regulations, EU, 53–56
Regulatory Decisions Committee (RDC), 39–43
regulatory Objectives, FSA, 33–36, 142–145
relevant person, 131, 161, 192
remuneration
   industry norms, 162, 245
   systems and controls, 126–127
repackagings
   see collective investment scheme
repo
   see stocklending
reporting
   client, to, 417
   regulator, self-reporting to, 40–41, 255–257
   trade, 413–414
   transaction, 414–415
request for quote (RFQ)
   see best execution
research, 25, 26
   advice, 82
   disclosures, 108
   financial promotions, 274
   'front running', 108
   market abuse, 329, 330, 333, 354, 359, 373, 375
   systems and controls, 108
   see insider dealing
research recommendation, 187

retail client
   see client
retail intermediaries
   see packaged products
right of action
   general law (contract, tortious), 246–247
   statutory, 165, 246, 299
risk factors (warnings), 284–289
risk-based supervision, 142–145
riskless principal
   see dealing
Rules, legal effect of, 50

safekeeping and administration
   see custody
sale and repurchase transaction
   see stocklending
Sale of Goods and Supply of Services Act, 306
SCARPS (structured capital at risk products), 292–293
securities
   collective investment schemes, 76–79
   convertibles, 67–69
   debt securities, 67–69
   depositary receipts, 69
   disclosure of information requirements, 330
   disclosure of interests in shares, 363 FN 137
   government, etc., securities, 68
   issuer of, 10–11
   listing of, 355
   offers to the public, 10–11, 24–25, 58, 265–270
   public offers, offers not to be trusted as, 10–11, 24–25, 58, 265–270
   shares, 65–67
   transferable securities, 265–270
   warrants, 69
Securities and Investments Board (SIB), 19, 20, 21
Self Regulating Organisations (SROs), 17–19, 114, 116
self-regulation, 17–19
self-reporting, 40–41, 255–257

459

senior management
  approved person, 132–139
  controlled functions, 123–125, 132–135
  liability, 137–139
  principle-based regulation, 132
  responsibilities, 135–137, 261
Serious Organised Crime Agency (SOCA), 314–315
share capital
  see companies
share options, 71–72
share warrant, 69
shares
  disclosure of interests in, 363 FN 137
  investment, as, 65–67
  listing of, 355
  offer to the public, 10–11, 24–25, 58, 265–270
  prospectus, 265–270
  public offers, offers not to be treated as, 10–11, 24–25, 58, 265–270
  transferable security, as, 265–270
Single Market, EU, 53–54, 326, 391
soft commission
  see conflicts of interest
solicitation
  see financial promotion
sophisticated investors
  expert clients, 236–239
  prospectuses, 269
special purpose vehicle (SPV), 233, 269
specialist (on exchange), 407
spinning, 189
spread bet
  see contract for differences
stabilisation rules, 245, 271, 339–342, 374
Statements of Principle for Approved Persons
  see APER
stock
  see companies
stocklending, 26, 83, 114, 202, 205, 207–208, 216, 220, 242, 245, 287, 288, 345, 359, 361, 362, 366, 386, 415

suitability
  application, 109
  appropriateness, 318–324
  Conduct of Business Rule, 309–318
  execution-only services, 318–320
  know-your-customer, 309–314
  Principle 9 (trust), 255, 307
  test, 314–318
SUP
8, 49
9.1.2, 49
9.2.5, 49
9.4.1, 49
10, 94
10.1.1, 140
10.1.7, 140
10.1.13, 140
10.1.13A, 133
10.1.13B, 133
10.1.13C, 133
10.1.6–10.1.15, 132
10.4–10.9, 132
10.7.2A, 134
10.7.4, 135
10.8.1, 133
10.9.5, 135
10.9.10, 133
10.10, 140
10.13.7, 134
10.13.12, 134
11, 94
12, 92, 93
13, 95
13A, 95, 104
14, 95
15, 256
15.3.3, 256
15.3.8, 256
15.3.11, 256
15.3.12, 256
15.3.13, 256
15.3.14, 256
17, 415–416
App. 1, 94
App. 3.6.2, 95
App. 3.6.7–3.6.9, 96
App. 3.9.5, 81
TP 8A, 8B, 133

super-equivalence
see gold plating
Supply of Goods and Services Act, 248–249
suspicious transactions, notification of
  market abuse, 374
  money laundering, 314–315
swap contract
  see contract for differences
SYSC
  1.1.1, 122, 123
  1.3.2–1.3.8, 227
  1.3.3, 105, 227
  1.3.10A, 141
  1.3.12, 165
  2.1.3, 123
  2.1.6, 123
  3.1.1A, 119
  3.1.6, 126
  3.1.8, 127
  3.1.9, 127
  3.2.20, 141
  4.1.1, 120, 122
  4.1.4, 122
  4.1.5, 120
  4.1.6–4.1.8, 123
  4.1.9, 125
  4.1.10, 120
  4.1.11, 125
  4.2.1, 133
  4.3.1, 122, 134
  4.3.2, 122
  5.1.1, 126
  5.1.2, 127, 131
  5.1.3, 127
  5.1.4, 127
  5.1.4A, 127
  5.1.6, 131
  5.1.7, 120
  5.1.8, 120
  5.1.12, 120
  6.1.1, 124
  6.1.2, 124
  6.1.3, 124, 131
  6.1.4, 124
  6.3, 123
  6.3.1, 315
  6.3.2–6.3.10, 315
  7.1, 120
  7.1.2–7.1.5, 120
  7.1.5, 131
  7.1.6, 125
  7.1.16, 120
  8.1.1, 129
  8.1.3, 129
  8.1.4, 129
  8.1.5, 129
  8.1.6, 129
  8.1.7, 130
  8.1.8, 130
  8.1.10, 129
  8.1.12, 130
  8.2.1, 131
  8.2.3, 131
  8.3.1, 131
  8.3.2–8.3.7, 131
  9.1.1, 141
  9.1.2, 141
  10.1.1, 105, 160, 227
  10.1.2, 105
  10.1.5, 162
  10.1.6, 165
  10.1.7, 141, 165
  10.1.8, 166
  10.1.9, 165, 166
  10.1.10, 165
  10.1.11, 165, 166
  10.1.12, 162
  10.1.13–10.1.15, 191
  10.2, 166
  10.2.1, 105, 227
  11–16, 120
  12.1.8, 120
  13, 120
  13.4.2, 256
  13.9, 130
  14.1.5, 141
  14.1.14, 120
  14.1.17, 120
  14.1.18, 120
  14.1.30–14.1.33, 120
  14.1.38–14.1.41, 125
  14.1.42–14.1.45, 125
  14.1.65, 120
  15.10.2, 374
  18, 140

Index

SYSC (*cont.*)
  application, 103–104
  Sched. 6, 49
  TP1, 119, 141
systematic internalising, 110, 387, 407–413
systems and controls
  anti-money laundering, 314–315
  application, 103–104
  apportionment and control, 121–123
  ATS, 419–420
  employees, 123–127, 132–141
  general rules, 117–121
  market abuse, 331, 375–376
  outsourcing, 127–131
  Principle (management and control), 117–118, 254, 256

takeovers, 54
  market abuse, 343, 351, 356, 358, 374, 376
taping, 388, 389, 390–391
TC
  1.1.1, 105, 127
  1.1.2, 105
  1.1.4, 127
  1–3, 127
  application, 108
terms of business
  amendments, 249–250
  client assets, 206–208
  content, 243–249, 275, 293, 310, 314, 382–383, 388, 394, 395
  enforcement, 251
  form, 249
  one-way/two-way consent, 251–253
  requirement, 241–243
  standard (unfair) terms, 158, 238, 241, 250–251, 259
territorial scope
  FSA rules, 99–110, 271, 272, 276, 279–280
  insider dealing, 327–328
  licensing, 71, 86–88
  market abuse, 350
  market manipulation, 338–339
  Principles, 258
third country firms/banks
  see non-EEA firms/banks
tied agent
  see appointed representative
timely execution, 381–382
tipping off
  insider dealing, 333
  market abuse, 358–359
total title transfer
  see client money
  see also custody
trade reporting, 413–414
training and competence, 105 127
transaction, 415
transaction reporting, 414–415
transferable securities, 265–270
trash and cash, 370
Treasury inquiries, 44–45
treating customers fairly (Principle 6)
  see Principles, Principle 6
trusts, trustees
  as clients, 234, 240–241
  conduct rules, 435–437
  exceptions from regulated activity, 89
  pension, 83
  regulated activity, 83, 89, 434
  systems and controls, 434, 435
  see also client money; custody

UCITS Directives, 59, 79
unauthorised person
  sanctions, 93
  test, 65–92
underwriting, 24–25, 79–82, 88–89, 90, 242, 245
unfair terms
  see terms of business, standard terms
unit trust scheme
  see collective investment scheme
unregulated collective investment scheme, 240, 245, 279, 432
unsolicited communication
  see financial promotion

volume overrides, 302
volume weighted average price (VWAP), 384, 413

wagering contracts, 76
waiver power, FSA's, 48–49
warrants, 69
wash trade, 361
way of business, activities carried on by, 70, 83, 92

website conditions, 249
whistleblowing, 140
writer
  see options